Neuroeconomics and the Decision-Making Process

Bryan Christiansen
PryMarke LLC, USA

Ewa Lechman
Gdansk University of Technology, Poland

A volume in the Advances in Psychology, Mental Health, and Behavioral Studies (APMHBS) Book Series

An Imprint of IGI Global

Published in the United States of America by
Business Science Reference (an imprint of IGI Global)
701 E. Chocolate Avenue
Hershey PA, USA 17033
Tel: 717-533-8845
Fax: 717-533-8661
E-mail: cust@igi-global.com
Web site: http://www.igi-global.com

Library of Congress Cataloging-in-Publication Data

Names: Christiansen, Bryan, 1960- editor. | Lechman, Ewa, editor.
Title: Neuroeconomics and the decision-making process / Bryan Christiansen
   and Ewa Lechman, editors.
Description: Hershey, PA : Business Science Reference, [2016] | Includes
   bibliographical references and index.
Identifiers: LCCN 2015050703| ISBN 9781466699892 (hardcover : alk. paper) |
   ISBN 9781466699908 (ebook : alk. paper)
Subjects: LCSH: Neuroeconomics. | Cognitive neuroscience. | Decision making.
   | Decision making--Physiological aspects. | Economics--Psychological
   aspects.
Classification: LCC QP360.5 .N4765 2016 | DDC 612.8/233--dc23 LC record available at http://lccn.loc.gov/2015050703

This book is published in the IGI Global book series Advances in Psychology, Mental Health, and Behavioral Studies (APMHBS) (ISSN: pending; eISSN: pending)

British Cataloguing in Publication Data
A Cataloguing in Publication record for this book is available from the British Library.

For electronic access to this publication, please contact: eresources@igi-global.com.

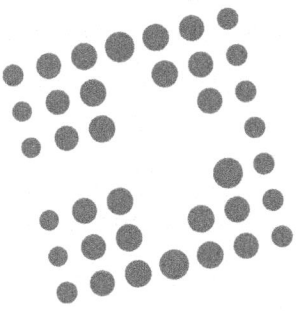

Advances in Psychology, Mental Health, and Behavioral Studies (APMHBS) Book Series

Bryan Christiansen
PryMarke, LLC, USA

ISSN: pending
EISSN: pending

MISSION

The complexity of the human mind has puzzled researchers and physicians for centuries. While widely studied, the brain still remains largely misunderstood.

The **Advances in Psychology, Mental Health, and Behavioral Studies (APMHBS)** book series presents comprehensive research publications focusing on topics relating to the human psyche, cognition, psychiatric care, mental and developmental disorders, as well as human behavior and interaction. Featuring diverse and innovative research, publications within APMHBS are ideally designed for use by mental health professionals, academicians, researchers, and upper-level students.

COVERAGE

- Substance Abuse
- Personality Disorders
- Trauma & Stress
- Anxiety
- Psychiatry
- Eating Disorders
- Addiction
- Treatment & Care
- Human Interaction
- Socialization

IGI Global is currently accepting manuscripts for publication within this series. To submit a proposal for a volume in this series, please contact our Acquisition Editors at Acquisitions@igi-global.com or visit: http://www.igi-global.com/publish/.

Titles in this Series

For a list of additional titles in this series, please visit: www.igi-global.com

www.igi-global.com

701 E. Chocolate Ave., Hershey, PA 17033
Order online at www.igi-global.com or call 717-533-8845 x100
To place a standing order for titles released in this series, contact: cust@igi-global.com
Mon-Fri 8:00 am - 5:00 pm (est) or fax 24 hours a day 717-533-8661

Editorial Advisory Board

Table of Contents

Detailed Table of Contents

Neuroeconomics is an emergent multidisciplinary field that strives to understand how and why humans make decisions. The field brings together behavioral methods and sophisticated computational theories from microeconomics, an understanding of emotional influences on behavior from psychology, and human functional neural imaging from neuroscience. This chapter presents the fundamentals of neuroeconomics, thus describing the concept of neuroeconomics; neuroimaging applications; neuroeconomics and loss aversion; neuroeconomics and temporal discounting; neuroeconomics of decision making in humans and animals; neuroeconomics, behavioral economics, and irrationality; neuroeconomics and utility theory; neural systems in economic decision making; neural systems in reward system; neural systems in cognitive control system; game theory, strategic interaction, and neuroeconomic studies; and the types of evidence about economic behavior.

This chapter investigates the development of neuroeconomics as a relative new sub-discipline in the fields of economics and behavioral science. After comparing paradigms of both classical and behavioral economics, the problem of the "conscious and rational consumer" is addressed in relation to more passive views of consumerism in neuroeconomics. Highlighting the most recent trends in neuroeconomics, the chapter also addresses the historical development of the discipline of neuroeconomics as an independent field of research within the fields of media and economics. The problem of new marketing strategies as well as the evolvement of neuroeconomics as an independent discipline in the age of digitalization is presented while considering the changing nature of the media industry.

Classical economics assumes human economic decision making is completely rational and dominated by self-interest. Behavior economics emerged to account for the fact that human economic preferences are often influenced by emotional and psychological factors leading to inconsistent, intransitive, and irrational decisions that fail to maximize utility and minimize cost and transcend only self-interest. Both rationality and emotions are seated in the human brain in the prefrontal cortex and limbic system, respectively. The brain imaging methods of neuroscience help in understanding the interplay between economic behavior and neural mechanisms. The human economic decision making behavior involves computational and neurobiological processes and is related to the psychological processes. Classical Economics, Psychology, and Neuroscience converge in Neuroeconomics to better understand and predict human economic decision-making. Neuromarketing is an emerging field that uses neuroscience techniques to understand economic preferences of consumers.

The purpose of this chapter is to explore the potential connection between neuroeconomics and the Central Language Hypothesis (CLH) which refers to the language placed within the subconscious mind of an individual. The CLH forwards that in the brains of bilingual and multilingual people, one language is more suppressive as it dominates reflexes, emotions, and senses. This central language (CL) is located at the centre of the limbic cortex of the brain. Therefore, when there is a stimulus on the limbic cortex (e.g., fear, anxiety, sadness), the brain produces the central language. The chapter begins with an Introduction followed by a Theoretical Framework. The next section discusses the neurolinguistic projection of the central language and includes the survey and the results used in this study. The Discussion section provides additional information regarding the questionnaire and the CLH, followed by Future Research Directions, Implications, and finally the Conclusion.

Assuming the meaning of intercultural competency is a crucial issue in multicultural societies and within business units as results of globalization, this chapter analyses cooperative attitude as a core component of intercultural competence. First, the chapter explains such terms as intercultural competence, cooperation, and culture, as well as the diffusion of cultures. Cooperation as a social value in strategic human resources management is also considered. Secondly, factors shaping cooperation (divided into two groups: cultural and biological) are discussed from a multidisciplinary perspective. Finally, the neuroeconomic dimension of cooperation is discussed with its subsequent socio-economic implications. The chapter concludes with recommendations regarding human choices resulting from individual ontogenetic processes (including cultural differences, genetic differences, and neural differences) and concludes on cooperative attitudes that are most likely culturally and biologically dependent, and which become a part of intercultural competence desired in a multicultural society and at the work place.

Managers in organizations are typically faced with changing and ambiguous signals in their operating environment. Based on interpretation of these signals, managers react with appropriate strategies. This chapter presents critical organizational issues in decision making process and its outcomes, including the manager's selective attention, interpretation, and reasoning of uncertain operating environment. In particular, the chapter first discusses why individual managers in the same organization who are faced with same environmental changes may differently interpret threat and opportunity aspects of these changes. Second, the chapter links outcomes of such interpretation to investigate different types of organizational actions. Third, the chapter drives into a greater depth to explore how the manager's experience and characteristics of the environment affect forms of reasoning in interpretation process and performance of subsequent organizational actions.

How diverse regions of the brain are coordinated to produce objective-directed decision is the essence of neuroeconomics. Indeed, the latter is a formal framework to describe the involvement of numerous brain regions including frontal, cingulate, parietal cortex, and striatum in economic and financial decision-making process. The purpose of this chapter is to explain the relationship between economic decision making and emotion on one hand, and the relationship between economic decision making and prefrontal cortex on the other hand.

This chapter is focused on the possibilities of game theory as a tool of strategists to interpret practical strategic decision-making situations. Simultaneously, there is a need to simplify presentation of game theory and consider the possibilities of mixed strategies. Practical game situations are relatively complex: even the rules of the game might change during the decision-making process, or at least there is need to change several times the strategy during the game, especially in the case of repeated game. This chapter shows some practical examples how to describe the strategic game situations in a manner relatively easy to understand.

Functional Magnetic Resonance Imaging (fMRI) is a very effective tool in neuromarketing. However, time limits, subject fatigue, fMRI costs, and participants' concentration are problematic. Conjoint analysis and its cards enable shortening the time and providing more attributes for evaluation. Conjoint analysis models of orthogonal matrices keep the amount of conjoint cards to a minimum which shortens the time spent in the fMRI machine and thus lowering costs. All conjoint cards are different and keep subjects concentrated during the test. fMRI is an efficient analyzing method of neuronal architecture and functions for the identification of the brain areas and networks. Conjoint analysis and fMRI are strong, combined methods to analyze customer needs and desires.

Oxana Karnaukhova, Southern Federal University, Russia
Inna Nekrasova, Southern Federal University, Russia

The chapter questions the applicability of the Efficient Market Hypothesis (EMH) for analysis of financial markets. The overall goal is to analyze methods of forecasting future prices of financial assets based on the concept of the fractal market structure and long-term memory of past prices. Fractals in the financial markets are interpreted either as investors with different investment horizons or as a configuration of the price movement on chart. This chapter examines the fractal structure of financial markets, nonlinear methods of analysis of financial markets, plasticity and long-term memory to long-term investment horizons of financial markets, fractal analysis of financial markets, new approaches to forecast prices of financial assets, which eliminate shortcomings of the linear paradigm.

Anastasia Y. Nikitaeva, Southern Federal University, Russia

This chapter substantiates the importance of improving management effectiveness of mesoeconomic systems in current economic conditions and the features of mesoeconomy as a management object which defines the high complexity of decision making at the meso level. There are approaches, methods, and technologies which provide support of the decision making process via the integration of formal methods for objective data analysis and methods of accounting to solve semi-structured complex problems of mesoeconomy. A cognitive approach, and an approach involving the integration of the On-Line Analytical Processing and Data mining technologies with methods of a multi-criteria assessment of alternative, in particular methods of Multi-Attribute Utility Theory are considered in the chapter. Cognitive mapping of interaction between state and business in a mesoeconomic system are included as a case-study.

Shefali Virkar, University of Oxford, UK

The purpose of this chapter is to examine the role of government in encouraging fiscal compliance from the theoretical perspective of the 'Ecology of Games'. Conceptual representations of human behaviour in formal complex institutions, located within Behavioural Economics Political Game Theory, presuppose it is possible for government agencies to strategically influence the behavioural preferences and consumption patterns of individual actors and groups in society. This study presents an empirical case concerned with the implementation and use of an electronic property tax collection system in Bangalore, India developed between 1998 and 2008.

Information which financial market participants use to make their decisions comes directly and indirectly from accounting. Although finance and accounting use the language of numbers which appear to be very clear and plain, it is obvious that sums presented in financial statements and then interpreted and used by financial managers and investors and other stakeholders are very subjective. The goal of this chapter is to pay attention to the implications of behavioral research in accounting and its new stream – neuroaccounting – for behavioral finance. It is argued that accounting should be considered by behavioral finance researchers because the product of accounting in the form of reports, statements, and different analyses represents not only economic standing of a company, but also those behind the scenes.

Economists, political scientists, and military analysts widely apply game theory techniques to analyze strategic decision making of players. The model is often adopted to analyze oligopolistic firms' actions, legal, and political negotiations, dating and mating strategies by couples, and competitive bidding in auctions. As a facet of neuroeconomics, game theory can highly complement the comprehension of human decision making processes. Although the model has been somewhat difficult for many readers, this chapter presents game theory with a high level of precision for easy understanding. The discourse presented in this chapter covers the different types of games, the approaches applied to predict games' outcomes, and general analysis of strategic choices. In its final section, the chapter underscores key aspects of auction and competitive bidding.

The purpose of this chapter is to examine why people are motivated to engage in luxury consumption, particularly in Asian countries. Purchases of global brands are increasingly popular among affluent society not only in Western nations, but also in other parts of the world. Global brands are normally associated with luxury brands from all categories of consumption goods such as cosmetics, handbags, electronic goods, cell phones and accessories, and watches among others. Previous studies have found that Western countries have clearly stated several key factors for consumers to purchase such luxury brands. Consumers in Asian markets are expected to engage in conspicuous consumption behavior to purchase global brands due to market demands and increasing income levels. Yet, such understanding is still much limited in the context of Asian consumers. Our work addresses this issue.

Foreword

Modern economics has in the recent years been often accused of ignoring the achievements of other scientific disciplines such as psychology and other fields of medical research, sociology, political sciences, or philosophy. Most mainstream economists did not accommodate them in the course of conducted research, thus missing an opportunity to reach more robust, more interesting, and sometimes more applicable conclusions. Additionally, a growing number of economists started using research tools typical for this scientific discipline to solve problems that were earlier typical for other disciplines (e.g., analyze human decisions regarding family or living location). Such attitude in itself does not constitute a scientific mistake, yet it cannot be applied indiscriminately as it may lead to results accommodating only certain perspectives such as the evaluation of strictly monetary factors. Critique of this approach may be noticed in accusations formulated in the recent years which led to the analysis of the problems labeled as 'economics imperialism' or 'economization of science'.

Nevertheless, simultaneously among some economists a trend opposite to the above-mentioned could have been observed, initially rather small and limited to certain universities and research institutes. One of its effects is the increasingly wider recognition and application of approaches characteristic for the 'neuroeconomics' category.

Fortunately, the division between economics and other disciplines which focus on similar research problems seems to be decreasing. Moreover, research methods and tools used by many economists are becoming more complex as they incorporate the widely recognized methods from other disciplines. This book, which I had a great pleasure to read, is an important step in this direction. It may be regarded as a sign of the deep change occurring in modern economics – maybe even a substantial shift in its paradigms . Authors present many different aspects of neuroeconomics and issues linked with this approach. As they show, methods of neuroeconomics may be applied to very distant economic topics, ranging from accounting through reaction of managers to media economics.

Neuroeconomics may be defined in various ways from very limited to a much wider field of interdisciplinary science covering various aspects linked with the processes occurring in the human organism and their impact on the undertaken actions. Authors of the presented chapters chose the second approach to the benefit of the reader. I strongly believe this book will of much interest and use to both scientists who may use the presented methods in their own research, and practitioners seeking fuller understanding of the decisions made by market participants (e.g., their clients) and impact on their situation. Furthermore, this book may be read by specialists from other disciplines than economics (or, more generally, business studies) who may use it as an inspiration for further studies and cooperation with researchers concentrating on the business studies.

There also some readings which will be especially interesting for people seeking an overview of the fundamentals of neuroeconomics and current trends in this new research field as well as comparisons between classical models and modern approaches. Another fascinating topic linked with neuroeconomics is different economic behavior patterns in various cultures. It should not be forgotten, though, that discussed issued are not limited to the decisions in the private sector – neuroeconomics, behavioral and game-theory approach apply to public sector as well, as proved in this book.

Increasing popularity of neuroeconomics may mean the dawn of seemingly outdated economic models based on assumptions excluding role of emotions in decision making. Results of the research presented in this book show that the updated models can be more convincing tools. It also proves that the topic of neuroeconomics is undertaken by scientists from different universities in various, often very distant countries; therefore, it may be regarded as a global trend not limited to a few places.

Chapters that seem particularly important in the context of the events in the global economy observed over the last few years are the ones devoted to the financial issues. The growing size of the financial system in comparison to other parts of the economy means understanding the actions of financial markets participants should be an especially important research topic. It often turns out that typical research methods used by economists fail to explain some of the observed phenomena e.g. behavior during times of market stress or transmission of shocks as well as some of the decisions made by investors or other people managing their personal assets. In such cases neuroeconomics can offer a number of useful tools and approaches, including the ones presented in this book: behavioral approach to accounting, neuroaccounting, decision making in finance (e.g., impact of several biases influencing investors), and discussion on the efficient market hypotheses – one of the most controversial topics among the financial academics and finance industry in the recent years.

I trust this valuable book is first in the series of groundbreaking publications, beneficial for the economists and researchers in other disciplines as well as the general public. I also firmly believe it will spark interest among many scientists and practitioners who will follow the route suggested by the authors.

Adam Marszk
Gdańsk University of Technology, Poland

Preface

Human life is one long decision tree – Sterelny

Neuroeconomics is a relatively new field which seeks to ground microeconomic theory regarding how the brain processes multiple alternatives in economic decision-making. As the study of the biological microfoundations of economic cognition and behavior, neuroeconomic research necessitates the investigation of neurobiology but not necessarily a departure from classical economic assumptions and theory. Following years of effort, neuroeconomics began in earnest as an interdisciplinary field in the 1990s combining neuroscience, experimental and behavioral econonics, and cognitive and social psychology.

As a social phenomenon, neuroecomics includes three distinct disciplines: behavioral economics, functional neuroanatomy, and computational learning theory. Since much neuroeconomic research today tends to focus on only one or two of these influences, the (sub)field appears to remain ununified, especially to the layperson. Paul M. Glimcher is considered the field's foremost methodological architect and in his 2009 book, *Neuroeconomics: Decision-Making and the Brain*, Glimcher and his colleagues cover a wide range of major topics related to neuroeconomics such as neoclassical and experimental economics, cognitive neuroscience, non-cooperative games, rational and irrational economic behavior, the neurobiology of judgment, decisions under uncertainty, emotion, and social preferences.

Since these key areas are already covered by established theorists, the purpose of our book is to provide some additional insights into neuroeconomics not normally covered such as conspicuous consumption, behavioral finance and neuroaccounting, media economics, the central language hypothesis in decision-making, mind mapping, and erratic decisions.

Chapter 1 presents the fundamentals of neuroeconomics, thus describing the concept of neuroeconomics; neuroimaging applications; neuroeconomics and loss aversion; neuroeconomics and temporal discounting; neuroeconomics of decision making in humans and animals; neuroeconomics, behavioral economics, and irrationality; neuroeconomics and utility theory; neural systems in economic decision making; neural systems in reward system; neural systems in cognitive control system; game theory, strategic interaction, and neuroeconomic studies; and the types of evidence about economic behavior.

Chapter 2 covers the development of neuroeconomics as a relative new sub-discipline in the fields of economics and behavioral science. After comparing paradigms of both classical and behavioral economics, the problem of the "conscious and rational consumer" is addressed in relation to more passive views of consumerism in neuroeconomics. Pointing out the most recent trends in neuroeconomics, the chapter also addresses the historical development of the discipline of neuroeconomics as an independent field of research within the fields of media and economics. The problem of new marketing strategies as well as the evolvement of neuroeconomics as an independent discipline in the age of digitalization is presented while considering the changing nature of the media industry.

Chapter 3 examines the rational, emotional, and neural foundations of economic preferences. Classical economics assumes that human economic decision making is completely rational and dominated by self-interest. Behavior economics emerged to account for the fact that human economic preferences are often swayed by emotional and psychological factors leading to inconsistent, intransitive and irrational decisions that fail to maximize utility and minimize cost and go beyond self-interest alone. Both rationality and emotions are seated in the human brain in the prefrontal cortex and limbic system respectively. The brain imaging methods of neuroscience help in understanding the interplay between economic behavior and neural mechanisms. Human economic decision making behavior involves computational and neurobiological processes and is related to the psychological processes. Classical Economics, Psychology and Neuroscience converge in Neuroeconomics to better understand and predict human economic decision-making.

Chapter 4 explores the potentially ground-breaking connection between neuroeconomics and the Central Language Hypothesis (CLH) which refers to the language placed within the subconscious mind of an individual. The CLH forwards that in the brains of bilingual and multilingual people, one language is more suppressive as it dominates reflexes, emotions, and senses. This central language (CL) is located at the centre of the limbic cortex of the brain. Therefore, when there is a stimulus on the limbic cortex (e.g., fear, anxiety, sadness), the brain produces the central language. The chapter begins with an Introduction followed by a Theoretical Framework. The next section discusses the neurolinguistic projection of the central language and includes the survey and the results used in this study. The Discussion section provides additional information regarding the questionnaire and the CLH, followed by Future Research Directions, Implications, and finally the Conclusion.

Chapter 5 analyzes cooperation attitude as a driver of contemporary socio-economic societies and organizations. The term of cooperation and culture begins the chapter and refers to intercultural competence becoming a core competence in multiethnic organizations. Furthermore, based on the assumption that difussion of cultures occurs, initiated by globalization, there is a concept of gene-culture co-evolution studies. Next, the cooperation as a social value in strategic human resources management is considered. Cooperation from a neuroeconomics perspective is then discussed. The chapter closes by examining further research implications and then providing the conclusion.

Chapter 6 discusses why individual managers in the same organization who are faced with same environmental changes may differently interpret threat and opportunity aspects of these changes. The chapter also links outcomes of such interpretation to investigate different types of organizational actions. Finally, the chapter further explores how the manager's experience and characteristics of the environment affect forms of reasoning in interpretation process and performance of subsequent organizational actions.

Chapter 7 explains the relationship between economic decision making and emotion in connection with the relationship between economic decision making and the prefrontal cortex. How diverse regions of the brain are coordinated to produce objective-directed decision is the essence of neuroeconomics. Indeed, the latter is a formal framework to describe the involvement of numerous brain regions including frontal, cingulate, parietal cortex, and striatum in economic and financial decision-making processes.

Chapter 8 covers the different types of games, the approaches applied to predict games' outcomes, and general analysis of strategic choices. The chapter underscores key aspects of auction and competitive bidding. As a facet of neuroeconomics, game theory can highly complement the comprehension of human decision making processes. Although the model has somewhat been difficult to many readers, this chapter attempts to present game theory with high level of precision for easy understanding.

Chapter 9 focuses on Functional Magnetic Resonance Imaging (fMRI) as a very effective tool in neuromarketing. Conjoint analysis cards shortens the time required to evaluate attributes related to factors such as fMRI costs, subject fatigue, and participant concentration. Orthogonal matrices keep the amount of conjoint cards to a minimum and shorten the time spent in the fMRI tube to lower costs. Conjoint analysis and fMRI are helpful and strong methods as combined to analyze customer needs and desires.

Chapter 10 questions the applicability of the Efficient Market Hypothesis (EMH) for the analysis of financial markets. The overall goal is to analyze methods of forecasting future prices of financial assets, basing on the concept of the fractal market structure and long-term memory of past prices. Fractals in the financial markets are interpreted either as investors with different investment horizons, or as a configuration of the price movement on chart. The chapter will shed light on the fractal structure of financial markets, nonlinear methods of analysis of financial markets, plasticity and long-term memory to long-term investment horizons of financial markets, fractal analysis of financial markets, and new approaches to forecast prices of financial assets, which eliminate shortcomings of the linear paradigm.

Chapter 11 study substantiates the importance of improving management effectiveness of meso-economic systems in current economic conditions and the features of mesoeconomy as a management object which defines the high complexity of decision making at the mesolevel. A cognitive approach, and an approach involving the integration of the On-Line Analytical Processing (OLAP) and Data Mining (DM) technologies with methods of a multi-criteria assessment of alternative, in particular methods of Multi-Attribute Utility Theory (MAUT) are considered in the chapter. Cognitive mapping of interaction between state and business in a mesoeconomic system are included as a case-study.

Chapter 12 presents an empirical case study concerned with the implementation and use of an electronic property tax collection system in Bangalore (India) developed between 1998 and 2008 to critically examine the role of government in encouraging fiscal compliance from the theoretical perspective of the 'Ecology of Games'.

Chapter 13 explores the implications of behavioral research in accounting and its new stream: neuroaccounting for behavioral finance. It is argued that accounting should be considered by behavioral finance researchers because the product of accounting in form of reports, statements and different analyses represents not only economic standing of a company, but also those behind the scenes including accountants and other participants of accounting processes.

Chapter 14 is focused on the possibilities of game theory as a tool of strategists to interpret practical strategic decision-making situations. Simultaneously, there is a need to simplify presentation of game theory and consider the possibilities of mixed strategies. Practical game situations are relatively complex since even the rules of the game might change during the decision-making process. This chapter shows some practical examples how to describe the strategic game situations in a manner that is relatively easy to understand.

Chapter 15 examines trends and patterns of conspicuous consumption behavior in Asian culture. Purchases of global brands are increasingly popular among affluent society not only in Western countries but also in other parts of the world. Global brands are normally associated with luxury brands from all categories of consumption goods such as cosmetics, handbangs, electronic goods, cell phones and accessories, computers, clothing, watches, shoes, and many more. Previous studies have found that Western countries have clearly stated several key factors for consumers to purchase such luxury brands. Consumers from the Asian market are expected to engage in conspicuous consumption behavior to purchase global brands due to the market demands and increasing income level. The study explores the concept of conspicuous consumption and material value in non-Western culture since this concept is widely studied in Western culture. By examining the conspicuous and materialism, the chapter explain why people are motivated to engage with luxury consumption especially among Asian countries.

Economics is ultimately a decision science, but the term "decision-making" means a wider bio-behavioral process incorporating both passive and active functions encompassing a broad range of cognitive complexity. We hope this book has provided some additional "food-for-thought" regarding the connection between neuroeconomics and decision-making for further research and discourse among academicians as well as practitioners.

Bryan Christiansen
PryMarke LLC, USA

Ewa Lechman
Gdansk University of Technology, Poland

REFERENCES

Anderson, E. (1988). Determinants of opportunistic behavior: An empirical comparison of integrated and independent channels. *Journal of Economic Behavior & Organization, 9*(3), 247–267. doi:10.1016/0167-2681(88)90036-4

Angeletos, G.-M., Laibson, D., Repetto, A., Tobacman, J., & Weinberg, S. (2001, Summer). The hyperbolic consumption model: Calibration, simulation, and empirical evaluation. *The Journal of Economic Perspectives, 15*(3), 47–68. doi:10.1257/jep.15.3.47

Craig, A. D. (2003). Interoception: The sense of the physiological condition of the body. *Current Opinion in Neurobiology, 13*, 500–505. doi:10.1016/S0959-4388(03)00090-4 PMID:12965300

Dadkhah, K. (2011). *Foundations of mathematical and computational economics* (2nd ed.). Berlin, Germany: Springer-Verlag. doi:10.1007/978-3-642-13748-8

Fumagalli, R. (2011). *Philosophical foundations of neuroeconomics: Economics and the revolutionary challenge from neuroscience.* (Unpublished Doctoral Dissertation). London School of Economics, London, UK.

Glimcher, P. W., Camerer, C. F., Fehr, E., & Poldrack, R. A. (2009). *Neuroeconomics: Decision-making and the brain.* London: Academic Press.

Glimcher, P. W., Dorris, M. C., & Bayer, H. M. (2005, August). Physiological utility theory and the neuroeconomics of choice. *Games and Economic Behavior, 52*(2), 213–256. doi:10.1016/j.geb.2004.06.011 PMID:16845435

Hannah, S. T., Waldman, D. A., Balthazard, P. A., Jennings, P. L., & Thatcher, R. W. (2013). The psychological and neurological bases of leader self-complexity and effects on adaptive decision-making. *The Journal of Applied Psychology, 98*(3), 393–411. doi:10.1037/a0032257 PMID:23544481

Hsu, M., Bhatt, M., Adolphs, R., Tranel, D., & Camerer, C. F. (2005, December 9). Neural systems responding to degrees of uncertainty in human decision-making. *Science, 310*(5754), 1680–1683. doi:10.1126/science.1115327 PMID:16339445

Kluckhohn, C. (1962). *Culture and behavior: Collected essays*. New York: The Free Press.

Martins, R. A., Kumar, K., Mukherjee, A., Nabin, M. H., & Bhattacharya, S. (2014). Decision-making in economics: Critical lessons from neurobiology. In B. Christiansen & M. Basılgan (Eds.), *Economic behavior, game theory, and technology in emerging markets* (pp. 46–56). Hershey, PA: IGI Global. doi:10.4018/978-1-4666-4745-9.ch004

Melnyk, S., & Tulusov, I. (2014). Modeling in economics and in the theory of consciousness on the basis of generalized measurements. *NeuroQuantology, 12*(2), 297–312. doi:10.14704/nq.2014.12.2.743

Ostrom, E. (2000). Collective action and the evolution of social norms. *The Journal of Economic Perspectives, 14*(3), 137–158. doi:10.1257/jep.14.3.137

Prendergast, C. (2008). Intrinsic motivation and incentives. *The American Economic Review, 98*(2), 201–205http://www.aeaweb.org/articles.php?doi=10.1257/aer.98.2.201.RetrievedonSeptember222014. doi:10.1257/aer.98.2.201

Şen, Z. (2013). Intelligent business decision-making in global organizations via fuzzy reasoning systems. In B. Christiansen & M. Basılgan (Eds.), *Economic behavior, game theory, and technology in emerging markets* (pp. 127–155). Hershey, PA: IGI Global.

Takahashi, T., Hadzibeganovich, T., Cannas, S. A., Makino, T., Fukui, H., & Kitayama, S. (2009). Cultural neuroeconomics of intertemporal choice. *Activitas Nervosa Superior Rediviva, 51*(1-2), 29–35. PMID:19675524

Tuluzov, I., & Melnyk, S. (2010). Physical methodology for economic systems modeling. *Electronic Journal of Theoretical Physics, 7*(24), 57–79.

Verplanken, R., & Holland, R. W. (2002). Motivated decision-making: Effects of activation and self-centrality of values on choices and behavior. *Journal of Personality and Social Psychology, 82*(3), 434–447. doi:10.1037/0022-3514.82.3.434 PMID:11902626

Wong, K. P. (2012). Optimal two-part pricing under cost uncertainty. *Managerial and Decision Economics, 33*(1), 39–46. doi:10.1002/mde.1559

Acknowledgment

We would like to thank all chapter authors for their excellent contributions regarding this publication effort, as well as all the Editorial Board members and chapter authors who took the time to review the following work during their busy schedules. Without your cooperation and assistance this publication would not have been possible.

Bryan Christiansen
PryMarke LLC, USA

Ewa Lechman
Gdansk University of Technology, Poland

Chapter 1
The Fundamentals of Neuroeconomics

Kijpokin Kasemsap
Suan Sunandha Rajabhat University, Thailand

ABSTRACT

Neuroeconomics is an emergent multidisciplinary field that strives to understand how and why humans make decisions. The field brings together behavioral methods and sophisticated computational theories from microeconomics, an understanding of emotional influences on behavior from psychology, and human functional neural imaging from neuroscience. This chapter presents the fundamentals of neuroeconomics, thus describing the concept of neuroeconomics; neuroimaging applications; neuroeconomics and loss aversion; neuroeconomics and temporal discounting; neuroeconomics of decision making in humans and animals; neuroeconomics, behavioral economics, and irrationality; neuroeconomics and utility theory; neural systems in economic decision making; neural systems in reward system; neural systems in cognitive control system; game theory, strategic interaction, and neuroeconomic studies; and the types of evidence about economic behavior.

INTRODUCTION

Neuroeconomics is an interdisciplinary field that incorporates psychology, economics, neuroscience, and computational science to investigate how people make decisions (Sharp, Monterosso, & Montague, 2012), and Davis (2010) states that the field is a new research program in economics in virtue of its adoption of neuroscience as a basis for the investigation of economic questions. Neuroeconomics focuses its approach in identifying some neuronal correlations specific to choices (Sebastian, 2014), and is the newest area of the economic sciences focusing on how the human brain interacts with its institutional and social environment to make economic decisions (McCabe, 2008).

Zak (2004) forwarded that neuroeconomics is a natural extension of bioeconomics, and the former is the study of evolved mechanisms that are in decision making at the neural level of the brain (Vromen, 2007). The application of conceptual structure and experimental techniques widely used in neuroscience to the study of economic behavior (Glimcher & Rustichini, 2004), neuroeconomics includes the

DOI: 10.4018/978-1-4666-9989-2.ch001

theoretical and methodological developments of cognitive neuroscience, computational neuroscience, psychology, and economics to accomplish the examinations of the brain processes when individuals make economically relevant decisions (Montague, 2007; Sanfey, Loewenstein, McClure, & Cohen, 2006).

The strength of this chapter is on the thorough literature consolidation of neuroeconomics. The extant literature of neuroeconomics provides a contribution to practitioners and researchers by describing a comprehensive view of the functional applications of neuroeconomics to appeal to the different segments of neuroeconomics in order to maximize the business impact of neuroeconomics in the decision-making process.

BACKGROUND

Neuroeconomics is a new field in economics (Glimcher, 2003; Montague & Berns, 2002), and its original program was to provide a test for a large number of competitive theories of decision making (Rustichini, 2009). Neuroeconomic methods combine behavioral economic experiments to parameterize aspects of reward-related decision making with neuroimaging techniques to record the corresponding brain activity (Sharp et al., 2012). In economics, the transfer of neuroscientific insights and methods led to the emergence of neuroeconomics (Hubert, 2010). Whereas traditional economic research explains behavior primarily through theoretical constructs such as utility or preferences, neuroscience considers the physiological aspects and somatic variables that affect decision making.

Neuroeconomics makes the positivistic assumption that the key to explaining human behavior is to understand the neural and physiological processes (Riedl, Hubert, & Kenning, 2010). Neuroeconomists recognize the specific brain activation during the perception of different marketing stimuli (Koenigs & Tranel, 2007). One of the most important intellectual challenges of neuroeconomic research is the translation of theoretical constructs into neurophysiological categories (Hubert, 2010). The integration of neuroscientific approaches and methods into economic research has led to the preliminary findings regarding economic marketing theory and practice (Kenning & Plassmann, 2005). In marketing research, the notion of neuroeconomics has gained attention because the interdisciplinary perspectives to explain the buying decisions are accepted in consumer research (Lee, Broderick, & Chamberlain, 2007).

THE FUNDAMENTALS OF NEUROECONOMICS

This section describes the concept of neuroeconomics; neuroimaging applications; neuroeconomics and loss aversion; neuroeconomics and temporal discounting; neuroeconomics of decision making in humans and animals; neuroeconomics, behavioral economics, and irrationality; neuroeconomics and utility theory; neural systems in economic decision making; neural systems in reward system; neural systems in cognitive control system; game theory, strategic interaction, and neuroeconomic studies; and the types of evidence about economic behavior.

Concept of Neuroeconomics

Neuroeconomics has its root in behavioral economics, a scientific subfield of economics that has adopted psychological research on social, cognitive, and emotional factors to better understand economic decisions (Mohr, Li, & Heekeren, 2010). Bermejo et al. (2011) stated that neuroeconomics is a new science that studies the brain processes involved in taking decisions, particularly related to economy. Neuroeconomics and neuromarketing are the emerging interdisciplinary fields at the interface between neuroscience, psychology, economics, and marketing (Sebastian, 2014).

Neuroeconomics relies on the two problematic steps; namely, the inference from brain activities to the engagement of cognitive processes in experimental tasks, and the presupposition that such inferred cognitive processes are relevant to economic theorizing (Bourgeois-Gironde, 2010). The first step only constitutes the reverse inference fallacy proper and ways to correct it include a better sense of the neural response selectivity of the targeted brain areas and a better definition of relevant cognitive ontologies for neuroeconomics. This second way allows the increased coherence between the cognitive processes involved in neuroeconomics experiments and the theoretical constructs of economics.

Economic decision making is a complex process of integrating and comparing the various aspects of the economically relevant options. Neuroeconomics has made the important progress in grounding these aspects of decision making in neural systems (Mohr et al., 2010). This progress includes the linking of the subfields of economics such as finance (Knutson & Bossaerts, 2007) and marketing (Plassmann, O'Doherty, & Rangel, 2007) with neuroscientific research methodologies. A wide range of studies in animals and humans have identified the neural mechanisms emphasizing the descriptions of value, reward, and risk, which are the important factors affecting economic behavior (Platt & Huettel, 2008; Rangel, Camerer, & Montague, 2008).

Economic decision making is considered as a type of value-based decision making, where the values of different actions are first compared, and the action selected is that corresponding to the highest value (Weber & Johnson, 2009). Two major competing classes of models in economic decision making have been proposed (d'Acremont & Bossaerts, 2008; Glimcher, 2008). The first class of models – utility based models – which includes the expected utility theory and the prospect theory (Kahneman & Tversky, 1979), proposes that decision makers first determine the value and the relative weight of each possible reward and then calculate the overall value of a choice option as the weighted sum of possible outcome values. The second class of models – namely risk-return models – proposes that decision makers first determine the expected reward of each of the alternatives and the associated risk (e.g., variance of rewards), and calculate the value of the alternative as the risk-corrected expected reward (Bell, 1995; Sarin & Weber, 1993).

Both classes of models consider both reward and risk, which is explicitly defined in risk-return models and implicitly influences the value of an alternative in utility-based models via the curvature of the utility function. However, a third factor influences the value of a choice alternative which is specified in the models of intertemporal choice (Kirby, 1997; Laibson, 1997). In addition to the factors that are explicitly specified in models of risky decision making, there are a number of additional second-order factors which do not directly affect the value. These include subject-related factors such as anticipatory emotions (Loewenstein, Weber, Hsee, & Welch, 2001), cognitive abilities, and object-related factors such as framing (Tversky & Kahneman, 1981). Cognitive abilities (e.g., working memory capacity and processing speed) influence the integration of information while estimating risk or expected reward (Mohr et al., 2010).

Neuroeconomics-derived theoretical predictions about the optimal adaptation in a changing environment provide an objective metric to examine psychopathology (Sharp et al., 2012). Neuroeconomics provides a multilevel research approach that combines performance (behavioral) measures with intermediate measures between behavior and neurobiology (e.g., neuroimaging) and uses a common metaphor to describe decision making across the multiple levels of explanation. The potential payoff of neuroeconomics has been debated in different fields (Glimcher, Camerer, Fehr, & Poldrack, 2008).

The most visible debate has been within economics with some economists arguing for the transformative potential of neuroeconomics (Camerer, 2007), and others arguing to keep economics mindless (Gul & Pesendorfer, 2008). Neuroeconomics seeks to ground microeconomic theory in details about how the brain works (Chorvat & McCabe, 2005; Zak, 2004). Glimcher (2004) stated that neuroeconomics can bring a critical inspection concerning economic models and economic behavior. The dopaminergic and serotoninergic brain systems have been identified as the important neurotransmitter systems involved in economic behavior (Mohr et al., 2010). Like dopamine, serotonin sustains significant changes during the adult lifespan (McEntee & Crook, 1991).

The perspectives of neuroeconomics-inspired models that have emerged in the economics literature (Brocas & Carrillo, 2008; Fudenberg & Levine, 2006) presumably argue in favor of the former neuro-economic concern. The extent to which neuroeconomics can inform consumer research (Egidi, Nusbaum, & Cacioppo, 2008), neuroscience (Camerer, 2008), psychology (Loewenstein, Rick, & Cohen, 2008), public policy (Hoffman, 2004), and basic business practices (Shane, 2009) is broadly recognized. Neuroeconomists have investigated several topics of interest to consumer researchers such as spending decisions (Knutson, Rick, Wimmer, Prelec, & Loewenstein, 2007), investment decisions (Kuhnen & Knutson, 2005), the price placebo effect (Plassmann, O'Doherty, Shiv, & Rangel, 2008), charitable giving (Harbaugh, Mayr, & Burghart, 2007), and self-control (Hare, Camerer, & Rangel, 2009). A great deal of contemporary decision research in economics, business, psychology, and neuroscience accepts the notion that emotions play a significant role in decision making (Reimann & Bechara, 2010).

Neuroimaging Applications

Neuroimaging includes the use of various techniques to either directly or indirectly image the structure and function of the nervous system. Neuroimaging is a relatively new discipline within medicine and neuroscience. In exploring the decision making process, a growing number of researchers use an array of tools that record the electrical activity and metabolic activity of the human brain and electroencephalograph (EEG), transcranial magnetic stimulation (TMS), functional magnetic resonance imaging (fMRI), positron emission tomography (Sebastian, 2014). These tools are utilized to explain the neurobiological mechanisms of the decision-making process (Pradeep, 2010; Zurawicki, 2010).

The investigation of whether neuroscientific methods can define the topics of interest to consumer researchers is acknowledged to some extent as described by the fMRI-based studies published in various marketing journals (Hedgcock & Rao, 2009). Neuroeconomic methods combine the behavioral economic experiments to parameterize the aspects of reward-related decision making with neuroimaging techniques to record the corresponding brain activity (Sharp et al., 2012). By explaining economic behavior and decision theory, an attempt is made to elaborate a model that explains in a more accurate way how people make decisions (Glimcher & Rustichini, 2004). Hsu et al. (2005) indicated that neuroeconomics has begun to abandon its near-exclusive reliance on fMRI data in favor of utilizing the multiple methods to better determine causality.

There has been a movement of experimental work on self-control in social psychology where it is primarily conceived as a limited capacity that functions like a muscle (Baumeister, Vohs, & Tice, 2007), although there are great limitations to this concept (Kurzban, 2011). Within systems-level neuroscience research, a common approach relies on simple model tasks taxing behavioral inhibition that are easily paired with neuroimaging such as go/no-go and stop-signal tasks (Monterosso, Piray, & Luo, 2012). Given a systematic mapping between brain function and brain structure, imaging data becomes simply another dependent variable that can be utilized to test between theories (Henson, 2005). Henson et al. (1999) used an imaging experiment to test a dual process model of recognition memory against a single process model.

Neuroeconomics and Loss Aversion

One phenomenon of particular interest to both consumer researchers (Novemsky & Kahneman, 2005) and neuroeconomists is loss aversion which refers to the tendency for losses to have greater hedonic impact than comparable gains. One interesting aspect of human decision making is a strong aversion to potential loss. Context effects refer to everything that biases an individual's affective forecast at the moment of the forecast such as the individual's environmental situation (Schwarz & Strack, 1999) and the motivational state (Buehler, McFarland, Spyropoulos, & Lam, 2007). Individuals fail to empathize with the requirements of their future selves, leading to a discrepancy between predicted utility and experienced utility (Lades, 2012).

Behavior in both risky and riskless contexts regularly reveals that individuals treat losses as if they were more effective than comparable gains (Rick, 2011). If losses are experienced no more intensely than comparable gains, then loss-averse behavior is misguided on both monetary and affective grounds (Kermer, Driver-Linn, Wilson, & Gilbert, 2006). In risky contexts, loss aversion can help to explain widespread risk aversion (Kahneman & Lovallo, 1993), as well as the so-called "St. Petersburg Paradox" (Camerer, 2005). In riskless contexts, loss aversion is normally advocated to explain the endowment effect (Thaler, 1980).

Loss aversion can help to analyze a broad range of phenomena, including the sunk cost fallacy, the attraction effect, the compromise effect, anticipated and experienced regret (Kardes, 1994), the status quo bias (Samuelson & Zeckhauser, 1988), brand choice (Hardie, Johnson, & Fader, 1993), labor supply (Camerer, Babcock, Loewenstein, & Thaler, 1997), the equity premium puzzle (Benartzi & Thaler, 1995), organ donation decisions (Johnson & Goldstein, 2003), and incumbency biases in elections (Quattrone & Tversky, 1988). Loss aversion is diminished for money or goods systematically allocated for exchange (Novemsky & Kahneman, 2005), gambles with small amounts of money (Harnick, Van Dijk, Van Beest, & Mersmann, 2007), gambles whose probabilities are concluded from outcome feedback (Erev, Ert, & Yechiam, 2008), and unattractive goods (Brenner, Rottenstreich, Sood, & Bilgin, 2007). Sellers with considerable marketplace experience (List, 2003) or influenced by incidental sadness (Lerner, Small, & Loewenstein, 2004) or positive mood (Zhang & Fishbach, 2005) tend to acknowledge reduced loss aversion.

Neuroeconomics and Temporal Discounting

Temporal discounting, at a behavioral level, refers to the intertemporal reward preferences often characterized by a decrease in reward value as a function of the delay to its receipt (Rachlin & Green, 1972). Bickel et al. (2007) stated that temporal discounting, considered as a measure of one's location on the continuum of impulsive decision-making to self-control, represents the interaction of these valuation systems and their associated neural networks. The neuroeconomic approach applies the mathematically tractable economic formalizations to the nervous system and focuses on basic economic concepts such as utility (Kable & Glimcher, 2007), risk (Platt & Huettel, 2008), and temporal discounting (Kim, Hwang, & Lee, 2008), thus providing quantitative frameworks for examining the neural mechanisms emphasizing cognitive processes.

Temporal discounting has been examined with tasks that arrange other sequences of questions, questionnaires, and single-item choice assessments (MacKillop, 2013). Bickel et al. (2014) explained that these procedures, although all measuring preferences for smaller sooner versus larger delayed rewards, have been referred to with a variety of different names including delay of gratification, delay discounting, impulsive choice, intertemporal choice, and time preference.

Neuroeconomics of Decision Making in Humans and Animals

Decision making refers to the process of using preferences, selecting and executing actions, and evaluating outcomes (Ernst & Paulus, 2005). Decision making requires the coordinated activity of motivational, emotional, and cognitive circuitry to weigh alternatives, take actions, and learn from feedback (McCabe, 2008). All animals and humans have an instinctive desire to explore their environment which requires neural mechanisms that detect rewards, identify punishments, and learn policies that map the predictive state representations onto a distribution of actions (McCabe, 2008).

Decision making includes preference formation, action selection, and execution and evaluation of outcomes (Sharp et al., 2012). Neuroeconomics, a discipline that marries the mathematical formalisms of classical economics, the psychophysical methods of behavioral economics, and contemporary neurosciences (Glimcher, 2009), provides a descriptive test of the functionality-based classification scheme for defining mechanistic pathologies in decision making (Kalenscher & van Wingerden, 2011).

In designing a cognitive neuroscience experiment, the experimenter must decide whether or not to study human or nonhuman brains (McCabe, 2008). Nonhuman brains are often used as models of the human brain based on the evolutionary hypothesis that the human brain evolved over time by extending homologous functions, and computations, in predecessor brains (Gazzaniga, Ivry, & Mangun, 2002). In nonhuman brains, the experimenter can use the lesion experiments, genetic manipulations, neuronal stimulation of specific neurons, and single-cell recordings methods to measure neuronal signals and neuronal connectivity in order to reconstruct neuronal mechanisms and learn how they compute (Gazzaniga et al., 2002).

Concerning the single-unit recordings methods in animals and neuroimaging in humans, the striatal dopaminergic signaling is critical for reward-related processing, motivation, and learning (Montague, Hyman, & Cohen, 2004). The dysfunctional dopaminergic signaling disrupts the reward anticipation in drug addiction (Schultz, 2011). Morris et al. (2006) indicated that the firing rates of midbrain dopamine neurons compute economic decision parameters (e.g., reward probability, reward delay, and reward uncertainty). Dopaminergic signaling is included in assessing the economic costs and benefits of upcoming rewards.

Neurons in rodent nucleus accumbens encode anticipated reward benefits without encoding response costs to achieve the reward (Gan, Walton, & Phillips, 2010). The nucleus accumbens has a significant role in the cognitive processing of motivation, pleasure, and reinforcement learning, and thus has significant role in addiction. The economic computations by the mesolimbic dopamine system contribute to addiction and other motivation-related disorders (Chang, Barack, & Platt, 2012).

Temporal discounting describes a time-dependent devaluation of economic value (Green & Myerson, 2004), and is a phenomenon observed across multiple species including rodents, monkeys, and humans

(Hwang, Kim, & Lee, 2009). When provided an option to choose an immediate but smaller reward over a larger reward with a longer delay, animals reliably prefer the immediate option (Myerson & Green, 1995). Addicted individuals discount more than non-addicted individuals (Schultz, 2011). Single-unit recordings in monkeys demonstrate that neurons in the striatum mediate computations underlying temporal discounting (Cai, Kim, & Lee, 2011).

Cardinal et al. (2001) indicated that the rats with nucleus accumbens lesions display severe difficulty in choosing a delayed reward option in an intertemporal choice task, suggesting a critical role of nucleus accumbens in computing economic values of rewards in time. Parkinson et al. (1999) stated that the nucleus accumbens lesions do not abolish the reward sensitivity altogether but impair the implementation of an optimal strategy as if these animals cannot accurately compute temporally discounted utility to guide decisions. Neural correlates of temporal discounting are found in the prefrontal cortex (Kim & Lee, 2011).

Neuroeconomics, Behavioral Economics, and Irrationality

Behavioral economics has its roots in the law of demand which states that the demand for a commodity decreases in a mathematically defined manner as its unit price increases (Hursh, 1984). Rowland et al. (2008) indicated that economists have used behavioral economics concepts to understand economies and consumer behavior, and it has become clear that groups of humans do not function in an economically optimal manner, defined, for example, as paying the least possible unit price among an array of choices. Behavioral economics emerges against the backdrop of the dominant normative approach to economic modeling recognized as the rational choice theory (Monterosso et al., 2012). Economic evaluation is often complicated by quality or perceived quality of goods, or too many concurrent choices (Wansink, 2004). The field of consumerism is the study of why people make particular choices in the particular markets (Dagevos, 2005).

Bickel et al. (2012) indicated that modern behavioral economic and neuroeconomic approaches consider addiction to function, in part, as a possible valuation disorder wherein normal decision-making mechanisms become dysfunctional, resulting in pathological reward processing. The study of human choice behavior and the neurobiology has received attention in recent neuroimaging studies (Padoa-Schioppa & Assad, 2006). Neuroeconomics seeks to understand the neural basis of decision making (Glimcher, 2003). In some situations, humans strongly deviate from statistical optimality in their judgments, and exhibit inconsistent or irrational preferences (Summerfield & Tsetsos, 2015).

Humans choosing among economic alternatives are often unduly swayed by irrelevant contextual factors, leading to inconsistent or intransitive decisions that fail to maximize potential reward (Kahneman, Slovic, & Tversky, 1982). Rationality is operationalized with a small set of minimum requirements that need to be satisfied for behavior to be coherent and orderly over time (Arrow, 1986). When measurement of brain function became affordable and accessible, many behavioral economists welcomed the idea of incorporating brain data into modeling, in the hope that modeling could be improved by identifying neurobiological gears between input and output. Irrational economic behavior can arise if the brain computes and represents stimulus value relative to the context provided by other previously (Stewart, Chater, & Brown, 2006) or currently available options (Louie, Khaw, & Glimcher, 2013).

Behavioral economists have collaborated with neuroimaging researchers seeking to identify brain correlates of behavioral economic phenomena, especially the sources of irrationality (Breiter, Aharon, Kahneman, Dale, & Shizgal, 2001). Concerning irrationality, the deficiencies in many contexts motivated a breakaway group of economists and psychologists to pay special attention to irrationality to develop more descriptively accurate alternatives (Camerer & Loewenstein, 2004). These divergences include non-normative probability weighting (Edwards, 1954), incomplete search of option space (Simon, 1967), reference dependence in utility judgments (Kahneman & Tversky, 1979), weighing delays nonuniformly (Laibson, 1997), and emotional state dependent utility (Loewenstein, 1996).

Neuroeconomics and Utility Theory

Although decision makers are reported to have difficulties in making comparisons among multidimensional decision outcomes, economic theory assumes a unidimensional utility measure (Witt & Binder, 2013). The decision makers' difficulties can be explained once the motivational aspects of utility (e.g., wanting) are disentangled from the experiential ones (e.g., liking) and the features of the different brain processes involved are recognized (Witt & Binder, 2013). At the essence of microeconomic theorizing lies the concept of individual preferences. It is the outcome of a century-long transformation of utility theory and its core notions (Bruni & Sugden, 2007).

In behavioral economics (Winkielman & Berridge, 2003), the two qualities of utility as motivator and experienced reward are identified with the concepts of wanting and liking, respectively. The motivational aspect of choosing an action can be identified with the notion of wanting (Berridge, 1999), which relates to appetite or incentive motivation in biology. The incentive value of an action (e.g., the reward) expected in terms of enjoying pleasures or relief from pain related to the forward looking preferences. Unless entirely random, the choice of an action is contingent on some form of expectations (Kahneman, Wakker, & Sarin, 1997). The wanting and liking features are not causally independent of each other and possess different neural correlates (Knutson & Peterson, 2005).

Without going into the details of brain imaging (e.g., EEG, TMS, fMRI, and positron emission tomography), studies on reward processing have opened up to some extent what was previously a "black box"; namely, the brain activities that are triggered when an individual encounters a rewarding object (McClure, York, & Montague, 2004). By considering how pleasure is coded in the brain (Kringelbach & Berridge, 2010), the neurobiology of reward can differentiate between the three psychological components of reward (Berridge & Kringelbach, 2008). The components are the learning, liking, and wanting. Individual organisms learn that goal objects are rewarding because of their affective (hedonic) qualities and because of the incentive salience (the wanting) that is attached to these hedonic qualities. All three component parts (learning, liking, and wanting) are mediated by the interactive neural systems (Witt & Binder, 2013).

While different tasks in general activate different brain regions, rewarding stimuli seem to consistently activate the same specific regions. Dopamine systems project from the ventral tegmental area to the nucleus accumbens (i.e., a part of the ventral striatum), amygdala, and frontal cortex and from the substantia nigra to the dorsal striatum (Becker & Meisel, 2007). The substantia nigra is a brain structure located in the mesencephalon (midbrain) that plays an important role in reward, addiction, and movement.

Besides these core areas, the orbitofrontal cortex (i.e., a part of the prefrontal cortex), the ventral pallidum, and the ventral striatum play an important role as the brain substrates of reward processing. The orbitofrontal cortex has been found to receive the direct input from primary taste and olfactory cortices as well as from higher-order visual and somatosensory areas (Kringelbach, 2005). It is an ideal place for the storage of reward values of sensory stimuli (McClure et al., 2004). The amygdala seems to be involved in processing the intensity of positive and negative stimuli. The ventral striatum plays an important role concerning rewards because of its connection with the mesencephalic (midbrain) dopamine system and the orbitofrontal cortex and amygdala (Holland & Gallagher, 1999).

The release of the neurotransmitter dopamine from the ventral tegmental area on the nucleus accumbens has been recognized as the mediating pleasure (Salamone, Correa, Farrar, & Mingote, 2007). The release of dopamine does not seem relevant for generating liking (Robinson & Berridge, 2003). Activation or suppression of mesolimbic dopamine systems does not change the liking of sweet tastes (Leyton, 2010). Lesions that eliminate dopamine in the nucleus accumbens do not impair the liking either (Berridge & Robinson, 1998). Dopamine plays a role in reward processing by mediating the wanting and learning (Caplin & Dean, 2008).

Neural Systems in Economic Decision Making

Evidence from a range of fMRI studies indicates that the ventral striatum and the ventromedial prefrontal cortex are implicated in the representations of reward (Elliott, Newman, Longe, & Deakin, 2003). These brain regions are not only shown to code for the reward itself at the time of its delivery, but also activated by reward-predicting stimuli in the anticipation of reward (Preuschoff, Bossaerts, & Quartz, 2006). In the context of risk processing, many studies have shown the following four key regions to be involved: the anterior cingulate cortex, the anterior insula, the dorsolateral prefrontal cortex, and the ventral striatum (Rushworth & Behrens, 2008). The anterior insula plays an important role in affective influences on decision making (Winkielman, Knutson, Paulus, & Trujil, 2007) and is related to the aversive emotions such as disgust (Adolphs, 2002). Risk-related activity in the anterior insula can reflect the processing of affective responses to risk, as suggested by some theories on risk (Loewenstein et al., 2001).

Basic neuroeconomic games allow for the modeling of the effects of beliefs and affect on reward processing (Sharp et al., 2012). Delgado et al. (2005) used a neuroeconomics game (e.g., trust task) to show that prior social and emotional information on trust game partners modulates reward responses in the brains of healthy adults. Sharp et al. (2011) showed that the modulation of insula responses is absent in the brains of boys with externalizing behavior problems. King-Casas et al. (2008) indicated that the norms used in perception of social gestures are pathologically perturbed among individuals with the borderline personality disorder, with differential insula activation in these patients compared with normal control subjects. The contribution of neuroeconomics games is the largest in the domain of social interaction (King-Casas & Chiu, 2012) where social-cognitive research with traditional methods has struggled to find ways to reach the real-life social interaction with ecological validity.

Neuroeconomics has started investigating the effect of delayed rewards resulting in partly ambiguous results (Ballard & Knutson, 2009). Neuroeconomic tasks are designed to more closely mirror the physical mechanisms of reward processing by tapping directly into utility functions while outcome uncertainty during anticipation in a monetary reward task is probed (Knutson, Bhanji, Cooney, Atlas, & Gotlib, 2008). Declerck et al. (2013) indicated that the motivation to cooperate generated by the reward system in the brain (extending from the striatum to the ventromedial prefrontal cortex), is modulated by two neural networks: a cognitive control system (centered on the lateral prefrontal cortex) and a social cognition system (including the temporo-parietal junction, the medial prefrontal cortex, and the amygdala) that processes trust and threat signals.

The mesolimbic reward system is formed by dopaminergic projections emanating from cell groups in the ventral tegmental area in the midbrain which loop through the limbic nuclei, the dopamine-rich nucleus accumbens in the ventral striatum, and connect to the ventromedial prefrontal cortex (Tekin &

Cummings, 2002). This medial dopaminergic pathway is applied to facilitate the affective and appetitive behavior (Schultz, 2002) and incentive motivation (Depue & Collins, 1999). It is activated when people receive or expect to receive a reward (Tricomi, Rangel, Camerer, & O'Doherty, 2010).

The ventromedial prefrontal cortex is implicated when subjects make an active choice and select the most valuable option (Rangel & Hare, 2010) and has been recognized to have a more general role in response selection and action planning (Schoenbaum, Setlow, & Ramus, 2003). Hare et al. (2008) stated that the brain region acts as an information aggregator, comparing and selecting the best option from a set of alternatives. However, the brain region responds to the reward value of a single item, when there is no choice required and no immediate alternative with which to compare (Knutson, Taylor, Kaufman, Peterson, & Glover, 2005).

Neural Systems in Reward Systems

The reward, called experienced utility in economics, is unidimensional as regards its neural correlates, lending support to the unidimensional measure for utility. Reward is processed along a single final common pathway in brain regions (McClure et al., 2004). The brain converts multidimensional payoff records into one single common currency (Kringelbach & Berridge, 2010). The plausibility of the common currency hypothesis of reward does not seem to be affected (Leknes & Tracey, 2008). The neural currency is the foundation of experiencing the reward associated with the goal objects (Witt & Binder, 2013). Basic research on the neuromodulation of reward processing (Schultz, 2006) indicates that economic decision making (e.g., reward processing) is influenced by dopamine (Fiorillo, Tobler, & Schultz, 2003).

While dopamine is associated with incentive motivation and wanting, the intense pleasurable feelings, gratification, and liking systematically involve the opioids and the gonadal steroids oxytocin and vasopressin (Declerck et al., 2013). In the striatum, the nucleus accumbens shell has been recognized as a site of integration of incentive information because it receives projections from many corticolimbic structures and contains opiate and oxytocin receptors (Depue & Morrone-Strupinsky, 2005). Functional interactions between dopamine and opioids (Depue & Morrone-Strupinsky, 2005) and between dopamine and oxytocin (Skuse & Gallagher, 2008) contribute to the hedonic effects accompanying reward, but these contributions appear to be independent of dopamine's role in assessing the salience of reward cues (Depue & Morrone-Strupinsky, 2005).

Fehr and Camerer (2007) indicated there is the extensive overlap of activation in the striatum between rewards for oneself (e.g., receiving or expecting a sum of money) and rewarding others (e.g., voluntarily giving money away). Izuma et al. (2010) confirmed with an fMRI experiment that the ventral striatum is activated when publically donating money to charity as well as when privately receiving money. For the brain, extrinsic lucrative rewards are equivalent to the intrinsic affective rewards stemming from socially motivated decisions (Declerck et al., 2013). Within the medial system, the ventromedial prefrontal cortex is well-positioned to serve as an interface between emotional and motivational processes, and therefore to shape the anticipation of reward. Being a highly connected integration center, it represents what a current choice is worth to the decision makers (Fellows, 2007) in accordance with their own moral goals (Hare et al., 2009). Regarding the emotional input of the ventromedial prefrontal cortex, Tekin and Cummings (2002) indicated that the medial system mediates the empathic and motivated behavior.

Dopamine neurotransmission in the reward system plays a critical role in the process of evaluating whether or not on its value, the cooperative decisions making can be maintained or interrupted to be replaced by decisions that lead to more satisfying outcomes (Declerck et al., 2013). The dopamine-rich caudate nucleus, previously linked to learning and memory, is an essential component in the reinforcement of actions potentially leading to reward (Tricomi, Delgado, & Fiez, 2004). The dopamine-rich caudate nucleus is involved in updating information to either modify future behavior in accordance with environmental changes, or to keep the status quo as long as expectations are met (Delgado, 2007). Decisions to donate effectively activate the oxytocin-rich subgenual area that is a brain region connected to the mesolimbic dopamine reward system related to the social attachment formation (Bartels & Zeki, 2004).

Both ventral striatum and dorsal striatum integrate inputs from other networks, including regions located in the lateral prefrontal cortex implicated in cognitive control (Staudinger, Erk, Abler, & Walter, 2009), and the temporal parietal junction included in the social cognition (Hare, Camerer, Knoepfle, & Rangel, 2010). Baumgartner et al. (2008) stated that the activity in the dorsal striatum can be developed by oxytocin or by information regarding the trustworthiness of others. Oxytocin, the neurotransmitter involved in the trusting behavior (Kosfeld, Heinrichs, Zak, Fischbacher, & Fehr, 2005), can interact with dopamine release in the ventral striatum to affect the social motivation (Skuse & Gallagher, 2008).

Neural Systems in Cognitive Control System

Paralleling the medial dopaminergic system, which is related to the forming expectations of reward, runs a lateral dopaminergic pathway that originates in a different population of cells in the ventral tegmental area and connects the substantia nigra in the midbrain with the dorsal striatum and stimulates the lateral regions of the prefrontal cortex (Tekin & Cummings, 2002). This lateral system evolved in full more recently during primate evolution and supports the executive functions which are crucial to adapt the goal-directed behavior to the changing environmental contingencies (Previc, 2009). The dorsolateral prefrontal cortex is an essential component of the working memory and executive functions (Miller & Cohen, 2001) and provides the cognitive capacities needed to resolve the conflict generated by the mixed intentions of a social dilemma (Carter & van Veen, 2007). An additional function of the dorsolateral prefrontal cortex is to provide the impulse control to resist the immediate selfish dedication in order to acknowledge the greater cooperative benefits at a later time (McClure et al., 2004).

Working in harmony with the dorsolateral prefrontal cortex, the dorsal anterior cingulate cortex is included in the conflict monitoring whenever there are the competing motives such as those presented in the social dilemmas (Carter, Botvinick, & Cohen, 1999). The dorsal anterior cingulate cortex is located in the posterior medial part of the frontal cortex and interconnected with the dorsolateral prefrontal cortex and the ventral striatum (Alexander, DeLong, & Strick, 1986). The human orbitofrontal cortex is an important brain region for the processing of rewards and punishments, which is a prerequisite for the emotional and social behaviors which contribute to the evolutionary success of humans (Kringelbach & Rolls, 2004). McClure et al. (2004) hypothesized that the discrepancy between the short-term and long-term choices in human time discounting reflects the differential activation of distinguishable neural systems. McClure et al. (2004) measured the brain activity of participants as they made an array of intertemporal choices between early and later monetary rewards. The early rewards have a lower value than the later rewards (McClure et al., 2004).

Game Theory, Strategic Interaction, and Neuroeconomic Studies

Game theory is the formal study of decision making where several players must make choices that potentially affect the interests of other players. Game theory provides models, known as games, to study the interactions with formalized incentive structures (Braeutigam, 2005). Such games are of profound theoretical importance in economics where individual wishes to model the processes in which the opti-mality of a course of economic action is affected by decision makers and competitors (Glimcher, 2002). Game theory relates to strategic thinking implicit in the notion of equilibrium and common knowledge of rationality (Griessinger & Coricelli, 2015). The emergence of bounded rationality models (Gigerenzer & Selten, 2002) and the behavioral game theory provide a theoretical framework in order to solve the neural roots of strategic reasoning and emphasize the decision-making mechanisms involved in social interaction. Game theory defines the strategic interactions as games representing decisions between agents where individual's payoffs depend on the other's actions, thus extending the model of individual's decision making to the understanding of the interactions in multi-agents situations (Griessinger & Coricelli, 2015).

The Nash Equilibrium, also called strategic equilibrium, is a list of strategies, one for each player, which has the property that no player can unilaterally change his or her strategy and obtain a better payoff. Several experimental and empirical studies show behavioral responses that deviate from the prescription of standard game theory and report the evidence of non-equilibrium play (Costa-Gomes, Crawford, & Broseta, 2001). Equilibrium play in normal form games corresponds to a distinctive pattern (in terms of transitions in the visual information acquisition between own and other player's payoffs), and any deviation generates non-equilibrium responses. Quantal response equilibrium (QRE) belongs to a class of bounded rationality models that relaxes the assumption of the best response and considers errors in choices, keeping the assumption of statistically accurate beliefs and equilibrium responses (McKelvey & Palfrey, 1995). QRE theory has several features in common with findings in recent neuroeconomics literature on noisy and stochastic choice (Haile, Hortacsu, & Kosenok, 2008). QRE can be reduced to a form of bounded accumulation models (Dickhaut, Rustichini, & Smith, 2009), a class of models that has been proven relevant to capture under a common theoretical framework stochasticity in value-based decision, reaction time, and visual fixation (Krajbich, Armel, & Rangel, 2010).

Neuroeconomic studies of coordination games have taken advantage of the established correlations between the populations of neurons in various brain areas and the mental processes in an attempt to validate theoretical models of how people solve the coordination problems (Bourgeois-Gironde, 2010). Coricelli and Nagel (2009) identified the neural substrates of strategizing in the beauty contest games. The successful strategic reasoning in that game effectively correlates with neural activity in the medial prefrontal cortex (Coricelli & Nagel, 2009). Jeankins et al. (2008) examined the repetition suppression of a brain region in cognitive tasks that consist in the introspection of individual's own mental states versus inferences about whether other people are having similar mental states. The neural bases of the human mentalizing ability have immediate neuroeconomic importance in order to clarify the cognitive basis of strategizing as it is captured by game theory (Singer & Fehr, 2005).

Sanfey et al. (2003) investigated by the neural basis of economic decision making in the ultimatum game by using the fMRI. The subjects act as responders in a game where they can either accept or reject an offer made by a proposer who decides how to split a given sum of money between the two. Standard utility theory (Frank, 2003) predicts that the responders accept any offer in this game, on the grounds that any monetary gain is better than none. The unfair offers have a significant chance of being rejected when the proposer is a human being as opposed to a computer (Sanfey et al., 2003). Activity in anterior insula is significantly increased for the rejected unfair offers, suggesting a key role for the emotion in choice and decision making (Braeutigam, 2005).

Smith et al. (2002) utilized the positron emission tomography to study neuronal responses in subjects choosing between risky games (i.e., known payoffs with well-defined probabilities) and ambiguous games (i.e., known payoffs with undefined probabilities). The main finding in that study is a behavioral interaction effect between outcome structure (e.g., risk and ambiguity) and payoff structure (e.g., loss and gain). The interaction effect observed in that study is contrary to standard economic reasoning, where individual assumes the evaluations of outcomes and payoffs to be independent (Braeutigam, 2005). McCabe et al. (2001) applied the fMRI to study the neuronal mechanisms indicating the cooperation in the two-person reciprocal exchange. The observations made in that study suggest that in a game of trust and reciprocity, the cooperative subjects considerably exhibit more activity in the frontal pole (e.g., Brodmann area 10 in neural systems) than non-cooperative players. The main finding in that study can bear on the studies of pervasive developmental disorders (e.g., autism) associated with deficits in theory of mind processes (Siegal & Varley, 2002).

Rilling et al. (2004) tested the possible role of the dopamine prediction error in evaluating the outcome of a cooperative decision in the fMRI experiment using the prisoner's dilemma paradigm. The prisoner's dilemma is a classic non-zero sum game often used to investigate cooperation in evolutionary biology, social psychology, and behavioral economics. Two players have to independently choose to cooperate (C) or defect (D) and will be awarded a sum of money in the function of the choices that they make. There are the four possible outcomes of the game: both players cooperate (CC); both players defect (DD), player 1 cooperates and player 2 defects (CD), or vice versa (DC).

The payoffs for these different outcomes are such that DC > CC > DD > CD. When played only once, DC is the dominant strategy because, irrespective of the strategy of the other player, a rational player has no incentive to deviate from this choice. The brain contrasts between reciprocated and unreciprocated cooperation indicated that only reciprocated cooperation activated the ventral striatum and the ventro-medial prefrontal cortex (Declerck et al., 2013). This activity reflects a positive prediction error (i.e., the discrepancy between reward estimate and actual outcome) from which the player can learn whether to keep on cooperating or to switch to a different strategy (Declerck et al., 2013).

The intrinsically rewarding value of cooperation without remuneration has been illustrated with fMRI. Decety et al. (2004) compared the neural correlates of cooperation and competition during a computer game whereby players had to construct a target pattern either alone, with another person (cooperation) or against another person (competition). Compared to competition, cooperation is associated with increased activity in the ventromedial prefrontal cortex and the posterior cingulate cortex. Decety et al. (2004) interpreted these results to be consistent with prepositions that people seek cooperation because it is socially more rewarding than competing. Krajbich et al. (2009) stated that the role of the ventromedial prefrontal cortex in generating positive affect from social interaction is confirmed by a study of patients with the ventromedial prefrontal cortex lesions.

The ventromedial prefrontal cortex patients are less generous and less trustworthy in a battery of economic games concerning the inability to experience social emotions (Bechara & Damasio, 2005). The hedonic rewards deriving from cooperation result from the fact that many people are intrinsically motivated to cooperate out of fairness considerations (Tabibnia & Lieberman, 2007). People are motivated to make decisions they consider to be morally right (Declerck et al., 2013). Moral judgments whether or not it is right to seize the life of one person to save several others activate the ventromedial prefrontal cortex. Patients with the ventromedial prefrontal cortex lesions are more likely to authorize utilitarian responses (Young & Koenigs, 2007).

Types of Evidence about Economic Behavior

Neuroeconomics provides three types of evidence regarding economic behavior as follows: (1) evidence which suggest the influence of new variables that are implicit, underweighed, or missing in the rational choice theory; (2) evidence which show mechanisms that implement the rational choice (e.g., utility maximization and the Bayesian integration of information), typically in tasks that are highly sculpted to make decisions that are useful for survival across species (e.g., vision, food, sex, and safety); and (3) evidence which support the kinds of variables and parameters introduced in behavioral economics in terms of time discounting, ambiguity aversion, nonlinear probability weighting, and limited strategic thinking. Firstly, the goal at the evidence for new psychological variables is to show that understanding biology and the brain can make fresh predictions about observed choices. Debates between rational choice and behavioral models usually revolve around psychological constructs, such as loss aversion (Kahneman & Tversky, 1979), the role of learning and limited strategic thinking, a preference for immediate rewards, and precise preferences over social allocations, which have not been observed directly.

Secondly, the evolution regarding evidence for the rational choice principles has either created neural circuits which reach the Bayesian rational choice, or learning mechanisms that generate the Bayesian rational choice with sufficient experience in a stationary environment, putting to use the highly developed capacities for sensory evaluation (e.g., vision, taste, and smell), memory, and social imitation. Platt and Glimcher (1999) found the remarkable neurons in monkey's lateral intraparietal cortex correlated with the expected value of juice rewards, triggered by a monkey's eye movement (Bayer & Glimcher, 2005). Deaner et al. (2005) stated that monkeys can reliably negotiate the juice rewards with exposure to the visual images.

Thirdly, the behavioral economics principles concerning evidence for behavioral economics principles explain the four areas in which neuroscience has established the tentative neural foundation for ideas from behavioral economics which are derived from experiments and field data. The four areas of behavioral economics principles involve time discounting, ambiguity aversion, nonlinear probability weighting, and limited strategic thinking.

1. Time discounting: Extensive experiments with animals, and later with humans, established that the discount factor put on future rewards is closer to a hyperbola, $1/(1+kt)$, than an exponentially-declining discount factor δ^t.
2. Ambiguity aversion: In subjective expected utility theory, the willingness to take bets on events is taken to reveal subjective probabilities of those events. The Ellsberg Paradox showed that for a small majority of subjects, when two events are equally likely but poorly understood, the revealed decision weights seem to combine judgment of likelihood and an additional factor which leads to an aversion to betting under ambiguity.
3. Nonlinear probability weighting: In the expected utility theory, the utilities of gamble outcomes are weighted by their probability p. But many experimental studies suggest that people actually weight probabilities nonlinearly with a function $\pi(p)$, overweighting low probabilities and underweighting probabilities close to the certainty effect.
4. Limited strategic thinking: In game theory, players are in equilibrium when they guess correctly what other players will do. When their beliefs about other players' strategies match the actual strategies others choose. Camerer et al. (2004) described an alternative cognitive hierarchy theory in which

players use various steps of strategic thinking. Some step-0 players randomize, other step-1 players anticipate randomization and best-respond to it, step-2 players best-respond to a mixture of step-0 and step-1 players, and so on. Since the highest-step players anticipate correctly the distribution of what other players will do, their beliefs are in equilibrium, but the beliefs of lower-step thinkers are not in equilibrium because they do not guess correctly what higher-step players will do.

FUTURE RESEARCH DIRECTIONS

The strength of this chapter is on the thorough literature consolidation of neuroeconomics. The extant literature of neuroeconomics provides a contribution to practitioners and researchers by describing a comprehensive view of the functional applications of neuroeconomics to appeal to the different segments of neuroeconomics in order to maximize the business impact of neuroeconomics in the decision-making process. The classification of the extant literature in the domains of neuroeconomics will provide the potential opportunities for future research. Future research direction should broaden the perspectives in implementation of neuroeconomics to be utilized in the knowledge-based organizations.

Practitioners and researchers should acknowledge the applicability of a more multidisciplinary approach toward research activities in implementing neuroeconomics in terms of knowledge management-related variables (e.g., knowledge-sharing behavior, knowledge creation, organizational learning, learning orientation, and motivation to learn). It will be useful to bring additional disciplines together (e.g., strategic management, marketing, finance, and human resources) to support a more holistic examination of neuroeconomics in order to combine or transfer existing theories and approaches to inquiry in this area.

CONCLUSION

This chapter presented the fundamentals of neuroeconomics, thus describing the concept of neuroeconomics; neuroimaging applications; neuroeconomics and loss aversion; neuroeconomics and temporal discounting; neuroeconomics of decision making in humans and animals; neuroeconomics, behavioral economics, and irrationality; neuroeconomics and utility theory; neural systems in economic decision making; neural systems in reward system; neural systems in cognitive control system; game theory, strategic interaction, and neuroeconomic studies; and the types of evidence about economic behavior.

Research in neuroeconomics has revealed the potential representations of value and costs within the brain. Understanding how the brain uses information about uncertainty when making decisions, and the brain circuits and chemicals involved in that process, effectively form the foundation for this emerging field. Studying the brain's decision-making processes using a combination of techniques from the fields of psychology, neuroscience, and economics, neuroeconomics determines the practical understanding of the brain's decision-making processes, thus challenging age-old assumptions to support more tailored research, treatment options, and greater insight into how and why judgments are formed.

Regarding neuroeconomics, the studies of decision making in social environments have explained the emotional components of decision making that may help to explain some deviations from optimal decision making in humans. Neuroeconomics brings together behavioral methods and sophisticated computational theories from microeconomics, an understanding of emotional influences on behavior from psychology, and human functional neural imaging from neuroscience. It is essential for modern organizations to understand their neuroeconomics applications and develop a strategic plan to regularly check their practical advancements of neuroeconomics toward achieving improved organizational performance.

REFERENCES

Adolphs, R. (2002). Neural systems for recognizing emotion. *Current Opinion in Neurobiology, 12*(2), 169–177. doi:10.1016/S0959-4388(02)00301-X PMID:12015233

Alexander, G. E., DeLong, M. R., & Strick, P. L. (1986). Parietal organization of functionally segregated circuits linking basal ganglia and cortex. *Annual Review of Neuroscience, 9*(1), 357–381. doi:10.1146/annurev.ne.09.030186.002041 PMID:3085570

Arrow, K. J. (1986). Rationality of self and others in an economic system. *The Journal of Business, 59*(4), S385–S399. doi:10.1086/296376

Ballard, K., & Knutson, B. (2009). Dissociable neural representations of future reward magnitude and delay during temporal discounting. *NeuroImage, 45*(1), 143–150. doi:10.1016/j.neuroimage.2008.11.004 PMID:19071223

Bartels, A., & Zeki, S. (2004). The neural correlates of maternal and romantic love. *NeuroImage, 21*(3), 1155–1166. doi:10.1016/j.neuroimage.2003.11.003 PMID:15006682

Baumeister, R. F., Vohs, K. D., & Tice, D. M. (2007). The strength model of self-control. *Current Directions in Psychological Science, 16*(6), 351–355. doi:10.1111/j.1467-8721.2007.00534.x

Baumgartner, T., Heinrichs, M., Vonlanthen, A., Fischbacher, U., & Fehr, E. (2008). Oxytocin shapes the neural circuitry of trust and trust adaptation in humans. *Neuron, 58*(4), 639–650. doi:10.1016/j.neuron.2008.04.009 PMID:18498743

Bayer, H. M., & Glimcher, P. W. (2005). Midbrain dopamine neurons encode a quantitative reward prediction error signal. *Neuron, 47*(1), 129–141. doi:10.1016/j.neuron.2005.05.020 PMID:15996553

Bechara, A., & Damasio, A. R. (2005). The somatic marker hypothesis: A neural theory of economic decision. *Games and Economic Behavior, 52*(2), 336–372. doi:10.1016/j.geb.2004.06.010

Becker, J. B., & Meisel, R. L. (2007). Neurochemistry and molecular neurobiology of reward. In A. Lajtha & J. D. Blaustein (Eds.), *Handbook of neurochemistry and molecular neurobiology* (pp. 739–774). New York, NY: Springer–Verlag. doi:10.1007/978-0-387-30405-2_20

Bell, D. E. (1995). Risk, return, and utility. *Management Science, 41*(1), 23–30. doi:10.1287/mnsc.41.1.23

Benartzi, S., & Thaler, R. H. (1995). Myopic loss aversion and the equity premium puzzle. *The Quarterly Journal of Economics, 110*(1), 73–92. doi:10.2307/2118511

Bermejo, P. E., Dorado, R., Zea-Sevilla, M. A., & Menéndez, V. S. (2011). Neuroanatomy of financial decisions. *Neurologia (Barcelona, Spain), 26*(3), 173–181. doi:10.1016/j.nrl.2010.09.015 PMID:21163202

Berridge, K. C. (1999). Pleasure, pain, desire, and dread: Hidden core processes of emotion. In D. Kahneman, E. Diener, & N. Schwarz (Eds.), *Well-being: The foundations of hedonic psychology* (pp. 525–557). New York, NY: Russell Sage Foundation.

Berridge, K. C., & Kringelbach, M. L. (2008). Affective neuroscience of pleasure: Reward in humans and animals. *Psychopharmacology*, *199*(3), 457–480. doi:10.1007/s00213-008-1099-6 PMID:18311558

Berridge, K. C., & Robinson, T. E. (1998). What is the role of dopamine in reward: Hedonic impact, reward learning, or incentive salience? *Brain Research Reviews*, *28*(3), 309–369. doi:10.1016/S0165-0173(98)00019-8 PMID:9858756

Bickel, W. K., Jarmolowicz, D. P., Mueller, E. T., Gatchalian, K. M., & McClure, S. M. (2012). Are executive function and impulsivity antipodes? A conceptual reconstruction with special reference to addiction. *Psychopharmacology*, *221*(3), 361–387. doi:10.1007/s00213-012-2689-x PMID:22441659

Bickel, W. K., Koffarnus, M. N., Moody, L., & Wilson, A. G. (2014). The behavioral- and neuro-economic process of temporal discounting: A candidate behavioral marker of addiction. *Neuropharmacology*, *76*, 518–527. doi:10.1016/j.neuropharm.2013.06.013 PMID:23806805

Bickel, W. K., Miller, M. L., Yi, R., Kowal, B. P., Lindquist, D. M., & Pitcock, J. A. (2007). Behavioral and neuroeconomics of drug addiction: Competing neural systems and temporal discounting processes. *Drug and Alcohol Dependence*, *90*, S85–S91. doi:10.1016/j.drugalcdep.2006.09.016 PMID:17101239

Bourgeois-Gironde, S. (2010). Is neuroeconomics doomed by the reverse inference fallacy? *Mind & Society*, *9*(2), 229–249. doi:10.1007/s11299-010-0076-z

Braeutigam, S. (2005). Neuroeconomics: From neural systems to economic behaviour. *Brain Research Bulletin*, *67*(5), 355–360. doi:10.1016/j.brainresbull.2005.06.009 PMID:16216681

Breiter, H. C., Aharon, I., Kahneman, D., Dale, A., & Shizgal, P. (2001). Functional imaging of neural responses to expectancy and experience of monetary gains and losses. *Neuron*, *30*(2), 619–639. doi:10.1016/S0896-6273(01)00303-8 PMID:11395019

Brenner, L., Rottenstreich, Y., Sood, S., & Bilgin, B. (2007). On the psychology of loss aversion: Possession, valence, and reversals of the endowment effect. *The Journal of Consumer Research*, *34*(3), 369–376. doi:10.1086/518545

Brocas, I., & Carrillo, J. D. (2008). The brain as a hierarchical organization. *The American Economic Review*, *98*(4), 1312–1346. doi:10.1257/aer.98.4.1312

Bruni, L., & Sugden, R. (2007). The road not taken: How psychology was removed from economics, and how it might be brought back. *The Economic Journal*, *117*(516), 146–173. doi:10.1111/j.1468-0297.2007.02005.x

Buehler, R., McFarland, C., Spyropoulos, V., & Lam, K. C. H. (2007). Motivated prediction of future feelings: Effects of negative mood and mood orientation on affective forecasts. *Personality and Social Psychology Bulletin*, *33*(9), 1265–1278. doi:10.1177/0146167207303014 PMID:17586732

Cai, X., Kim, S., & Lee, D. (2011). Heterogeneous coding of temporally discounted values in the dorsal and ventral striatum during intertemporal choice. *Neuron, 69*(1), 170–182. doi:10.1016/j.neuron.2010.11.041 PMID:21220107

Camerer, C. F. (2005). Three cheers–psychological, theoretical, empirical–for loss aversion. *JMR, Journal of Marketing Research, 42*(2), 129–133. doi:10.1509/jmkr.42.2.129.62286

Camerer, C. F. (2007). Neuroeconomics: Using neuroscience to make economic predictions. *The Economic Journal, 117*(519), C26–C42. doi:10.1111/j.1468-0297.2007.02033.x

Camerer, C. F. (2008). Neuroeconomics: Opening the gray box. *Neuron, 60*(3), 416–419. doi:10.1016/j.neuron.2008.10.027 PMID:18995815

Camerer, C. F., Babcock, L., Loewenstein, G., & Thaler, R. (1997). Labor supply of New York City cabdrivers: One day at a time. *The Quarterly Journal of Economics, 112*(2), 407–441. doi:10.1162/003355397555244

Camerer, C. F., Ho, T. H., & Chong, J. K. (2004). A cognitive hierarchy model of games. *The Quarterly Journal of Economics, 119*(3), 861–898. doi:10.1162/0033553041502225

Camerer, C. F., & Loewenstein, G. (2004). Behavioral economics: Past, present, future. In C. F. Camerer, G. Loewenstein, & M. Rabin (Eds.), *Advances in behavioral economics* (pp. 3–51). Princeton, NJ: Princeton University Press.

Caplin, A., & Dean, M. (2008). Dopamine, reward prediction error, and economics. *The Quarterly Journal of Economics, 123*(2), 663–701. doi:10.1162/qjec.2008.123.2.663

Cardinal, R. N., Pennicott, D. R., Sugathapala, C. L., Robbins, T. W., & Everitt, B. J. (2001). Impulsive choice induced in rats by lesions of the nucleus accumbens core. *Science, 292*(5526), 2499–2501. doi:10.1126/science.1060818 PMID:11375482

Carter, C. S., Botvinick, M. M., & Cohen, J. D. (1999). The contribution of the anterior cingulate cortex to executive processes in cognition. *Reviews in the Neurosciences, 10*(1), 49–57. doi:10.1515/REVNEURO.1999.10.1.49 PMID:10356991

Carter, C. S., & van Veen, V. (2007). Anterior cingulate cortex and conflict detection: An update of theory and data. *Cognitive, Affective & Behavioral Neuroscience, 7*(4), 367–379. doi:10.3758/CABN.7.4.367 PMID:18189010

Chang, S. W. C., Barack, D. L., & Platt, M. L. (2012). Mechanistic classification of neural circuit dysfunctions: Insights from neuroeconomics research in animals. *Biological Psychiatry, 72*(2), 101–106. doi:10.1016/j.biopsych.2012.02.017 PMID:22440615

Chorvat, T. R., & McCabe, K. (2005). Neuroeconomics and rationality. *Chicago-Kent Law Review, 80*(3), 1235–1255.

Coricelli, G., & Nagel, R. (2009). Neural correlates of strategic reasoning in medial prefrontal cortex. *Proceedings of the National Academy of Sciences of the United States of America, 106*(23), 9163–9168. doi:10.1073/pnas.0807721106 PMID:19470476

Costa-Gomes, M., Crawford, V., & Broseta, B. (2001). Cognition behavior in normal-form games: An experimental study. *Econometrica*, *69*(5), 1193–1235. doi:10.1111/1468-0262.00239

d'Acremont, M., & Bossaerts, P. (2008). Neurobiological studies of risk assessment: A comparison of expected utility and mean-variance approaches. *Cognitive, Affective & Behavioral Neuroscience*, *8*(4), 363–374. doi:10.3758/CABN.8.4.363 PMID:19033235

Dagevos, H. (2005). Consumers as four-faced creatures: Looking at food consumption from the perspective of contemporary consumers. *Appetite*, *45*(1), 32–39. doi:10.1016/j.appet.2005.03.006 PMID:15921822

Davis, J. B. (2010). Neuroeconomics: Constructing identity. *Journal of Economic Behavior & Organization*, *76*(3), 574–583. doi:10.1016/j.jebo.2010.08.011

Deaner, R. O., Khera, A. V., & Platt, M. L. (2005). Monkeys pay per view: Adaptive valuation of social images by rhesus macaques. *Current Biology*, *15*(6), 543–548. doi:10.1016/j.cub.2005.01.044 PMID:15797023

Decety, J., Jackson, P. L., Sommerville, J. A., Chaminade, T., & Meltzoff, A. N. (2004). The neural bases of cooperation and competition: An fMRI investigation. *NeuroImage*, *23*(2), 744–751. doi:10.1016/j.neuroimage.2004.05.025 PMID:15488424

Declerck, C. H., Boone, C., & Emonds, G. (2013). When do people cooperate? The neuroeconomics of prosocial decision making. *Brain and Cognition*, *81*(1), 95–117. doi:10.1016/j.bandc.2012.09.009 PMID:23174433

Delgado, M. R. (2007). Reward-related responses in the human striatum. *Annals of the New York Academy of Sciences*, *1104*(1), 70–88. doi:10.1196/annals.1390.002 PMID:17344522

Delgado, M. R., Frank, R. H., & Phelps, E. A. (2005). Perceptions of moral character modulate the neural systems of reward during the trust game. *Nature Neuroscience*, *8*(11), 1611–1618. doi:10.1038/nn1575 PMID:16222226

Depue, R. A., & Collins, P. F. (1999). Neurobiology of the structure of personality: Dopamine, facilitation of incentive motivation, and extraversion. *Behavioral and Brain Sciences*, *22*(3), 491–569. doi:10.1017/S0140525X99002046 PMID:11301519

Depue, R. A., & Morrone-Strupinsky, J. V. (2005). A neurobehavioral model of affiliative bonding: Implications for conceptualizing a human trait of affiliation. *Behavioral and Brain Sciences*, *28*(3), 313–395. doi:10.1017/S0140525X05000063 PMID:16209725

Dickhaut, J., Rustichini, A., & Smith, V. (2009). A neuroeconomic theory of the decision process. *Proceedings of the National Academy of Sciences of the United States of America*, *106*(52), 22145–22150. doi:10.1073/pnas.0912500106 PMID:20080787

Edwards, W. (1954). The theory of decision making. *Psychological Bulletin*, *51*(4), 380–417. doi:10.1037/h0053870 PMID:13177802

Egidi, G., Nusbaum, H. C., & Cacioppo, J. T. (2008). Neuroeconomics: Foundational issues and consumer relevance. In C. P. Haugtvedt, P. M. Herr, & F. R. Kardes (Eds.), *Handbook of consumer psychology* (pp. 1177–1214). New York, NY: Psychology Press.

Elliott, R., Newman, J. L., Longe, O. A., & Deakin, J. F. (2003). Differential response patterns in the striatum and orbitofrontal cortex to financial reward in humans: A parametric functional magnetic resonance imaging study. *The Journal of Neuroscience, 23*(1), 303–307. PMID:12514228

Erev, I., Ert, E., & Yechiam, E. (2008). Loss aversion, diminishing sensitivity, and the effect of experience on repeated decisions. *Journal of Behavioral Decision Making, 21*(5), 575–597. doi:10.1002/bdm.602

Ernst, M., & Paulus, M. P. (2005). Neurobiology of decision making: A selective review from a neurocognitive and clinical perspective. *Biological Psychiatry, 58*(8), 597–604. doi:10.1016/j.biopsych.2005.06.004 PMID:16095567

Fehr, E., & Camerer, C. F. (2007). Social neuroeconomics: The neural circuitry of social preferences. *Trends in Cognitive Sciences, 11*(10), 419–427. doi:10.1016/j.tics.2007.09.002 PMID:17913566

Fellows, L. K. (2007). Advances in understanding ventromedial prefrontal function. *Neurology, 68*(13), 991–995. doi:10.1212/01.wnl.0000257835.46290.57 PMID:17389302

Fiorillo, C. D., Tobler, P. N., & Schultz, W. (2003). Discrete coding of reward probability and uncertainty by dopamine neurons. *Science, 299*(5614), 1898–1902. doi:10.1126/science.1077349 PMID:12649484

Frank, R. H. (2003). *Microeconomics and behavior*. London, UK: McGraw–Hill/Irwin.

Fudenberg, D., & Levine, D. K. (2006). A dual-self model of impulse control. *The American Economic Review, 96*(5), 1449–1476. doi:10.1257/aer.96.5.1449

Gan, J. O., Walton, M. E., & Phillips, P. E. (2010). Dissociable cost and benefit encoding of future rewards by mesolimbic dopamine. *Nature Neuroscience, 13*(1), 25–27. doi:10.1038/nn.2460 PMID:19904261

Gazzaniga, M., Ivry, R., & Mangun, G. (2002). *Cognitive neuroscience*. New York, NY: W. W. Norton & Company.

Gehring, J. W., & Willoughby, A. R. (2002). The medial frontal cortex and the rapid processing of monetary gains and losses. *Science, 295*(5563), 2279–2282. doi:10.1126/science.1066893 PMID:11910116

Gigerenzer, G., & Selten, R. (2002). *Bounded rationality: The adaptive toolbox*. Cambridge, MA: MIT Press.

Glimcher, P. W. (2002). Decisions, decisions, decisions: Choosing a biological science of choice. *Neuron, 36*(2), 323–332. doi:10.1016/S0896-6273(02)00962-5 PMID:12383785

Glimcher, P. W. (2003). *Decisions, uncertainty and the brain: The science of neuroeconomics*. Cambridge, MA: MIT Press.

Glimcher, P. W. (2004). *Decisions, uncertainty, and the brain: The science of neuroeconomics*. Cambridge, MA: MIT Press.

Glimcher, P. W. (2008). Understanding risk: A guide for the perplexed. *Cognitive, Affective & Behavioral Neuroscience, 8*(4), 348–354. doi:10.3758/CABN.8.4.348 PMID:19033233

Glimcher, P. W. (2009). *Neuroeconomics: Decision making and the brain*. London, UK: Academic Press.

Glimcher, P. W., Camerer, C. F., Fehr, E., & Poldrack, R. A. (2008). Introduction: A brief history of neuroeconomics. In P. W. Glimcher, C. F. Camerer, E. Fehr, & R. A. Poldrack (Eds.), *Neuroeconomics: Decision making and the brain* (pp. 1–12). London, UK: Academic Press.

Glimcher, P. W., & Rustichini, A. (2004). Neuroeconomics: The consilience of brain and decision. *Science*, *306*(5695), 447–452. doi:10.1126/science.1102566 PMID:15486291

Green, L., & Myerson, J. (2004). A discounting framework for choice with delayed and probabilistic rewards. *Psychological Bulletin*, *130*(5), 769–792. doi:10.1037/0033-2909.130.5.769 PMID:15367080

Griessinger, T., & Coricelli, G. (2015). The neuroeconomics of strategic interaction. *Current Opinion in Behavioral Sciences*, *3*, 73–79. doi:10.1016/j.cobeha.2015.01.012

Gul, F., & Pesendorfer, W. (2008). The case for mindless economics. In A. Caplin & A. Shotter (Eds.), *The foundations of positive and normative economics* (pp. 3–39). Oxford, UK: Oxford University Press. doi:10.1093/acprof:oso/9780195328318.003.0001

Haile, P. A., Hortacsu, A., & Kosenok, G. (2008). On the empirical content of quantal response equilibrium. *The American Economic Review*, *98*(1), 180–200. doi:10.1257/aer.98.1.180

Harbaugh, W. T., Mayr, U., & Burghart, D. R. (2007). Neural responses to taxation and voluntary giving reveal motives for charitable donations. *Science*, *316*(5831), 1622–1625. doi:10.1126/science.1140738 PMID:17569866

Hardie, B. G. S., Johnson, E. J., & Fader, P. S. (1993). Modeling loss aversion and reference dependence effects on brand choice. *Marketing Science*, *12*(4), 378–394. doi:10.1287/mksc.12.4.378

Hare, T. A., Camerer, C. F., Knoepfle, D. T., & Rangel, A. (2010). Value computations in ventral medial prefrontal cortex during charitable decision making incorporate input from regions involved in social cognition. *The Journal of Neuroscience*, *30*(2), 583–590. doi:10.1523/JNEUROSCI.4089-09.2010 PMID:20071521

Hare, T. A., Camerer, C. F., & Rangel, A. (2009). Self-control in decision-making involves modulation of the vmPFC valuation system. *Science*, *324*(5927), 646–648. doi:10.1126/science.1168450 PMID:19407204

Hare, T. A., O'Doherty, J., Camerer, C. F., Schultz, W., & Rangel, A. (2008). Dissociating the role of the orbitofrontal cortex and the striatum in the computation of goal values and prediction errors. *The Journal of Neuroscience*, *28*(22), 5623–5630. doi:10.1523/JNEUROSCI.1309-08.2008 PMID:18509023

Harnick, F., van Dijk, E., van Beest, I., & Mersmann, P. (2007). When gains loom larger than losses: Reversed loss aversion for small amounts of money. *Psychological Science*, *18*(12), 1099–1105. doi:10.1111/j.1467-9280.2007.02031.x PMID:18031418

Hedgcock, W., & Rao, A. R. (2009). Trade-off aversion as an explanation for the attraction effect: A functional magnetic resonance study. *JMR, Journal of Marketing Research*, *46*(1), 1–13. doi:10.1509/jmkr.46.1.1

Henson, R. N. A. (2005). What can functional neuroimaging tell the experimental psychologist? *Quarterly Journal of Experimental Psychology*, *58*(2), 193–233. doi:10.1080/02724980443000502 PMID:15903115

Henson, R. N. A., Rugg, M. D., Shallice, T., Josephs, O., & Dolan, R. (1999). Recollection and familiarity in recognition memory: An event-related fMRI study. *The Journal of Neuroscience, 19*(10), 3962–3972. PMID:10234026

Hoffman, M. B. (2004). The neuroeconomic path of the law. *Philosophical Transactions of the Royal Society of London. Series B, Biological Sciences, 359*(1451), 1667–1676. doi:10.1098/rstb.2004.1540 PMID:15590608

Holland, P. C., & Gallagher, M. (1999). Amygdala circuitry in attentional and representational processes. *Trends in Cognitive Sciences, 3*(2), 65–73. doi:10.1016/S1364-6613(98)01271-6 PMID:10234229

Hsu, M., Bhatt, M., Adolphs, R., Tranel, D., & Camerer, C. F. (2005). Neural systems responding to degrees of uncertainty in human decision-making. *Science, 310*(5754), 1680–1683. doi:10.1126/science.1115327 PMID:16339445

Hubert, M. (2010). Does neuroeconomics give new impetus to economic and consumer research? *Journal of Economic Psychology, 31*(5), 812–817. doi:10.1016/j.joep.2010.03.009

Hursh, S. R. (1984). Behavioral economics. *Journal of the Experimental Analysis of Behavior, 42*(3), 435–452. doi:10.1901/jeab.1984.42-435 PMID:16812401

Hwang, J., Kim, S., & Lee, D. (2009). Temporal discounting and inter-temporal choice in rhesus monkeys. *Frontiers in Behavioral Neuroscience, 3*(9), 1–13. PMID:19562091

Izuma, K., Saito, D. N., & Sadato, N. (2010). Processing of the incentive for social approval in the ventral striatum during charitable donation. *Journal of Cognitive Neuroscience, 22*(4), 621–631. doi:10.1162/jocn.2009.21228 PMID:19320552

Jeankins, A., Neil Macrae, C., & Mitchell, J. (2008). Repetition suppression of ventromedial prefrontal activity during judgments of self and others. *Proceedings of the National Academy of Sciences of the United States of America, 105*(11), 4507–4512. doi:10.1073/pnas.0708785105 PMID:18347338

Johnson, E. J., & Goldstein, D. (2003). Do defaults save lives? *Science, 302*(5649), 1338–1339. doi:10.1126/science.1091721 PMID:14631022

Kable, J. W., & Glimcher, P. W. (2007). The neural correlates of subjective value during intertemporal choice. *Nature Neuroscience, 10*(12), 1625–1633. doi:10.1038/nn2007 PMID:17982449

Kahneman, D., & Lovallo, D. (1993). Timid choices and bold forecasts: A cognitive perspective on risk taking. *Management Science, 39*(1), 17–31. doi:10.1287/mnsc.39.1.17

Kahneman, D., Slovic, P., & Tversky, A. (1982). *Judgment under uncertainty: Heuristics and biases.* Cambridge, UK: Cambridge University Press. doi:10.1017/CBO9780511809477

Kahneman, D., & Tversky, A. (1979). Prospect theory: An analysis of decisions under risk. *Econometrica, 47*(2), 263–291. doi:10.2307/1914185

Kahneman, D., Wakker, P. P., & Sarin, R. (1997). Back to Bentham? Explorations of experienced utility. *The Quarterly Journal of Economics, 112*(2), 375–405. doi:10.1162/003355397555235

Kalenscher, T., & van Wingerden, M. (2011). Why we should use animals to study economic decision making: A perspective. *Frontiers in Neuroscience, 5*(82), 1–11. PMID:21731558

Kardes, F. R. (1994). Consumer judgment and decision processes. In R. S. Wyer & T. K. Srull (Eds.), Handbook of social cognition (pp. 399–466). Hillsdale, NJ: Lawrence Erlbaum Associates.

Kenning, P., & Plassmann, H. (2005). NeuroEconomics: An overview from an economic perspective. *Brain Research Bulletin, 67*(5), 343–354. doi:10.1016/j.brainresbull.2005.07.006 PMID:16216680

Kermer, D. A., Driver-Linn, E., Wilson, T. D., & Gilbert, D. T. (2006). Loss aversion is an affective forecasting error. *Psychological Science, 17*(8), 649–653. doi:10.1111/j.1467-9280.2006.01760.x PMID:16913944

Kim, S., Hwang, J., & Lee, D. (2008). Prefrontal coding of temporally discounted values during intertemporal choice. *Neuron, 59*(1), 161–172. doi:10.1016/j.neuron.2008.05.010 PMID:18614037

Kim, S., & Lee, D. (2011). Prefrontal cortex and impulsive decision making. *Biological Psychiatry, 69*(12), 1140–1146. doi:10.1016/j.biopsych.2010.07.005 PMID:20728878

King-Casas, B., & Chiu, P. H. (2012). Understanding interpersonal function in psychiatric illness through multiplayer economic games. *Biological Psychiatry, 72*(2), 119–125. doi:10.1016/j.biopsych.2012.03.033 PMID:22579510

King-Casas, B., Sharp, C., Lomax-Bream, L., Lohrenz, T., Fonagy, P., & Montague, P. R. (2008). The rupture and repair of cooperation in borderline personality disorder. *Science, 321*(5890), 806–810. doi:10.1126/science.1156902 PMID:18687957

Kirby, K. N. (1997). Bidding on the future: Evidence against normative discounting of delayed rewards. *Journal of Experimental Psychology: General, 126*(1), 54–70. doi:10.1037/0096-3445.126.1.54

Knutson, B., Bhanji, J. P., Cooney, R. E., Atlas, L. Y., & Gotlib, I. H. (2008). Neural responses to monetary incentives in major depression. *Biological Psychiatry, 63*(7), 686–692. doi:10.1016/j.biopsych.2007.07.023 PMID:17916330

Knutson, B., & Bossaerts, P. (2007). Neural antecedents of financial decisions. *The Journal of Neuroscience, 27*(31), 8174–8177. doi:10.1523/JNEUROSCI.1564-07.2007 PMID:17670962

Knutson, B., & Peterson, R. (2005). Neurally reconstructing expected utility. *Games and Economic Behavior, 52*(2), 305–315. doi:10.1016/j.geb.2005.01.002

Knutson, B., Rick, S., Wimmer, G. E., Prelec, D., & Loewenstein, G. (2007). Neural predictors of purchases. *Neuron, 53*(1), 147–156. PMID:17196537

Knutson, B., Taylor, J., Kaufman, M., Peterson, R., & Glover, G. (2005). Distributed neural representation of expected value. *The Journal of Neuroscience, 25*(19), 4806–4812. doi:10.1523/JNEUROSCI.0642-05.2005 PMID:15888656

Koenigs, M., & Tranel, D. (2007). Prefrontal cortex damage abolishes brand-cued changes in cola preference. *Social Cognitive and Affective Neuroscience, 3*(1), 1–6. doi:10.1093/scan/nsm032 PMID:18392113

Kosfeld, M., Heinrichs, M., Zak, P. J., Fischbacher, U., & Fehr, E. (2005). Oxytocin increases trust in humans. *Nature, 435*(7042), 673–676. doi:10.1038/nature03701 PMID:15931222

Krajbich, I., Adolphs, R., Tranel, D., Denburg, N. L., & Camerer, C. F. (2009). Economic games quantify diminished sense of guilt in patients with damage to the prefrontal cortex. *The Journal of Neuroscience, 29*(7), 2188–2192. doi:10.1523/JNEUROSCI.5086-08.2009 PMID:19228971

Krajbich, I., Armel, C., & Rangel, A. (2010). Visual fixations and the computation and comparison of value in simple choice. *Nature Neuroscience, 13*(10), 1292–1298. doi:10.1038/nn.2635 PMID:20835253

Kringelbach, M. L. (2005). The human orbitofrontal cortex: Linking reward to hedonic experience. *Nature Reviews Neuroscience, 6*(9), 691–702. doi:10.1038/nrn1747 PMID:16136173

Kringelbach, M. L., & Berridge, K. C. (2010). *Pleasures of the brain*. New York, NY: Oxford University Press.

Kringelbach, M. L., & Rolls, E. T. (2004). The functional neuroanatomy of the human orbitofrontal cortex: Evidence from neuroimaging and neuropsychology. *Progress in Neurobiology, 72*(5), 341–372. doi:10.1016/j.pneurobio.2004.03.006 PMID:15157726

Kuhnen, C. M., & Knutson, B. (2005). The neural basis of financial risk taking. *Neuron, 47*(5), 763–770. doi:10.1016/j.neuron.2005.08.008 PMID:16129404

Kurzban, R. (2011). *Why everyone (else) is a hypocrite: Evolution and the modular mind*. Princeton, NJ: Princeton University Press. doi:10.1515/9781400835997

Lades, L. K. (2012). Towards an incentive salience model of intertemporal choice. *Journal of Economic Psychology, 33*(4), 833–841. doi:10.1016/j.joep.2012.03.007

Laibson, D. (1997). Golden eggs and hyperbolic discounting. *The Quarterly Journal of Economics, 112*(2), 443–477. doi:10.1162/003355397555253

Lee, N., Broderick, A. J., & Chamberlain, L. (2007). What is "neuromarketing"? A discussion and agenda for future research. *International Journal of Psychophysiology, 63*(2), 199–204. doi:10.1016/j.ijpsycho.2006.03.007 PMID:16769143

Leknes, S., & Tracey, I. (2008). A common neurobiology for pain and pleasure. *Nature Reviews Neuroscience, 9*(4), 314–320. doi:10.1038/nrn2333 PMID:18354400

Lerner, J. S., Small, D. A., & Loewenstein, G. (2004). Heart strings and purse strings: Carryover effects of emotions on economic decisions. *Psychological Science, 15*(5), 337–341. doi:10.1111/j.0956-7976.2004.00679.x PMID:15102144

Leyton, M. (2010). The neurobiology of desire: Dopamine and the regulation of mood and motivational states in humans. In M. L. Kringelbach & K. C. Berridge (Eds.), *Pleasures of the brain* (pp. 222–243). New York, NY: Oxford University Press.

List, J. A. (2003). Does market experience eliminate market anomalies? *The Quarterly Journal of Economics, 118*(1), 41–71. doi:10.1162/00335530360535144

Loewenstein, G. F. (1996). Out of control: Visceral influences on behavior. *Organizational Behavior and Human Decision Processes*, *65*(3), 272–292. doi:10.1006/obhd.1996.0028

Loewenstein, G. F., Rick, S., & Cohen, J. D. (2008). Neuroeconomics. *Annual Review of Psychology*, *59*(1), 647–672. doi:10.1146/annurev.psych.59.103006.093710 PMID:17883335

Loewenstein, G. F., Weber, E. U., Hsee, C. K., & Welch, N. (2001). Risk as feelings. *Psychological Bulletin*, *127*(2), 267–286. doi:10.1037/0033-2909.127.2.267 PMID:11316014

Louie, K., Khaw, M. W., & Glimcher, P. W. (2013). Normalization is a general neural mechanism for context-dependent decision making. *Proceedings of the National Academy of Sciences of the United States of America*, *110*(15), 6139–6144. doi:10.1073/pnas.1217854110 PMID:23530203

MacKillop, J. (2013). Integrating behavioral economics and behavioral genetics: Delayed reward discounting as an endophenotype for addictive disorders. *Journal of the Experimental Analysis of Behavior*, *99*(1), 14–31. doi:10.1002/jeab.4 PMID:23344986

McCabe, K. A. (2008). Neuroeconomics and the economic sciences. *Economics and Philosophy*, *24*(3), 345–368. doi:10.1017/S0266267108002010

McCabe, K. A., Houser, D., Ryan, L., Smith, V., & Trouard, T. (2001). A functional imaging study of cooperation in two-person reciprocal exchange. *Proceedings of the National Academy of Sciences of the United States of America*, *98*(20), 11832–11835. doi:10.1073/pnas.211415698 PMID:11562505

McClure, S. M., York, M. K., & Montague, P. R. (2004). The neural substrates of reward processing in humans: The modern role of fMRI. *The Neuroscientist*, *10*(3), 260–268. doi:10.1177/1073858404263526 PMID:15155064

McEntee, W. J., & Crook, T. H. (1991). Serotonin, memory, and the aging brain. *Psychopharmacology*, *103*(2), 143–149. doi:10.1007/BF02244194 PMID:2027916

McKelvey, R., & Palfrey, T. (1995). Quantal response equilibria for normal form games. *Games and Economic Behavior*, *10*(1), 6–38. doi:10.1006/game.1995.1023

Miller, E. K., & Cohen, J. D. (2001). An integrative theory of prefrontal cortex function. *Annual Review of Neuroscience*, *24*(1), 167–202. doi:10.1146/annurev.neuro.24.1.167 PMID:11283309

Mohr, P. N. C., Li, S. C., & Heekeren, H. R. (2010). Neuroeconomics and aging: Neuromodulation of economic decision making in old age. *Neuroscience and Biobehavioral Reviews*, *34*(5), 678–688. doi:10.1016/j.neubiorev.2009.05.010 PMID:19501615

Montague, P. R. (2007). Neuroeconomics: A view from neuroscience. *Functional Neurology*, *22*(4), 219–234. PMID:18182129

Montague, P. R., & Berns, G. S. (2002). Neural economics and the biological substrates of valuation. *Neuron*, *36*(2), 265–284. doi:10.1016/S0896-6273(02)00974-1 PMID:12383781

Montague, P. R., Hyman, S. E., & Cohen, J. D. (2004). Computational roles for dopamine in behavioural control. *Nature*, *431*(7010), 760–767. doi:10.1038/nature03015 PMID:15483596

Monterosso, J., Piray, P., & Luo, S. (2012). Neuroeconomics and the study of addiction. *Biological Psychiatry, 72*(2), 107–112. doi:10.1016/j.biopsych.2012.03.012 PMID:22520343

Morris, G., Nevet, A., Arkadir, D., Vaadia, E., & Bergman, H. (2006). Midbrain dopamine neurons encode decisions for future action. *Nature Neuroscience, 9*(8), 1057–1063. doi:10.1038/nn1743 PMID:16862149

Myerson, J., & Green, L. (1995). Discounting of delayed rewards: Models of individual choice. *Journal of the Experimental Analysis of Behavior, 64*(3), 263–276. doi:10.1901/jeab.1995.64-263 PMID:16812772

Novemsky, N., & Kahneman, D. (2005). The boundaries of loss aversion. *JMR, Journal of Marketing Research, 42*(2), 119–128. doi:10.1509/jmkr.42.2.119.62292

Padoa-Schioppa, C., & Assad, J. A. (2006). Neurons in the orbitofrontal cortex encode economic value. *Nature, 441*(7090), 223–226. doi:10.1038/nature04676 PMID:16633341

Parkinson, J. A., Olmstead, M. C., Burns, L. H., Robbins, T. W., & Everitt, B. J. (1999). Dissociation in effects of lesions of the nucleus accumbens core and shell on appetitive pavlovian approach behavior and the potentiation of conditioned reinforcement and locomotor activity by D-amphetamine. *The Journal of Neuroscience, 19*(6), 2401–2411. PMID:10066290

Plassmann, H., O'Doherty, J., & Rangel, A. (2007). Orbitofrontal cortex encodes willingness to pay in everyday economic transactions. *The Journal of Neuroscience, 27*(37), 9984–9988. doi:10.1523/JNEUROSCI.2131-07.2007 PMID:17855612

Plassmann, H., O'Doherty, J., Shiv, B., & Rangel, A. (2008). Marketing actions can modulate neural representations of experienced pleasantness. *Proceedings of the National Academy of Sciences of the United States of America, 105*(3), 1050–1054. doi:10.1073/pnas.0706929105 PMID:18195362

Platt, M. L., & Glimcher, P. W. (1999). Neural correlates of decision variables in parietal cortex. *Nature, 400*(6741), 233–238. doi:10.1038/22268 PMID:10421364

Platt, M. L., & Huettel, S. A. (2008). Risky business: The neuroeconomics of decision making under uncertainty. *Nature Neuroscience, 11*(4), 398–403. doi:10.1038/nn2062 PMID:18368046

Pradeep, A. K. (2010). *The buying brain: Secrets for selling to the subconscious mind.* Hoboken, NJ: John Wiley & Sons.

Preuschoff, K., Bossaerts, P., & Quartz, S. R. (2006). Neural differentiation of expected reward and risk in human subcortical structures. *Neuron, 51*(3), 381–390. doi:10.1016/j.neuron.2006.06.024 PMID:16880132

Previc, F. H. (2009). *The dopaminergic mind in human evolution and history.* Cambridge, UK: Cambridge University Press. doi:10.1017/CBO9780511581366

Quattrone, G. A., & Tversky, A. (1988). Contrasting rational and psychological analyses of political choice. *The American Political Science Review, 82*(3), 719–736. doi:10.2307/1962487

Rachlin, H., & Green, L. (1972). Commitment, choice, and self-control. *Journal of the Experimental Analysis of Behavior, 17*(1), 15–22. doi:10.1901/jeab.1972.17-15 PMID:16811561

Rangel, A., Camerer, C. F., & Montague, P. R. (2008). A framework for studying the neurobiology of value-based decision making. *Nature Reviews Neuroscience*, *9*(7), 545–556. doi:10.1038/nrn2357 PMID:18545266

Rangel, A., & Hare, T. (2010). Neural computations associated with goal-directed choice. *Current Opinion in Neurobiology*, *20*(2), 262–270. doi:10.1016/j.conb.2010.03.001 PMID:20338744

Reimann, M., & Bechara, A. (2010). The somatic marker framework as a neurological theory of decision-making: Review, conceptual comparisons, and future neuroeconomics research. *Journal of Economic Psychology*, *31*(5), 767–776. doi:10.1016/j.joep.2010.03.002

Rick, S. (2011). Losses, gains, and brains: Neuroeconomics can help to answer open questions about loss aversion. *Journal of Consumer Psychology*, *21*(4), 453–463. doi:10.1016/j.jcps.2010.04.004

Riedl, R., Hubert, M., & Kenning, P. (2010). Are there neural gender differences in online trust? An fMRI study on the perceived trustworthiness of eBay offers. *Management Information Systems Quarterly*, *34*(2), 397–428.

Rilling, J. K., Sanfey, A. G., Aronson, J. A., Nystrom, L. E., & Cohen, J. D. (2004). Opposing BOLD responses to reciprocated and unreciprocated altruism in putative reward pathways. *Neuroreport*, *15*(16), 2539–2543. doi:10.1097/00001756-200411150-00022 PMID:15538191

Robinson, T. E., & Berridge, K. C. (2003). Addiction. *Annual Review of Psychology*, *54*(1), 25–53. doi:10.1146/annurev.psych.54.101601.145237 PMID:12185211

Rowland, N. E., Vaughan, C. H., Mathes, C. M., & Mitra, A. (2008). Feeding behavior, obesity, and neuroeconomics. *Physiology & Behavior*, *93*(1/2), 97–109. doi:10.1016/j.physbeh.2007.08.003 PMID:17825853

Rushworth, M. F., & Behrens, T. E. (2008). Choice, uncertainty and value in prefrontal and cingulate cortex. *Nature Neuroscience*, *11*(4), 389–397. doi:10.1038/nn2066 PMID:18368045

Rustichini, A. (2009). Neuroeconomics: What have we found, and what should we search for. *Current Opinion in Neurobiology*, *19*(6), 672–677. doi:10.1016/j.conb.2009.09.012 PMID:19896360

Salamone, J., Correa, M., Farrar, A., & Mingote, S. (2007). Effort-related functions of nucleus accumbens dopamine and associated forebrain circuits. *Psychopharmacology*, *191*(3), 461–482. doi:10.1007/s00213-006-0668-9 PMID:17225164

Samuelson, W., & Zeckhauser, R. (1988). Status quo bias in decision making. *Journal of Risk and Uncertainty*, *1*(1), 7–59. doi:10.1007/BF00055564

Sanfey, A. G., Loewenstein, G., McClure, S. M., & Cohen, J. D. (2006). Neuroeconomics: Cross-currents in research on decision-making. *Trends in Cognitive Sciences*, *10*(3), 108–116. doi:10.1016/j.tics.2006.01.009 PMID:16469524

Sanfey, A. G., Rilling, J. K., Aronson, J. A., Nystrom, L. E., & Cohen, J. D. (2003). The neural basis of economic decision-making in the ultimatum game. *Science*, *300*(5626), 1755–1758. doi:10.1126/science.1082976 PMID:12805551

Sarin, R. K., & Weber, M. (1993). Risk-value models. *European Journal of Operational Research, 70*(2), 135–149. doi:10.1016/0377-2217(93)90033-J

Schoenbaum, G., Setlow, B., & Ramus, S. J. (2003). A systems approach to orbitofrontal cortex function: Recordings in rat orbitofrontal cortex reveal interactions with different learning systems. *Behavioural Brain Research, 146*(1/2), 19–29. doi:10.1016/j.bbr.2003.09.013 PMID:14643456

Schultz, W. (2002). Getting formal with dopamine and reward. *Neuron, 36*(2), 241–263. doi:10.1016/S0896-6273(02)00967-4 PMID:12383780

Schultz, W. (2006). Behavioral theories and the neurophysiology of reward. *Annual Review of Psychology, 57*(1), 87–115. doi:10.1146/annurev.psych.56.091103.070229 PMID:16318590

Schultz, W. (2011). Potential vulnerabilities of neuronal reward, risk, and decision mechanisms to addictive drugs. *Neuron, 69*(4), 603–617. doi:10.1016/j.neuron.2011.02.014 PMID:21338874

Schwarz, N., & Strack, F. (1999). Reports of subjective well-being: Judgmental processes and their methodological implications. In D. Kahneman, E. Diener, & N. Schwarz (Eds.), *Well-being: The foundations of hedonic psychology* (pp. 61–84). New York, NY: Russell Sage Foundation.

Sebastian, V. (2014). New directions in understanding the decision-making process: Neuroeconomics and neuromarketing. *Procedia: Social and Behavioral Sciences, 127*, 758–762. doi:10.1016/j.sbspro.2014.03.350

Shane, S. (2009). Introduction to the focused issue on the biological basis of business. *Organizational Behavior and Human Decision Processes, 110*(2), 67–69. doi:10.1016/j.obhdp.2009.10.001

Sharp, C., Burton, P., & Ha, C. (2011). "Better the devil you know": A preliminary study of the differential modulating effects of reputation on reward processing for boys with and without externalizing behavior problems. *European Child & Adolescent Psychiatry, 20*(11/12), 581–592. doi:10.1007/s00787-011-0225-x PMID:22038344

Sharp, C., Monterosso, J., & Montague, P. R. (2012). Neuroeconomics: A bridge for translational research. *Biological Psychiatry, 72*(2), 87–92. doi:10.1016/j.biopsych.2012.02.029 PMID:22727459

Siegal, M., & Varley, R. (2002). Neural systems involved in "theory of mind.". *Nature Reviews Neuroscience, 3*(6), 463–471. PMID:12042881

Simon, H. A. (1967). The logic of heuristic decision making. In N. Rescher (Ed.), *The logic of decision and action* (pp. 1–20). Pittsburgh, PA: University of Pittsburgh Press.

Skuse, D. H., & Gallagher, L. (2008). Dopaminergic–neuropeptide interactions in the social brain. *Trends in Cognitive Sciences, 13*(1), 27–35. doi:10.1016/j.tics.2008.09.007 PMID:19084465

Smith, K., Dickhaut, J., McCabe, K., & Pardo, J. V. (2002). Neuronal substrates for choice under ambiguity, risk, gains, and losses. *Management Science, 48*(6), 711–718. doi:10.1287/mnsc.48.6.711.194

Staudinger, M. R., Erk, S., Abler, B., & Walter, H. (2009). Cognitive reappraisal modulates expected value and prediction error encoding in the ventral striatum. *NeuroImage, 45*(3), 713–721. doi:10.1016/j.neuroimage.2009.04.095 PMID:19442745

Stewart, N., Chater, N., & Brown, G. D. A. (2006). Decision by sampling. *Cognitive Psychology*, *53*(1), 1–26. doi:10.1016/j.cogpsych.2005.10.003 PMID:16438947

Summerfield, C., & Tsetsos, K. (2015). Do humans make good decisions? *Trends in Cognitive Sciences*, *19*(1), 27–34. doi:10.1016/j.tics.2014.11.005 PMID:25488076

Tabibnia, G., & Lieberman, M. D. (2007). Fairness and cooperation are rewarding: Evidence from social cognitive neuroscience. *Annals of the New York Academy of Sciences*, *1118*(1), 90–101. doi:10.1196/annals.1412.001 PMID:17717096

Tekin, S., & Cummings, J. L. (2002). Frontal–subcortical neuronal circuits and clinical neuropsychiatry: An update. *Journal of Psychosomatic Research*, *53*(2), 647–654. doi:10.1016/S0022-3999(02)00428-2 PMID:12169339

Thaler, R. H. (1980). Toward a positive theory of consumer choice. *Journal of Economic Behavior & Organization*, *1*(1), 39–60. doi:10.1016/0167-2681(80)90051-7

Tricomi, E. M., Delgado, M. R., & Fiez, J. A. (2004). Modulation of caudate activity by action contingency. *Neuron*, *41*(2), 281–292. doi:10.1016/S0896-6273(03)00848-1 PMID:14741108

Tricomi, E. M., Rangel, A., Camerer, C. F., & O'Doherty, J. P. (2010). Neural evidence for inequality-averse social preferences. *Nature*, *463*(7284), 1089–1091. doi:10.1038/nature08785 PMID:20182511

Tversky, A., & Kahneman, D. (1981). The framing of decisions and the psychology of choice. *Science*, *211*(4481), 453–458. doi:10.1126/science.7455683 PMID:7455683

Vromen, J. J. (2007). Neuroeconomics as a natural extension of bioeconomics: The shifting scope of standard economic theory. *Journal of Bioeconomics*, *9*(2), 145–167. doi:10.1007/s10818-007-9021-6

Wansink, B. (2004). Environmental factors that increase the food intake and consumption volume of unknowing consumers. *Annual Review of Nutrition*, *24*(1), 455–479. doi:10.1146/annurev.nutr.24.012003.132140 PMID:15189128

Weber, E. U., & Johnson, E. J. (2009). Mindful judgment and decision making. *Annual Review of Psychology*, *60*(1), 53–85. doi:10.1146/annurev.psych.60.110707.163633 PMID:18798706

Winkielman, P., & Berridge, K. C. (2003). Irrational wanting and subrational liking: How rudimentary motivational and affective processes shape preferences and choices. *Political Psychology*, *24*(4), 657–680. doi:10.1046/j.1467-9221.2003.00346.x

Winkielman, P., Knutson, B., Paulus, M., & Trujil, J. L. (2007). Affective influence on judgments and decisions: Moving towards core mechanisms. *Review of General Psychology*, *11*(2), 179–192. doi:10.1037/1089-2680.11.2.179

Witt, U., & Binder, M. (2013). Disentangling motivational and experiential aspects of "utility" – A neuroeconomics perspective. *Journal of Economic Psychology*, *36*(1), 27–40. doi:10.1016/j.joep.2013.02.001

Young, L., & Koenigs, M. (2007). Investigating emotion in moral cognition: A review of evidence from functional neuroimaging and neuropsychology. *British Medical Bulletin*, *84*(1), 69–79. doi:10.1093/bmb/ldm031 PMID:18029385

Zak, P. J. (2004). Neuroeconomics. *Philosophical Transactions of the Royal Society of London. Series B, Biological Sciences, 359*(1451), 1737–1748. doi:10.1098/rstb.2004.1544 PMID:15590614

Zhang, Y., & Fishbach, A. (2005). The role of anticipated emotions in the endowment effect. *Journal of Consumer Psychology, 15*(4), 316–324. doi:10.1207/s15327663jcp1504_6

Zurawicki, L. (2010). *Neuromarketing: Exploring the brain of the consumer.* Berlin, Germany: Springer–Verlag. doi:10.1007/978-3-540-77829-5

ADDITIONAL READING

Benhabib, J., & Bisin, A. (2005). Modeling internal commitment mechanisms and self-control: A neuro-economics approach to consumption–saving decisions. *Games and Economic Behavior, 52*(2), 460–492. doi:10.1016/j.geb.2004.10.004

Bernheim, B. D. (2009). On the potential of neuroeconomics: A critical (but hopeful) appraisal. *American Economic Journal: Microeconomics, 1*(2), 1–41. doi:10.1257/mic.1.2.1

Burgos, J. E., & Garcia-Leal, O. (2015). Autoshaped choice in artificial neural networks: Implications for behavioral economics and neuroeconomics. *Behavioural Processes, 114*, 63–71. doi:10.1016/j.beproc.2015.01.010 PMID:25662745

Camerer, C. F., Loewenstein, G., & Prelec, D. (2004). Neuroeconomics: Why economics needs brains. *The Scandinavian Journal of Economics, 106*(3), 555–579. doi:10.1111/j.0347-0520.2004.00377.x

Caplin, A., Dean, M., Glimcher, P. W., & Rutledge, R. B. (2010). Measuring beliefs and rewards: A neuroeconomic approach. *The Quarterly Journal of Economics, 125*(3), 923–960. doi:10.1162/qjec.2010.125.3.923 PMID:25018564

Chau, B. K., Kolling, N., Hunt, L. T., Walton, M. E., & Rushworth, M. F. (2014). A neural mechanism underlying failure of optimal choice with multiple alternatives. *Nature Neuroscience, 17*(3), 463–470. doi:10.1038/nn.3649 PMID:24509428

Doya, K. (2008). Modulators of decision making. *Nature Neuroscience, 11*(4), 410–416. doi:10.1038/nn2077 PMID:18368048

Emonds, G., Declerck, C. H., Boone, C., Vandervliet, E., & Parizel, P. (2011). Comparing the neural basis of strategic decision-making in people with different social preferences: An fMRI study. *Journal of Neuroscience, Psychology, and Economics, 4*(1), 11–24. doi:10.1037/a0020151

Ernst, M. (2012). The usefulness of neuroeconomics for the study of depression across adolescence into adulthood. *Biological Psychiatry, 72*(2), 84–86. doi:10.1016/j.biopsych.2012.02.027 PMID:22727458

Fehr, E., & Rangel, A. (2011). Neuroeconomic foundations of economic choice: Recent advances. *The Journal of Economic Perspectives, 25*(4), 3–30. doi:10.1257/jep.25.4.3 PMID:21595323

Gigerenzer, G., & Gaissmaier, W. (2011). Heuristic decision making. *Annual Review of Psychology, 62*(1), 451–482. doi:10.1146/annurev-psych-120709-145346 PMID:21126183

Glimcher, P. W., Dorris, M. C., & Bayer, H. M. (2005). Physiological utility theory and the neuroeconomics of choice. *Games and Economic Behavior, 52*(2), 213–256. doi:10.1016/j.geb.2004.06.011 PMID:16845435

Gul, F., & Pesendorfer, W. (2009). A comment on Bernheim's appraisal of neuroeconomics. *American Economic Journal: Microeconomics, 1*(2), 42–47. doi:10.1257/mic.1.2.42

Hartley, C. A., & Phelps, E. A. (2012). Anxiety and decision-making. *Biological Psychiatry, 72*(2), 113–118. doi:10.1016/j.biopsych.2011.12.027 PMID:22325982

Kable, J. W., & Glimcher, P. W. (2009). The neurobiology of decision: Consensus and controversy. *Neuron, 63*(6), 733–745. doi:10.1016/j.neuron.2009.09.003 PMID:19778504

Kolling, N., Wittmann, M., & Rushworth, M. F. S. (2014). Multiple neural mechanisms of decision making and their competition under changing risk pressure. *Neuron, 81*(5), 1190–1202. doi:10.1016/j.neuron.2014.01.033 PMID:24607236

Lee, D. (2008). Game theory and neural basis of social decision making. *Nature Neuroscience, 11*(4), 404–409. doi:10.1038/nn2065 PMID:18368047

Matsushima, T., Kawamori, A., & Bem-Sojka, T. (2008). Neuro-economics in chicks: Foraging choices based on amount, delay and cost. *Brain Research Bulletin, 76*(3), 245–252. doi:10.1016/j.brainresbull.2008.02.007 PMID:18498937

Paulus, M. P. (2007). Decision-making dysfunctions in psychiatry: Altered homeostatic processing? *Science, 318*(5850), 602–606. doi:10.1126/science.1142997 PMID:17962553

Rangel, A., & Clithero, J. A. (2012). Value normalization in decision making: Theory and evidence. *Current Opinion in Neurobiology, 22*(6), 970–981. doi:10.1016/j.conb.2012.07.011 PMID:22939568

Rilling, J. K., & Sanfey, A. G. (2011). The neuroscience of social decision-making. *Annual Review of Psychology, 62*(1), 23–48. doi:10.1146/annurev.psych.121208.131647 PMID:20822437

Ross, D. (2008). Two styles of neuroeconomics. *Economics and Philosophy, 24*(3), 473–484. doi:10.1017/S0266267108002095

Sobel, J. (2009). Neuroeconomics: A comment on Bernheim. *American Economic Journal: Microeconomics, 1*(2), 60–67. doi:10.1257/mic.1.2.60

Spinella, M., Yang, B., & Lester, D. (2008). Prefrontal cortex dysfunction and attitudes toward money: A study in neuroeconomics. *Journal of Socio-Economics, 37*(5), 1785–1788. doi:10.1016/j.socec.2004.09.061

Tom, S. M., Fox, C. R., Trepel, C., & Poldrack, R. A. (2007). The neural basis of loss aversion in decision-making under risk. *Science, 315*(5811), 515–518. doi:10.1126/science.1134239 PMID:17255512

Vlaev, I., Chater, N., Stewart, N., & Brown, G. D. A. (2011). Does the brain calculate value? *Trends in Cognitive Sciences, 15*(11), 546–554. doi:10.1016/j.tics.2011.09.008 PMID:21983149

von Neumann, J., & Morgenstern, O. (2007). *Theory of games and economic behavior*. Princeton, NJ: Princeton University Press.

Wyart, V., de Gardelle, V., Scholl, J., & Summerfield, C. (2012). Rhythmic fluctuations in evidence accumulation during decision making in the human brain. *Neuron, 76*(4), 847–858. doi:10.1016/j.neuron.2012.09.015 PMID:23177968

KEY TERMS AND DEFINITIONS

Behavioral Economics: The study of the effects of social, cognitive, and emotional factors on the economic decisions of individuals and institutions and the consequences for market prices, returns, and the resource allocation.

Decision Making: The cognitive process resulting in the selection of a course of action among several alternative scenarios.

Game Theory: A model of optimality taking into consideration not only benefits less costs, but also the interaction between participants.

Loss Aversion: People's tendency to strongly prefer avoiding losses to acquiring gains.

Nash Equilibrium: A stable state of a system that involves several interacting participants in which no participant can gain by a change of strategy as long as all the other participants remain unchanged.

Neuroeconomics: An interdisciplinary field that seeks to explain human decision making, to analyze the ability to process multiple alternatives, and to choose an optimal course of action.

Neuroscience: The scientific study of the nervous system.

Utility Theory: A theory used in economics that holds the belief that an item or service's utility is a measure of the satisfaction that the consumer will derive from the consumption of that particular good or service.

Chapter 2
Neuroeconomics and Media Economics

Dinçer Atli
Penn State University, USA, & Uskudar University, Turkey

Mehmet Yilmazata
Undersecretariat of Turkish Treasury, Turkey

ABSTRACT

This chapter investigates the development of neuroeconomics as a relative new sub-discipline in the fields of economics and behavioral science. After comparing paradigms of both classical and behavioral economics, the problem of the "conscious and rational consumer" is addressed in relation to more passive views of consumerism in neuroeconomics. Highlighting the most recent trends in neuroeconomics, the chapter also addresses the historical development of the discipline of neuroeconomics as an independent field of research within the fields of media and economics. The problem of new marketing strategies as well as the evolvement of neuroeconomics as an independent discipline in the age of digitalization is presented while considering the changing nature of the media industry.

INTRODUCTION

While treatises and writings on subjects regarding economic activities have existed at least since the Classical Ages, the emergence of economics as a separate scientific field is often credited to Adam Smith's milestone publication on *The Wealth of Nations* in 1776. Economists assume that Smith's book should be seen as the first step in the classical period of economic theory. In his treatise, Smith described a number of phenomena critical for understanding choice behavior and the aggregation of choices into market activity. These were, in essence, psychological insights (Glimcher, Camerer, Fehr, & Poldrack, 2009).

Neuroeconomics is the question of how the brain and not "the enlightened consumer" makes economic decisions and seeks to explore the mechanisms of decision-making which classic economists view not as conscious value judgments but merely computational processes. The goal of neuroeconomics is not only the understanding but also the prediction of strategic choices made by the consumer (Houser & Kevin, 2008). Since the late 1990s, several converging trends in behavioral and natural sciences as well

DOI: 10.4018/978-1-4666-9989-2.ch002

as social sciences have provided common ground for the "birth" of neuroeconomics (Glimcher, Camerer, Fehr, & Poldrack, 2009). In a rather traditional definition, neuroeconomics is more or less subordinated to behavioral economics which uses empirical evidence regarding the limits of computation, the free mind, and "greed". Nevertheless, neuroeconomics hopes to inspire new theories and approaches in a multidisciplinary research environment (Camerer, 2008).

Given that background, the study of media and communications has traditionally been dominated disciplines outside the sphere of economy from a scientific point of view. This might be true from a purely theoretical approach, but omits that economics has proven to be a highly relevant factor in understanding how media conglomerates and the mainstream media are operating as commercial, profit orientated players. The media economics area of inquiry emerged strongly in the 1970s and has more breadth and depth than many who are unfamiliar with its literature assume, and is based on a variety of economic theories and analysis methods (Picard, 2006).

According to Conen and Padua-Schioppa (2015), the brain processes information regarding economic decisions within the offer cells of the orbitofrontal cortex (OFC). Nevertheless, both authors stress that clinical and statistical data regarding the offer cells are yet to be improved in order to establish more certain outcomes (Conen & Padua-Schioppa, 2015). In addition, neuroeconomics strives to explore the function of the brain and use information in order to gather statistical proof for the measure of preferences. Furthermore, statistical proof will improve if more and reliable data is collected; in that aspect, neuroeconomics strives to link social theory with hard prove natural science evidence (Camerer, Bhatt, & Hsu, 2007).

Within the field of behavioral science, neuroeconomics focuses on the mediation of choices and valuation of consumption alternatives; it researches computational processes in specific brain areas and contributes with "hard data" gained from research within medical and psychological science. (Sun, 2012). Neurological reflexes are measured as emotional responses which in become economic decisions; again, neuroeconomics seeks to establish scientific background information in order to integrate it into economic theory (Burton & Shah, 2013). The business operations of corporations and smaller players in the media firms are to be evaluated in the context of given market conditions, technological alternatives, the regulatory and legal environment, and their anticipated financial implications (Owers, Carveth, & Alexander, 2004). Besides those factors, international trade, business strategies, pricing policies, competition and industrial clusters have to be analyzed if to be put in to the context of neuroeconomics, as those are having a deep impact on media corporations and industries (Doyle, 2002). Within this context, this chapter of the book is dealing with the potential impacts of neuroeconomics on economic processes in the field of media.

MODERN ECONOMICS AND NEUROECONOMICS

One of the key concepts of classical economics is the research of the gain of maximum value from limited sources centered on the concept of the "homo oeconomicus" with the consumer treated as rational actor. Thus, the rational actor thrives to maximize his profits based on self-interest (Fey, 1936). We must consider that early theorists did not construct "economic man" as a merely theoretic metaphor, but instead placed him in charge of representing real life economic actors (Bidlingmaier, 1973). The wish to maximize profit encourages competition, itself channeling collective ambitions towards socially desirable ends, resulting in the "common good and common welfare" being maximized by individual economic actor's wishes to enhance their profit (Adam Smith, 2001). In his definition of wealth creation, Smith (1723-1790), in accordance with the "Zeitgeist" of the 18th century, embraces the maximization of assets through the enhancement of capital goods in order to promote future investment, not just relying on consumption driven economic growth (Rothbard, 2006).

We should add, however, that the concept of the economic actor using "perfect" and flawless information regarding his decision has been challenged in mainstream economics for some time. In his groundbreaking paper on efficient markets theory, Yale economist Robert Shiller challenges the concept of "perfect markets", pledging to consider psychological factors as "biased self-attribution"(Shiller, 2003). The important point is to notice that the individual mind is considered an independent variable by the proponents of behavioral finance, thus paving the way for more exotic concepts as neuroeconomics.

An even more radical criticism of the concept of "perfect" information as a cornerstone of economic decision making is supported by Nassim Nicholas Taleb. Taleb actually regards factual information only as limited indicator for future decisions in a sense that neither the collection of vast research data nor historical references can actually point out established patterns of market (or other) behavior (Taleb, 2011). In that sense, neuroeconomics as an aspiring discipline is also criticized of trying to impose patterns of natural science on social science related studies.

Neuroeconomics, as opposed to classical economic postulates, takes it as a matter of fact that nonconscious decisions (i.e., neurologic reflexes are deciding over a passive consumers set of decisions). Shortly, one decisive paradigm of economics – the rational actor – is left out in neuroeconomics. Just like postulated by sub-disciplines of disciplines of neurology or psychology, only stimulating effects will contribute towards the sustainable upholding of neurologic signals (i.e., positive feelings). In addition, investment results only continue to motivate the individual investor if they continue to reward the investor with higher returns. Otherwise, the motivation to invest accumulated capital towards future positive returns (emotional and financial gain) in material or ideal terms (i.e., the rewarding thought of profiting from the "right decision") will diminish over time. Therefore, neuroeconomics is focusing on the perpetual enhancement of returns (Santos, 2009).

In research trends on neuroeconomics, it is possible to identify certain patterns that establish proximity towards other areas of research, especially psychology, neurology, and behavioral economics. As an example, Camerer stresses that psychology began to disappear from university economics departments in the early 20th century. Advances in neurosciences at the end of the 20th century made it possible to link those areas again, but economists seemed to be skeptical about applying those findings in their research. Camerer (2005) highlights that finance with its myriads of observations on price movements might profit from neuroeconomics in order to establish a more satisfactory theoretical base regarding patterns and trends of price changes. Neuroscience might also be helpful in explaining the human factor in the labor market (i.e., the phenomenon of wages being "sticky" in downward movements). Camerer et al. (2005) hopes to shed more light on the rational choice model while employing neuro science in combination with economic theory.

In his groundbreaking monograph, *Foundations of Neuroeconomics*, Glimcher (2009) explicitly stresses the importance of re-applying psychology in economics. Furthermore, he focuses on the limits of behavioral economics when applied towards neoclassical models. Glimcher's most remarkable contribution to the field might be his straightforward plaidoyer for an interdisciplinary synthesis between natural and social sciences. According to Glimcher, the "human choice factor" has to be researched in conclusion with so-called "hidden elements" that are influencing those choices. In order to proof his theory, Glimcher developed his "because" models, testing mathematical models that are used in neoclassical economics by comparing them with psychological and neurobiological data on their applicability or-non-applicability. In a nutshell, according to that model neuroeconomics is about "linking brain, mind and choice" (Glimcher, 2011).

In a similar manner, Politser (2008) attempts to simplify the reader's view of neuroeconomics by stressing the evaluation of specific elements of choice used while making decisions. Stressing neuronal processes, he links the concepts of neuroeconomic "passive" decision factors with the postulates of classical economics, critically analyzing paradigms. The enhancement of returns in consideration of the investment undertaken as a fundamental part of economic efforts remains unchallenged in traditional as well as in alternative (i.e., neuroeconomic theory). The main point of dispute is the role of the actor as independent agent or as a mere executer of external stimulations.

Nevertheless, neuroeconomics does not discourage the postulate of classical and neoclassical economics regarding the actor as an active agent seeking profit per se. The theoretical framework only tries to link actions to neurological factors that are establishing behavioral patterns leading to conscious or subconscious activity of any kind. When we take a closer look at neuroeconomics, we might even recognize an effort towards applying the principles of natural science-biology/neurology/medicine, etc., towards the discipline of economics. The "dismal science" (economics) which, while borrowing heavily from another branch of natural sciences (mathematics) remains firmly rooted in social science.

Maybe the most important novelty of neuroeconomics is not only the interdisciplinary approach, but also that the firm will use testable models from the field of neurology to integrate them into the variables that are defining economic questions. Therefore, we must recognize that classical and neoclassical economics applies mathematical models to verify various thesis and postulates regarding the development of prices, stocks, financial models, the job market, etc. At the end of the day, the biggest problem remaining is that all those models, while sometimes borrowing from mathematical analysis, remain within the frame of socially-defined paradigms.

As an example, while Keynes (1971) founded his criticism on classical economic theory defining wages in free labor markets as elastic, with his supply based models Keynes developed the theory of sticky wages. As can be seen, defenders of either one or the other point of view might apply research variables and be willing to test them with models; nevertheless, no absolute scientific certainty can be assigned regarding the respective fundamentals (Keynes, 1971).

It should be stated, though, that even the terminology applied to the field of neuroeconomics has not been left unchallenged. There has been a rather critical approach whether the term "Neuro-" itself should be applied to all kind of research fields; Muzur and Rincic (2013) reflect whether the adaption of the term "neuro" does justify the evaluation of the respective field of study as a separate science in terms of definition. Within that context, they highlight that not only the relatively late adaption of the term "neuroeconomics" in 2003 should be evaluated from a critical distance, they also judge that the mere use of the prefix "neuro" in the fields of neuroeconomics rather sounds "like an awkward caricature". Muzur and Rincic (2013) furthermore state that the use of the prefix neuro rather seems to serve the purpose of applying new labels to certain sub-field of science in order to gain attention.

To summarize the state of neuroeconomics and its relation to the media, it might be concluded that the ever growing commercialization and rising importance of revenues gained through advertising has made a lasting impact on the self-reflection of media itself. Advertisement, digitalization, and customer-tailed/targeted advertisements are no longer mere aspects of traditional journalism. While marketing strategies are concentrating to develop advertising strategies according to potential customer's digital usage patterns, psychology is manifesting itself in the targeting strategy as well. Therefore, neuroeconomics is likely to gain more prominence among marketing experts among the media community.

Supported by research gains in the disciplines of neurology and psychology, the digitalization of media will change the face of media economics as well. The media industry will be forced to remain committed to the maximization of profit, using neuroeconomic patterns to their utmost advantage.

HISTORICAL INCLINATIONS IN MEDIA ECONOMICS

The rise of mass and corporate media paved the way for the study of media economics which emerged during the 1950s. Media industries provided all of the fundamentals required to study the economic process. Content providers, presenting information and entertainment, became the suppliers though advertisers and consumers created the demand side of the market (Albarran, 2004). The study of media and related topics has been controlled by the question of establishing societal values, patterns, and relevant backgrounds for the content defined as "news". Economics or applied strategies of economy and management have always been an aspect regarding the administration of media companies; nevertheless from an intellectual point of view media scholars have started to pay closer attention to the subject (Doyle, 2002).

Communications departments in universities and colleges did not concentrate on media economics in a specific way before the 1980s. Nevertheless, the subject was addressed partially within the boundaries of the subject of political economy during the late 1960s and 1970s. Thus, media scholars have largely ignored researching the deep links between economics and their own discipline; however, it should be noted that media and communications studies were resting more or less on the back of sociology, history, psychology, and political science disciplines. What is more surprising is the fact that even business executives working in the media have largely ignored the fact that their respective industries were full-fledged enterprises (Picard, 2006). According to contemporary sources, Canadian academics and research institutes tend to focus on culture and politics, while the field of journalism seems to be frowned upon as nonprofessional skill related courses (Hoskins, McFadyen, & Finn, 2004).

Media economics enhanced and become more visible after the "soul searching" following the infamous the stock market crash called "Black Monday" in 1987 after which business enterprises started to re-think and re-organize their structures. The media industry took its' fair share during the hastily arranged, takeovers, breakups, mergers and acquisitions (Alexander, Owers, Carveth, Hollifield, & Greco, 2004). In the present time, due to rising insecurity after the debt crisis and market shake-up, media economics has become an ever more valuable tool of analysis for professionals as well as for academics. Rising market volatility, problems regarding the financing and operational challenges in the era of digitalization, and media companies are forced to encounter several challenges in order to stay alive (Owers, Rod, & Alexander, 2004).

It has been noted that around the new millennium a greater emphasis on researching the reciprocity between the media and the markets has shown itself in studies regarding big media conglomerates, mergers and acquisitions, as well as strategies of choice. In addition, media economics has evolved towards being recognized as a part of full programs of study since the 1990s in Executive MBA or related Master's programs, as well as PhD (doctoral) programs in countries such as Finland, Switzerland, the USA, Spain, or the United Kindom (Picard, 2006).

THE ECONOMIC CHARACTERISTICS OF THE MEDIA INDUSTRY

As management and financing issues are an everyday reality for media organizations, a closer view of economics as a discipline is necessary. Media organizations are usually described as economic actors in pursuit of maximizing profits while trying to fulfill their business objectives to the utmost level of satisfaction, focusing on enhancing efficiency, profit, and their respective market share (Ingenhoff & Koelling, 2012). Media organizations are organized in lieu with the classical theory of the company and many like commercial entities in any fields as "primarily geared towards maximizing profits and satisfying shareholders" (Doyle, 2002). From a legal point of view, media companies are treated according to antitrust regulations and economic performance requirements (Ozanich & Wirth, 2004; Doyle, 2002).

Media economics is often still treated by academia as a non-independent branch of media and economics. Accumulating the principles of media and communications studies and amalgamating themselves with the research of economic principles, the findings are applied by companies that are active in the fields of media or advertising (Owers et al., 2004). Economics has been described as "the study of how people make choices to cope with scarcity" (Parkin et al., 1997, p. 8; Doyle, 2002). The term media broadly comprises companies that are operating, owning or promoting the production, or emanation and distribution of media in different forms. As examples we can use broadcasting stations or networks, program production and distribution facilities, cable television systems or networks, in addition to more traditional media providers as newspaper and book publishers (Ozanich & Wirth, 2004).

Media economics helps us to realize the happenings and functions of media companies as economic organizations (Albarran, 2004). Thus, the student of media economics will engage himself with the interaction and changing face of economic factors shaping the decisions of media professionals, managers, or investors that own assets in the field of media (Doyle, 2002). In a nutshell, media economics actively researches the impact of economic decisions and factors related to media, determining the limits of emanating information with a commercial background (Picard, 2006). In short, media economics borrows from the field of sociology, confronting it with economic forces as international trade, business strategy, pricing policies, competition and industrial concentration (Doyle, 2002). However, media economics is a sub-branch of industrial organization, employing applied microeconomic tools to research markets and their impact on the economy as a whole. In addition, the major context in the consideration of media economics has been the industrial organization model (Tirole, 1988; Wildman, 2006; Caves 1987; Lacy & Bauer, 2006).

Definitions of media economy include the study of how media companies function across different points of activity through the use of concepts, theories, and principles draw from macroeconomic and microeconomic angles. Media companies are primarily profit-oriented and incorporate business entities directly or indirectly active in the distribution, production, or marketing of relevant information in a professional manner (Albarran, 2010). From another perspective, media economics is concerned with how media companies meet the informational and entertainment wants and needs of audiences, advertisers, and society with existing resources. In this realm, media economics refers to the business actors and financial activities of companies producing and selling output into the different media sectors (Picard, 1989; Doyle, 2002).

In that manner, media economics is distinctive among other sectors. Due to the open and covered profound social and political influence employed by powerful media corporations, public opinion is heavily influenced and sometimes even created by those conglomerates; political and cultural, even moral values attitudes and voting behavior is influenced by the media (Napoli, 2003). Furthermore, many media industries do function in what has been referred to by Picard (1989) as a "dual product" marketplace (p. 17-19). Media companies are mainly generating two products: content (newspaper copy, magazine articles, television programs, etc.) and audiences.

Additionally, even if this is a subject of much controversy, media output might also be classified as 'cultural' good (Albarran, 2004; Doyle, 2002). In political science, media has often been referred to as the "fourth estate" controlling the activities of state institutions, politicians, the judiciary, and even the business world. Moreover, media companies are usually operating as oligopolies. While in the past the actual sale of newspapers, media products etc. Might have been the main source of income, right now advertising might be classified as the "life blood" of the media (Doyle, 2002; Ingenhoff & Koelling, 2012).

In this regard, four predominant forces affect the interaction of economy with the media: globalization, regulation, technology, and social aspects (Albarran, 2010). Marx himself stated that new transportation and communication technologies were enabling capital to reach or build up distant markets, resulting in the globalization of world trade, as well as the global expansion of capital (Fuchs, 2011). Media economics, within the field of economy, has leaned itself towards the concepts of microeconomics. In short, micro-and macroeconomics are concerned with the study of small and large organizations, economic processes, and decisions. Therefore, economic processes are heavily influenced by the level of organization of the respective society; likewise, the environment for the operation of media companies is also set by the structures aforementioned (Alexander et al., 1998; Albarran, 2010).

If we research media economics under the aspect of microeconomic theory, we must also consider one of the basic concepts of economic research: economies of scale which are a highly prevalent feature of the media industry. The important aspect for the media economy is that marginal costs are of critical importance for the process of producing a product in tangible form (Albarran, 2004; Doyle, 2002). However, economies of scope are also to be found in the media, as the nature of media products is in a way that they are reformat able (Doyle, 2002). Additionally, advertising is of critical importance in the media economy. For example, in the US revenues cover virtually all broadcast media and 70% to 80% of revenues for newspapers (Shaver, 2004).

THE RELATIONSHIP BETWEEN NEUROECONOMICS AND MEDIA ECONOMICS

According to Albarran (2010), the concept of "media economics" is a holistic approach towards the economic policies and practices of media firms and industries. One of the distinctive characteristics of the media industry is its evolving character and the changing nature of their respective markets and industries. We might add that the media economy did change faster over time. After the introduction of widely circulated print media serviced by professional news agencies, the age of digitalization in the 21th century made the nature of change even more visible and did accelerate its pace. In addition, media economics is described as an effort to show out the role of media as an economic institution, taking into account the role of globalization in an ever-evolving network of media industries. Albarran (1998) also sees research on media economics as providing an alternative to mainstream mass media and an opportunity to take an interdisciplinary approach towards mass communication research.

The concept of media economics and neuroeconomics might be classified as "newcomers" in the field of behavioral and economic research. Evaluating paradigms of media economics in comparison with the meta scientific definition of economics, we have to establish a point of reference regarding the relevant definitions. As economics, or, with the words of the great but controversial 19th century historian, Thomas Carlyle, the "dismal science" has been interpreted under quite heterogeneous theoretical aspects, we choose to implement the "classics" of economic theory in order to balance establish a point of reference for comparisons with media economics (Harlow & Carter, 2003).

Media economics as such does have a clear and consistent structure within the sub-disciplines of business and media studies. Within that scope, the main focuses do lie on generating profits, managing the logistical, technical, and journalistic and management issues of a media company and last but not least generating a product in form of news and information. It might be said that profit is on the center of the whole concept since in order to provide the "idealistic" goal of generating independent news, the financial aspects have to be secured. In that sense, neuroeconomics contributes to the field of media economics as the focus on the rational generation of preferences helps to establish a customer base, with the reader or user as "consumer".

Generally speaking, the term media economics is usually associated with the profit margins of media outlets which include the fee of the "product" itself (i.e., the price of the respective publication advertising revenues, etc.). Nevertheless, it must be attempted to establish a more holistic approach towards media economics in the age of digitalization. Therefore, we must ask the following questions:

- Will media economics as a relatively young sub-category on the field of media related economic and business studies be able to survive the next step of digitalization?

Terms such as "Web 2.0" and the so-called "internet of things" suggest that the customer will become less and less dependent on traditional media outlets as an "agent" of information supply. If it is assumed that the next step in the development of social media deems media less and less important as an asset and reduces the journalist as well as media corporations more to the role of a "scout", providing the consumer with information and advertisement "tailored" to his very own need,

- Will media economics stay alive as a more or less visible and centralized field of research?

As the ever increasing power of computing has begun to place arithmetical programs increasingly into the driver seat in detecting customer expectations, how far will traditional media related companies be able to control the flow of information?

If it is assumed that information will not become totally autonomous and generated by non-human sources, media economics will be there to stay with us for a long time.

Nevertheless, as the media itself, it may very well be changing its face according to trends which are set in the digital economy. To give an example, one of the principles of traditional economic thought as formulated by Say is the positive correlation between demand and supply. To speak with the early economist, Say: "A product is no sooner created than it, from that instant, affords a market for other products to the full extent of its own value" (Wood & Kates, 2000, p. 126). Implied to media economics, we can assume that the structure of the media may become less and less centralized; nevertheless, even a changed content will always have its very own customers.

If adapted to neuroeconomics, it can be stated that generating stimulating effects through advertising will create neurologic signals (i.e., positive feelings) that maximize the (assumed) profit for both parties. Nevertheless, this feeling, whether assumed or real, has to be of a perpetuate character: this means that the investor must be provided with ever enhancing returns (Houser & McCabe, 2008). Otherwise, any possible motivation to further invest accumulated capital towards the mere possibility to gain future positive returns (i.e., for the media consumer to gain information that presumably helps him enriching himself) will be diminished over time.

CONCLUSION

We might declare that media economics as well as neuroeconomics are very much a product of the criticism of mainstream economics, as well as the search for new answers regarding new strategies of marketing and sales psychology in a changing environment. The global debts and financial markets crisis of 2008 led to questions regarding the principles of the information value of economic date and the principle of efficient market theory. Of course, neuroeconomics as a theory has been the subject of a growing community of scholars and academicians; nevertheless, it seems to possess a certain attractiveness due to the fact that it tries to integrate more research variables into the field than other sub disciplines of economics and psychology. Regarding the media, neuroeconomics seem to be a rewarding tool of analysis as the digitalization of media contributes to personalized marketing strategies.

REFERENCES

Albarran, A. B. (1998). Media economics: Research paradigms, issues, and contributions to mass communication theory. *Mass Communication & Society*, *1*(3-4), 117–129. doi:10.1080/15205436.1998.9677852

Albarran, A. B. (2004). Media economics. In E.J.D. McQuail, P. Schlesinger, & D. Wartella (Eds.), *The SAGE handbook of media studies* (pp. 291–308). Sage.

Albarran, A. B. (2010). *The Media Economy*. New York: Routledge.

Alexander, A., Owers, J., Carveth, R., Hollifield, C. A., & Greco, A. (2004). In A. Alexander, J. Owers, R. Carveth, C. A. Hollifield, & A. Greco (Eds.), *Media Economics Theory and Practice* (pp. 7–9). Mahwah, NJ: Lawrence Erlbaum Associates, Inc.

Bidlingmaier, J. (1973). *Unternehmerziele und Unternehmerstrategien*. Wiesbaden: Springer Verlag. doi:10.1007/978-3-322-87901-1

Burton, E., & Shah, S. (2013). *Behavioral Finance: Understanding the Social, Cognitive, and Economic Debates*. New York: John Wiley & Sons.

Camerer, C., Loewenstein, G., & Prelec, D. (2005). Neuroeconomics: How neuroscience can inform economics. *Journal of Economic Literature*, *43*(1), 9–64. doi:10.1257/0022051053737843

Camerer, C. F. (2008). The Potential of Neuroeconomics. *Economics and Philosophy*, *24*(03), 369–379. doi:10.1017/S0266267108002022

Camerer, C. F., Bhatt, M., & Ming, H. (2007). Neuroeconomics. In B. S. Frey & A. Stutzer (Eds.), *Economics and Psychology: A Promising New Cross-Disciplinary Field* (pp. 113–151). Boston, MA: MIT Press.

Conen, K. E., & Padua-Schioppa, C. (2015). Neuronal variability in orbitofrontal cortex during economic decisions. *Journal of Neurophysiology, 114*(3), 1367–1381. doi:10.1152/jn.00231.2015 PMID:26084903

Doyle, G. (2002). *Understanding Media Economics*. Thousand Oaks, CA: Sage. doi:10.4135/9781446279960

Fey, A. (1936). *Der Homo Oeconomicus in der klassischen Nationalökonomie und seine Kritik durch den Historismus*. Limburg: Limburger Vereindruckerei G.m.b.H.

Fuchs, C. (2011). Foundations of critical media and information studies. *Routledge Advances in Sociology, 384*. doi:10.4324/9780203830864

Glimcher, P. W. (2011). *Foundations of neuroeconomic analysis*. New York: Oxford University Press.

Glimcher, P. W., Camerer, C. F., Fehr, E., & Poldrack, R. A. (2009). Introduction: A Brief History of Neuroeconomics. In *Neuroeconomics Decision Making and The Brain* (pp. 1–12). San Diego, CA: Elsevier Inc.

Harlow, B., & Carter, M. (Eds.). (2003). *Archives of Empire-Volume II. The Scramble for Africa*. Durham, NC: Duke University Press. doi:10.1215/9780822385035

Hoskins, C., McFadyen, S., & Finn, A. (2004). *Media Economics: Applying Economics to New and Traditional Media*. http://doi.org/.<ALIGNMENT.qj></ALIGNMENT>10.4135/9781452233109

Houser, D., & Kevin, M. (2008). Introduction to Neuroeconomics. In D. Houser & M. Kevin (Eds.), *Neuroeconomics* (pp. 15–21). London, UK: Emerald Group Publishing Limited. doi:10.1016/S0731-2199(08)20014-2

Ingenhoff, D., & Koelling, A. M. (2012). Media governance and corporate social responsibility of media organizations: An international comparison. *Business Ethics (Oxford, England), 21*(2), 154–167. doi:10.1111/j.1467-8608.2011.01646.x

Keynes, J. M. (1971). The collected writings of John Maynard Keynes: *The General Theory of Employment, Interest, and Money* (vol. 7). London: Macmilian.

Lacy, S., & Bauer, J. M. (2006). Future Directions for Media Economics Research. In A. B. Albarran, S. M. Chan-Olmsted, & O. Wirth (Eds.), *Handbook of Media Management and Economics* (pp. 655–674). Mahwah, NJ: Lawrence Erlbaum Associates, Inc.

Muzur, A., & Rinčić, I. (2013). Neurocriticism: A contribution to the study of the etiology, phenomenology, and ethics of the use and abuse of the prefix neuro. *JAHR-European Journal of Bioethics, 4*(7), 545–555.

Napoli, P. M. (2013). *Audience economics: Media institutions and the audience marketplace*. Columbia University Press.

Owers, J., Rod, C., & Alexander, A. (2004). An Introduction to Media Economics Theory. In N. G. Alison, J. Alexander, J. Owers, R. Carveth, C. Ann, & A. Hollifield (Eds.), *Media Economics Theory and Practice* (pp. 3–49). Mahwah, NJ: Lawrence Erlbaum Associates.

Ozanich, G. W., & Wirth, M. O. (2004). Structure and Change: A Communications Industry Overview. In A. Alison, J. Owers, R. Carveth, H. C. Ann, & N. G. Albert (Eds.), *Media Economics Theory and Practice* (pp. 69–85). Mahwah, NJ: Lawrence Erlbaum Associates.

Parkin, M., Powell, M., & Matthews, K. (1997). *Economics* (3rd ed.). London: Addison-Wesley Longman.

Picard, R. G. (2006). Historical Trends and Patterns in Media Economics. In A. B. Albarran, S. M. Chan-Olmsted, & O. Wirth (Eds.), *Handbook of Media Management and Economics* (pp. 23–37). Mahwah, NJ: Lawrence Erlbaum Associates, Inc.

Politser, P. (2008). *Neuroeconomics: A Guide to the New Science of Making Choices*. New York: Oxford University Press. doi:10.1093/acprof:oso/9780195305821.001.0001

Santos, L. R., & Keith Chen, M. (2009). The evolution of rational and irrational economic behavior: evidence and insight from a non-human primate species. *Neuroeconomics–Decision Making and the Brain*, 81-93.

Shaver, M. A. (2004). The Economics of the Advertising Industry. In A. Alexander, J. Owers, R. Carveth, C. A. Hollifield, & A. N. Greco (Eds.), *Media Economics Theory and Practice* (pp. 249–265). Mahwah, NJ: Lawrence Erlbaum Associates, Inc.

Shiller, R. J. (2003). From Efficient Markets Theory to Behavioral Finance. *The Journal of Economic Perspectives*, *17*(1), 83–104. doi:10.1257/089533003321164967

Sun, R. (2012). *Grounding Social Sciences in Cognitive Sciences*. Cambridge, MA: MIT Press.

Taleb, N. (2011). *Der Schwarze Schwan, Die Macht höchst unwahrscheinlicher Ereignisse*. München: DTV.

Tirole, J. (1988). *The theory of industrial organization*. Cambridge, MA: MIT Press.

Wildman, S. S. (2006). Paradigms and Analytical Frameworks in Modern Economics and Media Economics. In Handbook of Media Management and Economics (pp. 67–90). Mahwah, NJ: Lawrence Erlbaum Associates, Inc.

Wirth, M. O., & Bloch, H. (1995). Industrial organization theory and media industry analysis. *Journal of Media Economics*, *8*(2), 15–26. doi:10.1207/s15327736me0802_3

Wood, J. C., & Kates, S. (2000). *Jean-Baptiste Say: critical assessments of leading economists* (Vol. 5). Taylor & Francis.

KEY TERMS AND DEFINITIONS

Economics: Is the social science that seeks to describe the factors, which determine the production, distribution and consumption of goods and services.

Homo Oeconomicus: Term coined by John Stuart Mill, describing humans acting within economic processes as rational and self-interested actors.

Industry: "An industry is a group of firms producing the same principle product or service" Porter (1980:7).

Media Economics: Is a holistic approach towards the economic policies and practices of media firms and industries.

Media: Consist of every broadcasting and narrowcasting medium such as newspapers, magazines, TV, radio, billboards, direct mail, telephone, fax, and internet.

Neuroeconomics: Is an interdisciplinary field that seeks to explore the mechanisms of decision-making, which are not seen by proponents of Neuroeconomics, not as conscious value judgments but merely computational processes.

Neuroscience: Is a multidisciplinary science field that is concerned with the study of the structure and function of the brain and nervous system.

Chapter 3
Rational, Emotional, and Neural Foundations of Economic Preferences

Harish C. Chandan
Argosy University, USA

ABSTRACT

Classical economics assumes human economic decision making is completely rational and dominated by self-interest. Behavior economics emerged to account for the fact that human economic preferences are often influenced by emotional and psychological factors leading to inconsistent, intransitive, and irrational decisions that fail to maximize utility and minimize cost and transcend only self-interest. Both rationality and emotions are seated in the human brain in the prefrontal cortex and limbic system, respectively. The brain imaging methods of neuroscience help in understanding the interplay between economic behavior and neural mechanisms. The human economic decision making behavior involves computational and neurobiological processes and is related to the psychological processes. Classical Economics, Psychology, and Neuroscience converge in Neuroeconomics to better understand and predict human economic decision-making. Neuromarketing is an emerging field that uses neuroscience techniques to understand economic preferences of consumers.

INTRODUCTION

Classical economics and game theory assume that human economic decision-making is motivated *only* by self-interest and utility maximization through rational choice in a context of scarce resources. The assumption is that humans utilize all the information available in the market to decide without being influenced by biases and emotions and then act in a logical and rational manner. They weigh risk and return factors by considering the *likelihood* of an outcome and the *value* of the outcome to maximize benefits while minimizing the costs. However, in real life, individuals do *not* always make rational, utility-maximizing decisions. People do deviate from rationality in a systematic manner and have biases. The biases, rules of thumb, or heuristics and emotions often overpower rational thinking and result in irrational behavior (Kahneman, 2003a, b).

DOI: 10.4018/978-1-4666-9989-2.ch003

Economic decision-making is often influenced by unconscious biases, implicit assumptions, and errors in judgment. These systematic biases have origins in human psychology. Human economic decisions are often influences by contextual and psychological factors leading to inconsistent, intransitive, and irrational decisions that fail to maximize utility and minimize cost (Summerfield & Tsetos, 2015). Behavior economics emerged to account for the cognitive biases, heuristics, emotions, and other psychological processes which often override reason unconsciously and automatically. Behavior economics and social neuroscience converged in neuroeconomics to better understand and predict human economic behavior realistically (Popescu & Nica, 2014). Neural activity causally determines economic choices and the neural computations necessary for making economic choices are stochastic (Corsani, 2013). Thus, economic decision-making has roots in economics, psychology and social neuroscience.

This chapter reviews the rational, emotional, and neural foundations of economic decisions. First, the classical perspective of rational choice in economic decision-making is presented and bounded rationality in real-life economic decisions is discussed. The special human capacity to represent others' intentions, beliefs and desires (i.e., mentalizing or the theory of mind – TOM) is discussed and the relationship between economic preferences and the big five personality traits are explored. The role of emotions, biases, and rules of thumb or heuristics in economic decision-making is reviewed leading to behavioral economics or behavioral finance. The neural perspective of economic decision-making that involves mentalizing and empathy is presented. This integrative neuroeconomic view allows one to better understand the human economic decision making in a way that combines rational, emotional, psychological, social and neural mechanisms. The promise and ethics of neuromarketing are discussed. Finally, policy implications and suggestions for future research are discussed.

CLASSICAL ECONOMIC DECISION MAKING: RATIONAL CHOICE AND UTILITY MAXIMIZATION

Classical economics studies individual and aggregate human economic decision-making and behavior. The individual decisions that people and businesses make regarding the allocation of resources and prices of goods and services (considering taxes and regulations created by governments) is called microeconomics which focuses on supply and demand and investigates how a specific company could maximize its production so it could lower prices and better compete in its industry. The aggregate human economic decision-making is covered in macroeconomics which studies the behavior of the economy as whole and not just specific companies.

Macroeconomics views economy-wide phenomena such as gross domestic product (GDP) and how it is affected by changes in unemployment, national income, rate of growth, and price levels. For example, macroeconomics would examine how a change in net exports would affect a nation's capital account or how GDP would be affected by unemployment rate. An understanding of both microeconomic and the macroeconomic behavior is required to create policies for social equity and justice. Due to the social nature of humans, individual economic decision making behavior is influenced by aggregate economic decision-making. For example, when an influential investor sells his stock for a particular company, smaller investors tend to do the same even though they did not know the reasons that led the influential investor to sell. This irrational behavior is called "herding" which is covered in behavior economics (Kudryavtsev, et al., 2013).

Economic decision-making can be regarded as a problem-solving activity leading to a solution that is considered satisfactory by the individual. This involves individuals selecting one option from many available options based on cost-benefit analysis. According to the rational choice theory in classical economics, people make decisions by reasoning to maximize benefits while minimizing costs. A rational decision is made by considering the 'likelihood' of a potential outcome and the 'value' of the outcome. The individual chooses the outcome that represents a higher 'value' for the *combined* effect of the 'likelihood' and the 'value' (i.e., the product of 'likelihood' and 'value') (Samuelson, 1983).

However, in real life, consumers take risks based on what appears to be a likely future outcome in an instance of random chance such as in a coin toss. Their logic is based on seeing the same outcome occur several times in a row and assuming a different outcome is due. This logic is not rational since the odds are independent and remain the same for either outcome in every instance. This is known as the "gambler's fallacy" (Ayton & Fischer, 2004).

Classical economics is based on the assumption that humans always make rational decisions to maximize expected utility. However, the rational choice assumption is one of the limitations of classical economics. Some examples of irrational economic behavior include *gambler's fallacy*, *groupthink*, and *herding*. For example, if some influential person sells his stocks at the hint of a financial decline, others decide to do the same out of fear of an economic collapse. People may rationally understand that selling their stock may not make sense for them in the long-term. They sell it anyway because everyone else is doing the same thing. This has its basis in the human emotions and mirror neurons: "monkey see, monkey do". Due to groupthink and herding, people follow whatever is popular at the time, thinking as a group of people instead of as individuals (Moorhead & Montanari, 1986).

In the framework of utility maximization, the assumption is that humans behave rationally and make optimal choices. However, the concept of utility is *subjective* and is a measure of the satisfaction the individual will derive from the consumption of a particular item or service. An individual's subjective perception of utility is difficult to assess. Since utility cannot be measured directly, it has to be inferred from the observed individual choice. These revealed preferences appear in people's willingness to pay for a product or service. The subjective nature of economic preferences means the concept of utility does not necessarily always involve receiving the most monetary or material benefit because the satisfaction received could be purely emotional. For example, while it would be more financially lucrative for an executive to remain at a company rather than to retire early, it would still be considered rational behavior for her to seek an early retirement if she feels the benefits of retired life outweigh the utility from the pay check that she receives (Simon, 1955).

An individual's concept of utility is shaped by preferences such as background risk, time, and social preferences. These preferences, in combination with expectations of future events, perceptions, beliefs, strategic consideration, prices, and constraints shape behavior. People usually face several risks and the interaction between them can affect the willingness to bear any one of them. Social preference captures the idea that an individual's utility does not depend only on his own material payoff, but that it is also shaped by others' behavior and material payoff. Social preferences include altruism and negative and positive reciprocity. Trust describes an individual's beliefs about others' trustworthiness combined with a preference to take social risks (Fehr, Fischbacher, & Kosfeld, 2005). Time preference describes how an individual trades off utility at different point in time (Frederick et al., 2002).

BOUNDED RATIONALITY: ECONOMIC DECISION MAKING IN REAL LIFE

The human mind is finite and is bound by cognitive limits. Humans do not have access to unlimited information to solve problems, nor do they have all the time in the world to ponder them. The theory of bounded rationality states people are not always able to obtain all the information they would need to make the best possible decision. The decision-making process involves information gathering, evaluating alternatives, and deciding on an optimal choice. In an information-rich world, a wealth of information creates a poverty of attention and a need to allocate that attention efficiently among the overabundance of information sources that might consume it.

Contrary to the principles of classical economics, individuals do not seek to maximize their benefit from a particular course of action since they cannot assimilate and digest all the information that would be needed to achieve such a thing. They do not obtain access to all the information required, but even if they could, their minds would be unable to process it properly. Instead of trying to maximize utility, the human mind seeks what is called "satisficing" – a combination of two words: "satisfy" and "suffice". People in many different situations seek something that is satisfactory and "good enough", rather than maximizing benefit (Kahneman, 2003a).

Simon's concept of bounded rationality suggests that the concept of utility or self-interest may be bounded as well. Due to subjective perception of the concept of utility, humans struggle to analyze problems *objectively* when the outcomes directly affect themselves. They view the economic choices through a "frame" of personal experience warped by social or cultural bias. The subjective perception of utility and the concept of bounded rationality result in humans coming up with their own 'rules of thumb', or "heuristics," when making quick decisions. The economic decisions that are made with relatively simple 'rules of thumb' do not make excessive demands upon one's thinking. While it is inherently rational to do so, the rules themselves and the behavior they lead to may not be. Heuristics are inherently irrational. In addition to utility maximization, other factors may drive consumers' economic choices such as altruism or self-control (Kahneman, 2003b).

Two additional examples of irrational economic preferences include mental accounting and retail therapy. The concept of mental accounting illustrates how people behave irrationally by placing greater value on some dollars than others even though all dollars have the same value. They might drive to another store to save $10 on a $20 purchase, but they would not drive to another store to save $10 on a $1,000 purchase Another example of irrational behavior is retail therapy in which consumers shop impulsively on credit to improve their mood. The field of behavioral economics is based on the idea that individuals often make irrational decisions and explores why they do so (Thaler, 1999).

PSYCHOLOGICAL AND EMOTIONAL FACTORS IN DECISION MAKING: BEHAVIORAL ECONOMICS

The classical perspectives on economics and securities assume that everyone takes full account of the available information in the market and behaves rationally. However, behavior economists have identified a large number of situations in which people deviate from the rational choice theory of standard economics and make decisions based on *psychological* elements (Kahneman, 1994; Brahmana et al., 2012).

An example is the rejection of low offers from the other person in the ultimatum game where a pair of partners must split the money in order to keep it. Rationally, accepting the low offer would enrich the person, but he is enraged at the unfairness of the low offer and rejects it even though he will not have the money he would have if he had accepted it. The person rejects the offer even though it is not in his self-interest to get pleasure at the thought of punishing the person who made the unfair offer. Such anomalies that occur in economic life cannot be explained by conventional economic theories. Therefore, the emergence of behavioral economics provides realistic psychological foundations to enhance the explanatory power of economics (Tversky & Kahneman, 1986).

Behavioral economics has been applied to many areas such as macroeconomics, labor economics, finance, and marketing. Behavioral economics integrates social, cognitive, and emotional factors in understanding economic decisions and considers the effect of emotions and psychology on economic decision-making (i.e., how emotions and thoughts affect monetary decisions) (Heukelom, 2007). Behavioral economics combines the rational perspective with psychological perspective that includes the role of emotions.

Emotions play a very significant role in economic decision-making. The use of heuristics (rules of thumb) and influence of framing on economic decisions cannot be explained based on rational choice alone. Emotion or intuition influences human decision-making and actions. The human brain has both rational and emotional centers that come into play for understanding offers, making choices, and taking actions. In terms of decision-making, the human brain can respond automatically fast (System I) or deliberately slow (System II). System I corresponds to unconscious, automatic processing leading to quick, intuitive response to a problem. System II corresponds to deliberate and slow response. It monitors the quality of answers provided by System I, considers the pros and cons, and sometimes can correct or override the decision from System I (Kahneman, 2003a, b).

Pure neoclassical economic theory uses mathematical models and a few basic assumptions like rational choice and maximizing utility. Behavior economics theory allows for variance in consumer logic and behavior, but behavioral economists cannot rely as heavily on mathematical models to predict outcomes. Instead, they collect real world data on past consumer behavior and conduct experiments involving real transactions to gauge how consumers might behave in future situations. The goal in collecting such data is to eliminate unlikely outcomes so that the likely ones come into focus. Although not as exact of a science compared to using mathematical equations, behavioral economists often manage to make startlingly accurate economic predictions. Economists have found that making realistic assumptions about human nature generally leads to a more precise result (Kahneman & Thaler, 1991).

Nevertheless, behavioral economics has succeeded in explaining market anomalies where neoclassical economics could not. For instance, it has been used to examine the roles played by human greed and fear in the 2008 global financial crisis. The promise of windfall profits lead financial companies to create and sell highly complex credit default swaps without fully understanding their risk. When the stock market crashed, fear drove usually adventurous hedge fund investors to withdraw their money from the market, even when they could have bought good stocks at record-low prices. Behavioral economics can explain other phenomena as well, such as why some prices or wages refuse to change with market forces -price stickiness, why stock markets perform worse on Mondays (the "calendar effect"), and why some investors choose to hold onto poorly performing stocks while selling high-performing ones (the "disposition effect") (Singh, 2009).

Rational economics suggests that people's choice of an economic behavior should not change over time. However, people act more impatiently when making decisions about shorter-term options than longer-term ones. For example, people will often pay extra for express delivery of a desirable but non-essential item that is in stock, but not for one that is out-of-stock and, therefore, will not be deliverable until later.

When people are offered an option for immediate reward, limbic structures are activated significantly more than when both options in the choice involved future delivery. The selection of the latter option was associated with significantly greater prefrontal cortex activity than the choice of the immediate one. Behavioral economics also deals with more complicated constructs like prospect theory of risky choice, hyperbolic time discounting, level-k models of games, and social preferences corresponding to internal rewards based on what happens to other agents (Volk et al., 2012).

PSYCHOLOGICAL BIASES AND HEURISTICS IN ECONOMIC DECISION MAKING

Globally, two commonly observed current market behaviors include excessive trading and the tendency to disproportionately hold on to losing investments while selling winners. Excessive trading is rooted in human emotion, overconfidence bias, and ease of trading due on-line trading. The tendency to hold on to losers while selling winners is rooted in loss aversion bias. Theoretically, markets are efficient but in practice, the biased crowd behavior of the investors can move the stock price. Human biases are rooted in their beliefs and are mostly unconscious. The human perception of reality is very subjective and unique based on one's past experiences. There are many biases affecting decision-making abilities and causing people to make irrational decisions.

An example of a bias is *anchoring and adjustment* where the decision is unduly influenced by initial information that shapes our view of subsequent information. Another example is *availability bias*, which is the tendency for some items that are more readily available in memory to be judged as more frequently occurring. For example, someone who watches a lot of movies about terrorist attacks may think the frequency of terrorism to be higher than it actually is. Due to *loss-aversion bias*, a loss of $100 hurts more than the joy of gaining $100. Another example is the *recency bias* in which people pay more attention to recent information to make decisions and ignore the more distant information even though it may be more important. These psychological biases lead to market anomalies and investor behavior that is not reconciled with the traditional finance paradigms (Park & Sohn, 2013).

Some of the ideas in behavioral economics include rule of thumb, framing, and market inefficiencies. People generally act on "rules of thumb" as opposed to rational thought. The *heuristics* (rule of thumb) and *framing* in making economic preferences cannot be explained by a purely rational approach. An example of a rule of thumb is "you get what you pay for", which is mostly true. However, sometimes a cheaper product is as good as or even better than an expensive version. It would be rational in this case to buy the cheaper product of equal quality. Most people, however, would buy the more expensive product, thinking it is superior.

Framing represents how a problem is presented and influences people's thoughts on a problem. An example is the higher sales of a product when the discount is presented as 75% versus $3 even though the discounted amount is the same in both cases. The third idea in behavioral economics is market inefficiencies which explain outcomes when something other than the expected happens market efficiency is the idea that price of a stock reflects all the known information available about a stock. No investor knows what will happen to the price before all of the other investors. Market inefficiency is anything that happens to challenge that idea, in a non-rational way (Table 1). For example, by selling overvalued stocks, and using that money to buy undervalued stocks, if done correctly, investors can make a lot of money this way, even if it does not seem rational (Kahneman & Tversky, 1979).

Table 1. Psychological Biases in Economic Decision Making (Adapted from Kahneman & Tversky, 1974, 1991, 2002; Kudryavtsev et al., 2013)

Bias	Description
Heuristic bias	'Rules of thumb' to make quick decisions.
Loss Aversion Bias	Actions are focused on avoiding loss rather than trying to make gains
Framing bias	This is best avoided by using numeracy with absolute measures of efficacy
Recency bias	Paying more attention on more recent information and either ignore or forget more distant information
Anchoring bias	Decisions are unduly influenced by initial information that shapes our view of subsequent information.
Group think bias	Peer pressure to conform to the opinions held by the group.
Confirmation Bias	Selective search for evidence, People tend to be willing to gather facts that support certain conclusions but disregard other facts that support different conclusions. Individuals who are highly defensive in this manner show significantly greater left prefrontal cortex activity as measured by EEG than do less defensive individuals, Premature termination of search for evidence, People tend to accept the first alternative that looks like it might work.
Choice-supportive bias	People distort their memories of chosen and rejected options to make the chosen options seem more attractive.
Primacy bias	Paying more attention to the first set of information
Repetition bias	A willingness to believe what one has been told most often and by the greatest number of different sources.
Source credibility bias	A tendency to reject a person's statement on the basis of a bias against the person, organization, or group to which the person belongs. People preferentially accept statement by others that they like
Correspondence bias	People tend to assume that outcomes are caused by dispositional factors, for example a person's constitution or personality, even when the actual cause is due to situational factors, for example, luck or coincidence

Research on the biases of risk-aversion and seeking is mainly focused on the choices about risk to oneself. The choices about risks to a group of others include biases of inequality aversion or fairness. Several of the same biases of risky decision-making also apply to the choices about inequality aversion or fairness suggesting that similar heuristics are being employed. This means that decisions about fairness are being made in very similar ways even though there is no personal risk involved. People will often feel differently about identical outcomes because of the presentation of how that outcome is reached. The framing and reference points matter in choices about fairness and inequality (Michaelson, 2015).

BIG FIVE PERSONALITY TRAITS AND ECONOMIC PREFERENCES

Personality traits are the relatively enduring patterns of thoughts, feelings, and behaviors that reflect the tendency of an individual to respond in certain ways under certain circumstances. The big five domains of psychological personality constructs include: openness, conscientiousness, extraversion, agreeableness, and neuroticism. Openness represents individual differences in the tendency to be open to new aesthetic, cultural, and intellectual experiences. Conscientiousness represents the tendency to be organized, responsible, and hard working. Extraversion represents the quality of being more outgoing, gregarious, sociable and openly expressive. Agreeableness represents the tendency to act in a cooperative, unselfish manner. Neuroticism represents a chronic level of emotional instability and proneness to psychological distress (Roberts, 2006).

Both economic preferences and personality traits predict a wide range of life outcomes. If the economic preferences and personality traits are closely linked, they are expected to be substitutes in explaining heterogeneity in behavior. However, if economic preferences and personality traits capture different aspects of behavior, the two measurement systems may have complementary predictive power for important life outcomes. In other words, the economic preferences and personality traits, individually or jointly, may explain life outcomes. Data from incentivized laboratory experiments and representative samples found only low degrees of association between economic preferences and personality.

However, on regressing life outcomes – such as labor market success, health status and life satisfaction, earnings, unemployment, and education – simultaneously on preference and personality measures, it was found that economic preferences and personality are complementary constructs when it comes to explaining heterogeneity in important life outcomes and behavior. However, no clear picture emerges regarding the relationship between measures of personality and economic preferences (Becker et al., 2012).

A core element of economic theory is the assumption of stable preferences. This assumption was tested in public goods games by repeatedly eliciting cooperation preferences in a fixed subject pool over a period of five months. It was found that cooperation preferences are very stable at the aggregate level, and, to a smaller degree, at the individual level, allowing us to predict future behavior fairly accurately. Furthermore, these results provide evidence on the psychological foundations of cooperation preferences. The personality dimension 'Agreeableness' is closely related to both the type and the stability of cooperation preferences. (Volk, Thoni, & Ruigrok, 2012).

SOCIAL FACTORS INFLUENCING ECONOMIC PREFERENCES: THEORY OF MIND

Economics and game theory assume that people are capable of predicting the actions of others. This requires people to be able to understand others' motives and beliefs and view the perspective of others. The capacity to represent others' intentions, beliefs, and desires is referred as mentalizing or the theory of mind (TOM) mentioned earlier and is a special intelligence that can assess not only one's own desires and beliefs, but also those of others. Economic TOM entails a hierarchy of beliefs: "I know my preferences, and I have beliefs about your preferences, beliefs about your beliefs about my preferences". Humans have an ability to view an economic situation from the other person's perspective based on their understanding of the motives and beliefs of others. Human economic preferences are based on both self-interest and regards for others.

People with a well-developed TOM have a better understanding of how other people think, feel, and react and can take this into account when making a decision resulting in a greater sense of fairness. They have a better understanding of how their decisions impact others (Robalino & Robson, 2012). TOM requires one to be able to understand the intentions, beliefs and desires of others, share their feelings, and predict their behavior regarding their economic decisions. The ability to share others' feelings or to empathize has consequences regarding one's own economic preferences. In addition, one's own emotions, biases, framing and heuristics influence the economic preferences and decision-making.

Sometimes the human decision-making process is a psychological one dictated by emotions. Some anomalies like heuristics and framing that occur in economic decision-making cannot be explained by conventional economic theories using rational choice. Empathy is the ability to understand another person's perceptions on a deep level without reference to one's own perceptions—which may be a culminating feature of TOM development. However, economists do not have any direct insight into empathy and its interactions with one's own economic decision-making (Singer & Fehr, 2005).

The human mind is an adaptive classification system in which the external stimuli is ordered and classified in terms of neural connections that are the result of biological inheritance and individual's past experiences unique to the individual. The ongoing classification and coding processes in the human mind create neural connections that allow the individual to continuously update a model of the environment as experienced by the individual and leads to economic preferences, decisions, and behavior.

Hayek's (1952) TOM and his economic theory helped develop modern cognitive and behavioral economics where the effect of cognitive biases on economic behavior is recognized. Entropy TOM is an economic theory of mind in which the value and cost of information processing is integrated into the overall picture of economic decision-making (Chen, 2011). Behavioral economics emerged to account for these anomalies by integrating social, cognitive, and emotional factors in understanding economic decisions (Kahneman, 2003a). Behavioral economics combines the rational perspective with psychological perspective that includes the role of emotions and personality attributes.

Evolutionary psychology provides a means of explaining constructs that deal with mental capacities like TOM and Machiavellian or social brain. Hayek's (1952) TOM shows how human codify information and use dispersed knowledge to make economic choices. TOM deals with a mental capacity that allows one to be able to read others' behaviors, linguistic and non-verbal cues, and analyzes their intentions. To have a social brain means being able to assess, compete with and, where necessary, outwit others. TOM states that humans have the innate ability to intuitively understand one's own and other people's minds or mental states which include thoughts, beliefs, perceptions, knowledge, intentions, desires, and emotions.

Human behavior is influenced by these mental states. This ability to recognize one's own state of mind and those of others is central to human consciousness. The understanding that others have mental states different from one's own makes it possible to infer what others are thinking and to predict their behavior (Loasby, 2004).

Entropy TOM is an economic theory of mind in which the value and cost of information processing is integrated into the overall picture of economic decision-making and includes a theory of judgment which provides a common framework to integrate behavioral and informational theories of investment. The theory of judgment provides a quantitative link between investors' judgment and their trading activities. It offers a simple and unified understanding of patterns in market activities and investor behaviors (Chen, 2011).

The cognitive ability of TOM develops by degrees from infancy through childhood and adolescence into adulthood. It forms a basis for a child's acquisition of language and the development of appropriate social behavior and skills. It includes the ability to understand that the representations generated in one's mind do not necessarily reflect the real world and that other people may hold different representations. Mind is involved in all aspects of daily living and social interactions. It underlies learning and teaching and the ability to follow directions and understand socially based information. Mind skills are essential for working cooperatively. They also underlie the ability to manipulate and deceive others.

A lack of mind skills is considered by many to be a core deficit in autism (Singer & Fehr, 2005). In interactive decision-making, TOM reasoning is not of a low level in all competitive game settings. Individuals display effective TOM reasoning, reflecting realistic assumptions about their opponents in both competitive and relatively simple games (Goodie et al., 2012). Human judgment and decision-making involve both cognitive and emotional. In risk perception and decision-making, one must extend beyond the deliberate, rational evaluation of the various alternatives to see if it feels right. Intuition and affect play an important role in decision-making (Bohm & Brun, 2008).

NEURAL MECHANISMS OF ECONOMIC DECISION MAKING –NEUROECONOMICS

Human economic decision-making is rooted in emotional, rational, and neural mechanisms. Both reason and emotion reside in the brain and their interaction leads to economic preferences (Miller & Cohen, 2001). Economic, goal-directed decision-making behavior has basis in neurobiological and computational processes in the human brain and is causally determined by the neural activity in human brain. The neural computations necessary for making choices are stochastic (Corsani, 2013). Based on neurobiological evidence, human behavior is motivated by seeking gain and avoiding loss. During anticipation of gain versus loss, different neural circuits may generate emotion since the computational and neurobiological processes behind the goal-directed decision-making and behavior are also related to the psychological processes (Cohen, 2005). Neuroscience studies provide insight into human economic preferences and decision-making by linking the neural mechanisms to the cognitive and psychological processes in the human brain. Neuroeconomics seeks to explain human decision-making in an integrative way by combining the neural, emotional, and cognitive mechanisms in the human brain.

Economic decision-making involves the ability to process multiple alternatives to determine a course of action that leads to gain and avoids loss. The perspectives of classical, experimental and behavioral economics, cognitive and social psychology, neurobiology, endocrinology, mathematics, and computer science are combined together in the interdisciplinary field of neuroeconomics which seeks to explain human economic decision-making behavior in an integrative fashion in terms of neural mechanisms, cognition, and emotion. Using a combination of tools from many fields, Neuroeconomics avoids the shortcomings that arise from a single perspective approach (Fehr & Rangel, 2011).

Neuroeconomics uses brain imaging to investigate processes of economic decision-making that involves the computation and the comparison of decision values underlying goal-directed behavior (Popescu & Nica, 2014). The neurons in the orbitofrontal cortex (OFC) encode values of the choices available and the choice made. The individual must quickly estimate the reward value of the stimulus and predict when the reward will occur. The rational or self-interest focused decision-making is related to this prior processing of the expected reward or punishment. Emotions provide quick, automatic ways to react to new situations through rules of thumb and heuristics.

Humans do have the capacity to override the quick emotional response to a new situation and develop a delayed rational response. This capacity resides in the prefrontal cortex which is the most recently evolved part of human brain that supports higher cognitive processes. The limbic system is responsible for emotional reactions. The role of emotion in human behavior is rooted in our evolutionary past and is helpful for survival even today through the quick fight or flight response. Dopamine is the key neurotransmitter in the limbic system for reward processing which allows humans to engage in "approach" type behaviors. Serotonin is important in the "avoidance" type behaviors (Schultz, 2006).

Non-invasive brain stimulation and imaging techniques provide insight into the neural networks involved in the decision-making and generation of choices. The regions of brain activation while making these decisions provide insight into human economic preferences (Glimcher et al., 2008). Understanding the neural implementation of the psychological processes involved in economic decision-making provides insight into the cognitive and motivational processes driving human behavior. Experimentally-induced variations in neural activity in specific regions of people's brain changes people's willingness to make an economic decision. Neurological change influences the mental state, but relating the change to mental state is difficult because the latter is not directly observable (Hunter, 2013).

The human brain is best understood as a confederation of two mechanisms- cognition (reason) in the prefrontal cortex and emotion in the limbic system. The prefrontal cortex has the reasoning abilities and the capacity for cognitive control. It has the ability to guide thought and action in association with abstract goals or intentions, especially when this requires overcoming countervailing habits or reflexes. A human decision can be viewed as a joint decision by a committee of emotion and reason. Cognition has the ability to guide the thought and action in association with abstract goals or intentions especially when it requires overcoming emotional reactions. Cognition and emotion usually act together and guide human behavior.

At times, emotion competes with cognition offering a different evaluation of the same situation and emotion can override reason quickly and unconsciously. Humans do have the capacity to override the quick emotional response to a situation and develop a delayed rational response. This capacity resides in the prefrontal cortex which is the most recently evolved parts of our brain that supports higher cognitive processes whereas the role of emotion is rooted in our evolutionary past and is helpful for survival through the quick fight or flight response.

The parts of the brain that decide approach/avoidance behavior in survival settings are also involved in financial decision making. In brain imaging studies, activation in the nucleus accumbens is a positive predictor of choosing a risky asset. Activation in the Anterior Insula is a positive predictor of choosing the risk-neutral asset. Excessive activation in these areas causes deviations from optimal choice of a risk-neutral asset and correlates with making risk-seeking and risk-averse investments (Kuhnen & Knotson, 2005).

Economic decision-making assumes that people are capable of predicting others' actions through mentalizing and empathy. Mentalizing allows one to predict others' intentions, beliefs, desires and motives and make choices that promote self-interest. Empathy represents the capacity to share the feelings of others. Through mentalizing and empathy, people are able to view the economic transactions from the perspectives of both the self-interest and from other participant's perspective. Neuroscience provides insight into the neural mechanisms underlying mentalizing and empathy. The ability to mentalize develops in humans by age five and is impaired in adults with autism. Using a wide range of stimuli representing the intentions, beliefs, and desires of others, brain imaging studies reveal that the same part of the medial prefrontal lobe called anterior paracingulate cortex is involved when mentalizing about the thoughts, intentions or beliefs of others or when people are attending to their own states. The ability to empathize allows one to make decisions that also consider the interests of others. Due to empathy, humans can share their feelings and emotions in the absence of any direct emotional stimulation to themselves. The neuroscientific model of empathy suggests that observation of another person in a particular emotional state automatically activates a representation of that state in the observer with its associated autonomic and somatic responses (Singer & Fehr, 2005).

The empathic responses can be measured using functional Magnetic Resonance Imaging (fMRI). The automatic empathic response does not require conscious effortful processing but can be inhibited or controlled (Preston & de Waal, 2002). In the automatic empathic response, there is active engagement of some explicit judgments about others' feelings and one represents the goals of others in terms of one's own goals without even being aware of it. There are individual differences in empathic abilities. People with stronger empathic abilities are better predictors of others' motives and actions and are more likely to exhibit altruistic behaviors (Singer, et al., 2004).

Social neuroscience provides insights into the theory of mind or 'mentalizing' the neural mechanisms underlying our capacity to understand others' intentions, beliefs, and desires and capacity to share the feelings of others (i.e., empathy). Empathy and mentalizing are useful to individuals to make self-interested choices because one is able to predict others' actions more accurately. While pursuing self-interest, empathy allows one to be considerate of others and encourages other-regarding behavior. Neuroscientific empathy experiments indicate that the same affective brain circuits are automatically activated when we feel pain and others feel pain (Frith & Frith, 2003).

Using Positron Emission Tomography (PET) and fMRI, it has been shown that the perception and production of motor action has a common code in the brain (Grezes & Decety, 2001). Brain activity studies in choice tasks and belief formation tasks have established that a part of the medial prefrontal lobe called the anterior paracingulate cortex is involved in mentalizing others' beliefs, thoughts, and intentions of others. The same area is involved when people are attending to their own mental states – thoughts, beliefs, and intentions (Singer & Fehr, 2005).

Another finding is that the neural mechanisms underlying our ability to represent others' goals and intentions by the mere observation of their motor actions. The neural basis for imitation has been found to be the "mirror neurons". The discovery of mirror neurons demonstrates that a translation mechanism is present in the brain and is automatically elicited when viewing others' actions. This mirror system might underlie our ability to share others' mental states providing us with automatic simulation of their actions, goals, and intentions (Gallagher & Frith, 2003).

Neuroeconomics aims to discover mechanisms of economic decisions, and express them mathematically to explain and predict observed choice. The economic, psychological, and neural levels of explanation can be linked. The neural evidence is quite strong for a process of learning valuations through prediction error, and a simple model of neural valuation and comparison that corresponds to random utility. Neuro-imaging studies of decision-making have generally related neural activity to objective measures (such as reward magnitude, probability or delay), despite choice preferences being subjective. However, economic theories posit that decision-makers behave as though different options have different subjective values.

Using fMRI, it has been shown that the neural activity in several brain regions—particularly the ventral striatum, medial prefrontal cortex and posterior cingulate cortex—tracks the revealed subjective value of delayed monetary rewards. This similarity provides unambiguous evidence that the subjective value of potential rewards is explicitly represented in the human brain. Neuroscientific discoveries can constrain and guide the models of economic preferences and the economic behavior can shape our understanding of the brain (Singer & Fehr, 2005).

In summary, although expected utility (EU) and the concept of rational agents are still being used in mainstream economics there is growing awareness about the role of emotions in economic decision making. Behavioral economics emerged by integrating social, cognitive, and emotional factors in understanding economic decisions. Neuroeconomics adds another layer by using neuroscientific methods in understanding the interplay between economic behavior and neural mechanisms. The economic preferences of time, risk, reciprocity, trust, and altruism have a neural basis. Neural activity has causal effects on economic behavior. The brain areas that generate emotional states also process information about risk, rewards and punishment. This suggests that emotions influence financial decisions. Positive emotional states such as excitement induce people to take risks and to be confident about their ability to evaluate investment options. Negative emotions like anxiety have the opposite effect on risk taking.

Emotions change behavior by changing risk preferences as well as learning (Kuhnen & Knutson, 2011). Activation in the Nucleus Accumbens is a positive predictor of choosing a risky asset. Activation in the Anterior Insula is a positive predictor of choosing the riskless event. Excessive activation in these areas causes deviations from optimal choice of a risk-neutral agent. It correlates with making risk-seeking and risk-averse mistakes (Kuhnen & Knutson, 2005). One can exogenously change one's risk taking behavior by triggering the brain areas that process emotions.

Anticipation of viewing highly rewarding stimuli promotes financial risk taking. This effect is partially mediated by increased Nucleus Accumbens activation. Neuroeconomics has contributed to our understanding of financial investing and consumer behavior (Knutson, et al., 2008).

NEUROMARKETING: ADVERTISING, MARKETING, AND BRAND LOYALTY

Neuromarketing is the application of neuroscience techniques to understand the decision processes of consumers in marketing, advertising, and brand loyalty. It involves scanning a consumers' brain using fMRI and recording their responses to stimuli to draw conclusions about how to sell to customers more effectively (Lindstrom, 2010). The purchasing behavior is determined at both conscious and subconscious levels. The traditional conscious measures such as surveys and focus groups miss the subconscious contribution which is 75% to 95%. To understand the subconscious level contribution towards the consumer purchasing behavior, one has to use neuroscience techniques.

Neuromarketing focuses on the reward system placed at the heart of the midbrain, which is related to release of dopamine. This motivates humans for simple behaviors like seeking food or sex or complex behaviors like choosing a brand, a taste, or an investment. Dopamine induces subjective feelings of pleasure and positive emotions. Cultural objects like cars that reflect a degree of wealth and social status and money activate the reward system. The human brain gets activated differently by gain or loss, both during anticipation and receiving (Touhami et al., 2011).

Just like in medicine, a placebo can be 30% effective; there is a marketing placebo effect. An unconscious expectation about the relationship between price and quality is an example of a marketing placebo effect. A change in price can affect neural representations on experiences pleasantness and effectiveness of a product (Shiv et al., 2005). Increasing the price of the same wine increases subjective reports of flavor pleasantness as well as blood-oxygen-level dependent activity in medio orbitofrontal cortex which is the brain area associated with experienced pleasantness during experiential tasks. This can be measured using the functional brain imaging techniques (Plassmann et al., 2008).

Using brain imaging, the neural circuits that are involved in identifying a brand preference have been identified. The preference of a brand is based on two factors including the intrinsic components of a product and "branding". The "branding" plays a key role in the mechanism of preference which influences buying behavior and brand loyalty (Plassman, Kenning, & Ahler, 2007). Two separate systems are involved in generating brand preference. When the judgments are based solely on sensory information (e.g. taste), the ventromedial prefrontal cortex (VMPFC) is involved. When the judgments are based on sensory and cultural information, hippocampus, dorsal prefrontal cortex and the midbrain are activated. In a taste test where the subjects knew that they were tasting coke, there was significant more activation than that for Pepsi. However, in blind taste tests, both coke and Pepsi tasting led to similar activation (McLure et al., 2004).

There is a debate about the ethics of neuromarketing. The critics of neuromarketing question the its ethics and recommend focusing on the heart rather than involving the brain. In spite of ethical concerns, neuromarketing is here to stay to provide insights into human cognition and emotion. Neuroscience techniques are just instruments to better understand our wants, drives and motivations. We have an ethical responsibility not to use neuromarketing to manipulate consumers. (Flores, Baruca, & Saldivar, 2014).

Table 2. Companies and the Purpose of Neuromarketing Research (adapted from Flores, Baruca and Saldivar, 2014; Babu and Vidyasagar, 2012)

Company	Industry	Neuromarketing Research Purpose
Microsoft	Technology/Software	Consumers' satisfaction and frustration in their interaction with computers
EBay	Online auction	Ad campaigns
Frito-Lay (Pepsi Co)	Food	Commercials, Products and Packaging
Daimler	Automotive	Consumer reaction to car headlight characteristics
Hyundai	Automotive	Consumer reaction when viewing a sports car
Viacom	Media	Consumer reaction to advertising
Neurofocus	Research	Conducted neuromarketing research for Google, Chevron and Walt Disney
Delta Airlines	Airlines	Understanding customer travel experience

The most promising application of neuromarketing may be in product development before the product is released in the marketplace (Ariely & Berns, 2010). Table 2 lists the companies that use neuromarkeitng for various purposes ranging from customer satisfaction, ad campaigns and packaging design.

SUMMARY AND IMPLICATIONS FOR SOCIAL POLICIES

The human economic decision-making is an integrative social process involving interaction of reason, emotion, feelings, and the ability to mentalize and empathize in the human mind. The human mind is a complex and *adaptive* classification system since it is modified by both a process of natural selection in forming the organism's set of neural connections and by individual's life experiences. To make sense of the world, human mind classifies and orders the external information inputs in terms of neural connections that are the result of the biological inheritance of the individual and the individual's unique past experiences.

The individual views the world through the lens of his or her past experiences. This information classification process in the human mind is dynamic and contextual. The order attributed to each particular information input depends on the other inputs that arrive with it. The inputs include both rational and psychological aspects. There is no one-to-one relationship between each given stimulus and the sensory order which is unique for each person. The sensory order depends on the external stimulus and the specific neural system involved in the process. Each individual has a unique neural system although there are common features among individuals. The ongoing classification and coding processes create neural connections that allow the individual to continuously update a model of the environment as experienced by the individual, and leads to economic preferences, decisions, and behavior (Ambrosino, 2014).

Classical economics which is based on rational choice and utility maximization does not adequately explain human economic decisions in real life. Instead of conducting due diligence to gather all the information available to make rational economic decisions, people make decisions based on their emotions, biases, and social influences. In other words, economic decisions are based on rational, emotional, social and neural factors. Behavioral economics emerged to account for the effect of emotions, biases, heuristics, and psychology on economic decision-making. The body's response to the external stimuli begins with emotions and feelings.Human mind begins at the level of feelings. Even with intact reason, if emotions are impaired, humans are not able to make good decisions.

Emotions are central to the life-regulating processes of humans. "We are not thinking machines that feel, we are feeling machines that think". Feelings are mental experiences of body states, which arise as the brain interprets emotions. The self-concept of humans emerges from emotions and feelings (Jason, 2014).

Behavioral economics includes both the rational and emotional aspects of economic decision-making which seeks to unite the basic principles of classical economics with the realities posed by human psychology. Behavioral economics has been applied to many areas including macroeconomics, labor economics, finance, and marketing. Behavioral finance combines the individual economic behavior with group economic behavior that includes social influence. Human economic decisions are influenced by what others do. Stock prices move up and down without any substantial change in the fundamentals of the companies.

People trade in herds and that influences stock prices. Behavioral economics includes the social factors including people's ability to predict others' intentions that influence self-interested economic preferences (Singh, 2009). The root cause of the 2008 financial crisis was a psychological phenomenon, not a fundamental one. Risk-seeking behaviors were evident in loss-dominant markets while excessive optimism and confirmation bias drove the crisis (Shefrin, 2009, 2000; Park & Sohn, 2013; Sadeghnia & Habibniko, 2013).

The interaction of behavioral economics with social neuroscience led to the development of neuro-economics which seeks to explain human economic decision making in an integrative way by combining insights from psychology, economics, and neuroscience. From a neuroscientific perspective, human decision-making is computational and involves the ability to process multiple alternatives and to follow a course of action. Economic preferences are the result of individuals assigning *values* to the offered choices in their brain (Fehr & Rangel, 2011). The brain imaging methods of neuroscience help in understanding the interplay between economic behavior and neural mechanisms.

Human economic decision-making combines rational and intuitive involving cognition and emotion which are seated in the prefrontal cortex and limbic system respectively in the human brain. Economic decision-making reflects the interaction of automatic and controlled parts of human brain. The automatic system is fast, unconscious, and emotional and requiring little effort while the controlled system is slow, rational, and deliberate and requires effort. People rely on rules of thumb or heuristics to make fast, automatic judgments especially when they are pressed for time, under cognitive load, in a good mood or lacking motivation (Sanfey & Chang, 2008). Understanding neural mechanisms contributes to our understanding of economic decision-making and studying economic behavior has the potential to contribute to understanding of neural mechanisms. Some of the criticisms of neuroeconomics include exaggeration of new findings, misuse of brain imaging data and poor testing of hypotheses (Craver & Alexandrova, 2008; Rubinstein, 2008).

In addition to self-interested rational and emotional economic decisions, humans do make *other-regarding* or altruistic economic decisions. Social neuroscience provides insight into the neural mechanisms that underlie the human capacity to predict others' actions (*mentalize*) and share feelings of others (*empathy*). The ability to mentalize promotes self-interested behavior and the ability to empathize promotes the other-regarding behavior or altruism. Rationality, emotions, and the ability to mentalize and empathize, are all seated in the human brain (Singer & Fehr, 2005).

The understanding of the interaction between emotion and cognition has great relevance to economists, sociologists, and policy makers. The social policies are aimed at protecting the society from emotional responses that may have served us well in our evolutionary past, but can interfere with the smooth functioning of modern society. The development of human capacity for rational thought has given rise to powerful technologies that can threaten human survival if human behavior is guided by the emotions alone (Cohen, 2005).

The findings from behavioral economics and judgment and decision making highlight many behavioral impediments including lack of self-control, emotions, and choice architecture that influence the savings behavior of individuals which impacts financial security in retirement. Policy makers can use this information to incentivize savings in the short-term, reframing the decision-context and shifting reference points to help individuals save more and spend less (Knoll, 2010).

Future research on neural mechanisms for economic decision-making can focus on gender and generation differences in the responses to the same stimuli. Another area for future research would be to understand the differences in the neural mechanisms in economic decision making for the labor force and the owners of the capital to get insight into the income-inequality issues that can generate social unrest. Insights into customer satisfaction, ad campaigns and packaging through Neuromarketing can help the firms and customers alike. Understanding the rational, emotional and neural mechanisms in economic decision-making enables us to predict human behavior at both the micro and macroeconomic levels.

REFERENCES

Ambrosino, A. (2014). A Cognitive Approach to Law and Economics: Hayek's Legacy. *Journal of Economic Issues*, *48*(1), 19–48. doi:10.2753/JEI0021-3624480102

Ariely, D., & Berns, G. S. (2010). Neuromarketing: The Hope and Hype of Neuroimaging in Business. *Nature Reviews. Neuroscience*, *11*(4), 284–292. doi:10.1038/nrn2795 PMID:20197790

Ayton, P., & Fischer, I. (2004). The Hot Hand Fallacy and the Gambler's Fallacy: Two Faces of Subjective Randomness? *Memory & Cognition*, *32*(8), 1369–1378. doi:10.3758/BF03206327 PMID:15900930

Babu, S. S., & Vidyasagar, T. P. (2012). Neuromarketing: Is Campbell in Soup? *The IUP Journal of Marketing Management*, *9*(2), 76–100.

Becker, A., Deckers, T., Dohmen, T., Falk, A., & Kosse, F. (2012). *The Relationship Between Economic Preferences and Psychological Personality Measures*. Retrieved On January 8, 2015, from: http://www.iame.uni-bonn.de/people/thomas-dohmen/iza-dp-6470

Bohm, G., & Brun, W. (2008). Intuition and Affect in Risk Perception and Decision Making. *Judgment and Decision Making*, *3*(1), 1–4.

Borghans, L., Duckworth, A. L., Heckman, J. J., & Ter Weel, B. (2008). The Economics and Psychology of Personality Traits. *The Journal of Human Resources*, *43*(4), 972–1059. doi:10.3368/jhr.43.4.972

Brahmana, R. K., Hooy, C. W., & Ahmad, Z. (2012). Psychological Factors on Irrational Financial Decision Making. *Humanomics*, *28*(4), 236–257. doi:10.1108/08288661211277317

Chen, J. (2011). The Entropy Theory of Mind and Behavioral Finance. *The IUP Journal of Behavioral Finance*, *8*(4), 6–39.

Cohen, J. D. (2005). The Vulcanization of the Human Brain: A Neural Perspective on Interactions between Cognition and Emotion. *The Journal of Economic Perspectives*, *19*(4), 3–24. doi:10.1257/089533005775196750

Corsani, A. (2013). Rent and Subjectivity in Neoliberal Cognitive Capitalism. *Knowledge Cultures*, *1*(4), 67–83.

Craver, C. F., & Alexandrova, A. (2008). No Revolution Necessary: Neural Mechanism For Economics. *Economics and Philosophy*, *24*(03), 381–406. doi:10.1017/S0266267108002034

Fehr, E., Fischbacher, U., & Kodfeld, M. (2005). Neuroeconomic Foundations of Trust and Social Preferences: Initial Evidence. *The American Review*, *95*(2), 346–351.

Fehr, E., & Rangel, A. (2011). Neuroeconomic Foundations of Economic Choice- Recent Advances. *The Journal of Economic Perspectives*, *25*(4), 3–30. doi:10.1257/jep.25.4.3 PMID:21595323

Flores, J., Baruca, A., & Saldivar, R. (2014). Is Neuromarketing Ethical? Consumers Say Yes, Consumers Say No. *Journal of Legal. Ethical and Regulatory Issues*, *17*(2), 77–91.

Frederick, S., Lowenstein, G., & O'Donoghue, T. (2002). Discounting and Time Preference: A Critical Review. *Journal of Economic Literature*, *40*(1), 351–401. doi:10.1257/jel.40.2.351

Frith, U., & Frith, C. D. (2003). Development and Neurophysiology of Mentalizing. *Philosophical Transactions of the Royal Society of London. Series B, Biological Sciences*, *358*(1431), 459–473. doi:10.1098/rstb.2002.1218 PMID:12689373

Gallagher, H. L., & Frith, C. D. (2003). Functional Imaging of Theory of Mind. *Trends in Cognitive Sciences*, *7*(2), 77–83. doi:10.1016/S1364-6613(02)00025-6 PMID:12584026

Glimcher, P. W. Colin, Camerer, E. F., Fehr, E., & Poldrack, R. A. (2008). Introduction: A Brief History of Neuroeconomics. In P. Glimcher, E. Fehr, C. Camerer, & R. A. Poldrack (Eds.), Neuroeconomics: Decision Making and the Brain (pp. 1-12). London: Academic Press.

Goodie, A. S., Doshi, P., & Young, D. L. (2012). Levels of Theory-of-Mind Reasoning in Competitive Games. *Journal of Behavioral Decision Making*, *25*(1), 95–108. doi:10.1002/bdm.717

Grezes, J., & Decety, J. (2001). Functional Anatomy of Execution, Mental Simulation, Observation and Verb Generation of Actions: A Meta Analysis. *Human Brain Mapping*, *12*(1), 1–19. doi:10.1002/1097-0193(200101)12:1<1::AID-HBM10>3.0.CO;2-V PMID:11198101

Hayek, F. A. (1952). *The Sensory Order*. Chicago: Chicago University Press.

Heukelom, F. (2007). *Kahneman and Tversky and the Origin of Behavioral Economics*. Tinbergen Institute Discussion Paper, TI 2007-003/1. Retrieved on May 9, 2013, from: http://www.tinbergen.nl

Hunter, M. (2013). Creativity and Making Connections: The Patchwork of Entrepreneurial Opportunity. *Psychological Issues in Human Resources Management*, *1*(2), 7–51.

Jason, P. (2014). Questions and Answers with Antonio Damasio. *MIT's Technology Review, 117*(4), 48–51.

Kahneman, D. (1994). New Challenges to the Rationality Assumption. *Journal of Institutional and Theoretical Economics, 150*(1), 18–44.

Kahneman, D. (2003a). Perspective on Judgment and Choice: Mapping Bounded Rationality. *The American Psychologist, 58*(9), 697–720. doi:10.1037/0003-066X.58.9.697 PMID:14584987

Kahneman, D. (2003b). Maps of Bounded Rationality: Psychology for Behavioral Economics. *The American Economic Review, 93*(5), 1449–1475. doi:10.1257/000282803322655392

Kahneman, D., & Thaler, R. (1991). Economic Analysis and the Psychology of Utility: Applications to Compensation Policy. *The American Economic Review, 81*(2), 341–346.

Kahneman, D., & Tversky, A. (1974). Judgment Under Uncertainty: Heuristics and Biases. *Science, 185*(4157), 1124–1131. doi:10.1126/science.185.4157.1124 PMID:17835457

Kahneman, D., & Tversky, A. (1979). Prospect Theory: An Analysis of Decision Under Risk. *Econometrica, 47*(2), 313–327. doi:10.2307/1914185

Kahneman, D., & Tversky, A. (1991). Loss Aversion in Riskless Choice: A Reference Dependent Model. *The Quarterly Journal of Economics, 106*(4), 1039–1061. doi:10.2307/2937956

Kahneman, D., & Tversky, A. (Eds.). (2002). *Choices, Values and Frames*. Cambridge, MA: Cambridge University Press.

Knoll, M. A. Z. (2010). The Role of Behavioral Economics and Behavioral Decision- Making in Americans' Retirement Savings Decisions. *Social Security Bulletin, 70*(4), 1–23. PMID:21261167

Knutson, B., Wimmer, G. E., Kuhnen, C. M., & Winkielman, P. (2008). Nucleus Accumbens Activation Mediates the Influence of Reward Cues on Financial Risk Taking. *Neuroreport, 19*(5), 509–513. doi:10.1097/WNR.0b013e3282f85c01 PMID:18388729

Kudryavtsev, A., Cohen, G., & Hon-Snir, S. (2013). Rational or Intuitive: Are Behavioral Biases Correlated Across Stock Market Investors? *Contemporary Economics, 7*(2), 31–53. doi:10.5709/ce.1897-9254.81

Kuhnen, C. M., & Knutson, B. (2005). The Neural Basis for Financial Risk Taking. *Neuron, 47*(5), 763–770. doi:10.1016/j.neuron.2005.08.008 PMID:16129404

Kuhnen, C. M., & Knutson, B. (2011). The Influence of Affect on Beliefs, Preferences, and Financial Decisions. *Journal of Financial and Quantitative Analysis, 46*(3), 605–626. doi:10.1017/S0022109011000123

Lindstrom, M. (2010). *Buy Ology: Truth and Lies about Why We Buy*. New York: Broadway Books.

Loasby, B. J. (2004). Hayek's Theory of the Mind. *Evolutionary Psychology and Economic Theory. Advances in Austrian Economics, 7*, 101–134. doi:10.1016/S1529-2134(04)07006-1

McLure, S. M., Li, J., Tomlin, D., Cypert, K. S., Montague, L. M., & Montague, P. R. (2004). Neural Correlates of Behavioral Preference for Culturally Familiar Drinks. *Neuron, 44*(2), 379–387. doi:10.1016/j.neuron.2004.09.019 PMID:15473974

Michaelson, Z. (2015). Biases in Choices About Fairness: Psychology and Economic Inequality. *Judgment and Decision Making*, *10*(2), 198–203.

Miller, E. K., & Cohen, J. K. (2001). An Integrative Theory of Prefrontal cortex Function. *Annual Review of Neuroscience*, *24*(1), 167–202. doi:10.1146/annurev.neuro.24.1.167 PMID:11283309

Moorhead, G., & Montanari, J. R. (1986). An Empirical Investigation of the Groupthink Phenomenon. *Human Relations*, *39*(5), 399–410. doi:10.1177/001872678603900502

Park, H., & Sohn, W. (2013). Behavioral Finance: A Survey of the Literature and Recent Development. *Seoul Journal of Business*, *19*(1), 3–42.

Plassman, H., Kenning, P., & Ahlert, A. (2007). Why Companies Should Make Their Customers Happy: The Neural Correlates of Customer Loyalty. *Advances in Consumer Research. Association for Consumer Research (U. S.)*, *34*, 735–739.

Plassman, H., O'Deherty, J., Shiv, B., & Rangel, A. (2008). Marketing Actions can Modulate Neural Representations of Experienced Pleasantness. *Proceedings of the National Academy of Sciences of the United States of America*, *105*(3), 1050–1054. doi:10.1073/pnas.0706929105 PMID:18195362

Popescu, G. H., & Nica, E. (2014). Neuroeconomic Models of Decision Making. *Knowledge Horizons – Economics*, *6*(1), 63–66.

Preston, S. D., & de Waal, F. B. M. (2002). Empathy: Its Ultimate and Proximate Bases. *Behavioral and Brain Sciences*, *25*(1), 1–72. PMID:12625087

Robalino, N., & Robson, A. (2012). The Economic Approach to theory of mind. *Philosophical Transactions of the Royal Society of London. Series B, Biological Sciences*, *367*(1599), 2224–2233. doi:10.1098/rstb.2012.0124 PMID:22734065

Roberts, B. W. (2006). Personality Development and Organizational Behavior. In B. M. Staw (Ed.), *Research on Organizational Behavior* (pp. 1–41). Amsterdam: Elsevier Science/ JAI.

Rubinstein, A. (2008). Comments on Neuroeconomics. *Economics and Philosophy*, *24*(03), 485–494. doi:10.1017/S0266267108002101

Sadeghnia, M., & Habibniko, A. (2013). Behavioral Finance and NeuroFinance and Research Conducted in This Area. *IJCRB*, *4*(12), 793–801.

Sanfey, A. G., & Chang, L. J. (2008). Multiple Systems in Decision Making. *Annals of the New York Academy of Sciences*, *1128*(1), 53–62. doi:10.1196/annals.1399.007 PMID:18469214

Schultz, W. (2006). Behavioral Theories and the neurophysiology of reward. *Annual Review of Psychology*, *57*(1), 87–115. doi:10.1146/annurev.psych.56.091103.070229 PMID:16318590

Shefrin, H. (2000). *Beyond Greed and Fear: Understanding the Behavioral Finance and the Psychology of Investing*. Boston, MA: Harvard Business School Press.

Shefrin, H. (2009). How Psychological Pitfalls Generated the Global Financial Crisis. In L. Siegel (Ed.), *Understanding the Global Financial Crisis*. Boston, MA: Harvard Business School Press. doi:10.2139/ssrn.1523931

Shiv, B., Carmon, Z., & Ariely, D. (2005). Placebo Effects of Marketing Actions: Consumers may Get What They Pay For. *JMR, Journal of Marketing Research, 42*(4), 383–393. doi:10.1509/jmkr.2005.42.4.383

Simon, H. (1955). A Behavioral Model of Rational Choice. *The Quarterly Journal of Economics, 69*(1), 99–188. doi:10.2307/1884852

Singer, T., & Fehr, E. (2005). Neuroscientific Foundations of Economic Decision Making – the Neuroeconomics of Mind Reading and Empathy. *The American Economic Review, 95*(2), 34–345. doi:10.1257/000282805774670103

Singer, T., Seymour, B., O'Doherty, J. P., Kaube, H., Dolan, R. J., & Frith, C. D. (2004). Empathy for Pain Involves the Affective but not Sensory Components of Pain. *Science, 303*(5661), 1157–1162. doi:10.1126/science.1093535 PMID:14976305

Singh, R. (2009). Behavioral Finance – The Basic Foundations. *ASBM Journal of Management, II*(1), 89–98.

Summerfield, C., & Tsetsos, K. (2015). Do Humans Make Good Decisions? *Trends in Cognitive Sciences, 19*(1), 27–34. doi:10.1016/j.tics.2014.11.005 PMID:25488076

Thaler, R. (1999). Mental Accounting Matters. *Journal of Behavioral Decision Making, 12*(3), 183–206. doi:10.1002/(SICI)1099-0771(199909)12:3<183::AID-BDM318>3.0.CO;2-F

Touhami, Z. O., Benlafkih, L., Jiddane, M., Cherrah, Y., Malki, O. E., & Benomar, A. (2011). Neuromarketing: Where Marketing and Neuroscience Meet. *African Journal of Business Management, 5*(5), 1528-1532.

Tversky, A., & Kahneman, D. (1986). Rational Choice and the Framing of Decisions. *The Journal of Business, 59*(4), S251–S278. doi:10.1086/296365

Volk, S., Thoni, C., & Ruigrok, W. (2012). Temporal stability and psychological Foundations of co-operation preferences. *Journal of Economic Behavior & Organization, 81*(2), 664–676. doi:10.1016/j.jebo.2011.10.006

KEY WORDS AND DEFINITIONS

Behavioral Economics: It combines the rational perspective of classical economics with the psychological perspective that includes the role of emotions and biases.

Big Five Personality Traits: They are five domains of psychological personality traits that are the relatively enduring patterns of thoughts, feelings and behaviors that reflect the tendency to respond in certain ways under certain circumstances and affect outcomes.

Bounded Rationality: People have cognitive limits and they are not always able to obtain all the information available they need to make the best possible decisions.

Emotional Response: An automatic response based on fight or flight response.

Heuristics: Rules of thumb people use as a short cut to make a decision in lieu of rational thought.

Neuroeconomics: It uses brain-imaging techniques of neuroscience to understand rational and emotional economic decision-making in humans.

Neuromarketing: Application of neuroscience techniques like brain imaging to understand the decision processes of consumers in marketing, advertising and brand loyalty.

Rational Choice: A choice arrived at using logic and reason alone.

Theory of Mind or Mentalizing: The capacity to represent others' intentions, beliefs and desires.

Utility: A subjective perspective of the benefits of a choice.

Chapter 4

Central Language Hypothesis in the Decision–Making Process

Duygu Buğa
Independent Researcher, Turkey

ABSTRACT

The purpose of this chapter is to explore the potential connection between neuroeconomics and the Central Language Hypothesis (CLH) which refers to the language placed within the subconscious mind of an individual. The CLH forwards that in the brains of bilingual and multilingual people, one language is more suppressive as it dominates reflexes, emotions, and senses. This central language (CL) is located at the centre of the limbic cortex of the brain. Therefore, when there is a stimulus on the limbic cortex (e.g., fear, anxiety, sadness), the brain produces the central language. The chapter begins with an Introduction followed by a Theoretical Framework. The next section discusses the neurolinguistic projection of the central language and includes the survey and the results used in this study. The Discussion section provides additional information regarding the questionnaire and the CLH, followed by Future Research Directions, Implications, and finally the Conclusion.

INTRODUCTION

The purpose of this chapter is to explore the potential connection between the field of neuroeconomics and the author's Central Language Hypothesis (CLH) which refers to the language placed within the subconscious mind of an individual. A relatively new area of economics involving the human mind and choice, neuroeconomics combines behavioural economics and neuroscience to investigate the variables affecting decision-making within an economic context (Glimcher, 2002, 2004, 2009; Verplanken & Holland, 2002). This chapter attempts to demonstrate a potential link between the Central Language (CL) concept and decision-making via a qualitative study with 30 multilingual and bilingual individuals from various linguistic backgrounds. It is envisioned this work can be used for further research in neuroeconomics and possibly in other fields such as cognition, psycholinguistics, and child development (Groome, 2014; Neufeld, 2007; Field, 2003; Liben & Müller, 2015).

DOI: 10.4018/978-1-4666-9989-2.ch004

Contemporary globalism is characterized by numerous worldwide changes occurring in economic, social, natural, and technological areas (Denktas-Sakar, et. al., 2014). As such, the dynamics involved in a wide variety of human activities such as economic development, international management, or education have necessarily changed since the dawn of the new millennium (Anderson & Wong, 2013; Friedman, 2009). How we perceive the world within the context of these activities is influenced by the language(s) we speak and understand. The author proposes the CLH is at the core of this statement, especially with regards to decision-making and economic choice based at least in part on the Sapir-Whorf Hypothesis (SWH) which is also referred to as the Whorfian Hypothesis (Kay & Kempton, 1984; Conen & Padua-Schioppa, 2015).

A controversial theory championed by the German-born linguist Edward Sapir first in 1929 and later with his student Benjamin Whorf, a chemical engineering graduate of Massachusetts Institute of Technology (MIT), the SWH states there are certain thoughts of an individual in one language that cannot be understood by those who live in another language, and the way people think is strongly affected by their native language(s). The theory is based on the two principles of *linguistic relativity* and *linguistic determinism*. *Linguistic relativity* states that people who speak different languages perceive and think about the world differently as thought is encoded linguistically (Boroditsky, 2001; Godart et al., 2015). *Linguistic determinism* refers to the fact that our thinking is determined by our language (de Cruz, 2009). As a result, language leads thought and what or how one thinks can be associated with the language used (Cengoz et al., 2001; Kemp, 2009; Nisbett, 2003). Multilingualism is an established field of research in linguistic studies that can be approached from different perspectives such as psycholinguistic, educational, neurolinguistic, and sociolinguistic angles (Garcia-Mayo, 2012, p. 129). The SWH raises a key question regarding multilingualism (Perlovsky, 2009; Kecskes & Albertazzi, 2007; Pavlenko, 2005):

- What language is the most effective on multilingual and bilingual people if any particular language has a different effect on an individual?

The critical point is that it is necessary to identify the dominant languages of multilingual and bilingual individuals to understand how they see the world and how their thoughts are shaped (de Angelis & Dewaele, 2009). The CLH is being forwarded in this chapter to answer the issues relevant to the question above.

Within the realm of multilingualism and bilingualism is the interesting concept of the Third Culture Kid (TCK) conceived in the 1960s by the sociologist Dr. Ruth Useem of Michigan State University in the USA (Lyttle, 2009). While studying the effects of extended overseas residence on British expatriates in India, Dr. Useem noticed their children were developing identities separate from both their parents and their contemporaries back in the United Kingdom. Dr. Useem eventually coined the term TCK following her study in India, and today TCKs are referred to as those who are born in one country (the "passport country") but raised during their formative years in another country (Pollock, 2001). Most TCKs are inherently bilingual or multilingual due to the very nature of their background. It should be noted that the term Third Culture Individual (TCI) is now more commonly used in the extant literature than TCK so as to include adults as well as children.

It is a fact that multilinguals and bilinguals outnumber monolinguals in the world (Tucker, 1999). Therefore, this chapter contributes to the extant literature regarding language and neuroeconomics by providing initial evidence for future research. The reader should consider the following proposition for the remainder of this chapter:

P1: *A central language (CL) is a key component to decision-making in neuroeconomics*

Process of Centralizing a Language in the Human Brain

Based in part on results from the qualitative survey, the author claims there is one language which is more suppressive in the subconscious mind of bilingual and multilingual individuals who are capable of speaking at least two languages fluently. However, when it is observed in specific conditions (e.g., in sorrow or other feelings which trigger the limbic cortex of the brain), it is clear these individuals tend to produce one language more than other native ones. Through efficient exposure, one language begins to be more dominant than other native languages and it eventually eclipses the other(s) by capturing the reflexes, emotions, and subconscious mind of a person. This is referred to as the Central Language (CL).

The CL is located at the centre of the limbic cortex of the brain. Via high exposure, the mind structures a language as CL which can be observed in reflexive situations and in other situations associated with the subconscious. An example can include when there is a stimulus in the limbic lobe (e.g., fear, anxiety, sadness) forcing the brain to produce the CL which culminates in the first utterance of an individual related to the person's CL. One of the most substantial features of the CL is its changeability. If there is sufficient exposure to another language, the CL of an individual can potentially transform into a new one. Sustained exposure to another language is the key to this transformation.

There exists a dichotomy between the CL and the mother tongue in that the latter is the first language acquired at home, but the CL may be the second language as well. Additionally, the CL is just one for an individual, but there can be more than one native language; therefore, there should not be any dichotomy between the notion of a native language and the CL. As such, the mother tongue of a bilingual/multilingual person might be her/his CL or vice versa. A bilingual/multilingual person might not be very competent or fluent in his/her CL, so it is not always easy to identify the CL of an individual. In some cases, simply the lexicons of a language might be dominant and an individual might use code switching; nonetheless, this does not mean it is the person's CL because high exposure may cause code switching/code mixing (Molinsky, 2007).

Understanding the concept in detail requires extending the view of the CL theory to comprehend how the CL mechanism occurs in the human brain. Figure 1 shows the Limbic lobe which is a region situated on the medial surface of each cerebral hemisphere. It has distinctive portions such as amygdale, hypothalamus, olfactory bulb, septal nuclei, and some thalamic nuclei. The Limbic lobe processes the emotional stimuli so it has an effective and substantial role in formation of the CL within the brain.

An individual can have more than one language on the level of a native one, and mastering multiple languages is common in much of the world (Flynn et al., 2005; Wood, 1988, 1998; Gass & Selinker, 2008). In the Limbic lobe of the brain is the Cingulate Cortex which is involved with emotion formation and processing, learning, and memory as is the CL that influences human reflexes. A CL can be seen clearly in *reflexive utterances* and *self-utterances* (talking inwardly). A person's reflexive and self-utterances are key factors to determine the CL of a bilingual or multilingual person, although there

Figure 1. Stages of structure of Central Language within the subconscious mind

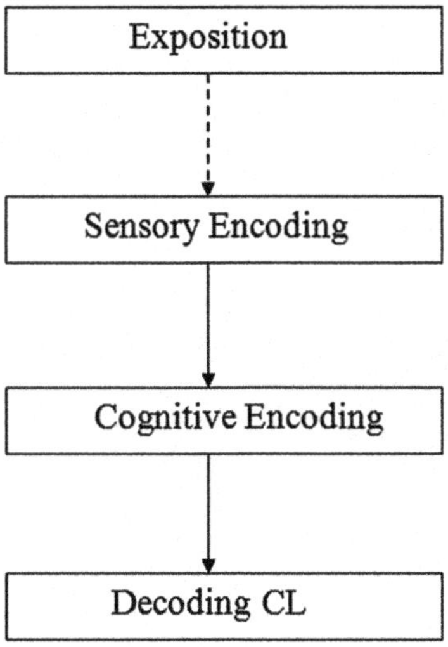

```
┌─────────────────────────────┐
│         Exposition          │
└─────────────────────────────┘
              ┆
              ▼
┌─────────────────────────────┐
│      Sensory Encoding       │
└─────────────────────────────┘
              │
              ▼
┌─────────────────────────────┐
│     Cognitive Encoding      │
└─────────────────────────────┘
              │
              ▼
┌─────────────────────────────┐
│        Decoding CL          │
└─────────────────────────────┘
```

are other factors involved as well. Dreams are one way in which to understand the CL of an individual. People who talk in dreams while sleeping provide clues regarding the CL since dreams are related to the subconscious mind. However, analysing Broca's area (anterior speech cortex) and Wernicke's area (posterior speech cortex) is useful in understanding the CL process because anterior and posterior speech cortices are responsible for language production and comprehension.

Yule (2010) indicated:

The anterior speech cortex is described more usually as Broca's area. Paul Broca, a French surgeon, reported in the 1860s that damage to this specific part of the brain was related to extreme difficulty in producing speech. It was noted that damage to the corresponding area on the right hemisphere had no such effect. This finding was first used to argue that language ability must be located in the left hemisphere and since then has been treated as an indication that Broca's area is crucially involved in the production of speech.

Regarding the posterior speech cortex or Wernicke's area, Yule added:

Carl Wernicke was a German doctor who, in the 1870s, reported that the damage to this part of the brain was found among patients who had speech comprehension difficulties. This finding confirmed the left hemisphere location of language ability and led to the view that Wernicke's area is part of the brain crucially involved in the understanding of speech.

As a result, those parts of brain have indispensable roles in language production and processing so nuclei of them can be examined in CL production and by observing them that way, concrete proofs might be obtained (figure 2).

Figure 2. Limbic Lobe

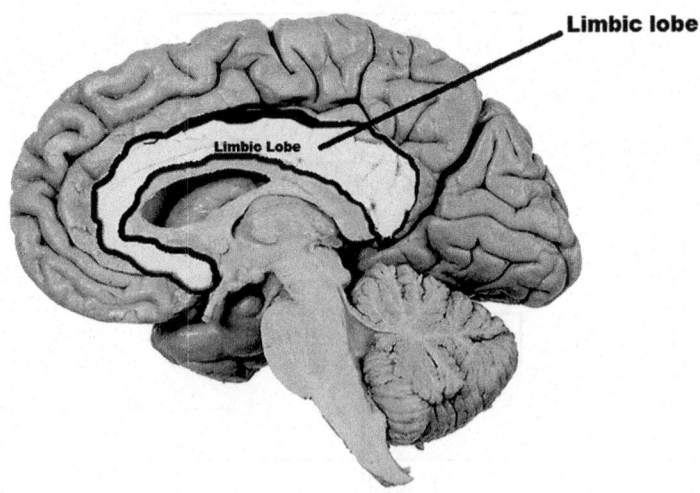

THEORETICAL FRAMEWORK

Literature Review

Harley (2008) states the concept of bilingualism has an extended definition:

If a speaker is fluent in two languages, then they are said to be bilingual. The commonly held image of a bilingual person is of someone brought up in a culture where they are exposed to two languages from birth. It is not necessary for them to be equally fluent in both languages, but at least they should be very competent in the second one. Some people are trilingual, or even multilingual. This definition of bilingualism is a little vague as it depends on what we mean by "fluent". It is perhaps best to think of proficiency in multiple languages as lying on a continuum, rather than being an either-or idea. Some authorities (e.g., Bialystock, 2001) distinguish between productive bilingualism (speaks can produce and understand both languages) and receptive bilingualism (speakers can understand both languages, but have more limited production abilities) (p.153-154).

The two parts of bilingualism include *simultaneous bilingualism* and *sequential bilingualism* (Flynn et al., 2005; Harley, 2008). The former means learning the first language (L1) and the second language (L2) simultaneously, while sequential bilingualism occurs when L2 is acquired after L1. Sequential bilingualism appears mostly in early childhood due to globalization and immigration. Furthermore, there is another definition of the bilingualism in recent studies. The term ''bilingual'' refers to all those people who use two or more languages or dialects in their everyday lives (Grosjean, 1994). In this case, the term "language" includes the dialects as well as the system of symbols and rules to communicate. Furthermore, Grosjean (1989) states that considering bilingualism as "two monolinguals in one person" is not a correct notion.

Fabbro (2001) added:

Indeed, bilinguals do not necessarily need to have a perfect knowledge of all the languages they know to be considered as such. The extremist view of the "perfect" bilingual derives from a language culture which is essentially monolingual. Bilinguals acquire and use their languages for different purposes, in different domains of life and with different people. For example, a Canadian born in Quebec may acquire Quebecois as mother tongue (L1) and use it with his or her family and friends; standard French as a second language (L2), being the official language of education; and English as a third (L3) language, the latter not being used everyday but, for example, to write scientific manuscripts or give lectures at international congresses. Irrespective of the degree of knowledge this person has of these three languages, he or she should definitely be considered a bilingual.

There is a correlation among Cognitivist and Constructivist thought and the process of CL. An individuals' mind and subconscious mind form a substantial basis for the CLH. Internal mental processes of mind are the core of cognitivist thought; in other words, cognitivism or nativism emphasizes the mind and cognition which is why it is a pathway for the CL. Additionally, perception and ideas are indispensable matters to obtain input and produce output and this approach is the core of the CL process because it is precisely structured in cognition. Chomsky (2007) states the language acquisition mechanism is an innate process. In other words, psychology has an indispensable role over language and its acquisition (Chomsky, 1977).

More generally, I think that the long-range significance of the study of language lies in the fact that in this study it is possible to give a relatively sharp and clear formulation of some of the central questions of psychology and to bring a mass of evidence to bear on them (Chomsky, 2006).

Constructivism is a multidisciplinary approach based on collaboration and learning in the social environment (Goldberg, 2002). In other words, constructivism emphasizes the nurture for the learning and, in this case, the CLH uses some critical matters from the constructivism as a foundation. Social life and collaboration bring about the language usage more and it means that also constructivist thought takes a considerable part of processing of the CL in the mind because exposition is the first stage of processing CL inside the mind and considerable amount of exposition is taken from the environment and social interaction such as negotiation and collaboration. This is why constructivism is a critical element in the CLH which also emphasizes that language localization differs from monolingual individual to the bilingual or multilingual individual.

Gordon and Ledoux (2008) discuss the study regarding the localization of language in the brain cortex:

Another divergence from the classic neurological model comes from the finding of a high degree of individual variability in the localization of essential language sites in cortex. Although most (not all) patients show an area of language localization anteriorly in frontal regions and posteriorly in temporal regions, the exact location of these areas varies widely. For some patients, language areas are identified within traditional Broca's and Wernicke's areas (although, as mentioned, rarely across these entire regions); for others, language regions may be slightly adjacent to these centers, and some patients will not show representation near these centers at all. Ojemann et al. (1989), in a review of cortical stimulation results of 117 patients tested at their center, showed that the area of greatest overlap of interference effects during naming across patients was the inferior posterior frontal cortex (Broca's area). But even at this site, 21% of the 82 patients tested with stimulation during naming did not show interference effects. Of the other 34 zones in which stimulation effects were tested, none was shown to lead to disruption of naming in more than 50% of the patients tested. The prediction of the precise location of language-essential cortex in any individual patient based on anatomical landmarks alone is therefore impossible with current methods. (p.175)

Furthermore, another aspect shows differences in localization of language in the brain of women and men. Women were more likely than men to have language areas only in the frontal lobes; that is, women were more likely to show greater precision of cortical representation of language than were men (Ojemann, 1991). In that case, we can discuss and analyse the physical settlement of the CL.

Is there any Relationship between Central Language Process and Behaviourism?

The CL is formed by the emission of the senses so output from the Limbic lobe is a clue of the CL. Additionally, the Limbic lobe is located between the Frontal lobe and Parietal lobe of the brain. That is to say, the limbic lobe has nuclei of the Frontal lobe and Parietal lobe. Sensory situations cause production of CL so the Limbic lobe is eclipsed by the CL. However, there might be a quandary about the CL and behaviouristic approach so that CL may be produced when the person obtains a stimulus from the external world such as shock, fear, anxiety, or other intense emotional conditions (Grillon & Davis, 1997; Lerner & Tiedens, 2006).

NEUROLINGUISTIC PROJECTION OF CENTRAL LANGUAGE

The neurolinguistic perspective states that brain lobes have multifunctional roles in language comprehension and production (Stemmer, 2006; Skills and Functions Associated with the Lobes of the Brain, 2015; The Anatomy of the Brain, 2015). Functions and skills of the brain lobes provide a rudimentary picture regarding the biological structuring of the CL (The Brain and Its Functions, 2015) (see figure 3).

Figure 3. Broca's area and Wernicke's area

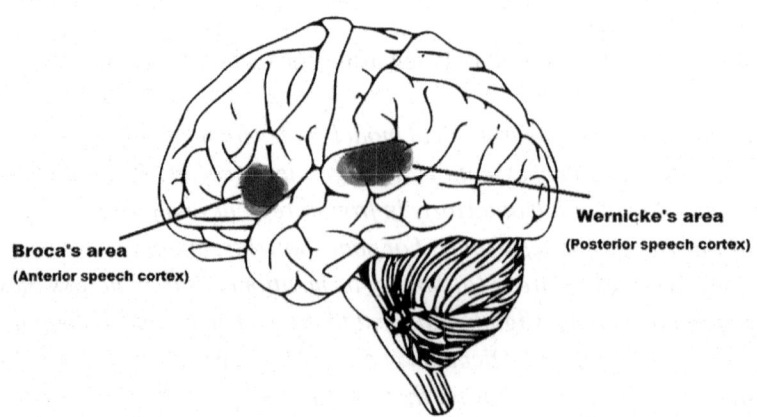

Frontal Lobe

- Attention
- Decision making
- Emotional, social, sexual control
- Expressive language
- Verbal expression
- Judgement
- Spontaneity
- Problem solving
- Motivation
- Motor integration
- Voluntary movement
- Sequencing

Occipital Lobe

- Reading (the perception and
- recognition of printed words)
- Visual perception
- Visual processing

Temporal Lobe

- Behaviour (aggressive)
- Face recognition
- Short-term memory
- Receptive language
- Language comprehension
- Musical awareness
- Selective attention
- Object categorisation
- Locating objects

Parietal Lobe

- Academic skills
- Awareness of body parts
- Eye-hand coordination
- Tactile perception (touch)
- Spatial orientation
- Object naming
- Right / left organisation
- Visual attention

Cerebellum

- Balance and equilibrium
- Eye movement
- Coordination of voluntary movement
- Gross and fine motor coordination
- Postural control

Brain Steam

- Arousal and sleep regulation
- Balance and movement
- Autonomic nervous system (heart rate, breathing, temperature, etc.)
- Level of alertness
- Swallowing food and fluid

Figure 4 shows the CL processes in the Frontal, Temporal, and Parietal lobes of the brain so that the limbic lobe lies along the Parietal, Frontal and Temporal lobes. Hence, the Limbic lobe in which senses and emotional phenomena are formed is the core of the CL; the Limbic cortex ought to be considered predominantly in the CL process. Considering those factors, the author developed a survey for 30 multilingual and bilingual people from different parts of the world (Table 1 and 2).

DISCUSSION

There are distinct questions in the survey based on psychology and the subconscious mind. The survey regarding psychological issues was prepared to enable monitoring of the subconscious mind of inter-

Figure 4. CL processes of the brain

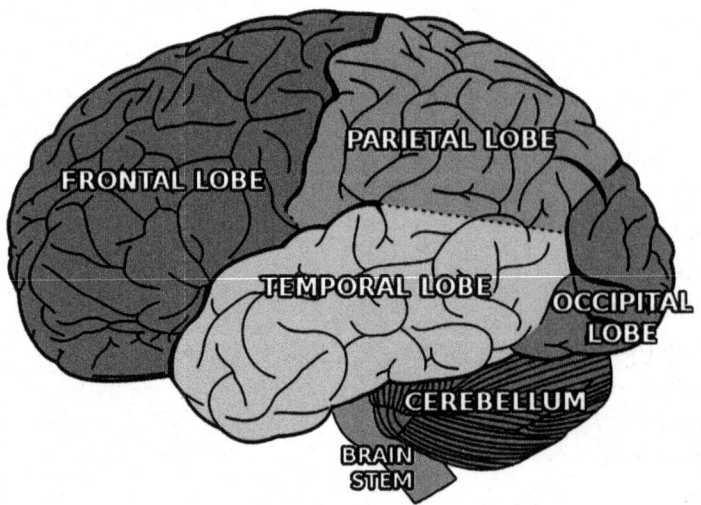

Table 1. Sample of the Central Language Identification Survey

Age:
Languages spoken as native languages:
Origin:
QUESTIONS
    1. When you witness a shocking situation (e.g., A terrible crash or a bloody body on the floor) which language do you use abruptly and directly to show your reaction
    2. Imagine that you are in court and blamed for killing a friend of you, but you are innocent and you will defend yourself, they will understand you whichever language you use. Think about your native languages and which one would you prefer to defend yourself?
    3. Imagine that you are in a wooden house alone and that is a jungle your house is in. Sky is hazy and you go out to wander, and while walking you notice a tiger running towards you. What would be your first word in this situation? Imagine the atmosphere and then jot down the word directly, *do not translate it into English.*
    4. In which language do you pray?
    5. Which language do you use *mostly* in your dreams while sleeping?
    6. Which language do you use in your daily life? How often do you use it and why do you prefer to use that language? Discuss it please by giving reasons. (e.g., I am Turkish but I use Italian at school because I live in Italy and mostly my friends are Italian at school however when I come home I turn back to Turkish, I speak Turkish with my family even though they can speak Italian fluently.)
    7. What language do you use to talk inwardly?
    8. Which language did you first acquire? (Your mother language)

Table 2. Compiled Results of the Survey

Names / Age/ First language	Native Languages	In Shocking Sit.1	To Defend Own Self Better	In Shocking Sit. 2	Language to Pray	Language in Dreams	Language in Daily Life	Inward Language
I / 22 / Turkish	Turkish & Dutch	Dutch	Dutch	Dutch	Turkish	Dutch	Dutch-Turkish	Dutch
II/ 21/ Turkish	Turkish & English	English	English	English	English-Turkish	English-Turkish	Turkish	Turkish
III/ 23/ Greek	Greek & Dutch	Greek	Greek	Greek	Greek	Greek	Greek-Dutch	Greek
IV/23/ Turkish	German & Turkish	German	Turkish	German	Turkish	Turkish	Turkish	Turkish
V/26/ Kurdish	Turkish & Kurdish	Kurdish	Turkish	-	Turkish	Kurdish	Kurdish	Kurdish
VI/26/Japan	Turkish & Japan	Japan	-	Japan	Japan	Japan	Turkish	Turkish
VII/26/ Kurdish	Turkish & Kurdish	Kurdish	Turkish	Turkish	Kurdish	Turkish-Kurdish	Turkish	Turkish
VIII/55/ Zazaki	Zazaki & Turkish	Turkish	Turkish	Turkish	Turkish	Turkish	Turkish	Turkish
IX/ 21/ Kurdish	Turkish & Kurdish	Turkish	Turkish	Turkish	Turkish	Turkish	Turkish	Turkish
X/ 21/ Turkish	Albanian & Turkish	Turkish	Turkish	Turkish	Turkish	Turkish	Turkish-Albanian	Turkish-Albanian
XI/24/ Galician	Galician & Spanish	Galician	Galician	Spanish	Galician	Spanish	Spanish	Galician
XII/22/ Turkish	German & Turkish	Turkish	German	Turkish	Turkish	Turkish	Turkish-German	Turkish
XIII/22/ Turkish	German & Turkish	Turkish	Turkish	Turkish	Turkish	Turkish	German	Turkish

continued on following page

Table 2. Continued

Names / Age/ First language	Native Languages	In Shocking Sit.1	To Defend Own Self Better	In Shocking Sit. 2	Language to Pray	Language in Dreams	Language in Daily Life	Inward Language
XIV/23/ Turkish	German & Turkish	German	Turkish	German	Turkish	Turkish	Turkish	Turkish
XV/21/Urdu	Urdu & German	German	German	German	German	German	German-Urdu	German
XVI/36/ Turkish	Turkish & German	German	German	German	Turkish	German	German-Turkish	German
XVII/49/ Zazaki	Zazaki & Turkish	Zazaki	Turkish	Zazaki	Zazaki	Turkish	Turkish	Turkish
XVIII/36/ Turkish	German & Turkish	German	German	German	Turkish	-	German	-
XIX/24/ Cantonese	Cantonese & Mandarin &English	Mandarin	Mandarin	English	Cantonese	Cantonese	Cantonese	Mandarin
XX/23/ Cantonese	Cantonese & Mandarin & English	Cantonese	Cantonese	English	Cantonese	Cantonese	Cantonese	Cantonese
XXI/24/ Mandarin	Mandarin & English	Mandarin	Mandarin	Mandarin	Mandarin	English	English	Mandarin-English
XXII/21/ Urdu	German & Urdu	German	German	German	German	German	German	German
XXIII/27/ Arabic	Turkmen & Arabic & English & Turkish	English	Turkish	Turkish	Arabic	Turkish	English	Turkish
XXIV /20/ Azerbaijani	Azerbaijani & Russian	Russian	Azerbaijani	Russian	Azerbaijani	Azerbaijani	-	-
XXV/23/ Greek	Greek & Dutch	Greek	Greek	Greek	Greek	Greek	Dutch	Greek
XXVI/21/ Dutch	Dutch & English & Arabic	English	English	English	-	English	English	English
XXVII/35/ Arabic	Arabic & Turkish	Turkish	Turkish	Turkish	Arabic	Turkish	Turkish	Turkish
XXVIII/65/ Georgian	Georgian &Turkish	Turkish	Turkish	Turkish	Turkish	Turkish	Turkish	Turkish
XXIX/30/ Ukranian & Russian	Russian & Ukranian & English	Russian	Russian	English	Russian	Russian	English	Russian
XXX/38/ Uzbek & Turkish	Uzbek & Turkish& Russian	Uzbek	-	Turkish	Uzbek-Turkish	Turkish	Uzbek-Turkish	Uzbek -Turkish

The identity of the interviewees are reserved

viewees in terms of emotional and reflexive reactions. This accounts for the highlighted columns in the table to show solid information about the CL of the interviewees. This is important because questions of the answers on those highlighted columns are simply and directly related to reflexive and emotional reactions to ascertain the CL. Furthermore, answers on highlighted columns demonstrate the discrepancy between the First Language (i.e., mother tongue) and the CL.

In some cases, the first language of individual is at the same time her/his CL or is different from her/his CL due to individual differences because each person is unique; therefore, the psychology of an individual differs from each other. The author developed other concrete demonstrations to reveal the variety of CL. For instance, during the research phase there was an opportunity to observe four people for an extended period due to the fact that the bilingual individuals are from the author's family. Therefore, the author could observe all aspects of their daily lives including their reflexive and emotional utterances spontaneously. These four individuals are referred to in the table as VIII, XVII, XIII, and XIV.

An unusual experience included a retired teacher (referred to as XXVIII in Table 1) showing how the language first acquired and used beyond Lenneberg's Critical Period Hypothesis of 1967 might be invalid in the mind of person over an extended period of time later (Hurford, 1991; Snow & Hofnagel-Höhle, 1978):

I was born in Georgia. My mother is Georgian but my father is Turkish. My mother and father divorced and I lived with my mother until the age of 5 in Georgia. My first language is Georgian and it was the only language I knew. Later, my father and mother returned to each other; however, I did not speak Turkish so I could not speak Turkish with my father. We moved to Turkey after a period of time and I began school in Turkey so it was necessary to learn Turkish. I have lived in Turkey since then and it is interesting to note that I cannot speak Georgian even though I spoke the language fluently until 5 years of age.

The experience forwards a contradiction about the notion of the mother tongue. Is it possible to forget completely one's first language which one knew through the age of five years? This demands an investigation regarding the notion of a mother tongue.

What are 2D and 3D Effects in the Brain?

Reading the written form of a situation and anticipating an inexperienced utterance mean a a so-called "2D effect" in the brain because imagining a situation without experiencing it is half-truth and differs from utterances in experienced situations. Moreover, anticipating utterances in inexperienced situations just by imagining cannot dominate the limbic lobe of the brain and an individual cannot feel herself/himself in these situations exactly. In that case, there is little influence on the brain; thus, the 2D effect.

It is clear that 3D objects are more realistic than 2D objects, so 3D effect refers to real life-like experience. Real life experiences always provide absolute and concrete data about psychology, so the experiment to identify the CL of a person should be based on real life like situations so as to obtain real life like utterances of a person. Furthermore, by conducting a "3D effect" experiment the participant can experience a specific situation to trigger his/her subconscious mind. The result is unconscious utterances which is key to identify the CL. To identify the CL of an individual requires triggering the limbic lobe which includes emotions.

POTENTIAL IMPLICATIONS

There are at least two potential implications in this initial study for neuroeconomics. First, the fully developed CLH could influence areas connected to neuroeconomics such as marketing or decision-making theory which could impact the results of neuroeconomic study in general. One example can include impulse purchases (e.g., chewing gum or cigarette lighters) at the Point-of-Sale (POS) in a retail store which is connected directly to consumer behavior. Second, the CLH could assist neuroeconomic academics to better understand the relatively understudied area of decision-making processes of multilinguals and TCIs. This can extend beyond issues such as marketing or economic choice to include considerations such as managerial decision-making or even brain surgery. The possibilities are numerous.

FUTURE RESEARCH DIRECTIONS

It is necessary to investigate the notion of a mother tongue to progress the CLH. Furthermore, multilingual and bilingual individuals should be observed and tested in real-life-like environments in which they should be unconscious during the testing process to obtain valid and reliable results regarding the 3D effect in the brain. Since the CLH is multidisciplinary, a cognition-based study related to psychology, linguistics, psycholinguistics, neurolinguistics, and neuroscience, academics should develop this hypothesis via mathematical models to explain the occurrence and processes of the CL in the human mind. Mathematical descriptions are needed to provide concrete proofs and base it upon computational items. Last, but not least, this brain-based study must be improved with regards to linguistics, psychology, cognitive science, and neuroscience as the brain is a mysterious treasure which remains largely underexplored and unknown to mankind.

CONCLUSION

In this chapter we have explored the potential impact of the CLH on neuroeconomics and related areas such as consumer behavior and (psycho)linguistic study. The Introduction provided a basis for the remainder of the chapter by including the need for this study as well as some general concepts such as the Sapir-Whorf Hypothesis, linguistic determinism and relativity, TCIs/TCKs, and the processing of a CL in the human brain. The Theoretical Framework included a Literature Review that touched upon the concepts of sequential and simultaneous bilingualism, cognitivist and constructivist thought, and the localization of language in the brain which supported the Proposition provided in the Introduction. The section on Neurolinguistic Projection of Central Language covered the survey used in this study as well as an in-depth description of the human brain. The Discussion section provided input for the Potential Implications and Future Research Directions part of this study.

The CLH has been developed by considering multilingualism and bilingualism within today's globalization and the concept of the TCI/TCK. We have seen via the survey that the CL emitted under pressure does not necessarily always equate to the mother tongue or first language of an individual, and that the CL can potentially influence the decision-making processes of an individual as it is an established

Figure 5. Medial view of major subdivisions of cortex

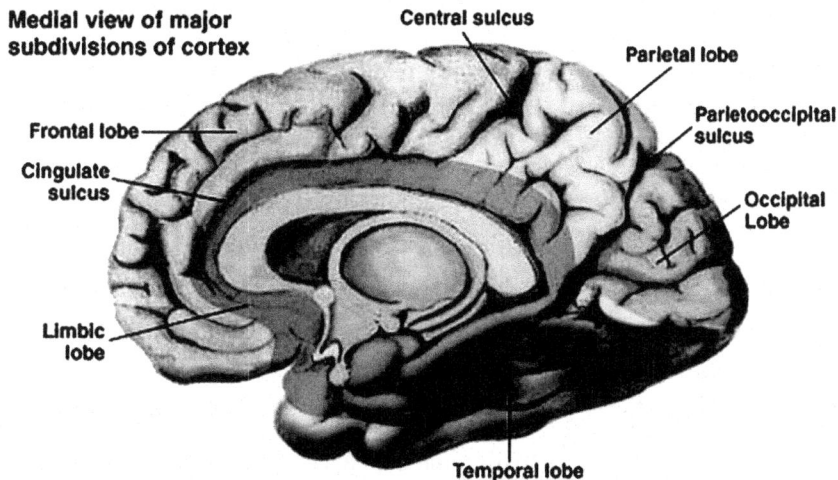

fact that language leads thought which was mentioned in the Introduction. The CL of multilingual and bilingual persons can change over time due to significant exposure in a different environment such as an extended move to another country in which a different language is generally spoken (e.g., from Brazil to China or Russia). The significance of this statement is potentially huge since it suggests decision-making processes can change for a particular individual depending on her or his location over time as mentioned in Nisbett (Figure 5) (2003).

REFERENCES

Andersen, B., & Wong, D. (2013, February). *The new normal: Competitive advantage in the digital economy*. London: Big Innovation Centre. Retrieved on September 11, 2014, from: http://www.biginnovationcentre.com/Assets/Docs/The%20New%20Normal.pdf

Boroditsky, L. (2001). Does Language Shape Thought? Mandaring and English speaker's conception of time. *Cognitive Psychology, 43*(1), 1–22. doi:10.1006/cogp.2001.0748 PMID:11487292

Cenoz, J., Hufeisen, B., & Jessner, U. (Eds.). (2001). *Cross-linguistic Influence in Third Language Acquisition: Psycholinguistic Perspectives*. Clevedon, UK: Multilingual Matters.

Chomsky, N. (1977). *Essays on Form and Interpretation*. Amsterdam: Elsevier Science, Ltd.

Chomsky, N. (2006). *Language and Mind* (3rd ed.). London: Cambridge University Press. doi:10.1017/CBO9780511791222

Chomsky, N. (2007). *Of Minds and Language*. London: Cambridge University Press.

Coello, Y., & Bartolo, A. (Eds.). (2013). *Language and Action in Cognitive Neuroscience*. New York: Psychology Press.

Conen, K. E., & Padua-Schioppa, C. (2015). Neuronal variability in orbitofrontal cortex during economic decisions. *Journal of Neurophysiology, 114*(3), 1367–1381. doi:10.1152/jn.00231.2015 PMID:26084903

de Angelis, G., & Dewaele, J. M. (2009). The development of psycholinguistic research on crosslinguistic influence. In L. Aronin & B. Hufeisen (Eds.), *The Exploration of Multilingualism*. Amsterdam: John Benjamins. doi:10.1075/aals.6.04ch4

de Cruz, H. (2009). Is Linguistic Determinism An Empirically Testable Hypothesis? *Logique & Analyse, 208*, 327–341.

Denktas-Sakar, G., Karatas-Cetin, C., & Saatcioğlu, O. Y. (2014). Discovering the Nexus between Market Orientation and Open Innovation: A Grounded Theory Approach. In B. Christiansen, S. Yıldız, & E. Yıldız (Eds.), *Transcultural Marketing for Incremental and Radical Innovation* (pp. 1–42). Hershey, PA: IGI Global. doi:10.4018/978-1-4666-4749-7.ch001

Fabbro, F. (2001). The Bilingual Brain: Bilingual Aphasia. *Brain and Language, 79*(2), 201–210. doi:10.1006/brln.2001.2480 PMID:11712844

Field, J. (2003). *Psycholinguistics: A Resource Book for Students*. New York: Routledge.

Flynn, S., Foley, C., & Vinnitskaya, I. (2005). New Paradigm for the Study of Simultaneous vs. Sequential Bilingualism. *Proceedings of the 4th International Symposium on Bilingualism* (pp. 768-774). Somerville, MA: Cascadilla Press.

Friedman, G. (2009). *The Next 100 Years: A Forecast for the 21st Century*. New York: Anchor Books.

Garcia-Mayo, M. D. P. (2012). Cognitive Approaches to L3 Acquisitions. *International Journal of English Studies*. Retrieved on July 4, 2015, from http://files.eric.ed.gov/fulltext/EJ975723.pdf

Gass, M. S., & Selinker, L. (2008). *Second Language Acquisition* (3rd ed.). New York: Routledge Press.

Glimcher, P. W. (2002). Decisions, decisions, decisions: Choosing a biological science of choice. *Neuron, 36*(2), 323–332. doi:10.1016/S0896-6273(02)00962-5 PMID:12383785

Glimcher, P. W. (2004). *Decisions, uncertainty, and the brain: The science of neuroeconomics*. Cambridge, MA: MIT Press.

Glimcher, P. W. (2009). *Neuroeconomics: Decision making and the brain*. London: Academic Press.

Godart, F. C., Maddux, W. W., Shipilov, A. V., & Galinsky, A. D. (2015). Fashion With a Foreign Flair: Professional Experiences Abroad Facilitate The Creative Innovations of Organizations. *Academy of Management Journal, 58*(1), 195–220. doi:10.5465/amj.2012.0575

Goldberg, M. F. (2002). *15 School questions and discussion: From class size, standards, and school safety to leadership and more*. Lanham, MD: Scarecrow.

Grillon, C., & Davis, M. (1997). Effects of stress and shock anticipiation on prepulse Inhibition of the startle reflex. *Psychophysiology, 34*(5), 511–517. doi:10.1111/j.1469-8986.1997.tb01737.x PMID:9299905

Groome, D. (2014). *An Introduction to Cognitive Psychology: Processes and Disorders* (3rd ed.). New York: Psychology Press.

Grosjean, F. (1989). Neurolinguists, beware! The bilingual is not two monolinguals in one person. *Brain and Language, 36*(1), 3–15. doi:10.1016/0093-934X(89)90048-5 PMID:2465057

Grosjean, F. (1994). Individual bilingualism. In R. E. Asher (Ed.), *The encyclopedia of langauge and linguistics* (pp. 1656–1660). Oxford, UK: Pergamon Press.

Harley, A. T. (2008). *The Psychology Of Language* (3rd ed.). New York: Psychology Press.

Hurford, J. R. (1991). The evolution of the critical period for language acquisition. *Cognition, 40*(3), 159–201. doi:10.1016/0010-0277(91)90024-X PMID:1786674

Kay, P., & Kempton, W. (1984). *What is the Sapir-Whorf Hypothesis?* Arlington, TX: American Anthropological Association.

Kecskes, I., & Albertazzi, L. (Eds.). (2007). *Cognitive Aspects of Bilingualism*. Amsterdam: Springer. doi:10.1007/978-1-4020-5935-3

Kemp, C. (2009). Defining multilingualism. In L. Aronin & B. Hufeisen (Eds.), *The exploration of multilingualism* (pp. 11–26). Amsterdam: John Benjamins. doi:10.1075/aals.6.02ch2

Lerner, J. S., & Tiedens, L. Z. (2006). Portrait of the angry decision maker: How appraisal tendencies shape anger's influence on cognition. *Journal of Behavioral Decision Making, 19*(2), 115–137. doi:10.1002/bdm.515

Liben, L. S., & Müller, U. (2015). *Handbook of Child Psychology and Developmental Science*. New York: Wiley & Sons, Inc.

Lyttle, A. D. (2009). *Making Sense of Cultural Complexity: An Experimental Study of Third Culture Individuals' Interpersonal Sensitivity as a Result of Intercultural Adaptation*. (Unpublished Master's Thesis). University of Liberty.

Molinsky, A. (2007). Cross-Cultural Code-Switching: The Psychological Challenges of Adapting Behavior in Foreign Cultural Interactions. *Academy of Management Review, 32*(3), 622–640. doi:10.5465/AMR.2007.24351878

Neufeld, R. W. J. (2007). *Advances in Clinical Cognitive Science: Formal Modeling of Processes and Symptoms*. Washington, DC: American Psychological Association. doi:10.1037/11556-000

Nisbett, R. (2003). *The Geography of Thought: How Asians and Westerners Think Differently...and Why*. New York: Free Press.

Ojemann, G. A. (1991). Cortical organization of language. *The Journal of Neuroscience*. PMID:1869914

Pavlenko, A. (2005). *Emotions and Multilingualism*. Boston: Cambridge University Press.

Perlovsky, L. (2009) Language and Emotions: Emotional Sapir-Whorf Hypothesis. *Article of Neural Networks,* 518-526. Retrieved on May 9, 2015, from, http://www.leonid-perlovsky.com/new-materials/9,%20NN,%20Emotional%20SWH.pdf

Pollock, D. (2001). *Third Culture Kids: The Experience of Growing Up Among Worlds*. London: Nicholas Brealey Publishing.

Skills and Functions Associated with the Lobes of the Brain. (n.d.). Retrieved on April 3, 2015, from: http://www.abiireland.ie/docs/BrainLaminate.pdf

Snow, C. E., & Hoefnagel-Höhle, M. (1978, December). The Critical Period for Language Acquisition: Evidence from Second Language Learning. *Child Development*, *49*(4), 1114–1128. doi:10.2307/1128751

Stemmer, B. (2006). *Imaging Brain Lateralization, Words, Sentences, and Influencing Factors in Health, Pathological, and Special Populations*. Amsterdam: Elsevier, Ltd.

The Anatomy of the Brain. (2015). Retrieved on April 12, 2015, from: http://psychology.about.com/od/biopsychology/ss/brainstructure_2.htm

The Brain and Its Functions. (2015). Retrieved on April 9, 2015, from: http://mybrainonline.ca/?page=3

Tucker, R. G. (1999). A Global Perspective on Bilingualism and Bilingual Education. *Carnegie Mellon University Digest*. Retrieved on May 3, 2015, from: http://eric.ed.gov/?id=ED435168

Verplanken, R., & Holland, R. W. (2002). Motivated decision-making: Effects of activation and self-centrality of values on choices and behavior. *Journal of Personality and Social Psychology*, *82*(3), 434–447. doi:10.1037/0022-3514.82.3.434 PMID:11902626

Wood, D. J. (1988). *How Children Think and Learn*. Oxford, UK: Blackwell.

Yule, G. (2010). *The Study of Language* (4th ed.). London: Cambridge University Press. doi:10.1017/CBO9780511757754

ADDITIONAL READING

Barcroft, J. (2002). Semantic and structural elaboration in L2 lexical acquisition. *Language Learning*, *52*(2), 323–363. doi:10.1111/0023-8333.00186

Berlyne, D. E. (1975). Behaviorism? Cognitive Theory? Humanistic Psychology? To Hull With Them All. *Canadian Psychological Review*, *16*(2), 69–80. doi:10.1037/h0081798

Cao, F., Rickles, B., Vu, M., Zhu, Z., Chan, H., & Harris, L. (2013). Early-stage visual processing predicts retention in second language learning. *Journal of Neurolinguistics*, *26*, 440–461. doi:10.1016/j.jneuroling.2013.01.003 PMID:23798804

Cenoz, J., & Gorter, D. (2011). A holistic approach to multilingual education: Introduction. *Modern Language Journal*, *95*(3), 339–343. doi:10.1111/j.1540-4781.2011.01204.x

Clement, R., Gardner, R. C., & Smythe, P. C. (1980). Social and individual factors in second language acquisition. *Canadian Journal of Behavioural Science*, *12*(4), 293–302. doi:10.1037/h0081081

Fabbro, F. (1999). *The Neurolinguistics of Bilingualism: An Introduction*. New York: Psychology Press.

Fabbro, F., Urgesi, C., & Marini, A. (2012). Clinical Neurolinguistics of Bilingualism. In M. Faust (Ed.), *The Handbook of the Neuropsychology of Language*. New York: Blackwell Publishing.

Gardner, R. C., & Smythe, P. C. (1975). Motivation and second-language acquisition. *Canadian Modern Language Review*, *31*, 218–230.

Grimshaw, G. M., Adelstein, A., Bryden, M. P., & MacKinnon, G. E. (1998). First-Language Acqusition in Adolescence: Evidence for a Critical Period for Verbal Language Development. *Brain and Language*, *63*(2), 237–255. doi:10.1006/brln.1997.1943 PMID:9654433

Ingram, J. C. L. (2007). *Neurolinguistics: An Introduction to Spoken Language Processing and its Disorders*. London: Cambridge University Press. doi:10.1017/CBO9780511618963

Levelt, W. J. M. (2013). *A History of Psycholinguistics: The Pre-Chomskyan Era*. London: Oxford University Press.

Long, M. H., & Porter, P. A. (1985). Group work, interlanguage talk and second language acquisition. *TESOL Quarterly*, *19*(2), 207–227. doi:10.2307/3586827

Schouten, A. (2009). The Critical Period Hypothesis: Support, Challenge, and Reconceptualization. Teachers College, Columbia University, *Working Papers in TESOL and Applied Linguistics*, Vol. 9, No. 1

Traxler, M. J., & Gernsbacher, M. A. (Eds.). (2006). *Handbook of Psycholinguistics* (2nd ed.). London: Elsevier.

Tremblay, P. F., & Gardner, R. C. (1995). Expanding the motivation construct in language learning. *Modern Language Journal*, *79*(4), 505–520. doi:10.1111/j.1540-4781.1995.tb05451.x

VanPatten, B., & Williams, J. (Eds.). (2007). *Theories in second language acquisition: An introduction*. Mahwah, NJ: Lawrence Erlbaum Associates Publishers.

Wei, L., & Moyer, M. G. (Eds.). (2008). *Research Methods in Bilingualism and Multilingualism*. New York: Blackwell Publishing. doi:10.1002/9781444301120

KEY TERMS AND DEFINITIONS

Central Language (CL): The language placed within the subconscious mind of an individual.

Lenneberg's Critical Period (LCP): The LCP is a controversial hypothesis which states that the first few years of life is the crucial time in which an individual can acquire a first language if presented with adequate stimuli. If language input does not occur during this period, the individual will never achieve a full command of language—especially grammatical systems.

Linguistic Determinism: The concept that our thinking is determined by our language.

Linguistic Relativity: The concept that people who speak different languages perceive the world differently as thought is encoded linguistically.

Neurolinguistic Projection: The fact that brain lobes have multifunctional roles in language comprehension and production.

Sequential Bilingualism: Learning a second language (L2) after the first language (L1).

Simultaneous Bilingualism: A person who learns L1 and L2 at the same time.

Third Culture Kid (TCK): An individual born in one country (the "passport country") but raised during the formative years in another country. Also referred to as a Third Culture Individual (TCI).

Chapter 5

Cooperation as a Core Component of Intercultural Competence:
A Neuroeconomic Perspective

Ewa Matuska
Higher Hanseatic School of Management, Poland

Alina Landowska
SWPS University of Social Sciences and Humanities, Poland

ABSTRACT

Assuming the meaning of intercultural competency is a crucial issue in multicultural societies and within business units as results of globalization, this chapter analyses cooperative attitude as a core component of intercultural competence. First, the chapter explains such terms as intercultural competence, cooperation, and culture, as well as the diffusion of cultures. Cooperation as a social value in strategic human resources management is also considered. Secondly, factors shaping cooperation (divided into two groups: cultural and biological) are discussed from a multidisciplinary perspective. Finally, the neuroeconomic dimension of cooperation is discussed with its subsequent socio-economic implications. The chapter concludes with recommendations regarding human choices resulting from individual ontogenetic processes (including cultural differences, genetic differences, and neural differences) and concludes on cooperative attitudes that are most likely culturally and biologically dependent, and which become a part of intercultural competence desired in a multicultural society and at the work place.

INTRODUCTION

The ability and willingness to act cooperatively is the very foundation of civilisation. Being 'cooperative' today is more valuable than ever before. Participants, partners, or simply team members in an effective consensus process should strive to reach the best possible decision for all of its members and the group as a whole rather than competing for personal preferences. The propensity to cooperate helps in building

DOI: 10.4018/978-1-4666-9989-2.ch005

a connection between individuals and/or groups of people, although sometimes the reason why a person or group elects to cooperate with others is because they want to have influence– to get back the support others for their own objectives. Working together to accomplish a mutual goal means extending a hand to others in the organization. It is an extremely effective way of influencing others. Building cooperative connections may involve collaboration (figuring out what you will do together), consultation (finding out what ideas other people have) and alliances (drawing on whoever already supports you or has the credibility you need).

Economic discourse traditionally uses a cooperation concept to explain the obvious benefits that are derived from the combination of joint activities of different groups of suppliers (e.g., workers, farmers, etc.) and consumers, embracing production, distribution, or trade. In terms of management, cooperation is defined as "the interaction of two or more persons or organizations directed toward a common goal which is mutually beneficial, or a an act or instance of working or acting together for a common purpose or benefit (i.e., joint action)" (House, 2005). Clearly, there are many research studies, especially in reference to so-called 'high performance work organizations' (HPWOs), documenting the positive effect of 'cooperation like' terms including: collaboration, teamwork, trust, commitment and mutual help offered by employees during day-to-day work (Kozlowski, Gully, Nason & Smith, 1999).

In today's globalized reality, the role of cooperation in terms of economic and management perspectives is obviously multiplied. Nobody can imagine implementing any modern innovation without the earlier process of multilevel cooperation that involves the engagement of different experts, suppliers, business supporters, and the involvement of different organizations, including research bodies activities, or expectations verbalized by groups of customers. However, within mainstream academic discussions lies the argument as to which is better for effective teamwork: cooperation (working with others) or competition (between coworkers), and if so, what proportion of these two behaviour-traits would be appropriate to achieving effectiveness in the workplace (Rosenbaum et al., 1980).

The debate asummes that both competitive and collaborative 'behaviours' are equally important in different work situations: competitive attitude is useful when people are working independently, but collaborative attitude is more rewarding when people are interdependent (Beersma et al., 2003). The value of competition in work performance cannot be undervalued. But, changes required from contemporary organizations individual-based structures, as well as team-based structures (Allred, Snow & Miles, 1996) and as a consequence internal cooperative behaviour cannot be overestimated. This creates a challenging condition for strategic human resource management processes (Becker & Huselid, 2006). The need to be 'cooperative' in intercultural societies and multinational corporations in times of high migration flows become a challenge. From a globalization point of view, it is important to maximize economic benefits that skilled migrants can provide, but on the other hand,it is necessary to develop intercultural competence for particular employees to benefit from that.

This chapter addresses the following issues: *Why intercultural competency starts to be so urgently needed worldwide and what are its distinctive features? What will happen with a particular cultures' uniqueness when inter-cultural paradigm will be continuously broadened and intensively developed?*

The chapter introduces discourse in sociology, ethnology, psychology, and behavioural economy about cooperation within the framework of intercultural competence. Importance is placed on neuroeconomic research dedicated to factors involved in the shaping and dissemination of cooperative attitudes, as well as decision-making processes directed at collaborative,as opposed to selfish, or hostile goals (Blizinsky& Chiao, 2010; Gintis, 2011).The perspective which suggests that cooperation is determined not only culturally, but also genetically, shines a completely new light onto social behaviours. And if this is the case (i.e., humans are born to cooperate), a completely new approach should also be applied to economics.

First, cultural differences (Hofstede, 2001) are used as a starting point to explain necessary revision of bipolar individualism *versus* cooperative dimensions in times of post-national business (Witte, 2012). The massive worldwide transfer of business cultures developed in economically rich and innovative regions to so-called "catching-up" or developing regions obviously implies obligatory intercultural cooperation. Being cooperative becomes one of the most universal and required skills of current and future organizations composed of intercultural teams. Following this trend, researchers postulate that cooperation among individuals/teams/societies is a core attitude of intercultural competency which also facilitate the adaptation of challenging macro- and micro-economic changes.

Second, reseach indicates factors shaping cooperation delivered by recent multidisciplinary (mostly anthropological, psychological, neurological and genetic) studies that explain the mechanisms of human behaviour (decision-making) and cognition, including business operations (Glimcher, 2010; Hickok, 2014). The neurological orientation in economics, which started with the discovery of mirror neurons in the 1990s, was redefined by the breakthrough work of Kahneman and Tversky (2000) and Kahneman (2011) who argued that human reasoning is distorted by systematic biases. Since that time, the hitherto paradigm of mostly rational behavior of *homo economicus* was challenged and also – the role of emotions and motivation started to be emphasized in analysis and modeling of social-organizational behaviour (Winter, 2014).The understanding of cooperation in terms of "gene–culture co-evolution" (GCC) (Blizinsky& Chiao, 2010; Gintis 2011) opens new perspective for business strategies in the future.

The chapter conludes with emphasis on the key role of cooperation in a globalized world. Extending presence of multiethnic societies undoutedly also implies the need of dissemination of intercultural competence. Challenges of contemporary economy demands for cooperation which should be perceived as a value, both for individuals as well as for societies.

BACKGROUND

Perception of cultural differences, both in a society and in the work environment, should not be seen as a barrier, but instead as an advantage and opportunity to use the strengths of each culture. This requires the development of tolerance, multicultural awareness, and the constant development of the intercultural competence of employees in an organisation. The "competence" (or a "competency", "competences" in plural), as a general notion, is strictly connected with the efficacy of work and, because of it, "competence management" represents the main stream of contemporary human resources management concepts (Matuska, 2015). Successful performance in modern organizations depends on employees' ability to adapt to a changing environment, where the major factor is an individual's acquired competency and conditions for its development. In a work context, *competence* (or *competency*) means mostly the ability of an individual to do a job properly. Competence in a broad sense can be viewed as the ability (that cannot be observed directly, but only by activities) to adequately and successfully combine and perform necessary activities in any contexts to achieve specific tasks or objectives (Stracke 2011).

Many authors (e.g., Spencer & Spencer, 1993; Athey & Orth, 1999; Chen & Naquin, 2006) agree that the definition of 'competency' should consider at least three dimensions: 1) knowledge, 2) abilities (skills), and 3) attitudes. Personal competences are only observable when performing tasks or activities. And only behavioural acts (not potentials) can be objectively observed and measured. Surely, one of such observable behaviour is cooperation. The question then is what kind of competence determines cooperation?

Intercultural Competence

Among the so-called "key competences" as recommended by the European Parliament in 2006 for lifelong learning in the context of the challenges of the contemporary labour market (EU Official Journal, 2006) is also the enumeration of the competence of "cultural awareness and expression" (European Parliament, 2006). Alternatively, this competence is known as "intercultural competence" (ICC) or multicultural competence. According to Wiseman (2003), *"Intercultural competence involves the knowledge, motivation, and skills needed to interact effectively and appropriately with members of different cultures"*. This definition, one of the simplest, corresponds with the overall definition of competency. Within the scope of various definitions of ICC, there is an overall agreement that ICC represents a complex phenomenon.

Some authors specify multiple components of ICC including: a) variety of characteristics or traits; b) three areas or domains; c) four dimensions; d) proficiency in at least one second language; e) various levels of a longitudinal and developmental process (Rathje, 2007). The basic requirements for intercultural competence can be conceptualized as a balance among four elements: 1) *Knowledge*– about other cultures and other people's behaviours; 2) *Empathy* – understanding the feelings and needs of other people; 3) *Self-confidence*–knowledge of one's own desires, strengths, weaknesses, and emotional stability; 4) *Cultural identity* – knowledge of one's own culture. What connects those elements is a culturally defined value system, which includes cooperation as its core value.

In Figure 1, we present a schema with components of "intercultural competence" determined by cooperation as a value. This value is surely developed by the impact of a person's own culture. But the value can also be facilitated via other traits, including biological aspects.

ICC can be seen generally as a trinomial behavioural construct which develops over a lifetime, and which can also be seen a cardinal feature for effective social adaptation of individuals and groups. It is worth noting that intercultural competence is not acquired automatically, but instead needs to be learned, practiced, and maintained throughout a lifetime (Council of Europe, 2010). More importantly, it is not a have-or-have-not proposition; instead, it is a matter of degree (Nardon, Steers, & Sanches-Runde, 2013). Essentially, intercultural competence represents the capacity to work successfully across different cultures (Blaškova & Blaško, 2015). The management of multicultural teams is usually perceived as problematic, as a cultural diversity that can become obsolete when employees are directed by various motives, values, social rules and habits and they have to substitute these drivers with the priorities of effective work performance (Sinha, 2008). However, multicultural teams are proved to be more creative than their mono-cultural counterparts (Stahl, Mäkelä, Zander, & Maynevski, 2010). Indeed, cultural challenges are not barriers, if managers and team members are able to recognize and choose the right strategy to avoid imposing single-culture-based approaches on multicultural situations (Brett, Behfar, & Kern, 2006).

The multicultural competence of an individual acting within an organization can be developed by the aims of a competence management system used as part of a strategic human resources management. When individual multicultural competences are identified, an organization can focus its human resources management functions on behaviours that are most relevant to successful performance and on

Figure 1. Intercultural competence schema Source: own elaboration

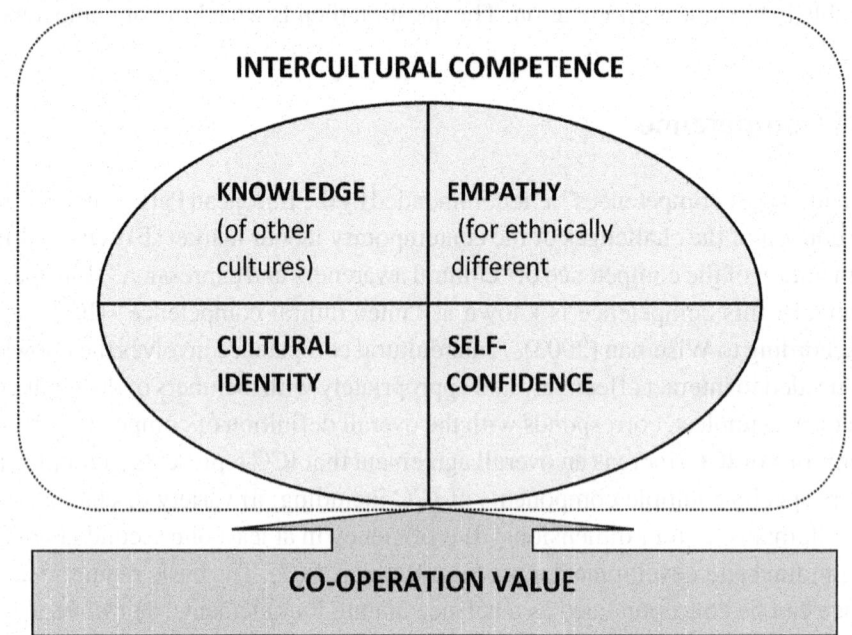

eliminating non-accepted cultural differences (Keršienė & Savanevičienė, 2005). Only when dimensions of organizational culture and those of national culture such as orientation to time, style of communication, personal space, competitiveness and worldview have been successfully adapted to their working practices to reflect the team members' background realities, can teams actually gained the added value of their multiculturalism (Sinha, 2006).

The main responsibility of an organization on creating intercultural competence lies on its leadership. First, managers should be multi-culturally competent. The most valuable, universal sub-competencies of a multicultural team leader are identified by two main personal characteristics (Blaškova & Blaško, 2015):

1. **Tolerance:** The ability of hindsight, wisdom and a peaceful, conflict-free access to individuals, groups, and the tackling of unusual and complicated situations.
2. **Flexibility:** The ability of provide an immediate and appropriate response to a situation and possible misunderstandings.

The importance of intercultural competence in a business – related cooperation is also stressed by Riether (2014) in his book, "Business Cooperation – cultural Integration as Key factor – Reasons for Failing and improving chances for success". In this book, Riether presented a Communication – Relationship – Trust model (CRT model) that enumerated just communication skills, the ability to build relationship and to create trust, as the essential factors that enable good cooperation. The "cultural integration" of any community is not only to understand others, but also to accept and to integrate the behaviour of others with one's own cognitive representation.

Diffusion of Cultural Differences and its Impact

The term 'culture' typically evokes images of fine art and fashion, but historically anthropologists have characterized culture as a complex of beliefs, values, behaviours and traditions associated with a particular population. Moreover, culture is all of the information that individuals acquire from others though a variety of social learning processes including teaching and imitation (Boyd & Richerson, 1982). The fidelity of cultural transmission is often sufficiently high for culture to act as an inheritance system (Boyd & Henrich, 2002).

Additionally, culture changes with time as it is a system of continuous modifications (Matsumoto, 1990). Humans inherit their social behaviour culturally, and cooperative attitude and behaviour serve as excellent examples. The scale of human cooperation is to assume that humans are not solely self-interested and that during the process of choice-making, individuals balance changes in their own welfare against changes in the welfare of others (Henrich at al., 2005).

Culture, in an expansive sense, builds an interactive aggregate of common characteristics that influence group's or society's response to its environment (Hofstede, 2001). Thus, today, globalization has advanced and is expressed, among others, in the increased mobility of people and in the natural mixing of cultures. It is further reflected in changes within business sectors, where members of different cultures are challenged to communicate and collaborate. All of it undoubtedly promotes the ability of humans and societies to understand and act together with 'others'.

A large amount of collected scientific literature have shown the vital differences between cultures, including anthropological, ethnographical, historical, sociological, psychological, economic, political, etc. Cultures are different not only between continents or nations, but also within the same community, and even within the same family. In the reality of globalized business, differences in culture can be seen both as a cost and as an opportunity (Mac-Dermott & Mornah, 2015). Academics and practitioners widely discuss the pros and cons of the multiplicity of various cultural communities co-existing within the settings of internationally operating businesses and networks (Sodenberg & Holden, 2002). Additionally, the phenomenon of multicultural organizational culture is recognized in the field of management, especially in terms of human resource management techniques (Keršienė & Savanevičienė, 2005).

Culture is also frequently interpreted as the predominant system of beliefs and values held in a group, it binds its members and shapes its identity (Cole, 1988). It is also controlled by reward systems, policies, and procedures based on specified patterns and rules of accepted and demanded behaviour. Thus, culture closely refers to cooperation within a society/ group. However, according to Hofstede (2001), culture "exists only by comparison", thus only comparing (benchmarking) cultures delivers proof for its existence.

Today, a well-established view on the stability and inevitability of national cultural differences seems to enter certain process of diffusion. It is caused by new technological dissemination, intensive worldwide development of social networks, and workforce mobility. During times of globalization and intense intercultural transmission, the concept that culture will always stay different should probably be revised. Following this assumption, well granted socio-economic theories about national cultural differences; for example, Hofstede's concept of six dimensions should also be re-interpreted.

In 1967, Hofstede, an industrial organizational psychologist in the Netherlands, embarked on a project of unprecedented magnitude. Under his direction, a collection of questionnaire data was initiated at all of the sites around the world where IBM operated. Participants in this research were employees of the major multinational corporation, across a wide range of occupational levels and a variety of job descriptions. Over 116,000 questionnaires were administered in two rounds of data collection in 72 countries. Equivalent versions of this questionnaire were developed in 20 languages.

The objective of the study was to compare the employees' values pertaining to their employment, and which was set across countries by means of standardized self-report paper-and-pencil scales. This mass of data thus were subjected to factor analysis which yielded four factors/dimensions, which Hofstede labelled as follows:1) *power distance; 2) uncertainty avoidance; 3) individualism-collectivism; and 4) masculinity-femininity*. In addition to these four original labels, Hofstede added a fifth dimension in the 1990s as a result of a research which was originally conducted by Michael Bond on Chinese employees and managers. That dimension, based on Confucian dynamism, was called *long-term* versus *short term orientation* and was applied to 23 countries. These five dimensions are used as "5-D model" – a popular measure used for comparing national the culture patterns of countries. In the 2010, a sixth dimension, called *indulgence-restraint* was added, based on Michael Minkov's analysis of the World Values Survey data for 93 countries. Each of the six dimensions is measured by a specific index, Hofstede defines as follows:

- **Power Distance (PDI):** Refers to the acceptance of inequality in the exercise of authority as well as in wealth, status, and privilege. High scorers in power distance endorse obedience as a cardinal value and are prepared to justify inequality as the established or natural order of things that is universal and immutable; low scorers endorse egalitarianism and informality.
- **Uncertainty Avoidance (UAI):** Describes societies in which discomfort is prominently experienced in settings, situations or contexts that lack clarity or structure. Persons high in uncertainty avoidance seek guidance and rules and often find them in precedent, tradition, and ritual. At the low end of distribution on this variable, people thrive on ambiguity, improvisation, and surprise.
- **Individualism – Collectivism (INV):** Is a bipolar dimension. The individualistic end of the continuum describes societies in which social ties are loose and individual strivings and aspirations are considered paramount. In collectivistic societies, integration into family, society, and nation is deemed to be the normal order of existence, and personal goals and preferences are subordinated to those of the larger entity.
- **Masculinity-Femininity (MAS):** Pertains to the distribution of emotional roles between the two genders. In masculine cultures male and female roles are clearly differentiated; in feminine cultures, overlap between male and female roles is the rule. Moreover, male cultures are tough-minded and prize-performance oriented; female cultures are marked by tender-mindedness and assign a high value to caring.
- **Long-Term Orientation (LTO):** This can be interpreted as dealing with society's search for "virtue". In societies with a long-term orientation, people believe that truth depends very much on situation, context, and time. They show an ability to adapt traditions to changed conditions, a strong propensity to save and to invest, thriftiness, and perseverance in achieving results. Societies with a Short-Term Orientation generally have a strong concern with establishing the absolute „truth". They are normative in their thinking. They exhibit great respect for traditions, a relatively small propensity to save for the future, and a focus on achieving quick results.
- **Indulgence – Restraint Orientation (IVR):** Where *indulgence* –stands for a society that allows relatively free gratification of basic and natural human drives related to enjoying life and having fun; and *restraint* – stands for a society that suppresses gratification of needs and regulates it by means of strict social norms.

The above-described culture descriptors help to understand the specificity and uniqueness of different cultures. The background for this variety is delivered by a means of cooperation and trust, and is involved in the internal life of particular communities. Thus, cooperation and trust are culturally determined, and in turn they emerge in differing degrees in different cultures (Fukuyama, 1995). Hofstede's input surely delivered an important theoretical frame for understanding and benchmarking cultures, but it was first appreciated as a very practical and useful tool in conducting international business, and during informal meetings that involve people from different cultures.

However, if following Hofstede argument that *"culture exists only by comparison"*, then scores of indexes' achieved by particular countries on every dimension are relative, and are true only when societies/ nations are compared to each other. But how can multicultural community is characterized precisely? In that context, the following hypothesis can be considered:

1. *If any "national" business model* acts globally and influences another "national" model for longer time, it probably will also change local existing "old" national patterns of making business, and may even change the common social behaviour of the nation;
2. *The cultural patterns* of an existing community will not only change by the assimilation of the new influences, but rather will interact with "new comers" causing the new comers to react in ways that will accommodate to the new surroundings;
3. *The diffusion of distinctive national culture patterns* elaborated by ages in different geographic localizations, and creating a new form of "collective international cultures".

Collective international cultures as a new socio-economic phenomenon resulting from globalization require continuous development of people's intercultural competence based on cooperation attitude. It is equally important for both contemporary societies and business units.

Factors Shaping Cooperation

Cooperation is the term that has long been used and is widely accepted to describe behaviour in the animal kingdom (Allee, 1951), not just in humans. Many examples of animals or plants demonstrate benefits gained from mutual symbiosis; they cooperate both with other members of their own species, and also with members of other species, simply because of mutual benefits. Humans' cooperation has its old history (Tomasello, Carpenter, Call, Behne, & Moll, 2005) and more complicated backgrounds. Oxford English dictionary technically defines cooperation and collaboration as synonyms.

Other sources distinguish between both terms (as well between other similar terms as: teamwork, partnership, coordination, communication, trust), and signal their structure, meaning, and intention as conceptually different, and thus they also need separate theories of explanation (D'Amour, Ferrada-Videla, Rodriguez, & Beaulieu, 2005). In the extant management literature, the term "collaboration" is more frequently used and it consists of two morphemes of Latin origin: prefix *co* what means (together), and the verb *laborare* (to work). Thus, "collaboration" can be interpreted as "working together", while a "cooperation" is commonly defined as a process of groups of organisms working or acting together for their common/mutual benefit, as opposed to working in competition or for individual benefit.

Multilevel conceptualization of collaboration, published by members of a research team from the University of Central Florida (Bedwell et al., 2012), is mostly used in terms of strategic human resources management (SHRM). It assumes that collaboration has various understandings and definitions, partly

Figure 2. Cooperation components and functions in terms of HRM. Source: Matuska E. & Landowska A. Cooperation asa core competency. The neuro - economic approach (2015, p. 132)

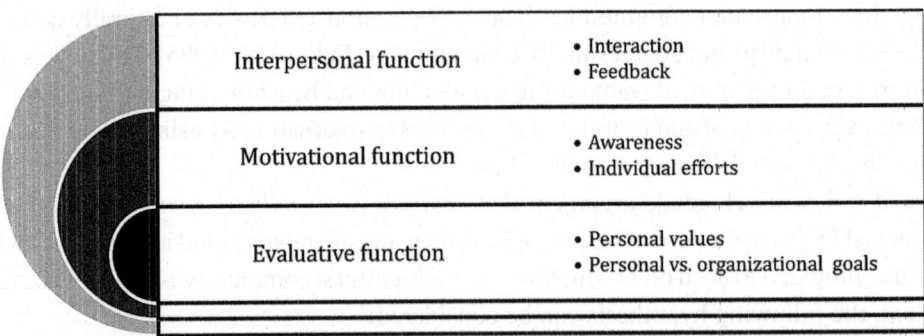

overlapping, done by different disciplines – both social as biological. Collaboration is commonly seen as a form of interaction, but needs an integration of particular observations into a conceptually homological network.

Thus, the authors propose to see collaboration as a super-ordinate construct which subsumes and overlaps with several related variables, including cooperation as subordinated element. All of them are included into space of collaboration, but varying on levels of coordination, depending on task and the size of the entities involved. In other words, team orientation describes the extent to which individuals are predisposed to work well with others; the extent to which they are cooperative. Following Bedwell et al. (2012), other authors assume a cooperation to be a subordinate construct of organizational collaboration.

It is the main attitudinal construct that helps to facilitate the process of collaboration. Cooperation, thus is defined here as an individually held attitude (by individual employee or team) that is required for overall effective collaboration (Bedwell et al., 2012). Moreover, authors propose to extract three main features of cooperation and referred three different functions of organizational processes to them (see Figure 2). These main features or components and corresponding functions of cooperation are as follows:

1. *Cooperation includes the kind of reciprocal interaction* between its different sides. Seeing that cooperation can be perceived as "dyadic" process, usually through examining the dynamics of interactions between" (Pinto, Pinto, & Prescott, 1993). This constitutes *an interpersonal function of cooperation;*
2. *Cooperation means the conscious effort of employees on fixed work tasks.* Cooperation is understood as the "wilful contribution of an employee to the successful completion of interdependent organizational tasks" (Wegner, 1995). This feature illustrates a *motivational function of cooperation;*
3. *Cooperation is the attitudinal construct* "describing the extent to which entities are concerned about the overall goal rather than individual goals" (Salas, Sims, & Burke, 2005). This describes *an evaluative function of cooperation.*

Summarizing the above considerations, the specific features of cooperation (interpreted as a subordinated component of work collaboration) implies three specific functions of cooperation: interpersonal, motivational, and evaluative. As presented earlier, some authors try to make distinct differences between cooperation and collaboration, and put them both into interrelations. Following such interpretation, it should be clearly stated that cooperation is first and foremost an attitude – it accents the processual attributes demonstrated during work activity (smooth and cordial interaction between different individuals/groups); and then a collaboration – it focuses more on achiving common results expected as planned effects of common work.

The investigation of the benefits of cooperative organizational behavior is a major research topic in most micro-economic researches. According to opinions of specialists, cooperation firstly improves company performance, but also boosts employees' well-being (Campion, Medsker& Higgs, 1993; Cohen & Ledford, 1994; White, Hill, McGovern, Mills, & Smeaton, 2003). The focus on internal cooperation is seen as a process of common learning that accompanies a work activity was started in the1970s.

Since that time, the context of "joint learning activities" and "project-based learning" has emerged as a research area. It was inspired by fast dissemination of democratic styles of management, and through a major shift of work content of regular workers. Work shifted from mostly technical processes, individual performance and subordinate behavior, to completely new forms: intellectual processes, teamwork and self-managing processes, including decision making.

The knowledge-based economy announced in the 1990s has started to place the main competitive asset on information. Consequently, the processes of sharing and dissemination knowledge during a work activity has started to be crucial. The prevalence of human resources quality and their interactive effects (nor quantity) was put in a focus. And it still remains, especially when a common use of ITC and social communication media in everyday's work is considered. Thus, the value of internal and external cooperation is currently recognized as also important. Cooperation attitudes are simply necessary to confront the most critical contemporary challenges for organizations.

Moreover, cooperative attitude could be defined as a predisposition or a tendency to respond (positively or negatively) to a certain idea, object, person, or situation. Attitude influences an individual's choice of action, and responses to challenges, incentives, and rewards (together called stimuli). Four major components of attitude are considered: (1) Emotions or feelings; (2) Cognitive: beliefs or opinions held consciously; (3) Connotative: inclination for action; (4) Evaluative: positive or negative response to stimuli. All those components are culturally dependent as number of recent research of different disciplines shown such as anthropology, ethnology, psychology, biology, and genetics.

Tom, Tyler, and Blader (2001) differentiate between two forms of cooperative behaviour: discretionary cooperative behaviour and mandated cooperative behaviour. Mandated cooperation occurs when people engage in behaviour that is dictated or required by a group's rules or norms. The terms and guidelines of the behaviour are prescribed by some rules or policy of the group (often social norms). In contrast, discretionary behaviour is that which is not directly required by the rules or norms of group membership. Such behaviour is "voluntary" because is not specifically required by group rules or norms and is not directly linked to incentives or sanctions. Thus, this distinction between types of cooperative behaviour involves the nature of the behaviour involved. Mandated behaviour originates from external sources (group rules), while discretionary behaviour originates with the group members themselves.

Cooperation Being Culturally Dependent

Among primates, humans are recognized as the most cooperative species because humans live in cultures (social cultures) constituted by all kinds of cooperative institutions and social practices with shared goals and differentiated roles (Boyd & Richerson, 2005). It might be assumed that primate cognition in general was driven mainly by social competition. Additionally, the cognitive skills of humans needed to create complex technologies, cultural institutions and systems of symbols were probably constituted by social cooperation (Tomasello, Carpenter, Call, Behne, & Moll, 2005).

As the mathematical biologist Martin Nowak declared in an overview of the evolution of cooperation: "Perhaps the most remarkable aspect of evolution is its ability to generate cooperation in a competitive world. Thus, we might add 'natural cooperation' as a third fundamental principle of evolution beside mutation and natural selection" (Nowak, 2006). After years of promoting fierce competition as a key argument for organizational efficiency and productivity, today there is a growing evidence that evolution may favour people who cooperate and societies that include such promising individuals (Dawkins, 2006; Bowles, 2006; Benkler, 2011).

Such an approach challenges conventional economic thinking and requires re-defining of many assumption in order to function well in economic models. Still 'natural cooperation' principle competes with 'self-interested humans', which are more valuable for market-oriented organizations, because of creation of demand. Cultural evolution researchers have taken many of the same methods, tools, and concepts that biologists have developed so far to explain biological diversity and complexity and used them to explain similar diversity and complexity in cultural evolution. As a result, several important forces were observed that can lead to cultural evolution mechanisms, such as random errors in teaching or acquiring items of culture, statistical effects in small populations, and the effect of using different cultural variants on an individual's survival and reproduction (Boyd, Henrich, & Richerson, 2010).

Several other forces driving cultural evolution are found as very distinctive ones from the forces of genetic evolution, and derive from the fact that culture can be transmitted through social networks (Findlay, Hansell & Lumsden, 1989; Broesch & Henrich, 2011) in ways that are much more complex than even gene transmission in genetic systems (Richerson & Ross, 2014). Many studies on the evolution of human culture have emphasized the non-genetic transmission of skills and information across generations via imitation and other forms of social learning. It had its origin in the cooperative group activities and communication in which much of human social interaction occurs, and in which many new cognitive skills are generated.

If cumulative cultural evolution of humans requires faithful transmission in a kind of cultural ratchet across generations (Efferson, Lalive, & Fehr, 2008; Henrich, 2008; Henrich & McElreath, 2003), then it also requires innovations. Additionally, many such acts of cultural creation emerge from collaborative activities in which groups of individuals accomplish things that no one individual could have accomplished on their own. Humans generate new cultural variants by other processes such as individual learning, and recombination of existing ideas or techniques (Gil-White & Henrich, 2001; Henrich & McElreath, 2007).

It is generally best for society as a whole if everyone within it cooperates, and moral teachings can broadly be thought of as guidelines designed to influence individuals to sacrifice their own interests in favour of the interests of the group. Many, if not most, moral and ethical questions have the prisoner's dilemma aspects. Since society has an interest in moving people toward cooperation, social norms tend to develop to influence people to cooperate. The Golden Rule is an example of a widely followed ethical rule that increases cooperation. If one exists in a society where people generally follow the Golden Rule, he or she may be able to cooperate with the confidence that one would be defected. Additionally, religions usually have moral codes designed to increase cooperation among members. Social norms punishing or shunning defectors also work to increase cooperation.

The societies with the greatest cooperation and with the most effective norms promoting cooperation tend to be the most historically outbred societies. Although it is a winning strategy for everyone in society to cooperate, it is a losing strategy for a person to cooperate with someone who is going to defect. If one person follows the Golden Rule and another follows a strategy of pure self-interest, the self-interested party will consistently defect and the Golden Rule follower will be a loser. This is the fundamental flaw of strict universalism – it is ultimately suicidal. If social norms that cause people to cooperate break down, defection becomes more and more common.

Another multi-level selection theories stress that the so-called 'strong reciprocity' could be the basis of human cooperative interactions (Fehr & Gächter, 2002), which is additionally supported by the so-called 'cultural group selection' (Richerson & Boyd, 2005). All theories suggest that human cooperation seems to be something very different. Many different processes have been included which had not been studied earlier.

Cooperation Being Biologically Dependent

Human cooperative nature until now had not been usually explained by traits of socialization, but research in neuroeconomics proves its additional neurological and genetic backgrounds (Rilling et al., 2002). Evolutionary biologists and psychologists have found neuronal and possibly genetic evidence of a human predisposition to cooperate, which is expressed in human genome responding and adapting to cultural environment (Laland, Odling-Smee, & Myles, 2010). This approach is summarized in the well-known "gene-culture co-evolution theory" by such authors as Chiao and Blizinsky, (2010), Gintis (2011) or Chudek et al. (2013), which influences most current research in the topic of cooperation.

The idea of co-evolution of genes and culture creates new pattern for understanding human behaviour, which evolves, but could not have evolved only through the action of natural selection of genes. Modern human behaviour seems to be the product of many hundreds of generations of the interplay between the genetic and cultural inheritance systems. It surely also counts in case of cooperative behaviour. For example, Boyd and Richerson (1982) and Henrich and Richerson (2003) have conducted studies that searched for the explanation of the evolution of behaviours that allow humans to create cooperative social groups with non-relatives.

Human bodies are biologically stable across time, but lately, an emerging research is demonstrating that external social conditions, especially human's subjective perceptions of those conditions, can influence their most basic internal biological processes and it is called the "expression of genes" (Orphanides & Reinberg 2002). This research on human social genomics has begun to identify the types of genes that are subject to social-environmental regulation, the neural and molecular mechanisms that mediate the effects of social processes on gene expression, and the genetic polymorphisms that moderate individual differences in genomic sensitivity to social context.

The molecular models resulting from this research provide new opportunities for understanding how social and genetic factors interact to shape complex behavioural phenotypes and its eventual tendency to diseases. This research also shows new agents influencing the evolution of the human genome. And at the same time, it confronts the fundamental belief that humans' molecular makeup is relatively stable and impermeable to social-environmental influence. On that basis, the evolutionists (i.e., Henrich et al., 2003) indicate much more. Groups, which interact infrequently, can evolve very different cultural traditions and institutions.

The ones with cultures that enable or encourage their members to behave more effectively will thrive at the expense of groups that are less culturally well endowed. Moreover, groups that developed traditions of punishing selfish behaviour to the group as a whole may well have been more successful than groups that tolerated more individualistic behaviour. Genes that encourage cooperation could have arisen in such groups because the culture would have favoured individuals who were more docile and willing to behave in accordance with existing cultural norms.

It is expected that repeated co-evolutionary cycles could drastically modify the psychological mechanisms that influence human social interaction. The research shows how social influences regulate gene expression on an individual level. The question arises regarding how they may also be involved in gene expression at a collective group level.

There are also a number of empirical evidences which present a process of social signal transduction involving a meta-genomic system in which individual genomes operate differently depending on the presence of other people and their (subjectively perceived) implications for individual fitness outcomes such as reproduction and survival (Cole, Hawkley, Arevalo, & Cacioppo, 2011; Slavich, Way, Eisenberger & Taylor, 2010; Kauffman, 1993). All of it suggests the existence of a kind of human "meta-genome" which acts as a system that is likely to generate complex emergent properties as transcriptional dynamics propagated through networks of genomes.

If the human genome is so dynamic and susceptible to the influence of cultural environment, it may consequently encode a wide variety of "potential biological selves", and which "biological self" is achieved depends on the social conditions we experience over our life course. Functional genomics studies of Slavich and Cole (2013) have shown that although DNA codes for the production of a wide variety of proteins that affect human functioning, our genetic code does not always result in the production of these proteins. It rather appears as though certain genes can be "turned on" and "turned off" by different social-environmental conditions.

Additionally, it has been demonstrated that some social-environmental factors (e.g., social isolation, social rejection) can influence the activity of not just a couple of genes, but broad sets of hundreds of genes (i.e., gene profiles or gene programs). It has long been known that social-environmental conditions can shape complex behavioural phenotypes and be susceptibility to disease and longevity (Cohen, Janicki-Deverts, & Miller, 2007). An example of that is social isolation which is associated with increased risk for mortality (Holt-Lunstad, Layton, & Smith, 2010; House, 2001; House, Landis, & Umberson, 1988; Virchow, 1848/2006). Some biological (mostly neuronal) traits of cooperative behaviour are also explored on the background of behavioural economics and neuroeconomy.

Neuroeconomic Dimension of Cooperation

In the confrontation with last global economic crisis, it was undoubtedly confirmed that economic models do not provide a satisfying theory of how individuals (managers, regular workers, customers) and organizations act on the market and how they make decisions. The crucial input of psychologists (Kahneman & Tversky, 2000) discovered set of cognitive errors and biases that shape individual judgments of self-interested people during decision-making processes. This work stopped the hitherto assumptions about the exclusive rational behaviour of *homo economicus*, and the role of emotions and motivation started to be emphasized (Winter, 2014).

Kahneman's research (2011) explains the neuronal mechanism of human thinking and decision-making by postulating that people comprehend the world by making use of two fundamentally different modes of thoughts: System 1 called "fast", which is guided by intuitions, associations, metaphors and impressions, and System 2 called "slow", which is guided by focus, deliberation and effort. This seems to be the key knowledge for managers and organizations – how to adequately use emotions during decision-making, how to facilitate creativity and innovations, how to analyse occurred errors, how to facilitate cooperation and built commitment and trust to organization, etc.

In terms of motivation, economists have generally operated on the assumption that people are motivated to maximize their own personal self-interest – defined in terms of material gains and losses. The findings herein show that people are motivated by a broader range of goals than is easily explained via material self-interest – that is, by people's concerns about incentives and sanctions. Those seeking to best understand how to motivate cooperation should focus their attention upon social motivations of behaviour, so far commonly neglected in economics.

Traditional economics is well-focused on formulating predictions of human choice given preferences, incentives, and feasibility constraints. Used by this discipline, mostly quantitative methodology, lack of deeper understanding the mechanisms of human behaviour, including psychological and biological background, results with usually not sufficiently proved and narrow interpretation of *homo economicus* behaviour projections, including decision making, or cooperation. It has not yet been established that any complete and coherent economic concept explaining motives, barriers, or typical contents of human cooperation exists.

The confrontation of this challenge can help neuroeconomics which uses a combination of research methods coming from different fields of studies including: neuroscience, experimental and behavioural economics, cognitive and social psychology, theoretical biology, computer science and mathematics. Neuroeconomics actually brings the process of studying human's cooperative behaviour to a completely new and higher level of analysis. The basis for consideration about background of cooperation offers the results obtained from research dedicated to human decision making – the main scientific topic of neuroeconomics.

Cooperation also means decision making– people can choose common activity or oppositely, they can decide to act as separate individuals. To cooperate or not to cooperate is actually also a kind of decision making. Humans' decisions always are made under some conditions, usually complex, and not fully controlled. They obviously consist of objective elements (which are easy to recognize and describe), but those "objective reality" is interpreted in a subjective, individual, or team influenced, mood. Thus, the crucial issue is to consider individual conditions of human's decisions. Those individual conditions include neurological aspects, as well as the influence of social (culture) interactions.

In psychology, sociology, and in many other disciplines, behavioural human studies search for determinants of different pro-social interactions including: altruism, cooperation, or antisocial interactions, such as aggression, punishing others or self-punishment, and many others. The traditional area of clinical psychology has since a long time collected data of clinical symptoms of damaged brain and carefully describes the differences between behavioural results coming from damage of particular parts of CNS. In the same discipline, there also exists the scope of well-documented results of studies on behavioural aspects of different brain neurotransmitters and bio-chemicals (for example, dopamine and others).

In neuroeconomics, the special neural imaging method is used to map which area of human brain is active during a particular decision-making process. All of this has brought also a new light on brain's determinants of cooperation. The assumption that cooperative behaviour, including cooperation during work activity, has an important neurological background has already been confirmed by a large of number of experimental research conducted during the last decade.

This work documents that behaving in accordance with well-acquired social norms such as cooperating, activates the brain's reward-anticipatory circuits in the same manner as does the obtaining of direct cash payment (i.e., Tabibnia, Satpute & Lieberman, 2008).This discovery addresses the issue of cooperation, and have prompted recent studies (Brown & Richerson, 2014) to develop the following conclusions:

- *Complying with norms "feels good"* influences the brain in the same way as the act of receiving rewards (as getting money does);
- *Punishing by really hurting defectors*(physically or monetarily) activates relative brain reward circuits more than symbolism of the punishments;
- *Activations of the brain's reward circuitry* in cited experiments allow the prediction behavioural outcomes – cooperation or lack thereof.

Discoveries that the motivation to cooperate can be generated by the reward system in the brain are also confirmed by recent results which suggest this effect can be modulated by two separate neural networks (Declerck et al., 2013):

- *A cognitive control system* (centred on the lateral prefrontal cortex) that processes extrinsic cooperative incentives, and/or
- *A social cognition system* (including brain structures such as: superior temporal sulcus, anterior medial frontal cortex and amygdala) that processes trust signals.

The above conclusions regarding independent modulators influencing the incentives for cooperation have recently been updated by a growing body of neuroimaging data. They also reconcile the apparent paradox between economic (cooperation) versus social (trust) rationality in the extant literature (Declerck, Boone, & Emonds, 2013). In line with this, Sanfey, Loewenstein, McClure, and Cohen (2006) describe dual information processing which occur in the mind. The concept consists of automatic (emotional) and controlled (deliberative) processes. This concept certainly corresponds to Kahneman's idea of the two ways of human thinking: slow and fast.

Cooperation as an attitude has both emotional and cognitive parts. Today, they are usually interpreted as complimentary psychological processes. Many neurobiological studies based on the modern technique of neuroimaging reveal that apparently irrational decisions are correlated with the emotional part of the brain (Shiv, Loewenstein, & Bechara, 2005). Although emotions are no direct part of preferences of cooperative or non-cooperative behaviour, they easily confuse primary preference-oriented behaviour and can lead to irrationality in the case of non-optimizing decision-making.

It has also been clearly stated in a recent research that individual differences in cooperation may reflect variation in neural sensitivities. Mirror neurons and neural mirror systems produce an emotion of 'sympathy work' in the same way as when the subject performs an act emotionally and when the subject observes others showing an identical emotion. There is a harmony between being active *"when the action is performed and also when it is observed"* (Glimcher & Rustichini, 2004). Described results and observations can be concluded in line with the purposes of modelling cooperative attitude on organizational behaviour:

1. The positive emotions experienced during work activity will facilitate a cooperative behaviour;
2. The negative emotions experienced during work activity will facilitate non-cooperative (selfish, hostile, rivalry etc.) behaviour.

Indeed, the knowledge that the emotional atmosphere experienced at work influences work performance is not new in terms of behavioural economics or human resources management theories, but this time it is confirmed by experimental methods and explained through a neurobiological theory. The crucial impact both for behavioural economics and for strategic human resources management is that reward-related brain areas connect the brain's responses to the measurement of utility. Based on the existing research, evidences that can be assumed for purposes of modelling desirable cooperative attitude at work include:

- *Self-regarding individuals* (oriented on economic rationality) are more responsive to extrinsic co-operative incentives, and therefore, rely more on cognitive control to consider possible individual benefits from hypothetical cooperative decisions, whereas
- *Other – regarding individuals* (oriented on social rationality) are more sensitive to trust signals in order to avoid betrayal and recruit relatively more brain activity in the social cognition system.

Neuroeconomic research helps to understand how neuronal and brain processes are activated during work activity and how they determine the cooperative or non-cooperative attitude of teamwork. This brings a completely new kind of arguments for explaining the repercussions associated with competitiveness and innovativeness.

SOLUTIONS AND RECOMMENDATIONS

Diversity usually reduces social bonds and trust, but also brings new inspirations and a promise of innovation. Owing to the rapid growth of multicultural societies and countries, ever stronger international migration flows, and the accelerated development of digital technologies, cultural diversity is becoming the principal challenge of our times. Cultural diversity is understood not only as the common heritage of mankind, which needs to be protected and promoted, but also as a resource, which needs to be managed.

Sociology and economy are today two very sensitive areas that are fast changing, together with increment in diversity. The extending of multi-ethnicity of communities and organizations needs new approaches and instruments. First, it is necessary to have better understanding of different cultures and the use of the heritage and potentials of different cultures. The role of intercultural competence is evident and this competence should be widely nurtured and disseminated. The basis for this competence is cooperation; thus, the cooperative behaviour should be reinforced via integration programs and its promotion should be included as the stable part of general social/labour market policy.

Recent studies deliver a new set of parameters that is available both to sociologists and economists, which might be defined as an input. These parameters are diversified and cover both cultural as well as biological markers. Neuroeconomics provides new data in addition to those available from theoretical, empirical, and experimental research on human behaviour. It has been known for a long time which specific brain areas are active when we act in specific ways. The practicality of this knowledge becomes evident when it is used during the modelling of desirable patterns of behaviours, such as cooperation. Moreover, genetics argue that humans' predisposition to cooperate is culturally interdependent. All of this creates more complex environment, which is challenged by economists. Hence, it is necessary to find some "navigation system" in today's turbulent times, and it can only be achieved through commonly shared values. One of most universal values seems to be simply cooperation.

FUTURE RESEARCH DIRECTIONS

The fact that social-environmental factors may induce changes in the expression human genes represents a new paradigm on gene-culture interplay. These two factors are no longer independent of each other, which lead to the provision of new insights into how culture and biology interact. It should be clearly stated that we are just beginning to understand how genomic activity differs as a function of the full range of positive and negative social conditions that humans' experience.

GCC is rapidly growing as an interdisciplinary field. As an explanatory concept of human behaviour, it will certainly play an important role in linkages between socio-cultural and genetic theories. Combining neuroeconomics and GCC may result in completely new understanding of organizational and economic behaviour. If 'cooperation', which plays a key role in socio-economic development is recognized as a cultural dependent factor opposite to societies, different economic behaviour might be expected in different societies as cultural economics expects. Thus, it is necessary to deepen a multidisciplinary research on cooperation and its factors with special focus on its organizational and economic consequences.

For a long time, economics has neglected interactions among economic behaviour and other human behaviours. Recent empirical data resulting from neuroscientific and genetic methods are challenges that economics faces today. Identifying more clearly the implications of human choices, as well as reasons of human choices associated with their background (including cultural differences, genetic difference, neural differences), seems to be further expanding and validating, which allows economist to negate, modify, or extend existing economic theories. New research explaining innovativeness and competitiveness should also address intercultural issues in order to respond to more complex social realities and to seek how to improve overall productivity performance within their respective domains.

CONCLUSION

In a globalizing world in which geographical boundaries are becoming increasingly less relevant, the demands on our social and communication skills are changing rapidly. Global community is reflected across many cross-cultural assumptions, values, and behaviours. Moving from a mono-cultural perspective to a multicultural one requires, first, observation and knowledge, and then the adoption of new knowledge about cultures. It implies withholding judgment about those who appear to be different in the society, and learning to respect others for who they are. Intercultural competence goes beyond this, since it requires people with different nationalities, backgrounds, languages, ethnicities and religions to learn to work together and to collaborate in an effective way.

Anthropologists and ethnologists reciprocally explain how cooperation depends on culture understood as social norm transmitter where asocial learning process occurs. Genetics argue that humans' predisposition to cooperate is dependent on culture. Psychologists and neurologists document the big psycho-nervous efforts human beings use to adapt to the current "turbulent" and insecure times of work and life. All of this creates a complex environment with which economists and managers must contend. As one of the young disciplines, neuroeconomics is a new source with promising data that verifies all data that have been collected so far through theoretical, empirical, and experimental research on human behaviour.

It delivers information about potential customer-behaviour as well as knowledge about potential employees – information, which is no longer simulation based. Its value increases in particular in human resource management, which focuses on selecting cooperative candidates. Cooperation, which is also culturally dependent, becomes a part of intercultural competence desired in multicultural work places, and is necessary to the achievement of a peaceful multi-ethnic, and coexisting societies.

REFERENCES

Allee, W. C. (1951). *Cooperation among animals, with human implications: A revised and amplified edition of the social life of animals.* New York: Schuman.

Allred, B. B., Snow, C. C., & Miles, R. E. (1996). Characteristics of managerial careers in the 21st century. *The Academy of Management Executive, 10*(4), 17–27.

Becker, B. E., & Huselid, M. A. (2006). Strategic human resources management: Where do we go from here? *Journal of Management, 32*(6), 898–925. doi:10.1177/0149206306293668

Bedwell, W. L., Wildman, J. L., Diaz Granados, D., Salazar, M., Kramer, W. S., & Salas, E. (2012). Collaboration at work: An integrative multilevel conceptualization. *Human Resource Management Review, 22*(2), 128–145. doi:10.1016/j.hrmr.2011.11.007

Beersma, B., Hollenbeck, J. R., Humphrey, S. E., Moon, H., Conlon, D. E., & Ilgen, D. R. (2003). Cooperation, competition, and team performance: Toward a contingency approach. *Academy of Management Journal, 46*(5), 572–590. doi:10.2307/30040650

Benkler, Y. (2011). The Unselfish Gene. *Harvard Business Review, 89*(7–8), 77–85. PMID:21800472

Blaškova, M., & Blaško, R. (2015).Tolerance and flexibility as crucial competences of multicultural team leader. In *Proceedings of Scientific Papers, 12th International Scientific Conference Human Potential Development.* Klaipeda: Klaipeda University Press. Retrieved on May 14, 2015, from: http://frcatel.fri.uniza.sk/hrme/ConfHPM/index.html\

Bowles, S. (2006). Group competition, reproductive leveling, and the evolution of human altruism. *Science, 314*(5805), 1569–1572. doi:10.1126/science.1134829 PMID:17158320

Boyd, R., & Richerson, P. J. (1982). Culture transmissionand the evolution of cooperative behavior *Human Ecology, 10*(3), 325–351. doi:10.1007/BF01531189

Brett, J., Behfar, K., & Kern, M. (2006). Managing Multicultural Teams. *Harvard Business Review, 84*(11), 84–91. PMID:17131565

Brown, G. R., & Richerson, P. (2014). Applying evolutionary theory to human behaviour: Past differences and current debates. *Journal of Bioeconomics, 16*(2), 105–128. doi:10.1007/s10818-013-9166-4

Campion, A., Medsker, G. J., & Higgs, C. (1993). Relation between work group characteristics and effectiveness: Implications for designing an effective work group. *Personnel Psychology, 46*(4), 823–850. doi:10.1111/j.1744-6570.1993.tb01571.x

Chan, K. W., & Mauborgne, R. (2015). *Blue Ocean Strategy, Expanded Edition: How to Create Uncontested Market Space and Make the Competition Irrelevant.* Boston, MA: Harvard Business Review Press.

Chiao, J. Y., & Blizinsky, K. D. (2010). Culture–gene coevolution of individualism–collectivism and the serotonintransporter gene. In *Proceedings of the Royal Society B: Biological Sciences* (vol. 277, pp. 529–537). Retrieved on September 11, 2013, from: http://rspb.royalsocietypublishing.org/content/277/1681/529

Cohen, S., Janicki-Deverts, D., & Miller, G. E. (2007). Psychological stress and disease. *Journal of the American Medical Association*, *298*(14), 1685–1687. doi:10.1001/jama.298.14.1685 PMID:17925521

Cohen, S. G., & Ledford, G. E. (1994). The effectiveness of self-managing teams: A quasi-experiment. *Human Relations*, *47*(1), 13–43. doi:10.1177/001872679404700102

Cole, G. A. (1988). *Personnel Management. Theory and Practice* (2nd ed.). London: D.P. Publications, Ltd.

Cole, S. W., Hawkley, L. C., Arevalo, J. M., & Cacioppo, J. T. (2011). Transcript origin analysis identifies antigen-presenting cells as primary targets of socially regulated gene expression in leukocytes. In *Proceedings of the National Academy of Sciences of the United States of America* (vol. 108, pp. 3080–3085). Retrieved on May 9, 2015, from: http://www.ncbi.nlm.nih.gov/pmc/articles/PMC3041107/

Council of Europe. (2010). *White Paper on Intercultural Dialogue: Living together as equals in dignity. Report of the Group of Eminent Persons of the Council of Europe*. Strasbourg: Council of Europe Publishing.

D'Amour, D., Ferrada-Videla, M., Rodriguez, L. S. M., & Beaulieu, M. D. (2005). The conceptual basis for interprofessional collaboration: Core concepts and theoretical frame works. *Journal of Interprofessional Care*, *19*(1), 116–131. doi:10.1080/13561820500082529 PMID:16096150

Dawkins, R. (2006). *The Selfish Gene (30th anniv. ed.)*. Oxford, UK: Oxford University Press.

Declerck, C. H., Boone, C., & Emonds, G. (2013). When do people cooperate? The neuroeconomics of prosocial decision making. *Brain and Cognition*, *81*(1), 95–117. doi:10.1016/j.bandc.2012.09.009 PMID:23174433

Efferson, C., Lalive, R., & Fehr, E. (2008). The coevolution of cultural groups and in groupfavoritism. *Science*, *321*(5897), 1844–1849. doi:10.1126/science.1155805 PMID:18818361

European Commission (2006). *Recommendation of the European Parliament and of the Council of 18 December 2006 on key competences for lifelong learning*. Official Journal 2006/962/EC.

Fehr, E., & Gächter, S. (2002). Altruistic punishment in humans. *Nature*, *415*(6868), 137–140. doi:10.1038/415137a PMID:11805825

Findlay, C. S., Hansell, R. I., & Lumsden, C. J. (1989). Behavioral evolution and biocultural games: Oblique and horizontal cultural transmission. *Journal of Theoretical Biology*, *137*(3), 245–269. doi:10.1016/S0022-5193(89)80072-4 PMID:2811392

Fukuyama, F. (1995). *Trust: The Social Virtues and the Creation of Prosperity*. New York: Free Press.

Gintis, H. (2010). Gene–culture coevolution and the nature of human sociality. In *Proceedings of the Royal Society B: Biological Sciences* (vol. 366, pp. 878–888). Retrieved on October 7, 2013, from: http://rspb.royalsocietypublishing.org

Glimcher, P., & Rustichini, A. (2004). The consilience of brain and decision. *Science*, *306*(5695), 447–452. doi:10.1126/science.1102566 PMID:15486291

Glimcher, P. W. (2010). *Foundations of Neuroeconomic Analysis*. Oxford, UK: Oxford University Press. doi:10.1093/acprof:oso/9780199744251.001.0001

Henrich, J. (2008). A cultural species. In M. Brown (Ed.), *Explaining Culture Scientifically* (pp. 184–210). Seattle, WA: University of Washington Press.

Henrich, J., Bowles, S., Boyd, R. T., Hopfensitz, A., Richerson, P. J., & Sigmund, K. (2003). Group report: The cultural and genetic evolution of human cooperation. In P. Hammerstein (Ed.), *Genetic and Cultural Evolution of Cooperation* (pp. 445–468). Cambridge, MA: MIT Press.

Henrich, J., & Boyd, R. (2002). On modeling cognition and culture. Why cultural evolution does not require replication of representations. *Journal of Cognition and Culture*, *2*(2), 87–112. doi:10.1163/156853702320281836

Henrich, J., Boyd, R., Bowles, S., Camerer, C., Fehr, E., Gintis, H., & Tracer, D. et al. (2005). Economic man in cross-cultural perspective: Behavioral experiments in 15 small-scale societies. *Behavioral and Brain Sciences*, *28*(6), 795–855. doi:10.1017/S0140525X05000142 PMID:16372952

Henrich, J., & Broesch, J. (2011). On the nature of cultural transmission networks: Evidence from Fijian villages for adaptive learning biases. *Philosophical Transactions of the Royal Society of London. Series B, Biological Sciences*, *366*(1567), 1139–1148. doi:10.1098/rstb.2010.0323 PMID:21357236

Henrich, J., & Gil-White, F. (2001). The Evolution of Prestige: Freely conferred deference as a mechanism for enhancing the benefits of cultural transmission. *Evolution and Human Behavior*, *22*(3), 165–196. doi:10.1016/S1090-5138(00)00071-4 PMID:11384884

Henrich, J., & McElreath, R. (2003). The Evolution of Cultural Evolution. *Evolutionary Anthropology*, *12*(3), 123–135. doi:10.1002/evan.10110

Henrich, J., & McElreath, R. (2007). Dual Inheritance Theory: The Evolution of Human Cultural Capacities and Cultural Evolution. In R. Dunbar & L. Barret (Eds.), *Oxford Handbook of Evolutionary Psychology* (pp. 555–570). Oxford, UK: Oxford University Press. doi:10.1093/oxfordhb/9780198568308.013.0038

Hickok, G. (2014). *The Myth of Mirror Neurons: The Real Neuroscience of Communication and Cognition*. New York: W.W. Norton & Company.

Hofstede, G. (2001). *Culture's Consequences: Comparing Values, Behaviors, Institutions and Organizations across Nations*. Thousand Oaks, CA: Sage Publications.

Hofstede, G., Hofstede, G. J., & Minkov, M. (2010). *Cultures and Organizations: Software of the Mind. Revised and expanded* (3rd ed.). New York: McGraw-Hill.

Holt-Lunstad, J., Smith, T. B., & Layton, J. B. (2010). Social relationships and mortality risk: A meta-analytic review. *PLoS Medicine*, *7*(7), e1000316. doi:10.1371/journal.pmed.1000316 PMID:20668659

House, J. S. (2001). Social isolation kills, but how and why? *Psychosomatic Medicine*, *63*(2), 273–274. doi:10.1097/00006842-200103000-00011 PMID:11292275

House, J. S., Landis, K. R., & Umberson, D. (1988). Social relationships and health. *Science, 241*(4865), 540–545. doi:10.1126/science.3399889 PMID:3399889

Kahneman, D. (2011). *Thinking Fast And Slow - The Neuroscience Behind Good Decision-Making.* New York: Penguin Books.

Kahneman, D., & Tversky, A. (Eds.). (2000). *Choices, values and frames.* New York: Cambridge University Press.

Kauffman, S. A. (1993). *The origins of order: Self-organization and selection in evolution.* New York: Oxford University Press.

Keršienė, K., & Savanevičienė, A. (2005). Defining and Understanding Organizational Multicultural Competence. *The Engineering Economist, 2*(42), 45–52.

Kozlowski, S. W. J., Gully, S. M., Nason, E. R., & Smith, E. M. (1999). Developing adaptive teams: A theory of compilation and performance across levels and time. In D. R. Ilgen & E. D. Pulakos (Eds.), *The changing nature of work performance: Implications for staffing, personnel actions, and development* (pp. 240–292). San Francisco, CA: Jossey-Bass.

Laland, K., Odling-Smee, J., & Myles, S. (2010). How culture shaped the human genome: Brinding genetics and the human sciences together. *Nature Reviews. Genetics, 11*(2), 137–148. doi:10.1038/nrg2734 PMID:20084086

Mac-Dermott, R., & Mornah, D. (2015). The Role of Culture in Foreign Direct Investment and Trade: Expectations from the GLOBE Dimensions of Culture. *Open Journal of Business and Management, 3*(01), 63–74. doi:10.4236/ojbm.2015.31007

Matsumoto, D. (1990). Cultural Similarities and Differences in Display Rules. *Motivation and Emotion, 14*(3), 195–214. doi:10.1007/BF00995569

Matuska, E. (2015). Competence Management in frame of human capital management. In A. Sokół (Ed.), *Managing diversity in the organization. Creativity- Competence- Knowledge- Trust* (pp. 51–76). London: Sciemcee Publications.

Matuska, E., & Landowska, A. (2015). Cooperation as a core competency. The neuro-economic approach. In *Proceedings of Scientific Papers, 12ᵗʰ International Scientific Conference Human Potential Development* (pp. 136-148). Klaipeda: Klaipeda University Press. Retrieved on June 2, 2015, from: http://frcatel.fri.uniza.sk/hrme/ConfHPM/index.html\

Nardon, L., Steers, R. M., & Sanches-Runde, C. J. (2013, May 9). Developing Multicultural Competence. *The European Business Review.* Retrieved on November 11, 2014, from: http://www.europeanbusinessreview.com/?p=1386

Nowak, M. A. (2006). Five rules for the evolution of cooperation. *Science, 314*(5805), 1560–1563. doi:10.1126/science.1133755 PMID:17158317

Orphanides, G., & Reinberg, D. (2002, February 22). A Unified Theory of Gene Expression. *Cell, 108*(4), 439–451. doi:10.1016/S0092-8674(02)00655-4 PMID:11909516

Pinto, M. B., Pinto, J. K., & Prescott, J. E. (1993). Antecedents and consequences of project team cross-functional cooperation. *Management Science, 39*(10), 1281–1297. doi:10.1287/mnsc.39.10.1281

Rathje, S. (2007). Intercultural Competence: The Status and Future of a Controversial Concept. *Journal for Language and Intercultural Communication, 7*(4), 254–266. doi:10.2167/laic285.0

Richerson, P. J., & Boyd, R. (2005). *Not by genes alone. How culture transformed human evolution.* Oxford, UK: Oxford University Press.

Richerson, P. J., Boyd, R., & Henrich, J. (2010). Gene-culture coevolution in the age of genomics. In *Proceedings of National Academy of Science of the United States of America.* Retrieved on January 22, 2013, from: http://www.pnas.org/content/107/Supplement_2/8985.full

Richerson, P. J., Boyd, R., & Henrich, J. (2003). Cultural evolution of human cooperation. In P. Hammerstein (Ed.), *Genetic and Cultural Evolution of Cooperation* (pp. 357–388). Berlin: MIT Press.

Riether, W. (2014). *Business Cooperation cultural Integration as Key Factor.* Saarbruecken: AV Akademikerverlag.

Rilling, J. K., Gutman, D. A., Zeh, T. R., Pagnoni, G., Berns, G. S., Clint, D., & Kilts, C. D. (2002). A Neural Basis for Social Cooperation. *Neuron, 35*(2), 395–405. doi:10.1016/S0896-6273(02)00755-9 PMID:12160756

Rosenbaum, M., Moore, D., Cotton, J., Cook, M., Heiser, R., Shovar, N., & Gray, M. (1980). Group productivity and process: Pure and mixed reward structures and task interdependence. *Journal of Personality and Social Psychology, 39*(4), 626–642. doi:10.1037/0022-3514.39.4.626

Ross, C. T., & Richerson, P. J. (2014). New frontiers in the study of human cultural and genetic evolution. *Current Opinion in Genetics & Development, 29,* 102–109. doi:10.1016/j.gde.2014.08.014 PMID:25218864

Salas, E., Sims, D. E., & Burke, C. S. (2005). Is there "big five" in teamwork? *Small Group Research, 36*(5), 555–599. doi:10.1177/1046496405277134

Sanfey, A. G., Loewenstein, G., McClure, S. M., & Cohen, J. D. (2006). Neuroeconomics: Cross-Currents in Research on Decision-Making. *Trends in Cognitive Sciences, 10*(3), 108–116. doi:10.1016/j.tics.2006.01.009 PMID:16469524

Shiv, B., Loewenstein, G., & Bechara, A. (2005). The Dark Side of Emotions? *Brain Research. Cognitive Brain Research, 23*(1), 85–92. doi:10.1016/j.cogbrainres.2005.01.006 PMID:15795136

Sinha, R. (2006). *Key Factors of Multicultural Team Management & Leadership.* Retrieved on April 1, 2010, from: http://ezinearticles.com/?Key-Factors-of-Multicultural-Team-Management-and-Leadership&id=293829

Sinha, R. (2008). *Managing Multicultural Teams.* Icfai University Press.

Slavich, G. M., & Cole, S. W. (2013). The Emerging Field of Human Social Genomics. *Clinical Psychological Science, 1*(3), 331–348. doi:10.1177/2167702613478594 PMID:23853742

Slavich, G. M., Way, B. M., Eisenberger, N. I., & Taylor, S. E. (2010). Neural sensitivity to social rejection is associated with inflammatory responses to social stress. In *Proceedings of the National Academy of Sciences of the United States of America* (vol. 107, pp. 14817–14822). Retrieved on July 4, 2013, from: http://www.ncbi.nlm.nih.gov/pmc/articles/PMC2930449/

Soderberg, A. M., & Holden, N. (2002). Rethinking Cross Cultural Management in a Globalizing Business World. *International Journal of Cross Cultural Management, 2*(1), 103–121. doi:10.1177/1470595802002001091

Stahl, G. K., Mäkelä, K., Zander, L., & Maynevski, M. L. (2010). A Look at the Bright Side of Multicultural Team Diversity. *Scandinavian Journal of Management, 26*(4), 439–447. doi:10.1016/j.scaman.2010.09.009

Stracke, Ch. M. (2011). Competence Modeling for Innovations and Quality Development in E-Learning: Towards learning outcome orientation by competence models. In *Proceedings of World Conference on Educational Multimedia, Hypermedia and Telecommunication 2011*. Retrieved on March 13, 2014, from: http://www.qed-info.de/downloads

Tabibnia, G., Satpute, A. B., & Lieberman, M. D. (2008). The sunny side of fairness – reference for s activates self-control fairness activates reward circuitry (and disregarding unfairnescircuitry). *Psychological Science, 19*(4), 339–347. doi:10.1111/j.1467-9280.2008.02091.x PMID:18399886

Tom, R., Tyler, T. R., & Blader, S. L. (2001). Identity and Cooperative Behavior in Groups. *Group Processes & Intergroup Relations, 4*(3), 207–226. doi:10.1177/1368430201004003003

Tomasello, M., Carpenter, M., Call, J., Behne, T., & Moll, H. (2005). Understanding and sharing intentions: The ontogeny and phylogeny of cultural cognition. *Behavioral and Brain Sciences, 28*(05), 675–735. doi:10.1017/S0140525X05000129 PMID:16262930

Virchow, R. (2006). Report on the typhus outbreak of Upper Silesia. *Social Medicine, 1*(1), 11–27. (Original work published 1848).

Wegner, D. M. (1995). A computer network model of human transactive memory. *Social Cognition, 13*(3), 319–339. doi:10.1521/soco.1995.13.3.319

White, M., Hill, S., McGovern, P., Mills, C., & Smeaton, D. (2003). High performance – management practices, working hours and work-life balance. *British Journal of Industrial Relations, 41*(2), 175–195. doi:10.1111/1467-8543.00268

William, B. (2003).Cross-Cultural and Intercultural Communication. Thousand Oaks, CA: Sage.

Winter, E. (2014). *Feeling Smart: Why Our Emotions Are More Rational Than We Think*. New York: Public Affairs.

Wiseman, R. L. (2003). Intercultural Communication Competence. In W. B. Gudykunst (Ed.), *Cross-Cultural and Intercultural Communication* (pp. 191–208). Thousand Oaks, CA: Sage.

Witte, A. (2012). Making the Case for a Post-National Cultural Analysis of Organizations. *Journal of Management Inquiry, 21*(2), 141–159. doi:10.1177/1056492611415279

KEY TERMS AND DEFINITIONS

Collaboration: The word "collaboration" consists of two morphemes of Latin origin: prefix *co* what means (together), and the verb *laborare* (to work) and represents action of working together.

Co-Operation: An attitude being a result of interpersonal, motivational and evaluative functions individually defined in ontogenetic process, also a part of collaboration in case of teamwork.

Cultural Pattern: An orientation, which underlie most common behaviour of culture group members, and which is transmitted through social learning.

Intercultural Competence: A set of knowledge, skills and attitudes towards other cultures, which facilitate mutual cooperation in multiethnic society.

Intercultural Communication: A communication that aims to share information across members representing different cultural groups, when social interaction occurs, and in which many new cognitive skills are generated.

Multicultural Society: A society, in which many cultural groups co-exist.

Social Rationality: A rationality, which implicates individual's choices and predictions under uncertainty with focus on social contexts.

Chapter 6
Managerial Reactions to Ambiguous Environmental Changes:
Attention, Reasoning, and Erratic Decisions

Wiboon Kittilaksanawong
Saitama University, Japan

ABSTRACT

Managers in organizations are typically faced with changing and ambiguous signals in their operating environment. Based on interpretation of these signals, managers react with appropriate strategies. This chapter presents critical organizational issues in decision making process and its outcomes, including the manager's selective attention, interpretation, and reasoning of uncertain operating environment. In particular, the chapter first discusses why individual managers in the same organization who are faced with same environmental changes may differently interpret threat and opportunity aspects of these changes. Second, the chapter links outcomes of such interpretation to investigate different types of organizational actions. Third, the chapter drives into a greater depth to explore how the manager's experience and characteristics of the environment affect forms of reasoning in interpretation process and performance of subsequent organizational actions.

1. INTRODUCTION

Organizations are required to adapt to environmental changes to survive and prosper. The adaptations are largely influenced by how managers interpret these environmental changes (Daft & Weick, 1984; Thomas, Clark, & Gioia, 1993). Managers in organizations are typically faced with challenges of interpreting changing and ambiguous signals in their operating environment. Based on their interpretation, managers formulate and implement appropriate strategies in response to these signals (Dutton, Fahey, & Narayanan, 1983). The effectiveness of these strategies on organizational performance is thus largely determined by the extent to which the strategies are fit with the environment (Miles & Snow, 1978). Because signals in the environment are often complex and ambiguous, managers appear to simply categorize

DOI: 10.4018/978-1-4666-9989-2.ch006

them into a salient form of either threats or opportunities (Dutton & Jackson, 1987). The importance of these categorizations lies in their link to strategic decision making process and subsequent organizational actions (Dutton & Jackson, 1987; Thomas et al., 1993). In addition to perceptions of the environment, actions of an organization are also influenced by its characteristics such as strategic orientations and resource slack (Chattopadhyay, Glick, & Huber, 2001).

Going more deeply into the decision making process, strategic decisions and organizational actions are often the result of the manager's attention, interpretation, and analogical reasoning (Dutton et al., 1983; Ocasio, 1997). Attention and interpretation are so intertwined that there is no meaningful distinction between them (Cho & Hambrick, 2006). Managerial attention to environmental changes strongly influences how firms behave (Ocasio, 1997). Attention refers to noticing and interpreting of various stimuli in the environment (Ocasio, 1997). Analogical reasoning is relevant when the present new situation that requires interpretation has both similarities and dissimilarities vis-à-vis the manager's prior experience. It builds on the manager's past experience in a similar circumstance to draw inferences about the present new and partially-known situation (Miller & Lin, 2015). In particular, managers focus on and respond to only certain aspects of their environment (Ocasio, 1997). Thereafter, they try to map their past similar experience onto the present partially-known situation to identify an appropriate analogy as a plausible inference for subsequent organizational actions.

High quality decision making and organizational actions via such attention and analogical reasoning processes are usually obtainable in stable and consistent environments (March, 1982). However, in reality, organizations seldom experience such environments as they usually have to adapt to ambiguous environmental changes. Strategic decision making, particularly in rapidly changing environments, can thus be highly unpredictable and, in response to these changes, is at times inconsistent. This inconsistency, at times even with limited new information, is simply because managers make erratic decisions (Mitchell, Shepherd, & Sharfman, 2011). These erratic decisions are influenced by cognitive and environmental factors.

This chapter presents critical organizational issues in the strategic decision making process and outcomes with respect to the manager's attention, interpretation, and reasoning of ambiguous environmental changes. In particular, we first discuss why managers in the same organization who are faced with same environmental changes may interpret threat and opportunity aspects of these changes differently, taking into account structural distance of the changes, perception of organizational capability, and domain-specific experience (Barreto & Patient, 2013). Second, we link outcomes of such interpretation to investigate organizational actions in terms of externally versus internally directed actions, taking into account organizational characteristics such as strategic orientation and resource slack (Chattopadhyay et al., 2001). Third, we drive into a greater depth to investigate how the manager's experience and environmental signals in terms of hostility and dynamism affect forms of reasoning in interpretation process and performance of subsequent organizational actions (Miller & Lin, 2015; Mitchell et al., 2011).

2. THEORETICAL BACKGROUND

According to attention-based view, firms can be viewed as systems of structurally distributed attention of individuals (Ocasio, 1997). Organizational behaviors are thus determined by how attention of decision makers in the organization is channeled and distributed. In particular, strategic choices of these decision makers depend on issues and answers that they focus their attention on. Such attention is associated with biased interpretation where individual managers in an organization assign varying weights to contrasting aspects of the same stimuli (Cho & Hambrick, 2006). Therefore, individual managers in an organization may have different interpretations on the same stimuli. This interpretation is context-specific and it depends on characteristics of the stimuli and the individual who direct attention (Ocasio, 1997).

Managers interpret exogenous ambiguous signals by paying attention to their salient aspects in terms of an opportunity versus a threat (Dutton & Jackson, 1987; Ocasio, 1997). Which of these two salient aspects (e.g., threat and opportunity) of environmental signals individual managers are likely to pay more attention to depends on their attentional drivers (Ocasio, 1997). These drivers include social, economic, cultural, and cognitive factors that influence allocation of time, effort, and attentional focus of individual managers in an organization.

Based on strategic issue diagnosis theory (Dutton et al., 1983), individual managers' political interests and cause-effect beliefs can interact with characteristics of the environmental change to influence the interpretation. Managers are likely to pay more attention to particular aspects of such change when the change poses a potential threat to their political interests in terms of status, power, and control of resources. Cause-effect beliefs are understandings of effects of external environment and strategic inputs on organizational performance. Managers also use such beliefs to make sense of environmental changes and to selectively focus on certain aspects of these changes.

The assessment of future events, according to construal level theory, depends on individual considerations of desirability and feasibility of their outcomes (Liberman & Trope, 1998). Desirability refers to the degree of attraction or aversion that an individual attributes to outcomes of an event. Feasibility refers to the degree of ease with which an individual can reach outcomes of an event. For a given environmental change, a manager's political interests will therefore crate a more positive attitude toward that change when expected outcomes of that change satisfy those interests (Barreto & Patient, 2013). Likewise, a manager's cause-effect beliefs will therefore create a more positive belief toward that change when reaching expected outcomes of that change is feasible based on such beliefs (Barreto & Patient, 2013). Therefore, managers with political interests and cause-effects beliefs that create more positive attitudes and beliefs about an environmental change are likely to perceive opportunity aspects more salient while those with more of such negative attitudes and beliefs are likely to perceive threat aspects more salient (Barreto & Patient, 2013).

These perceived threats and opportunities are associated with urgency, difficulty, and high stakes (Dutton & Jackson, 1987). Threats are involved with an unfavorable circumstance where losses are likely and one has little control, and opportunities are associated with a favorable circumstance where gains are likely and one has a reasonable amount of control. To predict organizational responses to environmental threats and opportunities, the threat rigidity hypothesis (Staw, Sandelands, & Dutton, 1981) suggests that organizations appear to exhibit rigidity to act on something new, when faced with economic adversity or threats because of constraints in terms of information, control, and resources. Managers faced with threats are likely to perceive that they have little control over the circumstance that potentially yields a negative outcome. Threat perceptions can also heighten concerns about organizational efficiency. To mitigate such negative perceptions, managers are likely to respond to these threats by acting in less risky domains internal to organizations where they have a greater amount of control.

Prospect theory (Kahneman & Tversky, 1979), however, appears to contradict the explanation of such organizational responses. Actual decision making of individuals is not always rational as individuals are likely to frame decision alternatives as either gains or losses. However, their perception of losses from these alternatives tends to be more pronounced than gains. Importantly, individuals are likely to be risk averse when faced with gains and be risk seeking when faced with losses. In particular, managers in favorable or opportunity situations feel that they have more to lose than to gain, and thus are likely to be risk-averse. On the contrary, managers in unfavorable or threat circumstances feel that they have little to lose and thus are likely to be risk-seeking.

3. MANAGERIAL ATTENTION AND INTERPRETATION

Managers in organizations are usually overwhelmed with information that goes beyond their capability to attend to and to process all at once. They are faced with ongoing challenges of interpreting such information, which is changing in nature and coming from both inside and outside of their organization. Importantly, managers are able to attend to, interpret, and respond to only certain aspects of information in their organizational environment (Ocasio, 1997). Based on individual biases, they often assign varying weights to and interpret contradictory aspects of the same environmental signal. Managerial attention to a particular organizational issue is thus associated with context-specific and biased interpretation (Cho & Hambrick, 2006).

Environmental information is often ambiguous, containing both threat and opportunity aspects (Dutton & Jackson, 1987). Whether managers are more likely to attend to threat or opportunity aspects of the environment depends largely on social, economic, cultural, and cognitive factors. Particularly, these factors influence the extent to which managers allocate time, effort, and attentional focus to each of these two environmental aspects (Dutton & Jackson, 1987; Ocasio, 1997).

To understand why managers in the same organization who are faced with same environmental signals may interpret threat and opportunity aspects differently, we need to know characteristics of the focal organization and its environment. Such selective attention is influenced by individual managers' assessments of desirability and feasibility (Barreto & Patient, 2013; Liberman & Trope, 1998). The attentional drivers that capture variation in desirability and feasibility are structural distance of environmental signals and perception of organizational capability respectively.

3.1 Structural Distance from Environmental Change

Managers pay different levels of attention to aspects of an organization's environment because of their structural position within the organization (Ocasio, 1997). Different structural positions are associated with varying interests of stakeholders involved in these positions. Managers are therefore likely to give more weight to certain aspects of environmental changes at the expense of other aspects. Whether managers within a firm would assign more weight to threat aspects than to opportunity aspects of an environmental change or vice versa depends on the distance between their structural position and the locus of direct impact from that change (Barreto & Patient, 2013).

In the presence of an ambiguous environmental change, managers in a structurally shorter distance from the change are more likely to interpret such change as threat while those in a structurally longer distance from that change are more likely to interpret it as opportunity (Barreto & Patient, 2013). In particular, when the distance is short, managers are likely to perceive that their interests are at a greater risk and possible losses are more salient. Therefore, they tend to focus more on what they currently have rather than look for what they could have in the future (Samuelson & Zeckhauser, 1988). When the distance is long, however, managers have more latitude to prepare and to draw on what they could have in the longer term to counter with such changes.

3.2 Perception of Organizational Capability

Firm resources and capabilities can direct managers to differently interpret aspects of an environmental change (Ocasio, 1997). Managers, however, have different perceptions of their organizational capability even if they belong to an organization that holds same resources and capabilities. This perceived capability is essentially determined by the extent to which each manager perceives their firm as holding the resources and capabilities that can sufficiently address requirements from the environmental changes (Dutton & Duncan, 1987).

In the presence of an ambiguous environmental change, managers with higher levels of perceived organizational capability are more likely to interpret such change as opportunity while those with lower levels of perceived organizational capability are more likely to interpret that change as threat (Barreto & Patient, 2013). In particular, when the perceived capability is high, managers are likely to form more positive early beliefs toward congruent opportunity aspects of the change. When the perceived capability is low, managers are likely to form more negative early beliefs toward incongruent threat aspects of that change.

Managers who possess greater and better-organized knowledge in a specific domain are likely to have more confidence in their beliefs related to that domain (Fischer & Budescu, 2005). Such domain-specific knowledge can indirectly affect the manager's attention toward threat and opportunity aspects of a given related environmental change. In particular, domain-specific knowledge tends to strengthen the positive effect of perceived capability on opportunity interpretation and also strengthen its negative effect on threat interpretation of an environmental change (Barreto & Patient, 2013).

These attentional drivers (e.g., structural distance from environmental change and perception of organizational capability) exert their pressure on managerial interpretation of environment in a hierarchical manner depending on the importance of events (Hubner, Steinhauser, & Lehle, 2010). Events are classified as superordinate when they are more central and essential and subordinate when they are peripheral and less essential to an organization (Barreto & Patient, 2013). Structural distance from environmental change is therefore superordinate because it directly affects the manager's interests, whereas perception of organizational capability is subordinate because it reflects the manager's beliefs about the firm's ability to address and handle the changes.

Accordingly, variations in the structural distance from environmental change have a priority and dominant effect on the interpretation of the change regardless of variations in the perceived capability (Barreto & Patient, 2013). In particular, a long structural distance to environmental changes tends to strengthen the manager's attention toward the opportunity aspects and weaken the attention toward the threat aspects regardless of the level of perceived capability. A high level of perceived capability may strengthen the manager's attention toward the opportunity aspects and weaken the attention toward the threat aspects only when the distance from the environmental changes is structurally short.

4. ORGANIZATIONAL ACTIONS AND MANAGERIAL INTERPRETATION

The simple categorizations of environmental information into either threat or opportunity aspects allow organizations to further process and respond to strategic issues related to environmental changes (Chattopadhyay et al., 2001; Dutton & Jackson, 1987). Because both threat and opportunity aspects of the environment are associated with urgency, difficulty, and high stakes, they are likely to evoke some organizational actions (Dutton & Jackson, 1987).

Organizational actions toward such environmental changes are broadly classified into whether they are directed externally or internally (Cook, Shortell, Conrad, & Morrisey, 1983; D'Aveni & MacMillan, 1990). Externally directed organizational actions are aimed at modifying the environment. Managers are often required to operate in new business domains where they have less control. These actions are generally riskier and more difficult to implement and control (Dutton & Jackson, 1987). On the contrary, internally directed organizational actions are aimed at adapting an organization to environmental changes. Managers are often required to operate in existing largely known business domains where they have a relatively larger amount of control. These actions are generally less risky and easier to implement and control (Cook et al., 1983; Dutton & Jackson, 1987).

4.1 Reduction or Enhancement of Control vs. Loss or Gain Situations

Organizational actions in response to either threat or opportunity interpretation are subject to characteristics of environmental events. These events are largely categorized as reduction or enhancement of control versus loss or gain situations (Chattopadhyay et al., 2001). In the events that are directly related to the reduction or enhancement of control, managers who interpret their environment as threats are likely to perceive that they have little control over the situation. This perception intensifies concerns about the organization's efficiency (Staw et al., 1981).

To mitigate such perceived control-reducing threats, managers are likely to respond to associated strategic issues in domains internal to their organization over which they have a greater amount of organizational control (Chattopadhyay et al., 2001; Thomas et al., 1993). This organizational response is usually done by initiating internally directed risk-averse actions (Dutton & Jackson, 1987). On the contrary, managers who interpret their environment as opportunities are likely to perceive that they have a greater sense of control over the situation with potential gains (Dutton & Jackson, 1987). Managers faced with such control-enhancing opportunities are likely to initiate externally directed actions, which might otherwise be perceived as too risky (Dutton & Jackson, 1987; Thomas et al., 1993).

In the events that are directly related to the loss or gain of tangible resources, mangers in favorable situations are likely to be risk-averse because they feel that they have more to lose than to gain from these situations (Kahneman & Tversky, 1979). On the contrary, managers who are in unfavorable circumstances are likely to be risk-seeking because they feel that they have less to lose than to gain from these situations. Thus, managers who interpret their environment as threats are likely to respond to associated strategic issues with externally directed risk-seeking actions (Chattopadhyay et al., 2001), while those who interpret their environment as opportunities are likely to respond with internally directed risk-averse actions (Fiegenbaum & Thomas, 1988; Wiseman & Gomez-Mejia, 1998).

The effects of threat and opportunity interpretation on externally or internally directed organizational actions are contingent upon organizational characteristics in terms of strategic orientation such as product-market development versus domain defense and organizational resource slack (Chattopadhyay et al., 2001). In particular, variations in an organization's adoption of such strategic orientation and use of resource slack are also shaped by the manager's perceptions of strategic issues in the environment.

4.2 Strategic Orientation

Organizations that focus on developing new products or markets are likely to pursue externally directed actions while those that emphasize on domain defense are likely to pursue internally directed actions

(Chattopadhyay et al., 2001). The effectiveness of the former largely depends on the extent to which the organization can control or modify the external environment, whereas that of the latter relies on the extent to which the organization can increase its efficiency through standardization of internal organizational processes (Miles & Snow, 1978).

When faced with control-reducing threats, managers are likely to respond to the associated strategic issues with well-known and familiar organizational actions (Staw et al., 1981). However, for organizations that emphasize a product-market development, managers tend to pursue externally directed actions such as expanding in new markets or introducing new products to mitigate such control-reducing threats (Chattopadhyay et al., 2001). When faced with control-enhancing opportunities, managers are likely to go beyond their usual routines regardless of their organization's strategic orientation (Staw et al., 1981). Organizations that emphasize product-market development may, therefore, be even more likely to pursue such externally directed actions.

The effects of likely gain and loss situations are likely to be independent of organizational context such as strategic orientations (Fiegenbaum & Thomas, 1988; Kahneman & Tversky, 1979). In particular, managers who are faced with threats of likely losses are more likely to engage in externally directed risk-seeking actions. Such externally directed actions may be reinforced when the organization pursues product-market development strategy. Lacking such strategic orientation, the likelihood of externally directed actions may be reduced. Managers who are faced with opportunities of likely gains are likely to engage in internally directed risk-averse actions. Such internally directed actions are likely to be reinforced when the organization pursues domain defense strategy.

4.3 Organizational Resource Slack

Organizations holding more resource slack have greater flexibility to implement strategic actions in response to strategic issues in their environment (Cyert & March, 1963). Resource slack allows organizations to relax their internal control and to be more involved in externally directed actions that are otherwise considered highly uncertain and risky. When holding lower levels of resource slack, organizations are thus likely to pursue internally directed less risky actions, which require lower levels of resource slack.

When faced with control-reducing threats, organizations that possess higher levels of resource slack are likely to focus even more on internal processes to gain even more control over the situation by initiating internally directed actions (Chattopadhyay et al., 2001; Staw et al., 1981). Resource slack also provides the cushion for organizations to be able to spend time waiting until such threats are gone away or are at a manageable level (Dutton & Duncan, 1987). Without sufficient resource slack, organizations may be more sensitive to changing environment because of lacking resources to buffer the associated threats (D'Aveni & MacMillan, 1990). These organizations may have to engage in more externally directed problemistic search actions to adapt to the environment and survive from the threats (Cyert & March, 1963; Dutton & Duncan, 1987).

Opportunities often lead organizations to depart from their usual actions (Dutton & Jackson, 1987). With higher levels of resource slack, organizations may relax internal control and engage more in externally directed actions because resource slack buffers them from uncertainty and risk associated with these actions (Nohria & Gulati, 1996). In response to control-enhancing opportunities, organizations with higher levels of resource slack may therefore be more motivated to engage in even more risky externally directed actions to explore and exploit such opportunities in their environment. Without sufficient resource slack, organizations may engage in internally directed actions, which are mainly aimed at politically commanding a share of scarce resources to exploit such opportunities in the environment (Cyert & March, 1963).

When faced with likely loss situations, organizations are likely to take externally directed risky actions because they feel that they have less to lose than to gain from these situations (Kahneman & Tversky, 1979). With higher levels of resource slack, organizations may have even more latitude to pursue such risky actions (Chattopadhyay et al., 2001; Wiseman & Gomez-Mejia, 1998). Without sufficient resource slack, organizations are thus likely to pursue internally directed actions, which are less costly and less risky, aiming at tightening control in their existing business domains and improving efficiency (Cook et al., 1983).

When faced with likely gain situations, organizations are likely to be risk-averse and pursue internally directed actions because such opportunities are typically associated with a degree of uncertainty and risk (Kahneman & Tversky, 1979). Organizations are likely to feel that they have more to lose than to gain from these situations. Particularly, organizations with higher levels of resource slack may choose to forgo such external opportunities because the availability of resource slack allows them to sit back and afford to be risk-averse. Organizations without sufficient resource slack however may instead choose to take greater risk associated with externally directed actions and problemistic search to acquire additional resources (Cyert & March, 1963).

These organizational actions are the outcome of the manager's analogical reasoning processes (Miller & Lin, 2015). Along these processes, to facilitate organizational learning and effective actions, managers scan the environment to selectively collect relevant data and then interpret to give meaning to these data (Daft & Weick, 1984). Such interpretation transforms a variety of information associated with aspects of the environmental changes into an integrated and holistic understanding.

5. ANALOGICAL REASONING AND ERRATIC DECISIONS

The analogical reasoning processes of managers require that characteristics of the current situation be compared with those of past organized knowledge to arrive at classifications of the situation based on the degree to which they are matched (Dutton & Jackson, 1987; Markman & Moreau, 2001). This inference yields hypotheses that guide current organizational actions to exploit perceived opportunities or to mitigate threats in the changing environment (Dutton et al., 1983). The accuracy of such inference therefore critically influences strategic actions and organizational performance. Excessive optimism or pessimism about the organization's prospects may lead to inappropriate strategic actions and poor organizational performance.

Analogical reasoning has different forms including satisficing match, best available match, and exact match (Miller & Lin, 2015). The reasoning processes are involved with specifying possible analogies from past memories, comparing these analogies to the current problems, selecting an analogy, and deriving inferences (Markman & Moreau, 2001). In dynamic environments, best available match and exact match as opposed to satisficing match are likely to improve the accuracy of interpretation over time (Miller & Lin, 2015). Past distant experiences through satisficing match may be useful in early periods when the complexity of environment is low. However, organizations should try to unlearn past distant experiences in favor of investing heavily in the learning of more recent dynamic environments through best available match or exact match.

For new entrants, investing heavily for learning in dynamic environments may lead to poor organizational outcomes in the short run. However, over time, they can attain better organizational performance derived from accumulated knowledge and experience in coping with dynamism in the environment (Miller & Lin, 2015). Decision makers with limited experience in their complex operating environment should employ the best of what they know, rather than wait for what they should ideally know to address the problems.

While in the short run, applying well known past experiences can reduce volatility of organizational outcomes relative to heavily investing for learning in the dynamic environment, this lower risk alternative also comes at the expense of organizational performance in the long run (Miller & Lin, 2015). Therefore, organizations in dynamic environments are required to tradeoff between their operating performance and risk when deploying past experiences and investing in learning to address problems in the short and long term, respectively.

5.1 Metacognition

The quality of analogical reasoning is associated with ability of managers to understand their own thinking. This ability is determined by the manager's metacognition. Metacognition refers to the ability to understand a given situation in relation to one's own cognitions (Haynie, Shepherd, Mosakowski, & Earley, 2010). A manager's inconsistent judgments for the same circumstance are erratic decisions which are the result of erroneous beliefs of one's own cognitions and lack of awareness in one's own decision-making processes. A person has a metacognitive experience if that person feels a particular task is difficult to understand and then draws on past experience to inform decision frameworks for present new, but related situations (Haynie et al., 2010). Therefore, managers with more metacognitive experiences are likely to better apply their previous decision-making processes to address the current decision tasks, thereby improving quality of their decision making.

Managers tend to use metacognitive experiences when the situations are complex and thus require careful consideration (Flavell, 1979). By using metacognitive experiences to address the current decision tasks, managers can verify the usefulness of their decision-making processes, thereby allowing them to improve quality of their thinking processes (Flavell, 1979). The use of metacognitive experiences, over time, allows managers to accumulate important knowledge and gain better control of their decision-making processes, thereby reducing the likelihood of making erratic decisions (Mitchell et al., 2011).

Managers possessing more metacognitive experiences are thus less likely to make erratic strategic decisions. Because thinking processes of individual managers are embedded in the broader external environment, quality of their judgments will rely not only on their metacognitive experiences and ability to understand their own thinking and decision making, but also on their perception of the environmental context.

5.2 Hostile and Dynamic Environment

The extent to which managers make erratic strategic decisions is influenced by their perceived experience in hostile and dynamic environments (Dutton & Duncan, 1987). In hostile environments, decision makers may not be able to sufficiently carry out cognitive processes to arrive at a stable decision (Staal, Bolton, Yaroush, & Bourne, 2008). Managers may not be able to take sufficient past, present, and future alternatives into consideration. In particular, such a threatening environment worsens information processing ability of decision makers, thus leading to inconsistent decision outcomes (Staal et al., 2008). Managers are therefore likely to make more erratic strategic decisions in an environment with greater hostility (Mitchell et al., 2011).

Dynamic environments are highly unstable and unpredictable (Dutton & Duncan, 1987). In these environments, managers hardly comprehend the relationship between means and ends of the situation, so they are required to concurrently draw on multiple cognitive processes at a given time (Gilbert & Osborne, 1989). Managers may thus be less aware of their own inconsistencies between current and previously established preferences in decision making processes (March, 1982; Ocasio, 1997). In an environment with greater dynamism, managers are thus likely to make more erratic strategic decisions.

In an environment that is characterized by both hostility and dynamism, managers are likely to perceive a higher risk of failure and a greater uncertainty about sources of such failure. They tend to be anxious about highly uncertain threats (Freeman & Freeman, 2008). Because available data about environmental threats are not sufficient, managers are likely to utilize minimal data in their decision making processes (Freeman & Freeman, 2008). Such decision making processes are thus unlikely to yield thoroughly thoughtful and logical decision alternatives. The erratic strategic decisions due to hostile environments are thus likely to be more pronounced with a combination of high environmental dynamism.

6. DISCUSSION AND CONCLUSION

Managers play the critical role in diagnosis of strategic issues in their company's operating environment. This diagnosis is conducted through their attention and interpretation of organizational data and stimuli and their analogical reasoning (Barreto & Patient, 2013; Chattopadhyay et al., 2001; Miller & Lin, 2015). Because individual managers are different in their attention to opportunity versus threat aspects of the environment, managers within the same organization and environment may also differ in their interpretation of these two environmental aspects (Barreto & Patient, 2013). Such attention is shaped by individual managers' divergent desirability and feasibility considerations (Barreto & Patient, 2013; Miller & Lin, 2015). In particular, the results of such interpretation processes in terms of threat and opportunity are contingent upon structural distance of the manager from the environmental signals, perception of organizational capability, and characteristics of the organizational environment.

Organizational actions are largely influenced by such threat or opportunity interpretation. However, threat aspects of the environment are likely to be more pronounced than opportunity aspects in managerial decision making (Chattopadhyay et al., 2001). In particular, control-reducing threats lead to more conservative internally directed actions whereas likely losses lead to riskier externally directed actions. When faced with a control-reducing threat, managers are likely to act in domains in which their organization has the greatest control including implementation of well-known strategies (Staw et al., 1981). However, they will be risk-seeking when their organization is faced with a loss prospect (Kahneman & Tversky, 1979). Organizational actions in response to control-enhancing and likely gain opportunities are however rather equivocal (Chattopadhyay et al., 2001). When faced with opportunities, organizations may focus more on developing and exploiting new ideas and technologies rather than taking any actions in response to control-enhancing or likely gain opportunities (Dutton & Jackson, 1987).

Organizations are likely to pursue externally directed riskier actions when they are faced with external events that threaten their distinctive resources and capabilities. When managers place greater emphasis on product-market development instead of domain defense, organizational actions are likely to be externally rather than internally directed because their capabilities lie in gaining control over the external environment through building new products and markets (Chattopadhyay et al., 2001). These externally directed actions are likely to be more salient to deal with control-reducing threats which lower their control over the external environment.

Because threat aspects of the environment are likely to be more pronounced than opportunity aspects in managerial decision making, organizational resource slack appears to provide managers the resources necessary to respond to control-reducing threats and likely losses (Chattopadhyay et al., 2001). In particular, organizations with more resource slack are likely to respond to control-reducing threats with internally directed actions while respond to threats of likely losses with externally directed actions. Organizational resource slack however may not always influence organizational actions to respond to control-enhancing and likely gain opportunities. In such case, organizations may use resource slack to implement actions that are independent of the outcome of managerial interpretation.

In dynamic environments, managerial interpretations as discussed above are likely to be more accurate when organizations pursue analogical reasoning in the form of best available or exact match rather than satisficing match (Miller & Lin, 2015). While these forms of reasoning may worsen performance of organizational actions in the short run, they promote experiential learning and, over time, improve accuracy of the reasoning and thus organizational performance in the long run (Miller & Lin, 2015). Experiential learning is indeed fundamental to the accuracy of reasoning and interpretation of environmental signals. Therefore, organizations should unlearn past distant experiences, which often mislead them to pursue a satisficing form of reasoning for the sake of short-term organizational performance.

When environmental unpredictability is not very high, organizations should pursue reasoning in the form of best available match rather than exact match (Miller & Lin, 2015). In such circumstance, managers should deploy the best of what they know instead of waiting for all of what they should ideally know. Managers may pursue satisficing match only in early periods with low environmental volatility (Miller & Lin, 2015). In particular, satisficing form of reasoning, while stabilizing organizational performance in the short run relative to reasoning in the form of best available and exact match, comes at the expense to organizational performance in the long run.

Strategic decision making processes are critical to organizational outcomes. However, these processes are often inconsistent and thus erratic. Erratic decisions are engendered from the manager's lacking of metacognitive experiences in the decision domains and in the characteristics of environment (Mitchell et al., 2011). Such metacognitive experiences decrease the extent to which managers make erratic strategic decisions.

Environmental hostility increases the extent to which managers make erratic strategic decisions. However, in dynamic environments, managers may, over time, invest in learning to accumulate experience in these environments to the extent that such experience reduces erratic strategic decisions (Zollo & Winter, 2002). Environmental dynamism may thus provide organizations with learning opportunities that potentially mitigate such adverse effects of environmental hostility (Mitchell et al., 2011). In environments with greater hostility, managers may thus be able to reduce erratic strategic decisions when they have accumulated more experience through investing in learning from dynamic environments (Mitchell et al., 2011). However, without such learning opportunity (e.g., in low levels of environmental dynamism), the hostility aspects of environment are likely to exert a more salient negative effect on organizational decision making processes.

Managers should be aware that individuals in an organization may be unconsciously biased in strategic decision making. Managers may be able to reduce the biases by seeking more ideas from outside of their own organizations. Organizations often rely on their past experiences and apply these to current strategic decision making. Such local search may paralyze efforts of individuals and organizations to explore and develop new solutions for long-term performance. While recognizing the importance of past experience, managers should increase the number of alternatives, and utilize them to complement decision making.

However, managers should also be cautious that investing in new and unfamiliar alternatives may turn out to be not useable, excessively delaying responses and causing significant costs. In an uncertain organizational environment, managers should not forgo such opportunities but consider strengthening their capabilities by implementing experiments. Experiments allow an organization to learn and gain experience that potentially becomes alternatives and guidelines for encountering new challenges in the future.

ACKNOWLEDGMENT

This work was supported by JSPS KAKENHI Grant Number 15K03694.

REFERENCES

Barreto, I., & Patient, D. L. (2013). Toward a theory of intraorganizational attention based on desirability and feasibility factors. *Strategic Management Journal*, *34*(6), 687–703. doi:10.1002/smj.2029

Chattopadhyay, P., Glick, W. H., & Huber, G. P. (2001). Organizational actions in response to threats and opportunities. *Academy of Management Journal*, *44*(5), 937–955. doi:10.2307/3069439

Cho, T. S., & Hambrick, D. C. (2006). Attention as the mediator between top management team characteristics and strategic change: The case of airline deregulation. *Organization Science*, *17*(4), 453–469. doi:10.1287/orsc.1060.0192

Cook, K., Shortell, S., Conrad, B., & Morrisey, M. (1983). A theory of organizational response to regulation: The case of hospitals. *Academy of Management Review*, *8*(2), 193–205. PMID:10263058

Cyert, R., & March, J. (1963). *A Behavioral Theory of the Firm*. Englewood Cliffs, NJ: Prentice-Hall.

D'Aveni, R., & MacMillan, I. (1990). Crisis and the content of managerial communications: A study of the focus of attention of top managers in surviving and failing firms. *Administrative Science Quarterly*, *35*(4), 634–657. doi:10.2307/2393512

Daft, R. L., & Weick, K. E. (1984). Toward a model of organizations as interpretation systems. *Academy of Management Review*, *9*(2), 284–295.

Dutton, J., & Jackson, S. (1987). Categorizing strategic issues: Links to organizational action. *Academy of Management Review*, *12*(1), 76–90.

Dutton, J. E., & Duncan, R. B. (1987). The creation of momentum for change through the process of strategic issue diagnosis. *Strategic Management Journal*, *8*(3), 279–295. doi:10.1002/smj.4250080306

Dutton, J. E., Fahey, L., & Narayanan, V. K. (1983). Toward understanding strategic issue diagnosis. *Strategic Management Journal*, *4*(4), 307–323. doi:10.1002/smj.4250040403

Fiegenbaum, A., & Thomas, H. (1988). Attitudes towards risk and the risk-return paradox: Prospect theory explanations. *Academy of Management Journal, 31*(1), 85–106. doi:10.2307/256499

Fischer, I., & Budescu, D. V. (2005). When do those who know more also know more about how much they know? The development of confidence and performance in categorical decision tasks. *Organizational Behavior and Human Decision Processes, 98*(1), 39–53. doi:10.1016/j.obhdp.2005.04.003

Flavell, J. H. (1979). Metacognition and cognitive monitoring: A new area of cognitive-developmental inquiry. *The American Psychologist, 34*(10), 906–911. doi:10.1037/0003-066X.34.10.906

Freeman, D., & Freeman, J. (2008). *Paranoia: The Twenty-First Century Fear.* Oxford, UK: Oxford University Press.

Gilbert, D. T., & Osborne, R. E. (1989). Thinking backward: Some curable and incurable consequences of cognitive busyness. *Journal of Personality and Social Psychology, 57*(6), 940–949. doi:10.1037/0022-3514.57.6.940

Haynie, J. M., Shepherd, D., Mosakowski, E., & Earley, P. C. (2010). A situated metacognitive model of the entrepreneurial mindset. *Journal of Business Venturing, 25*(2), 217–229. doi:10.1016/j.jbusvent.2008.10.001

Hubner, R., Steinhauser, M., & Lehle, C. (2010). A dual-stage two-phase model of selective attention. *Psychological Review, 117*(3), 759–784. doi:10.1037/a0019471 PMID:20658852

Kahneman, D., & Tversky, A. (1979). Prospect theory: An analysis of decision under risk. *Econometrica, 47*(2), 263–291. doi:10.2307/1914185

Liberman, N., & Trope, Y. (1998). The role of feasibility and desirability considerations in near and distant future decisions: A test of temporal construal theory. *Journal of Personality and Social Psychology, 75*(1), 5–18. doi:10.1037/0022-3514.75.1.5 PMID:11195890

March, J. G. (1982). Theories of choice and making decisions. *Society, 20*(1), 29–39. doi:10.1007/BF02694989

Markman, A. B., & Moreau, C. P. (2001). Analogy and analogical comparison in choice. In D. Gentner, K. J. Holyoak, & B. N. Kokinov (Eds.), *The Analogical Mind: Perspectives from Cognitive Science.* Cambridge, MA: MIT Press.

Miles, R. E., & Snow, C. C. (1978). *Organizational Strategy, Structure, and Process.* New York: McGraw-Hill.

Miller, K. D., & Lin, S. J. (2015). Analogical reasoning for diagnosing strategic issues in dynamic and complex environments. *Strategic Management Journal, 36*(13), 2000–2020. doi:10.1002/smj.2335

Mitchell, J. R., Shepherd, D. A., & Sharfman, M. P. (2011). Erratic strategic decisions: When and why managers are inconsistent in strategic decision making. *Strategic Management Journal, 32*(7), 683–704. doi:10.1002/smj.905

Nohria, N., & Gulati, R. (1996). Is slack good or bad for innovation? *Academy of Management Journal, 39*(5), 1245–1264. doi:10.2307/256998

Ocasio, W. (1997). Towards an attention-based view of the firm. *Strategic Management Journal, 18*(S1), 187–206. doi:10.1002/(SICI)1097-0266(199707)18:1+<187::AID-SMJ936>3.3.CO;2-B

Samuelson, W., & Zeckhauser, R. (1988). Status quo bias in decision making. *Journal of Risk and Uncertainty, 1*(1), 7–59. doi:10.1007/BF00055564

Staal, M. A., Bolton, A. E., Yaroush, R. A., & Bourne, L. E. Jr. (2008). Cognitive performance and resilience to stress. In B. J. Lukey & V. Tepe (Eds.), *Biobehavioral Resilience to Stress*. Boca Raton, FL: CRC Press.

Staw, B., Sandelands, L., & Dutton, J. (1981). Threat rigidity effects in organizational behavior: A multilevel analysis. *Administrative Science Quarterly, 26*(4), 501–524. doi:10.2307/2392337

Thomas, J., Clark, S., & Gioia, D. (1993). Strategic sensemaking and organizational performance: Linkages among scanning, interpretation, action, and outcomes. *Academy of Management Journal, 36*(2), 239–270. doi:10.2307/256522 PMID:10125120

Wiseman, R., & Gomez-Mejia, L. (1998). A behavioral agency model of managerial risk taking. *Academy of Management Review, 23*(1), 133–153.

Zollo, M., & Winter, S. G. (2002). Deliberate learning and the evolution of dynamic capabilities. *Organization Science, 13*(3), 339–351. doi:10.1287/orsc.13.3.339.2780

Chapter 7
Economic Decision Making, Emotion, and Prefrontal Cortex

Salim Lahmiri
ESCA School of Management, Morocco

ABSTRACT

How diverse regions of the brain are coordinated to produce objective-directed decision is the essence of neuroeconomics. Indeed, the latter is a formal framework to describe the involvement of numerous brain regions including frontal, cingulate, parietal cortex, and striatum in economic and financial decision-making process. The purpose of this chapter is to explain the relationship between economic decision making and emotion on one hand, and the relationship between economic decision making and prefrontal cortex on the other hand.

INTRODUCTION

Understanding and explaining human decision-making process is approached differently in economics and neuroscience. For instance, traditional economic theory explains behaviour primarily through theoretical foundations such as utility, preferences, and axioms. On the other side, neuroscience considers the physiological aspects and somatic variables that affect decision-making. In recent years, neuroeconomics has emerged as a multidisciplinary research area that integrates knowledge from neuroscience, psychology, and economics to better understand economic decision-making and to specify more accurate models of choice and decision. Multiple options always characterize decisional situations by multiple options, each carrying potential rewards, risks and related outcome probabilities.

Therefore, real life decision making requires the ability to make decisions effectively. The purpose of the chapter is to explain the relationship between economic decision making and emotion on one hand, and the relationship between economic decision making and prefrontal cortex on the other hand. In particular, based on a brief literature review, we aim to present the role of psychological factors, especially emotions, in economic decision making and presenting cortex regions involved in financial decision making. We essentially focus on physiological and neuroimaging aspects of economic and financial decision making. The chapter is organized as follows. Section 1 focuses on economic decision making and emotion. Section 2 covers economic decision making and the prefrontal cortex. Section 3 provides directions for future works as suggested in the literature. Section 3 presents the Conclusion.

DOI: 10.4018/978-1-4666-9989-2.ch007

Economic Decision Making and Emotion

Classical and neoclassical economics states that decisions are made based on valuable information and cost-benefit analysis. In particular, the main purpose in making a decision is to maximize the gains or outcome expected value expressed as a linear multiplicative relationship between probability and utility. Basically, classical economic theory assumes that all agents are aggregating and weighing information accurately and consistently. However, in real life problems, individuals have not been found to make decisions following a normative model (Beach & Lipshitz, 1993). In addition, human decision making process is affected by heuristics, biases, and framing effects (Tversky & Kahneman, 1974). More importantly, it involves psychological factors; especially emotions (Bechara et al., 2000; Bechara et al., 2002). Therefore, classical economic theory fails to explain human behaviour and decision-making.

Several psychological biases have been proposed in economic literature to explain economic decision making process including theory of beliefs (Barberis & Thaler, 2003), belief perseverance (Barberis & Thaler, 2003; Rabin, 1998), confirmatory bias (Rabin, 1998), overconfidence (Barberis & Thaler, 2003), optimism (Barberis & Thaler, 2003), representativeness (Barberis & Thaler, 2003; Kahneman, 2003), prototype heuristics (Kahneman, 2003), law of small numbers (Rabin, 1998), conservatism (Barberis & Thaler, 2003), anchoring and adjustment (Barberis & Thaler, 2003; Kahneman, 2003; Rabin, 1998), and availability biases (Barberis & Thaler, 2003; Kahneman, 2003). They are described in Table 1.

However, the most studied factor is emotion. Indeed, According to Somatic Marker Hypothesis (Bechara et al., 2000; Bechara et al., 2002), decision-making is a process guided by emotions. It provides a neuroanatomical and cognitive framework for decision-making and suggests that the process of decision-making depends on neural substrates that regulate homeostasis, emotion, and feeling. In order to investigate decision making process in neuroeconomics, a series of brain imaging modalities are used to record electrical activity and metabolic activity of the human brain including electroencephalograph (EEG), transcranial magnetic stimulation (TMS), functional magnetic resonance imaging (fMRI), and positron emission tomography (PET). These modalities help understanding and explaining neurobiological mechanisms of the decisional process (Pradeep, 2010). Indeed, at anatomical level, neuronal activation

Table 1. Biases in financial decision making

Biases	Description
Theory of beliefs	How agents form their expectations in the market
Belief perseverance	People form their own hypotheses and are likely to less attentive to information which contradicts their hypotheses
Confirmatory bias	People are influenced by initial judgements. They tend to use information to affirm their initial hypotheses
Overconfidence	Estimated quantities or probabilities are affected by overconfidence
Optimism	People's unrealistic positive view about themselves
Representativeness	People tend to determine something by the characteristics of the group or class to which it belongs.
Prototype heuristics	Broader view of the representativeness heuristic
Law of small numbers	People exaggerate the behaviour of small samples
Conservatism	Hesitation of many investors to act on new information
Anchoring and adjustment	Values are estimated similar to the initial values of uncertain quantities
Anchoring and adjustment	Probability of an event is estimated based on memories and personal experiences

is observed in caudate nucleus in relation with satisfaction (de Quervainet al., 2004), and in the ventral striatum related to exhibitions of trust in an investment game (King-Casas et al., 2005). In general, emotional process is associated with activation in ventral tegmental, nucleus accumbens, ventromedial frontal, orbitofrontal, anterior cingulated cortex, and amygdala and insular cortex (Dalgleish, 2004).

The relationship between the cortex regions was also investigated to understand the decision making process. For instance, by examining communication across brain regions to examine motivational decision making, evidence was discovered of intercommunication between associative regions, mainly within the prefrontal cortex, and striatum, insula, cingulated cortex and amygdale (Alexander & Brown, 2011; Andersen & Cui, 2009; Clark, 2010; Kable & Glimcher, 2009; Rangel & Hare, 2010; Wallis & Kennerley, 2010). In addition, these works related subcomponents of decision making processes to specific brain regions (Alexander & Brown, 2011; Andersen & Cui, 2009; Clark, 2010; Kable & Glimcher, 2009; Rangel & Hare, 2010; Wallis & Kennerley, 2010). In particular, dorsal and ventral lateral prefrontal cortices and parietal lobe are implicated in integrative computation of expected value.

However, ventromedial and dorsomedial prefrontal cortices and adjacent orbitofrontal cortex are involved in abstract value representation. Univariate data analysis is the most common technique to establish direct relationships between specific economic variables and regional brain activity. However, they treat each region in isolation rather in dynamical framework where it is assumed to interplay with other regions. Therefore, multivariate techniques are becoming more popular to study the dynamic connectivity between cortical nodes. In this regard, several approaches have been used in the literature; including psychophysiological interaction (PPI) tests (Friston et al., 1997), dynamic causal modeling (Friston et al., 2003; Stephan et al., 2007), and graph-based network analysis (Camara et al., 2009; Zamora-López et al., 2010). These methods are described in Table 2.

Using univariate analysis to study financial decision making tasks, Camara et al., (2008) found that activity in the ventral striatum is closely mirrored by responses across the insula, amygdala, hippocampus, and orbitofrontal cortex during reward processing. Hare et al. (2010) concluded that ventromedial prefrontal cortices activity integrated inputs from the anterior insula and temporal cortex to reflect the amount donated during a study of charitable giving. Park et al. (2011) found that sub-genual cingulate and amygdale are coupled when monetary rewards are linked to physical pain.

In a recent study, Minati et al. (2012) used graph-based network analysis and concluded that: (i) expected value is positively correlated with activity within medial prefrontal and occipital cortices; (ii) value-sensitive effective connections are arranged as a unitary characterized by dense connectivity and high shortest-path centrality; (iii) observed effective connectivity effects are highly pertinent to dichotomous gain/loss comparisons. For a summary of cortex regions involved in decision-making making process, we have adapted Table 3 from Gutnik et al. (2006) to show cortex regions along with their functional classifications.

Table 2. Methods descriptions in economic decisional task

Methods	Description
Psychophysiological interaction (PPI)	It tests for the changes in the (physiological) influence of a given source region on the activity of a second target region as a result of a specific external (psychological/economic/financial) factor.
Dynamic causal modeling	It is used to gain quantitative estimates of the magnitude and direction of causal interaction between brain regions when decision-maker is subject to external perturbation.
Graph-based network analysis	When decision-maker is peforming a task, its brain areas are parcelled PPI is applied across parcels to identify networks of connections modulated by relevant economic factors.

Table 3. Decision-making functions of brain areas (adapted from Gutnik et al., 2006)

Area of Brain	Subregion	Function
Prefrontal cortex	Orbitofrontal cortex /ventromedial	Incentive gain, best-guess estimation
	prefrontal cortex	Reversal learning
	Dorsolateral prefrontal cortex	Manipulation of decision-related information and conscious; deliberation during decision-making; working memory functions; Decision-making under uncertainty
	Anterior cingulate cortex	Cognitive conflict processing
Amygdala		Reward recognition; perception of emotion; emotion in general
Basal ganglia	Mesolimbic and mesocortical dopaminergic pathways	Reward and addiction and their decision processing
	Prefrontal serotonergic pathways	Reinforcement-driven learning and decision-making

Economic Decision Making and Prefrontal Cortex

The prefrontal cortex is one of the human brain regions that attract attention of researchers in economic and financial decision making given its role in executive functions such as reasoning, planning and decision-making (Spinella et al., 2007). For instance, individuals with neurological insults to prefrontal systems often show poor financial management (Spinella et al., 2007), and healthy individuals consistently show activation of prefrontal systems during financial tasks (Spinella et al., 2007). Table 4 shows the results of neuroimaging in financial decision processing.

Table 4. Prefrontal–subcortical systems in response to monetary reward and punishment

Study	Impulse and Region
Delgado et al. (2000)	Rewards activate nucleus accumbens.
Elliott et al. (2000)	Ventral striatum activated during reward but not during punishment.
Knutson et al. (2000)	Monetary rewards and punishments activate the caudate and putamen
O'Doherty et al, (2001)	Monetary rewards activate the orbitofrontal cortex
O'Doherty et al, (2001)	Magnitude of orbitofrontal activation correlates with the magnitude of rewards and punishments.
O'Doherty et al, (2001)	Medial prefrontal cortex also responds to monetary rewards
Knutson et al. (2001)	Activation of the ventromedial prefrontal cortex when reward was contrasted against non-reward outcomes
Gehring & Willoughby (2002)	Increases in cerebral blood flow and electrophysiological activation is observed in the medial prefrontal cortex during both monetary rewards and punishments
Gehring & Willoughby (2002)	After loss, choice is riskier and yields greater loss-related activity in the medial prefrontal cortex.
Elliott et al. (2000)	Subcallosal regions of the medial prefrontal cortex activated during monetary reward
Ernest et al (2002)	Monetary decision making causes predominantly right-sided activation across multiple prefrontal Areas: dorsolateral, orbitofrontal, anterior cingulated.
Elliott et al. (2003)	Striatal and brainstem monoamine structures activated in response to financial reward.

In order to examine the relationship between self-rated executive functions and personal income, Spinella et al. (2007) administered a sample of subjects under study the Barratt Impulsiveness Scale (Patton et al., 1995) which is a self-rating scale that measures three factors (Patton et al., 1995): non-planning (orientation towards the present rather than the future), motor impulsivity (or acting without thinking), and attentional impulsivity (lack of concentration). Spinella et al. (2007) found evidence of an inverse relationship between income and total impulsiveness, and that association remains significant after controlling for sex, age and education. In addition, they found that the motor impulsivity was the subscale with the most consistent associations. Therefore, they concluded that self-rating measure of executive dysfunction is inversely correlated with income.

In order to study other aspects of financial behaviour, Spinella et al. (2007) examined the relationship between prefrontal systems and credit card debt. They found that credit card debt is related to the ability to mentally track finances. They concluded that a prefrontal system is involved in executive functions that relate to financial behaviour. Since damage in prefrontal cortex affects negatively short and long-term decision making (Spinella et al., 2008), the authors collected information from a sample of individuals about their attitudes toward money and credit cards and a measure of their possible diminished neural functioning. In particular, the purpose was to study the relationship between measures of prefrontal cortical functioning and credit card and money attitudes by using the frontal systems behaviour scale.

The latter was developed by Grace et al. (1999) in order to evaluate behavioural and personality traits associated with the function of the prefrontal cortex. Grace et al. (1999) found that traits and habits associated with psychological impairment due to prefrontal cortical dysfunction are significantly associated with credit card and money attitudes and behavior. In particular, subjects with high scores on the measure of prefrontal cortical dysfunction consider money as a means to impress and influence others and as a symbol of success. In addition, subjects with high scores had hesitancy, doubt and suspicion regarding money transactions. Finally, they consider money as a source of worry and anxiety and were less concerned with producing financial security for the future Grace et al. (1999).

More recently, Cloutier and Gyurovski (2014) investigated ventromedial prefrontal cortex (VMPFC) activity during impression formation of individuals varying on distinct dimensions of social status. For instance, participants were asked to form an impression of the targets, but were not instructed to explicitly evaluate them based on social status. They found evidence of interaction of status dimension and level in ventromedial prefrontal cortex. In particular, results from functional magnetic resonance imaging (fMRI) showed evidence of preferential response to targets with higher compared to lower moral status as previously demonstrated, and also greater response to targets with lower compared to higher financial status.

Evans and Hampson (2014) examined if sex differences on cognitive tasks dependent on the prefrontal cortex. In particular, they examined the idea that the prefrontal cortex is sexually differentiated by comparing men's and women's performance on tasks which are associated to activation in discrete regions of the frontal cortex. Results from three experiments (self-ordered Pointing, Iowa gambling task, probabilistic reversal learning task) showed that functions carried out by the ventromedial prefrontal cortex and orbitofrontal cortex are sexually differentiated in humans. Ricardo et al. (2015) tested if resting state connectivity may predict choice behaviour in monetary exchange game. The experimental results from twenty-nine healthy adults resting state fMRI showed an increased functional connectivity between the salience (bilateral insula/ anterior cingulate) and central executive (dorsolateral prefrontal cortex/ posterior parietal cortex) networks significantly predicted the monetary choice.

In summary, results found in Spinella et al. (2007, 2008) are in accordance with prior studies (Goel, 1997; Ernest et al., 2002) confirming that prefrontal systems play a role in specific aspects of finances including income and credit card use.

FUTURE RESEARCH DIRECTIONS

There are several directions for future research in the context of prefrontal cortex and financial decision making. For instance, Spinella et al. (2008) recommended identifying which financial attitudes and decisions are associated with prefrontal cortex dysfunction and which are not. In addition, Spinella et al. (2008) recommended examining the association between neuropsychological measures of brain dysfunction and decision-making using econometric tests that economist under conditions of risk and uncertainty. Furthermore, Spinella et al. (2008) suggested investigating the association between abnormal electrcoencephalograms and income and other economic variables.

Because of its interdisciplinary character and approaches, neuroeconomics are now gaining attention in marketing and consumer research to explain buying-decisions. Indeed, as a contiguous to neuroeconomics, neuromarketing combines neuroscience, economics and psychology (Lee et al., 2007) to study price perception, processing and storage (Plassmann et al., 2008), present effects such as framing or anchoring (Deppe et al., 2007), examining advertising appeal (Kenning et al., 2007), studying product policy (Stoll et al., 2008) and analyzing of buying-decisions (Grosenick, Greer, & Knutson, 2008).

CONCLUSION

Economic theory is based on the fact that the economic agent is rational, self-interested, unemotional, and it seeks to maximize utility. However, it was observed that agent always deviate from rationality and show some decision biases or anomalies. Consequently, neuroeconomics has emerged as a multidisciplinary science to analyze economic decision and behaviour from a neurobiological perspective by using advanced neuroscientific methods; including procedures for measuring electromagnetic activity of the brain and those sensitive to changes of cerebral blood flow or metabolism. In this regard, studies have shown that prefrontal cortex is significantly associated with financial decision making process. In addition, the latter is highly affected by emotions.

REFERENCES

Alexander, W. H., & Brown, J. W. (2011). Medial prefrontal cortex as an action-outcome predictor. *Nature Neuroscience*, *14*(10), 1338–1344. doi:10.1038/nn.2921 PMID:21926982

Andersen, R. A., & Cui, H. (2009). Intention, action planning, and decision making in parietal–frontal circuits. *Neuron*, *63*(5), 568–583. doi:10.1016/j.neuron.2009.08.028 PMID:19755101

Barberis, N., & Thaler, R. (2003). A survey of behavioral finance. In G. M. Constantinides, M. Harris, & R. M. Stulz (Eds.), *Handbook of the Economics of Finance*. Amsterdam: Elsevier.

Beach, L. R., & Lipshitz, R. (1993). Why classical decision theory is an inappropriate standard for evaluating and aiding most human decision making. In G. A. Klein & J. Orasanu (Eds.), *Decision making in action: models and methods*. Westport, TX: Ablex Publishing.

Bechara, A., Damasio, H., & Damasio, A. R. (2000). Emotion, decision-making, and the orbitofrontal cortex. *Cerebral Cortex, 10*(3), 295–307. doi:10.1093/cercor/10.3.295 PMID:10731224

Bechara, A., Tranel, D., & Damasio, A. R. (2002). The *somatic marker hypothesis and decision-making*. In F. Boller & J. Grafman (Eds.), *Handbook of neuropsychology: Frontal lobes, 7(2)*. Amsterdam: Elsevier.

Camara, E., Rodriguez-Fornells, A., & Münte, T. F. (2008). Functional connectivity of reward processing in the brain. *Frontiers in Human Neuroscience, 2*, 19. doi:10.3389/neuro.09.019.2008 PMID:19242558

Camara, E., Rodriguez-Fornells, A., Ye, Z., & Münte, T. F. (2009). Reward networks in the brain as captured by connectivity measures. *Frontiers in Neuroscience, 3*(3), 350–362. doi:10.3389/neuro.01.034.2009 PMID:20198152

Clark, L. (2010). Decision-making during gambling: An integration of cognitive and psychobiological approaches. *Philosophical Transactions of the Royal Society of London. Series B, Biological Sciences, 365*(1538), 319–330. doi:10.1098/rstb.2009.0147 PMID:20026469

Cloutier, J., & Gyurovski, I. (2014). Ventral medial prefrontal cortex and person evaluation: Forming impressions of others varying in financial and moral status. *NeuroImage, 100*, 535–543. doi:10.1016/j.neuroimage.2014.06.024 PMID:24936688

Dalgleish, T. (2004). The emotional brain. *Nature Reviews. Neuroscience, 5*(7), 583–589. doi:10.1038/nrn1432 PMID:15208700

de Quervain, D. J. F. et al.. (2004). The neural basis of altruistic punishment. *Science, 305*(5688), 1254–1258. doi:10.1126/science.1100735 PMID:15333831

Delgado, M. R., Nystrom, L. E., Fissell, C., Noll, D. C., & Fiez, J. A. (2000). Tracking the hemodynamic responses to reward and punishment in the striatum. *Journal of Neurophysiology, 84*, 3072–3077. PMID:11110834

Deppe, M., Schwindt, W., Pieper, A., Kugel, H., Plassmann, H., Kenning, P., & Ringelstein, E. B. et al. (2007). Anterior cingulate reflects susceptibility to framing during attractiveness evaluation. *Neuroreport, 18*, 1119–1123. PMID:17589310

Elliott, R., Friston, K. J., & Dolan, R. J. (2000). Dissociable neural responses in human reward systems. *The Journal of Neuroscience, 20*, 6159–6165. PMID:10934265

Elliott, R., Newman, J. L., Longe, O. A., & Deakin, J. F. (2003). Differential response patterns in the striatum and orbitofrontal cortex to financial reward in humans: A parametric functional magnetic resonance imaging study. *The Journal of Neuroscience, 23*, 303–307. PMID:12514228

Ernst, M., Bolla, K., Mouratidis, M., Contoreggi, C., Matochik, J. A., Kurian, V., & London, E. D. et al. (2002). Decision-making in a risk-taking task: A PET study. *Neuropsychopharmacology, 26*(5), 682–691. doi:10.1016/S0893-133X(01)00414-6 PMID:11927193

Evans, K. L., & Hampson, E. (2015). Sex differences on prefrontally-dependent cognitive tasks. *Brain and Cognition*, *93*, 42–53. doi:10.1016/j.bandc.2014.11.006 PMID:25528435

Friston, K. J., Buechel, C., Fink, G. R., Morris, J., Rolls, E., & Dolan, R. J. (1997). Psychophysiological and modulatory interactions in neuroimaging. *NeuroImage*, *6*(3), 218–229. doi:10.1006/nimg.1997.0291 PMID:9344826

Gehring, W. J., & Willoughby, A. R. (2002). The medial frontal cortex and the rapid processing of monetary gains and losses. *Science*, *295*(5563), 2279–2282. doi:10.1126/science.1066893 PMID:11910116

Goel, V., Grafman, J., Tajik, J., Gana, S., & Danto, D. (1997). A study of the performance of patients with frontal lobe lesions in a financial planning task. *Brain*, *120*(10), 1805–1822. doi:10.1093/brain/120.10.1805 PMID:9365372

Grace, J., Stout, J. C., & Malloy, P. F. (1999). Assessing frontal behavior syndromes with the Frontal Lobe Personality Scale. *Assessment*, *6*(3), 269–284. doi:10.1177/107319119900600307 PMID:10445964

Grosenick, L., Greer, S., & Knutson, B. (2008). Interpretable classifiers for fMRI improve prediction of purchases. *IEEE Transactions on Neural Systems and Rehabilitation Engineering*, *16*(6), 539–548. doi:10.1109/TNSRE.2008.926701 PMID:19144586

Gutnik, L. A., Hakimzada, A. F., Yoskowitz, N. A., & Patel, V. L. (2006). The role of emotion in decision-making: A cognitive neuroeconomic approach towards understanding sexual risk behaviour. *Journal of Biomedical Informatics*, *39*(6), 720–736. doi:10.1016/j.jbi.2006.03.002 PMID:16759915

Hare, T. A., Camerer, C. F., Knoepfle, D. T., & Rangel, A. (2010). Value computations in ventral medial prefrontal cortex during charitable decision making incorporate input from regions involved in social cognition. *The Journal of Neuroscience*, *30*, 583–590. PMID:20071521

Kable, J.W., & Glimcher, P.W. (2009). The neurobiology of decision: Consensus and controversy. *Neuron*, *63*, 733–745.

Kahneman, D. (2003). Maps of Bounded Rationality: Psychology for Behavioral Economics. *The American Economic Review*, *93*(5), 1449–1475. doi:10.1257/000282803322655392

Kenning, P., Plassmann, H., & Ahlert, D. (2007). Applications of functional magnetic resonance imaging for market research. *Qualitative Market Research*, *10*(2), 135–152. doi:10.1108/13522750710740817

King-Casas, B. et al.. (2005). Getting to know you: Reputation and trust in a two-person economic exchange. *Science*, *308*(5718), 78–83. doi:10.1126/science.1108062 PMID:15802598

Knutson, B., Adams, C. M., Fong, G. W., & Hommer, D. (2001). Anticipation of increasing monetary reward selectively recruits nucleus accumbens. *The Journal of Neuroscience*, *21*, RC159. PMID:11459880

Knutson, B., Westdorp, A., Kaiser, E., & Hommer, D. (2000). FMRI visualization of brain activity during a monetary incentive delay task. *NeuroImage*, *12*(1), 20–27. doi:10.1006/nimg.2000.0593 PMID:10875899

Lee, N., Broderick, A. J., & Chamberlain, L. (2007). What is 'neuromarketing'? A discussion and agenda for future research. *International Journal of Psychophysiology*, *63*(2), 199–204. doi:10.1016/j.ijpsycho.2006.03.007 PMID:16769143

Minati, L., Grisoli, M., Seth, A. K., & Critchley, H. D. (2012). Decision-making under risk: A graph-based network analysis using functional MRI. *NeuroImage, 60*(4), 2191–2205. doi:10.1016/j.neuroimage.2012.02.048 PMID:22387471

O'Doherty, J., Kringelbach, M. L., Rolls, E. T., Hornak, J., & Andrews, C. (2001). Abstract reward and punishment representations in the human orbitofrontal cortex. *Nature Neuroscience, 4*(1), 95–102. doi:10.1038/82959 PMID:11135651

Park, S. Q., Kahnt, T., Rieskamp, J., & Heekeren, H. R. (2011). Neurobiology of value integration: When value impacts valuation. *The Journal of Neuroscience, 31*(25), 9307–9314. doi:10.1523/JNEUROSCI.4973-10.2011 PMID:21697380

Patton, J. H., Stanford, M. S., & Barratt, E. S. (1995). Factor structure of the Barratt impulsiveness scale. *Journal of Clinical Psychology, 51*(6), 768–774. doi:10.1002/1097-4679(199511)51:6<768::AID-JCLP2270510607>3.0.CO;2-1 PMID:8778124

Plassmann, H., O'Doherty, J., Shiv, B., & Rangel, A. (2008). Marketing actions can modulate neural representations of experienced pleasantness. *Proceedings of the National Academy of Sciences of the United States of America, 105*(3), 1050–1054. doi:10.1073/pnas.0706929105 PMID:18195362

Pradeep, A. K. (2010). *The buying brain: Secrets for selling to the subconscious mind*. John Wiley & Sons.

Rabin, M. (1998). Psychology and Economics. *Journal of Economic Literature, 36*, 11–46.

Rangel, A., & Hare, T. (2010). Neural computations associated with goal-directed choice. *Current Opinion in Neurobiology, 20*(2), 262–270. doi:10.1016/j.conb.2010.03.001 PMID:20338744

Ricardo, C., Andrew, J. G., Gutman, D. A., & Kilts, C. D. (2015). Organization of intrinsic functional brain connectivity predicts decisions to reciprocate social behavior. *Behavioural Brain Research*. doi:10.1016/j.bbr.2015.07.008

Spinella, M., Yang, B., & Lester, D. (2007). Lester D. Prefrontal systems in financial processing. *Journal of Socio-Economics, 36*(3), 480–489. doi:10.1016/j.socec.2006.12.008

Spinella, M., Yang, B., & Lester, D. (2008). Prefrontal cortex dysfunction and attitudes toward money: A study in neuroeconomics. *Journal of Socio-Economics, 37*(5), 1785–1788. doi:10.1016/j.socec.2004.09.061

Stephan, K. E., Harrison, L. M., Kiebel, S. J., David, O., Penny, W. D., & Friston, K. J. (2007). Dynamic causal models of neural system dynamics: Current state and future extensions. *Journal of Biosciences, 32*(1), 129–144. doi:10.1007/s12038-007-0012-5 PMID:17426386

Stoll, M., Baecke, S., & Kenning, P. (2008). What they see is what they get? An fMRI-study on neural correlates of attractive packaging. *Journal of Consumer Behaviour, 7*(4-5), 342–359. doi:10.1002/cb.256

Tversky, A., & Kahneman, D. (1974). Judgement under uncertainty: Heuristics and biases. *Science, 185*(4157), 1124–1131. doi:10.1126/science.185.4157.1124 PMID:17835457

Wallis, J. D., & Kennerley, S. W. (2010). Heterogeneous reward signals in prefrontal cortex. *Current Opinion in Neurobiology, 20*(2), 191–198. doi:10.1016/j.conb.2010.02.009 PMID:20303739

Zamora-López, G., Zhou, C., & Kurths, J. (2010). Cortical hubs forma module formulti sensory integration on top of the hierarchy of cortical networks. *Frontiers in Neuroinformatics*, *4*, 1. PMID:20428515

ADDITIONAL READING

Anselme, P. (2015). Does reward unpredictability reflect risk? *Behavioural Brain Research*, *280*, 119–127. doi:10.1016/j.bbr.2014.12.003 PMID:25496783

Bereczkei, T., Papp, P., Kincses, P., Bodrogi, B., Perlaki, G., Orsi, G., & Deak, A. (2015). The neural basis of the Machiavellians' decision making in fair and unfair situations. *Brain and Cognition*, *98*, 53–64. doi:10.1016/j.bandc.2015.05.006 PMID:26093237

Canessa, N., Pantaleo, G., Crespi, C., Gorini, A., & Cappa, S. F. (2014). The impact of egocentric vs. Allocentric agency attributions on the neural bases of reasoning about social rules. *Brain Research*, *1581*, 40–50. doi:10.1016/j.brainres.2014.06.001 PMID:24928617

Dixona, M. L., & Christoff, K. (2014). The lateral prefrontal cortex and complex value-based learning and decision making. *Neuroscience and Biobehavioral Reviews*, *45*, 9–18. doi:10.1016/j.neubiorev.2014.04.011 PMID:24792234

Yasuno, F., Matsuoka, K., Kitamura, S., Kiuchi, K., Kosaka, J., Okada, K., & Kishimoto, T. et al. (2014). Decision-making deficit of a patient with axonal damage after traumatic brain injury. *Brain and Cognition*, *84*(1), 63–68. doi:10.1016/j.bandc.2013.11.005 PMID:24316983

KEY TERMS AND DEFINITIONS

Economic Decision Making Process: Identifying and selecting appropriate actions or sequence of actions to achieve an ideal solution.

Economic/Financial Reward: Outcome or benefit of an economic/financial decision.

Financial Gambles: A tool to investigate how motivational decisions are reached in the presence of risk.

Functional Magnetic Resonance Imaging: It is a technique for measuring brain activity by detecting the changes in blood oxygenation and flow that occur in response to a specific neural activity.

Magnetic Resonance Imaging: It is a medical imaging technique used in radiology to detect structural anatomy of the body. In particular, it makes pictures of organs and structures inside the body.

Neuroeconomics: A discipline used to apply findings from neuroscience to the study of economic behaviour.

Prefrontal Cortex: The most anterior portions of the frontal lobe.

Risk: It is a known probability distribution of possible outcomes.

Uncertainty: It refers to an unknown probability distribution of possible outcomes.

Chapter 8
The Role of the Mixed Strategies and Selective Inflexibility in the Repeated Games of Business:
Multiple Case Study Analysis

Rauno Rusko
University of Lapland, Finland

ABSTRACT

This chapter is focused on the possibilities of game theory as a tool of strategists to interpret practical strategic decision-making situations. Simultaneously, there is a need to simplify presentation of game theory and consider the possibilities of mixed strategies. Practical game situations are relatively complex: even the rules of the game might change during the decision-making process, or at least there is need to change several times the strategy during the game, especially in the case of repeated game. This chapter shows some practical examples how to describe the strategic game situations in a manner relatively easy to understand.

INTRODUCTION

Contemporary business literature on game theory emphasizes simple game situations in which each player has only one possible move to maximize her/his benefit in the game. This one-shot game principle is easy to learn and understand and, therefore, a popular tool in areas such as business education (Dekker & Van Rooy, 2000). However, practical strategic game situations between the firms contain several steps, rounds and phases and even the rules of the business game are possible to change during the game periods. However, the traditional tools and applicability of game theory have met some criticism among philosophers as in Grüne-Yanoff & Lehtinen (2010).

DOI: 10.4018/978-1-4666-9989-2.ch008

This chapter highlights some problems associated with game theory and its applicability in business, especially strategic form games which simplify the game situations of real life because of their restricted visualization into mainly four-fold or nine-fold tables, depending on the number of the available strategies of the players. However, the extensive form games allow wider repertoire of moves and decision-paths which illustrate the game situations. Though relatively flexible visualization of extensive form games, their weight as evidence is limited in the situations where the game arena or rules of the game are changing. Supergames consider repeated game situations. Again, however, the basic assumption is that the payoffs and the structure and the rules of the game are fixed.

This study also emphasizes the fact that the actual business life game situations are flexible and even the "rules of the game" are changing (e.g., due to changes in business environment such as in legislation). Therefore, the flexibility of the strategy is important instead of "here I stand" –strategy, or at least selective inflexibility (cf. Dixit & Nalebuff, 1991). More specifically, this chapter considers the following features of the games in actual business life such as:

1. Thought some game situations are temporal one-shot games, they might have long-term reflections on the business arena in the future.
2. Most of the business games are repeated games; that is, the firms will meet each other in the same kinds of circumstances.
3. Because most of the business games are repeated games, typically strategic function form do not provide platform which is adequate for analysis.
4. Though the games are repeated games, it is possible that rules of the game will change during the game process. Then the solution methods of repeated game do not fit to actual game situation.

Mixed strategies describe the situations in which the strategies of the players are flexible. Thus, these strategies fit relatively well to the actual business life situations, but the challenge is that the rules of the game and circumstances of the business environment are assumed to be constant. In business activities, the repeated game is a typical relationship between two (or more) competing firms. Often the game theoretic perspectives of repeated game are focused on one solution, which might be (e.g., collusion equilibrium) (Rusko, 2005; Niyato & Hossain, 2008). Another possibility, after long-term collusion equilibrium, is that some of the colluding firms will cheat and deviate from the collusion to achieve temporally the higher market share and profit. This cheating will lead into the punishment with the perfect competition equilibrium, which might last several periods or even forever (Green & Porter, 1984; Rotemberg, & Saloner, 1989).

This kind of perspective does not entertain the possibility of mixed strategies. By intentionally changing the strategies in the game during the specific series of moves, it is possible to obtain an outcome compared to a pure strategy policy. This chapter will introduce differences between one-shot games and repeated games – and, in the case of repeated games, the differences between pure strategy and mixed strategy policy. We especially consider the possibilities of flexible strategy compared to a pure strategy by using real life business examples from several industries. The visualization of the outcomes are based on the figures with pure strategies and possible area of outcomes of mixed strategies, which are based on the allotment of probabilities; the visualization based on coalition function form (see, e.g., Gardner, 1995; Ferguson, 2005); and on the sets of feasible payoffs (Bennett, Ragland, & Yolles, 1998).

Although hundreds or even thousands of allotted pairs of probabilities of moves, some areas in the set of feasible payoffs are nearly impossible to achieve unintentionally, but often the careful intentional mixed strategy policy will produce higher outcomes to the players of the game. This chapter will show some illustrative examples.

The aim of this chapter is to present the remarkable opportunities of mixed strategies in business using illustrative visualization to increase the accessibility of practitioners about the outcomes of the game theoretical perspectives. Generally, game theoretical frameworks and outcomes are conceived difficult to adapt among business practitioners. This chapter aims to fill in this gap using visual tools and describing business life examples in the analysis.

The organization of this chapter is the following: after the Introduction follows some basic concepts of game theory, especially pure strategy and mixed strategy with several illustrative game examples. Then, this chapter includes descriptions about the exploited methodology. The next section presents cases from business and some outcomes. The outcomes are interpreted more carefully in the discussions and conclusion. Finally, there are some ideas for further studies.

BASICS OF GAME THEORY: PURE STRATEGIES AND MIXED STRATEGIES

Game theory is strongly focused on the Nash equilibrium. In business education, a simple tool to introduce the logic of Nash equilibrium is based on illustrative examples such as the Prisoners Dilemma which provides applications that have often been used in the literature of management and business (e.g., the branches of construction project management) (Barough et al., 2012), international law (Ohlin, 2012), and in economic zone development (Ling et al., 2014). There are several versions of the Prisoner's Dilemma, but our version follows the illustration of Brams (1993, p. 567): There are two suspected criminals and they are given the following consequences:

If one confesses and the other remains silent, the confessor goes free (the best payoff of 4) and the silent suspect gets a 10-year sentence (the worst payoff of 1); if both confess, they get five-year sentences (the next-worst payoff of 2); and if both remain silent, they get one-year sentences (the next-best payoff of 3)

The solution for this game is Nash equilibrium. The game situation using strategic-form presentation is depicted in Table 1.

The simple rule to locate the Nash solution is the following: *In the Nash equilibrium none of the players are willing to change his/her strategy alone* (see, e.g., Duarte et al., 2012; Angelides & Sofokleous, 2013). Following this rule, Suspect 1 wants to change his move from a to c, where his payoff is 4 (instead of 3). Additionally, Suspect 2 wants b instead of a in which he obtains 4 as a payoff. Similarly, Suspect 2 wants to change his move from c to d in order to get 2 instead of 1. In addition, Suspect 1 wants to change his move from b to d where his payoff is 2 instead of 1. However, none of the players

Table 1. Prisoner's Dilemma (cf. Brams, 1993)

		Suspect 2	
		Remains Silent	**Confess**
Suspect 1	remains silent	(3,3) a	(1,4) b
	confess	(4,1) c	(2,2) d

are willing to change their strategy from point d where both of the Suspects "confess" – a strategy with payoffs 2 (Table 2). This strategy combination (d) is Nash equilibrium because neither Suspect 1, nor Suspect 2 is willing alone to change his strategy.

Thus, in this kind of non-cooperative game the players end in the solution which is not the best one. In Nash equilibrium (d), both of the players have 2 as payoff because of their "confession" strategy. Point a {remains silent, remains silent} is better for both of these players, but impossible because it is not in Nash-equilibrium. In cooperative games, the solution is that both of the players remain silent.I

In repeated games, also referred to as a "supergame" (Radner et al., 1986; Engle-Warnick & Slonim, 2006), the players which meet the same situation repeatedly cooperate having "remains silent" as their strategy. That is, their payoffs are 3 in each round. If one of the players deviate having confess as a strategy, then he obtains in this round 4 and counterparty gets 1, but counterparty will not trust on the cooperation anymore and chooses "confess" as his strategy in the future. Both of the players know this situation and they choose the confess strategy after this deviation several rounds, or forever, if they do not negotiate to obtain again cooperative solution in the future. If Player 2, for example, changes his strategy from the collaborative solution during round 3, then the drains of payoffs are:

$$(3,3) + (3,3) + (1,4) + (2,2) + (2,2) + (2,2) + \dots$$

Sometimes pure strategies will not provide optimal solution in the repeated games. This means that in order to achieve optimal solution, the players must cooperate by changing their strategies in turn. This kind of activity is called a mixed strategy (Gardner, 1995; Yin, et al., 2012). Thus, it is possible to achieve, on the average, higher long-turn payoffs compared with pure strategy solutions. Table 3 demonstrates an example.

The game introduced in Table 3 provides the situation, where the optimal solution in cooperative game is to change the strategies in turn. Following this perspective, players contract that they will use only strategy combinations a and d in turn. Suppose that they start with a, that is combination {cooperate, cooperate}, and then they have d: {compete, compete} and after that a, d, a, d, a, d, …. In other words, the drains of payoffs are:

$$(3,1) + (1,3) + (3,1) + (1,3) + (3,1) + (1,3) + \dots$$

Table 2. Prisoner's Dilemma and moves

		Suspect 2	
		Remains Silent	**Confess**
Suspect 1	remains silent	(3,3) a	(1,4) b
	confess	(4,1) c	(2,2) d

Table 3. The game with mixed strategy equilibrium (p and q are probabilities)

		Player 2	
		Cooperate (C) *q*	**Compete (No)** *1-q*
Player 1	cooperate (C) *p*	(3,1) a	(0,0) b
	compete (No) *1-p*	(0,0) c	(1,3) d

On average both of the players will get per round $(1+3)/2 = 2$, which result is impossible to achieve following a pure strategy policy. To achieve this mixed strategy equilibrium, players need to contract. Incidentally, it is impossible to get as high as 2 as payoff to the players.

(Non-cooperative) mixed strategy solution is possible to calculate using probabilities, as in:

$E(U1)= p[3q]+(1-p)[1-q]=4pq-p-q+1$; Max $dE(U1)/dp =0 => q = ¼ = 0.25$

$E(U2)= q[p]+(1-q)3[1-p]= 4qp-3q-3p+3$; Max $dE(U2)/dq =0 => p = ¾ = 0.75$

Mixed strategy solution means that:

$E(U1)= 4*0.75*0.25- 0.75-0.25 +1 = 0.75$

and:

$E(U2)=4*0.25*0.75-3*0.25-3*0.75+3=0.75,$

which is not a satisfactory result to the players. Players should cooperate and obtain on the average 2 instead of 0.75 in each round of the game. Incidentally, combination (2,2) is impossible to achieve. Let us ballot 500 times the combination of probabilities *p* and *q* using excel with interval [0,1} and place these probabilities into equations EU1 and EU2. As a result we get the situation depicted in Figure 1. Figure 1 shows it is impossible to achieve (2,2) and the focal point of the results is near the point (0.75,0.75).

Already this simple example shows that compromise provide higher benefits compared with pure strategies. Thus, the companies, which meet each other repeated game arena, should be ready to co-ordinate their moves and strategies in business game situations. Instead, via the "here I stay" strategy (Dixit & Nalebuff, 1992) it might be profitable to follow emergent strategy: that is, readiness to change strategies according to the changing business environment and context.

Figure 1. Results of the ballot (500 times)

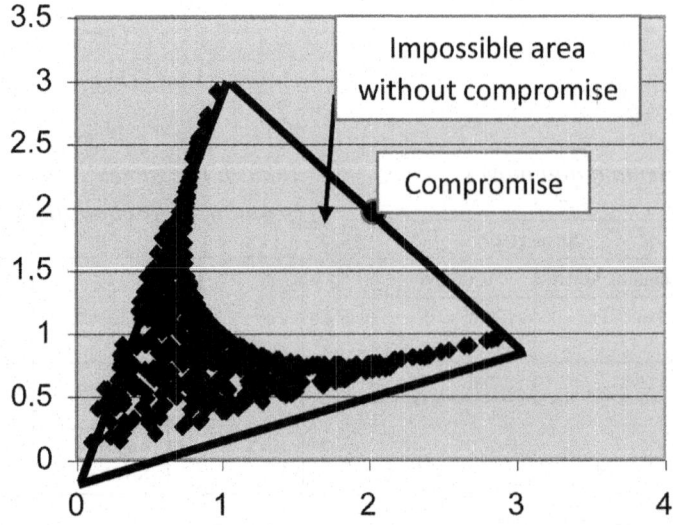

METHODOLOGY

Despite some exceptions (Barougha et al., 2012; Ohlin, 2012), typical game theoretical studies leans on quantitative mathematical justifications and simulations (Vogel et al., 2006; Kebritchi et al., 2010). The analysis in this chapter partly follows these traditions. However, this paper exploits, qualitative and textual reasoning in addition to quantitative justification which is partly based on business case descriptions. In other words, this study follows a case study strategy which often covers several complementary methods in order to achieve the aims of the research (Yin, 1983; Eriksson & Kovalainen, 2008).

The purpose of this chapter is to consider the applicability of the game theory perspectives generally and using case study examples from business life. These examples emphasize the situations which show the needed flexibility of the business strategies. Even the rules of the game can change during the strategic game process of the players in business life. Because we introduce, following the aims of the chapter, several cases which show the need to have mixed or flexible strategies instead of pure strategies, this study is possible to be interpreted as a multi-case study (c.f. Poon & Swatman, 1999; Mettler & Rohner, 2009).

The introduced cases are the following: a) Rovio and Supercell relationships in game industry, b) NUMMI –project between Generals Motors and Toyota and c) Development work of Nokia and Motorola in China at the beginning of Millennium.

CASES AND OUTCOMES

Case 1: Two Firms from the Game Industry, Rovio and Supercell

Two competing Finnish firms of the game industry, Rovio and Supercell, have several joint public activities. They are active organizers of the monthly evening events of the Finnish game developers. Finnish game firms have joint recruit systems for game developers such as GamePro arranged by Suomen Pelinke-hittäjät ry and Neogames, in which Rovio and Supercell and about 20 other game firms are involved (Rusko, 2015). Furthermore, Rovio and Supercell cooperate in the forms of mega events, such as Slush, Northern Europe's biggest startup event, with 1,200 participating companies. Finland has demoscenes, computer art subculture that specializes in producing demos which contain audio-visual presentations that run in real-time on a computer. The main goal of a demo is to show off programming, artistic, and musical skills. However, the demosceners did not try to reach an outsider public. Furthermore, the de-mosceners never had to bother with official copyright laws (Carlsson, 2009), which enabled prototypes to be developed quickly in the industry (Rusko, 2015).

However, these two firms – Rovio and Supercell – are independent with own totally different ownership structure. Thus, the main strategy between them is competition. The above described collaboration practices are temporal and related to particular events in the game industry. In other words, both Rovio and Supercell have continuously two different strategies: competition strategy and collaboration strategy. In the events both of these firms are following collaboration strategy, but otherwise both of these firms have a collaborative strategy.

Thus, the strategy of the firms is linked with the context and timing: during and especially at the events the strategy is collaborative, but otherwise mainly competitive. This situation is possible to describe following strategic form presentation in a four-fold table (Table 4). However, in addition to two strategies of the players (competition, collaboration), the context also has two stages: during the event and outside the event. Table 4, and especially 5, actually describes the entire situation but omits the possibility that the firms will also cooperate outside the events, that there are other forms of collaboration as well. Actually, both of the firms have four strategies: competition (all time)/No collaboration; Competition (during the times of events)/Collaboration other times; Competition (all time, except events)/Collaboration during events; and Collaboration (all time) (Table 6).

Table 6 explains that many of the combinations of the strategic form game between Rovio and Supercell are difficult to estimate. Table 5 assumes, however, that collaboration in the forms of innovation events provides extra benefits to the participating game enterprises such as Rovio and Supercell in the forms of Research and Development (R&D) (see Rusko, 2015).

Figure 2 considers the same game situation between Rovio and Supercell using extensive form presentation.

In the extensive form games the order of the players is known. In Figure 2, the order of the decisions is not critical because Rovio is able to notice the moves of N and Supercell. Therefore, it does not matter whether Supercell or Rovio moves first if the players can notice the moves. During the time of event, solution is *{participate, participate}* and payoffs are (3,3). This is also in Nash equilibrium and sub-game perfect equilibrium, which is possible to find following e.g. backward induction –principle (Shubik, 1970; Gardner & Ostrom, 1991; Rich, 2015).

The case description will not speak out the periods and contexts which are not linked with events. Thus, Figure 2 does not define the outcomes of these periods. However, generally we can assume that the firms are following competition strategies, which is in this case combination *{No, No}*, but outcomes are unknown. Even Figure 2 in the case of all completed outcomes will not describe all possible strategic game situations between Rovio and Supercell. It presents only part of the story: generally Supercell and Rovio have also other strategies such as collaboration, competition –combination. In other words, game theory is able to focus only one case at a time, not the entire story. Therefore, the combination of different stories, where the player is involved in potentially provides perspective about the whole strategic field of player. The strategies of the firms are more like emergent than deliberative in this manifold field of strategies. Strategic form games oversimplify the content and context of strategizing.

Table 4. Strategic form illustrations of the Rovio-Supercell –case

Supercell		Rovio	
		Competition	Collaboration
	Competition	Main strategy (excluding joint events)	
	Collaboration		Demoscenes, Slush, monthly evening events

Table 5. Strategic form illustrations of the Rovio-Supercell-case

Supercell		Rovio	
		Competition (do not participate in the events)	Collaboration (participates in the events)
	Competition (do not participate in the events)	1,1	0,2
	Collaboration (participates in the events)	2,0	3,3

Table 6. Strategic form illustrations of the Rovio-Supercell-case

		Rovio			
		Competition (all time)	**Competition during the times of events (Collaboration other times)**	**Competition all time, except events (Collaboration during events)**	**Collaboration (all time)**
Supercell	Competition (all time)	1,1	?, ?	0,2	?, ?
	Competition during the times of events (Collaboration other times)	?, ?	?, ?	?, ?	?, ?
	Competition all time, except events (Collaboration during events)	2,0	?, ?	3,3	?, ?
	Collaboration (all time)	?, ?	?, ?	?, ?	?, ?

Figure 2. The Rovio and Supercell case in the extensive form game description.

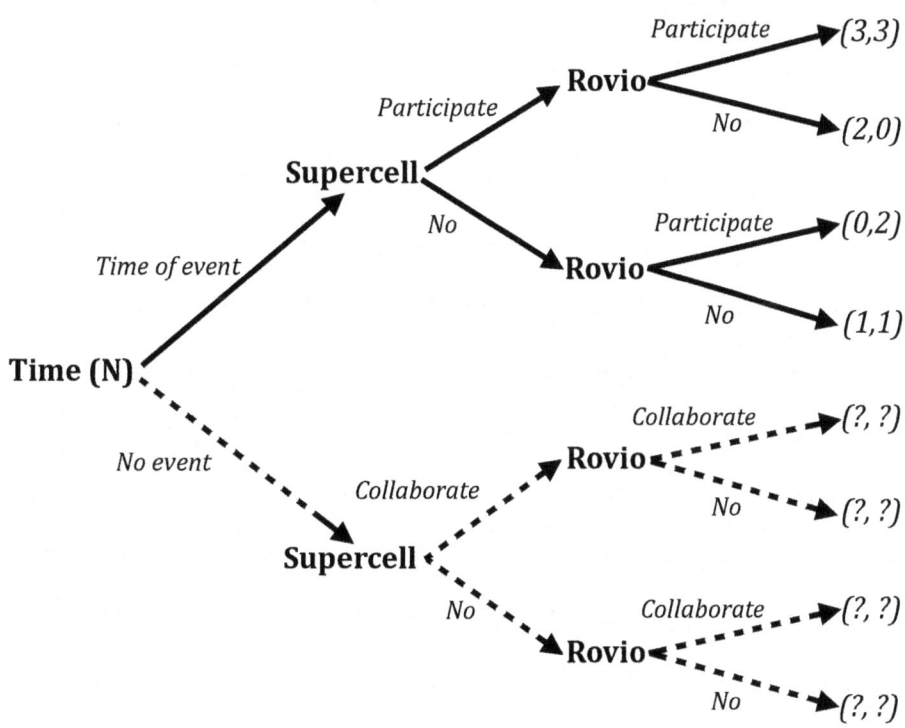

In everyday business life the forum and rules of the game are changing according to time and context of the game situation. One descriptive example is NUMMI between Toyota and General Motors in the 1990s, and another is the game situation between mobile phone companies Nokia and Motorola in China (Luo, 2004a,b). These two cases resemble the case between Supercell and Rovio because also in these cases the alternative strategies are whether to "cooperate" or "compete". Furthermore, both of these cases contain the situation, where the context has effects on the chosen strategy.

Case 2: NUMMI –Project between Toyota and General Motors

Generally, the alliances between competing car producers are popular way to improve the firm's position in the market. NUMMI joint venture is only one example.

The NUMMI project was implemented in California, USA during the period 1984-2010. The NUMMI joint venture provided benefits for both of the participants: to GM as an opportunity to learn about low-cost lean manufacturing from Toyota, and Toyota familiarized with North America as a potential market area and also gained its first manufacturing base in North America and a chance to implement its production system in an American work force environment. There were two kinds of value: high-quality, efficiently produced cars, and the learning that accrued to the partners. (Doz & Hamel, 1998).

From the game theoretical perspective, the NUMMI-case resembles the Rovio-Supercell collaboration. Most of the time Rovio and Supercell are competitors, but during events they have relatively strong collaborative activities. However, these events last only one or two days. In the case of NUMMI, the collaboration lasted for several decades. At the same time, Toyota and General Motors experienced tough competition with each other. In the NUMMI, case the context is not based on timing but rather another context: project, which progress basing on collaboration in California plant, while otherwise Toyota and General Motors had hard competition. Table 7 describes the situation.

The NUMMI case also shows there is a need to have diversified strategies. Although competition is the main strategy in the game between General Motors and Toyota, it is not the only one – it is not the "Here I stand" – strategy. The NUMMI case is part of the emergent strategies of Toyota and General Motors. The participants of NUMMI case assumes that counterparty will cooperate in the actions associated with NUMMI, but compete in the activities outside the NUMMI case. If one of the players deviate from these positions, especially follow competing strategy in the activities NUMMI case, the future of the Joint Venture would be treated. Actually, in long term projects such as NUMMI, there are repeated game situation, where continuously counterparties assume that both of the players will follow

Table 7. Two general strategies of Toyota and General Motors

Toyota		Generals Motors	
		Competition	**Collaboration**
	Competition	Main strategy (excluding e.g. NUMMI-case)	
	Collaboration		Joint plants and activities, such as NUMMI -case

Table 8. Two strategies of NUMMI joint venture

NUMMI joint venture	Generals Motors		
Toyota		Competition	Collaboration
	Competition	2,2	4,1
	Collaboration	1,4	3,3

collaborate –strategy. It is also possible to consider alone NUMMI case between these firms. Then we obtain the situation depicted in Table 8.

If one of the players deviates, then counterparty will also deviate from the collaboration. Then, the drains of payoff are following (assuming that player 1 deviates first (during fourth round), as in:

$$(3,3) + (3,3) + (3,3) + (4,1) + (2,2) + (2,2) + (2,2) + \dots$$

Competition strategy during the collaborative project endangers the future of the whole project as the equation above demonstrates. The benefits (if project is creating value to the both of the players) are smaller after deviation and probably the total net benefits are due to deviation, an easily negative one.

Case 3: NUMMI Project between Nokia and Motorola

At the beginning of new Millennium Nokia and Motorola cooperated with each other with the local government in order to establish new production units in China. Luo (2004a, b) introduced this case where two competing firms (Nokia and Motorola) in China are cooperating to develop the infrastructure of China with the local authorities. The main aim of this coopetition is to obtain conditions which enable production of (in this case) mobile phones in China. Luo (2005) describes cooperation in the following manner: "cooperating to create a bigger business pie, while competing to divide it up" (see Brandenburger & Nalebuff, 1996). Yadong Luo (2004a, b) noticed this cooperation and called these actions to be as coopetition activities in which the competing firms cooperate with each other. Because of collaboration between competitors and the government of China, this situation is can be referred to as a multifaceted coopetition (Rusko, 2014a, b), where are more than two counterparties in the coopetition activity (see Rusko, 2015).

Case 3 between Nokia, Motorola, and local governments in China resembles Case 1 and Case 2 in which the strategy depends on the context. Both Nokia and Motorola needed new solutions to achieve lean production of mobile phones near the promising new markets in China. The infrastructure and education of labor force have to be suitable for mobile phone production. In order to achieve these targets, both Nokia and Motorola developed together facilities and education possibilities in certain areas of China with the help of local authorities. (Luo, 2004a, b). After this collaboration, the subsidiaries of Nokia and Motorola had competition situation with each other. The situation is depicted in Table 9.

Table 9 shows the situation, where one fixed strategy does not provide the highest possible payoffs to players. This case fits well with the coopetition principle above: "cooperating to create a bigger business pie, while competing to divide it up". Again, there is the need to follow emergent strategy instead of the fixed "here I stand" strategy.

Table 9. Case Nokia and Motorola.

In the Chinese Market	Motorola		
Nokia		Competition	Collaboration
	Competition	Main strategy after development work focused on facilities and education	
	Collaboration		Local joint development work before founded mobile phone plants.

DISCUSSIONS AND CONCLUSION

This chapter shows the importance of flexibility in business strategies. Especially important is the context and timing. The strategies of the players are related to the context. In particularly, during the exceptional phases of business the strategy is different from the typical phases of business. These exceptional phases do not have to be in any phases of crisis which is possible. The contexts where strategic choices differ from the ordinary are in this study based on:

1. Events, such as demoscenes in the game industry;
2. General developing phases before competition, such as the development work of Nokia and Motorola at the beginning of millennium in China;
3. Although the NUMMI case had several reasons, also important is the emergency because of general problems in the industry, such as the strategic alliances in automobile industry during the recessions of 2007-2011.

Especially examples from automobile and mobile phone industries fit the perspectives of Mintzberg et al. (2005) about changing periods between configuration phases and transformation phases. The development work happens during configuration phases and competition during transformation phases. At least the decision about NUMMI in the mid 1980s has been made in relatively constant business environment, although some other strategic alliances of automobile industry have underlying emergence state. Collaboration between mobile phone companies in China, while preparing by investments suitable conditions for mobile phone manufacturing, happened mostly during relatively constant configuration phases and after that started transformation phases with reciprocal hard competition activities between subsidiaries in China. (Luo, 2004 a, b).

Typically, collaborative activities, such as strategic alliances, are based on the assumption that partners of the alliance will gain from the alliance equally during the different phases of partnership (Doz & Hamel, 1998). However, the introduced mixed strategy policy of the companies allows the assumption that the highest benefits of the companies will rotate among the partners of the collaboration –or at least the firms are ready to have "peaceful" events and phases with lower payoffs because temporal reasons, such as investments in development work or in research & development activities (see Rusko, 2015).

The outcomes of the analysis show the importance of the coordinated mixed strategies among the members of the alliance. Furthermore, the flexibility of the strategy is important instead of "here I stand" strategy, or at least selective inflexibility (cf. Dixit & Nalebuff, 1991). The partners of "the game" must be prepared to co-operate events during those periods in which the outcomes are asymmetric.

The analysis based on three case study examples coming from game industry, mobile phone industry, and automobile industry. All these cases showed the importance of emergent strategy policy with flexible strategies where the context is the underlying feature during the time the firms are deciding their strategy. All these cases contained only two strategies: competition and collaboration. Both of these strategies seemed to be relevant alternative, even simultaneously depending on the context, where decisions have been made. This chapter intended to simplify and to make more practical the principles of game theory.

However, the challenge to improve the breakthrough activities of game theory to business is still challenging. Further studies need various perspectives and cases in the way to familiarize game theory to the business practitioners.

This study provides several managerial implications; in addition to fact that chapter showed the possibilities to interpret practical strategic situations using game theory, this study showed that strategists of the companies have to prepare changes in their strategies. One long-term strategy will not necessarily produce the best possible outcome. Furthermore, in order to avoid the outcomes, such as the equilibrium of the prisoner's dilemma, managers and strategists of the companies need to take into the account also cooperative solutions, which might be based on the pure strategy combination or the mixed strategy combination. The latter also requires flexibility in the strategy-making process. Furthermore, strategists have to follow the whole game and its environment: it is also possible that the "rules of the game" will change due to changing business environment. Such situations presuppose new careful analysis, which map new strategic situations in the market. All of these examples show the importance of flexibility in the strategic game situations of the business life.

Furthermore, this chapter showed several themes for further studies. Generally, game theory is mainly based on quantitative analysis, which provides only abstruse information for the needs of the managers and strategists of the companies. There is a general need to develop game theoretical forms to present practical business life situations that is strategic games, in a way, which is easier to interpret in practice. This chapter showed only some examples about this perspective. Game theorists must develop their capabilities to transfer game theoretical presentations and solutions into real life situations. This study presented that this is possible; however, the possibilities of research in this perspective is nearly unlimited.

REFERENCES

Angelides, M. C., & Sofokleous, A. A. (2013). A game approach to optimization of bandwidth allocation using MPEG-7 and MPEG-21. *Multimedia Tools and Applications*, *62*(1), 287–309. doi:10.1007/s11042-011-0981-0

Barough, A. S., Shoubi, M. V., & Skardi, M. J. E. (2012). Application of game theory approach in solving the construction project conflicts. *Procedia: Social and Behavioral Sciences*, *58*, 1586–1593. doi:10.1016/j.sbspro.2012.09.1145

Bennett, L. L., Ragland, S. E., & Yolles, P. (1998). Facilitating international agreements through an interconnected game approach: The case of river basins. In Conflict and cooperation on trans-boundary water resources (pp. 61-85). New York: Kluwer Academic Publishers.

Brams, S. J. (1993). Theory of moves. *American Scientist*, 562–570.

Carlsson, A. (2009). The forgotten pioneers of creative hacking and social networking–Introducing the demoscene. In *Re: live Media Art Histories 2009 conference proceedings*, (pp. 16-20).

Dekker, P., & Van Rooy, R. (2000). Bi-directional optimality theory: An application of game theory. *Journal of Semantics*, *17*(3), 217–242. doi:10.1093/jos/17.3.217

Dixit, A., & Nalebuff, B. (1991). *Thinking Strategically*. New York: WW Norten & Company. Inc.

Doz, Y. L., & Hamel, G. (1998). *Alliance advantage: The art of creating value through partnering.* Boston: Harvard Business Press.

Duarte, P. B., Fadlullah, Z. M., Vasilakos, A. V., & Kato, N. (2012). On the partially overlapped channel assignment on wireless mesh network backbone: A game theoretic approach. *Selected Areas in Communications. IEEE Journal on*, *30*(1), 119–127.

Engle-Warnick, J., & Slonim, R. L. (2006). Inferring repeated-game strategies from actions: Evidence from trust game experiments. *Economic Theory*, *28*(3), 603–632. doi:10.1007/s00199-005-0633-6

Eriksson, P., & Kovalainen, A. (2008). *Qualitative Methods in Business Research*. Thousand Oaks, CA: SAGE Publications, Ltd. doi:10.4135/9780857028044

Ferguson, T. (2005). *Game theory: Games in coalitional form*. Retrieved July 24, 2015, from: http://www.math.ucla.edu /~tom/Game_Theory/coal.pdf

Gardner, R. (1995). *Games for business and economics*. New York: John Wiley & Sons.

Gardner, R., & Ostrom, E. (1991). Rules and games. *Public Choice*, *70*(2), 121–149. doi:10.1007/BF00124480

Green, E. J., & Porter, R. H. (1984). Noncooperative collusion under imperfect price information. *Econometrica*, *52*(1), 87–100. doi:10.2307/1911462

Grüne-Yanoff, T., & Lehtinen, A. (2010). Philosophy of game theory. *Philosophy of Economics, 13*, 467-513.

Kebritchi, M., Hirumi, A., & Bai, H. (2010). The effects of modern mathematics computer games on mathematics achievement and class motivation. *Computers & Education*, *55*(2), 427–443. doi:10.1016/j.compedu.2010.02.007

Ling, C., Na-na, Y., & Yun-shan, S. (2014). The application of game theory in the Hercynian economic development. In *Management Science & Engineering (ICMSE), 2014 International Conference on* (pp. 794-799). IEEE.

Luo, Y. (2004a). A coopetition perspective of MNC–host government relations. *Journal of International Management*, *10*(4), 431–451. doi:10.1016/j.intman.2004.08.004

Luo, Y. (2004b). *Coopetition in international business*. Copenhagen, Denmark: Copenhagen Business School Press.

Luo, Y. (2005). Toward coopetition within a multinational enterprise: A perspective from foreign subsidiaries. *Journal of World Business, 40*(1), 71–90. doi:10.1016/j.jwb.2004.10.006

Mettler, T., & Rohner, P. (2009). E-procurement in hospital pharmacies: An exploratory multi-case study from Switzerland. *Journal of Theoretical and Applied Electronic Commerce Research, 4*(1), 23–38.

Mintzberg, H., Ahlstrand, B., & Lampel, J. (2005). *Strategy Safari: A Guided Tour Through The Wilds of Strategic Managament.* New York: Simon and Schuster.

Niyato, D., & Hossain, E. (2008). Competitive pricing for spectrum sharing in cognitive radio networks: Dynamic game, inefficiency of nash equilibrium, and collusion. Selected Areas in Communications. *IEEE Journal on, 26*(1), 192–202.

Ohlin, J. D. (2012). Nash Equilibrium and International Law. *European Journal of International Law, 23*(4), 915–940. doi:10.1093/ejil/chs060

Poon, S., & Swatman, P. (1999). An exploratory study of small business Internet commerce issues. *Information & Management, 35*(19), 9–18. doi:10.1016/S0378-7206(98)00079-2

Radner, R., Myerson, R., & Maskin, E. (1986). An example of a repeated partnership game with discounting and with uniformly inefficient equilibria. *The Review of Economic Studies, 53*(1), 59–69. doi:10.2307/2297591

Rich, P. (2015). Rethinking common belief, revision, and backward induction. *Mathematical Social Sciences, 75*, 102–114. doi:10.1016/j.mathsocsci.2015.03.001

Rotemberg, J. J., & Saloner, G. (1989). Tariffs vs quotas with implicit collusion. *The Canadian Journal of Economics. Revue Canadienne d'Economique, 22*(2), 237–244. doi:10.2307/135666

Rusko, R. (2005). The effects of a demand shock upon the market prices of the exported paper and pulp. *Forest Policy and Economics, 7*(3), 423–435. doi:10.1016/j.forpol.2003.08.002

Rusko, R. (2014a). Coopetition for Organizations. In M. Khosrow-Pour (Ed.), *Encyclopedia of Information Science and Technology* (3rd ed.). Hershey, PA: IGI Global.

Rusko, R. (2014b). Mapping the perspectives of coopetition and technology-based strategic networks: A case of smartphones. *Industrial Marketing Management, 43*(5), 801–812. doi:10.1016/j.indmarman.2014.04.013

Rusko, R. (2015). New business model: Intentional and unintentional degree one and degree two consumer coopetition in a branch of the Finnish game industry. *International Journal of Business Environment, 7*(3), 219. doi:10.1504/IJBE.2015.071221

Shubik, M. (1970). Game theory, behavior, and the paradox of the prisoner's dilemma: Three solutions. *The Journal of Conflict Resolution, 14*(2), 181–193. doi:10.1177/002200277001400204

Vogel, J. J., Vogel, D. S., Cannon-Bowers, J. A. N., Bowers, C. A., Muse, K., & Wright, M. (2006). Computer gaming and interactive simulations for learning: A meta-analysis. *Journal of Educational Computing Research, 34*(3), 229–243. doi:10.2190/FLHV-K4WA-WPVQ-H0YM

Yin, R. K. (1983). *Case Study Research: Design and Methods* (3rd ed.). Thousand Oaks, CA: Sage Publications.

Yin, Z., Jiang, A. X., Tambe, M., Kiekintveld, C., Leyton-Brown, K., Sandholm, T., & Sullivan, J. P. (2012). TRUSTS: Scheduling randomized patrols for fare inspection in transit systems using game theory. *AI Magazine, 33*(4), 59–72.

KEY TERMS AND DEFINITIONS

Collusion Equilibrium: An equilibrium between colluding firms from which none of the firms can not deviate without punishment of the competing firms.

Mixed Strategy: A strategy, where the players of the game change their pure strategies following particular probabilities in their moves.

Nash Equilibrium: In Nash equilibrium none of the players are willing to change his/her strategy alone.

One Shot Game: A game, where is only one move for each player.

Prisoner's Dilemma: Non-cooperative game situation in which the equilibrium of the game causes unpleasant outcome to the players. This outcome is the Nash equiliubrium.

Pure Strategy: A strategy in which a player will choose only one (same) move even though in the case of repeated game.

Repeated Game: A game where the players have several rounds, and therefore, moves.

Supergame: A repeated game.

Chapter 9
Conjoint Analysis with fMRI:
A Novel Analytical Approach to Neuromarketing

Jarmo Heinonen
Laurea University of Applied Sciences, Finland

ABSTRACT

Functional Magnetic Resonance Imaging (fMRI) is a very effective tool in neuromarketing. However, time limits, subject fatigue, fMRI costs, and participants' concentration are problematic. Conjoint analysis and its cards enable shortening the time and providing more attributes for evaluation. Conjoint analysis models of orthogonal matrices keep the amount of conjoint cards to a minimum which shortens the time spent in the fMRI machine and thus lowering costs. All conjoint cards are different and keep subjects concentrated during the test. fMRI is an efficient analyzing method of neuronal architecture and functions for the identification of the brain areas and networks. Conjoint analysis and fMRI are strong, combined methods to analyze customer needs and desires.

INTRODUCTION

Functional Magnetic Resonance Imaging (fMRI) is a very effective tool in neuromarketing research and analysis. However, as subjects cannot remain long inside the fMRI tube, there is the need for a method to shorten the research time. For researchers, limited time, subject fatigue (Nakagawa et al., 2013), fMRI costs (Sample & Adam, 2003), and the ability to keep subjects concentrated (Laufs & Tagliazucchi, 2014) are problematic. Regarding the last issue, one answer or solution may be conjoint analysis and its cards which allow shortening the time by providing more attributes for analysis regarding products and services. There is a way to improve fMRI research techniques by implementing a mixed method approach through conjoint analysis. This chapter introduces these two methods and describes the advantages of this type of research.

Conceptually, conjoint analysis should be examined holistically because it is not limited to just one method but rather combines different procedures. The fMRI is the most efficient method compared to other neuromarketing methods of analysis of neuronal architecture and functions. EEG or MEG may be applied, but they do not provide the deep data on human brain functioning as does the fMRI. As conjoint

DOI: 10.4018/978-1-4666-9989-2.ch009

analysis reveals the most meaningful attributes and their subgroups for the product or service, the fMRI connect these particular attributes (from conjoint cards) in the subjects' brain. Conjoint analysis and fMRI combined provide a helpful and effective method to analyze customer needs and desires.

Data Collecting Process in Conjoint Analysis

Conjoint analysis can be used as providing methodology for operationalizing the conceptual basis in a conjoint measurement framework (DeSarbo, Huff, Rolandelli, & Choi, 1994; Karabatsos, 2001). A prestudy must be conducted to find relevant attributes for the analysis, and these attributes can be discussed beforehand with customers, employees, or managerial staff. Sometimes the attributes are discussed with employees rather than with customers. In this manner, employees are involved in the study contributing with their own ideas about meaningful attributes concerning customers. On the other hand, researchers may find good attributes by themselves.

The Attributes in Conjoint Analysis

Of the attributes all the factor levels could be discrete, but one of them should be a continual factor. The discrete factor levels could be categorical and no assumption should made about the relationship between the factor and final scores or ranks. Continual factors sometimes demonstrate linear relationship which means the scores or ranks are expected to be linearly related to the factor. For example, price is ideal for the continual factor because if a person has learned to be loyal to a specific brand, the level of arousal he experiences in a purchasing situation may be quite low, and the individual simply selects the preferred brand and disregards the price. However, if the desired item is not available, high degrees of arousal capacity would remain the same although the actual level of arousal differs. It is only the degree to which the arousal capacity is activated in a specific situation that is dependent on the purchasing experience and on the situational characteristics on that occasion (Rajaniemi, 1992, p. 70).

Buyers are not all similar in their preferences and different preferences may require different product design responses. This, of course, enforces market segmentation and product differentiation. More specifically, the underlying principle is that if discernibly different buyer groups exist, special attention should be paid to the need for correspondingly differentiated product designs. The more important the differentiating characteristics of the buyer groups, the more important it is to take these characteristics into account in designing products.

The following relationship is also unveiled: the higher the level of product design testing among buyers, the greater the likelihood of identifying buyer's perceptions. Additionally, the more attributes are identified, the more effective the product design development process; the ease of segmenting buyers on the basis of attributes, and the desirability of design differentiation. The early identification of buyer-perceived attribute gaps may lead to identification of designer-caused attribute gaps (and vice versa) (Zaltman, LeMasters, & Heffring, 1982, pp. 129–135). Anttila (1990) highlighted that "only those particular product attributes which are salient or determinant to an individual should be used in the multiattribute model. The salient product attributes affect most significantly the total evaluation of the product in a brand choice situation. The choice among alternative brands is then assumed to be based on the salient attributes" (p. 107).

A choice between unattractive alternatives proves more difficult than choosing between two attractive alternatives. According to Nagpal and Krishnamurthy (2008), this is due to the nature of the task at hand. The task of choosing involves the attractiveness judgment which is more compatible with attractive alternatives than with unattractive ones. Hence, reframing the task to assure the conformity with the negative selection leads to compatibility between alternative valence and task reduces the decision time and the difficulty while strengthening the attribute recalls. (Zurawicki, 2010, p. 128). In real life, consumers have certainly more than two options from which to choose. As a matter of fact, we often face an abundance of choices from between and within the categories of products and services available. In very convincing terms, the renowned sociologist Schwartz (2005) addressed the choice overload and the related self-doubt, anxiety, and dread (not to mention the expense of time and energy) with which the consumers must cope. In numerous situations, it makes actually perfect sense to engage a consultant when facing a cornucopia of available goods.

There is another rule which independently guides the decider to save time and energy in narrowing down the search process. The corresponding mode of screening tends to focus on certain functionalities as well hedonic attributes, which matter most for the particular buyer or user. Since regret in contrast to mere disappointment is a self-evaluative judgment implying a potential error, there is some merit in the post-decision information search which may uncover the cause of miscalculation (Shani, Tykocinski, & Zeelenberg, 2008). Such an approach which would be typical of consumers whose goal is to learn from past mistakes. Yet, coping with regret suggests a possibility of the opposite standpoint. It is much easier to justify one's purchase decisions when relatively little information is available after the action took place.

Interestingly, while consumers might be willing to gather as much relevant data as possible before making a decision, after the purchase they gain time savings and are emotionally spared when ignoring additional information about the alternatives (Mishra, Shiv, & Nayakankuppam, 2008). Is there a connection between the size of the consideration set and the intensity of regret? Su, Chen, and Zhao (2009) believe so. In their experiments, which parallel Desmeules' (2002) mentioned above, the larger the set the more it hurts the decision makers to realize that it included a superior foregone option. However, when the better option was not originally a part of self-generated evoked set, this effect was far less pronounced. It is as if the unrecognized winner out of the larger pool of viable competitors is held in greater regard.

Orthogonality in Conjoint Cards

Virtually all conjoint applications reported in the extant literature, orthogonal arrays are used to implement full profile presentations (Green, Helsen, & Shandler, 1988, p. 392; Green & Srinivasan, 1978). An orthogonal array is a subset of all possible combinations that still allows estimation of the part-worth's for all main effects. Interactions in which the part-worth for a level of one factor depends on the level of another one are assumed to be negligible. In an orthogonal array, each level of one factor occurs with each level of another factor with equal or at least proportional frequencies, assuring independence of the main effects (SPSS, 1995). For example, if we have three main attributes and they all have five attribute levels, then 243 combinations would result ($=3^5$). The problem of ranking or evaluating each of these 243 objects is by no means easily resolved. In a factorial design, the 3^5 would still require 81 combinations.

On the other hand, an orthogonal array of only 27 combinations could test main effects for even a 3^{13} factorial design (Green, 1984). Orthogonality helps decreasing the number of questionnaire cards. The use of fractional factorial designs is a very common way to avoid respondent fatigue. Since the number of profiles presented increases multiplicatively with the number of attributes and levels, an approach that reduces the task for respondents seems attractive (Grover & Vriens, 2006; Reibstein, Bateson, & Boulding, 1988). Huber (1987), Karakaya and Awasti (2014) have suggested that the use of orthogonal designs may provide a higher degree of robustness over various task simplifications (e.g., ignoring levels and/or entire attributes), that subjects may employ in coping with the job of profile evaluation.

In particular, orthogonal designs could guard against possible sources of misspecification error that may occur when various simplifying decision strategies are employed (Green et al., 1988). The orthogonal contrasts which define effects and interactions can be readily determined from a table of orthogonal polynomials. The advantage of using orthogonal polynomials contrasts to define effects and interactions arises from the fact that orthogonal polynomials are so constructed that it is a term of any other term. This property of independence permits to compute individual regression coefficient independently, and also facilitates testing the significance of each coefficient (Green & Rao, 1971; Green & Srinivasan, 1978).

Reliability and Validity in Conjoint Analyses

The popularity of conjoint analysis appears to derive at least in part from its presumed superiority in reliability and validity over simpler, less expensive techniques such as collecting self-explicated attribute weights (Grover & Vriens, 2006; Leigh, MacKay, & Summers, 1984, p. 456). Leigh et al. (1984) report the results of a study designed to compare the test-retest reliability and predictive validity of several alternative techniques with that of self-explicated weights under the condition of all attributes being dichotomous. The findings fail to demonstrate greater reliability and validity for the conjoint analysis techniques considered.

There have been studies demonstrating a trial to investigate whether the number of factors presented, affects the method's reliability (Malhotra, 1982; Scott & Wright, 1976). All these studies allow concluding that as the number of factors increases, the method's reliability is reduced. However, it should be noted that all these studies have focused on the full profile approach and have ignored other data collection procedures (Reibstein et al., 1988).

The most important finding in the Reibstein, Bateson, and Bouldings (1988) study is that attribute set reliability is very high. The attribute set reliability is so high that it implies designing a conjoint study one does not have to be overly concerned with having all the attributes included in the design. Their study shows that if one possesses the key attributes included of which other attributes are or, are not also included, it will have minimal bearing (Reibstein et al. 1988). The conjoint method, across a variety of methods of data collection and across a number of product categories, appears to be reliable in an absolute sense. One can also rest fairly assured that the nature of the attributes selected has a minimal (significance) on the techniques reliability (Reibstein et al., 1988, p. 284).

In some conjoint studies, many (or all) of the attributes may be monotonic meaning that most of respondents order the attribute levels the same way; that is, "more is better". Examples include product durability, length of guarantee, price, convenience of application, and so forth. In such cases, some profiles could dominate others in an orthogonal array (i.e., some profiles may be at least as good as the dominated profile on all attributes and strictly better on at least one attribute). Although this situation would make the preference task easier to perform, in the real marketplace, buyers would not be likely to find dominance's; and even if dominances were found, buyers would be presumed to recognize them and to eliminate dominated options at the outset (Green et al., 1988).

Marketers consider product offerings as bundles of benefits (Lancaster, 1966). According to such approach, on one hand products incorporate features which are functional, measurable, and easily verifiable (e.g., gas mileage of a car model), while on the other hand, the attributes are more pleasure-oriented.

In that context, some hypotheses suggest that meeting these functional performance standards generates the satisfaction; while fulfilling the hedonic aspirations enhances the feeling of delight (Chitturi, Raghunathan, & Mahajan, 2008).

Huber and Hansen (1986) found that the predictive accuracy of profile pairs that were balanced to exhibit small differences in utility actually produced higher internal validity (even though the choices were more difficult to concluding points of Huber and Hansen's (1986, p. 163)) study is of particular interest: 1.) Thus, having trouble in deciding between alternatives appears to lead to greater richness in response and greater correspondence with subsequent choice, rather than the reverse option. 2.) It is reasonable to expect that more complex holdout choices would be best predicted by conjoint tasks that elicit analogously complex processing. In contrast to the above findings, the results of the Green et al. (1988) study provide no empirical support for higher internal validity when the model used to make up the validation set of stimuli is also applied to construct the calibration stimuli.

If one chooses to use a full-profile conjoint, results provide two suggestions on how its performance can be improved (Huber, Wittink, Fiedler, & Miller, 1993). First, the sensitivity of the full profile's predictive validity to the number of attributes reinforces the recommendation by Green and Srinivasan (1990) that a hybrid conjoint or ACA (Adaptive Conjoint Analysis) can be used when the number of attributes exceeds six. Secondly, the order effect found indicates that full profile is likely to be more effective when it is preceded by a warm-up task that familiarizes respondents with the attributes and their levels (Huber et al., 1993).

Conjoint Models

According to Green and Srinivasan (1990), there are three measuring structures in conjoint analysis: the compositional (self-explicated) approach, decompositional (conjoint analysis), and compositional/decompositional (e.g. hybrid, ACA). *Compositional* methods ask respondents to assess values for attribute levels, and use these values to build up preferences for attribute bundles or profiles (Huber, 1987). *Decompositional* methods begin with overall evaluations of objects defined on multiple attributes and derive values for attribute levels from these evaluations. With either method one can predict choice from a broad range of alternatives specified by the domain of the original attributes. Once individual choice has been modelled, the prediction of choice shares in simulators has been of great value to managers as a way to estimate the impact of a change in product formulation and/or price (Green & Srinivasan, 1990; Huber et al., 1993).

Both decompositional and compositional methods typically take judgment as inputs. These judgments are often assumed to be intervally scaled measures of preferences or of the importance of attributes. What one cares most about is choice, the selection of one brand from a set of available alternatives. Though this distinction between judgment and choice may at first appear to involve merely substituting categorical choice for an assessment of degree of preference, numerous researchers have stressed the differences in the psychological demands of judgment and choice (Huber et al., 1993). The hybrid models (Green, 1984) and the Adaptive Conjoint Analysis (ACA) model (Johnson, 1987) collect a limited number of full or partial profiles that serve as ways to refine self-explicated part-worths (ACA) or estimate additional group-level parameters (hybrid models). Because these approaches have fewer data demands than other conjoint methods, they have received extensive commercial application.

The Brain and fMRI

Taking advantage of conjoint analysis and fMRI can be a function of two approaches. First, the advances in the analysis of neuronal architecture and functions performed by different areas provide a hint to neuromarketers as to the foci of investigation on the cognitive, affective and behavioral reactions of the consumers. Clearly, the identification of the brain areas and networks which prove the most promising candidates to reflect various phenomena pertaining to buying brings a sense of direction in the applied experimental studies.

Secondly, and more importantly, advances in neuroscience help to understand the intricacies of people's feelings and thinking in every day's life when choosing and using resources. As a matter of fact, consumption is the essence of life and most human activities can be interpreted as such. This means that in terms of desires and ways to deal with them, marketers can learn much about the machinery which drives the customers from a broader perspective offered by neuroscience. At the same time marketing scholars are well advised to reach beyond the contributions which specifically deal with the neuronal aspects of the selection and purchasing of goods (Zurawicki, 2010, p. 242).

Consumers live in a world where not all the information is readily available (at least not instantaneously despite the internet). Consequently, our cognition might agonize over the best strategy. When faced with uncertainty and ambiguity, logic and conscious deliberation can only help to an emotional experience and it does not surprise that the somatic "hunches" are recruited to select the apparently optimal option. Indeed, it was shown (Bechara & Damasio, 2005; Hsu, Bhatt, Adolphs, Tranel, & Camerer, 2005) that the evaluation of ambiguous as opposed to risky choices involves different areas of the brain. Among the regions more active under conditions of ambiguity as opposed to risk the amygdala, the orbito frontal cortex (OFC) and the dorsomedial pre-frontal cortex (PFC).

By contrast, the dorsolateral striatum is preferentially activated during the risky condition. As the dorsal striatum is implicated in reward prediction, the result indicates that ambiguity reduces the anticipated reward of decisions. In the words of Overskeid (2000), when facing doubt people opt for the solution which feels the best and reduces the fear of unknown – laying a foundation of the intuitive decision-making. However, even if people pride themselves for being rational and logical, they still cannot defuse the emotions.

Logical evaluation of pros and cons helps people to make rational choices between different kinds of products or services. Sharot, Martino and Dolan (2009) point out that difficult choices between seemingly equivalent options are predetermined by more precise neural estimates computed in the brain even during the imaginary tasks. Second, talking oneself into a done deal is not just a symptom of self-persuasion and *ex post* rationalization – liking what one has for the sake of the peace of mind. It also reflects a genuine emotional form of the endowment effect as following the re-appraisal in the brain reward area. (Zuravicki 2010, pp. 105-161).

Coricelli, Critchley, Joffily, O'Doherty, Sirigu, and Dolan (2005) point to the role of the OFC which is strongly involved in both the experience and the anticipation of regret – an affectionate response upon learning what would have happened if a different decision was made. One confirmation is that the patients with damage to OFC do not experience regret while at the same time they perfectly capable of feeling anger and disappointment over the outcome of a decision (Camille et al., 2004). Other areas implicated in the emotion of regret are ACC and the hippocampus suggesting that one of the functions of regret is to remember the wish to retract and learn from that experience. The fact that the same pattern of the OFC activation occurs 1) when the regret is experienced following the unfavorable outcome and 2) before making a subsequent new decision in the same domain (for example, a new gamble) suggests that people are effected by possible regret already at the moment of elaborating new decisions (Coricelli et al., 2005).

Assuming that regret expresses lack of confidence in one's own competence and also derives from the feeling of responsibility for consequences of the choice made, factoring regret into mental calculations preceding the selection of an alternative does act as analgesic to sadness for not having done things differently. The introspective sensation of anticipatory regret emerges further as a control in pursuit of the best emotional result under circumstances. In cases when the fear of regret looms large and compounds the unpleasantness of difficult choices, the consumer tends to avoid making the decision altogether. Emulating in real life the choices of others – it presupposes that he decider has some feelings towards the opinion leaders – proves not only a pretty common but also an efficient rule of thumb. From the academic view this tendency, however, raises concern about the circularity of such an explanation is in turn, and one has to explain who and how influences the leaders.

It is also relevant that prices tend to be subject to the contagion effect not unlike the carryover phenomena cited earlier with respect to products. In particular, the presence of the extremely high-priced items can increase the reservation price for the less costly related product as well as for the product category as a whole (Krishna, Wagner, & Yoon, 2006).The so called "money illusion" posits that by simply changing the nominal representation of income, or dept for that matter, without changing the actual purchasing power, the average buyer feels like having more to spent (Shafir, Diamond, & Tversky, 1997). Indeed, a recent experiment confirmed that just increasing al the catalogue prices and the spending allowance by the same high proportion correlated with the greater activation in the ventromedial orbito frontal cortex (VMOFC) – the brains' reward processor (Weber, Rangel, Wibral, & Falk, 2009).

When prefeelings about the future develop, structures like the nucleus accumbens (NAcc) and the anterior regions of the ventral striatum excite correspondingly with the anticipation of the pleasant events, whereas simulation of painful future events distinctively activates the amygdala and/or the posterior ventral striatum. Therefore, a homeostatic balance of both systems might be important for generating adequate expectations under uncertainty (i.e., for the outcomes comprising both the rewarding and punishing elements) (Yacubian et al., 2006).

It follows from the previous comments that the simulations for the future may prove inaccurate not only due to the unknown/new facets of the impeding scenarios. Another factor of relevance relates to the distorted memories of the past to be discussed later. Additionally, in simulating things to happen people have a natural tendency to consider a "big picture" with limited attention to unessential details. The key elements are likewise retrieved from the memory. In reminiscing on past vacation it could be the image of the pristine palm beach, spacious hotel room with the ocean view, and a rich buffet table. Following such a model, the secondary or tertiary features (getting beach towels, booking excursions) may be simply omitted. Yet, the unessential event components impact the hedonic sum total of the experience.

Assuming that most events consist of a rather limited selection of the extremely positive or negative essential attributes and also comprise numerous moderately positive or negative essential attributes and also comprise numerous moderately positive and moderately adverse inessential attributes, the event's overall hedonic value would emerge as a weighted average of all those elements. Because simulations omit essential features, people tend to predict that good events will be worse than they actually turn out to be. Indeed, from the neurological perspective Tom, Fox, Trepel, and Poldrack (2007) showed that the degraded connectivity between the midbrain dopamine neurons and the brain stem serotonin and the brain stem serotonin system contributes to the increase of the emotionally influenced overvaluation of both gains and losses (Zurawicki, 2010).

Money as Continuous Attribute

Under practical circumstances shopping on an empty as opposed to a full stomach is a totally different experience. Low energy level (physical and psychological) makes controlling behavior much more laborious and likely to fail (Faber & Vohs, 2004). In a similar token, impulse buying may be more common at the end of the shopping trip or after a long day of decision-making. The mechanism of self-regulation in the human brain only begins to be understood. It is normally implemented by a neural circuit comprising various prefrontal regions, including the ventrolateral pre frontal cortex (VLPFC), and the subcortical limbic structures including the amygdala and striatum. Based on the extensive literature review, Cohen and Lieberman (2010) concluded that the VLPFC is engaged when a person attempts self-controlling regardless of whether it comes to motor response inhibition, dominating one's risky behavior, delaying gratification, regulating emotion, inhibiting memory or suppressing thoughts.

Certainly, avoiding intellectual exhaustion or reducing its scope is very crucial for the decision makers regardless of the context. Intriguing for our purpose are the consequences of consumer decision-making while in the depleted state. It has been argued that in such a case, consumers have a tendency to conserve effort and are less inclined to compromise. They concentrate on just one attribute (e.g., the lowest price), use only partial information, succumb to the dominance effect, or simply preserve the *status quo* and do not make a selection (Masicampo & Baumeister, 2008). Depletion influences also the memory aspect of consumer decisions – it significantly reduces the "self-choice" effect. However, the latter usually makes people remember better the choices they made themselves compared to the items chosen for them by others, such a tendency does not apply to decisions made during the depleted state suggesting that the exhausted mind uses a simplified selection process that produces a weaker memory mark (Baumeister, Sparks, Stillman, & Vohs, 2008).

Engelman, Capra, Noussair, and Berns (2009) noticed that in a lab experiment consisting of the expert financial advice (as opposed to the case of no such help); the subjects demonstrated a lesser activity in the areas involved in calculating the effects of the probability on the expected payoff. The affected network comprised the anterior cingulate cortex (ACC), dorsolateral pre frontal cortex (DLPFC), thalamus, medial occipital gyrus, and the anterior insula. As Seymor and McClure (2008) argue, there is a connection between the fact that people tend to value the options and prices in the relative rather than absolute terms and display strong sensitivity to exemplar and price anchors on the one hand and the functioning of the reward processing in the brain on the other. The relative valuation method may be necessary to represent values accurately given the limits of neuronal coding. In addition, the fluctuating perceptions of value may reflect the role of expectations in determining value based upon all the available information as confirmed by recent findings. The relevant studies point to the pre frontal cortex (PFC), striatum, and VMOFC when it comes to scaling of value (Seymour & McClure, 2008).

The Research and the Research Frame

Attributes are collected via open questions in a questionnaire as a pretest. By coding these answers, it is possible to reveal the most obvious attributes for conjoint cards. In the fMRI tube, the subjects will see the same conjoint cards as the preference group (Figure 1).

In the full-concept – also known as full-profile method – the subject is asked to rank, order, or score a set of profiles, or cards, according to its preference. In each of these profiles, all factors of interest are represented and a different combination of factor levels (features) appears. In this way, a full concept

Figure 1. Research frame

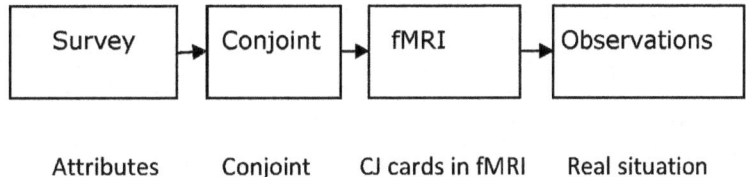

(that is, a complete product or service) is described on each profile. The respondent's task is to rank or score each profile from most to least preferred, most to least likely to purchase, or some other preference scale. From these rankings or scores, conjoint analysis derives utility scores for each factor level. These utility scores, analogously to regression coefficients, are called part-worth's and can be used to find the relative importance of each factor (Suleiman, Troitzsch, & Gilbert, 2012).

In Green and Srinivasan's (1990) overview of conjoint analysis, the most useful method in fMRI will be the preference model will be a parth-worth model, the data collection method full profile method, the stimulus set construction fractional factorial design, the stimulus presentation verbal and numerical description, the measurement scale for the dependent variable rating and ranking scales, and the estimation method metric method (multiple regression). Thus, conjoint analysis will easily combine with fMRI, resulting in the biggest differences between the stimulus presentation answering forms (i.e., cards (Figure 2).

The conjoint cards (Figure 2) will be shown inside the fMRI tube on a screen individually. Subject will choose the suitable percentage level with a sliding potentiometer operated by finger. The percentage will be the same as the participant preference for given bundle of attributes. For example conjoint card might consist of attributes regarding a new car and the subject should choose how likely she would like to buy it. There might be words: color (the main attribute) yellow (the sub-attribute); engine size (main attribute) 1.8 liter (sub-attribute); brand (main attribute) ford (sub-attribute). The next conjoint card will show different sub-attributes and the subject will then give preference percentage for the ongoing cards.

Technically speaking, the fMRI is scanning structural and functional imaging data analysis and can be performed by using Statistical Parametric Mapping (SPM) software. The SPM software package has been designed for the analysis of brain imaging data sequences. The sequences can be series of images from different cohorts, or time-series from the same subject. The functional data of each participant are going to be motion-corrected, coregistered with the structural data, and then spatially normalized into the standard MNI (Montreal Neurological Institute) space. The MNI space is the same as the grey

Figure 2. Task: Conjoint cards, main attributes and attribute levels

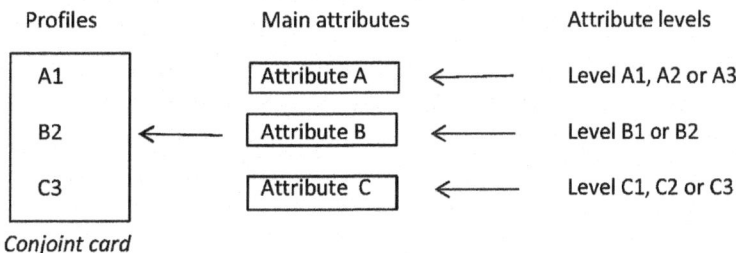

shadow behind brain figures, thus helping researchers to place markers in the correct anatomical position. The data could be smoothed in the spatial domain using a Gaussian kernel and all statistical analyses conducting by means of the general linear model. Cluster analysis and general linear model are typically used statistical methods with fMRI. Each experimental condition will be generated on the basis of the hemodynamic response functions implemented in SPM.

The fMRI is based on studying the vascular response in the brain to neuronal activity and can be used to study mental activity. It is most commonly performed using blood oxygenation level-dependent (BOLD) contrasts (Lindquist, Loh, Atlas, & Wager, 2009). This BOLD-contrast imaging is used in fMRI to observe different areas of the brain, which are found to be active at the moment. When analyzing the shape of the estimated hemodynamic response function (HRF), summary measures of psychological interest can be extracted and used to infer information of the underlying brain metabolic activity. The analysis for the entire group could be performed by computing linear t-contrast for each subject individually. All task-related effects can be reported at $p < 0.05$ corrected for multiple comparisons by means of the conservative FWE (family wise error) procedure implemented in SPM. Only those activation clusters exceeding a spatial extent threshold of 80 voxels (2*2*2 mm) should be reported where the voxel is the same as a three dimensional pixel.

Normally MR imaging will commence with the acquisition of the structural scans, followed by the experimental paradigm and functional scans. Before MR imaging will be performed, the tasks should be demonstrated and practiced outside the scanner. The total time of the fMRI test session per subject will normally take approximately 30-45 minutes and the total time about one hour per subject.

FUTURE RESEARCH DIRECTIONS

Neuromarketing is one field of neuroscience and customer relationships. Neuroeconomics and neuro-management research may benefit from combining conjoint analysis with fMRI. There are numerous opportunities (e.g., customer vs. employee, business to business, etc.) in future research, which might broaden the perspective for human decision-making.

CONCLUSION

This chapter described the concept of combined conjoint analysis and the fMRI technique. Subjects' exhaust and also managing fMRI use costs with limited amount of material for the research call for a method to shorten the time and also keeps the subjects awake and focused. Conjoint cards enable to use more attributes for subjects to evaluate, compared normal questionnaire.

Customers might not know by themselves how they make their decisions to buy. There is always emotion and previous decisions. Conjoint analysis is a good analyzing tool for products or services and precisely its attributes and sub-attributes. Conjoint will reveal which main attributes (e.g., color or price or model) means most for the customer and which one from sub-attributes of the specific main attribute they prefer most (e.g., yellow, green, blue or red). Full or partial profiles conjoint analysis that serve as ways to refine self-explicated part-worths (Adaptive Conjoint Analysis) or estimate additional group-level parameters (hybrid models) are needed.

However, simultaneously to revealing the best combination between the attributes, it should be known which of those attributes makes the customers really act. fMRI may solve this challenge. In our brain, the greater activation in the VMOFC, the brains' reward processor (Weber et al., 2009) show if particular attribute have bigger effect than the others like the difference between conjoint cards and their attributes. On the contrary value may reflect the role of expectations in determining value based upon all the available information. The studies point to the PFC, striatum, and VMOFC when customers are scaling value (Seymour & McClure, 2008). But how can we predict when we do not have all the information? If there are new attributes such as new color, model, type, or even new instructions to use? By using conjoint cards we can differentiate every piece (attributes) from each other from the product and calculate its utilities. Different cards and their utility scores can be calculated and fMRI show the activity in the brain between these cards.

Avoiding intellectual exhaustion or reducing its scope is very crucial for the consumer in the decision-making process. Customers have a tendency to conserve effort and are less inclined to compromise by concentrating on just one attribute, partial information, the dominance effect, or do not make a selection (Masicampo & Baumeister, 2008). By revealing these salient attributes – such as price – with conjoint cards and comparing the results to fMRI's markers from the brain there may be a good base for marketers to choose those attributes that they should concentrate on in their targeted market or marketing segments.

For fMRI researchers, subjects fatigue (Nakagawa et al., 2013), fMRI costs (Sample & Adam, 2003), and how to keep subjects concentrated (Laufs & Tagliazucchi, 2014) are problematic. Conjoint analysis models use orthogonal matrices to keep the amount of conjoint cards as minimum as possible. This will shorten the time in fMRI tube and keep the costs low. All conjoint cards are different except for those which will be used for significant tests to keep subjects alert and focused during the test.

Lancaster (1966) said that product can be seen as bundles of benefits and in the same way we can see products or services as a variety of different kinds of attributes. Conjoint analysis will distinguish the attributes from each other and evaluate their utilities or significance for customers. fMRI enables to find out how strong is the feeling for these attributes – and in which part of the brain the stimulus is created. The latter will indicate do they hate it (response in amygdala) or prefer (marker in striatum) to buy.

REFERENCES

Anttila, M. (1990). *Consumer price perception and preferences: a reference price model of brand evaluation and a conjoint analysis of price utility structures*. Helsinki.

Baumeister, R. F., Sparks, E. A., Stillman, T. F., & Vohs, K. D. (2008). Free will in consumer behavior: Self-control, ego depletion, and choice. *Journal of Consumer Psychology*, *18*(1), 4–13. doi:10.1016/j.jcps.2007.10.002

Bechara, A., & Damasio, A. R. (2005). The Somtic Marker Hypothesis: A Neural Theory of Economic Decision. *Games and Economic Behavior*, *52*(2), 336–372. doi:10.1016/j.geb.2004.06.010

Camille, N., Coricelli, G., Sallet, J., Pradat-Diehl, P., Duhamel, J.-R., & Sirigu, A. (2004). The involvement of the orbitofrontal cortex in the experience of regret. *Science*, *304*(5674), 1167–1170. doi:10.1126/science.1094550 PMID:15155951

Cattin, P., & Wittink, D. R. (1982). Commercial Use of Conjoint Analysis: A Survey. *Journal of Marketing*, *46*(3), 44. doi:10.2307/1251701

Chitturi, R., Raghunathan, R., & Mahajan, V. (2008). Delight by Design: The Role of Hedonic Versus Utilitarian Benefits. *Journal of Marketing*, *72*(3), 48–63. doi:10.1509/jmkg.72.3.48

Cohen, J. R., & Lieberman, M. D. (2010). The common neural basis of exerting self-control in multiple domains. In *Society to Brain: The New Sciences of Self-Control* (pp. 141–162). New York: Oxford University Press. doi:10.1093/acprof:oso/9780195391381.003.0008

Coricelli, G., Critchley, H. D., Joffily, M., O'Doherty, J. P., Sirigu, A., & Dolan, R. J. (2005). Regret and its avoidance: A neuroimaging study of choice behavior. *Nature Neuroscience*, *8*(9), 1255–1262. doi:10.1038/nn1514 PMID:16116457

de Bont, C. J. P. M. (1992). *Consumer Evaluations of Early Product-concepts*. Delft University Press.

DeSarbo, W. S., Huff, L., Rolandelli, M. M., & Choi, J. (1994). Service Quality: New Directions in Theory and Practice. In *On the Measurement of Perceived Service Quality: A Conjoint Analysis Approach* (pp. 201–223). Thousand Oaks, CA: SAGE Publications, Inc.

Desmeules, R. (2002). Desmeules / The Impact of Variety on Consumer Happiness The Impact of Variety on Consumer Happiness: Marketing and the Tyranny of Freedom. *Academy of Marketing Science Review*, (12): 1–33.

Engelmann, J. B., Capra, C. M., Noussair, C., & Berns, G. S. (2009). Expert Financial Advice Neurobiologically "Offloads" Financial Decision-Making under Risk. *PLoS ONE*, *4*(3), e4957. doi:10.1371/journal.pone.0004957 PMID:19308261

Faber, R. J., & Vohs, K. D. (2004). To buy or not to buy?: Self-control and self-regulatory failure in purchase behavior. In R. F. Baumeister & K. D. Vohs (Eds.), *Handbook of self-regulation: Research, theory, and applications* (pp. 509–524). New York: Guilford Press.

Green, P. E. (1984). Hybrid Models for Conjoint Analysis: An Expository Review. *JMR, Journal of Marketing Research*, *21*(2), 155. doi:10.2307/3151698

Green, P. E., Helsen, K., & Shandler, B. (1988). Conjoint Internal Validity under Alternative Profile Presentations. *The Journal of Consumer Research*, *15*(3), 392–397. doi:10.1086/209177

Green, P. E., & Rao, V. R. (1971). Conjoint Measurement for Quantifying Judgmental Data. *JMR, Journal of Marketing Research*, *8*(3), 355. doi:10.2307/3149575

Green, P. E., & Srinivasan, V. (1978). Conjoint Analysis in Consumer Research: Issues and Outlook. *The Journal of Consumer Research*, *5*(2), 103–123. doi:10.1086/208721

Green, P. E., & Srinivasan, V. (1990). Conjoint Analysis in Marketing: New Developments with Implications for Research and Practice. *Journal of Marketing*, *54*(4), 3. doi:10.2307/1251756

Grover, R., & Vriens, M. (2006). *The Handbook of Marketing Research: Uses, Misuses, and Future Advances*. SAGE Publications.

Holbrook, M. B. (1994). The Nature of Customer Value: An Axiology of Services in the Consumption Experience. In *Service Quality*. Thousand Oaks, CA: SAGE Publications. doi:10.4135/9781452229102.n2

Hsu, M., Bhatt, M., Adolphs, R., Tranel, D., & Camerer, C. F. (2005). Neural Systems Responding to Degrees of Uncertainty in Human Decision-Making. *Science, 310*(5754), 1680–1683. doi:10.1126/science.1115327 PMID:16339445

Huber, J. (1987). Conjoint Analysis: How we got here and where we are. In *Proceedings of the Sawtooth Software Conference on Perpetual Mapping, Conjoint Analysis, and Computer Interviewing* (pp. 237–252). Ketchum, ID: Sawtooth Software.

Huber, J., & Hansen, D. (1986). Testing the impact of dimensional complexity and affective differences of paired concepts in adaptive conjoint analysis. *Advances in Consumer Research. Association for Consumer Research (U. S.), 14*, 159–163.

Huber, J., Wittink, D. R., Fiedler, J. A., & Miller, R. (1993). The Effectiveness of Alternative Preference Elicitation Procedures in Predicting Choice. *JMR, Journal of Marketing Research, 30*(1), 105. doi:10.2307/3172517

Johnson, R. M. (1987). Adaptive Conjoint Analysis. *Sawtooth Software Conference on Perpetual Mapping, Conjoint Analysis, and Computer Interviewing* (pp. 253–265). Ketchum, ID: Sawtooth Software.

Karabatsos, G. (2001). The Rasch model, additive conjoint measurement, and new models of probabilistic measurement theory. *Journal of Applied Measurement, 2*(4), 389–423. PMID:12011506

Karakaya, F., & Awasthi, A. (2014). Robustness and sensitivity of conjoint analysis versus multiple linear regression analysis. *International Journal of Data Analysis Techniques and Strategies, 6*(2), 121. doi:10.1504/IJDATS.2014.062461

Krishna, A., Wagner, M., Yoon, C., & Adaval, R. (2006). Effects of Extreme-Priced Products on consumer Reservation Prices. *Journal of Consumer Psychology, 16*(2), 176–190. doi:10.1207/s15327663jcp1602_8

Lancaster, K. J. (1966). A New Approach to Consumer Theory. *Journal of Political Economy, 74*.

Laufs, H., & Tagliazucchi, E. (2014). Beware of sleep during resting state fMRI. *F1000Posters, 5*(806).

Leigh, T. W., MacKay, D. B., & Summers, J. O. (1984). Reliability and Validity of Conjoint Analysis and Self-Explicated Weights: A Comparison. *JMR, Journal of Marketing Research, 21*(4), 456. doi:10.2307/3151471

Lindquist, M. A., Loh, J. M., Atlas, L. Y., & Wager, T. D. (2009). Modeling the Hemodynamic Response Function in fMRI: Efficiency, Bias and Mis-modeling. *NeuroImage, 45*(1Suppl), S187–S198. doi:10.1016/j.neuroimage.2008.10.065 PMID:19084070

Malhotra, N. K. (1982). Structural Reliability and Stability of Nonmetric Conjoint Analysis. *JMR, Journal of Marketing Research, 19*(2), 199–207. doi:10.2307/3151620

Masicampo, E. J., & Baumeister, R. F. (2008). Toward a Physiology of Dual-Process Reasoning and Judgment: Lemonade, Willpower, and Expensive Rule-Based Analysis. *Psychological Science, 19*(3), 255–260. doi:10.1111/j.1467-9280.2008.02077.x PMID:18315798

Mishra, H., Shiv, B., & Nayakankuppam, D. (2008). *The Blissful Ignorance Effect: Pre Versus Post Action Effects on Outcome-Expectancies Arising from Precise and Vague Information (SSRN Scholarly Paper No. ID 1158496).* Rochester, NY: Social Science Research Network.

Nagpal, A., & Krishnamurthy, P. (2008). Attribute Conflict in Consumer Decision Making: The Role of Task Compatibility. *The Journal of Consumer Research, 34*(5), 696–705. doi:10.1086/521903

Nakagawa, S., Sugiura, M., Akitsuki, Y., Hosseini, S. M. H., Kotozaki, Y., & Miyauchi, C. M. et al. (2013). Compensatory Effort Parallels Midbrain Deactivation during Mental Fatigue: An fMRI Study. *PLoS ONE, 8*(2), e56606. doi:10.1371/journal.pone.0056606 PMID:23457592

Overskeid, G. (2000). The slave of the passions: Experiencing problems and selecting solutions. *Review of General Psychology, 4*(3), 284–309. doi:10.1037/1089-2680.4.3.284

Rajaniemi, P. (1992). *Conceptualization of product involvement as a property of a cognitive structure.* Acta Wasaensia, Vaasa.

Reibstein, D., Bateson, J. E. G., & Boulding, W. (1988). Conjoint Analysis Reliability: Empirical Findings. *Marketing Science, 7*(3), 271–286. doi:10.1287/mksc.7.3.271

Rust, R. T., & Oliver, R. L. (Eds.). (1994). *Service quality: new directions in theory and practice.* Thousand Oaks, CA: Sage Publications.

Sample, I., & Adam, D. (2003). *The brain can"t lie.* Retrieved June 11, 2015, from: http://www.theguardian.com/science/2003/nov/20/neuroscience.science

Schwartz, B. (2005). *The Paradox of Choice: Why More Is Less.* New York: Harper Perennial.

Scott, J. E., & Wright, P. (1976). Modeling an Organizational Buyer's Product Evaluation Strategy: Validity and Procedural Considerations. *JMR, Journal of Marketing Research, 13*(3), 211. doi:10.2307/3150730

Seymour, B., & McClure, S. M. (2008). Anchors, scales and the relative coding of value in the brain. *Current Opinion in Neurobiology, 18*(2), 173–178. doi:10.1016/j.conb.2008.07.010 PMID:18692572

Shafir, E., Diamond, P., & Tversky, A. (1997). Money Illusion. *The Quarterly Journal of Economics, 112*(2), 341–355. doi:10.1162/003355397555208

Shani, Y., Tykocinski, O. E., & Zeelenberg, M. (2008). When ignorance is not bliss: How feelings of discomfort promote the search for negative information. *Journal of Economic Psychology, 29*(5), 643–653. doi:10.1016/j.joep.2007.06.001

Sharot, T., Martino, B. D., & Dolan, R. J. (2009). How Choice Reveals and Shapes Expected Hedonic Outcome. *The Journal of Neuroscience, 29*(12), 3760–3765. doi:10.1523/JNEUROSCI.4972-08.2009 PMID:19321772

Su, S., Chen, R., & Zhao, P. (2009). Do the size of consideration set and the source of the better competing option influence post-choice regret? *Motivation and Emotion, 33*(3), 219–228. doi:10.1007/s11031-009-9127-3

Suleiman, R., Troitzsch, K. G., & Gilbert, N. (2012). *Tools and Techniques for Social Science Simulation.* New York: Springer Science & Business Media.

Tom, S. M., Fox, C. R., Trepel, C., & Poldrack, R. A. (2007). The neural basis of loss aversion in decision-making under risk. *Science, 315*(5811), 515–518. doi:10.1126/science.1134239 PMID:17255512

Weber, B., Rangel, A., Wibral, M., & Falk, A. (2009). The medial prefrontal cortex exhibits money illusion. Proceedings of the National Academy of Sciences, pnas.0901490106. doi:10.1073/pnas.0901490106

Yacubian, J., Gläscher, J., Schroeder, K., Sommer, T., Braus, D. F., & Büchel, C. (2006). Dissociable systems for gain- and loss-related value predictions and errors of prediction in the human brain. *The Journal of Neuroscience, 26*(37), 9530–9537. doi:10.1523/JNEUROSCI.2915-06.2006 PMID:16971537

Zaltman, G., LeMasters, K., & Heffring, M. (1982). *Theory construction in marketing: some thoughts on thinking*. Toronto: John Wiley & Sons Canada, Limited.

Zeithaml, V. A. (2009). *Delivering Quality Service*. New York: Free Press.

Zeithaml, V. A., Parasuraman, A., & Berry, L. L. (1990). *Delivering Quality Service: Balancing Customer Perceptions and Expectations*. London: Simon and Schuster.

Zurawicki, L. (2010). *Neuromarketing*. Berlin: Springer Berlin Heidelberg. doi:10.1007/978-3-540-77829-5

ADDITIONAL READING

Glimcher, P. W. (2010). *Foundations of Neuroeconomic Analysis*. Oxford: Oxford University Press. doi:10.1093/acprof:oso/9780199744251.001.0001

Vriens, M. (1995). *Conjoint Analysis In Marketing*. Capelle a/d Ijssel: Labyrint Publication

Wallisch, P., Lusignan, M., Benayoun, M., Baker, T. I., Dickey, A. S., & Hatsopoulos, N. G. (Eds.). (2009). *Front Matter. Matlab for Neuroscientists* (pp. i–iii). London: Academic Press.

KEY TERMS AND DEFINITIONS

Attribute: Is the classical term used in conjoint analysis for characteristics of target qualities. *Attribute levels* are characteristics for this given attribute. Attributes can be discrete (descriptive, nominal) or continuous (numeral).

Conjoint Card: Is the classical term used in conjoint analysis to denote data collecting questionnaires from target group.

Data Collection Method: In conjoint analysis is trade-off method or the full-profile method.

Estimation Method: In conjoint analysis is metric method (multiple regression), nonmetric method (LINMAP, MONANOVA, PREFMAP, Johnson's nonmetric algorithm) or choice-probability-based method (logit, probit).

Fulfillment: Implies that a satiation level is known, as in the basic needs of water, food, and shelter. Observers of human behavior, however, understand that each of these need levels can be (and frequently is) exceeded in various ways. Thus, consumer researchers have moved away from the literal meaning of fulfilment or satisfaction and now pursue this concept as the consumer experiences and describes it.

Model of Preference: In conjoint analysis is vector model, ideal point model, part-worth model or mixed model. *Part-worth* model is assumed to be an additive function of values (worth's) of its components (i.e., attribute levels).

Stimulus Set Construction: For the full-profile method in conjoint analysis is fractional factorial design or full factorial design. In *fractional factorial design* only a fraction of the master design is reflected in the attribute profile. *Full factorial design* present all possible attribute combinations.

Utility: Is the classical term used in conjoint analysis to denote estimated results. In this text utility corresponds to perceived service or products and their attributes.

Value: Is the customers overall assessment of the utility of a product based on perceptions of what is received and what is given. Value of any product (i.e., any good, service, event or idea) depends upon its role in providing services that create some consumption experience. No consumption experience is likely to be interpretable as displaying only one pure type of value. Rather, each instance of consuming behaviour tends to engage various kinds of value and thereby to blur the distinctions among them. Value varies among the people who make evaluations. Value is situational, value is relativistic in the sense that it depends on the context which a value judgments occurs.

Chapter 10
Plasticity and Memory in the Financial Markets

Oxana Karnaukhova
Southern Federal University, Russia

Inna Nekrasova
Southern Federal University, Russia

ABSTRACT

The chapter questions the applicability of the Efficient Market Hypothesis (EMH) for analysis of financial markets. The overall goal is to analyze methods of forecasting future prices of financial assets based on the concept of the fractal market structure and long-term memory of past prices. Fractals in the financial markets are interpreted either as investors with different investment horizons or as a configuration of the price movement on chart. This chapter examines the fractal structure of financial markets, nonlinear methods of analysis of financial markets, plasticity and long-term memory to long-term investment horizons of financial markets, fractal analysis of financial markets, new approaches to forecast prices of financial assets, which eliminate shortcomings of the linear paradigm.

INTRODUCTION

This chapter discusses applicability of the Efficient Market Hypothesis (EMH) for the analysis of financial markets. The overall goal is to analyze methods of forecasting future prices of financial assets based on the concept of the fractal market structure and long-term memory of past prices. Fractals in the financial markets can be interpreted either as investors with different investment horizons or as a configuration of the price movement on the chart.

The need to explore the EMH is initiated by the idea that traditional analytical methods used in practice and in academia are based on the linear paradigm and exclude the fractal structure of the market. This paradigm postulates that in the situation of external influences' absence, any system, including markets, seeks balance: demand equals supply, everything is stable, and trends do not appear accidentally. Linear theory is based on the proposition that markets have no memory: news is announced then markets react and forget immediately. However, this theory does not match our every-day reality of the financial markets.

DOI: 10.4018/978-1-4666-9989-2.ch010

On the contrary, recent research confirms ineffectiveness of the financial markets. This inefficiency is verified by existence of the so-called market anomalies "calendar anomalies", "price anomalies", "effect size", "effect of the news", and so forth. Such anomalies indicate the long-term memory existing in the financial markets. In these circumstances, the hypothesis of the Fractal Market Hypothesis (FMH) has been reassessed and used as the background of the analysis for the chapter.

Interestingly, on the border between the conflicts of opposing forces, one can find not nascent chaotic, disordered structures, but instead a spontaneous rise of the higher level self-organization. Moreover, the structure of such self-organization is of new kind, irrelevant to the older Newton scheme. As soon as markets have a long-term memory at the long-term investment horizons, the past behavior of price influences its future value. The intrigue lies in the fact that if the assumption of random movement in prices in the capital markets is incorrect, most of the current theories, empirical research, and methodological approaches are rendered useless. New methods must displace older methods which do not involve independence of variables and normality distribution of variables. These new methods should include fractals and nonlinear dynamics which are being applicable to real data and demonstrate greater efficiency.

Within the theory of markets, the nonlinear paradigm includes the concept of long-term memory: events that may affect the markets for a long time, and perhaps infinitely. The modern linear paradigm allows only the possibility of short-term memory, in the best case, in submartingal form. Inability of a linear system is due to the fact that the statistical deterministic systems allow a small degree of freedom. This fact significantly limits their ability to adapt; they are forced to give way to competitors in the development.

This chapter will attempt to answer the following issues:

- Fractal structure of financial markets
- Nonlinear methods of analysis of financial markets
- Plasticity and long-term memory to long-term investment horizons of financial markets
- Fractal analysis of financial markets
- New approaches to forecast prices of financial assets which eliminate shortcomings of the linear paradigm

Therefore, the practical significance lies in the intention to equip academics and practitioners with new methods and tools for analysis and forecasting future development and dynamic of the financial markets.

THEORETICAL FRAMEWORK

Analysis of the key theoretical concepts explaining financial market behavior should begin with the founding father of the traditional theory of market, Loui Bachelier (1964). In 1900 he attempted to defend his doctorate thesis titled, *Theory of Speculation*, in which the basic question of price development was articulated. Most approaches of that time centered on the simple cause-answer scheme: if an event happens, prices react with a definite and expected result. Such connection could be easily observed after an event, but could hardly be predicted in advance. Bachelier has chosen another way to explain this phenomenon by attempting to apply theory probability to financial market development and to estimate the probability of price instability via a set of factors. He discovered existing analogy between heat dispersion within a substance (or Brownian movement of molecules in water) and fluctuation of bonds costs.

By comparing them, he demonstrated that diagramming monthly or annual fluctuations created the so-called Gaussian curve. In the centre of the curve, a large number of small changes is grouped around while a few of big changes are spread on edges. Bachelier used the Brownian movement description to create an analogous equalization for probability of price fluctuations. The risk of buying bonds was considered a standard deflection in the Gaussian curve.

This theory was applied in practice when Bachelier calculated the profit probability for a buyer of a 45-day call (with a mistake of one percent). Although by 1900 several books about financial markets had already been published, this sphere of economics was not considered a research field. Therefore, Bachelier did not earn his doctorate degree; however, some 50 years later his dissertation was discovered, and on its foundation the theory of markets, investment, and finance was created. Harry Max Markowitz (1952) used Bachelier's results to create a theory of portfolio. The idea was as follows: If there are two portfolios of investments, the variant with the maximum expected average profitability and minimal dispersion (risk) must be chosen.

For calculation of the average mean value, the expected profit for each type of stocks in a portfolio is multiplied with the weight coefficient. The dispersion is calculated using correlation activities between stocks. On the base of this theory, the follower of Markowitz William Sharp developed the Capital Active Pricing Model (CAPM) to help calculate the threshold value of the expected delivery enclosure of investments and to make a decision (Sharp, 1964).

In the 1970s when the new type of market was born (the market of calls), Black and Scholes (1973) moved further toward classic financial theory and created a Equation for the calculation of call cost. Today, this Equation (with some corrections) is used by corporate financiers while buying unexpected risk insurance. In the same period, Fama (1976) established the law of the Brownian movement in financial markets. He Equationted the hypothesis of the effective market and demonstrated the correlation between effective market activities and Brownian movement. The hypothesis came from the idea that in the ideal market, the securities cost completely reflect information, which could predict future events. In financial markets, the number of buyers is equal to the number of sellers. In such circumstances, both buyer and seller agree upon a price referred to as "the right price". To extend this idea to the fund market as a whole, one can conclude the common market price also should be "right".

In other words, considering available information the published stock price should reflect the best common market of future profit. However, following the fund market crisis of 1987, which did not comply with the standard model of financial risk, the new method Value at Risk (VaR) was established. In the beginning it was used by a group of financial institutions in the USA, and only in 1994 was this method openly published by financiers of JPMorgan Chase & Company. In 1997, this method appeared in the field of vision of state institutions in Europe and the USA which were responsible for regulation and control over financial activities. For a state, it was extremely convenient instrument to control market risks in trade portfolios banks, investment, and insurance companies.

Therefore, this method has spread among financial institutions throughout the world. The method called Expected Shortfall or Conditional Value at Risk (CVaR) was first employed in the beginning of the 2000s as an alternative to the VaR method. It was linked with the fact that the popular VaR has some shortcomings. The core shortcoming is underestimation of risks in case, if waste distribution has so called "heavy tails". Heavy-tailed distribution means probability distribution which tails are not exponentially bounded. Synonimous terms are the fat-tailed, the long-tailed distributions, and together with the heavy-tailed distributions are used to describe the subexponential distributions. The Shortfall is a more conservative risk measure than the VaR. For the same level of probability, this method demands to reserve greater capital, but at the same time this measure can more accurately estimate risks in case of "heavy tails".

Today, the methods for the analysis and prediction of financial market behavior are borrowed from neuroeconomics and have become extremely popular. Many economists believe neuroeconomics as an interdisciplinary field in its broadest sense is a neurobiology of decision-making (decision neuroscience) (Glimcher & Rustichini, 2004; Rilling et al., 2008). It combines neuroscience, economics, psychology, and other disciplines to form the basis of new knowledge about mechanisms of decision-making and helps to simulate the behavior of humans and animals.

It is important to note that neuroeconomics focuses on the study of the neurobiological mechanisms of the simplest (perceptual) solutions, as well as on the nature of irrationality on causes of stronger emotional response to a loss than to acquisition (loss aversion) (Tom et al., 2007). Temporal discounting has been intensively studied; namely, the causes of disproportional preference of momentary interest in comparison with interest in deferred time (McClure et al., 2004). For the research of financial market memory, the most interesting is the study of brain mechanisms determining subjective utility in the selection process of possible alternatives, the search for an answer of how the human brain considers risks when making financial decisions. This aspect also links with consumer behavior (Knutson et al., 2005; Kuhnen & Knutson, 2005); namely, the perception of price and advertising (Klucharev et al., 2011; Plassmann et al., 2008).

RESEARCH QUESTION

The irrational behavior of investors which does not fit into traditional regulatory economic theory is the result of evolutionary selection embodied in the structure and function of neural nets of the brain. This irrational behavior is expressed in the so-called market anomalies. In turn, market anomalies confirm existence of the fractal structure of financial markets and a long-term memory. In neuroeconomic theory, the greatest potential in terms of applicability to the financial markets analysis is in the Fractal Market Hypothesis (FMH). In the FMH framework, financial markets may be considered an analogue of neural brain networks, and fractals (investors with different investment horizons) as an analogue of neurons.

To assume that investment decisions can be predicted on the basis of analysis of the information impact on various neurons (fractals), the disclosure of relevant neural mechanisms opens new horizons in understanding the nature of the investors' behavior in financial markets. For this reason, market anomalies should the subject of further consideration on the basis of comparative analysis of the FMH and classical Efficient Market Hypothesis (EMH) as mentioned in the Introduction.

METHODOLOGY

The applicability of basic assumptions of the EMH model and normality of distribution of price changes in financial markets should first be questioned. EMH researchers interested in fund markets discovered a number of anomalies, thus giving rise to some doubts about the assumptions of normality. One such anomalie was discovered in 1964 by Osborne in his study of the density function of profits in the stock market; namely, the tails of this function are thicker than a size of normally distributed value. However, Osborne did not pay any attention to this issue.

Fama (1965) discovered while studying daily profits that profits have a negative asymmetry: the greater number of observations was concentrated in the left tail than in the right. Moreover, tails of distribution are thicker and the peak of average value is much higher than predicted by normal distribution. This fact was later verified by other research. For instance, in 1997 the Dow-Jones index during the same day fell by 7.7% with the lowest probability. In July, 2002, the index fell three times in seven days with the lowest probability. On October 19, 1987, the index fell by 29.2% which was the worst trading day in the 20th century. According to the standard model of financial theory, such an event could occur in less than one event per 10^{50}.

The applicability of the EMH should also be examined. Following Fama's publications, much research was devoted to fortuity of movements in share prices on the stock market in order to demonstrate efficiency of the capital market. Contrarily, recent research confirms inefficiency of different capital markets by discovery of so-called market anomalies. Basic anomalies on fund markets can be divided into following types:

1. **Calendar Anomalies:** These are effects influencing the anomaly of price behavior and being dependent on timely, calendar, and seasonal factors. Typical calendar anomalies are effect of month, effect of a weekday, effect of pre-holidays and holidays, effect of weekends, effect of the New Year, mid-month effect, mid-day effect, full moon effect, and seasonal effect. Calendar anomalies are revealed not only in fund markets, but also on resource, monetary markets, etc. Some of them are about degeneration, but some are sustainable. The brightest and frequently pronounced is "the effect of January": during at least the past 70 years, an excess of the average stock returns in January over their profitability in other months has been observed. On the New York Stock Exchange, the size of excess is about three percentage points. In the last 25 years, this stock exchange also demonstrates "the week day effect": namely, on Mondays dividend yield almost always has a negative value. For instance, the Russian stock market demonstrates that trading sessions on Monday start with "sagging", which confirms the presence of "the beginning of the week effect" on the Russian stock market.

2. **The Size Effect:** It is considered that small-cap stocks tend to behave better than the larger stocks with the same risk indicators. One of such research follows this anomaly during the period 1926-1980. Based on the size of the companies listed on market, all stocks were divided into quintiles. The quantile with the smallest capitalization yield exceeds the yield in other quintiles, as well as the indices yield. This effect became very popular in press and academic journals, such as the *Journal of Financial Economics*. The company Dimensional Fund Advisors (DFA) provided a research of the stock portfolio of small-cap companies and found abnormally high returns that differ from predicted by the model CAPM. But after publication of the results abnormally high (due to "the size effect") revenues in the US market gradually began to decrease, and more recent studies have recorded statistically insignificant or significantly smaller revenues compared with the period 1926-1980s.

3. **Price Anomalies:** Trade ideas, based on price anomalies, are one of the most widespread. There are a lot of confirmations of the fact that investors often overestimate growth prospects of companies or underestimate the market value of companies. It occurs because pricing strategies bring higher revenues due to mistakes of typical investor, and not because they are potentially more risky. There are at least two well-known examples of price anomalies. The first one is low coefficient P/B (Price/ Balance sheet profit). The research of this phenomenon embraced almost all stocks at

NYSE, AMEX and NASDAQ during the period 1963 – 1990s. Stocks were divided into 10 groups using the coefficient P/B and have been ranged. It was discovered that income securities with the worst P / B superior income securities with the best P / B in each decile by 8% to 21.4%. The second example as low coefficient P/E (Price/Yield) demonstrates that stocks with a low P / E have an increased yield in comparison with a high P / E stocks. Some research on this matter has been conducted on the USA bond market.

The share prices of various companies from 1973 to 1993 were analyzed. These shares were divided into quintile, based on indicators of the P / E, and profitability for each group compared with the average. It was found that the profitability of the group with the lowest P / E significantly exceeds average results of the year and the quarter in particular. Moreover, the increased yield was detected for securities on which the release of positive corporate news was distributed, as well as for securities with negative releases. It means that any news, positive or negative, will impact positively on the securities with low P / E and negatively - on securities with high P/E.

It is important to look closely at the applicability of some assumptions of the classic financial theory based on the EMH. The first assumption is that all investors are rational. The theory supposes that having all necessary information about stocks or bonds individual investors make the correct choice, thus leading to maximum personal wealth and happiness. They never ignore important information and their behavior is always rational. However, behavioral economics a study of human behavior on the financial market has denied this assumption.

Emotions make people interpret information in a wrong way, thus leading to distortion in estimation of the probability of winning and making wrong decisions. For instance, if offered a choice regarding a roll of coins tails, a person will obtain 200 rubles, and in a roll of an eagle the individual will obtain nothing; or by refusing the offer he will earn $100. Most people prefer the second option because they consider it more reliable. However, if we change the rules of the game and assume that a roll of the coin results in tails, a person loses 200 rubles, and the eagle obtains nothing, or simply refuses to play and pays $100. Research indicates that most players prefer the first option.

These two games are a mirror of each other, so in terms of the classic theory a person in both cases should make the same decision. But the typical decision is explained due to the fact that the defeat is perceived as more painful than winning, so the individual is ready to choose the riskier option in order to have the opportunity not to lose a single dollar. This example shows that the mechanism of choosing in the decision-making process is based on operation of parallel neuronal systems. An automatic involuntary system provides a quick response to changing conditions, but it often fails and leads to an economically suboptimal solution.

This system arose before any other system of decision-making and often poorly adapted to modern economic realities. Perhaps that is why it was the need for forming any system which would adjusted the activities of involuntary mechanisms. To understand mechanisms of human behavior on the one hand, psychic automatism of human irrationality should be considered. On the other hand, the role of rational decision-making mechanisms should not be exaggerated.

The second important assumption within the classic economic theory is that all investors act similarly. According to this idea, all investors have the same goals and the same investment horizons. Having the same information they make the same decisions. But in reality, this assumption does not work properly. Since people are different, their preferences are not the same: one can buy stocks and keep them for 30 years, but another buys and sells every day, speculating on the market.

The third assumption is that the price is constantly changing. The classic financial theory supposes that share prices or exchange rates move continuously from one value to another, they cannot jump on a few items at once. In the reality prices constantly change. Often these changes are not sufficient and occur when brokers rounded prices, skipping the intermediate values. Large jumps are rarer and may occur, for example, when there is a quantitative mismatch of orders to buy and sell shares, so the players begin to rapidly raise or lower the price until equilibrium is established.

The fourth assumption is that the price changes are similar to the Brownian movement. The bulk of price fluctuations on the market take place in a rather small range, and major changes are very rare, and the frequency of their occurrence decreases very rapidly. After studying the behavior of the Dow Jones index for 100 years, Mandelbrot discovered that actual fluctuations in the index are far beyond the Brownian model and on this basis proposed that the standard financial model is wrong. Mandelbrot proposed using the FMH instead of the EMH and was the first person who fixed the fact of market persistence – the ability of a state to exist longer than the process which created it. According to him, financial markets have a long-term memory (Mandelbrot, Benoit, & van Ness, 1968).

Further development of Mandelbrots' concepts was conducted by Greene and Fielitz (1977) by proving presence of a long-term dependence in prices of the stocks in the New York Stock Exchange. Booth, Kaen, and Koveos (1982) also confirmed that some financial data have a long-term memory. Helms et al. (1984) based his analysis on prices on futures and also proved the fact of market persistence. The concepts of the FMH were actively popularized by Peters (1991, 1994). The FMH theory combines fractals and other concepts from chaos theory with traditional quantitative methods to explain and predict the market behavior. FMH considers the daily randomness of the market and anomalies such as market crashes and stampedes.

The FMH is based on the following principles:

1. The market is stable when it consists of investors, who cover a large number of investment horizons. This ensures there is ample liquidity for traders.
2. The information set is more related to market sentiments and technical factors in the short term than in the longer term period. As investment horizons increase, long-term fundamental information dominates.
3. If an event occurs which questions the validity of fundamental information, long-term investors either stop participating in the market or begin trading based on the short term information set. When the overall investment horizon of the market shrinks to a uniform level, the market becomes unstable.
4. Prices reflect a combination of short–term technical trading and long–term fundamental valuation.
5. If a security has no tie to the economic cycle, then there will be no long–term trend. Trading, liquidity, and short-term information will dominate.

The FMH states that information is valued according to the investment horizon of an investor. As soon different investment horizons value information differently, the diffusion of information is also uneven. In a moment of time, prices may not reflect all available information, but only information which is important to a specific investment horizon. The FMH applies an economic and mathematical structure to the fractal market analysis so it is possible to understand the behavior of markets.

Although a sufficient number of studies are devoted to the problem of market persistence and long-term memory, there is no unified methodology. This causes further development of this issue, especially in the context of long-term memory identification and methodology of market persistence estimation.

LONG-TERM MEMORY AND PLASTICITY AS BASIC PROPERTIES IN THE FRACTAL STRUCTURE OF FINANCIAL MARKETS

The precise definition of the fractal is absent in the extant scholarly literature. Usually it is pointed out that "fractal" came from the Latin "fractus" and close to the English word of fraction or fractional. Therefore, from the mathematic point of view, fractal is a plurality with a fractional (fractal) dimension. The fractal dimension characterizes the way how an object or a time series fills space. In addition, it describes the structure of an object when the zoom factor is changing or while zooming the subject. Under zoom factor the scope escalation is meant. For physical (or geometric) fractals, such conversion occurs in space. The fractal dimension of the time series measures how rugged is the time series itself. The direct line should have a fractal dimension equal to its classical geometrical (Euclidean) dimension.

The fractal dimension D is a critical dimension, in which measure changes its value from 0 to ∞. Nevertheless, the topological dimension (the Lebesgue dimension) is always an integer, so for its D can take the following values:

1. D = 0 for a point;
2. D = 1 for a line (e.g., an ellipse, a square);
3. D = 2 for a surface (e.g., a square area);
4. D = 3 for an area (e.g. acube).

The fractal dimension of random time series is 1.5 and represents a zoom function changing over time. The fractal dimension of the time series is extremely important because it recognizes that the process may be somewhere between deterministic (the line with fractal dimension of D = 1) and random (fractal dimension of D = 1,5). The statistics of time series with fractal dimensions different from 1.5, is in great extent deviant from the Gaussian statistics, and not necessarily located within the normal distribution.

Fractal is an attractor (a limit and a goal) for the movement of the chaotic system. Why are these notions identical? In a strange attractor as well as in a fractal while increasing it reveals more details (i.e., it triggers the principle of self-similarity). As much as the size of the attractor is changed it is always in the same proportion. The time series is considered fractal when it exhibits a statistical self-similarity; namely, this property is enjoyed by all ranks of financial assets quotations. The self-similarity could be seen during reading ordinary graphs. For instance, it is impossible to distinguish minute, hourly, and daily charts of any product because they are similar and monotonous. In technical analysis, a typical example of a fractal is "Elliott Waves" which construction is also based on the principle of self-similarity.

An additional idea rooted in fractality regards non-integer dimensions which are usually referred to as a one-dimensional, two-dimensional, or three-dimensional integer world. However, there may be a non-integer dimension such as 2.58 (i.e., located between two-axe and three-axe dimensions). Mandelbrot (1968) called such dimensions fractals. This idea originates from the opinion that the three-dimensional measurement of the real sphere or cube is inadequate, as soon as in the real world it could be hardly found a perfect sphere or a cube, without scratches or any other inaccurateness. In order to describe complex objects, other measurements should exist. Such measurement of incorrect fractal shapes introduces the concept of a fractal dimension.

From the point of view of classical Euclidean geometry, a crumpled sheet of paper will be a three-dimensional sphere. However, in reality it is still only a two-dimensional sheet of paper even if it is crumpled. Hence, it can be assumed that the new object will have a dimension greater than two but less than three. It hardly fits the Euclidean geometry, but can be well described by fractal geometry which argues that the new object will be located in the fractal dimension equal approximately to 2.5 (i.e., will have a fractal dimension of about 2.5). The physical meaning of this dimension is very simple in that in the classical three-dimensional space, some parts remain empty because of gaps and holes naturally presented in a crumpled sheet of paper.

When applying this theory to the financial markets, we can assume that markets are characterized by various degrees of plasticity defined as the capacity to take and retain form. This definition means that markets can be molded to various degrees in terms of their shapes and functions, and that they are able, to various degrees to retain such changes in their properties even after the molding effort ceases. Thus, plasticity is a dual construct since it requires both fluidity defined as the capacity to take form, and stability defined as the capacity to retain form. All markets are plastic even though their degree of plasticity can change. Therefore, the interplay between fluidity and stability helps us understand market dynamics in more detail.

The term "market plasticity" encapsulates the dynamic and socially constructed nature of markets better than other available terms. Expressions such as "dynamics", "development", and "evolution" lean more toward the process of market change than the characteristics of markets that allows dynamics. Other constructs such as "change" and "fluidity" neglect what is arguably a critical facet of market dynamics, namely its dual character of both fluidity and stability.

There are two important consequences of the plastic character of markets as defined above. First, the ability to retain form allows markets to give form to other entities by, for example, affecting the shape of a particular exchange object, the mode of a specific economic exchange, or the characteristics of an exchange agent. Markets are thus performative in the broad sense of the term (Law & Urry, 2004). Second, the ability to take form allows markets to host multiple forms simultaneously. As actors enact "their" market, markets tend to multiply into overlapping versions (Kjellberg & Helgesson, 2006).

In the natural sciences, plasticity is a construct used to describe suppleness and deformation in various contexts. For example, in physics plasticity is defined as a deformation of a material undergoing nonreversible changes in shape in response to forces applied (Bigoni, 2012; Lubliner, 2008). In biology, the term "plasticity" is most often used to discuss "phenotypic plasticity"; that is, the ability of organisms to alter their phenotypes (observable characteristics) in response to changes in the environment (West-Eberhard, 1989). "Neuroplasticity" is the capability of the cerebral cortex to alter its physical structure and functional organization (Pascual-Leone et al., 2005).

Systems theory differentiates between structural and organizational plasticity. The former refers to a social system's ability to drift toward greater congruence through recurring perturbations, while the latter refers to the system's ability to neutralize external structural changes by making internal structural changes (Forrester, 1961; Maturana, 1978; Sterman, 2000). In philosophy, Malabou (2008, 2010) discusses the concept of plasticity with reference to a three-fold definition: (a) the capacity to receive form; (b) the capacity to give form; and (c) the powerful rupture or annihilation of all forms (possibly inspired by the notion of plastic explosives). In the social sciences, the plasticity construct is used less often and as a more peripheral concept than in the natural sciences. For example, in sociology, the term "plasticity" is loosely referred to as variability (Turner et al., 1995); hence, the difficulty of describing, defining, or demarcating the boundaries of something (Donaldson, 1987).

Two explicit uses of the term plasticity can be detected in economics. First, Alchian and Woodward (1988) use asset plasticity "to indicate that there is a wide range of discretionary, legitimate decisions within which the user may choose" (p.69). This characteristics is said to explain which resources are vulnerable to morally hazardous exploitation; hence, giving agents opportunities to bias their actions toward their own interests. Second, Strambach (2010) discusses the notion of institutional plasticity, emphasizing that institutions are both enabling and restraining. Their plasticity character is linked to interpretative flexibility, which in turn depends on the sanctions (e.g., social and legal) associated with a particular institution.

Because actors take action in situations where firm, industry, regional, national, and international institutions overlap, there are opportunities for new combinations of earlier institutional components. Finally, complementarity between institutions is identified as having an ambiguous role, with contributing to both stability (via lock in) and fluidity (through accumulation of incremental changes). In marketing, Alderson (1957, p. 277) used the term plasticity to signify the potentiality for remolding and subsequently responding differently. However, the plasticity concept does not belong to the core lexicon used by organization theorists or strategy researchers.

During the literature review, five main facets of plasticity were identified: the abilities to take form, retain form, give form, annihilate form, and change function. These facets are to compare our proposed definition of plasticity (market plasticity) with definitions of other identified meanings and use of the term; most of existing plasticity conceptions emphasizes the duality of taking and retaining form. Malabou's (2008, 2010) definition of plasticity is the most extensive, because it also acknowledges performative and destructive forces of plasticity. Additionally, plasticity definitions, being rooted in the natural sciences, differentiate between the plasticity of form and the plasticity of function. However, differentiating structural and functional plasticity becomes increasingly challenging when investigating social phenomena.

THE HURST INDEX AS A MEASURE FOR THE FRACTAL STRUCTURE AND LONG-TERM MEMORY OF FINANCIAL MARKETS

The main method of the fractal time series study is R/S-analysis or the method of rescaled range. It was suggested by the hydrologist Harold Edwin Hurst (1951) who in the mid-20th century worked at the Nile dam project (p. 205). The task was to calculate the required volume of the dam reservoir, filling of which occurred due to various natural sources: rainfalls, floods, etc. Usually, in such cases, hydrologists start with the assumption that the water level in the river is a random series where the value of the water level in the following years do not depend on the previous ones. But having read about floods in the last 800 years, Hurst discovered the following regularity: the year the high water level is usually followed by another year with a high level, and the year with a low level of water by another year with low levels. It appeared like a cycle with an unpredictable period. A standard statistical analysis revealed no significant correlations between observations, so Hurst had to develop his own methodology.

There are at least two variations of fractal dimension – D and A. The fractal dimension D (where D is the dimension of time track – an assessment of the degree of affectation series) is defined due to Equation 1:

$$D = 2 - H \tag{1}$$

Mandelbrot and van Ness (1968) has demonstrated that the fractal dimension is the reciprocal value of the Hurst exponent (H). For instance, if H = 0.5, the fractal dimension is equal to 2 (1/0.5), and if H = 0.8, the fractal dimension is equal to 1.25 (1/0.8). Therefore, the fractal dimension of Mandelbrot A (where A is the dimension of the probability space – estimationof the thickness of tails in the probability density function) is calculated due to Equation 2:

$$A = 1 / H \tag{2}$$

The Hurst exponent can be defined on the interval $[0,1]$, and is calculated within the following limits:

$0 \leq H < 0,5$ – Data is fractal, the FMH is confirmed, «heavy tails» of distribution, antipersistent series, negative correlation in instruments of value changes, pink noise with frequent changes in direction of price movement, trading in the market is more risky for an individual participant;

$H = 0,5$ – Data is random, the EMH is confirmed, movement of asset prices is an example of the random Brownian motion (Wiener process), time series are normally distributed, lack of correlation in changes in value of assets (memory of series), white noise of independent random process, traders cannot «beat» the market with any trading strategy;

$0,5 < H \leq 1$ – Data is fractal, the FMH is confirmed, «heavy tails» of distribution, persistent series, positive correlation within changes in the value of assets, black noise, the trend is present in the market.

Hurst took the Equation from Einstein's work on Brownian motion of particles as a reference point per Equation 3:

$$R = \sqrt{T}, \text{ где} \tag{3}$$

where R – the distance covered by a Brownian particle in time T; T – time index.

According to this Equation, a Brownian particle moved by a distance equal to the square root of time spent on this movement. If $H = 0,5$, a system runs in the time T the same distance as a Brownian particle. With large values of H a system goes a considerable distance in the same time T in comparison with a Brownian particle. The Hurst exponent calculation can be carried out according to the following Equation (4, 5):

$$R \backslash S = (aN)^{H}, \text{ consequently} \tag{4}$$

Table 1. The values of the variations of the fractal dimension

Hurst Index (H)	$H \approx 0$	$H = 0,5$	$H = 1$
Fractal Dimension D	$D \approx 2$	$D = 1,5$	$D = 1$
Fractal Dimension A	$A \to \infty$	$A = 2$	$A = 1$
	Straight line	Random Series	Infinite Linear Trend

$$H = \frac{\log(R \setminus S)}{\log(aN)} \text{, where} \tag{5}$$

H – The Hurst index;

S – The mean-squar deviation of an observations series x;

R – The amplitude of the accumulated deviations Zu;

N – The number of observation periods;

a – The given constant, a positive number. Hurst has empirically calculated this constant for relatively short-term time series of natural phenomena. The constant is $0,5$.

Even using $0,5$ as the constant, with a small number of observations N the Hurst index tends to evaluate random series as persistent (having a trend), overstating H. Therefore, for further research it is more reliable to use the constant as $a = \pi / 2$ (6).

$$S = \sqrt{\frac{1}{N} \sum_{i=1}^{N} \left(Xi - X\right)^2} \text{, где} \tag{6}$$

X – the arithmetic mean of a set of observations x for N periods (7):

$$X = \frac{1}{N} \sum_{i=1}^{N} Xi \tag{7}$$

The amplitude of the accumulated deviation is the most important element in the Equation for calculating the Hurst index. It is calculated as follows Equation (8):

$$R = \max(Zu) - \min(Zu), \tag{8}$$

where Zu - accumulated deviation of series x from the average value X (9):

$$Zu = \sum_{i=1}^{u} (Xi - X) \tag{9}$$

Eric Naiman has improved the Hurst Equation for those cases, when sampling of random variables is represented by a small number of observations (Naiman, 2011) (10):

$$H_T = \frac{\log\left(\dfrac{R}{S_T}\right)}{\log\left(\pi * \dfrac{N}{2}\right)} (-0,0011 * ln(N) + 1,0136) \tag{10}$$

It is visible from the Equation of the Hurst index that there some influential factors, namely: an increase of the oscillation amplitude R, reduction of the arithmetic mean deviation S, reduction of the number of observations N.

As it is observed, the dynamics of market prices corresponds to the Hurst index (H) much higher than $0,5$. In other words, the dynamics of market prices and macroeconomic indicators is not accidental, and there are at least two good reasons for this situation. First, information about the market is not immediately considered in the prices. This occurs, inter alia, because of unbalanced access of different market players to the same information. Second, over time, the influence of information is reduced. Therefore, a well-known psychological phenomenon as memory of market is demonstrated. The memory of market can be characterized in four words – the market is inertial. This thesis could be justified via the FMH. The Hurst index is seen helpful to calculate fractal dimension, so it should be interpreted as the necessary element of the FMH.

The Hurst index could be also used as a measure of volatility of the data series. Peters (1994) highlights in his *Fractal Market Analysis: Applying Chaos Theory to Investment and Economics* that in the analysis of stock risks it is preferable to use the fractal dimension instead of the standard deviation. The standard deviation is good while it characterizes variability of random series. If to deal with market as a stochastic process, in this case the use of standard deviation as the main characteristics of risk values is justifiable enough. If to admit that market is not stochastic, but chaotic, fractal dimension as a measure of non-linearity of price movements is much better suited.

Why does an effect of the price inertia in relation to the previous motion appear in the financial markets? This fact can be explained based on the psychology of human memory. The Hurst index of over $0,5$ also confirms the presence of non-volatile memory market – the present depends on the past and the future depends on the present.

As some of the contemporary research of human memory has demonstrated, people daily "lose" up to 25 percent of the information already received. Under the information we refer not only to knowledge acquisition, but also to psychological experiences associated with the process of obtaining such knowledge. For example, if on Monday the market had a strong increase in prices, a trader in that day, of course, remembers the full scope of information related to price increases and is under the impression of such growth. On Tuesday, the trader will retain in memory about 75% of the psychological emotions of the previous day, and of a specific content, which caused a rise in prices. On Wednesday, the percentage of memories will fall to 50%, on Thursday up to 25%, and on Friday will leave only a slight trace of memories.

The percentage of forgetting may vary depending on events in subsequent days. If on Tuesday the rise in prices continues, it will intensify the impression of Monday, and on Wednesday the increase on Monday and Tuesday will be a spectacular event in memory of a trader. The percentage of memory will be more than 75%. If on Tuesday price will decline, on the contrary, the events of Monday will lose their weight more than 50% by Wednesday. That is why the memory of trader must be considered in one continuous chain of events where the latest events will be given greater weight. It reminds us of the calculation of the exponential moving average. Since in the second and third day (Tuesday and Wednesday in our example) the trader remembers most of events of the first day, then this memory will impose a significant imprint on his actions during these days.

Few dare to sell in a strong bull market without sufficient reason. However, after a strong movement a fear of sales will be affected for several days, gradually weakening its impact on a trader. In reality, it often happens that a strong move on Friday is continued on Monday, sometimes grabbing the first half of Tuesday. Strong price changes on Tuesday/Wednesday and weaken by Thursday/Friday. Knowing this and understanding the reasons for such a behavior of the market, one can avoid hasty actions and stop working with the trend. Understanding of market inertia allows us to make an important remark: an investor will better understand the market if he learns to consider it through the eyes of an average trader who largely bases actions on previous market developments. This does not mean the descend level of knowledge of an average trader.

STUDY OF THE AVAILABILITY OF THE FRACTUAL STRUCTURE AND LONG-TERM MEMORY OF THE CURRENCY MARKET WITH THE HURST INDEX

Another example of the long-term memory influence is the currency market activities. Let us calculate the Hurst index for the currency pair EUR / USD with closing prices, the range - 1 day, the number of observations – 20 1. Those who calculate the Hurst index, based on market prices, often stand the arising question of what ranks to explore – data series or data changes. For instance, it could be the logarithm of the current value to the previous one which is usually used in the analysis of market quotations. Analysis has shown that the normalized logarithmic scale of random series of changes is much smaller than the scale of the normalized logarithmic linear (rising or falling) series changes.

As the result, the Hurst index calculated on the logarithms of linear series changes reach huge quantities. Therefore, if we take a series of data that evince some signs of trending, calculate logarithms changes on it, the Hurst exponent of such series will be well above 1. That is why it will be used the classic model of the Hurst index calculation according to the initial data series. The results of our calculations are shown in Table 2.

The results of calculation demonstrate that the market has short-term memory within the short time interval, as H = 0.5964. Further, we have chosen more longitude interval of one year and made the same calculation for the currency pair EUR/USD. The interval is equal to 1 week, the number of observations – 53. The results of calculations are presented in Table 3.

The results demonstrate that the market has memory in the long-term interval, which is equal to 1, the Hurst index is higher and constitutes 0.6999. Thus, our calculations show that market events and economic indicators are not random. This conclusion was reached for all the calculated data series at different time intervals. The market is inert and has a memory. Moreover, the longer the interval, the more pronounced the market memory. This confirms the validity of the FMH which is seen as an alternative to the EMH. Since the Hurst index can be helpful for calculating fractal dimension, it is considered a necessary element of the FMH.

CONCLUSION AND RECOMMENDATIONS

Key concepts of the classical financial theory (e.g., pricing model CAPM, portfolio theory of Markowitz, Black-Scholes Equation), on which are built the vast majority of methods used in the practice of commercial and investment banks, investment funds, insurance companies and other financial institutions around the world, are based on the assumption that the feasibility of the efficient market hypothesis. If earlier anomalies and sharp stock market crashes have caused debates of supporters and opponents of

Table 2. Hurst exponent calculation results on the closing prices of the currency pair EUR / USD (N=20)

Date	Close Price	$(x_i - X)$	$\Sigma(x_i - X)$
May, 4 2014	1,38719	0,0037	0,0037
May, 2 2014	1,38714	0,0037	0,0074
May, 1 2014	1,38699	0,0035	0,0109
April, 30 2014	1,38682	0,0034	0,0143
April, 29 2014	1,38130	-0,0022	0,0121
April, 28 2014	1,38520	0,0017	0,0139
April, 27 2014	1,38392	0,0005	0,0143
April, 25 2014	1,38366	0,0002	0,0145
April, 24 2014	1,38270	-0,0008	0,0138
April, 23 2014	1,38172	-0,0017	0,0120
April, 22 2014	1,38071	-0,0027	0,0093
April, 21 2014	1,37917	-0,0043	0,0050
April, 20 2014	1,38143	-0,0020	0,0030
April, 18 2014	1,38158	-0,0019	0,0011
April, 17 2014	1,38109	-0,0024	-0,0013
April, 16 2014	1,38240	-0,0011	-0,0023
April, 15 2014	1,38111	-0,0023	-0,0047
April, 14 2014	1,38156	-0,0019	-0,0066
April, 13 2014	1,38473	0,0013	-0,0053
April, 11 2014	1,38869	0,0052	0,0000
Arithmetic mean X	**1,383456**	**Maximum**	**0,0145**
Standard deviation S	**0,0027**	**Minimum**	**-0,0066**
Scope R	**0,0145-(-0,0066)=**		**0,0211**
Normalized scope R/S	**0,0211/0,0027=**		**7,8148**
Log(R/S)	**Log(7,8148)=**		**0,8929**
Log(N*π/2)	**log(20*3,1416/2)=**		**1,4971**
Hurst index H	**0,8929/1,4971=**		**0,5964**
Calculation R/ST	**7,8148*0,998752+1,051037 =**		**8,8561**
Log(R/ST)	**Log(8,8561)=**		**0,9472**
Hurst index HT	**0,9472/1,4971*(-0,0011*Ln(20)+1,0136) =**		**0,6392**

Table 3. Hurst exponent calculation results on the closing prices of the currency pair EUR / USD (N=53)

Date	Close Price	$(x_i - X)$	$\Sigma(x_i - X)$
February, 1 2015	1,1316	-0,1740	-0,1740
January, 25 2015	1,1288	-0,1768	-0,3508
January, 18 2015	1,1208	-0,1848	-0,5357
January, 11 2015	1,1569	-0,1487	-0,6844
January, 4 2015	1,1842	-0,1214	-0,8058
December, 28 2014	1,2003	-0,1053	-0,9111
December, 21 2014	1,2176	-0,0880	-0,9991
December, 14 2014	1,2228	-0,0828	-1,0820
December, 7 2014	1,2462	-0,0594	-1,1414
November, 30 2014	1,2286	-0,0770	-1,2184
November, 23 2014	1,2452	-0,0604	-1,2788
November, 16 2014	1,2390	-0,0666	-1,3454
November, 9 2014	1,2524	-0,0532	-1,3987
November, 2 2014	1,2454	-0,0602	-1,4589
October, 26 2014	1,2525	-0,0531	-1,5120
October, 19 2014	1,2671	-0,0385	-1,5505
October, 12 2014	1,2763	-0,0293	-1,5798
October, 5 2014	1,2628	-0,0428	-1,6227
September, 28 2014	1,2517	-0,0539	-1,6766
September, 21 2014	1,2685	-0,0371	-1,7137
September, 14 2014	1,2829	-0,0227	-1,7364
September, 7 2014	1,2965	-0,0091	-1,7455
August, 31 2014	1,2951	-0,0105	-1,7561
August, 24 2014	1,3133	0,0077	-1,7484
August, 17 2014	1,3243	0,0187	-1,7297
August, 10 2014	1,3399	0,0343	-1,6954
August, 3 2014	1,3411	0,0355	-1,6599
July, 27 2014	1,3431	0,0375	-1,6225
July, 20 2014	1,3432	0,0376	-1,5849
July, 13 2014	1,3524	0,0468	-1,5381

continued on following page

Table 3. Continued

Date	Close Price	$(x_i - X)$	$\Sigma(x_i - X)$
July, 6 2014	1,3609	0,0553	-1,4828
June, 29 2014	1,3596	0,0540	-1,4288
June, 22 2014	1,3649	0,0593	-1,3696
June, 15 2014	1,3599	0,0543	-1,3153
June, 8 2014	1,3542	0,0486	-1,2667
June, 1 2014	1,3642	0,0586	-1,2081
May, 25 2014	1,3631	0,0575	-1,1506
May, 18 2014	1,3634	0,0578	-1,5381
May, 11 2014	1,3695	0,0639	-1,4828
May, 4 2014	1,3760	0,0704	-1,4288
April, 27 2014	1,3870	0,0814	-1,3696
April, 20 2014	1,3833	0,0777	-1,3153
April, 13 2014	1,3815	0,0759	-1,2667
April, 6 2014	1,3885	0,0829	-1,2081
March, 30 2014	1,3703	0,0647	-1,1506
March, 23 2014	1,3753	0,0697	-0,5064
March, 16 2014	1,3794	0,0738	-0,4326
March, 9 2014	1,3915	0,0859	-0,3468
March, 2 2014	1,3878	0,0822	-0,2646
February, 23 2014	1,3802	0,0746	-0,1900
February, 16 2014	1,3740	0,0684	-0,1216
February, 9 2014	1,3693	0,0637	-0,0579
February, 2 2014	1,3635	0,0579	0,0000
Arithmetic mean X	1,30562	**Maximum**	-0,0579
Standard deviation S	0,0769	**Minimum**	-1,7561
Scope R	-0,0579-(-1,7561)=		1,6982
Normalized scope R/S	1,6982/0,0769=		22,0816
Log(R/S)	Log(22,0816)=		1,344
Log(N*π/2)	Log(53*3,1416/2)=		1,9204
Hurst index H	1,344/1,9204=		0,6999
Calculation R/ST	22,0816*0,998752+1,051037=		23,1051
Log(R/ST)	Log(23,1051) =		1,3637
Hurst index HT	1,3637/1,9204*(-0,0011*Ln(20)+1,0136)=		0,7166

the EMH about the applicability of such an assumption, after the global crisis in 2008, it became clear that the EMH does not fully apply in practice. If considering financial markets as an analogue of the brain neural networks and fractals (e.g., investors with different investment horizons) as an analogue of neurons, the most interesting impact could be demonstrated by application of the FMH. The FMH is one the alternatives to the EMH. Our analysis verifies the fact of fractality in the most of contemporary markets. The classical methods of risk estimation do not take into account the fractal structure of the market, while this is the main advantage of the fractal approach.

The results of our calculations demonstrate that market events and economic indicators are not random phenomena. The market has a fractal structure and a long-term memory and plasticity. This conclusion has been reached for all data series in different time intervals. Therefore, the FMH can be applied successfully to economic phenomena. The assumption that investment decisions can be predicted based on the analysis of neural mechanisms of the information influence on fractals will allow to open new horizons in understanding of the investor behavior in financial markets. In order to understand the process of investment decision-making, the following scheme could be recommended:

1. On the first step, the Equationtion of a problem creates a view about the purpose and context of the decision. It integrates information about the internal conditions of the organism and environmental factors, such as famine or level of threat in the context of future action.
2. The next step is determined by the value or valuation of the choosing procedure with particular behavioral alternatives.
3. On the third step, alternative solutions are compared and the best solution is selected. This step is called action selection.
4. After implementation of a selected action the results are calculated and efficiency is evaluated.
5. The last step is training. Training means updating information stored in the memory, so that all subsequent steps would be implemented with greater efficiency.

REFERENCES

Alchian, A., & Woodward, S. (1988). The firm is dead; long live the firm: A review of Oliver Williamson's The Economic Institutions of Capitalism. *Journal of Economic Literature, 26*(1), 65–79.

Alderson, W. (1957). *Marketing Behavior and Executive Action, A Functionalist Approach to Marketing Theory*. Homewood, IL: Richard D. Irwin, Inc.

Bachelier, L. (1964). Theory of Speculation. In The Random Character of Stock Market Price. Cambridge, MA: MIT Press. (Originally published in 1900.)

Bigoni, D. (2012). *Nonlinear Solid Mechanics: Bifurcation Theory and Material Instability*. New York: Cambridge University Press. doi:10.1017/CBO9781139178938

Black, F., & Scholes, M. (1973). The Pricing of Options and Corporate Liabilities. *Journal of Political Economy, 81*(3), 637–654. doi:10.1086/260062

Booth, G. G., Kaen, F. R., & Koveos, P. E. (1982). R/S analysis of foreign exchange rates under two international monetary regimes. *Journal of Monetary Economics*, *10*(3), 407–415. doi:10.1016/0304-3932(82)90035-6

Donaldson, M. (1987). Labouring men: Love, sex and strife. *Journal of Sociology (Melbourne, Vic.)*, *23*(2), 165–184. doi:10.1177/144078338702300201

Eu, F. (1976). Foundations of Finance: Portfolio Decisions and Securities Prices. New York: Basic Books.

FOREX. (2014). Retrieved on February 2, 2015, from: http://ru.fxempire.com/currencies/eur-usd/tools/historical-data/

Forrester, J. W. (1961). *Industrial Dynamics*. Portland, OR: Productivity Press.

Greene, M. T., & Fielitz, B. D. (1977). Long-term Dependence in Common Stock Returns. *Journal of Financial Economics*, *4*(3), 339–349. doi:10.1016/0304-405X(77)90006-X

Helms, B. P., Kaen, F. R., & Rosenman, R. E. (1984). Memory in Commodity Futures Contracts. *Journal of Futures Markets*, *4*(4), 559–567. doi:10.1002/fut.3990040408

Hurst, H. E. (1951). Long-term Storage of Reservoirs: An Experimental Study. *Transactions of the American Society of Civil Engineers*, *116*, 770–799.

Kjellberg, H., & Helgesson, C.-F. (2006). Multiple Versions of Markets: Multiplicity and Performativity in Market Practice. *Industrial Marketing Management*, *35*(7), 839–855. doi:10.1016/j.indmarman.2006.05.011

Klucharev, V. A., Smidts, A., & Shestakova, A. N. (2011). Neuroeconomics. The Neurobiology of Decision-making. *Experimental Psychology*, *4*(2), 14–35.

Knutson, B., Taylor, J., Kaufman, M., Peterson, R., & Glover, G. (2005). Distributed Neural Representation of Expected Value. *The Journal of Neuroscience*, *25*(19), 4806–4812. doi:10.1523/JNEUROSCI.0642-05.2005 PMID:15888656

Kuhnen, C. M., & Knutson, B. (2005). The Neural Basis of Financial Risk Taking. *Neuron*, *47*(5), 763–770. doi:10.1016/j.neuron.2005.08.008 PMID:16129404

Law, J., & Urry, J. (2004). Enacting the Social. *Economy and Society*, *33*(3), 390–410. doi:10.1080/0308514042000225716

Malabou, C. (2010). *Plasticity at the Dusk of Writing: Dialectic, Destruction, Deconstruction*. New York: Columbia University Press.

Mandelbrot, B. B., & van Ness, J. W. (1968). Fractional Brownian Motion, Fractional Noises, and Application. *SIAM Review*, *10*(4), 422–437. doi:10.1137/1010093

Markowitz, H. M. (1952). Portfolio Selection. *The Journal of Finance*, *7*(1), 77–91.

Maturana, H. R. (1978). Biology of Language: The Epistemology of Reality. In G. A. Miller & E. Lenneberg (Eds.), *Psychology and Biology of Language and Thought*. New York: Academic Press.

McClure, S. M., Laibson, D. I., Loewenstein, G., & Cohen, J. D. (2004). Separate Neural Systems Value Immediate and Delayed Monetary Rewards. *Science, 306*(5695), 503–507. doi:10.1126/science.1100907 PMID:15486304

Osborne, M. F. M. (1964). Brownian Motion in the Stock Market. In P. Cootner (Ed.), *The Random Character of Stock Market Price*. Cambridge, MA: MIT Press.

Pascual-Leone, A., Amedi, A., Fregni, F., & Merabet, L. B. (2005). The Plastic Human Brain Cortex. *Annual Review of Neuroscience, 28*(1), 377–401. doi:10.1146/annurev.neuro.27.070203.144216 PMID:16022601

Peters, E. E. (1991). *Chaos and Order in the Capital Markets*. New York: John Wiley and Sons.

Peters, E. E. (1994). *Fractal Market Analysis: Applying Chaos Theory to Investment and Economics*. New York: John Wiley and Sons.

Rangel, A., Camerer, C., & Montague, P. R. (2008). A Framework for Studying the Neurobiology of Value-based Decision making. *Nature Reviews. Neuroscience, 9*(9), 545–556. doi:10.1038/nrn2357 PMID:18545266

Sharpe, W. F. (1964). Capital Asset Prices: A Theory of Market Equilibrium under Conditions of Risk. *The Journal of Finance, 19*(3), 425–442.

Sterman, J. D. (2000). *Business Dynamics: Systems Thinking and Modeling for a Complex World*. Chicago: McGraw Hill.

Strambach, S. (2010). Path Dependence and Path Plasticity: The Co-evolution of Institutions and Innovation. In R. Boschma & R. Martin (Eds.), *The Handbook of Evolutionary Economic Geography* (pp. 406–431). Cheltenham, UK: Edward Elgar. doi:10.4337/9781849806497.00029

Turner, B. S., Rowland, R., Connell, R. W., Waters, M., & Barbalet, J. M. (1995). Symposium: Human Rights and the Sociological Project. *Journal of Sociology (Melbourne, Vic.), 31*(2), 1–44. doi:10.1177/144078339503100201

West-Eberhard, M. J. (1989). Phenotypic Plasticity and the Origins of Diversity. *Annual Review of Ecology and Systematics, 20*(1), 249–278. doi:10.1146/annurev.es.20.110189.001341

ENDNOTE

[1] The data used for this calculation was retrieved at the FOREX - FXTMPIRE // http://ru.fxempire.com/currencies/eur-usd/tools/historical-data/

Chapter 11
Objective and Subjective Aspects of Decision-Making Support at the Mesoeconomic Level

Anastasia Y. Nikitaeva
Southern Federal University, Russia

ABSTRACT

This chapter substantiates the importance of improving management effectiveness of mesoeconomic systems in current economic conditions and the features of mesoeconomy as a management object which defines the high complexity of decision making at the meso level. There are approaches, methods, and technologies which provide support of the decision making process via the integration of formal methods for objective data analysis and methods of accounting to solve semi-structured complex problems of mesoeconomy. A cognitive approach, and an approach involving the integration of the On-Line Analytical Processing and Data mining technologies with methods of a multi-criteria assessment of alternative, in particular methods of Multi-Attribute Utility Theory are considered in the chapter. Cognitive mapping of interaction between state and business in a mesoeconomic system are included as a case-study.

INTRODUCTION

Today evolutionary development of national economies in the global economic environment greatly depends on the level of management efficiency in meso-economic systems. This is due to the fact that the meso-level of the economy acts as a kind of an economic space center, the connecting element between individual economic entities of micro-level and a higher macroeconomic level of state or suprastate governance. On one hand, at the meso-level there is an opportunity to fully realize the systematic approach to management and to create effective institutional mechanisms enhancing economic development, but on the other hand to provide adaptation of the mechanism of management to tasks and features in the functioning of specific economic systems. Thus, firstly at the meso-level there is a possibility to transmit

DOI: 10.4018/978-1-4666-9989-2.ch011

and implement managerial impulses of macro-level and through the stimulation of the formation and activation of certain economic ties and relations to achieve significant changes in the socio-economic development; and secondly, to adapt tools and institutes of development to the needs and the potential of concrete meso-economic systems, which are significantly different.

Together this allows considering meso-economies as a kind of development center which will create positive impulses that, in turn, will affect the entire hierarchical structure of the economy under condition of the effective management. Because of this and due to the binding of the economic potential to the specific areas and territories in the global economy, the formation of competitive advantages occurs mainly at the meso-level and the processes of globalization and regionalization or localization occur parallel.

The meso-economy is a complex, open, and dynamic socio-economic system. Thus, the specific features of meso-economic systems which are shown in the complexity of their structure, uncertainty, and unevenness of development, the inaccuracy of an assessment of parameters of such systems, differentiations of social and economic characteristics of components and subsystems, determines the complexity of making effective decisions in the managerial process. A significant number of tools have been developed in recent years to improve the efficiency of the decision-making process in economic systems of various levels.

However, in most cases the use of traditional tools of decision support at the meso-level is complicated either by insufficient data availability for analysis or the inability to rely only on objective indicators in managerial processes and so forth due to the importance to consider account the social (ecological/ethical/cultural) dimension of the development of meso-economic systems. Solving the problem of effectiveness of meso-economic management systems is possible through exploration of the targeted system and justification of decisions based on structuring of problems in complex and uncertain situations and the lack of statistical information about the current processes and phenomena.

This is possible by using methods and tools of neuroeconomics which allow encoding the subjective value of decision-making, determining the role of emotions in decision-making, investigating the interaction of emotional and rational mechanisms of decision-making, analyzing and modeling the basis of social and economic interaction and, thereby, overcoming the limitations of the classical economic theory and increasing the efficiency of decision-making processes at the meso-level.

This chapter focuses on explaining the approaches, methods, and technologies supporting management decisions at the meso-level of economy that take into account and integrate the objective and subjective aspects of managerial decision-making based on a combination of quantitative and qualitative procedures, including the analysis of possibilities of their application for the increase of management efficiency of meso-economic systems in modern economies.

BACKGROUND

Over the past 10 years, meso-economic systems were deeply investigated by a number of research projects (e.g., Gorelova, Matveeva, & Nikitaeva, 2007; Kleiner, 2011; Kolesnikov, 2009; Wolfram, Torsten, & Henning, 2015; Ng, 1987). The term "meso-economics" dates back to the 1980s when several economists began to question a bridge between two main economic paradigms in the mainstream economics: micro- and macroeconomics. The term "meso-economics" has two meanings. First, it reflects the subject sphere of research – the part of a national economy located in economic space between the macro- and micro levels. This sphere includes branches, markets, regions, major cross-sectoral economic systems, business networks and clusters grouped according to various criteria (Kleiner, 2011). However, meso-economics is the scientific discipline that studies this subject area and possesses specific approaches, methodology, and tools.

In some work devoted to meso-economic systems, the researchers focus on the formation of a unified theory of operation for all types of meso-economic systems, as well as the development of an integrated management methodology for the meso-economy. The creation of a methodological and methodical approach to the analysis and synthesis of meso-economic systems is most often based on the genetic characteristics of national economies and specific tasks of a certain period in its development (e.g., Kleiner, 2011; Druzhinin & Ionov, 2001; Inshakova & Samokhin, 2008). Along with general theoretical and methodological developments, significant amount of research is devoted to the study of specific types of meso-economic systems: regions, clusters, and industries; and development of managerial mechanisms and the technology for them (Amin,1999; Kleiner, 2011; Moulaert & Mehmood, 2010; Porter, 2001; Scott & Garofoli, 2007; Vázquez-Barquero, 2002).

Another perspective of the meso-economic systems consideration (especially clusters, networks and regions) suggests their study as various groups of institutionally-coordinated agents, interacting arenas and subpopulations of human agents, firms and other organizations. In accordance with this approach, the meso-economy is a complex system consisting of a large number of heterogeneous elements, interacting in nontrivial ways. Accordingly, the properties of meso-economic systems and forecasts of its development cannot be determined through analysis of these individual elements, but it requires a comprehensive study of the phenomenon of self-organization and behavioral processes (Wolfram, Torsten, & Henning, 2015, p. 421). This approach is closely connected to synergetic one for researching complex socio-economic systems (Knyazeva & Kurdyumov, 1999).

Considering the important role of meso-economy in ensuring successful economic development of the micro- and macroeconomic systems, a significant amount of research has been devoted to the development management of meso-economic systems (Granberg, 2005; Kiselyova, 2007; Kolesnikov, 2009). In scientific research on the development management of meso-economic systems, an important place has been occupied with cases and works revealing the specific features of meso-economies (Druzhinin, 2005; Puppim de Oliveira, Ali, 2011; Rodríguez-Pose & Comptour, 2011).

The understanding of the importance of effective management of meso-economic systems to ensure economic growth and development and simultaneously the complexity of decision-making process at the meso-level has led to the emergence of scientific activities aiming to develop novel approaches, models, and analytical tools for decision support in complex systems with semi-structured problems. Among these approaches, an important role is played by the cognitive mapping approach (Gorelova, Verba, & Zakharova, 2004; Knyazeva, & Kurdyumov, 1999; Vanwindekens, Stilmant & Baret, 2013; Gorelova, Matveeva, & Nikitaeva, 2007).

In addition, the development of decision making methods in complex socioeconomic systems has been implemented in other areas of researches in recent years. Despite active development of instrumentation and decision support systems based on quantitative data analysis (Lotov, Bushenkov, & Kamenev, 2004; Katsko, Krepishev, & Sennikova, 2011) and subjective methods of modeling the problem situation (Anich & Larichev, 1996; Pirlot & Bouyssou, 2009; Saati, 2008), integration of appropriate techniques, corresponding to meso-economic systems to improve the efficiency of their management development has not been sufficiently implemented.

Combining emotional (subjective) and rational (cognitive, objective) systems in the decision-making process recently has occurred in the course of research in neuroeconomics bringing together neuroscience, economic science, psychology, and several other disciplines (Klyucharev, Smits, & Shestakova, 2011). Studies on the duality of decision-making processes (Kahneman, 2003), mechanisms of subjective utility determination in the selection process out of the possible alternatives, risk account (Knutson, Taylor, Kaufman, Peterson, & Glover, 2005; Kuhnen & Knutson, 2005; Rangel, Camerer, & Montague, 2008), temporary discounting (McClure, Laibson, Loewenstein, & Cohen, 2004) are of particular importance in the context of the given research. However, for meso-economics and for improving the efficiency of decision-making at the meso-level, neuroeconomics, characterizing the peculiarities of emotional and rational systems of decision-making, is not used sufficiently.

Despite a considerable amount of research on the chosen area of interest, research on meso-economy management is mainly concentrated either on a strategic level of decision-making with help of methods of expert assessment and quality tools of strategic analysis, or on management of certain types of meso-economic systems or subsystems. This is largely determined by the complexity of decision-making formalization of procedures at the meso-level. There is an obvious lack of high quality of scientific papers on the development of methods of meso-economy management based on simultaneous consideration of objective and subjective characteristics of management process. The level of technological support of decision-making is insufficient for the effective management of complex socio-economic systems on the meso-level. In turn, research on the development of methods and tools to support managerial decision-making in complex systemsare more focused on the corporate sector of the economy and / or technological systems, and are insufficiently used in the management of various meso-economic systems.

Thus, sharing the attitude of researchers, highlighting the importance and complexity of effective management of the development of meso-economic systems, it is appropriate to focus in this chapter on identifying the specific characteristics of meso-economy as an object of management. The analysis of approaches, methods, and tools used in this area of research which consider the objective and subjective aspects of managerial decision-making, based on a combination of quantitative and qualitative procedures (methods of activating the thinking of experts and methods of formalization of complex systems, subjective methods of modeling the problem situation and quantitative data analysis) to improve the efficiency of the decision-making process at the meso-level.

MANAGEMENT OF MESO-ECONOMIC SYSTEMS: FEATURES AND TOOLS FOR DECISION-MAKING SUPPORT

Meso-Economy Features as an Object of Management

Theoretical studies and practical experience show that sustainable competitive advantages in the global economic system are largely dependent on geographically-localized factors (Amin, 1999). For example, studies by Enright (2000) show that out of 160 industrial clusters, more than 60% are world leaders and only about 20% are characterized by weak competitiveness. Comparable results were obtained in relation to the characteristics of the innovative capacity of clusters (Enright, 2000). Along with clusters other meso-economic systems demonstrate a higher level of competitiveness in today's global economy through the use of consolidated potential of businesses and synergies. The competition on the world market increasingly involves the regions but not the individual enterprises and organizations at the microlevel. In recent years, this has led to increasing attention of researchers to meso-economic systems of different types.

On one hand, meso-economic systems can be considered an intermediate level between the macro- and micro levels of an economy which can provide a transfer of administrative impulses from macro to microeconomic level and get an appropriate feedback. On the other hand, in some extent it is an independent system, existing in countries with a market economy. Meso-economy represents a part of national economy located in the economic space between macro- and micro level. While microeconomy studies empirically verify existing objects – firms, for example – and their behavior, and macroeconomy operates on the aggregated data and the designed objects modeling this or that aspect of interaction of groups of economic subjects, the meso-economy is compelled to serve as the conductor of various levels of hierarchy of the economic sphere and to work with diverse and very different objects.

In fact, the meso-level of the economy is considered a certain economic space center, an intermediate link (or rod) connecting economic agents on micro and macro level of national and/or supranational governance. Additionally, meso-economic systems have a fairly high level of independence and integrity. Their size, structure, resource availability, and functioning features allow application of a systematic approach to managing the economy to create effective strategies and institutional mechanisms of development while ensuring the adaptation of the managerial mechanism by objectives and specific features of functioning of the economic systems at the meso-level.

Modern researchers have identified four main components of meso-economy:

1. Branch meso-economy (branches and subsectors of a national economy).
2. Interindustry meso-economy (inter-industry vertical complexes, steady agrarian and industrial complexes or military industrial complex).
3. Regional meso-economy (regions, territorial clusters, and other regional groups of organizations).
4. Interregional meso-economy which is based on the territorial social and economic formations. (Kleiner, 2011, p. 6).

In this case, such economic systems as branches of industry, regions, large inter-sectoral economic complexes, industrial clusters, and agglomerations could be treated as meso-economic systems which belong to the class of socio-economic systems and contain active elements. This means their basic element is the human being; human activity determines the characteristics of all processes of functioning and development of such a system. Connection, due to which these systems exist, characterize the complex and contradictory relationships between people based on their interests, values, motives and attitudes.

For example, from an economic point of view building a nuclear power plant may become a rational way to solve the electricity shortage problem in the region as a meso-economic system. However because of a number of reasons (e.g., for fear of emergencies with nuclear reactors), the population of the region can prevent this decision, preferring a more expensive way to purchase energy from the neighboring regions.

In spite of a large variety all meso-economic systems have some common features:

- The presence of independent objects in their composition.
- The presence of a complex set of relations between objects, including elements of competition, cooperation, coordination, and co-evolution.

- The presence of many subjects, the development of which is non-linear, and the interaction has non-trivial character.
- Failure in determining the strategic priorities of development, based on formal criteria only.
- Absence of a single management center.

On this basis, it is possible to assume that it is inexpedient to apply directly the traditional methodology of macroeconomic modeling, based on concepts of perfect market or a planned regulation, either the methodology of microeconomic modeling, based on concepts of rational behavior of a subject and a choice for optimal solutions made by well-known criterion with given constraints for making effective decisions at the meso-economic level. Instruments of decision-making support at the meso-economic level should consider system characteristics of meso-economy, functioning on an integrated methodological platform of systemic, institutional, and evolutionary paradigms in economics (Kornai, 1998; Kleiner, 2011).

Meso-economy as a system is complex and can be characterized by a large number of elements and relations between them and the environment, different kinds of uncertainty, imprecision of quantitative and qualitative estimation of parameters in such systems, different levels and obviousness of the development, nonlinearity of processes inside the system, and many others. In this regard, the problem of forecasting and governance of complex systems development is being considered as semi-structured. Simultaneously, the need to establish effective governance mechanisms of meso-economic systems and the development of appropriate tools to support managerial decision-making process is becoming increasingly important.

The management of meso-economy from a system approach position assumes:

- Problems of meso-economy are defined with taking into account the relationship with systems of a higher level hierarchy which includes the considered system and with which it is linked by common goals.
- The purposes of meso-economy should be considered in connection with a system in general or with larger systems.
- Sustainable development of the system cannot be obtained by making small changes to existing accepted forms; it is based on planning, assessing and making decisions that involve new and positive changes for the system as a whole.
- The system approach and system paradigm are based on such methods of reasoning as the induction and synthesis, which are different from the methods of deduction, analysis and reduction, used to improve systems.
- Planning of the sustainable development of the meso-economic system represents a process in which the scheduler assumes the role of a leader, in order to lead, but not to be lead by someone (Gorelova, Zakharova, & Radchenko, 2006).

Thus, for effective system management of meso-economy, it is important to understand the specificity of its relationships and their mutual influence and to find, first of all, the points of the managerial influence, the activation of which will allow to achieve positive changes in terms of resource constraints in the system as a whole; secondly, to find ways for the effective activation of such points. This requires improving the model and analytical tools to support the corresponding decision-making. In such a case the process of decision-making at the meso-level cannot be fully formalized, as it heavily depends on the value orientations of individuals defining the strategy. However, the subjective approach to the decision making process in a given perspective may also not be sufficiently effective, because people without using appropriate analytical tools may not simultaneously take into account all the internal and external factors, affecting meso-economic development.

Meso-economy as a control object has its own peculiarities; thus, to accept effective administrative decisions it is important to use such methods and technologies that can identify patterns and characteristics of the appropriate system development and apply them to determining the strategic guidance and plans for their implementation, based on objective data and subjective preferences, use of the potential of economic and mathematical methods and human intuition, value preferences and experience of specific subjects of management.

Abilities to Integrate Objectively and Subjectively Focused of Decision-Making Process Support Instruments

Over the twentieth century, the complexity of managerial decision-making has continuously increased and is today higher than ever before. A rapidly changing world, including many interrelated subjects and objects, constantly provides new challenges for decision makers. This is especially important in meso-economic systems due to the fact that to provide for their successful development it is necessary to make non-standard decisions in conditions of uncertainty. One of the main actual directions of increasing of administrative activity efficiency is its automation. The main results of automation include improving the quality, rapidity and efficiency of management decisions, and increasing the efficiency of management as a specific type of activity. Automation of administrative activity is performed using the entire set of available methods and affects the entire range of management activities. An increasingly important role, respectively, in support of the activities of the subject of management is played by the decision support systems (DSS), allowing to estimate a set of various alternatives and to choose the best opportunity.

The results of several studies show that many systems of decision support for the management of meso-economic systems, of most interest are On-Line Analysis Processing technologies (OLAP) which are an adequate instrument of consideration for problems with a complex structure. OLAP class applications and technologies are designed to collect, store, and analyze multidimensional data in support of the management decision making process. To be considered an OLAP application, the DSS is also required to be a high-speed system.

An important feature of OLAP is the ability to analyze large volumes of data describing the studied object or process from different angles by providing analytics with tools for working with multidimensional data. The same quantitative characteristics can be described, represented and evaluated from different sides. The system must provide a multidimensional conceptual view of data, including full support for multiple hierarchies, as this is the most logical way to conduct strategic analysis. The data that the application works with are coming from transactional systems. On the basis of the analysis of these data the report with which the user works is under construction. This report is the main instrument for working with an OLAP application. Reports the user creates on his own, choosing dimensions, levels of aggregation, or receives regular reports with pre-defined structure. Thereafter, different analytical tools are used to the data selected for concrete research.

For example, analysis of information on innovative regional clusters can be conducted on such measurements of measures such as types of products, years, companies-participants of the cluster and such measurements of facts as cost, selling price, and the amount of goods sold. In OLAP applications, in addition to specific to OLAP methods, are methods used for the discovery of new knowledge such as Data Mining (DM) methods whch can be defined as the process of decision support based on the search of hidden patterns within the data (Parsaye, 1998).

Thus, the DM method is designed to detect previously unknown dependencies and works regardless of users, sometimes in fully automatic mode. As a rule, the application of this class handles very large volumes of data. DM methods focused on fulfilling the tasks of reporting, classifying, clustering, anomaly detection, induction rules, correlation, and regression analysis. In meso-economic systems, DM can solve a wide variety of tasks. For example, it can refer the regions of a particular cluster to increase the targeting of measures for economic policy or to optimize the selection of suppliers by product groups within the value chains for vertical clusters.

Actually, the OLAP application is to build a report that is a subset of the multidimensional cube and use in relation to them both OLAP-operations, and specific methods, for example, such as data mining. Analytical study of the problem with the use of DM is a specific process of obtaining new knowledge, built on the use of a variety of techniques which include decision trees, fuzzy logic methods, evolutionary programming, artificial neural networks, genetic algorithms, and other neuroeconomic methods.

A set of OLAP and DM methods used in combination are suitable for analysis of evidence and consideration of the problem situation from different sides, although it does not sufficiently supports the incorporation of subjective positions of decision-makers, and processing of information, bearing a qualitative assessment of objects. Therefore, it makes sense to use OLAP applications as a base platform for information-analytical support of decision making at the meso-level, but methodological apparatus of corresponding DSS should be expanded through the integration of technologies that allow taking into account subjective factors and parameters.

In other words, in the decision-making process in the meso-economic system the process of building a model of objective reality must followed by the process of creating the selection criteria based on their subjective assessment by the decision-maker. It is caused by the compliance of current state of economic system to the development purposes, and also the actually desirable future condition of the system is defined, eventually, by the person. However, the objective limits of human capacity for simultaneous assessment of multiple parameters determine the need for the application of specialized techniques.

In case of a large number of alternative criteria, the decision-makers' activity becomes so complicated that errors become inevitable. To solve problems with too much complexity for humans, multi-criteria methods for decision support are used. The model of preferences and policy of the decision makers is constructed using them. Methods based on models of subjective nature allow abstracting from the subject area and solve within a single algorithm the structured tasks of choosing between alternatives.

Widespread and repeated software implementation in the world theory and practice has received three approaches to multi-criteria assessment of alternatives in solving problems that lack of objective models:

- Analytical Hierarchy Process (AHP).
- Multi-Attribute Utility Theory (MAUT).
- ELimination Et Choix Traduisant la REalité (ELECTRE).

As the results of several studies show (Pletnyakov, 2012), the MAUT and AHP methods are the most promising for efficient working with a multidimensional OLAP-cube in the decision support system for making difficult decisions in relation to semi-structured problems. The process of using MAUT for working with OLAP-cube is fairly simple, in its framework each containing important for making decision cube dimension is evaluated using a utility function (Pletnyakov, 2012).

Using a combination of these objective and subjective approaches and their analytical units allows:

- Determining accurately the position of decision-makers on the importance of indicators and criteria. These methods give the opportunity to express a position of decision-makers with high precision and to obtain a correct idea of the meaning of the criteria in needs for building integrated indicators based on the views of several different decision makers in different positions.
- Choose the alternative that best meets the criteria. In case of finding the exact values of criteria it is a technical problem to be solved by the following the algorithm of the method.
- In case of a wrong choice to correct the importance of a particular criterion and to use the assessment of the importance of criteria in the future.

In fact, implementation of the proposed approach first permits the analyzing of information on the construction of objective models of meso-economy, its subsystems and problematic situations, and then providing instrumental support for the subjective assessment of validity, and selection of targets and criteria of their achievement by the decision maker. This provides the opportunity to actually combine formal mathematical methods as well as intuition and experience of the specific people. Initially, empirical knowledge is used as a source of information and at the decision-making stage, experience and knowledge about the importance of certain factors which are not amenable to formalization, are used by management.

A methodologically valid decision-making process has significant advantages over a choice made only on the basis of experience and intuition of experts or decision-makers. Even in case of the wrong choice, it is known by what criteria it was accepted and it is possible to conclude that the position was wrong. If the decision-maker wishes to follow intuition, it is possible to receive positive result but not information about how the decision differs taken earlier, and if different, in what direction. In case of successful adoption of solutions based on special calculation and analytical methods, the replication of successful experiences is possible. Therefore, it is possible to expect essential increases of efficiency of decision-making processes in general, in case of integration of the considered methods of support of decision-making within a uniform system.

In this manner, the use of OLAP and DM methodologies in combination with the MAUT allows analyzing objective data across different meso-economic parameters, identify hidden dependencies and patterns of its development in an automated process and take into account the subjective preferences of the decision-maker while choosing strategic guidelines. However, the use of appropriate technologies requires specific skills for decision-making process and comprehensive IT support. This approach is not the only one to solve the problem of efficiency increase in meso-economic decision-making by considering the simultaneous consideration of its objective and subjective components. A cognitive approach and tools of its practical implementation have significant potential in this context.

Potential of Cognitive Mapping in Support of the Meso-Economic Decisions-Making Process

A cognitive approach already discussed is a variant of integration of assessment methods of objective reality and subjective preferences of decision-makers which also permits simultaneous use of the potential of formal methods and expertise of the people to improve the process of decision making at the meso-level of the economy. Cognitive mapping is based on the methodological platform of epistemology, cognitive psychology, neurophysiology, anthropology, linguistics, information theory, decision theory, theoretical computer science, and the theory of artificial intelligence. It allows solving semi-structured problems by using intuition, experience, associative thinking and guesswork of experts, as well as providing a tool for transferring of such knowledge for quantitative calculations. Cognitive mapping focuses on the structuring knowledge of experts in a particular subject area and can be used in meso-economic decision making support systems development.

The technology of cognitive modeling allows defining possible and rational ways of management of a situation to provide the transition of purpose from initial negative states to positive. The technology of cognitive modeling allows meso-economic management to be proactive and avoiding potentially dangerous situations to be alarming and conflicting and, in case of their occurrence, to make rational decisions.

The main task of constructing cognitive models is to provide better understanding of an observed event, phenomenon, and process. Modeling sets to the researcher a certain scheme within which it is possible to test concrete hypotheses and, which allows predicting events. Cognitive models, based on the information processing scheme, are a heuristic construct used to organize the existing volume of literature, the stimulation of further research, coordination of research efforts and facilitate communication between scientists and decision makers. Cognitive models are based on conclusions drawn from observations. Their tasks are to provide intelligible representation of character of the observed, to help make predictions in the development of hypotheses, to develop mechanisms of managerial decision-making process.

The great advantage of a cognitive model is that it allows one to view the entire picture in details so as to integrate logic and imagination. Cognitive mapping consists of the following: the development of the structure of gained knowledge of the subject area (defined by a list of the main concepts of the subject area), the identification of relationships between concepts, and the definition of the relation of the subject area with the surrounding world. Thus, cognitive mapping is a convenient tool for the study of semi-structured problems, promotes better understanding and identifying contradictions and qualitative analysis of systems (Gorelova, Verba, & Zakharova, 2004).

The logical stages of cognitive model creation reflect consecutive transition from allocation of the basic factors characterizing a problem situation (including the target and operating factors) to a group of factors in the blocks forming tops or "concepts" of a cognitive map, further to definition of connections between factors, to identification of cause and effect chains, creation of a cognitive map and, at last, drawing up the equations of a cognitive model and checking its adequacy (Gorelova, Zakharova, & Radchenko, 2006). Cognitive modeling begins with the development of a cognitive map of the object. The cognitive map – a structural diagram of causal relationships in the system – is created to understand and analyze the behavior of a complex system.

Let the system consist of a set of the V separate elements. Two elements Vi and Vj of system on the scheme can be represented as separate points-tops and if the Vi element is connected with the Vj element by relationship of cause and effect, they should be connected by the focused arch. It is quite possible that consequences can be the cause of change of other factors. It is probable that consequences can be the cause of change of other factors. Cause and effect chains can be quite long and complicated. The causality analysis is required, for example, to predict the development of the situation, implementation of various schemes of management processes in the system. After creation of the cause-and-effect relationships, strategies of decision-making in a given subject area are defined.

Definition of elements of the object studied with a definite purpose and establishment of communications between elements is conducted with the help of experts by collecting and processing statistical information on the basis of studying of literary data via theoretical knowledge in a particular subject area. Cognitive structuring is resulted by development of the informal description of knowledge about a particular subject area which can be represented in the form of a diagram, graph, matrix, table, or text. The schemes of cause-and-effect relationships, interpreting the views and opinions of decision-makers, referred to as cognitive maps. The concept of cognitive maps – maps of cognition – is initial in the cognitive analysis and modeling of difficult situations (Gorelova, Matveeva, & Nikitaeva, 2007).

The cognitive map displays only the fact of existence of influence of factors at each other. Its main advantage is the ability to perform qualitative simulation. The complex nature of influences of factors, dynamics of changes of influences depending on change of a situation, temporary changes of factors are not displayed in a cognitive map. Considering all of these circumstances requires transition to the next level of structuration of information, displayed in a cognitive map (i.e., transition to a cognitive model is required). At the level of the cognitive model, each connection between factors of a cognitive map reveals to the corresponding equation which may contain both the quantitative (measured) variables, and qualitative (unchangeable) variables.

Process of cognitive modeling includes the following stages.

Stage One: The cognitive analysis of a difficult situation (immersion in a problem, identification of a problem) consists of a number of actions: statement of the problem and research objectives, the study of the current situation or process from the position of set goal; collection, systematization, analysis of existing statistical and qualitative information on problems (sources of information: statistical reports, documents, experts, media, private sources, etc.); the allocation of the main characteristic features of the process under study and identification of the relationships between them; determination of actions of the basic objective laws (e.g.,economic, social, political, ecological) of studied situation developments that will allow marking out objective dependences and tendencies in the processes happening in situations; definition inherent in the studied situation of requirements, conditions, restrictions; allocation of the main subjects connected with a situation, determination of their subjective interests in development of this situation that will allow to define possible changes in objective development of a situation, to allocate factors which subjects can really influence; definition of ways, mechanisms of action, implementation of economic and political interests of the main socio-political subjects that will allow to define further strategy of behavior and prevention of undesirable consequences of development of a situation.

Stage Two: Creation of a cognitive (graph) model of a problem situation consists of the following actions: allocation of the factors, according to experts characterizing a problem situation (allocation of the basic (main) factors describing a problem essence, allocation in total of basic factors of target factors, allocation in total of basic factors of the governing factors which will be a potential leverage over the situation in the model, definition of the factors - indicators reflecting and explaining development of processes in a problem situation and their influence on various spheres (e.g., economic, social, etc.); grouping of factors in blocks; the factors that characterize the area of the problem and defining processes in this area are combined in one unit; there may be options depending on the specifics of the problem, objectives of analysis, number of subjects, situations, etc. Allocation in the block certain group of integrated indicators (factors), on which change can be judged. The general tendencies in this sphere, allocation within the block of indicators – factors – characterizing tendencies and processes in this sphere; definition of connections between factors (definition of connections and interrelations between blocks of factors that will allow to define the main directions of influence of factors of different blocks at each other, definition of direct connections of factors in the block: definition of the direction of influences and interferences between factors (i.e., identification of a chain: "reason – consequence"), determination of character and extent of influence, definition of connections between factors of various blocks; the creation of a cognitive map (graph) of a given situation; drawing up equations of a cognitive model of the situation; checking of an adequacy of the model.

Stage Three: Modeling. Cognitive modeling of processes in a situation is represented in the form of cyclic procedure (Figure 1).

Knowledge regarding the studied problem is widening; hence, the initial model is constantly improving. Thus, a cognitive modeling toolkit allows conducting structural and dynamic studies of complex structured objects which include socio-economic systems of the meso-level, and identifying a causal links between their basic components. The practical significance of the presented approach is determined by the ability of the assessment of the meso-economic effects of management actions on the basis of scenario analysis to improve the quality and soundness of decisions. In other words, a cognitive approach allows defining the basic characteristics of meso-economic system and to simulate scenarios of its development to identify effective management decisions with regard to their impact on the system as a whole. Thus, one of the main features of the cognitive model is a construction of a unique cognitive model for each meso-economic system.

Figure 1. Procedures of cognitive modeling (Gorelova, Matveeva, & Nikitaeva, 2007)

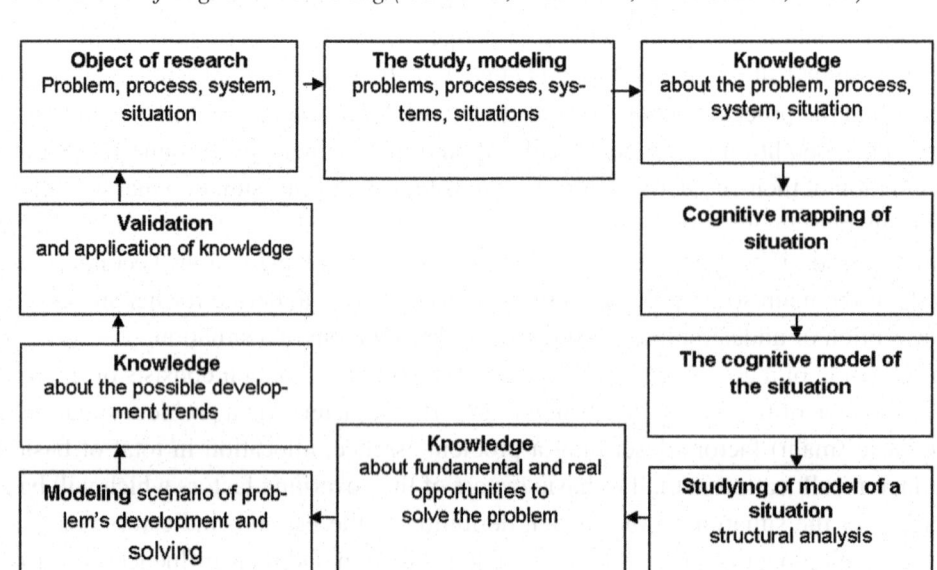

Cognitive Mapping of Interaction between State and Business in Meso-Economic System

Cognitive mapping of interaction between the state and business in meso-economic systems of the Southern Russian region will be presented as a case-study. The appropriateness of considering this case in our research is determined by the fact that a significant potential for improving the efficiency of development of meso-economic systems is incorporated in the space of partnerships between the state and business. Numerous examples of establishing public-private partnerships in developed and developing economies demonstrate significant positive effects for both participants of partnership relations and the economy as a whole due to the integration of capabilities and institutional resources of public and private structures.

Thus, the use of such forms of cooperation as business participation in the expertise of draft laws and regulatory impact assessment and creation of expert and advisory bodies, development of strategies and regional development programs, cross-sectoral personnel rotation, implementation of administrative reforms, leads to the improvement of state regulations which also includes the avoidance of redundant functions, adoption of balanced decisions, reduction of administrative barriers, improvement of the investment climate, growth of professional competencies among officials and improvement of public administration efficiency. Together, this helps to create an institutional environment that promotes effective economic development (Nikitaeva, 2007).

However, in some countries, including the modern Russian economy, the potential for cross-sectoral collaboration is significantly underutilized. Public-private partnership is not often a strategic priority since its potential is underestimated. Dependences between the proliferation of public-private partnerships and development of meso-economic systems are not clearly defined. Consideration of a meso-economic system of interaction between government and business as a subsystem of the regional economic system as a whole with the use of a cognitive approach will provide information to understand the essence of the occurring processes and form the basis for creating appropriate management decisions in the future.

Some results of study over the modern Russian system of interaction of state and business allow concluding that, on one hand, the main problems in the area under consideration is the class of semi-structured, the tendency of domination of the uncertain dependences, signs, and characteristics is observed. On the other hand, a number of effects, arising from the interaction between government agencies and commercial companies, are quantifiable, and requires determination of the relevant parameters and monitoring schemes. This gives the possibility of modeling the process of managing the interaction of state and business in the economic system of the region based on a combination of quantitative and qualitative procedures, and to increase the effectiveness of the adoption and implementation of management decisions aimed at the improvement of existing mechanisms of inter-sector cooperation through the development of an appropriate decision support systems.

To solve this problem, it is possible to use a cognitive approach assuming a combination on the basis of consecutive application of various methods of modeling of difficult systems including methods aimed at activating the use of intuition and experience of experts, and formalized representation methods of complex systems. The application of the cognitive approach allows building a systemic-functional model of interaction of state and business, which will present the main elements of the system in conjunction with the components of the economic system of the region and reflect the functional relationship between the factors determining the specificity of interaction between government and businesses in meso-economic projections.

It gives the opportunity to run a dynamic system behavior modeling of interaction between government and business with application of cyclic procedures according to the scenario approach. From the formal perspective the cognitive map (the basis of cognitive model) is a symbolic directed graph (digraph) as:

$$G = \langle V, E \rangle, \tag{1}$$

where: V is the set of tops, tops ("concepts") $V_i \in V$, i =1, 2,…, k are the elements of the studied system; E is a set of acrs, arcs $e_{ij} \in E$, i,j=1, 2, …, N represent the interrelation between tops V_i and V_j; the impact of V_i on V_j in the studied situation can be positive ("+"sign above the arc), when the increase (decrease) of one factor leads to an increase (decrease) in other negative ("- "sign above the arc), when the increase (decrease) of one factor leads to a decrease (or increase) in the other, or absent (0). Cognitive map G can be represented by a matrix of relations A_G.

A matrix of relationships A_G – is a square matrix, of which lines and columns are marked with tops of graph G, and on crossing of an i-line, j - column stand (or not) number one if the relation between the Vi and Vj elements exists (does not exist) like:

$$A_G = \left[a_{ij} \right]_{k \times k}, a_{ij} = \begin{cases} 1 \text{ if } V_i \text{ is connected with } V_j \\ 0 \text{ if } V_i \text{ is not connected with } V_j \end{cases} \tag{2}$$

Building a cognitive map of interaction between government and business was based on a consistent application of the methods of structuring the "top down" and "bottom-up". Initially a detailed study of selected consolidated blocks of factors and then aggregation of the selected indicators were conducted with the conservation cause-and-effect relationships of their mutual influence. The choice of the concepts of systemic-functional cognitive model of interaction between government and business in the economic system of the region and the determination of cause-effect chains requires some explanation.

The state in the considered context represents a complex of institutes and officials and includes public authorities, and also public institutions implementing functions of regulation, and functions of providing services and managing state property. State institutions and organizations are represented in the system, on one hand, as a key component of the management subsystem of the system of interaction, but on the other hand as the main subjects of cross-sectoral collaboration. The public authorities play a dominant role in the budget process, prioritization of the distribution in expenditure of the regional budget, providing, respectively, the impact on the quality and of the populations' well-being in the region.

In addition, the regulatory impacts of governmental structures significantly affect regional markets of goods and services. Legislative and rulemaking activity of the state bodies has a direct impact on the formation and development of the institutional environment of the region. State agencies performing the functions of providing services and managing state property, are the major stakeholders in the development of public-private partnerships, particularly in infrastructure, investment and social spheres.

The impact of public authorities on business companies is conducted through the formation of a specific institutional environment, the use of various forms and technologies of interaction with the business community and its individual representatives, as well as through direct and indirect financial incentives and the regulation of business actors at the expense of the regional budget. Thus, tax assignments of business make bulk of receipts of revenues of the regional budget that puts its fullness into direct dependence on activity of business firms. Another group of factors affecting the regional budget is associated with functionality of regional markets of goods and services, while the demand is determined by the population and by commercial companies (which play a leading role in shaping the supply in regional markets).

A component "business" includes the key performance indicators of business companies in the region, including profitability, production, number of enterprises and organizations, the number of people employed in this sector of the economy, etc. Separation of blocks of indicators of investments and innovations seems reasonable in the framework of a cognitive model. This is due to the fact that these two concepts, although closely linked with accomplishing their businesses, are most dependent on the activities of the regional authorities, the institutional environment of meso-economy, simultaneously providing a significant impact not only on the performance of commercial structures, but also on the competitiveness of the regional economy. Moreover, it is necessary to consider investment and innovative activity of state organizations and, among them, research and educational institutions.

A set of indicators "interaction of state and business" includes the basic principles, forms, and technologies of direct cooperation between the government and business structures, forming the core mechanism for the implementation of public-private partnerships. It is the interaction that influences the processes of transformation of the institutional environment, the success of business development and transformation in the governmental bodies under the influence of the feedback loop. Direct two-way connection of an interaction concept with the top of innovation is due to the stimulation of innovative activity in the result of joint efforts of actors from different sectors as well as provision of innovative forms and technologies of cooperation between state institutions and business.

Regional risks are considered in this model from several positions. First, from the point of view of economic entities: for business firms enterprise risks are in direct dependence on degree of uncertainty of the business environment that allows speaking about existence of the inverse functional connectivity of the regional risks of commercial companies, and the interaction between the state and business in the region (including information exchange). In turn, the assessment of enterprise risks of companies corresponds to decisions on innovative and investment activity of economic entities. Thus, it is necessary to emphasize that innovation and investment are factors enforcing risks emergence due to the nature of these phenomena. Secondly, internal and external risks of regional economy are considered, including economic, political, social, environmental, financial, investment, criminal, and legislative risks are in the number of regional risks.

It should be noted that functional relations of certain types of risks with other concepts of the cognitive map can be both direct and indirect. In particular, increases of investment productivity of businesses and creation of new industrial facilities in most cases have a negative impact on the environment of the regional socio-economic system, as it increases environmental risks. The creation of new jobs within the same sample contributes to the reduction of social risks in the region. Based on the analysis of existing information (in the form of quantitative and qualitative data) about the condition of the system of interaction between state and business in the context of a particular socio-economic system of the region, a list of factors and indicators that characterize the area of a cognitive map was offered.

1. Regional budget may be defined as: $X_1, x_1^i \in X_1, i = \overline{1, n_1}$, where:

   x_1^1 - balanced budget;

   x_1^2 - budget expenses;

x_1^3 - budget income;

x_1^4 - budget of development;

x_1^5 - the functioning budget;

x_1^6 - share of own income of the consolidated budget of the region in its full expenses;

x_1^7 - interbudgetary relations;

....

x_1^{n1} - other indicators.

2. Indicators of state organizations may be defined as: $X_2, x_2^i \in X_2, i = \overline{1, n_2}$, where

x_2^1 - integrity of systems of public administration in the region;

x_2^2 - quality of public administration;

x_2^3 - the number of officials;

x_2^4 - administrative reform;

x_2^5 - regional policy;

x_2^6 - population confidence in the authorities;

x_2^7 - the activities of state organizations performing the function of providing services;

x_2^8 - characteristics of state-owned assets in the social, educational, infrastructure and other spheres;

....

x_1^{n2} - other indicators.

3. Population of the region may be defined as: $X_3, x_3^i \in X_3, i = \overline{1, n_3}$, where:

x_3^1 - population;

x_3^2 - the number of economically active population;

x_3^3 - the unemployment rate;

x_3^4 - average income per capita;

x_3^5 - the standard of living;

x_3^6 - GDP per capita;

x_3^7 - national and cultural features;

x_3^8 - the coverage of social services;

....

x_3^{n3} - other indicators.

4. Regional markets for goods and services may be defines as: $X_4, x_4^i \in X_4, i = \overline{1, n_4}$, where:

x_4^1 - dynamics of prices in regional markets;

x_4^2 - supply and demand;

x_4^3 - saturation of the regional markets;

x_4^4 - types of branch markets;

....

x_4^{n4} - other indicators.

5. Institutional environment may be defineds as: $X_5, x_5^i \in X_5, i = \overline{1, n_5}$, where:

x_5^1 - legal environment;

x_5^2 - development of market economy institutions in the region;

x_5^3 - administrative barriers;

x_5^4 - the development of market infrastructure;

....

x_5^{n5} - other indicators.

6. Business may be defined as:: $X_6, x_6^i \in X_6, i = \overline{1, n_6}$, where:

    x_6^1 - the output of products and services;

    x_6^2 - basic production assets;

    x_6^3 - profit / loss;

    x_6^4 - the number and sizes of business entities;

    x_6^5 - branch structure;

    x_6^6 - exports and imports, interregional exchange;

    x_6^7 - the number of people employed in business structures;

    x_6^8 - average salary of employees;

    x_6^9 - corporate social responsibility;

    ....

    x_6^{n6} - other indicators.

7. Investments may be defines as: $X_7, x_7^i \in X_7, i = \overline{1, n_7}$, where:

    x_7^1 - the total value of investments in the region;

    x_7^2 - investments into fixed capital (fixed capital formation??);

    x_7^3 - the share of residents ' investments in the regional economy in the total value of investments;

    x_7^4 - sources of investment;

    x_7^5 - investment efficiency;

    ....

    x_7^{n7} - other indicators.

8. Innovation may be defined as:: $X_8, x_8^i \in X_8, i = \overline{1, n_8}$, where:

    x_8^1 - innovation activity of enterprises and organizations;

    x_8^2 - innovation-focused investments;

    x_8^2 - the structure and the number of types of innovation in the region

    ....

    x_8^{n8} - other indicators.

9. Interaction of state and business may be defined as: $X_9, x_9^i \in X_9, i = \overline{1, n_9}$, where:

    x_9^1 - the forms and technologies of interaction between government and businesses;

    x_9^2 - models of public-private partnership;

    x_9^3 - the role of business in making decisions at the meso-level;

    x_9^4 - organizational and infrastructure parameters of interaction;

x_9^5 - economical and administrative parameters of interaction;

x_9^6 - balance of private and public interests;

x_9^7 - information support of interaction;

....

x_9^{n9} - other indicators.

10. Risks may be defined as: $X_{10}, x_{10}^i \in X_{10}, i = \overline{1, n_{10}}$, where:

x_{10}^1 - economic risks;

x_{10}^2 - political risks;

x_{10}^3 - social risks;

x_{10}^4 - ecological risks;

x_{10}^5 - financial risks;

x_{10}^6 - investment risks;

x_{10}^7 - legal risks;

....

x_{10}^{n9} - other types and indicators of risks.

The purpose of the developed model is to research the influence of interaction between government and business on the economic system development in the region in order to determine the directions, scope, and power of managerial actions that ensure the desired change of the target factors, which are the concepts of "population", "regional budget", "business". Such earmarking of targeted factors requires some adjustment. First of all, it is consistent with these strategic goals of Russia's development as the improvement of people's welfare and poverty reduction on the basis of dynamic and sustainable economic growth, as well as the way to achieve the stated objectives, consisting in the solution of a problem of the dramatic increase in the competitiveness of three components: human rights, state institutions and business. The regional budget is selected as one of the main indicators of quality of activity of the regional public authorities.

Creating a cognitive map on which the interaction system of state and business are embedded in the economic system of the region. Due to the fact, that when making management decisions it is necessary to assess the full range of consequences of regulatory decisions, since the goal of management in the proposed context is the use of cross-sectoral collaboration as a mechanism for the successful development of meso-economic systems. In this case, and state organizations and business structures are both factors of governance in the framework of interaction management of the state and business and integral components of the regional economic system, whose functions go far beyond multi-sectoral partnerships. The cognitive map of the system interaction of state and business in the regional economic system, reflecting the basic, strongest dependencies of the analyzed phenomena is presented in Figure 2.

Type of the cognitive model most corresponding to the tasks solved in research taking into account the existing restrictions, is the vector functional graph (F-graph) which represents a tuple:

K=<G, X, F>, (3)

Figure 2. The cognitive map of the interaction between the state and business in the regional economic system

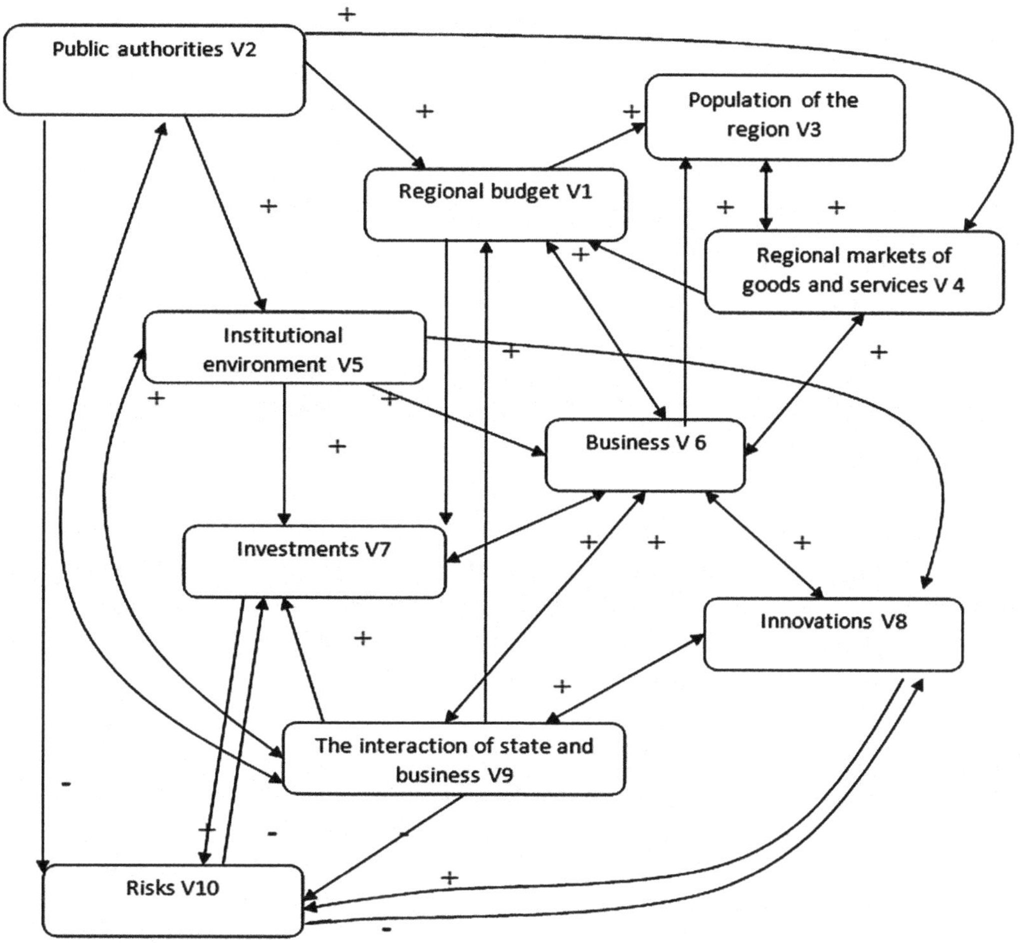

where:

1. G=<V,E> - vector graph;

2. X – set of parameters of tops V; X={X$^{(Vi)}$}, i=1,2,...,k, X$^{(Vi)}$={x$^{(i)}_g$}, g=1,2,...n$_i$; i.e. each top of the parameter vector is independent from each other and put in compliance X$^{(Vi)}$, (or one parameter x$^{(i)}_g$=x$_i$, if g=1); X:V→R, R – set of real numbers;

3. F=F(X,E)= F(x$_i$, x$_j$, e$_{ij}$) – the functionality of transformation of arches putting in compliance to each arch or a sign ("+", "-"), or weight coefficient ω$_{ij}$, or function f(x$_i$, x$_j$, e$_{ij}$) = f$_{ij}$ (Gorelova, G., Matveeva L., Nikitaeva A., 2007).

When choosing the sign dependence of the tops of the graph on the cognitive map the matrix of contiguity of the offered configuration of a cognitive map will look as follows:

	V1	V2	V3	V4	V5	V6	V7	V8	V9	V10
V1	0	0	1	0	0	1	1	0	0	0
V2	1	0	0	1	1	0	0	0	1	−1
V3	1	1	0	1	0	0	0	0	0	0
V4	1	0	1	0	0	1	0	0	0	0
R = V5	0	0	0	0	0	1	1	1	1	0
V6	1	0	1	1	0	0	1	1	1	0
V7	0	0	0	0	0	1	0	0	0	1
V8	0	0	0	0	0	1	0	0	1	1
V9	0	1	0	1	1	1	1	1	0	−1
V10	0	0	0	0	0	0	−1	−1	0	0

In the functional graph generated, perturbation coincides with the received perturbation and is equal to the sum of the elementary impulses acting on a top in the given time. Under the influence of various perturbations, the values of the variables at the tops of the graph may change; a signal received at one of the tops, is distributed along the chain to the other, amplifying or fading. The rule (PR) for the change of parameters in tops at the moment t_{n+1} (Gorelova, Zakharova, & Radchenko, 2006, pp. 203-208).

Let the x_i parameter depend on time (i.e. $x_i(t)$, t=1,2,3,...). Then it is possible to define the spread of perturbations on the graph (i.e., the transition of the system from state t-1 to t, t+1,…).

Let the value of $x_i(t+1)$ in the top v_i depend on $x_i(t)$ and from the tops adjacent to Vi. Let V_i be adjacent to V_j, let $p_j(t)$ – change in V_j top in t time point, then the influence of this change on the x_i parameter at the time of t will be described by the $\pm p_j(t)$ function depending on the sign of an arch connecting V_i and V_j. Generally, if there are some tops of Vj, adjacent to Vi, the spread of perturbation on the graph is determined by the rule defined as in:

$$x_i(t+1) = x_i(t) + \sum_{j=1}^{k-1} f(x_i, x_j \cdot e_{ij}) p_j(t),$$
(4)

where initial values of X(0) are knows in all tops and an initial vector of perturbation of P(0).

Modeling can be performed by steps or pulses. The essence of such modeling is that one of the vertices of the graph is set to a definite change. This activating top actualizes the whole system performance. Let present the f_{ij} function between tops V_j, V_i using the coefficients λ_{ji}, ω_{ji}, characterizing the sign (λ_{ji}: «+» or «-») and the degree of influence of ω_{ji} parameter of V_j top to the parameter of Vi top; replace the $p_j(t)$ function of influence of change in top of V_j, adjacent to V_i, with an impulse:

p(n) = x(n+1) – x(n), where x(n), x(n+1) – the values of the indicator in top V in the steps of the simulation at time t=n and follows t=n+1. Then the formula (4) is converted to the form:

$$x_i(n+1) = x_i(n) + \sum_{j=1}^{k-1} \lambda_{ji} \omega_{ji} [x_j(n+1) - x_j(n)],$$
(5)

In models of this type, the coefficients ω_{ij} characterizing the interaction of adjacent tops can be defined either by expert or statistical methods. The rule (PR) of change for parameters in the tops at the time of t_{n+1} if impulses came to t_n time point in tops:

$$x_i(t_{n+1}) = x_i(t_n) + \sum_{v_j:e=e_{ij} \in E}^{k-1} f(x_i, x_j, e_{ij}) P_j(t_n) + Q_i(t_{n+1}),$$
(6)

The impulse generated by the change of a parameter in top:

$$P_{v_i}(t_{n+1}) = \sum_{v_j:e=e_{ij} \in E}^{k-1} f(x_i, x_j, e_{ij}) P_j(t_n) + Q_i(t_{n+1}),$$
(7)

As in the f-graph the impulse in the pulse process is represented by the ordered sequence without reference to time, it is possible to use formulae "in n-th time". Then:

$$x_{v_i}(n+1) = x_{v_i}(n) + \sum_{v_j:e=e_{ij} \in E}^{k-1} f(x_i, x_j, e_{ij}) P_j(n) + Q_i(n+1)$$
(8)

$$P_{v_i}(n+1) = \sum_{v_j:e=e_{ij} \in E}^{k-1} f(x_i, x_j, e_{ij}) P_j(n) + Q_i(n+1)$$
(9)

The impulse process model is a tuple $<F, Q, PR>$ where the F – F-Graf, $F=<(V, E), X, W>$, $Q=Q(t_n)$ is a sequence of perturbations, PR – the rule of change of parameters. To use the impulse process model within a cognitive approach to assess the impact of management actions on target factors will make a plan of the experiment — the plan of filing a single initial pulse q_i in the top of the chain $q_i =+1$, $q_i = -1$, additional single impulses on various n - steps of the simulation (Table 1).

Table 1. The plan of making managerial impulses to the concepts of the interaction model of state and business in a meso-economic system of the region

No	Impulses q_i	Q - Vector of Pulses in the Top									
		V_1	V_2	V_3	V_4	V_5	V_6	V_7	V_8	V_9	V_{10}
11	q_9 (simple process)	0	0	0	0	0	0	0	0	+1	0
22	q_9 (simple process)	0	0	0	0	0	0	0	0	-1	0
33	q_5, q_9	0	0	0	0	+ 1	0	0	0	-1	0
44	q_5, q_9	0	0	0	0	- 1	0	0	0	+1	0
55	q_7 (simple process)	0	0	0	0	0	0	+1	0	0	0
66	q_{10}	0	0	0	0	0	0	0	0	0	-1
77	q_5, q_7, q_9	0	0	0	0	-1	0	-1	0	+1	0

The considered impulses in the practice can have rather accurate economical and administrative interpretation in a quantitative or qualitative form. For example, the single positive impulse in the concept "interaction of the state and business" can correspond to the adoption of the regional law on concessional agreements, stimulating implementation of public-private projects. The negative impulse in the same top can result in reduction of informational openness of public authorities.

To conduct this experiment developed by Radchenko & Gorelova software permitted the solution of all problems in a complex by implementing the methodology of cognitive modeling of meso-economic systems. Thus, emphasis is on the implementation of structural analysis functions: identifying patterns of development situations, identifying "good" and "bad" scenarios, the analysis of the various subsystems interaction and interacting components, search of mechanisms of influence in the management system. Algorithms of the using software are based on cognitive and scenario modeling, theory methods of graphs and the theory of systems.

Scenario One: When making a positive single impulse into V9 top – "Interaction of the state and business" through four cycles of the simulation there is a clear tendency of growth of the target factors, and the highest rates of positive dynamics characters for businesses whereas indicators of the regional budget and the population change more slowly, though with rather high rates (Figure 3).

Prolongation of the scenario with the set initial impulse of q9 = + 1 shows a continuation of observed trends (experiment was conducted to the 17th step of modeling).

Figure 3. Pulse processes at $q_9 = +1$

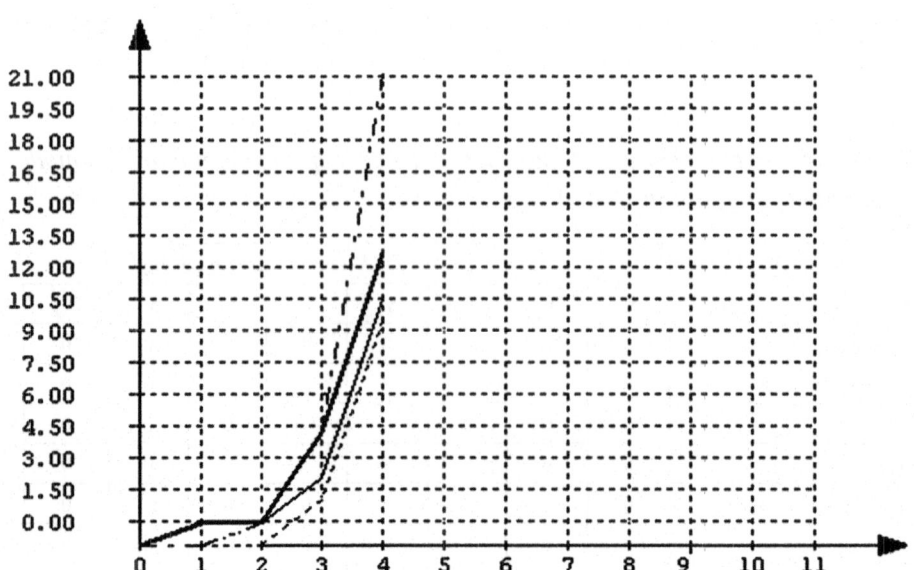

Scenario Two: Making of a negative single impulse into V9 top – "Interaction of the state and business" shows a mirror to the first scenario development of a situation (Figure 4).

Scenario Three: Characterizes development of a situation on conditions of simultaneous entering of a positive single impulse into top of V5 and a negative single impulse into V9 top. The simulation results show that if on the first steps impulses in relation to resulting factors partially compensate influence of each other, already at the fourth step the obvious tendency of a prevalence of negative consequences of deterioration of interaction of the state and business over the initial positive impulses brought on institutional environment of regional economy (for example, due to reduction of administrative barriers) as shown in Figure 5)

These tendencies only amplify further and if the institutional environment worsens slower rates, businesses and the regional budget react to the negative impulse brought in the corresponding top, rather strongly (Figure 6).

The dominant influence of changes of the parameters of V9 top allows for the concluison that improving of the efficiency of institutions in the region should be carried out in conjunction with improving of the interaction between government and business.

Figure 4. Pulse processes at q9 = - 1

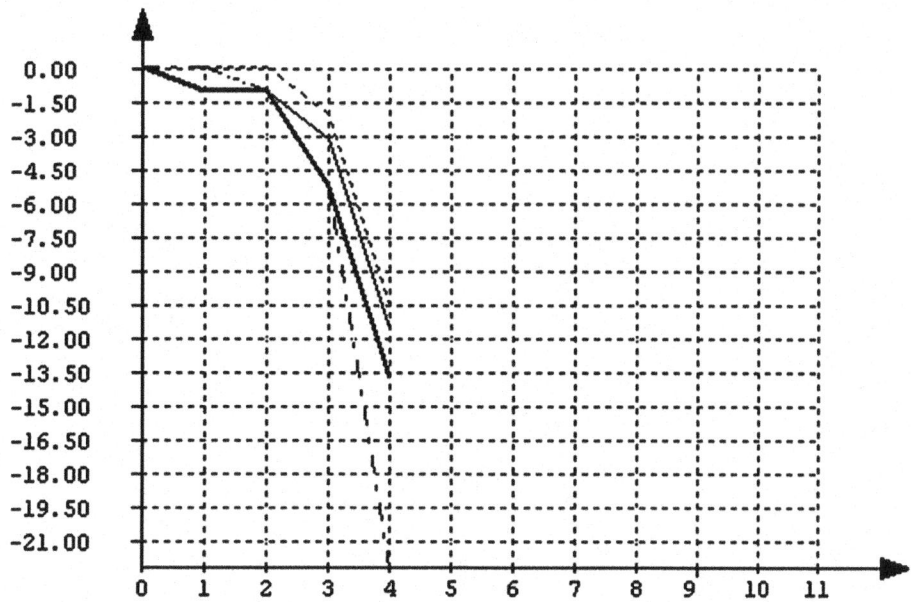

Figure 5. Pulse processes at $q_5 = + 1$, $q_9 = - 1$ (steps of modeling 1-4)

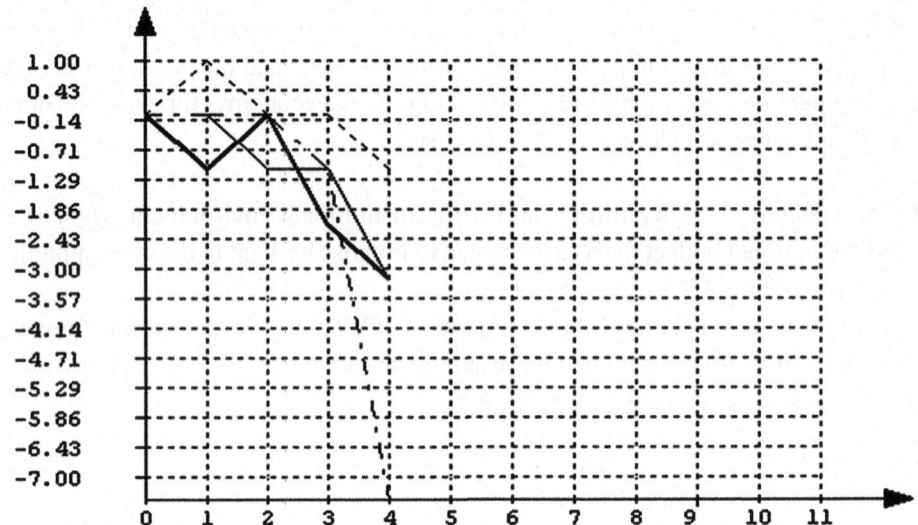

Figure 6. Pulse processes at $q_5 = + 1$, $q_9 = - 1$ (steps of modeling 1-5)

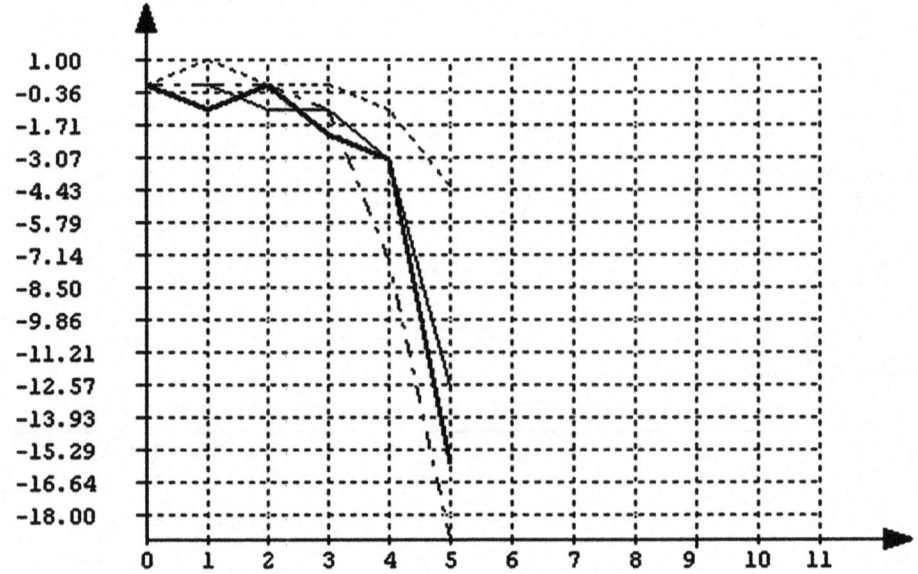

Scenario Four: Describes the changes of the target factors in the system of interaction between state and business, incorporated in the structure of meso-economic relations when entering a positive single impulse into V9 top ("interaction of the state and business") and negative – in V5 concept ("the institutional environment"). In reality this scenario may reflect a situation where the development and adoption of the development conception for regional innovation clusters is accompanied by a parallel deterioration of the fiscal environment of small and medium business conduction, which is observed in particular in the Rostov region of the Russian Federation.

That is actually the situation opposite to the previous set of impulses that is considered. Development of the scenario shows that already through two steps of modeling the institutional environment overcomes a negative initial impulse due to the positive role of interaction between the state and business, and further, all the tops show a positive trend (Figure 7).

Scenario Five: Entering of a positive single impulse into V7 top – "Investments". Simulated development of the situation shows that a negative relationship between tops "Interaction of state and business" and "Risks" implemented through the concept of "Business" positive correlation between tops V5 and V9, as well as other functional dependencies of a cognitive model can lead to a certain reduction of risk on some steps of modeling even on condition of increase in investment and innovation activity (Figure 8).

Figure 7. Pulse processes at $q_5 = -1$, $q_9 = +1$

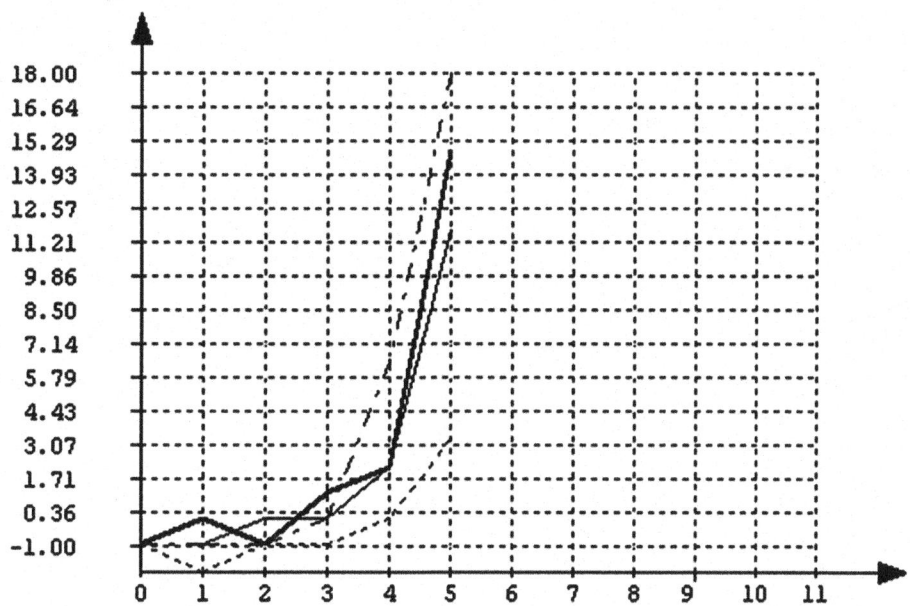

Figure 8. Pulse processes at $q_7 = 1$ (steps of modeling 1-4)

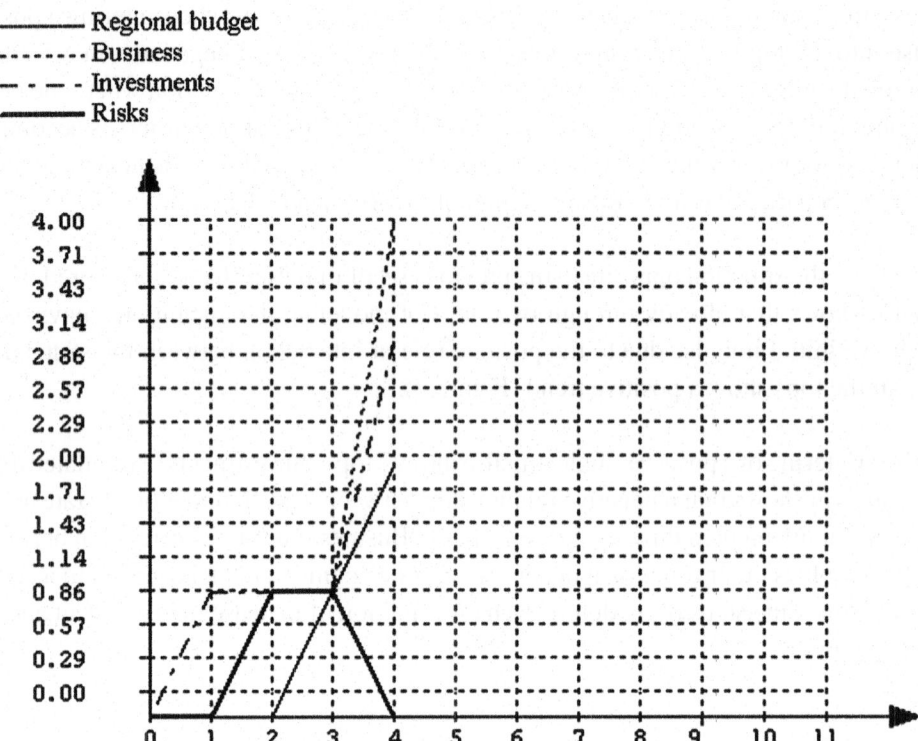

Target factors begin to respond to managerial influence corresponding to this version of events through two steps that reflects the time lag necessary in order that impulses came to the interconnected tops due to their transfer on arches of a cognitive map. It corresponds also to real economic practice when time for receiving return on investments is required. The steady growth of target factors at lower growth rates of risks is observed further (Figure 9).

Scenario Six: Reflects simultaneous entering of negative single impulses into V5, V7 tops and a positive single impulse in V9 top. The analysis of a situation in dynamics allows to conclude that in spite of the fact that on the first steps negative influence of managing factors (which received negative impulses) on business (as a target factor) is observed, since the third step of modeling the condition of the institutional environment in the region is leveled and growth of indicators of business is observed. The following step reflects positive dynamics and operating, and all target factors (Figure 10). Tendencies of growth of indicators of target tops remain at experimental prolongation.

The results of the conducted experiment provided an opportunity to draw some conclusions related to the specific behavior of the meso-economic system of interaction between state and business to the capabilities of the methodology applied to the scenario analysis.

First of all, it is important to note that positive and negative impulses in top "Interaction of the state and business" have stronger impact on a condition of target factors, than impacts on other concepts of a cognitive map. Moreover, at simultaneous entering of multidirectional impulses into the managing

Figure 9. Pulse processes at $q_7 = 1$ (steps of modeling 1-7)

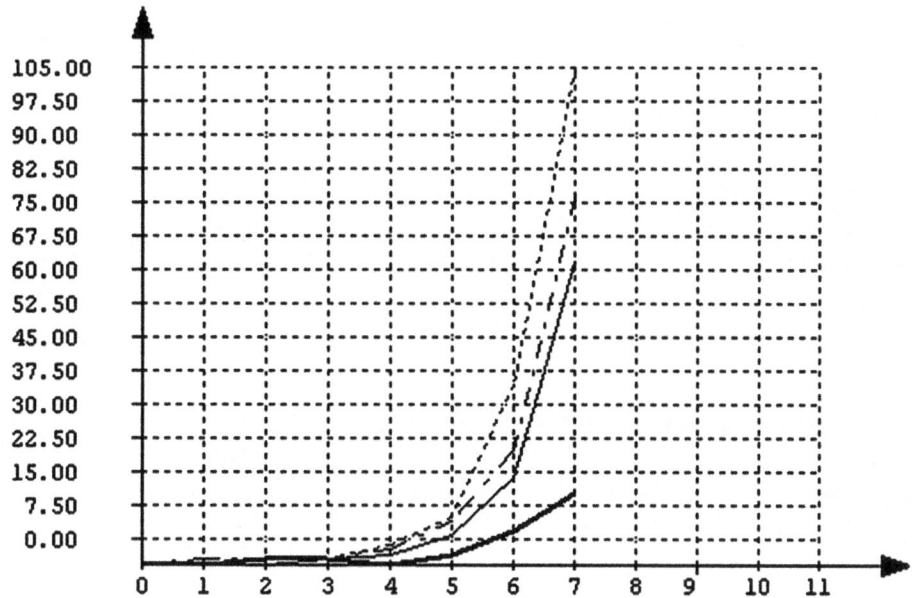

Figure 10. Pulse processes at $q_5 = -1$, $q_7 = -1$, $q_9 = +1$ (steps of modeling 1-5)

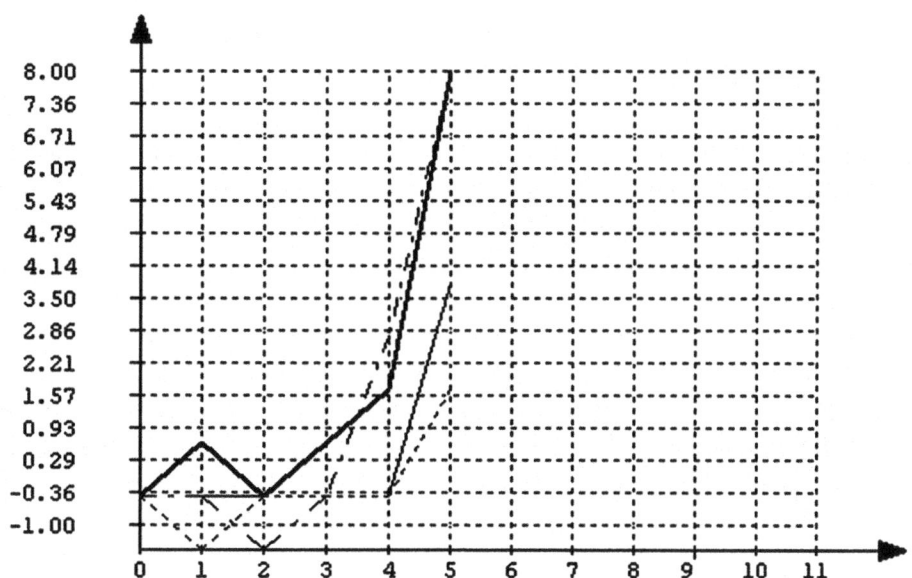

concepts, one of which is "Interaction of the state and business", through several steps of modeling (from two to five) changes of target indicators are caused by development tendencies of the relations of state and business. This demonstrates the importance of improving the efficiency of interaction between government and business in conjunction with the strategic management of the regional economy.

Using the proposed model allows to generate alternative options for management decisions regarding the interaction between government and business and to carry out the most effective, in the context of specific realities of the meso-economy. The practical significance of the model can be enhanced as a result of its development in accordance with the specific objectives of socio-economic systems in the areas that provide additional adjustment of the model as an element of the decision making mechanism based on the available empirical data:

- Detailing indicators of the concepts of cognitive maps, which characterize the components of the economic system of the region, and the definition of their values to improve the accuracy of calculations.
- Clarification of identified functional dependencies to determine the weights of the dependencies of the tops of the graph.
- Converting the model to determine ways of improving structural stability of the system.

The advantages of using the discussed methodology, based on a systematic and cognitive approach and adapted to the needs of meso-economy management, consist of the possibility to assess changes of target factors in the regional development on the basis of introducing impulses of various force, orientation and frequency, corresponding to certain governmental influences with economical and administrative interpretation.

It increases efficiency of the decision-making mechanism of meso-economic scale and assess the full range of consequences of regulatory impacts through the application of the model taking into account complexity and coherence of components of meso-economic systems in the conditions of uncertainty of an environment at limited volumes of reliable information for forecasting of development of a situation by statistical methods.

SOLUTIONS AND RECOMMENDATIONS

Since the dynamics of meso-economic systems, acting to some extent as cores / development centers and basis of modern global economy, in many ways determines the nature and pace of socio-economic development of national economies (being in many ways a conductor of regulating impulses of a control subject at national and supra-national levels, and also economic level of their implementation), an important role is given to the search of methods and tools to increase management efficiency of meso-economies of different types with consideration of their common characteristics and patterns of development.

To improve the effectiveness of decision-making support in meso-economic systems, it is desirable to apply approaches that combine methods of formal data work with the subjective information and personal preferences within uniform methodology. It can be the application of the approach, integrating the OLAP and Data mining technologies with methods of a multi-criteria assessment of alternatives, and also the use of cognitive approach, allowing to apply the methods, aimed at the activization of the use of intuition and expert experience, and methods of the formalized representation of complex systems, and also other approaches respecting the set requirements.

Thus, for the practical application of the given approaches and methods fundamental role is played by their implementation in the form of the decision support systems, since it greatly expands the number of users of the corresponding technologies. Nevertheless, even the available software applications, which are not always united on the platform of a unified support system for decision-making acceptance, can significantly improve the quality of decision-making at the meso-level through the application of these approaches. This requires the adoption of the conceptual framework of decision-making as a methodological background.

FUTURE RESEARCH DIRECTIONS

Currently, methods and technologies that will form the analytical apparatus of decision support systems are developing dynamically. Especially high dynamics of growth is shown by Business intelligence (BI) technologies, including OLAP technologies. While the fairly new, but increasing trend is the integration of different methods and technologies within a single software application, reflecting attempt of researchers to unite on a common methodological platform ways to work with objective and subjective aspects of solving semi-structured problems. However, not all of the considered methods can be used together.

Consequently, more research is needed to find the optimal combinations of approaches and methods, working with objective and subjective aspects of the decision-making process, and to identify areas of their convergence. In addition, the use of appropriate technologies requires a certain investment (in the development or acquisition of software) and ensures a sufficient level of staff for their practical application. Accordingly, it is important to study issues of evaluating the effectiveness of decision support systems with non-standard tools supporting the objective and subjective components of the decision making process.

Another point that should be taken into account when addressing issues of information and analytical support of decision making in meso-economic systems is associated with the tendency to strengthen the role of compatibility of information systems used in the modern world. All of these questions actually have set the trends for further research in this area.

CONCLUSION

Thus, meso-economic systems play an important role in the modern economic development, possessing also specific features as object of management. By combining and effectively using the potential of various economic entities, meso-economic systems have a great potential as points and centers of economic development and become important actors in the global competition. In addition the complexity of decision-making, in meso-economic systems (e.g., regions, clusters, agglomerations, industries, etc.) leads to of the use of appropriate tools and information technologies to support managerial decision-making processes. Appropriate tools should allow management entity to identify explicit and implicit patterns of development and the relationships of meso-economic systems, analyze reliable data and consider the subjective preferences of the decision maker, simulate possible scenarios of events during the implementation of specific management actions.

Using appropriate technologies, the decision support technologies should allow the user (expert, decision maker, etc.) working effectively with objective and subjective models of reality. It is possible, firstly, in case of application of the cognitive approach, to model meso-economic dynamics; and secondly, when integrated as part of the process of decision making, OLAP and Data mining technologies, and methods of multi-criteria evaluation of alternatives. The case study of the cognitive model construction has shown that its use helps to obtain non-trivial results. In particular, it shows that development of state-and-business cooperation in the region is able to neutralize a number of negative events which are associated with risk increase, deterioration of the institutional environment in meso-economy and have a stronger positive impact on the meso-economic dynamics even in comparison with development of such concepts as investments and innovations.

REFERENCES

Amin, A. (1999). An Institutionalist Perspective on Regional Economic Development. *International Journal of Urban and Regional Research, 23*(2), 365–378. doi:10.1111/1468-2427.00201

Anich, I., & Larichev, O. I. (1996). The ELEKTRA Method and the Problem of Acyclicity of Relations of Alternatives. *Automatics and Telemechanics, 8,* 108–118.

Druzhinin, A. G. (2005). *South of Russia in the late XX – early XXI century (economic-geographical aspects).* Rostov n/D: Publishing house of Rostov State University.

Druzhinin, A. G., & Ionov, A. C. (2001). *A Conceptual framework for the regionalization of the economy.* Rostov n/D: Publishing house of North-Caucasus scientific center of high school.

Enright, M. J. (2000). *Survey on the Characterization of Regional Clusters: Initial Results.* Working Paper, Institute of Economic Policy and Business Strategy. Hong Kong: University of Hong Kong.

Gorelova, G., Matveeva, L., & Nikitaeva, A. (2007). *Systematic approach and instruments of management in geographically localized economic systems of meso-level.* Rostov n/D: Publishing house of Southern Federal University.

Gorelova, G. V., Verba, V. A., & Zakharova, E. N. (2004). Cognitive models in intelligent systems to support management decisions. Herald of TSURE, 5, 35 - 39.

Gorelova, G.V., Zakharova, E.N., & Radchenko., S.A. (2006). *The study semi-structured problems of socio-economic systems cognitive approach.* Rostov-on-Don: Publishing house of Southern Federal University.

Granberg, A. G. (2005). *Strategy of development of macroregions of Russia.* Moscow: HSE.

Inshakova, E. I., & Samokhin, A. V. (2008). Sustainable development of the macroregion: Methodological and theoretical aspects of research. *Herald of Volgograd State University. Series 3, 1*(12), 80–85.

Kahneman, D. (2003). A perspective on judgment and choice: Mapping bounded rationality. *The American Psychologist, 58*(9), 697–720. doi:10.1037/0003-066X.58.9.697 PMID:14584987

Katsko, I. A., Krepishev, D.A., & Sennikova, A.E. (2011). Elements of the theory of multi-criteria decision making in system research. *Scientific Journal Proceedings of the Kuban State Agrarian University, 5*, 7-13.

Kiselyova, N. N. (2007). *Sustainable development of socio-economic system of the region: methodology of research, model, management.* Rostov-on-Don: Publishing house of Southern Federal University.

Kleiner, G. B. (Ed.). (2011). *Meso-economy of Development.* Moscow: Central Economics and Mathematics Institute RAS.

Klyucharev, V. A., Smits, A., & Shestakova, A. N. (2011). Neuroeconomics: The neurobiology of Decision-making. *Experimental Psychology, 4*(2), 14–25.

Knutson, B., Taylor, J., Kaufman, M., Peterson, R., & Glover, G. (2005). Distributed neural representation of expected value. *The Journal of Neuroscience, 25*(19), 4806–4812. doi:10.1523/JNEUROSCI.0642-05.2005 PMID:15888656

Knyazeva, S. N., & Kurdyumov, S. P. (1999). Synergetics in the context of sustainable development of complex systems. In C. A. Koptyug, V. M. Matrosov, & V. K. Levashov (Eds.), *A new paradigm of development of Russia (the complex problems of sustainable development)* (pp. 340–344). Moscow: Publishing House Academy.

Kolesnikov, Y.S. (2009). *Strategic planning for socio-economic development of region in the conditions of modernization.* Rostov-on-Don: Publishing house of Southern Federal University.

Kornai, J. (1998). *The System Paradigm.* William Davidson Institute Working Papers. Series 278. William Davidson Institute at the University.

Kuhnen, C. M., & Knutson, B. (2005). The neural basis of financial risk taking. *Neuron, 47*(5), 763–770. doi:10.1016/j.neuron.2005.08.008 PMID:16129404

Lotov, A. V., Bushenkov, V. A., & Kamenev, G. K. (2004). *Interactive decision maps. Approximation and Visualization of Pareto Frontier. In Appl. Optimization* (Vol. 89). Boston: Kluwer Academic Publishers.

McClure, S. M., Laibson, D. I., Loewenstein, G., & Cohen, J. D. (2004). Separate neural systems value immediate and delayed monetary rewards. *Science, 306*(5695), 503–507. doi:10.1126/science.1100907 PMID:15486304

Moulaert, F., & Mehmood, A. (2010). Analysing regional development and policy: A structural-realist approach. *Regional Studies, 44*(01), 103–118. doi:10.1080/00343400802251478

Ng, Y.-K. (1986). *Meso-economics: A Micro-Macro Analysis.* London: Harvester.

Nikitaeva, A.Y. (2007). *Theory and practice of management of interaction of the state and business: regional aspect.* Rostov-on-Don: Publishing house of Southern Federal University.

Parsaye, K. A. (1998). Characterization of Data Mining Technologies and Processes. *Journal of Data Warehousing, 1*, 13–18.

Pirlot, M., & Bouyssou, D. (2009). *Analysing the correspondance between strict and non-strict concordance relations.* Bonn: Allemagne.

Pletnyakov, V. A. (2012). *Research and analytical tools of strategic decision making in the economy.* Taganrog: Publishing house of TSURE.

Porter, M. E. (2001). Regions and the new economics of competition. In *Global City-Regions: Trends, Theory, Policy.* Oxford, UK: Oxford University Press.

Puppim de Oliveira, J. A., & Ali, S. H. (2011). Gemstone mining as a development cluster: A study of Brazil's emerald mines. *Resources Policy, 36*(2), 132–141. doi:10.1016/j.resourpol.2010.10.002

Rangel, A., Camerer, C., & Montague, P. R. (2008). A framework for studying the neurobiology of value-based decision making. *Nature Reviews. Neuroscience, 9*(7), 545–556. doi:10.1038/nrn2357 PMID:18545266

Rodríguez-Pose, A., & Comptour, F. (2011). Do clusters generate greater innovation and growth? An analysis of European regions. *Bruges European Economic Research Papers, 21.* Retrieved May 3, 2015, from: http://www.coleurope.eu/sites/default/files/research-paper/beer21.pdf

Saati, T. (2015). *Making decision with dependence and feedback links: Analytical network.* Moscow: LCI.

Scott, A. J., & Garofoli, G. (Eds.). (2007). Development on the Ground. Clusters, Networks and Regions in Emerging Economies. Routledge.

Vanwindekens, F. M., Stilmant, D., & Baret, Ph. V. (2013). Development of a broadened cognitive mapping approach for analysing systems of practices in social–ecological systems. *Ecological Modelling, 250,* 352–362. doi:10.1016/j.ecolmodel.2012.11.023

Vázquez-Barquero, A. (2002). *Endogenous Development: Networking, Innovation, Institutions and Cities.* London: Routledge. doi:10.4324/9780203217313

Wolfram, E., Torsten, H., & Henning, Sch. (2015). The Size Dimension of Complex Economies—Towards a Meso-Economics: The Size of Interaction Arenas and the Emergence of Meso-Platforms of Institutional Coordination. In *The Microeconomics of Complex Economies* (pp. 419–447). Bremen, Germany: University of Bremen.

KEY TERMS AND DEFINITIONS

Business Intelligence: Methods and tools to translate raw information into a convenient form for conducting business analysis and search of strategic development opportunities at the expense of processing large volumes of unstructured data.

Cognitive Mapping: Methodology which allows simultaneous use of potential of formal methods and expertise of the people to improve the process of decision making by structuring knowledge of experts in a particular subject area and using methods of complex system formalization.

Data Mining: The collective name used for designation of set of detection methods in earlier unknown, uncommon, practically useful and available for interpretation knowledge necessary for decision-making in various spheres of human activity.

Decision Support Systems (DSS): The interactive information system using data and models of a choice of decisions that provide users with convenient and efficient access to information resources and providing them with a variety of opportunities for processing information and decision-making.

Meso-Economics: The section of economic science connected with the study of behavior, the contents and essence of the intermediate systems, standing between micro and macroeconomic systems of national economy and having an important independent value.

Meso-Economy: Set of social and economic subsystems of the average level of economic hierarchy and the subsystems lying at lower levels of hierarchy, in particular, enterprises and their groups.

OLAP (Online Analytical Processing): A class of applications and technologies designed to collect, store and analyze multidimensional data in order to support management decision making processes.

The Decision Maker: The subject of the decision (the manager), empowered and responsible for the consequences of the taken and implemented management decisions.

The Decision-Making Theory: The field of knowledge studying the patterns of individuals to choose ways of solving different types of problems and ways of rational choice of the best of possible alternatives.

Chapter 12
Successfully Playing Games of Tax Compliance:
Government Agencies as Architects of Public Choice

Shefali Virkar
University of Oxford, UK

ABSTRACT

The purpose of this chapter is to examine the role of government in encouraging fiscal compliance from the theoretical perspective of the 'Ecology of Games'. Conceptual representations of human behaviour in formal complex institutions, located within Behavioural Economics Political Game Theory, presuppose it is possible for government agencies to strategically influence the behavioural preferences and consumption patterns of individual actors and groups in society. This study presents an empirical case concerned with the implementation and use of an electronic property tax collection system in Bangalore, India developed between 1998 and 2008.

INTRODUCTION

In evaluating the impact of any Government-sponsored public policy measure, it is important to know not only *whether* the initiative has resulted in an increase in absolute monetary revenues collected, but also *if* the project at hand has led to an improvement in the percentage of people complying with the proposed legal requirement. Tax compliance is a societal phenomenon that is hitherto difficult to explain. A large part of fiscal compliance hinges on citizen attitudes towards the government and towards tax burdens, and convincing the public that it is worth their while to pay taxes requires both a sustained campaign and concrete action on the part of the tax collecting authority. But what exactly drives people to pay their taxes? Is it the fear of being caught and penalised? Is it because they believe it is for the common good? Or it is because they follow what they think everyone else is doing?

Through the presentation of an empirical case study surrounding the implementation and use of an electronic property tax collection system in Bangalore (India), developed between 1998 and 2008, this

DOI: 10.4018/978-1-4666-9989-2.ch012

chapter critically examines both the role of Information and Communication Technologies (ICTs) in governmental reform processes and the contribution of such technologies to the deeper evolution of the social dynamics shaping e-government projects used to reform public sector institutions. Anchored in Behavioural Game Theory, and drawing on the theoretical perspectives of the 'Ecology of Games' and 'Design-Actuality Gaps' – both of which recognise the importance of a multitude of diverse motives and individualistic behaviour as key factors influencing organisational reform and institutional change – the research contributes not just to an understanding of the role of ICTs in public administrative reform, but also towards that emerging body of scholarship which is critical of managerial rationalism for an organization as a whole. It is also sensitive to an ecology of actors and their various motivations within the symbiotic organisation.

RESEARCH METHODOLOGY AND SOURCES OF EVIDENCE

The ultimate aim of this chapter is to contribute to the development of a conceptual framework that is relevant to policy discussions of e-government software platform design and maintenance within not only an Indian, but also a broader global context. In order to augment theoretical discussions of administrative reform in a digitised world, this chapter uses a case study to explore its central research issues, within which a mixed-methods approach employing a combination of qualitative and quantitative data was selected to inform and to strengthen the understanding of the relationships between the actors, inputs, and project outputs. Therefore, the goal of the study was to evolve ideas that could be generalised across similar situations and the research was consequently developed in the following steps:

- In-depth review of existing theoretical perspectives and literature surrounding corruption and tax evasion, ICTs and public administration, and property tax reform.
- Qualitative analysis of official documents;
- Collection and analysis of quantitative data relevant to the case;
- Developing case studies through in-depth personal interviews;
- Data analysis and interpretation;
- Preparation of conclusions and their validation;
- Recommendations for the future.

The use of mixed-method case study research is becoming increasingly popular in the social sciences, and is fast being recognised as a successful approach for investigating contemporary phenomena in a real-life context when the boundaries between phenomenon and context are not evident and where multiple sources of evidence present themselves (Yin, 2003). It was thus felt to be a particularly apt way of studying the nature and impact of actor actions, motivations and behaviours on e-government software platform conception and design, where the aim is not simply to judge whether the project at hand represents a success or failure, but is to understand the qualities inherent in the architecture that have made it so.

More precisely, case study research consists of a detailed investigation of phenomena within a given context, often with data being collected over a period of time. The aim of this approach is to provide the researcher with an all-round analysis of the surrounding environment and processes, in order that they might throw light on the theoretical issues being investigated (Eisenhardt, 1989). The phenomenon under examination is thus not isolated from its context; rather, it is of interest precisely because the aim is to observe and understand actor behaviour and/or organisational processes and their interplay with the surrounding environment. The use of a case study itself is, therefore, not as much a method as it is a *research strategy*, where the context is deliberately included as part of the overall design. Today, case studies are widely used in organisational research across the social sciences, indicating growing confidence in the approach as a rigorous research strategy in its own right (Hartley, 2005).

As research conducted by adopting this strategy is typically done in the field, the presence of too many observations and uncontrollable 'variables' makes the application of standard experimental or survey approaches infeasible. Further, information tends to be scattered and generally cannot be picked up using one single method (Eisenhardt, 1989). Case studies typically combine a number of data collection methods such as participant observation, direct observation, interviews, focus groups, ethnography, document analysis, questionnaires etc., where evidence may be quantitative or qualitative depending on the research issues at hand (Hartley, 2005). The approach is consequently flexible, allowing for new methods to be incorporated as new sources of data and new actors present themselves. The case study approach may thus be and has been used for various purposes – to provide a descriptive narrative, to generate new theory, or to test existing theory through the triangulation of data (Virkar, 2011).

For the larger study from which this chapter is drawn, 40 personal interviews were conducted over a 24-month period. The interviewees can be roughly divided into four groups based on their relationship to the case: Senior Civil Servants involved with the planning and implementation of the project, including current and former BBMP Commissioners, Deputy Commissioners for Revenue, and Revenue Officers, Revenue and Tax Officials, primarily Assistant Revenue Officers (AROs) responsible for the in-the-field collection and administration of property tax in the city, Software Developers involved in the conception, design, and implementation of the project, and Miscellaneous Actors including journalists and external consultants.

Twenty-seven subjects agreed to full-length interviews and to have their comments recorded. This included all six members of the project planning committee, one senior official involved with the implementation of the GIS, and 20 senior revenue officers involved with the system's application in the field. Additional informal interviews conducted face-to-face or over the email were also used to close gaps in knowledge or to follow up new information and anchor the interpretation of events and motives in the perceptions of participants. In addition to the recorded interviews, this chapter uses information and quotes obtained informally from people related to the project who did not wish to be interviewed formally or have their comments recorded.

Out of the 13 people in this category, 10 were junior revenue officials (Station Managers, Tax Inspectors and Accountants) working under the AROs interviewed, two were Revenue Officers supervising the overall administration of the Revenue Offices, and one person was a local correspondent from a leading national daily.

EXAMINING ICTs IN THE CONTEXT OF ORGANISATIONAL REFORM AND INSTITUTIONAL CHANGE

Any examination of the relationship between ICTs, organisational reform and institutional change may commence with the words of Nye (2002): "Technology affects society and government, but the causal arrows work in both directions. Technological change creates new challenges and opportunities for social and political organizations, but the response to those challenges depends on history, culture, institutions, and paths already taken or forgone."

Traditionally, political institutions have been seen as preconditions for civilised society, with students of politics being interested in how they work and how their organisation within a society impacts the lives of citizens (March & Olsen, 1989). Institutions may be defined as: "…the structure that humans impose on human interaction and therefore define the incentives that together with the other constraints (budget, technology, etc.) determine the choices that individuals make that shape the performance of societies and economies over time" (North, 1994, p. 1). Therefore, institutional change, according to Prats (2000), refers to the intentional or voluntary insertion of innovation into a current system through a sufficiently assumed transformation of its rules and internal games. Alterations of relative prices, such as information costs or technology changes, become the most important sources of institutional change.

Changes in relative prices, however, are motivated both by the transformation of actor perceptions regarding those changes as well as the alterations in behaviour that those perceptions give rise to; that is, by the construction of new mental models that result from the acquisition of learning and of skills that help interpret the new context. Institutional change generally occurs whenever an alteration in a relative cost is perceived by one or more group of actors as a win-win situation for that group or for all the participants involved. Such change thus depends chiefly on the actors' perceptions with respect to the gains (the payoffs) to be obtained. At the same time, it must be remembered that it is the existing institutions themselves that determine the nature and direction of the payoffs (North, 1994).

If, like Thomas and Bennis (1972), one understands organisational change within institutions as the deliberate design and implementation of a structural innovation, a policy, a new goal, or an operational transformation; it may be accepted that ICT applications could result in organisational changes (such as the efficient and speedy delivery of public services, increased proximity of services to the citizen, or simplification of formalities and requirements) that impact public management values. What is less clear, though, is how public sector ICT applications result in either formal or informal institutional alterations which are, to paraphrase North (1990), the reform of the rules of interactions within those structures or (more strictly speaking) of the constraints that humans impose on their political, economic, and social interactions (North, 1990, p. 3). This is largely due to the fact that the relationship between technology and institutional transformations has not yet been clearly defined.

In assuming that the manner in which ICT applications are being used depends on the type of institution they are adopted by, this researcher supports Fountain (2002) in upholding the claim that the potential benefits of implementing an e-government strategy will be and are strongly influenced by current institutions and incentive systems of government, as the direction and nature of these structural and infrastructural arrangements strongly influence and determine the evolution of the perceptions, choices, and behaviour of the actors involved in their day-to-day running (Virkar, 2011). ICTs in the public sector are thus designed, developed, adopted, and used according to the preferences and choices of government stakeholders and their interpersonal interactions which, in turn, have been shaped taking into consideration the formal and informal rules and constraints (or *institutions*) that circumscribe society together with the enforcement characteristics of both (Fountain, 2001).

However, it does not automatically lead one to necessarily state that technology transformations alter the *status quo* of the public organisations. According to Gascó (2003), Information and Communication technologies will give way to institutional change if the new skills and learning that governmental actors acquire change their perception about the potential gains that result from the new situation. In turn, the degree to which those perceptions may be altered depends on how much the workplace of that actor is affected by the new structures that result from ICT applications (Gascó, 2003).

The question is, then, what will motivate that change? Fountain and Osorio-Urzua (2001) identified three groups of institutional variables that would collectively influence not only whether a project would be undertaken at all, but also whether a new technology would be adopted by all the actors concerned, thereby giving rise to alterations in their perceptions of the given technology (Fountain & Osorio-Urzua, 2001). The first group consists of Technological Variables, which include the ability of a user-population to access ICTs, the quality of the user population's Internet use, the availability of an internal technological infrastructure, and the provision of technical skills to the government workforce. Fountain and Osorio-Urza argued that "...the quality of an agency's Information and Communication technology infrastructure and overall skill level are critical inputs to make-or-buy decisions".

The second group is that of Managerial Variables, in which are included the efficiency and effectiveness of the supply chain, the characteristics of the agency's culture, and its capacity to adapt to and manage change. Again, the authors argue that "...an agency that is well managed is likely to have a higher probability of success implementing either internal or outsourced e-government solutions". The final group, Political Variables, consists of the perceptions public servants have regarding potential labour cuts, administrative turnover, changes in executive direction generated by the development of e-government, the desire of political actors to be associated with e-government projects, budgetary resources, and the direction or orientation to long-term results. Only when all these variables and their interrelationships take place will both organisational and institutional change occur.

In summary, because Information Technology projects within the public sector result in new organisational forms that exploit new knowledge and give rise to work alterations, there is obviously a chance for institutional change to take place (Gascó, 2003). From this discussion, two areas of study present themselves as useful starting points for the analysis of the central research issues advanced within this chapter (Virkar, 2011):

- **Actor Perceptions:** Organisations and institutions both shape and are shaped by the use of technology, which is in turn influenced by changes in the perceptions of governmental actors towards that technology. Understanding actor preferences and opinions is thus key to determining the nature and direction of organisational reform and institutional change.
- **Project Outcome:** The design and implementation of a project must be carried out within the constraints of the current organisational and institutional set-up. In other words, the outcome of a project depends on the interaction between organisational and institutional realities and the project design. In turn, project outcome has an impact on the existing organisational and institutional framework.

THE HUMAN DIMENSION IN COMPUTER SYSTEM DESIGN AND IMPLEMENTATION: FROM HUMAN *FACTORS* TO HUMAN *ACTORS*

First coined by Camerer (2003), the term *Behavioural Game Theory* is effectively, today, a distinct discipline within that area of the social sciences concerned with how real people make decisions when confronted by, and whilst confronting, the various institutional mechanisms considered as assured across variants of prevailing game-theoretic models (Virkar, 2011); as discussed in forthcoming sections of this chapter. More particularly, Behavioural Game Theory attempts to understand just how psychological factors – such as *emotions*, *biases*, and *prejudices* – can help predict decision-making behaviour patterns across different social, political, and economic institutions (Innocenti & Sbriglia, 2008, p. 7). Further, studies and research involving Behavioural Game Theory focus especially on how real people actually play or live out theoretical games, and seek to add dimension to existing mathematical functions to make modelled behaviour more human-like (Williams, 2013).

The discipline as a whole, similar to the manner in which the subject matter contained within this thesis is treated, is interested predominantly in issues related to the framing of a decision, and to how the surrounding environment or arena of action can ultimately bias the sphere of human interaction(Williams, 2013). It is important to note that most behavioural game theorists are not attempting to discredit Game Theory in its purist form, especially through their insistence of the need to demonstrate the point of departure of real peoples' cognitive frameworks and behaviour from its base theoretical precepts; rather, it may be argued that behavioural game theorists are, instead, attempting to build a better theory of human decision-making that utilises pure Game Theory and its variants; both as a method of enquiry and as its foundational basis.

As academic scholarship and public dialogue surrounding the decline of social capital, and the role of the new Information and Communication Technologies in this dynamic, has expanded over the last couple of decades, a new medium – the Internet – has become prominent as the latest catalyst for the emergence of new socio-psychological environments globally. In this regard, some theorists and practitioners are extremely sanguine about the Internet and its impact on the psychology of individuals and communities within a society; many even assert that being "wired" has the potential to tighten existing social associations and to encourage community building (Coleman, 2005). In particular, individuals who use the Internet to explore interests, gather data, communicate with colleagues and friends, and send e-mail appear to be *more*, not less, socially and politically engaged (Chiu, 2006).

The design and implementation of complex computer systems, such as those that support e-government platforms, requires a better understanding in practitioner circles of the users of such networks and the settings in which they work. Part of the problem resides in the implicit treatment of ordinary people as unskilled, non-specialist users of technology and their networks comprising of elementary processes or *factors* that can be studied in isolation in a field laboratory setting (Bannon, 1991).

Although psychology has a long tradition of contributing to computer systems design and implementation, it has been a neglected discipline in scholarly circles and key issues such as those relating to the underlying values of the people involved in large-scale system design and their motivation in the work setting have been missed out in recent computer science-based scholarly analysis (Salvendy, 2012). Conceptualising and understanding people as *actors* in situations, on the other hand, with a set of skills and shared practices based on work experiences with others, requires a reorientation in the way in which the relationship between key elements of computer system design, namely people, technology, work requirements, and organisational constraints in work settings, is negotiated (Kuuti, 1996).

The use of the terms 'human factors' and 'human actors' gives us a clue as to how people in system design clusters are approached (Virkar, 2013). More particularly, the terms highlight the difference in how people and their contributions are perceived, the former connoting a passive, fragmented, depersonalised, somewhat automatic human contribution to the systems environment; the latter an active, controlling, involved one (Carayon et. al., 2012). More precisely, within the *human factor* approach, the human element is more often than not reduced to being another system component with certain characteristics that need to be factored into the design equation for the overall human-machine system (Czaja

& Nair, 2012). In doing so, the approach de-emphasises certain important elements of work design: the goals, values, and beliefs that technologists and system-users hold about life and work (Jacko et. al., 2012). By using the term *human actor*, emphasis is placed on users and developers as autonomous agents possessing the capacity to control, regulate, and coordinate their behaviour, rather than them being on par and analysed as mere information processing automatons (Proctor & Vu, 2012).

UNDERSTANDING ACTOR BEHAVIOUR WITHIN THE CONTEXT OF COMPLEX COMPUTER SYSTEMS

A detailed investigation of the actor interactions intrinsic to a networked computer system is, hence, considered central to the deeper understanding of a given complex e-government initiative, as well as to the development and maintenance of a designated network; it is important to precisely determine the impact that actor motivations and their associated strategic behaviours have on both the design and structure of an e-government system and on subsequent policy outcomes. In this respect, psychologists contend that human motivation must be understood as the product of the interaction between events and things in the social world and the interpretations of those things in people's psyches (Strauss, 1992). One approach, hence, to the study of the strategic motivation behind political e-participation and e-service provision begins by defining and examining the *motives* that prompt actors to interact and participate in decision- and policy- making processes on- and offline; not with reference to *internal stimuli* only, but also within the context of *external goals* that stem from a number of different *needs* or *base requirements* (D'Andrade, 1992).

This study assumes, in the manner of work conducted jointly by Tversky and Kahneman (Kahneman, 2003), that it is possible for government agencies to influence human actors' behavioural preferences, in guiding them towards the consumption of 'healthier' options more suited to the public good, by redesigning the environment within which these actors take both automatic and reflective decisions and make their individual choices. At its most basic, individuals choose between set *options* or given *alternatives* by weighing the *pros* and the *cons* of each prospective *choice* against an available or a perceived list of different *choice attributes* (Johnson et. al., 2012).

These choice attributes may either be important to attain in their own right, or pivotal when considered in combination with others as factors enabling decision-makers to achieve more fundamental objectives (Keeney, 1996). It follows from this, that the ideal decision may be said to incorporate all of the relevant choice attributes available to participating actors; and weights their salience in a fashion, and to a degree, that allows for *decision-* and *policy-makers* to achieve their objectives, and for professed *choice architects* to influence public behaviour thereby (Virkar, 2011; Johnson et. al., 2012).

A decision- or policy-maker becomes a choice architect *per force* when the administering legal authority facilitates the making of choices by the general public as one of its stated primary strategic objectives (Virkar, 2011); wherein individuals are directly guided into attending on and using attributes accurately, most particularly by adhering to the imparted universal public service principles of *parsimony*, *linearity*, *comparability*, and *evaluability* (Johnson et. al., 2012). In constructing a robust choice architecture, therefore, choice architects may choose to make some choice attributes, such as those with externalities that might otherwise be neglected, more salient to the target population than others; especially through the development and deployment of those theoretical frameworks and practitioner tools which advance the delineation (or *attribute translation*) and the structuring (or *attribute expansion*) of available choice options.

The key issue that needs to be understood, therefore, while studying the development of ICT platforms and their implementation in public sector organisations through an analysis of actor interactions is: *Why do people do what they do?* The key approach taken to understanding strategic behaviour is to look at the rationality of individual *actors*, rather than at human *factors*, or at the computer system network as a whole. This is largely, as discussed earlier, because human *actors* are driven by a combination of organisational and institutional roles and duties and calculated self-interest; with political, social, and economic interactions being organised around the *construction* and the *interpretation* of *meaning* as well as the *making of choices*. It can, hence, be extremely difficult to transplant new technologies and ways of working into organisations without a change in both jargon and mindset (March & Olsen, 1989).

Political actors, in particular, possess a complex set of goals including *power, income, prestige, security, convenience, loyalty* (to an idea, an institution or the nation), *pride* (in work well done), and a *desire to serve the public interest* (as the individual actor conceives it). According to Downs (1964), political actors range from being purely self-interested ('*climbers*' or '*conservers*', motivated entirely by goals which benefit themselves and their status quo rather than their organizations or the society at large) to having mixed motives ('*zealots*', '*advocates*' and '*statesmen*', motivated by goals which combine self-interest and altruistic loyalty with larger values). Through the discussion of property tax administration in the Indian context set out in previous sections, four sets of actors or choice architects and their motivations may be identified:

- **Local Politicians:** Are responsible for legislating on various aspects of tax administration. This group is usually motivated by the need to retain power and prestige, win votes, and advance career prospects within their respective parties. However, as they are easily held to account by the public, their chief actions in games of tax administration generally involve promoting policies that would be popular with the electorate whilst at the same time avoiding decisions that could result in electoral losses (Maskin & Tirole, 2004).
- **Senior Civil Servants:** Are motivated either by the need to increase power and prestige, or by convenience and security. As they are relatively more accountable to elected representatives than to the public, their actions generally consist of either embracing change that would increase their own spheres of influence or resisting any reform that they feel might reduce their present privileges (Downs, 1964). This may be done within themselves as a group, or through initiating interpersonal contacts with senior and junior officials from the adopting departments.
- **Senior and Junior Revenue Officials:** Responsible for the hands-on administration of the property tax within municipalities are, like their superiors, often motivated by the need to retain their own spheres of influence as well as by convenience and security (Virkar, 2011). Again, their actions consist chiefly of embracing or rejecting reform depending on their perceptions of benefit and loss.
- **Citizens:** Are chiefly concerned with maximising personal wealth and are generally influenced by political and socio-economic factors associated with paying tax. Current income levels, tax rates, and the degree of trust in government all play a part in inducing either voluntary compliance or tax avoidance behaviour (Kirchler, 2007).

Introducing e-government initiatives into public bodies is a tricky game to play, as computerization alters the work-load, work profile and content of the average public sector employee; impacting accountability, reducing the opportunities for exercising discretion, making performance more visible and flattening the hierarchy (Bhatnagar, 2004), and often forcing the need for retraining and retooling and sometimes creating redundancy. Many projects tend to face internal resistance from staff – particularly from the middle to lower levels of the civil service – with moves made to reengineer processes and effect back-end computerisation having a profound effect on the way civil servants perform their duties and perceive their jobs. Very often in developing countries, it is the fear of the unknown that drives this resistance, especially if the introduction of new technology results in a change of procedures and the need for new skills. Further, in corrupt service delivery departments, there may be pressure to slow down or delay the introduction of technology-led reforms due to the impending loss of additional income.

GAME THEORY FOR POLITICAL SCIENTISTS: THE ECOLOGY OF GAMES

From the turn of the century to the present, there has been a progressive movement away from the view that governance is the outcome of rational calculation to achieve specific goals by a unitary governmental actor, and in that context metaphors based on games have been extremely useful in developing new ways to think about the policy process. A look through the literature reveals that although many political games have been described by scholars within differing contexts, ranging from electoral politics to administrative functioning, there exists no comprehensive description of the public organization as a system of these various interactions.

The use of Game Theory and most other game metaphors (although differing widely in their orientation) have had, according to scholars, one major limitation for clarifying policy processes: they focus squarely on a single arena or field of action; be it a school, a county, a legislature, etc. Yet, by their very nature, policy making and implementation cut across these separate arenas, in both their development and impact (Firestone, 1989).

In e-government projects for instance, systems built by both public and private enterprises for use by government employees and citizens across different political constituencies must be enforced by legislative acts created and interpreted by national branches of government. In addition, actors at different levels of the policy system encounter divergent problems posed by the system in question and their actions are influenced by varied motives. What is needed, therefore, is a framework that goes beyond single games in order to focus on how games 'mesh or miss' each other to influence governance and policy decisions. One of the few efforts to look at this interaction and interdependence was Norton Long's (1958) discussion of "The Local Community as an Ecology of Games."

Rejected in favour of Behaviouralism and Rational Choice Theory – two approaches based on the assumption that individuals act autonomously as a result of either socio-psychological characteristics or due to rational calculations of their personal utility (Hechter & Kanazawa, 1997) – during the period immediately following World War II, Institutionalist approaches came into their own in the late 1980s under the guise of New Institutionalism as a result of a growing number of scholars attempting to describe and understand in concrete terms the political world around them (Peters, 2000). Contrary to both Behavioural Theory and Rational Choice Theory, New Institutionalists considered observable behaviour to occur and be understood solely within the context of institutions, leading to the creation and development of two new branches of theory, namely Rational Choice Institutionalism and Behavioural Institutionalism (Immergut, 1998).

Rational Choice Theory in particular depends for its analytical power on unhindered, utility-maximising individuals; and it would, at first glance, appear to be futile indeed to relate it to the idea of institutions and their constraining influence on actor behaviour (Peters, 2000). However, despite the individualistic basis underpinning the approach, a number of rational choice theorists have come to accept the first and foremost precept of the New Institutionalism, which is that most political life occurs within institutions, and that in order to provide a comprehensive explanation of politics, their theories must address questions regarding their nature and role (Tsebelis, 1990). There has, in consequence, been a flowering of rational choice literature on political institutions since the late 1980s, including work on legislatures (McCubbins, 1987), cabinets (Laver & Schofield,1990) and bureaucracies (Johnson & Libecap, 1994), and some economic theorists have even gone as far as to apply the idea of rational choice to the institution of marriage (Becker, 1991).

Furthermore, despite the possible contradictions put forward by March and Olsen (1989) in their work (March & Olsen, 1989), there are several approaches to institutions that depend on the underlying logic of rational choice approaches. Notable amongst these are Dunleavy's (1991) discussion of 'institutional public choice' and 'first principles public choice', Kenman's (1996) argument for the utility of 'institutional rational choice' and Fritz Scharpf's (1997) treatise on 'actor-centred institutionalism'.

The basic assumption is that not only may social phenomena be explained as the outcome of interactions amongst intentional actors – individual, collective, or corporate – but that these interactions are structured and outcomes are shaped by the characteristics of the institutional settings within which they occur (Scharpf, 1997). As the basic argument of rational choice approaches is that utility maximisation can and will remain the primary motivation of individuals, rational choice approaches to institutions all presume the same egoistic behavioural characteristics found in similar approaches to other aspects of political behaviour (Peters, 2000). However, the institutional variants of the approach focus attention on the importance of *institutions* as mechanisms for channelling and constraining individual behaviour.

Proponents of rational choice institutionalism hold that, as actors depend on socially constructed rules to orient their actions in otherwise chaotic social situations, institutions may be considered to have a key influence on not only the actors themselves but on the nature and direction of their interactions (Scharpf, 1997). Further, collective and corporate actors central to policy processes are institutionally constituted, as the institutions themselves may be said to "exist" only to the extent that the individuals acting within them are able to coordinate their choices within a common frame of reference that is constituted by institutional rules.

In addition, this approach identifies clear actors in each process, in direct contrast to other variations of institutional theories that deal with only sets of rules and norms (Peters, 2000). Thus, for models that combine rational choice concepts with institutional analysis, individual actors are still expected to manoeuvre in order to maximise personal utilities, but their actions are inherently constrained by the rule sets of the one or more or institutions within which they are operating.

Throughout this body of work, notes Peters (2000), institutions are conceptualised as collections of rules and incentives that establish the conditions for bounded rationality, thus establishing a 'political space' within which many interdependent political actors can function. Institutions define not only the membership of composite actors and the resources (both material and legal) that they may draw upon – thus defining the scope of their legitimate activities and the powers of the individuals who act for them – but also the purposes that they are to serve or the values that they are to consider in arriving at their choices (Scharpf, 1997). More particularly, institutions have explanatory value because sanctioned rules will reduce the range of potential behaviour by specifying required, prohibited, or permitted actions (Ostrom et. al., 1994).

While both Rational Choice and Behaviouralist approaches considered the actions of individual actors to be unfettered by both formal and informal institutions, instead making their own choices with preferences being viewed as exogenous to the political process (Simon, 1955), initial proponents of the New Institutionalism (most notably March and Olsen, who named the movement in 1984) highlighted the need to reassert some of the features of the old perspective (Hall & Taylor, 1996). As well as altering the theoretical perspectives of the discipline, this change in paradigm was also a response to a growing demand for the use of rigorous research methods in the social sciences and an equally strong push for a more explicit constitution of empirical political theory: both ideas then being seemingly incompatible with an institutional focus. In particular, March and Olsen (1984) argued that behavioural and rational choice approaches were characterised by five basic weaknesses:

- **Contextualism:** The tendency to subordinate political phenomena to societal phenomena by seeing politics as an integral part of society, but being less inclined to differentiate the polity from the rest of society;
- **Reductionism:** The propensity to see political phenomena as the aggregate consequences of individual behaviour, rather than linking political outcomes to organizational structures and rules of appropriate behaviour;
- **Utilitarianism:** The inclination to see action as the product of calculated self-interest without acknowledging the response of political actors to obligations and duties;
- **Functionalism:** Or the assumption that history is an efficient process moving towards equilibrium, leading to the smooth and untroubled evolution of the political process;
- **Instrumentalism:** Or the tendency to define decision-making and the allocation of resources as the central concerns of political life, paying less attention to the ways in which political life is organised around the development of meaning and identity through symbols, rituals, and ceremonies.

Building upon theories of Rational Choice, scholars such as Beinhocker (2006) and Gintis (2000) have proposed a vision of the economy and other socio-political institutions that falls within the purview of Complex Adaptive System theories in response to what they perceive to be the combined aridity of classical game theory and general equilibrium theory – both of which have been generally considered as the two most popular ways to describe the creation of wealth by actors within a social ecology. Viewing markets and other institutions as complex adaptive systems radically alters the analytical tools that may be deployed to model socio-economic and political behaviour within a given field of play (Gintis, 2006).

According to Gintis (2006), complex adaptive systems are almost a mirror inversion of neoclassical economic theories such as traditional game theories for, as Axel Leijonhufvud notes in Gintis, neoclassical theories model "smart people in unbelievably simple situations" whilst real-world situations involve "simple people [coping] with incredibly complex conditions" (Gintis, 2006, p. 2). Beinhocker (2006) offers the following useful summary of the differences between conventional game theories rooted in neoclassical models and complexity economics (cf. Davis, 2008):

- **Dynamics:** The complex economy is open and dynamic and generally far from equilibrium, whereas neoclassical economic models are far more static and closed.
- **Agents:** In a complex economy, actors have limited information and face high costs of information processing. Under appropriate conditions, these agents may develop non-optimal but highly effective heuristics for operating in complex environments. By contrast, agents operating in neoclassical economies are assumed to possess perfect information and are able to optimize at minimum cost.

- • **Networks:** Complex economic theory recognizes that actors participate in a number of sophisticated networks that allow them to compensate for having limited information and high information processing costs. This, as discussed earlier, is quite the contrary for actors operating under neoclassical conditions.
- • **Emergence:** Theories surrounding complex economies lend themselves to the modelling of macro-systems through an examination of individual agent-level behaviour. This is in contrast to neoclassical theories where the actions of individual actors may not be easily determined.
- • **Evolution:** The order and structuring of actor behaviour in complex economies is derived through evolutionary processes such as differentiation, selection, and amplification. Such concepts do not exist in classical game theory.

Furthermore, in considering institutions as biological systems, complex adaptive system theories also put forward the idea of "imitation" to explain socio-political and cultural evolution. Gintis (2000), for instance, demonstrates how individuals and groups with low pay-off strategies tend to switch from these to strategies used by more successful actors. The idea of change through imitation has also found use in behavioural economics and the modelling of actor behaviour within institutions, as well as the process of technological diffusion; thereby building on neoclassical approaches to game theory. However, overall there has been to date only a few contributions to the economic literature on behavioural change through imitation, and far less in other social science disciplines such as Politics and Sociology.

Additionally, Beinhocker emphasizes that behavioural economic research (Gintis, 2006) shifts focus away from more conventional neoclassical ideas of actor behaviour onto the actions of individual actors who are not purely self-centred in their social interactions within a group, but rather are (cf. Fehr & Gachter, 2002; and Beinhocker, 2006) a combination of *conditional co-operators* (who prefer to sacrifice personal goals for the sake of the larger good) and *altruistic operators* (who act to maintain the group's *status quo*). The chief 'embarrassment' of classical game theory, according to Gintis (2006), is thus its inability to explain why an individual actor or group would ever play a 'one-shot' game. What is needed, therefore, is a framework that goes beyond single games in order to focus on how games 'mesh or miss' each other to influence governance and policy decisions. One of the few efforts to look at this interaction and interdependence was Norton Long's (1958) discussion of "The Local Community as an Ecology of Games", whose key ideas will be dealt with in subsequent sections of this chapter.

The Ecology of Games framework, as first laid out by Long in the late 1950s, offers a New Institutionalist perspective on organisational and institutional analysis. As with most theories of New Institutionalism, it recognises that political institutions are not simple echoes of social forces, and that routines, rules and forms within organisations and institutions evolve through historically interdependent processes that do not reliably and quickly reach equilibrium (March & Olsen, 1989). Long developed the idea of the ecology of games as a way of reconciling existing debates about who governed local communities as he believed they had significant flaws.

The crucial insight in Long's theory however, was not the idea of games *per se* which, as has been discussed earlier, was already well developed, but his linking of that notion to the metaphor of an ecology (Firestone, 1989). Ecology as a concept relates to the interrelationships of species in their environment, allowing for numerous relationships amongst entities, and has been used to understand the relationships among individuals and more complex social systems. This speaks of a singular interdependence between different actors within a given territory. Although there may be other relationships as well, what is significantly missing is a single, rational, coordinating presence.

Games themselves are social constructs that vary over time and across social contexts (Crozier & Friedberg, 1980). Similar types of games might recur within similar social settings, but all games tend to be uniquely situated in place and time, and any typology of games that might emerge across a cumulative body of studies is likely to remain quite abstract. Despite this, Dutton (1992) has identified several key attributes which all games may share: first, every game has a set of goals, purposes, or objectives, with some games having multiple aims. Second, a game has a set of prizes, which may vary widely from profit to authority to recognition, and are distinct from the objectives of the players.

Third, games have rules that govern the strategies or moves open to players depending on the organisational or institutional settings within which they are played. Rules need not be public or fair (depending on whether public or private interests are involved), may change over time, and may or may not need consensus to be accepted. Finally, a game has a set of players, defined by the fact that they interact – compete or cooperate – with another in pursuing the game's objectives.

For Long, territories of strategic interaction (or fields of play) were defined quite literally by being local communities. Moved from the community context to the world of e-government design, adoption and implementation, territories may be diverse – from the inner circle of the project design team, through to the adopting organisation, the nation and finally the international policy arena – but the idea of each stage being a political community or a collection of actors whose actions have political implications is still very much applicable. The ecology of games metaphor thus provides us with a useful way to think about how the various players interact in making and carrying out administration and developing policy.

EXPERIMENTS IN STRATEGIC INTERACTION: CLASSIFYING BASIC GAME TYPES

There exist, in the extensive literature surrounding Game Theory – its variants and its metaphors – differences in the types of models that adapt contemporary conceptualisations of game-play to political analysis; contingent, especially, on the class and nature of game construct employed, or the scope and direction of human interaction studied therein (Virkar, 2011). Derived chiefly from the game-theoretic concept of Nash equilibrium (Nash, 1950), the predominant typographies of game-play might be advanced qualitatively (Dixit & Skeath, 2004; Williams, 2013), particularly through their depiction in a game table (also known as a *game matrix* or a *payoff table*); as follows *below*. Within this given matrix of strategic human behaviour, wherein each micro-arena is classified for the purposes of creating a viable basic taxonomy as a *game*, interactions may assume any permissible combination of available characteristics, or any feasible permutation thereof.

Normal-Form Games and Extensive-Form Games

There exists, at first glance, a distinction between *Normal-Form Games* and *Extensive-Form Games* (Virkar, 2011). Expressed in symbolic notation, Normal-Form Games are essentially mathematical constructs presented in tabular form, whereas Extensive-Form Games are illustrated typically by a game tree that depicts moves as progressing from one branch to another (Gintis, 2009). Framed in terms of qualitative analysis, this difference in formulation is indicative of, primarily, the variations prevailing between and within different decision-making environments (Dixit & Skeath, 2004).

Normal-form games, on the one hand, generally model situations in which decisions are made simultaneously, and wherein players are not necessarily aware of the strategies selected by other players while deciding on their own (Romp, 1997). Extensive-form games, on the other, allow for more dynamic game-play comprising of (near-) full information, and, again, containing elements of simultaneous choice.

Co-Operative (*Coalitional*) Games and Non- Co-Operative (*Procedural*) Games

A second basic game variant makes the distinction between strategic interactions that embody *co-operative* or *coalition-building behaviours*, on the one hand, and *non- co-operative* or *procedural- based human action*, on the other (Virkar, 2011). During Co-operative or Coalitional Games, players can communicate with each other and form binding coalitions and pacts, or agreements among members to co-ordinate any strategic action (Ordeshook, 1986). These interactions are based predominantly on predictions of how players will divide up rewards and aggregate pay-offs (Dixit & Skeath, 2004). A Non- Co-operative or Procedural Game, on the contrary, specifies all the possible actions for each individual participant or decision-maker; generally referred to, again, as a *player* (Ordeshook, 1986). Thus, during non- co-operative games, players cannot form binding ties and agreements, as they may or may not be able to communicate with each other in full (Chakravarty et. al., 2015). Dixit and Skeath (2004) have argued that non- co-operative games are more fundamental than co-operative games; which, unlike their non-co-operative counterparts, assume binding agreements whose provisions are difficult to enforce in the real world (Morrow, 1994).

Competitive Games and Non-Competitive Games

Strategic interactions may also be broadly classified into *competitive games* and into games that are not strictly competitive (or otherwise, known as *non-competitive games*) (Virkar, 2011). In a strictly Competitive Game, the rewards and payoffs to players sum either to zero, in what is commonly referred to as a *zero-sum game*, or they do not, in what is known as a *constant-sum game* (Dixit & Skeath, 2004). Overall, however, it is important to note that in *strictly competitive strategic interactions* there exists no opportunity for compromise or for joint gains (Brams, 2004). Other social situations are strictly non-competitive, and often involve co-ordination and co-operation. Non-Competitive Games or strictly non-competitive strategic interactions are usually either *variable-sum games* (Brams, 2004) or *non- zero-sum games* (Ordeshook, 1986); interactions in which the rewards and payoffs to the players involved are not either constant nor do not sum to zero (Virkar, 2011).

Pure- (*Dominant-*) Strategy Games and Mixed- Strategy Games

A distinction can also be drawn between Pure- or Dominant- Strategy Games and Mixed- Strategy Games (Williams, 2013); wherein, while taking a decision, a player might opt for *either* one dominant strategy choice over another (or over several others) (Gintis, 2009), *or* for a multiple strategy equilibrium (Brams, 2004) in order to achieve a particular outcome or set of outcomes, attain a specific goal or set of goals, or benefit from a singular reward or set of rewards (Virkar, 2011). *Pure- Strategy* or *Dominant Games*, therefore, involve players selecting or being able to select only *one strategy-choice option* from a menu of available strategy-choice options (Ordeshook, 1986). In contrast, *Mixed- Strategy Games* involve players opting for a *probabilistic multi-pronged strategy* (Camerer, 2003), selecting an optimum combination of behaviours and moves from a variety of different given alternatives; in order to maximise the potential afforded to them as rational actors from existing situational efficiencies, utilities, and economies of scale (Gintis, 2009).

Single-Shot (*Dynamic*) Games and Repeated (*One-Off*) Games

Another manner in which strategic political interactions might be conceptualised has been to think of them in terms of their regenerative frequency (Virkar, 2011). In this regard, interactions might occur either *once*, solely or *frequently*, at predictable or undefined intervals. Within this given framework, the idea of a Single-Shot or Dynamic Game refers to those interactions between people wherein players only interact with each other, or play the game in question, *once* (Romp, 1997). These games are usually *dynamic*- and/or *simultaneous-move games* (Virkar, 2011); in which the players involved within a given situation take decisions based on imperfect or asymmetric information (Dixit & Skeath, 2004).

Repeated Games of strategic interaction, on the other hand, involve a different conceptualisation of the time element (Ordeshook, 1986); with the game at hand being played *repeatedly* or *more than once* (Williams, 2013). In this respect, *Repeated Games* may be of one of two types (Virkar, 2011): *Finite Repeated Games*, in which an ending period is fixed; or *Infinite Repeated Games*, in which no ending period is defined. *Stage Games* are another variant of Repeated Games (Romp, 1997), wherein the term *stage* refers explicitly to a single period of time (Gintis, 2009).

Games of Complete (*Symmetric*) or Perfect Information and Games of Incomplete (*Asymmetric*) or Imperfect Information

Strategic human interactions can also be further sub-divided and classified according to the information that players possess concerning the structure of the game that they are involved with, and its content (Virkar, 2011). Firstly, in Games of Complete (Symmetric) or Perfect Information, players can, and are expected to, possess full knowledge about all aspects of the given game environment (Williams, 2013). Two informational constructs are used to model this knowledge (Dixit & Skeath, 2004): *complete information* (otherwise, called *symmetric*), a situation in which players know of in full the strategies involved, and are aware of the payoffs accruing to other participants within the set game context; or *perfect information*, a situation wherein a player knows and can therefore anticipate the moves of other players, and possesses a global comprehension of the given action and its history (Williams, 2013). In other words, everything about the given game structure – its strategies, key goals, rewards, payoffs, and moves – and its immediate environment is known by, and made known to, all players participating.

In contrast, in a situation of *imperfect* and *incomplete* (or *asymmetric*) *information*, players are not privy to knowledge concerned with all the relevant aspects of the given game of strategic interaction (Williams, 2013). In this context, the same two informational constructs, discussed above, apply (Virkar, 2011). Games of Imperfect Information imply that a player does not know of all the moves or actions permissible within in a game; whilst in Games of Incomplete (Asymmetric) Information, players lack exact knowledge of the strategies chosen by, and the exact payoffs accruing to, other players operating within the same game arena (Dixit & Skeath, 2004).

ASSESSING PROJECT OUTCOME: A DISCUSSION
OF THE DESIGN-ACTUALITY GAP MODEL

Like all political interactions, the behaviour of actors related to the design and uptake of e-government projects is circumscribed by the organisations and institutions within which they are played out, and by the range of actors taken from the individuals and groups directly and indirectly involved with the process of governance. The outcome of an e-government project therefore does not depend on a single project entity alone, and instead depends on the interaction between different actors in the process and the nature of the relationships between them. Gaps in project design and implementation can in reality be seen as expressions of differences arising from the interaction between different (often conflicting) actor moves and strategies, determined to a large extent by actor perceptions, and played out within the context of set circumstances.

Heeks (2003) concluded that the major factor determining project outcome was the degree of mismatch between the current realities of a situation (the 'where are we now') and the models, conceptions, and assumptions built into a project's design (the 'where the e-government project wants to get us'). From this perspective, e-government success and failure depends largely on the size of this *'design-actuality gap'*: the larger gap, the greater the risk of e-government failure, the smaller the gap, the greater the chance of project success. By examining numerous case studies related to ICTs and e-government failure in developing countries, Heeks (2002) identified three dominant categories of reported outcome: *total failure*, *partial failure*, and *success*.

- The first possible outcome is *total failure*, where a project is either never implemented or in which a new system is implemented but is almost immediately abandoned.
- A second possible outcome is the *partial failure* of an initiative, in which major goals are unattained or where there are significant undesirable outcomes. Cases range from straightforward underachievement to more complex "sustainability failures" of an initiative.
- Finally, one may see the *success* of an initiative, in which most actor groups attain their major goals and do not experience significant undesirable outcomes.

Heeks also identified three so-called 'archetypes of failure', situations when a large design-actuality gap, and consequently project failure, is likely to emerge: *Hard-Soft Gaps* (the difference between the actual, rational design of the technology and the actuality of the social context within which it operates), *Public-Private Gaps* (the mismatch that results when technology meant for private organisations is used in the public sector without being adequately adapted to the adopting organisation) and *Country Context Gaps* (the gap that arises when a system designed for one country is transferred unaltered into the reality of another).

The previous discussion reveals that although the strength of the Ecology of Games lies in its ability to identify and analyse the interrelationships between the different actors involved in the process of e-government system design and adoption, when taken alone it provides no insight into the consequences of this behaviour and its impact on project outcome. Similarly, the Design-Actuality Gap model is able to analyse structural weaknesses in a project's design but doesn't on its own provide an adequate explanation of the decision-making processes that led to such structural deficiencies in the first place. The results and analysis of this chapter will, therefore, rely on the two frameworks being used in combination to arrive at prescribed solutions and examples of best practice within the case study at hand. The advantage of using such an approach is that it allows the researcher to not only identify and analyse patterns of behaviour within the case under study, but also link decisions and actions to specific project outcomes.

PROPERTY TAX: DEFINITION, SCOPE, AND ADMINISTRATION

Property tax may be defined as a recurrent tax on real property (land and/or improvements) in urban areas (Dillinger, 1988). Just like other taxes, it may be considered as 'a compulsory transfer of money… from private individuals, institutions or groups to the government…[as] one of the principal means by which a government finances its expenditure' (Bannock et. al., 1987). Furthermore, Rosengard (1998) defines Property Tax as '…[an] *ad valorem* ("according to the value" tax, as opposed to a unit tax), *in rem* ("against the object" tax as opposed to a personal or *in personam* tax) levied on the ownership, occupation or development of land and/or buildings. Property taxes usually are assessed annually upon the capital value of a property, or upon proxies for capital value such as presumed or actual rental income. Taxes not confined to immovable property, such as net wealth taxes and general capital gains taxes, are not commonly classified as property taxes."

As a means of financing the recurrent cost of municipal services, the merits of the property tax are controversial. Property tax is appealing to local governments in developing countries for a number of reasons. First and possibly most importantly, it is a potential revenue generator, particularly given the high-income elasticity of property ownership in developing countries. It is a relatively stable source of income, and it is easy to implement slight adjustments and incremental rate changes. The tax is generally equitable and progressive for residential properties. It is hard to avoid legally due to the high visibility and relative immobility of property, with asset immobility also conferring a high degree of economic efficiency on the tax. It is clearly enforceable, particularly through the seizure and liquidation of property. The tax has the potential to enhance the local government agency's responsiveness to local priorities, particularly when used to finance local goods.

The performance and fairness of property taxation, however, depends to a large extent on how well the tax is administered, and property tax administration is difficult to reform. The tax is both highly visible and politically sensitive (Virkar, 2011). Unlike sales tax or excise duty, which are hidden in the selling price of goods and services in a manner whereby citizens are generally unaware of how much tax they are actually paying, it is easy to calculate one's property tax dues and citizens are generally completely aware of their tax liability for a given year. Further, unlike income tax where people are held liable according to their ability to pay, everyone who owns a property is required to pay property tax regardless of their income.

The tax is also unpopular because its calculation is (often correctly) perceived to be subjective, with revenue staff exercising enormous discretion during the assessment process. Additionally, tax laws regarding assessment and collection are often opaque, and redress from inaccurate valuation is generally a tedious process. In India, while the last four decades have seen a number of committees make recommendations about improving the property tax system, there has been a general inertia within the political class to implement any of the suggested reforms, and attempts made by municipal bodies to reform their property tax systems have often fallen short of stated intentions due to lack of legislative support.

GAMES OF TAX ADMINISTRATION: FROM CORRUPTION TO EVASION AND COMPLIANCE

The administration and collection of tax revenue invites several forms of malpractice – on the one hand, taxpayers may try to evade their legal liabilities, whilst on the other tax inspectors may solicit bribes in order to facilitate tax evasion or more generally abuse the authority of which they are entrusted (Hindriks et. al., 1999). A sizeable literature on tax evasion has evolved over the last few decades, which today includes a number of principal-agent-client models and game theory-based models, dating back to Allingham and Sandmo's (1972) seminal paper which proposes that in order to deter or reduce tax evasion, a tax administration needs to design an audit strategy whereby audits that compel taxpayers to disclose their true (as against reported) incomes are carried out by agents whose objectives are assumed to be in line with the goals of the tax administration (Allingham & Sandmo, 1972).

Such an argument, however, overlooks the role of those agents whose objectives may conflict with that of the administration, particularly within a hierarchical setup where a principal delegates a task to an agent, together with some discretion over certain decisions and within which there is subsequent room for collusion (Virkar, 2011).

Most recently, therefore, economists have moved to bridge this gap by developing models that incorporate the possibility of corruption in tax administration (Chander & Wilde, 1992). Collusive corruption in the tax system arises for two reasons: firstly, it is necessary for the government to delegate authority to tax officials who have the ability to obtain the necessary information to make the determination; and secondly, the government is unable to properly monitor its officials, a problem particularly acute in developing countries like India whose accounting and bookkeeping standards are relatively poor (Flatters & McLeod, 1995). Both these factors give rise to opportunities for collusion between taxpayers and inspectors, and bribes are either paid to tax inspectors in return for reductions in tax dues or to prevent officials from reporting a taxable income higher than true. Firm evidence on the extent of such practices is hard to come by, but a small literature initiated by Virmani (1987) and Chu (1990) exists, and anecdotal evidence abounds.

The flip-side of tax evasion – compliance – is as much a societal phenomenon that is difficult to explain. A large part of tax compliance hinges on citizen attitudes towards the government and tax burdens, and convincing the public that it is worth their while to pay taxes requires a sustained campaign and concrete action on the part of the tax collecting authority. But what exactly drives people to pay their taxes? Is it the fear of being caught and penalised? Is it because they believe it is for the common good? Or it is because they follow what they think everyone else is doing?

Economists see the problem of compliance as a rational decision made under uncertainty. This implies that cheating on taxes is a gamble; either paying off in the form of lower taxes or – with the probability of detection – ending in sanctions (Torgler, 2002). This view of taxpayer behaviour was first presented as a formal model by Allingham and Sandmo (1972), influenced by the economics-of-crime approach, which suggests that the level of tax compliance depends on the degree of enforcement (Becker, 1968). It is essential to recognise that this approach also concludes that an individual pays taxes because – and only because – of the fear of detection and punishment (Alm, 1998).

PROPERTY TAX ADMINISTRATION IN INDIA: THE CASE OF THE GREATER BANGALORE MUNICIPAL CORPORATION (BBMP)

The State of Karnataka is particularly interesting when studying the various games and interactions related to the use of Information Technology for public service reform within Indian government departments, as ongoing processes of change within different government agencies in the state have had the use of ICTs deeply implicated in them, and many government and quasi-government bodies have entered into partnerships with private and non-profit organisations. In recent years, there has been growing pressure placed by citizen groups, international agencies, and the local media on both city corporations and the state government to rationalise existing revenue collection structures and improve the collection of property tax in the field, both within cities and across the State at large.

In view of the need to turn property tax in to a productive tax instrument, the Greater Bangalore Municipal Corporation (BBMP) teamed up with a series of private and not-for-profit technology firms in partnerships which aimed to improve property tax collections across Bangalore city using computerised revenue records and Geographical Information Systems (GIS)-based property mapping. Against the background of technological innovation in the State, project planners decided to do away with the manual, paper-based system of property tax administration considering it to be increasingly archaic, opaque, and inefficient.

In particular, members of the core project group felt that property tax collections under the manual system had over the years suffered consistently from poor recordkeeping and bad information management practices, slow processing times, and overcomplicated assessment and payment procedures. This had, in turn, created frustration amongst taxpayers and resulted in increasingly low levels of tax compliance. The computerised property tax system was thus borne out of an ever-growing need to reform the old system of property tax administration in Bangalore city and to improve tax revenues and compliance through the improvement of back-office efficiency, the simplification of tax collection, and the reduction of money lost as a result of malpractice through the effective detection and deterrence of tax evasion. Concurrently planners were also spurred on by the need to enhance their own power, authority, and reputations with their respective spheres of influence and beyond.

This chapter focuses on the prevalence, significance, and impact of Extensive-Form Games in political institutions. In doing so, the research presented in the work adopts a behavioural approach to the study of Game Theory, one which attempts to add a human dimension to the basic rational player that is otherwise assumed. Nash (1950), in considering games as a mathematical constructs, defines the concept as that '...of an *n*-person game in which each player has a finite set of pure strategies and in which a definite set of payments to the *n* players corresponds to each *n*-tuple of pure strategies, one strategy being taken for each player. [sic.]...'(Nash, 1950, p. 48).

Broadly conceptualised, *an extensive-form game* may be defined as an arena of *competition* and/or *cooperation*, structured around a set of pre-defined *rules* and *assumptions* about how to *act* in order to *achieve* a particular *set of objectives*, with either *complete* and/or *perfect* information (Cf. Dutton, 1992; Virkar, 2011); in other words, a sphere of human interaction requiring a set of players (otherwise known as actors), a set of sequences of nodes (known as decision nodes or choice nodes), a base assumption of perfect recall (meaning that players cannot forget how they have moved or acted previously), and a set of outcomes for each sequence of choices (for which players possess a utility function already pre-defined) (Virkar, 2011).

These pre-conditional rules provide researchers with a standard way to create, to identify, and to recognise an extensive-form game; as also to enable them to understand and to analyse more clearly how rewards, payoffs, and profits are assigned (Gintis, 2009). The primary focus here, however, is on the *feelings* and *emotions* that are present during the various stages of human interaction and game-play, and is about how diverse *thinking and learning cognitive frameworks* feed into both decision-making and the eventual advancement of public policy (Virkar, 2011).

Interviews with key people involved with the design and implementation of the project, conducted between 2005 and 2009, brought to light a number of games or interactions operating at different levels or 'arenas', all of which had an impact – direct or indirect – on the effectiveness of the system and its eventual performance. These are outlined below (see tables 1-4):

Table 1. Project Planning Committee Games (Source: Author Analysis, 2010)

Games	Key Players	Key Objectives	Nature of Moves
The e-Government Movement	Various current senior *BBMP* officials, software providers.	Encourage *BBMP* departmental reform through the use of technology.	Positive Game Play
System Conception and Design c) Formation of the Core Project Planning Group d) Initial Design and Conception of the System	Various current senior *BBMP* officials, software providers. *BBMP* officials on the project planning committee, *eGovernments Foundation* representatives.	Take credit for the initial design idea and design process. Design and launch a successful system.	Negative Game Play Altruistic Game Play
Digital Democracy	Senior *BBMP* officials and *eGovernments Foundation* members.	Seek to influence the design of the *PTIS* to support their conception of democracy.	Negative Game Play

Table 2. BBMP Revenue Department Games (Source: Author Analysis, 2010)

Games	Key Players	Key Objectives	Nature of Moves
System Acceptance Games	Project planning group (Senior *BBMP* officials, software providers, external consultants), senior and junior revenue officials.	Get officials on the ground to accept and adopt the system.	Positive Game Play
Efficiency Games	Senior *BBMP* officials, Assistant Revenue Officers, and junior revenue staff.	Hold down costs and increase tax revenues by improving efficiency.	Positive Game Play
Management Control	Senior *BBMP* officials, Revenue officials.	Expand power and decisional control.	Negative Game Play
Game to Control Petty Corruption	Senior *BBMP* officials, Revenue officials.	Reduce revenue losses from petty corruption.	Negative Game Play
Revenue Office Politics	Revenue Officials, Assistant Revenue Officers, Station Managers, junior revenue staff.	Assert 'superior' status, to retain power and authority within the field office.	Negative Game Play

Table 3. Bangalore City Games (Source: Author Analysis, 2010)

Games	Key Players	Key Objectives	Nature of Moves
Image Building Game	*BBMP* officials, the media, citizens.	Improve image of the *BBMP* as an accountable, modern and responsive government agency.	Positive Game Play
Tax Compliance Game	*BBMP* officials, the media, citizens.	Encourage citizens to pay taxes through a mixture of carrot and stick initiatives.	Largely Positive Game Play

Table 4. National-level Games (Source: Author Analysis, 2010)

Games	Key Players	Key Objectives	Nature of Moves
The Innovation Game	*BBMP* officials, non-profit software providers	Introduce and be associated with a new idea, policy, or technology to improve the national image of the city and agency.	Positive Game Play
The Game for Business Competition	The *eGovernments Foundation* executive, associated software developers	Be associated with a successful project to gain national recognition.	Positive Game Play

WHAT'S IN A GAME? DISCUSSING E-GOVERNMENT SUCCESS AND FAILURE

This chapter sought to unravel the social dynamics shaping e-government projects used to reform public sector institutions. In particular, its chief aim was to analyse actor behaviour, motivations, and interactions surrounding the conception, development and maintenance of e-government software platforms facilitating these transformations. The principal approach of this research to the issues thrown up by these cross-sectoral interactions was the use of an empirical case study dealing with the design, implementation, and subsequent use of an electronic property tax system based in the Revenue Department of the Greater Bangalore Municipal Corporation (BBMP).

The overarching aim of the computerised system was to improve tax revenues and tax compliance through the streamlining of tax administration processes by increasing back-office efficiency, simplifying methods of tax payment, reducing the amount of money lost through petty corruption, and improving tax yields and citizen compliance through the speedy detection of tax evasion. Designers of the project sought to use automation and digitisation to improve data management in the revenue offices, reduce the use of discretion by government officials in revenue-related decisions, and make property tax collection processes more transparent.

In particular, the system sought to increase revenues from property tax through better quality data, quicker evaluations, greater computational accuracy, and positive psychological reinforcement; whilst at the same time reducing losses in revenue occurred as a result of back-office inefficiencies and fraudulent practices through the use of digital databases and GIS maps. However, as illustrated by the case study, the underlying motivations for the individual partners and actors within each of the participating organisations turned out in some instances to be widely divergent, resulting in several highly divisive and negative outcomes within the context of the project under study.

As the analysis in previous sections has shown, certain key games with local impacts get played out in different arenas between actors influenced by not only local but also national and international factors. An examination of interview data and other documents brought to light a number of games in different arenas, each involving key actors related to the project, whose interplay had a bearing on the project's eventual outcome. No single game can account for the ultimate outcome of the Revenue Department project at the time of writing, and instead the impact that the system has had on property tax administration can be best understood as an 'interacting set' or 'ecology' of games – as discussed in previous sections. Games that shaped the development and adoption of the system appear to have be layered or 'nested', with some contained within others.

Key games found to have significantly shaped the outcome of the system appear to have been played during the initial stages of the process, either during the time of its conception (in the form of positive and negative interactions between members of the project planning committee) or at the stage of internal implementation and adoption (in the form of friction between the core project team and the intended end-users such as the field officers), corroborating the findings of the quantitative data analysis set out in the previous section of this chapter. The only city-level game that had any significant impact on the project appeared to be the Tax Compliance game, played between the BBMP and the taxpayers of Bangalore. Other games at the city and national levels were primarily found to be ideological games and games centred around the interplay of market forces, thus having little direct bearing on the tax administration system and its eventual fate.

Questions remained, however, as to whether conflicting motivations and interests could be aligned to ensure win-win situations for all actors concerned and to promote the long-term sustainability of the project at hand. The discussion of the case study in previous sections also reveals that at the heart of each game lay a design-actuality gap, usually brought about from a power struggle stemming from a deep-seated mistrust between different actor groups. In particular, the case study demonstrates that gaps arise because those with the power and authority to take design or implementation decisions at different key stages of the process are usually unwilling to allow any initiative to go ahead that would give the other actor group(s) in the game more autonomy over the system or more control over their actions. Design-actuality gaps also arise when key actors refuse to acknowledge the impact that external, tangential factors and circumstances have on the shaping of decisions and government policy.

In recognising that design-actuality gaps open up and give way to unfavourable project outcomes if designers and top managers assume that localised outcomes result only from direct local influences, discounting the impact of other factors external to the project at hand, preliminary findings suggest that the project may at the time of writing be classed as a *partial failure* under Heeks' threefold categorisation.

However, as evidenced by the discussion, this so-called 'failure' is neither a straightforward case of the outright inability of project managers to achieve stated objectives nor is it a so-called 'sustainability failure'. Causes of failure to meet stated aims appear to be two-fold: manifested through Hard-Soft gaps, stemming from competitive and divisive moves made by actors in key games relating to the system's design and implementation that generated conflict and disharmony in later attempts by users to adopt the system, and Private-Public gaps, rooted in fierce competition and oftentimes rivalry between key executive members on both sides of the profit- non-profit divide that stemmed from their differing values, work cultures, and agendas.

SUCCESSFULLY PLAYING GAMES OF TAX COMPLIANCE: GOVERNMENT AGENCIES AS ARCHITECTS OF PUBLIC CHOICE

Based on the results of several key psychological studies, scholars Thaler and Sunstein (2009) discuss the psychology behind human choices and how these can be influenced by public agencies and others acting as so-called 'choice architects' (Virkar, 2011). Thaler and Sunstein conclude that when acting within a group, people are by-and-large conformists and often fall prey to what is known as 'collective conservatism' (Thaler & Sunstein, 2009, p. 63): the tendency of groups to stick to established patterns of behaviour even as new needs arise.

Collective conservatism is often a result of what is termed *pluralistic ignorance*; or, ignorance on the part of all or most about what other people think. As human beings spend time conforming to social norms and fashions, especially when they think that others are closely paying attention to what they are doing, collective conservatism has become an important parameter in the evaluation of the impact of any tax-related measure against which to determine whether a cross-section of people follow a practice or tradition, not because they like it or think it is defensible, but because they think others consider it acceptable and/or would like it, or not (Virkar, 2011).

Furthermore, while assessing the significance of tax-related administrative reform, it is important to know not only whether a given strategic intervention has resulted in an increase in absolute tax revenues collected, but also whether the change in policy discourse has resulted in an improvement in the percentage of people complying with the legal requirement. The BBMP meta-game to improve compliance has so far concentrated on encouraging property tax payments through increasing public awareness about the progress it has made in simplifying tax assessment procedures and facilitating tax payments, and by warning citizens about the risks they run if they do not comply with existing tax laws.

While these are no doubt important factors in encouraging citizens to file their returns on time (indeed, evidence has shown that citizen compliance appeared to respond to modifications in the tax administration process), too great an emphasis on non-compliance may in the long-run focus attention on the negative game of non-compliance itself and eclipse its potential benefits. This is because there is a general tendency for law-abiding citizens (not only in India, but also elsewhere) to believe that there are far more people who are able to easily break the law and evade their taxes than is actually the case.

Cynicism such as this is further compounded by limited faith in government, and impacts the efficacy of any system that those in power might put in place. A sustained awareness campaign that focuses on not only the achievements made by technology in the identification and apprehension of those citizens who do not comply, but which also touches on how the majority of citizens are benefitting by responding positively to its introduction, would go a long way in contributing to the success of the computerised system as an effective tool to improve tax revenues for the municipality.

CONCLUSION

Local government agencies across the developing world, being at the bottom of the fiscal food chain, generally face stringent resource constraints to improving their operations and service delivery. Property tax, for all its weaknesses, presents itself as a viable means of financing the recurrent costs of municipal services. If administering an existing property tax system is complex and often unpredictable, the reform of property tax administration is an equally difficult game to effectuate and to play; not only because of the tax's high visibility and political sensitivity, but because it is often played between a number of actors harbouring competing interests.

The penultimate section of this chapter highlighted the strategic interactions and interventions closely involved with property taxation and its eventual administration; together with a number of areas wherein the interaction of competing strategic games met with highly negative implications, and resulted in the emergence of design-actuality gaps that led to project targets not being fully met. The chapter identified lack of trust between different actors as a significant reason as to why they often chose to behave in a self-interested manner, rather than in more co-operative ways that could have benefitted all parties concerned. In particular, moves made by project planners and strategies adopted by those with authority within the BBMP were seen to have a profound influence on the moves and strategic interactions of junior employees situated elsewhere; and, in fact, were marked out as game changers in previous sections of this work.

What then makes people comply? And how can this understanding be harnessed by government agencies wishing to engage their populations in a win-win game? The theoretical basis for tax liability compliance, as observed within discussions of strategic action presented in this chapter, is that of *collective conservatism*; the idea that the social conundrums associated with the fulfilment of tax liabilities are fundamentally products of a process of collective definition instead of existing independently as a set of objective social arrangements with an intrinsic makeup, and wherein the principal tendency of individuals and groups is to remain attached to the collective past. It follows, hence, that if choice architects wish to shift strategic behaviour, they might simply change the manner in which they engage their employees and citizens in political games by drawing public attention on to what others within a given game environment are actually doing.

Through its chosen case study, this chapter took forward both discussions surrounding the analytical frameworks involved in the identification and evaluation of strategic behaviour concerning property tax administration and the application of technology therein, together with the idea that the development and implementation of ICT-for-development projects carry deep political implications; that, in summation, the politics of power and influence often drive the design of a project, that political reputations may be staked on the pre-supposed outcome, that opinions generally vary on whether certain aspects of a system are economically and politically viable or indeed desirable, that politics circumscribes what can and cannot be implemented, and that reactions to the reform of a property tax system always carry deep political implications.

REFERENCES

Allingham, M. G., & Sandmo, A. (1972). Income Tax Evasion: A Theoretical Analysis. *Journal of Public Economics*, *1*(3-4), 323–338. doi:10.1016/0047-2727(72)90010-2

Alm, J. (1998). *Tax Compliance and Administration*. Working Paper. University of Colorado at Boulder.

Bannock, G., Baxter, R. E., & Davis, E. (1987). *The Penguin Dictionary of Economics* (4th ed.). London: Penguin Books.

Bannon, L. J. (1991). From Human Factors to Human Actors: The Role of Psychology and Human Computer Interaction Studies in System Design. In J. Greenbaum & M. Kyng (Eds.), *Design At Work: Cooperative Design of Computer Systems* (pp. 25–44). Lawerence Erlbaum Associates Inc.

Becker, G. S. (1968). Crime and Punishment: An Economic Approach. *Journal of Political Economy*, *76*(2), 169–217. doi:10.1086/259394

Beinhocker, E. D. (2006). The Origin of Wealth: Evolution, Complexity and the Radical Remaking of Economics. Boston: Harvard Business School Press.

Bhatnagar, S. (2004). *E-Government: From Vision to Implementation*. New Delhi: SAGE Publications.

Brams, S. J. (2004). *Game Theory and Politics*. Mineola, NY: Dover Publications, Inc.

Bruhat Bangalore Mahanagara Palike. (2000). *Property Tax Self-Assessment Scheme: Golden Jubilee Year 2000*. Mahanagara Palike Council Resolution No. 194/99-2000.

Bruhat Bangalore Mahanagara Palike. (2007). *Assessment and Calculation of Property Tax Under the Capital Value System (New SAS): 2007- 2008*. Unpublished.

Camerer, C. F. (2003). *Behavioral Game Theory: Experiments in Strategic Interaction*. Princeton, NJ: Princeton University Press.

Carayon, P., Hoonakker, P., & Smith, M. J. (2012). Human Factors in Organizational Design and Management. In G. Salvendy (Ed.), *Handbook of Human Factors and Ergonomics* (4th ed.; pp. 534–552). John Wiley and Sons. doi:10.1002/9781118131350.ch18

Chakravarty, S. R., Mitra, M., & Sarkar, P. (2015). *A Course on Cooperative Game Theory*. New Delhi: Cambridge University Press.

Chander, P., & Wilde, L. (1992). Corruption in Tax Administration. *Journal of Public Economics*, *49*(3), 333–349. doi:10.1016/0047-2727(92)90072-N

Chiu, C. M., Hsu, M. H., & Wang, E. T. (2006). Understanding Knowledge Sharing in Virtual Communities: An Integration of Social Capital and Social Cognitive Theories. *Decision Support Systems*, *42*(3), 1872–1888. doi:10.1016/j.dss.2006.04.001

Chu, C.Y.C. (1990). Income Tax Evasion with Venal Tax Officials - the Case of Developing Countries. *Public Finance = Finances Publiques, 45*(3), 392-408.

Coleman, S. (2005). Just how risky is online voting? *Information Polity*, *10*(1), 95–104.

Crozier, M., & Friedberg, E. (1980). *Actors and Systems*. Chicago, IL: University of Chicago Press.

Czaja, S. J., & Nair, S. N. (2012). Human Factors Engineering and Systems Design. In G. Salvendy (Ed.), *Handbook of Human Factors and Ergonomics* (4th ed.; pp. 38–56). John Wiley and Sons. doi:10.1002/9781118131350.ch2

D'Andrade, R. G. (1992). Schemas and Motivation. In R. G. D'Andrade & C. Strauss (Eds.), *Human Motives and Cultural Modes* (pp. 23–24). Cambridge, UK: Cambridge University Press. doi:10.1017/CBO9781139166515.003

Dada, D. (2006). The Failure of E-Government in Developing Countries: A Literature Review. *The Electronic Journal on Information Systems in Developing Countries, 26*(7), 1–10.

Davis, P. (2008). Book Review: The Origins of Wealth: Evolution, Complexity, and the Radical Remaking of Economics. *The FINSIA Journal of Applied Finance, 1*(3), 48–50.

Dillinger, W. (1988). *Urban Property Taxation in Developing Countries.* World Bank Policy Research Working Paper Series, no. 41, 1988. Retrieved on June 14, 2008, from: http://ideas.repec.org/p/wbk/wbrwps/41.html

Dixit, A., & Skeath, S. (2004). *Games of Strategy* (2nd ed.). New York: W.W. Norton & Company, Inc.

Downs, A. (1964). *Inside Bureaucracy.* Boston, MA: Little Brown.

Dunleavy, P. (1991). *Democracy, Bureaucracy and Public Choice: Economic Explanations in Political Science.* London: Harvester Wheatsheaf.

Dutton, W. H. (1992). The Ecology of Games Shaping Telecommunications Policy. *Communication Theory, 2*(4), 303–324. doi:10.1111/j.1468-2885.1992.tb00046.x

Eisenhardt, K. M. (1989). Building Theories from Case Study Research. *Academy of Management Review, 14*(4), 532–550.

Fehr, E., & Gachter, S. (2002). Altruistic Punishment in Humans. *Nature, 415*(6868), 137–145. doi:10.1038/415137a PMID:11805825

Firestone, W. A. (1989). Educational Policy as an Ecology of Games. *Educational Researcher, 18*(7), 18–24. doi:10.2307/1177165

Flatters, F., & MacLeod, W. B. (1995). Administrative Corruption and Taxation. *International Tax and Public Finance, 2*(3), 397–417. doi:10.1007/BF00872774

Fountain, J. E. (2001). *Building the Virtual State: Information Technology and Institutional Change.* Washington, DC: Brookings Institution Press.

Fountain, J. E. (2002). A Theory of Federal Bureaucracy. In E. Kamarck & J. S. Nye Jr., (Eds.), *Governance. com: Democracy in the Information Age* (pp. 117–140). Washington, DC: Brookings Institution Press.

Fountain, J. E., & Osorio-Urzua, C. A. (2001). Public sector: Early stage of a deep transformation. In R. Litan & A. Rivlin (Eds.), *The Economic Payoff from the Internet Revolution* (pp. 235–268). Washington, DC: Brookings Institution and Internet Policy Institute.

Gascó, M. (2003). New Technologies and Institutional Change in Public Administration. *Social Science Computer Review, 21*(6), 6–14. doi:10.1177/0894439302238967

Gintis, H. (2000). *Game Theory Evolving: A Problem-Centered Introduction to Modeling Strategic Behavior.* Princeton, NJ: Princeton University Press.

Gintis, H. (2006). *The Economy as a Complex Adaptive System - A Review of Eric D. Beinhocker, The Origins of Wealth: Evolution, Complexity, and the Radical Remaking of Economics.* MacArthur Research Foundation Paper Series. Retrieved on September 30, 2011, from: http://www.umass.edu/preferen/Class%20Material/Readings%20in%20Market%20Dynamics/Complexity%20Economics.pdf

Gintis, H. (2009). *Game Theory Evolving: A Problem-Centered Introduction to Modeling Strategic Interaction* (2nd ed.). Princeton, NJ: Princeton University Press.

Hall, P. A., & Taylor, R. C. R. (1996). *Political Science and the Three New Institutionalisms.* MPIFG Discussion Paper 96/9.

Hartley, J. (2004). Case Study Research. In C. Cassell & G. Symon (Eds.), *Essential Guide to Qualitative Methods in Organisational Research* (pp. 323–333). London: SAGE Publications. doi:10.4135/9781446280119.n26

Hechter, M., & Kanazawa, S. (1997). Sociological Rational Choice Theory. *Annual Review of Sociology, 23*(1), 191–214. doi:10.1146/annurev.soc.23.1.191

Heeks, R. (2002). Information Systems and Developing Countries: Failure, Success and Local Improvisations. *The Information Society, 18*(2), 101–112. doi:10.1080/01972240290075039

Heeks, R. (2003). *Most eGovernment-for-Development Projects Fail: How Can the Risks be Reduced?* i-Government Working Paper Series, Paper No. 14, IDPM.

Hindriks, J., Keen, M., & Muthoo, A. (1999). Corruption, Extortion and Evasion. *Journal of Public Economics, 74*(3), 395–430. doi:10.1016/S0047-2727(99)00030-4

Immergut, E. M. (1998). The Theoretical Core of New Institutionalism. *Politics & Society, 26*(5), 5–34. doi:10.1177/0032329298026001002

Innocenti, A., & Sbriglia, P. (2008). *Games, Rationality and Behaviour: Essays on Behavioural Game Theory and Experiments.* New York, NY: Palgrave Macmillan.

Isaac-Henry, K. (1997). Development and Change in the Public Sector. In K. Isaac-Henry, C. Painter, & C. Barnes (Eds.), *Management in the Public Sector: Challenge and Change* (pp. 1–25). London: International Thomson Business Press.

Jacko, J. A., Yi, J. S., Sainfort, F., & McClellan, M. (2012). Human Factors and Ergonomic Methods. In G. Salvendy (Ed.), *Handbook of Human Factors and Ergonomics* (4th ed.; pp. 289–329). John Wiley and Sons. doi:10.1002/9781118131350.ch10

Johnson, E. J., Shu, S. B., Dellaert, B. G. C., Fox, C., Goldstein, D. G., Häubl, G., & Weber, E. U. et al. (2012). Beyond Nudges: Tools of a Choice Architecture. *Marketing Letters, 23*(2), 487–504. doi:10.1007/s11002-012-9186-1

Johnson, R. N., & Libecap, G. D. (1994). The Federal Civil Service System and the Problem of Bureaucracy. Chicago, IL: University of Chicago Press. doi:10.7208/chicago/9780226401775.001.0001

Kahneman, D. (2003). Maps of Bounded Rationality: Psychology for Behavioral Economics. *The American Economic Review, 93*(5), 1449–1475. doi:10.1257/000282803322655392

Keeney, R. L. (1996). Value-Focused Thinking: Identifying Decision Opportunities and Creating Alternatives. *European Journal of Operational Research*, *92*(3), 537–549. doi:10.1016/0377-2217(96)00004-5

Kenman, H. (1996). Konkordanzdemokratie und Korporatismus aus der Perspektive eines rationalen Institutionalismus. *Politische Vierteljahresschrift*, *37*, 494–515.

Kirchler, E. (2007). *The Economic Psychology of Tax Behaviour.* Cambridge, UK: Cambridge University Press. doi:10.1017/CBO9780511628238

Kuutti, K. (1996). Activity Theory as a Potential Framework for Human Computer Interaction Research. In B. A. Nardi (Ed.), *Context and Consciousness: Activity Theory and Human Computer Interaction* (pp. 17–44). Boston, MA: M.I.T. Press.

Laver, M., & Schofield, N. (1990). *Multiparty Government: The Politics of Coalition in Europe.* Oxford, UK: Oxford University Press.

Long, N. E. (1958). The Local Community as an Ecology of Games. *American Journal of Sociology*, *64*(3), 251–261. doi:10.1086/222468

March, J. G., & Olsen, J. P. (1984). The New Institutionalism: Organisational Factors in Political Life. *The American Political Science Review*, *78*(3), 734–749. doi:10.2307/1961840

March, J. G., & Olsen, J. P. (1989). *Rediscovering Institutions: The Organisational Basis of Politics.* New York: The Free Press.

Maskin, E., & Tirole, J. (2004). The Politician and the Judge: Accountability in Government. *The American Economic Review*, *94*(4), 1034–1054. doi:10.1257/0002828042002606

McCubbins, M. D., & Sullivan, T. (1987). *Congress: Structure and Policy.* Cambridge, UK: Cambridge University Press.

Morrow, J. D. (1994). *Game Theory for Political Scientists.* Princeton, NJ: Princeton University Press.

Nash, J. F. Jr. (1950). Equilibrium Points in n-Person Games. *Proceedings of the National Academy of Sciences of the United States of America*, *36*(1), 48–49. doi:10.1073/pnas.36.1.48 PMID:16588946

North, D. C. (1990). *Institutions, Institutional Change, and Economic Performance.* Cambridge, UK: Cambridge University Press. doi:10.1017/CBO9780511808678

North, D. C. (1994). Institutional Change: A Framework of Analysis. *Working Papers in Economics.* Retrieved on May 10, 2010, from: http://ideas.repec.org/p/wpa/wuwpeh/9412001.html#related

Nye, J. S. (2002). Information technology and democratic governance. In E. Kamarck & J. S. Nye Jr., (Eds.), *Governance.com: Democracy in the Information Age* (pp. 1–16). Washington, DC: Brookings Institution Press.

Ordeshook, P. C. (1986). *Game Theory and Political Theory: An Introduction.* Cambridge, UK: Cambridge University Press. doi:10.1017/CBO9780511666742

Ostrom, E., Gardner, R., & Walker, J. (1994). *Rules, Games and Common-Pool Resources.* Ann Arbor, MI: University of Michigan Press.

Peters, B. G. (2000). *Institutional Theory in Political Science: The New Institutionalism*. London: Continuum.

Proctor, R. W., & Vu, K.-P. L. (2012). Selection and Control of Action. In G. Salvendy (Ed.), *Handbook of Human Factors and Ergonomics* (4th ed.; pp. 95–116). John Wiley and Sons. doi:10.1002/9781118131350. ch4

Romp, G. (1997). *Game Theory: Introduction and Applications*. New York: Oxford University Press.

Rosengard, J. K. (1998). *Property Tax Reform in Developing Countries*. Boston, MA: Kluwer Academic Publications. doi:10.1007/978-1-4615-5667-1

Salvendy, G. (2012). *Handbook of Human Factors and Ergonomics* (4th ed.). John Wiley and Sons. doi:10.1002/9781118131350

Scharpf, F. W. (1997). *Games Real Actors Play: Actor-Centered Institutionalism in Policy Research*. Oxford, UK: Westview Press.

Simon, H. A. (1955). A Behavioural Model of Rational Choice. *The Quarterly Journal of Economics, 69*(1), 99–118. doi:10.2307/1884852

Strauss, C. (1992). Introduction. In R. G. D'Andrade & C. Strauss (Eds.), *Human Motives and Cultural Modes* (pp. 1–20). Cambridge, UK: Cambridge University Press. doi:10.1017/CBO9781139166515.002

Thaler, R. H., & Sunstein, C. R. (2009). *Nudge: Improving Decisions about Health, Wealth and Happiness*. London: Penguin Books, Ltd.

Thomas, J. M., & Bennis, W. G. (1972). *The Management of Change and Conflict: Selected Readings*. Harmondsworth, UK: Penguin Books.

Torgler, B. (2002). Speaking To Theorists and Searching for Facts: Tax Morale and Tax Compliance in Experiments. *Journal of Economic Surveys, 16*(5), 657–683. doi:10.1111/1467-6419.00185

Tsebelis, G. (1990). Nested Games: Rational Choice in Comparative Politics. Berkley, CA: University of California Press.

Virkar, S. (2011). *The Politics of Implementing e-Government for Development: The Ecology of Games Shaping Property Tax Administration in Bangalore City, India*. (Unpublished Doctoral Thesis). University of Oxford.

Virkar, S. (2013) Designing and Implementing e-Government Projects: Actors, Influences, and Fields of Play. In S. Saeed & C. G. Reddick (Eds.), Human-Centered Design for Electronic Government (pp. 88-110). Hershey, PA: IGI Global, Inc.

Virmani, A. (1987). *Indirect Tax Evasion and Production Efficiency. Development Research Department, Economics and Research Staff*. Washington, DC: World Bank.

Williams, K. C. (2013). *Introduction to Game Theory: A Behavioral Approach* (International Edition). New York, NY: Oxford University Press.

Yin, R. K. (2003). Applied Social Research Methods Series: *Case Study Research: Design and Methods* (vol. 5). London: SAGE Publications.

ADDITIONAL READING

Asquith, A. (1998). Non-elite Employees' Perceptions of Organizational Change in English Local Government. *International Journal of Public Sector Management*, *11*(4), 262–280. doi:10.1108/09513559810225825

Bahl, R. W., & Linn, J. F. (1992). *Urban Public Finance in Developing Countries*. New York: Oxford University Press.

Bellamy, C. (2000). The Politics of Public Information Systems. In G. D. Garson (Ed.), *Handbook of Public Information Systems* (pp. 85–98). New York: Marcel Dekker, Inc.

Ciborra, C. (2005). Interpreting e-government and development: Efficiency, transparency or governance at a distance? *Information Technology & People*, *18*(3), 260–279. doi:10.1108/09593840510615879

Cornwell, B., Curry, T. J., & Schwirian, K. P. (2003). Revisiting Norton Long's Ecology of Games: A Network Approach. *City & Community*, *2*(2), 121–142. doi:10.1111/1540-6040.00044

Datta, A. (1983). *Property Taxation in India*. New Delhi: Centre for Urban Indian Studies – The Indian Institute of Public Administration.

Fehr, E., & Gachter, S. (1998). Reciprocity and Economics: The Economic Implications of *Homo Reciprocans*. *European Economic Review*, *42*(3), 845–859. doi:10.1016/S0014-2921(97)00131-1

Friend, J. K., & Jessop, W. N. (2013). *Local Government and Strategic Choice: An Operational Research Approach to the Processes of Public Planning*. Abingdon: Routledge Press.

Jones, B. D. (2001). *Politics and the Architecture of Choice: Bounded Rationality and Governance*. Chicago: The University of Chicago Press.

Lewis, A. (1982). *The Psychology of Taxation*. Oxford: Martin Robertson & Company.

Macy, M. W., & Willer, R. (2002). From Factors to Actors: Computational Sociology and Agent-Based Modeling. *Annual Review of Sociology*, *28*(1), 143–166. doi:10.1146/annurev.soc.28.110601.141117

National Institute of Urban Affairs. (2004). *Reforming the Property Tax System. Research Study Series no. 94*. New Delhi: NIUA Press.

Newbery, D., & Stern, N. (1987). *The Theory of Taxation for Developing Countries*. New York: Oxford University Press.

Rose-Ackerman, S. (1978). *Corruption: A Study in Political Economy*. New York: Academic Press.

Skov, L. R., Lourenço, S., Hansen, G. L., Mikkelsen, B. E., & Schofield, C. (2013). Choice Architecture as a Means to Change Eating Behaviour in Self-Service Settings: A Systematic Review. *Obesity Reviews*, *14*(3), 187–196.

Chapter 13

Behavioral Stream in Polish Accounting:
Its Relation to Behavioral Finance and the Perspectives for Neuroaccounting Development in Poland

Nelli Artienwicz
University of Gdansk, Poland

ABSTRACT

Information which financial market participants use to make their decisions comes directly and indirectly from accounting. Although finance and accounting use the language of numbers which appear to be very clear and plain, it is obvious that sums presented in financial statements and then interpreted and used by financial managers and investors and other stakeholders are very subjective. The goal of this chapter is to pay attention to the implications of behavioral research in accounting and its new stream – neuroaccounting – for behavioral finance. It is argued that accounting should be considered by behavioral finance researchers because the product of accounting in the form of reports, statements, and different analyses represents not only economic standing of a company, but also those behind the scenes.

INTRODUCTION

Finance and accounting are both concerned with the financial aspects of a business or organization. However, the managers and employees in finance and accounting departments work in completely different manners. Accounting is concerned mainly with the recording of business transactions of a company, preparing financial statements and reports, reflecting the financial position of the company at a particular date, making sure all liabilities (especially taxes) are paid on time, and disseminating of information to managers, investors, and other stakeholders. Alternatively, finance focuses on making important financial decisions for an organization, directing investment activities, and developing financial strategies and plans for an organization.

DOI: 10.4018/978-1-4666-9989-2.ch013

Although finance and accounting use the language of numbers that seem to be very clear and plain, it is obvious that sums presented in financial statements and then interpreted and used by financial managers and investors and other stakeholders are very subjective. The subjectivity in the decision making process in this area is analyzed by two schools of behavioral research: behavioral finance and behavioral accounting. Behavioral trends in finance and accounting have been developing since the 1960s. However, their evolution is separate and little attention is paid to common research. Additionally, accounting theory and accounting results in the form of financial statements and reports seem to be taken for granted by economists and finance analysts and the role of accounting is hardly noticeable. The relationship between behavioral finance and behavioral accounting is very important and has not received sufficient attention in the past – neither in international nor in Polish literature.

Within behavioral schools of finance and accounting, new streams have emerged which seek to explain neuronal aspects of human decision making and behaviors. They are based on neuroeconomics which focuses on brain processes and neuroscientific discoveries. Despite criticism, neuroeconomics has become a well-established field of academic study. Neuroaccounting as a logical extension of the field, however, remains considerably less mainstream. Although the discussion about the "black box" is not a new one in accounting, not much research exists in this area and accounting both on the behavioral and neuronal level does not seem to be widely acknowledged or treated as a contributing area to neuro and behavioral trends in economics.

The aim of this chapter is to pay attention to the implications of behavioral research in accounting for finance theory and practice and to consider possibilities of development of neuroaccounting as the stream within behavioral accounting research in Poland. First, attention is paid to accounting itself and its behavioral aspects. Because accounting research in Poland falls into the "finance category" and behavioral trends both in finance and accounting are quite new issues in Polish research, in the next step behavioral accounting and behavioral finance are briefly compared both on the international and country level. Lastly, the base for interdisciplinary neuroresearch in accounting in Poland is analyzed. The study is based on a literature overview and internet-based research.

Background

In different branches of economic and finance, accounting appears to be a neglected "component" (Artienwicz, 2013). The most common definitions of accounting show accounting as a system that measures the results of an organization's economic activities and conveys this information to a variety of users (stakeholders). This system is, however, so fundamental for economic reality yet complex and hermetic that few outside accounting profession are able to fully appreciate it. Although its beauty and perfection has been praised by German poet Goethe, in the words of one of his characters as "one of the finest inventions of the human spirit" (Chambers & Dean, 2013, p. 144) and by British mathematician Cayley, who published a small booklet, *The Principles of Book-keeping by Double Entry,* in which he wrote:

The Principles of Book-keeping by Double Entry constitute a theory which is mathematically by no means uninteresting: it is in fact like Euclid's theory of ratios an absolutely perfect one, and it is only its extreme simplicity which prevents it from being as interesting as it would otherwise be. (Cayley, 1894, Preface)

The importance of accounting has always needed some strong defense (Belkaoui, 2004, p. 1). Nonetheless, accounting is a social phenomenon and it has arisen to meet social needs. It is an inevitable part of the enterprise because it gives a global picture of the course and results of the economic activities, reveals existing problems and provides the background data for decision-making processes in every enterprise (Kayanova, 2006). Traditional division of accounting includes financial accounting which provides external financial statements for general use and managerial accounting which provides internal reports tailored to the needs of managers inside the company. The accounting data helps with financial planning, reviewing the performance of the business (for example how to raise money for future projects, how to utilize the resources of the company so that company makes profit), and ensuring the business is meeting legal obligations such as tax reporting.

Accounting is not merely a type of practical business knowledge, but it is also an academic discipline. The theory of accounting encompasses research on accounting practice and results of this research in the form of theories, conceptions, models, and hypotheses. Accounting is an independent science; however, its borders are vague and it is not possible to determine exactly where accounting ends and other disciplines begin (Jaruga, 1997, p. 164). Accounting theory is treated as a set of principles which enables a better understanding of existing accounting practice, which creates notional structure for assessment of this practice and which points out the direction for developing of new methods and procedures (Babuśka, 2013, p. 28).

Accounting academics believe accounting is at the core of the economic sciences. The aggregation and appraisal of economic values would not have been possible if accounting had not existed. Accounting as a science develops theoretical framework for valuation and presentation of economic values which is then applied in accounting practice. Data produced by the accounting system (which includes also costing and taxation) is the basis for such disciplines as economics, statistics, and finance. At a general abstract level, finance principles and concepts are based on accounting information and use accounting information as a basis for their development (Ryan, Scapens, & Theobald, 2002). This is why considering accounting, and especially behavioral and neuro streams in this discipline, is important for finance and economy researchers as it can shed some new light on research issues.

Although accounting is frequently viewed as a highly analytical and dry discipline with very precise answers, it is in fact quite subjective financial knowledge about an organization. At each stage of producing accounting information, certain decisions must be made and these decisions are obviously made by humans. Behavioral accounting challenges simplistic assumptions of rational behavior and focuses on behavioral structure within which accountants function. Its basic objective is to explain and predict human behavior in all possible accounting contexts (Belkaoui, 1996, p. 148). It is concerned with the usefulness of reported data, material judgments, decision effects of alternative accounting procedures, and the impact of culture and language on the interpretation and application of accounting pronouncements (Hellmann, 2013).

Considering the traditional division of accounting – financial accounting (external reporting) and managerial accounting (internal reporting) – the scope of behavioral accounting is broad. Additionally, it may focus on two more areas: tax accounting and auditing. It may include the behavior of accountants, the effect of behavior on the construction and use of the accounting system, the influence of the accounting function on behavior and the influence of accounting information on those receiving that information (Ashton, 2013, p. 115).

Behavioral accounting research cannot be underestimated. Accounting is assumed to be action oriented; its purpose is to influence action (behavior) directly through the informational content of the message conveyed and indirectly through the behavior of accountants (Belkaoui, 2004, p. 368). Accounting information affects society and can be of great consequence. Some examples include the following (Wolk, Dodd, & Rozycki, 2012):

- Numbers presented in financial statements can affect dividend payments
- Financial ratios calculated on the basis of accounting values can affect the company's credit standing and, therefore, the cost of capital
- Numbers presented in financial statements of public companies can affect the stock price
- Accounting information helps evaluating the performance of management, which can affect salaries and bonuses and even retaining the job by individual managers

However, society cannot "see through" the accounting methods that have been employed, cannot see emotions, behavior patterns and cognitive processes of chief accountants, or members of the board of directors and auditors engaged in accounting function. Behavioral accounting constantly develops (Bloomfield, 2011). Some examples of research in different areas of behavioral aspects of accounting are presented in Table 1.

BEHAVIORAL ACCOUNTING VERSUS BEHAVIORAL FINANCE AND NEUROACCOUNTING RESEARCH IN POLAND

Behavioral Accounting in Comparison to Behavioral Finance: Worldwide and Polish Perspective

Research in both behavioral finance and behavioral accounting is growing and is helping in understanding the relationship between the decision-making processes and psychological aspects in finance and accounting. Behavioral finance challenges the concept of *homo oeconomicus* incorporated into traditional finance and aims at improving the understanding of financial markets and its participants by focusing on how people behave. Behavioral accounting aims at improving the understanding of decisions made by participants of accounting system while producing accounting information and non-accountants who are influenced by accounting reports and statements. These two branches of behavioral research have evolved separately as presented in Table 2.

Both behavioral finance and behavioral accounting attempt to explain how and why cognitive errors and other behavioral factors influence financial decisions. However, their character is different. Firstly, the main focus of behavioral finance is investors and markets, whereas the main area of interest in behavioral accounting is the accounting environment. Although the accounting environment includes capital markets, the perspective taken is different than that in behavioral finance. Secondly, decisions made within accounting function of an organization seem to be more down to earth and more orderly because of accounting and tax regulations which must be followed while performing accounting tasks and because the double-entry method used. This is true in financial aspects of accounting. In management accounting decisions are limited by the organizational structure of a company, still they are taken within the company and the processes researched are internal.

The two schools of behavioral research, although separate, are intertwined because both are concerned with financial reporting within capital markets and the behavior of investors. They study individual and group behavior caused by the communication of financial information. From the finance perspective, the

Table 1. Examples of behavioral accounting research

Year	Author	Research problem
Financial accounting		
Investor oriented		
1989	Davis	The effect of different types of graphic (bar charts, line graphs, pie charts and tables) on the accuracy and decision time of judgements about financial variables
1990	Kaplan, Pourciau & Reckers	The role of the President's Letter and Stock Advisory Service Information in interpreting the firm's financial statements and making decisions about the firm
2007	Pinsker	The effect of disclosure pattern (sequential versus simultaneous) and direction of information (positive/negative versus negative/positive) on non-professional investors' belief revisions
2012	Bailey & Sawers	How trust influences nonprofessional investor decisions under rules-based and principles-based standards
Accountant oriented		
1991	Street & Bishop	The motivational criteria of accountants--need for achievement, need for power, and need for affiliation
2002	Schwartz & Wallin	The relative effect of the available method of lying on the frequency of lying in fraudulent reports
2011	Bryant, Stone & Wier	Whether creativity is essential or antithetical to professional accounting work
2013	Cote, Latham & Sanders	The influence of individual characteristics on ethical choice in a financial reporting task
Management accounting		
1983	Lewis, Shields & Young	Framework for evaluating human judgments and prescribing decisions aids
1990	Murray	The relationship between participative budgeting and performance, variables that may moderate the effect of participation on performance are identified
2004	Chenhall	Cognitive and Affective Conflict in Early Implementation of Activity-Based Cost Management
2011	Nicolaou	The complementary nature of decision-facilitation and decision-influencing objectives of management accounting systems design as enabled by the use of integrated information systems in interorganizational settings
Auditing		
1985	Libby	The application of the availability heuristic in auditing domain
1986	Cushing & Loebbecke	Examination of audit methodologies (audit manuals) in large accounting firms
1990	Rebele & Michaels	antecedents to and consequences of role conflict and ambiguity experienced by independent auditors
2011	Hatfield, Jackson & Vandervelde	The effects of prior auditor involvement and client pressure on the magnitude of proposed audit adjustments.
Taxation		
1992	Pei, Reckers & Wyndelts	The effects of information presentation sequence, client preference and domain experience on tax professionals
2000	Samelson & Jeffrey	Accuracy of recall of declarative tax knowledge of tax accountants, and calibration of confidence in the accuracy of recall
2002	Newmark & Karim.	How a red-flag item, an unfavorable projection error and time pressure affect the aggressiveness of tax preparers' recommendations
2010	Hageman	The nature of tax preparers' confidence and how the introduction of a tax decision support system affects tax preparers' confidence levels

Table 2. Behavioral finance and behavioral accounting comparison on the international level

	Behavioral finance	Behavioral accounting
First formal paper	Slovic (1972), Psychological study of human judgment: implications for investment decision making, Journal of Finance	Devine (1960), *Research methodology* and *accounting* theory formation, The *Accounting* Review
Journals with primary focus on the field	• Behavioral & Experimental Finance eJournal (since 1997) • The Journal of Behavioral Finance (since 2003) formerly published as The Journal of Psychology and Financial Markets (since 2000) • The IUP Journal of Behavioral Finance (since 2004) • Review of Behavioural Finance (since 2009)	• Behavioral Research in Accounting (BRIA) (since 1989) • Advances in Accounting Behavioral Research (since 1998)
	• International Journal of Behavioural Accounting and Finance (since 2008)	
Recognized publications	• Thaler (ed.), Advances in Behavioral Finance, vol. 1 (1993) and II (2005) • Montier (2002), Behavioural Finance. Insights into Irrational Minds and Markets • Shefrin (2007), Behavioral Corporate Finance: Decisions that Create Value	• Schiff & Lewin (eds.) (1974), Behavioral aspects of accounting • Belkaoui (1989), Behavioral Accounting: The Research and Practical Issues • Arnold & Sutton (eds.), (1997), Behavioral Accounting Research: foundations and frontiers
Scope of research	Stock valuation, asset allocation, portfolio construction, corporate finance	Managerial control, participation in the budgetary process, accounting information processing, accounting information system design, auditing
Research subjects	Individual investors, corporate investors, analysts, business students	Accountants, auditors, investors, accounting students, managers

topic of how information is processed by investors and analysts is researched (e.g., DeBondt & Thaler, 1985, 1987; Abarbanell & Bernard, 1992; Bradshaw, 2000; Fisher & Statman, 2000). In accounting, the research issue is how accounting disclosure is used and the influence of accounting disclosure and different valuation methods on decisions made by financial statements users (Dyckman, 1964; Ball & Brown, 1968; Kida & Smith, 1998, Krishnan & Booker 2002; Hodge & Pronk, 2006). Some authors attempt to combine these disciplines together and compare their results (Ricciardi, 2004; Breitkreuz, 2009; Bloomfield, 2011).

As shown in the table, both schools of behavioral research are well-grounded on the international level. However, this situation is not reflected in Polish research. There is a large discrepancy between behavioral perspective when comparing behavioral finance and behavioral accounting in Poland. Behavioral finance seems to be an acknowledged branch of research which has been rapidly developing in recent years, whereas behavioral accounting is still in its infancy. A brief comparison of output of Polish behavioral finance and accounting is presented in Table 3. All titles have been translated from Polish into English.

The field of behavioral finance started its development about 10 years earlier than behavioral accounting, so the former is more influential than the latter. The books presented in the table in the behavioral finance column are either mainly or solely concerned with psychological aspects of the field, whereas books in behavioral accounting column just include psychological aspects as one of the themes among others and are the only books published in Poland covering the behavioral aspects of accountants and accounting processes.

The discrepancy is also evident when it comes to the number and scope of papers published. The results of queries using the Library's of Science search engine for the expression "behavioral finance"

Table 3. Behavioral finance and behavioral accounting in Poland

	Behavioral finance	**Behavioral accounting**
First paper that goes into psychological aspects of the field	Zielonka & Tyszka (1999), Modern finance: market efficiency or behavioral finance?	Hasik (2008), The Quality of Reporting Information in the Context of Behavioural Accounting Versus Economic Practice
Journals which in their scope include the field	Journal of Capital Market and Behavioral Finance (2014)	none
Recognized publications (books) in Polish	• Zaleśkiewicz (2003), Psychology of stock investor. Introduction to behavioral finance • Zielonka (2003), What is behavioral finance. A short introduction into psychology of financial markets • Szyszka (2009), Behavioral finance: the new approach to investing in capital market • Czerwonka & Gorlewski (2008), Behavioral finance, behaviors of investors and markets • Gajdka (2013), Behavioral finance: basic approaches and concepts.	• Dobija & Kucharczyk (ed.) (2009) Management accounting. Theory, practice, behavioral aspects. • Kabalski (2012), Some issues in application of International Financial Reporting Standards in Poland. Organisation, culture, personality, language.
Examples of papers	• Buczek (2006), Behavioral Finance and Investments in Equities • Kicia (2006), Personality Type and Risk Tolerance - Behavioral Finance Perspective • Antkiewicz (2008),The Psychological Dimension of Constructing Investment Portfolio and Markowitz Model • Dudzińska-Baryła & Michalska (2010), Turn-Of-The-Month Effect and behavioral aspects of decision making • Osińska, Pietrzak & Żurek (2011), Evaluation of Impact of Behavioral and Market Factors on Attitudes of Individual Investors in Polish Capital Market Using SEM Model • Czerwonka & Rzeszutek (2011), Analysis of Investment Behaviour of Stock Market Investors and Students of Business and Psychology from the perspective of Behavioural Finance • Dębniewska & Wojtowicz (2014), Influence of Current Public Information on the Investors Decisions in the Context of Behavioral Finance • Soliwoda (2014), Behavioural Approach and Economic Experiment in Agricultural Finance	• Kabalski, Wyganowska &Tobór-Osadnik (2012), International Financial Reporting Standards Versus Homo Sovieticus and Attitudes of Polish Accountants • Artienwicz (2013a), Behavioral Accounting as an Interdyscyplinary Field of Accounting and Behavioral Sciences • Gmińska & Magier-Łakomy (2014), The framing effect in economic decisions based on accounting information • Jaworska (2014), Behavioral Perspective in Accounting in the Light of Chosen Theories of Psychology of Motivation

and "behavioral accounting" are presented in Table 4. The Library of Science is maintained by the Centre for Open Science (part of the Interdisciplinary Centre for Mathematical and Computational Modelling at the University of Warsaw) which provides access to the largest collection of digital scientific resources in Poland. The Virtual Library of Science is accessible to all academic institutions in Poland, and Polish scientific databases and journals in open access. The query was executed on May 20, 2015. Two expressions were searched: "*rachunkowość behawioralna*" (behavioral accounting) and "*finanse behawioralne*" (behavioral finance) in several search fields.

Queries in the title were modified according to Polish grammatical rules so that no results were omitted. As expected, there are more publications concerning behavioral finance than behavioral accounting. What is alarming in these results is the "behavioral accounting" expression was not found in "keywords" section despite the fact that original papers concerning behavioral stream in accounting have this expres-

Table 4. Number of publications concerning behavioral finance and accounting in Poland in years 2000-2015 according to the Polish Library of Science

Expression	"Behavioral finance"	"Behavioral accounting"
keyword	85	0
title	16	3
any field	206	23

sion presented in keywords. Such a situation may make behavioral accounting underestimated in Poland, where the most important search engine does not seem to include the expression as worth considering.

Furthermore, behavioral accounting papers in Polish are mainly descriptive or introductionary in nature. By the end of 2014, there were only two papers that examined human behavior in accounting context (Kabalski, Wyganowska, & Tobór-Osadnik, 2012; Gmińska & Magier-Łakomy, 2014). The first paper examined whether the personality features of Polish accountants predisposed them to practicing accounting accurately according to International Financial Reporting Standards (IFRS) and how common personality type incompatible with international approach to accounting was among Polish accountants. The second paper covers managerial accounting and examines the existence and strength of the framing effect in managerial decisions based on accounting information.

Several papers try to build fundamentals for further research in behavioral accounting. Artienwicz (2011a) analyzed the scope of possible research on accountants' behavior within existing accounting paradigms. The paradigms suggested by Riahi-Belkaoui were used in this analysis. Jaworska (2014) presented psychological theories of motivation whose assumptions facilitate understanding why and what prompts accountants to choose a particular behavior. Artienwicz (2011b) associated accounting skills with three levels of intelligence: rational, emotional and spiritual. This is not much compared to behavioral finance in which many practical issues are covered such as the impact of psychological factors on propensity for risk, anchoring effect and the investment decisions on the stock market, personality type and sex, and their influence on the decision making processes.

Neuroaccounting: The New Aspect of Behavioral Research in Accounting and its Chances for Development in Poland

The development of noninvasive techniques to study brain activity in the last two decades of the 20th century created new possibilities for advances in the social sciences. From studying the human mind and behaviors in accountancy settings, the workings of "the black box" and the word "neuroaccounting" appeared as a natural consequence. Neuroaccounting could be defined as a new trend within behavioral accounting which is based on neuronal research.

Neuroaccounting lies at the intersection of experimental accounting research and neurobiology and neuropsychology. This interdisciplinary area combines neuroscience knowledge and technique to investigate the physiology of the neural circuits involved in the many kinds of decisions accountants must make. Not much work has been conducted in the new stream of neuroaccounting, but there are four publications worth mentioning.

Dickhaut, Basu McCabe, and Waymire (2010) developed the hypothesis that culturally evolved accounting principles can be explained by their consilience with how human brain evolved. The authors placed the brain as the central point in building economic institutions. They show that fundamental accounting principles have distinct parallels in brain behaviors. Brinberg & Ganguly (2011) discuss the reasons why neuroeconomics should be of interest to behavioral accounting researchers. They conclude, however, that a separate sub-field of neuroaccounting is not likely in the near future due mostly to practical reasons of complicated neurobiological knowledge needed to conduct research. The last two papers were published in 2014 in a special section of the November issue of *The Accounting Review* titled: "A forum on neuroscience and ultimate causation in accounting research", which attempted to present research on links between brain, human behavior, accounting and financial markets.

In the first paper, Barton, Berns, and Brooks (2014) using functional magnetic resonance imaging captured neural activity in the ventral striatum—a key area in the human brain's reward processing circuit—of 35 adult investors learning the earnings per share disclosed by 60 publicly traded companies. The results were consistent with prospect theory, as there was a strong neurobiological evidence of an asymmetric reaction to positive and negative earnings surprises. In the second paper, Farell, Goh, and White (2014) showed results of investigation of managers' brain activity and choices under fixed wage and performance-based contracts. Functional magnetic resonance imaging and traditional experiments were used.

Considering the output of behavioral accounting in Poland and the first steps of neuroaccounting worldwide, it does not seem unusual that there are no works that attempt to examine the human brain further in Polish accounting research. Some theoretical background for "neuro" in the context of economics and finance is present in Poland (Zaleśkiewcz, 2008; Krawczyk, 2011). As in case of behavioral streams in economics and finance, however, researchers seem to forget about the source for economic information which is accounting. Only one introductory paper on neuroaccounting has been published in Poland (Miązek, 2014). It describes the essence of the term "neuroaccounting" together with the reasons for the use of neurological research in economics. It also presents methods of measuring human brain activities.

The question whether neuroaccounting has an opportunity for development in Poland is still debatable. The small international output of the stream does not help the situation. The willingness of researchers to explore new topics and proceed along unknown paths of research is not strong in the accounting domain in Poland. The conservative approach of Polish researchers regarding new fields and paradigms can be lessened by invoking international developments and successes. This is not presently the case in neuroaccouting. Secondly, the condition of behavioral accounting itself must be taken into consideration. As it was presented earlier in this chapter, experimental research in accounting and creating practical studies in behavioral issues is something new in Poland. To conduct neuronal experiments, which are based on observable behaviours, first strenghthening the psychological aspects of Polish research in accounting is needed.

Thirdly, the access to special equipment and possibilities of cooperation with neuropsychologist and neurobilogists must be considered. This third factor, however, seems to possess potential. There are a total of 12 medical universities in Poland with proper research facilities. Neuronal research is especially conducted in Warsaw Medical University. Other institutions focusing on neuronal interdisciplinary research include the Nencki Institute of Experimental Biology of Polish Academy of Sciences (*Instytut Biologii Doświadczalnej Polskiej Akademii Nauk*), the Institute of Psychology of Polish Academy of Sciences (*Instytut Psychologii Polskiej Akademii Nauk),* and University of Social Sciences and Humanicies (*Szkoła Wyższa Psychologii Społecznej*).

The most important issue for neuroresarch in accounting to develop in Poland is strengthening its basis (i.e., behavioral research in accounting), especially experimental research. What seems to be also important is the attitude of psychologists and finance researchers towards the accounting discipline. Accounting is still taken for granted and the value of behavioral and potential neuronal research in this area and the results that may be of great value to behavioral finance and neuroeconomics are underestimated.

CONCLUSION

The financial and managerial accounting systems of today could not exist without humans whose behavior in the context of accounting is the subject of research in behavioral accounting. Behavioral accounting is an interdisciplinary field of research that derives from behavioral sciences, but it does not have a strong connection with behavioral finance which is much more popular among economists. Financial reporting is the final output of the accounting process. Financial statements exist to present a record for a specific period in a company's life and are supposed to give a fair picture of a company at a certain date. However, it also indirectly presents choices and preferences of persons involved in producing these statements.

Valuation methods are not merely "accounting constructs" as they have real impact on the values presented in financial statements. It is important for finance to fully understand financial reporting figures, not only classically but also behaviorally, to see the behavioral path which starts the moment the accounting system of an organization is designed and entries to the system are made, and ends the moment financial decisions are made in the market (i.e., decisions based *inter alia* on a prepared set of accounting information). The very important aspect of how people behave in production of accounting knowledge should be considered by finance researchers. If accounting information is a requirement for making financial decisions, behavioral insights about how accountants prepare such information are needed. A natural consequence of insights into the human psyche is the need to dig deeper into the human brain.

It could be argued that not only the behavior of financial practitioners might contribute to market inefficiency. On a global, abstract level, the inefficiency might reach deeper and its causes might also lay in the accounting systems and behavior of accountants. This way of viewing behavioral consequences of financial reporting makes the whole process even more subjective, uncertain, and contextual. However, what might help understand the deep reasons for behaviors is examining how the human brain functions in different accounting processes and decision making. For now, the expression that consists of "neuro" plus "accounting" is very fresh and not embedded in science.

Neuroscience can provide a foundational understanding of accounting principles, of creating accounting policies and choosing how to present information in financial statements. Neuroscience research can be the basis for specialized behavioral accounting experiments. The application of neuroscience in accounting can lead to deeper, multidisciplinary understanding of the financial processes within markets and organizations. The potential of neuroaccounting is huge as it is an undiscovered land with many research issues and outlets.

REFERENCES

Abarbanell, J. S., & Bernard, V. L. (1992). Tests of Analysts' Overreaction/ Underreaction to Earnings Information as an Explanation for Anomalous Stock Price Behavior. *The Journal of Finance*, *47*(3), 1181–1207. doi:10.1111/j.1540-6261.1992.tb04010.x

Antkiewicz, S. (2008). Kryteria o podłożu behawioralnym a klasyczna teoria Markowitza. *Studia i Prace Wydziału Nauk Ekonomicznych i Zarządzania Uniwersytetu Szczecińskiego*, *9*, 362–377.

Arnold, V., & Sutton, S. G. (Eds.). (1997). *Behavioral Accounting Research: foundations and frontiers.* Sarasota, FL: American Accounting Association.

Artienwicz, N. (2011a). Możliwości badania zachowania księgowych w świetle paradygmatów rachunkowości. *Prace i Materiały Wydziału Zarządzania Uniwersytetu Gdańskiego*, *1/2*, 355–364.

Artienwicz, N. (2011b). Sztuka pomiaru i komunikowania z perspektywy umiejętności księgowego. In Rachunkowość. Sztuka pomiaru i komunikowania (pp. 23-36). Warszawa: Oficyna Wydawnicza SGH.

Artienwicz, N. (2013). Rachunkowość behawioralna jako interdyscyplinarny nurt rachunkowości i społecznych nauk o zachowaniu. *Zeszyty Teoretyczne Rachunkowości*, *71*(127), 7–23.

Ashton, R. H. (2013). Historical Perspective on Behavioral Accounting Research. In R.H. Ashton (Ed.), The Evolution of Behavioral Accounting Research: An Overview (pp. 113-119). London: Routledge.

Babuśka, E. W. (2013). Teoria rachunkowości i jej miejsce w dyscyplinarnej strukturze nauk o kierowaniu organizacjami. *Zeszyty Teoretyczne Rachunkowości*, *71*(71(127)), 25–37. doi:10.5604/16414381.1061632

Bailey, W. J., & Sawers, K. M. (2012, Spring). In GAAP We Trust: Examining How Trust Influences Nonprofessional Investor Decisions Under Rules-Based and Principles-Based Standards. *Behavioral Research in Accounting*, *24*(1), 25–46. doi:10.2308/bria-50071

Ball, R., & Brown, P. (1968). An Empirical Evaluation of Accounting Income Numbers. *Journal of Accounting Research*, *6*(2), 159–178. doi:10.2307/2490232

Barton, J., Berns, G. S., & Brooks, A. M. (2014). The Neuroscience Behind the Stock Market's Reaction to Corporate Earnings News. *Accounting Review*, *89*(6), 1945–1977. doi:10.2308/accr-50841

Belkaoui, A. (1989). *Behavioral Accounting: The Research and Practical Issues.* New York: Quorum Books.

Belkaoui, A. (1996). *Accounting, a Multiparadigmatic Science.* Westport, CT: Greenwood Publishing Group.

Belkaoui, A. (2004). *Accounting theory.* London: Thomson Learning.

Birnberg, J. G., & Ganguly, A. R. (2012). Is Neuroaccounting Waiting in the Wings? An Essay. *Accounting, Organizations and Society*, *37*(1), 1–13. doi:10.1016/j.aos.2011.11.004

Bloomfield, R. (2011). Traditional Versus Behavioral Finance. In H. K. Baker & J. R. Nofsinger (Eds.), *Behavioral Finance: Investors, Corporations, and Markets.* New York: Wiley. doi:10.1002/9781118258415.ch2

Bradshaw, W. M. (2000). *How do analysts use their earnings forecasts in generating stock recommendations?* Harvard University Working Paper. Retrieved on November 10, 2014, from: www.researchgate.net

Breitkreuz, R. (2009). *Behavioral Accounting vs. Behavioral Finance. A comparison of the related research disciplines.* Univeristat St. Gallen. Accessed December 13, 2014, from: http://www.grin.com/en/e-book/129284/behavioral-accounting-vs-behavioral-finance

Bryant, S. M., Stone, D., & Wier, B. (2011). An Exploration of Accountants, Accounting Work, and Creativity. *Behavioral Research in Accounting, 23*(1), 45–64. doi:10.2308/bria.2011.23.1.45

Buczek, S. (2006). Finanse behawioralne a inwestowanie w akcje. *Współczesne problemy finansów, bankowości i ubezpieczeń w teorii i praktyce, 1*, 293-306.

Cayley, A. (1894). *The principles of book-keeping by double entry.* Cambridge University Press. Accessed April 1, 2015, from: https://archive.org/details/principlesofbook00caylrich

Chambers, R. J., & Dean, G. W. (2013). *Chambers on Accounting: Logic, Law and Ethics.* New York: Routledge.

Chenhall, R. H. (2004). The Role of Cognitive and Affective Conflict in Early Implementation of Activity-Based Cost Management. *Behavioral Research in Accounting, 16*(1), 19–44. doi:10.2308/bria.2004.16.1.19

Cote, J., Latham, C., & Sanders, D. (2013). Ethical Financial Reporting Choice: The Influence of Individual Characteristics. *Advances in Accounting Behavioral Research, 16*, 115–148. doi:10.1108/S1475-1488(2013)0000016010

Cushing, B. E., & Loebbecke, J. K. (1986). *Comparison of audit methodologies of large accounting firms.* Sarasota, FL: American Accounting Association.

Czerwonka, M., & Gorlewski, B. (2008). *Finanse behawioralne: zachowania inwestorów i rynku.* Warszawa: Szkoła Główna Handlowa - Oficyna Wydawnicza.

Czerwonka, M., & Rzeszutek, M. (2011). Analiza zachowań inwestycyjnych inwestorów giełdowych oraz studentów kierunków ekonomicznych i psychologicznych z perspektywy finansów behawioralnych. *Studia i Prace Kolegium Zarządzania i Finansów, 107*, 28–44.

Davis, L. (1989). Report format and the decision makers' task: An experimental investigation. *Accounting, Organizations and Society, 14*(5-6), 495–508. doi:10.1016/0361-3682(89)90014-7

De Bondt, W., & Thaler, R. H. (1985). Does the Stock Market Overreact. *The Journal of Finance, 40*(3), 793–805. doi:10.1111/j.1540-6261.1985.tb05004.x

De Bondt, W., & Thaler, R. H. (1987). Further Evidence on Investor Overreaction and Stock Market Seasonality. *The Journal of Finance, 42*(3), 557–581. doi:10.1111/j.1540-6261.1987.tb04569.x

Dębniewska, M., & Wojtowicz, K. (2014). Wpływ bieżących informacji na decyzje inwestorów w kontekście teorii finansów behawioralnych. *Prace Naukowe Wyższej Szkoły Bankowej w Gdańsku, 32*, 105–116.

Devine, C. (1960). Research methodology and accounting theory formation. *Accounting Review, 35*, 387–399.

Dickhaut, J., Basu, S., McCabe, K., & Waymire, G. (2010). Neuroaccounting: Consilience between the Biologically Evolved Brain and Culturally Evolved Accounting Principles. *Accounting Horizons*, *24*(2), 221–255. doi:10.2308/acch.2010.24.2.221

Dobija, D., & Kucharczyk, M. (Eds.). (2009). *Rachunkowość zarządcza: teoria, praktyka, aspekty behawioralne*. Warszawa: Wydawnictwa Akademickie i Profesjonalne.

Dudzińska-Baryła, R., & Michalska E. (2010). Efekt miesiąca a behawioralne aspekty podejmowania decyzji. *Metody i zastosowania badań operacyjnych, 10*, 54-75.

Dyckman, T. (1964). The Effects of Alternative Accounting Techniques on Certain Management Decisions. *Journal of Accounting Research*, *2*(1), 91–107. doi:10.2307/2490158

Farrell, A. M., Goh, J. O., & White, B. J. (2014). The Effect of Performance-Based Incentive Contracts on System 1 and System 2 Processing in Affective Decision Contexts: fMRI and Behavioral Evidence. *Accounting Review*, *89*(6), 1979–2010. doi:10.2308/accr-50852

Fisher, K., & Statman, M. (2000). Cognitive bias in market forecasts. *Journal of Portfolio Management*, *27*(1), 72–81. doi:10.3905/jpm.2000.319785

Gajdka, J. (2013). *Behawioralne finanse przedsiębiorstw: podstawowe podejścia i koncepcje*. Łódź: Wydawnictwo Uniwersytetu Łódzkiego.

Hageman, A. M. (2010). The role of confidence in tax return preparation using tax software. *Advances in Accounting Behavioral Research*, *13*, 31–57. doi:10.1108/S1475-1488(2010)0000013006

Hasik, W. (2008). Jakość informacji sprawozdawczych w kontekście rachunkowości behawioralnej a praktyka gospodarcza. *Prace Naukowe Akademii Ekonomicznej we Wrocławiu, 1199*, 20-27.

Hatfield, R. C., Jackson, S. B., & Vandervelde, S. D. (2011). The Effects of Prior Auditor Involvement and Client Pressure on Proposed Audit Adjustments. *Behavioral Research in Accounting*, *23*(2), 117–130. doi:10.2308/bria-10064

Hellmann, A. (2013). *Behavioral Accounting*. New York: Nova Science Publishers.

Hodge, F., & Pronk, M. (2006). The impact of expertise and investment familiarity on investors' use of online financial reporting information. *Journal of Accounting, Auditing & Finance*, *21*(3), 267–292.

Jaruga, A. (1997). Jarosław Wiaczesławowicz Sokołow: Rachunkowość. Od źródeł do naszych dni. *Zeszyty Teoretyczne Rady Naukowej, 42*, 12–16.

Jaworska, E. (2014). Perspektywa behawioralna w rachunkowości w świetle wybranych teorii psychologii motywacji. *Zeszyty Naukowe Uniwersytetu Szczecińskiego. Finanse. Rynki finansowe. Ubezpieczenia*, *70*, 49–58.

Kabalski, P. (2012). *Wybrane problemy stosowania Międzynarodowych Standardów Sprawozdawczości Finansowej w Polsce. Organizacja, kultura, osobowość, język*. Łódź: Wydawnictwo Uniwersytetu Łódzkiego.

Kabalski, P., Wyganowska, M., & Tobór-Osadnik, K. (2012). Międzynarodowe Standardy Sprawozdawczości Finansowej a homo sovieticus i postawy pracownicze polskich księgowych. *Zeszyty Teoretyczne Rachunkowości, 65*, 71–98.

Kajanova, J. (2006). The relationship between business finance and accounting. *VADYBA (Management), 2*, 58–64.

Kaplan, S. E., Pourciau, S., & Reckers, Ph. M. J. (1990). An Examination of the Effect of the President's Letter and Stock Advisory Service Information on Financial Decisions. *Behavioral Research in Accounting, 2*, 63–92.

Kicia, M. (2006). Cechy indywidualne a stosunek do ryzyka w świetle teorii finansów behawioralnych. *Współczesne problemy finansów, bankowości i ubezpieczeń w teorii i praktyce, 1*, 367-376.

Kida, T., Smith, J. F., & Maletta, M. (1998). The effects of encoded memory traces for numerical data on accounting decision making. *Accounting, Organizations and Society, 23*(5-6), 451–466. doi:10.1016/S0361-3682(98)00003-8

Krawczyk, M. (2011). Pożytek z neuroekonomii. *Decyzje, 15*, 43–59.

Krishnan, R., & Booke, M. (2002). Investors' use of analysts' recommendations. *Behavioral Research in Accounting, 14*(1), 129–156. doi:10.2308/bria.2002.14.1.129

Lewis, B. L., Shields, M. D., & Young, S. M. (1983). Evaluating human judgements and decisions aids. *Journal of Accounting Research, 13*(1), 271–285. doi:10.2307/2490947

Libby, R. (1985). Availability and the generation of hypotheses in analytic review. *Journal of Accounting Research, 23*(2), 648–667. doi:10.2307/2490831

Miązek, A. (2014). Neurorachunkowość jako nowoczesne podejście w rachunkowości. *Studia Oeconomica Posnaniensia, 2*(5), 75–83.

Montier, J. (2002). *Behavioural Finance. Insights into Irrational Minds and Markets.* New York: Wiley.

Murray, D. (1990). The Performance Effects of Participative Budgeting: An Integration of Intervening and Moderating Variables. *Behavioral Research in Accounting, 2*, 829–842.

Newmark, R. I., & Karim, K. E. (2002). The effects of red-flag items, unfavorable projection errors, and time pressure on tax preparers' aggressiveness. *Advances in Accounting Behavioral Research, 5*, 213–243. doi:10.1016/S1474-7979(02)05043-3

Nicolaou, A. I. (2011). Integrated Information Systems and Interorganizational Performance: The Role of Management Accounting Systems Design. *Advances in Accounting Behavioral Research, 14*, 117–141. doi:10.1108/S1475-1488(2011)0000014008

Osińska, M., Pietrzak, M. B., & Żurek, M. (2011). Ocena wpływu czynników behawioralnych i rynkowych na postawy inwestorów indywidualnych na polskim rynku kapitałowym za pomocą modelu SEM. *Przegląd Statystyczny, 58*, 175–194.

Pei, B., Reckers, P., & Wyndelts, R. (1992). Tax professionals' Belief Revision: The Effects of Information Presentation Sequence, Client Preference and Domain Experience. *Decision Sciences*, *23*(1), 175–199. doi:10.1111/j.1540-5915.1992.tb00383.x

Pinsker, R. (2007). Long series of information and nonprofessional investors' belief revision. *Behavioral Research in Accounting*, *19*(1), 197–214. doi:10.2308/bria.2007.19.1.197

Rebele, J. E., & Michaels, R. E. (1990). Independent Auditors Role Stress: Antecedent, Outcome, and Moderating Variables. *Behavioral Research in Accounting*, *2*, 124–153.

Riccardi, V. (2004). *A Risk Perception Premier: A Narrative Research Review of the Risk Perception Literature in Behavioral Accounting and Finance*. Golden Gate University.

Ryan, B., Scapens, R. W., & Theobald, M. (2002). *Research Method and Methodology in Finance and Accounting* (2nd ed.). Cornwall, UK: Mitcham Surrey International.

Samelson, D., & Jeffrey, C. (2000). Accuracy and calibration in professional judgment: A study of tax practitioners. *Advances in Accounting Behavioral Research*, *3*, 153–176. doi:10.1016/S1474-7979(00)03030-1

Schiff, M., & Lewin, A. Y. (Eds.). (1974). *Behavioral aspects of accounting*. Englewood Cliffs, NJ: Prentice Hall.

Schwartz, S. T., & Wallin, D. E. (2002). Behavioral Implications of Information Systems on Disclosure Fraud. *Behavioral Research in Accounting*, *14*(1), 197–221. doi:10.2308/bria.2002.14.1.197

Shefrin, H. (2007). *Behavioral Corporate Finance: Decisions that Create Value*. Boston: McGraw-Hill.

Slovic, P. (1972). Psychological study of human judgment: Implications for investment decision making. *The Journal of Finance*, *27*(4), 779–799. doi:10.1111/j.1540-6261.1972.tb01311.x

Soliwoda, M. (2014). Podejście behawioralne i eksperyment ekonomiczny w finansach rolnictwa. *Zagadnienia Ekonomiki Rolnej*, *1*, 57–77.

Street, D. L., & Bishop, A. C. (1991). An Empirical Examination of the Need Profiles of Professional Accountants. *Behavioral Research in Accounting*, *2*, 97–116.

Szyszka, A. (2009). *Finanse behawioralne: nowe podejście do inwestowania na rynku kapitałowym*. Poznań: Wydawnictwo Uniwersytetu Ekonomicznego.

Thaler, R. H. (Ed.). (1993). *Advances in Behavioral Finance* (Vol. 1). New York: Princeton University Press.

Thaler, R. H. (Ed.). (2005). *Advances in Behavioral Finance* (Vol. 2). New York: Princeton University Press.

Wolk, H. I., Dodd, J. L., & Rozycki, J. J. (2012). *Accounting theory. Conceptual Issues in a Political and Economic Environment* (8th ed.). London: Sage Publishing.

Zaleśkiewicz, T. (2003). *Psychologia inwestora giełdowego. Wprowadzenie do behawioralnych finansów*. Sopot: Gdańskie Wydawnictwo Psychologiczne.

Zaleśkiewicz, T. (2008). Neuroekonomia. *Decyzje, 9*, 29–56.

Zielonka, P. (2003). *Czym są finanse behawioralne, czyli krótkie wprowadzenie do psychologii rynków finansowych*. Warszawa: Narodowy Bank Polski.

Zielonka, P., & Tyszka, T. (1999). Nowoczesne finanse: Efektywność rynku czy finanse behawioralne? *Bank i Kredyt, 11*, 8–19.

KEY TERMS AND DEFINITIONS

Accountant: A practitioner of accounting, a person that is engaged in accounting processes which is the measurement, disclosure, or provision of assurance about financial information.

Accounting: The measurement, processing and communication of financial information about economic entities.

Behavioral Accounting: The study of the behavior of accountants and other participants of accounting processes as they communicate, understand and use accounting information.

Financial Reporting: The process of producing financial information in form of the reports, called statements, that disclose an organization's financial status to management, investors and other stakeholders.

Chapter 14
Game Theory

William Amone
Gulu University, Uganda

ABSTRACT

Economists, political scientists, and military analysts widely apply game theory techniques to analyze strategic decision making of players. The model is often adopted to analyze oligopolistic firms' actions, legal, and political negotiations, dating and mating strategies by couples, and competitive bidding in auctions. As a facet of neuroeconomics, game theory can highly complement the comprehension of human decision making processes. Although the model has been somewhat difficult for many readers, this chapter presents game theory with a high level of precision for easy understanding. The discourse presented in this chapter covers the different types of games, the approaches applied to predict games' outcomes, and general analysis of strategic choices. In its final section, the chapter underscores key aspects of auction and competitive bidding.

INTRODUCTION

Game theory has long been difficult to understand, probably because the model has always been presented in rather complex ways. This chapter presents the subject in its simplest form using practical examples and clear analyses of the theory of games with the hope that any ordinary person should be able to read, comprehend, and apply it to analyze situations involving conflicts or cooperation. This chapter covers the different types of games in game theory (static or dynamic, zero-sum or non-zero sum, cooperative or non-cooperative, etc.), the approaches used to predict outcomes of games, and it presents with examples how to analyze different types of games. In its final section, the chapter provides a comprehensive discussion of auction and competitive bidding.

BACKGROUND

The set of tools applied to analyze conflict and cooperation among players (such as firms or individuals) who decide strategically is called game theory. Game theory techniques are often applied to evaluate situations where individuals or organizations have conflicting objectives. Developed in the 1940s by

DOI: 10.4018/978-1-4666-9989-2.ch014

mathematician John von Neumann and economist Oskar Morgenstern, game theory formally describes games and predicts their outcomes conditional on the rules of the games, the information that players have and other factors. Each player adopts a plan (strategy) to compete with others (von Neumann & Morgenstern, 1944).

Any situation in which individuals must make strategic choices and in which the final outcome will depend on what each person chooses to do can be viewed as a *game.* All games have three basic elements: (1) players (2) strategies and (3) payoffs. Games may be *cooperative,* in which players can make binding agreements, or *non-cooperative,* where such agreements are not possible (Koutsoyiannis, 1979).

Economists use game theory when a player's optimal strategy depends on the actions of others, often described as ***strategic interdependence***. For example, telephone providers in most countries carefully monitor each other's behavior; since relatively few firms compete in such markets, each firm can influence the price, and hence the payoffs of rival firms. The need to consider the behavior of rival firms makes each firm's profit maximization decision more difficult than that of a monopoly or a competitive firm. A monopolist has no rivals, and perfect competitive firms ignore the behavior of individual rivals (Perloff, 2008). Game theory is therefore used to study oligopolistic behavior but not competitive or monopolistic behaviors.

Oligopoly markets are categorized depending on the characteristics of the market, such as the type of actions firms take, how the firms set quantity or prices, and whether firms act simultaneously or sequentially. The three poplar models of oligopoly are the Cournot model, the Stackelberg model, and the Bertrand model (Breitmoser, 2010).

In the Cournot model, firms simultaneously choose quantities without colluding. The firms have imperfect information about their rivals, so each chooses its output level before knowing what the other firm will choose. The quantity that one firm produces directly affects the profits of the other firm since the market prices depend on total (market) output. In choosing its strategy to maximize profits, each firm considers what it believes about the output the rival will sell.

In the Stackelberg model, a leader firm chooses its quantity and the follower firms independently choose their quantities. This type of situation where one firm acts before the other normally arises if one firm enters a market before another. The leader firm believes that once it sets its output, the rival (follower) must use its possible best response outputs to select its output. The leader therefore predicts what the follower will do before the follower acts.

Instead of setting quantities, in the Bertrand model, firms set prices and allow consumers to decide on the quantity to buy. The Bertrand model is similar to the Cournot model except that the strategic variable is price rather than quantity. The firms choose prices simultaneously and independently leading to a market equilibrium that is different form the Cournot or Stackelberg equilibra (Cumbul, 2012).

Game theory attempts to solve two problems: 1) *how to describe a game; 2) how to predict the game's outcome.* A game is described in terms of the players; its rules; the outcome (for example, who wins an auction); the payoffs to players corresponding to each possible outcome; and the information that players have about their rivals' moves. The rules of a game determine the timing of players' moves and the actions that players can choose at each move. A payoff function determines any player's payoff given the combination of actions by all players (Nicholson & Snyder, 2008).

Economists typically assume that players have common knowledge about the rules of the game, the payoff functions and other players' knowledge about these issues. In many games players have complete information about how payoffs depend on the strategies of all players. In some games, players have perfect information about players' previous moves.

Game theory is often applied to examine how a small number of firms or individuals interact. Economists, military analysts, and political scientists often use it to analyze players' strategic decision making. Thus, this chapter can particularly be very useful in analyzing the following:

- Oligopolistic firms' price and quantity setting, and their decisions.
- Legal and political negotiations, example in peace talks between two nations at war where each nation wants to arrange a settlement that benefits it more.
- Dating and mating strategies during courtship where both men and women may adopt complicated or sometimes deceitful strategies based on their own objectives.
- Interactions between polluters and those harmed by pollution.
- Competitive bidding in auctions.

ANALYSIS OF STATIC GAMES

- **Normal-Form Games:** A normal-form game (or a strategic form game) is a game in which the players choose their actions simultaneously. The games can be defined only by specifying the players, their strategies and the payoffs (Nicholson & Snyder, 2008).
- **Two-Person Zero-Sum Game:** Zero-sum games refer to games of pure conflict; they are played by two opponents with strictly opposite interests. The payoff of one player is the negative of the payoff of the other player (Halpern & Pass, 2015).
- **Certainty Model:** Consider a duopoly market in which each duopolist attempts to maximize his market share. Given this goal, whatever a firm gains (by increasing its market share) the other firm loses (due to the decrease in its share). Thus, any gain of one rival is offset by the loss of the other, and the net gain sums up to zero; hence, the name 'zero-sum game'. The model is based on the following assumptions:
    i.   The firms have a given, well-defined goal, such as maximization of the market share or maximization of profit.
    ii. Each firm knows the strategies open to it and its rival and it concentrates on these important strategies.
    iii. Each firm knows with certainty the payoffs of all combinations of the strategies being considered. This implies that a firm knows its total revenue, total cost, and total profit from each combination of strategies.
    iv. The action chosen by the duopolists do not affect the total size of the market.
    v.   The firms are rational. Each firm chooses its strategy 'expecting the worst from its rival', that is, they act in the most conservative way, expecting the rival to choose the best possible counter-strategy.
    vi. In the zero-sum games, there is no incentive for collusion, given assumption (iv) since the goals of the firms are diametrically opposed.

Using a payoff matrix of the two firms (Table 1 and 2), the equilibrium solution can easily be established. The payoffs (shares of the market) result from the adoption of any two strategies by the rivals. Assume that the two firms (Firm I and Firm II) each have four strategies open to it. The payoff matrices of the duopolists are shown in Tables 1 and 2.

Table 1. Payoff matrix of Firm I

		\multicolumn{4}{c}{**Firm I's strategies**}		
		A₁	**A₂**	**A₃**	**A₄**
Firm II's strategies	**B₁**	0.45	**0.60**	0.35	0.30
	B₂	0.70	0.85	0.30	0.55
	B₃	0.40	0.75	0.55	0.40
	B₄	0.85	0.65	0.80	0.20

Table 2. Payoff matrix of Firm II

		\multicolumn{4}{c}{**Firm I's strategies**}		
		A₁	**A₂**	**A₃**	**A₄**
Firm II's strategies	**B₁**	0.55	**0.40**	0.65	0.70
	B₂	0.30	0.15	0.70	0.45
	B₃	0.60	0.25	0.45	0.60
	B₄	0.15	0.35	0.20	0.80

In this simple model, the sum of the payoffs in corresponding cells of the two payoff tables add up to unity since the numbers in these cells represent market shares, and the total market is shared between the two firms. In the two-person zero-sum game, only one payoff matrix could be enough to analyze the game because the payoff table of Firm I contains indirectly information about the payoff of Firm II. However, both payoff tables have been shown, to enhance clarity on how to determine the equilibrium solution.

- **Choice of Strategy by Firm I:** Firm I examines the outcomes of each strategy open it. It analyses each column of its payoff matrix and finds the most favorable outcome of the corresponding strategy because the firm expects the rival to adopt the most advantageous action possible, as assumed earlier.

By carefully reviewing Table 1, if Firm I adopts A_1, the worst outcome that it may expect is a share of 0.40 (which will be realized if the rival adopts its most favorable strategy B_3). If Firm I adopts strategy A_2, the worst outcome will be a share of 0.60 (the best possible action for the rival is B_1). If Firm I adopts strategy A_3, the worst outcome will be a share of 0.30 (Firm II chooses its the best alternative, B_2). If Firm I adopts strategy A_4, the worst outcome will be a share of 0.20 (realized by action B_4 of Firm II). Among all these minima (that is among the above worst outcomes) Firm I chooses the maximum, the 'best of the worst.' This is called a maximin strategy because the firm chooses the maximum among the minima. In the current example the maximin strategy of Firm I is A_2, and it yields a share of 0.60.

- **Choice of Strategy by Firm II:** Firm II behaves in a similar way as Firm I. The only difference is that Firm II examines the rows of its payoff table because they are the rows that have its results (shares) for the possible strategies open to it. For each strategy (indicated by rows), Firm II finds the worst outcome (on the assumption that the rival will choose the best), and among these worst outcomes Firm II chooses the best. Thus, if Firm II uses its own payoff table, its behavior is a maximin behavior identical to the behavior of Firm I.

However, as stated earlier, in the zero-sum game only one payoff matrix is adequate for determining equilibrium solution. In the example, the first payoff table can be used not only by Firm I but also by Firm II. Using the first payoff table, the decision-making process of Firm II can be re-stated as follows. Firm II examines the rows of the payoff matrix of Firm I because these rows contain the information about the payoff of its strategies as well. For each strategy Firm II finds the maximum payoff (of Firm I) because this is the worst situation that Firm II will face if it adopts the strategy corresponding to that row.

Using the combined payoff matrix (Table 3), for strategy B_1 the worst outcome (for Firm II) is 0.6; for strategy B_2 the worst result is 0.85; for strategy B_3 the worst result is 0.75 and for strategy B_4 the worst

Table 3. Combined payoff matrix

		Firm I's strategies (maximin behavior)			
		A₁	**A₂**	**A₃**	**A₄**
Firm II's strategies	**B₁**	0.45	**0.60**	0.35	0.30
	B₂	0.70	0.85	0.30	0.55
	B₃	0.40	0.75	0.55	0.40
	B₄	0.85	0.65	0.80	0.20

outcome is 0.85. Among these maxima of each column-strategy Firm II will chose the strategy with minimum value, 0.6 in this case. Thus, the strategy of Firm II is a minimax strategy, since it involves the choice of a minimum among the unappealing maxima payoffs.

Although different terms are used for the choice of the two firms (maximin behavior of Firm I, minimax behavior of Firm II), the behvioural rule for both firms is the same: each firm expects the worst from its rival. In the example, the equilibrium solution is strategy A_2 for Firm I and B_1 for Firm II. This solution yields shares 0.60 for Firm I and 0.40 for Firm II. It is an equilibrium solution because it is the preferred one by both firms. This solution is called the 'saddle point', and the preferred strategies A_2 and B_1 are called 'dominant strategies' (Koutsoyiannis, 1979). Such equilibrium (saddle) solution may not exist if there is no payoff which is preferred by both firms simultaneously. Under certain mathematical conditions other solutions and strategy choices can be determined; the analysis of the resulting mixed strategies requires a slightly sophisticated exposition of utility theory and random selection which is beyond the scope of this chapter.

- **Uncertainty Model:** The assumption that each firm knows with certainty the exact value of the payoff of each strategy is unrealistic. A more feasible situation in the real world is that the firm, by adopting a certain strategy, may expect a range of results for each counter-strategy of the rival, each result with an associated probability (Koutsoyiannis, 1979). Thus, the payoff matrix is constructed so as to include the *expected value* of each payoff. The expected value is the sum of the products of the possible outcomes of a pair of strategies (adopted by the two firms) each multiplied by its probability:

$$\sum_{s=1}^{n} \text{gsi Ps } E(Q_{ij}) = q_{1i}P_1 + q_{2i}P_2 + \ldots + q_{ni}P_n$$

$$E(Q_{ij}) = \sum_{s=1}^{n} q_{si}P_s$$

where q_{si} = the sth of the n possible outcomes of strategy i of Firm I (given that Firm II has chosen strategy *j*). P_s = the probability of the sth outcome of strategy *i*.

The uncertainty zero-sum game assumes the following:

1. The firms maximize their expected payoffs.
2. Both firms assign the same probability to each pair of payoffs; they make the same judgment. This implies that the firms must have the same information and the same objective criteria with which

to evaluate the probabilities of the different payoffs; otherwise, the probability distribution of the payoffs will not be objective.

3.   The firms maximize their total utility, and the utility of each payoff is proportional to the value assumed by the payoff.

Hypothetically, consider that Firm I chooses strategy A_1 and Firm II reacts with strategy B_1. This pair of simultaneous strategies may yield the shares for Firm I each with a certain probability, as shown in Table 4.

Thus, the expected payoff of the pair of strategies A_1 and B_1 is

$$E(Q_{11}) = (0.00)(0.00) + (0.20)(0.15) + (0.40)(0.35) + \ldots + (0.80)(0.2) + (1)(0.01) = \mathbf{0.514}$$

Given the matrix of expected payoffs, the behavioral pattern of the firms is the same as in the certainty model. Firm I adopts the maximin strategy, it finds for each column the minimum expected payoff, and among these minima it chooses the one with the highest value. Firm II adopts the minimax strategy: it finds for each row the maximum expected payoff, and among the maxima it chooses the one with the smallest value (the minimum among the maxima).

Undoubtedly, the above assumptions are strong and unrealistic. Furthermore, the basic condition of the zero-sum game, that the 'gain' of one firm is equal to the 'loss' of the other, is rarely met in the real business world. Usually the gains are not offset by equal losses, so most games are non-zero sum. Only in the case of a share goal or very rare cases do we have zero-sum games. Poker and gambling are some examples of zero-sum games since the sum of the amounts won by some players equals the combined losses of the others. Others are games like chess and tennis, where there is one winner and one loser. In the subsequent sections, this chapter presents various forms of non-zero-sum games.

NON-ZERO-SUM GAMES

Example 1

Consider a duopolistic market in which the firms aim at profit maximization. Their products are close substitutes so that if their prices differ, the firm with the lower price supplies the largest part of the market. The firms would probably use prices as their means of competition. Assume that each firm can charge

Table 4. Probability for market shares of Firm I

Possible shares of Firm I for the pair of strategies A_1 and B_1	Probability of each share
0.00	0.00
0.20	0.15
0.40	0.35
0.60	0.29
0.80	0.20
1.00	0.01
	$\sum P_i = 1$

two prices (either $4 or $6), which are actually the two strategies open to the firms. The firms experience different cost structures and the market size depends on the rivals' combined action. Under these conditions, the payoffs of each firm's is expressed in terms of levels of profits as provided in Figure 1.

The payoff matrix shows the profits in thousand dollars that result from the strategies. If Firm1 chooses the higher price ($6), and Firm 2 chooses the lower price ($4), the profits are in the lower left hand corner of the payoff (profit) matrix; $\Pi_1=\$30$ (upper right number) and $\Pi_2=\$75$(lower left number). If the firms both choose the lower price strategy their profits are $\Pi_1=\$50$, and $\Pi_2=\$40$. Since the firms choose their actions simultaneously, each firm selects a strategy that maximizes its profits given what it believes the other firm will do.

The payoff matrix (Figure 1 shows that the lower price (P=$4) yields higher profits for both firms given the strategy of the rival; that is, P=$4 is a dominant strategy. Under these circumstances, there is a unique equilibrium price ($4) which will be adopted by both firms. Unfortunately, with this strategy both firms are in worse situation as compared to the alternative situation in which they choose the higher price (P=$6), since both realize a lower profit, and even the industry (joint) profit is not maximized ($\Pi_{P=4}=\$90 < \Pi_{P=6}=\$100$).

Using the duopoly example above, the behavioral rule is the same for both firms: each expects the worst from the rival. The choice of Firm 1 is a maximin strategy. If Firm 1 sets the price of $6, its minimum gain is $30, if it sets P=$4, its minimum profit is $50. Among these two minima the firm chooses the maximum or preferred strategy of P=$4. Similarly, the choice of Firm 2 is a maximin strategy.

Non Cooperative Games: The Prisoner's Dilemma

A game is considered non-cooperative if it is not possible to negotiate or agree with other participants and enter into some form of binding agreement. Non-cooperative games can often result into outcomes that are undesirable for the participants and for society. One example of such suboptimal solution is the "Prisoner's Dilemma" which refers to a game in which all players have dominant strategies leading to payoffs (profits or utility) that are inferior to what they could achieve if they cooperated and pursued alternative strategies (Petersen & Lewis, 1999). The model takes its name from the story of two people (suspected criminals) who were arrested for allegedly committing big bank robbery. However, the evidences were not adequate to make the robber charge stand unless one or both suspects confess (Koutsoyiannis, 1979).

Figure 1. Combined payoff matrix for a non-zero-sum game

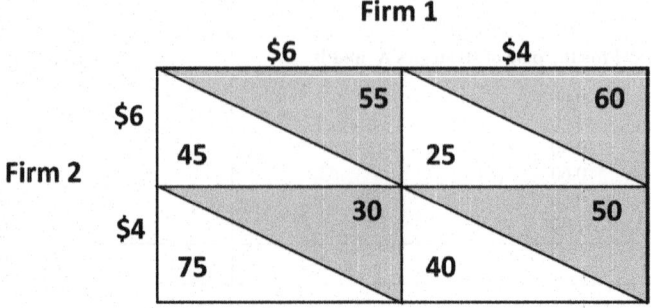

Example 2

Consider Evans and Eugene who have been arrested by police for allegedly committing a crime. The two suspects are separated and interrogated by the police (using fairly standard rules of law). One police officer tells Evans that if he does not confess and his friend does, he will be convicted for a major crime and put in jail for seven years, and his friend will go free. If they both confess, they both get only four years' jail. Evans is further told that if they all deny the claim or fail to talk, they will be convicted for a minor crime for which they will each serve only one year in jail. Meanwhile, another police officer is giving Eugene the identical offer from another room. The two suspects (players) cannot communicate with each other. Figure 2 shows the undesirable (negative) payoffs that result from the game.

Evans does not know if Eugene will confess or not. Due to lack of communication between the suspects and the uncertainty about the other suspect's loyalty, each of them will prefer to confess since it makes each better off regardless of the choice taken by the other. From the payoff matrix (Figure 2), confessing is a dominant strategy, although it leads to a worse position for the suspects. Both suspects confess and get four years in prison. This will happen yet it could be possible for both of them to get only one year in jail if they cooperated and did not confess or stayed silent. In this case, the suspects (players) are risk averse, they adopt a minimax decision criterion given that the outcomes are undesirable (Petersen & Lewis, 1999). The minimax approach involves minimizing the maximum jail sentence they could receive by confessing.

PREDICTING THE OUTCOME OF A GAME

The outcome of some games can be predicted using the belief that rational players will always avoid strategies that are dominated by others. In situations where this approach cannot foster the prediction of a game's outcome, another approach that assumes that players choose their "best response" to other players' actions can be applied. This chapter discusses the following three approaches of predicting the outcome of games.

- **Dominant Strategies Approach:** Any game's outcome can be precisely predicted as long as any player in the game has a dominant strategy. A dominant strategy is a strategy that produces a higher payoff than any strategy that a player can use for every possible combination of its rival's strategy (Perloff, 2008).

Figure 2. Prisoner's Dilemma game

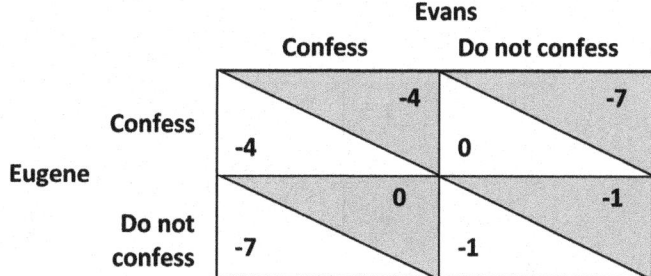

Example 3

Consider a two player game in which two companies, Dell Inc., and Apple Inc., are supplying a specific market with similar brands of laptop computers. The players (companies) have any two possible actions of supplying either 75,000 or 50,000 computers in a year. Each company can choose only one of the two options, and they both take action simultaneously. The payoff matrix (profit matrix) in figure 3 shows the profits in one million dollars for each of the possible combinations of the strategies open to the firms.

If Apple chooses the high output (Q=75), Dell's high output maximizes its profits (4>3). If Apple chooses the low output strategy (Q=50), Dell's high output strategy still maximizes its profits (5>4.5). Thus, the high output strategy is Dell's dominant strategy. By the same reasoning, Apple's high output strategy is also a dominant strategy. Since the high output strategy is the dominant strategy for both firms, the outcome of this game is the pair of high output strategies, $Q_{Dell} = 75 = Q_{Apple} = 75$. This is also a Prisoner's Dilemma game; all the players have dominant strategies that lead to profits that are inferior to what they could realize if they cooperated and pursued alternative strategies.

- **Iterated Elimination of Dominated Strategies:** In games where not all players have dominant strategies, it is not possible to precisely predict the game's outcome. Figure 4 shows the normal form representation of a game between Dell Inc. and Apple Inc. where they can each choose between three possible actions: supply 100,000, 75,000, or 50,000 computers per year in the market.

Figure 3. Profit matrix for quantity setting game: dominant strategy

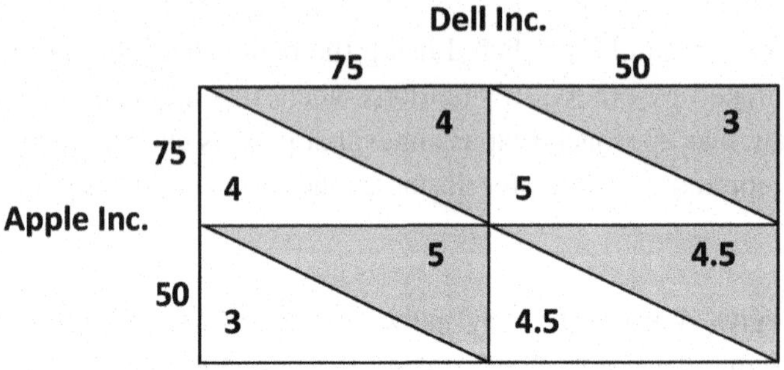

Figure 4. Profit matrix for quantity setting game: iterated dominance

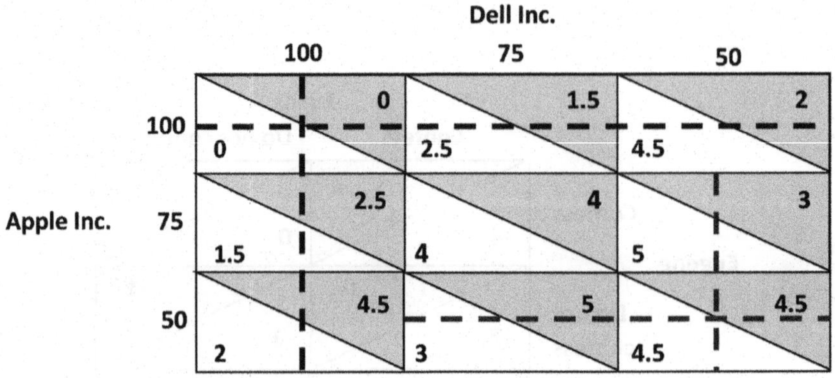

No firm has a strictly or single dominant strategy. Since it is clearly known that a firm cannot use a strategy that is strictly dominated by another, each strictly dominated strategy can be eliminated until a unique set of strategies is predicted as the outcome of the game.

The payoff matrix in Figure 4 shows that Dell's strategy of $Q_{Dell} = 100$ is strictly dominated by its alternative strategy of $Q_{Dell} = 75$. Regardless of which strategy Apple uses, $Q_{Dell} = 75$ produces a higher profit for Dell than does $Q_{Dell} = 100$. Similarly, Apple's strategy of $Q_{Apple} = 100$ is strictly dominated by its strategy of $Q_{Apple} = 75$. The firms will not use these dominated strategies, red lines should be drawn through the strategies to show that the firms will not use them.

The remaining matrix is the same as the 2×2 matrix in Figure 3, where the firms can produce either 75,000 or 50,000 computers per year. From the previous analysis of Figure 3, producing 50,000 computers is strictly dominated by producing 75,000 computers. Orange lines can again be drawn through the dominated strategies of the 2×2 matrix. Therefore, by elimination of strictly dominated strategies, it is possible to predict that the firms will each choose to produce 75,000 laptops per year. This approach is based on the belief that, players cannot choose strictly dominated strategies. It also assumes that players are payoff maximizers.

- **Best Response and Nash Equilibrium:** When the iterated elimination of strictly dominated strategies fails to predict a unique outcome, the best response or Nash equilibrium approach can be applied. For any given set of strategies chosen by rivals, a player wants to use its best response: the strategy that maximizes a player's payoff given its beliefs about its rivals' strategies. A dominant strategy is a best response to all possible strategies that a rival might use. Although a particular strategy might be a best response for some rival strategies but not for others, given that firms always choose their best response, it is possible to accurately predict the outcome of many games that cannot precisely be predicted using the iterated elimination of strictly dominated strategies (Perloff, 2008).

Economists often rely on a solution concept introduced by John Nash (1951) that is based on the belief that players use their best responses. A set of strategies is in Nash equilibrium if all the players use these strategies, no player can obtain a higher payoff by choosing a different strategy. If each player uses a Nash equilibrium strategy, then no player wants to deviate by choosing another strategy, a Nash equilibrium is thus self-enforcing. The Nash equilibrium is a stronger solution conception than the iterated elimination of strictly dominated strategies. Not all Nash equilibria can be determined using the iterated elimination of strictly dominated strategies. However, if the iterated elimination of strictly dominated strategies produces a solution consisting of a single pair of strategies, then that combination of strategies is the unique Nash equilibrium in the game.

Using the Dell-Apple example, (Figures 3 or 4), it can be illustrated that the pair of strategies chosen by iterated elimination of strictly dominated strategies is Nash equilibrium. By eliminating the dominated strategies, it becomes apparent that both firms want to set output at 75,000 computers. At that output level, neither firm wants to deviate from that proposed outcome. If Dell knew that Apple would supply 75,000 computers, Dell would not switch to 50,000 computers because its profit would fall from US$4 million to US$3 million.

By the same reasoning, Apple would not want to change strategies either. Therefore, given that the other firm chooses 75,000, the strategy of 75,000 computers is a firm's best response. Since neither firm wants to change strategies given that the other firm is playing its Nash equilibrium strategy, the pair of strategies $Q_{Dell} = Q_{Apple} = 75$ is a Nash equilibrium. For any other combination of strategies, one or the other firm would want to change its behavior; hence, none of the other strategy pairs is a Nash equilibrium.

MULTIPLE NASH EQUILIBRA, PURE AND MIXED STRATEGIES

In all the cases discussed above, it was assumed that each participant selects only one course of action. This approach is called pure strategy and it results into only one Nash Equilibrium (Peterson & Lewis, 1999). Imagine an entry game that has more than one Nash equilibrium in pure strategy, for such a game, besides using a pure strategy a player could use a mixed strategy by making a choice among possible actions according to the probabilities it assigns. A pure strategy assigns a probability of 1 to a single action, whereas a mixed strategy is a probability distribution over actions. An entry game has both pure and mixed strategy Nash equilibra (Perloff, 2008).

Consider two petroleum companies, Shell and Total contemplating to build gas stations in a market that originally never had a gas station. The Market has enough physical space for at most two stations. The profit matrix in Figure 5 presents the probable profits in million dollars. It shows that there is enough demand for only one station to profitably operate. From the table, if both firms enter each loses two million dollars. None of the firms has a dominant strategy, and each firm's best action depends on the action taken by the rival.

- **Pure Strategy:** This game has two Nash equilibra; Shell enters and Total does not enter, or Total enters and Shell does not. The equilibrium in which only one firm enters (either Shell or Total) is a Nash equilibrium because neither firm wants to change its behavior. If any firm deviated from such equilibrium, they would either earn nothing or even make losses. Note that the players do not know which Nash equilibrium would result because each cannot predict the rival's strategy unless they collude and agree to enforce their agreement. For instance, if Shell enters, it could pay Total to stay out of the market. Without an enforceable collusive agreement, even prior discussion between the firms is unlikely to help.
- **Mixed Strategies:** when both firms use similar mixed strategies, and they enter with probability of one-half, (say if a flipped coin comes up head), there would be a Nash equilibrium in mixed strategies as neither firms will want to change their strategies given that the other firm uses its Nash equilibrium mixed strategy. In the Shell-Total case, if both use mixed strategies, each of the four outcomes in the payoff matrix (Figure 5) is equally likely.

Figure 5. Simultaneous entry game

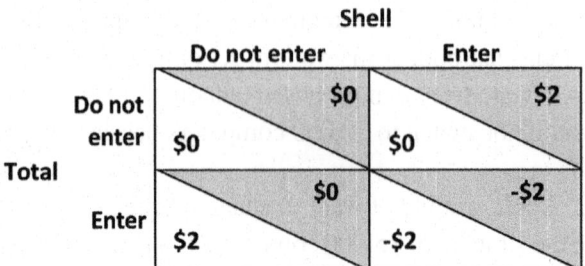

Shell has one-fourth (1/4) chance of earning \$2 or losing \$2, and one-half (1/2) chance of earning nothing. Shell's expected profit; its profit multiplied by the probability of the outcome is:

$$\text{Shell's expected profit: } \left(\$2 \times \frac{1}{4}\right) + \left(-\$2 \times \frac{1}{4}\right) + \left(\$0 \times \frac{1}{2}\right) = 0$$

If Total believes that Shell will use its equilibrium mixed strategy, it is indifferent as to which pure strategy it should use, or even any mixed strategy over these pure strategies. In these forms of symmetrical games, both players have the same probability of entering say θ. For Total to use a mixed strategy, it must be indifferent between entering or not entering if Shell enters with probability θ. Total's payoff from entering or not are given as;

$$\text{Entering } \left(\$2 \times \theta\right) + \left(-\$2 \times (1 - \theta)\right) = 4\theta - 2$$

$$\text{Not entering } \left(0 \times \theta\right) + \left(-0 \times (1 - \theta)\right) = 0$$

Equating these two expected profits, $4\theta - 2 = 0$, and solving gives us $\theta = \frac{1}{2}$

Therefore, both firms using mixed strategy where they enter with a probability of one-half is a Nash equilibrium.

Example 4: Battle of the Sexes

The battle of the sexes provides a classical example of a coordination game where two agents need to coordinate their actions but they have different preferences. Consider a couple contemplating how to spend their time over a weekend. They love to spend the weekend together, but have different preferences; the husband wants to watch football, but the wife prefers watching boxing. Since the couple likes to spend their time together, if they go separate ways, they will receive no utility. If they go together either to watch football or boxing, both will receive some form of utility, but one of them will actually enjoy the activity more. The description of this game in a strategic form is presented in Figure 6.

Figure 6. Battle of the sexes

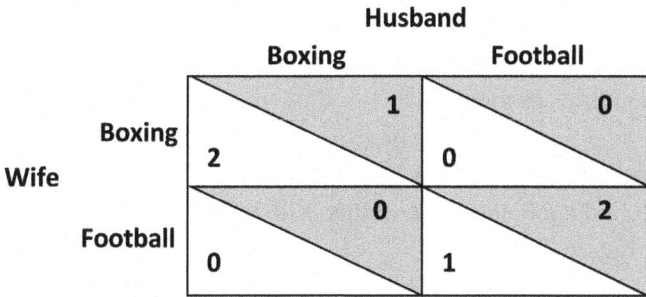

From the payoff matrix, if the couple does not spend their time together they receive no utility (0,0). If they both watch football, they all receive some utility but the husband enjoys more (1,2); similarly, if they both go for boxing the wife obtains higher utility (2,1). In this case, knowing the opponent's strategy will not help one to decide on their own course of action, and there is a possibility that an equilibrium may not be reached. This game has two pure strategy Nash equilibria (2,1 and 1,2) and one mixed strategy Nash equilibrium.

- **Calculating the Mixed Strategy Nash Equilibrium:** suppose both agents randomize, and the husband uses mixed strategy (S_h) with probability θ for football:

The expected utilities of the wife's actions are:

U_{Wife} (Football): $(0 \times \theta) + (1 \times (1 - \theta)) = 1 - \theta$

U_{Wife} (Boxing): $(2 \times \theta) + (0 \times (1 - \theta)) = 2\theta$

If the wife mixes between her two actions, they must have the same expected utility.

Thus $(1 - \theta) = 2\theta$

$$\theta = \frac{1}{3}$$

Therefore, when the husband uses a mixed strategy, he opts for football or boxing with the following probabilities:

$$Football = \frac{1}{3} \ Boxing = \frac{2}{3}$$

A similar calculation shows that if the wife uses mixed strategy, her probabilities are

$$Football = \frac{1}{3} \ Boxing = \frac{2}{3}$$

This model can be extended to analyze and solve various other conflicting situations, example resolving conflicts between countries or forces.

Question 1: Walter wants to support her daughter Georgina if she looks for work but not otherwise. Georgina wants to find a job only if her father will not support her life of indolence. Their payoff matrix is given in Figure 7.

Figure 7. Walter and Georgina

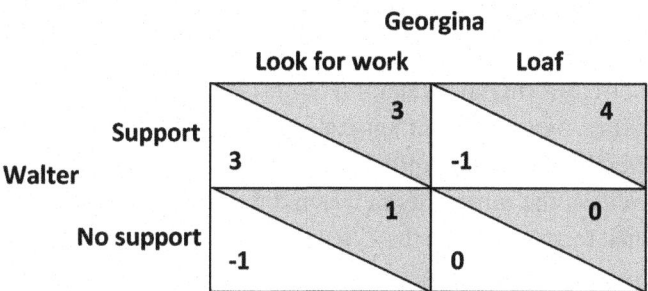

If Walter and Georgina choose their actions simultaneously, where are the pure or mixed strategy equilibra?

Hint: Check if any of the four pairs of pure strategies is a Nash Equilibrium. By calculating and equating the expected payoffs, determine the mixed strategy equilibrium.

Cooperative Games: Enforcing a Cartel

In cooperative games, it is possible to negotiate and enforce agreements that bind the participants in the game to a particular strategy (Nicholson & Snyder, 2008). Using Example 2 in our previous analysis, Evans and Eugene were in a non-cooperative game because each was unable to know what the colleague was going to do or say. If they were allowed to jointly decide on their strategies, and if each had the assurance that the colleague would not renege, none of them would have confessed. They could have avoided spending much time in jail.

Similarly, in the quantity setting Prisoner's Dilemma game between Dell Inc. and Apple Inc. (Example 3), if the firms had signed a binding contract pledging that they would use the low output strategy (Q = 50), both would have earned 4.5 million dollars, (1/2 million more) in profits.

DYNAMIC GAMES

In static normal form games, the players move simultaneously and only once, so they have imperfect information. On the flipside, in dynamic games the players move sequentially or simultaneously but repeatedly overtime, so a player has perfect information about other players' previous moves. Rather than using the normal form, dynamic games can be analyzed in their extensive form. Extensive form games specify the number of players, the sequence in which players make their moves, the actions they can take at each move, the information that each player has about the rival's previous moves and the payoff function over all possible strategies (Perloff, 2008). This chapter presents two types of dynamic games: sequential games and repeated games.

Sequential Game

Sequential games are those in which players make moves at different times or in turn. Consider a two-stage game played once (e.g., in a single period). In the first stage, Player one moves, in the second stage

Player two moves, and the game ends with the players receiving payoffs based on their actions. A good example of such a game is the Stackelberge Model (Breitmoser, 2010).

- **Game Tree:** The normal-form representation of this game (Figure 4) does not capture the sequential nature of the firms' moves. To demonstrate the role of sequential moves, the *extensive-form diagram* or *game tree* has been used in Figure 8 which shows the order of the firms' moves, each firm's possible actions at the time of its move, and the resulting profits at the end of the game. In contrast to the normal form games, in the extensive form games the players choose their actions in an order, so there is a time dimension. A game tree is a graphical illustration of a game on extensive form (Nicholson & Snyder, 2008). Figure 8 presents the Stackelberg game tree; it shows the order of the firms' moves, their possible actions, and the resulting profits.

From the figure, each box is a point of decision by one of the firms, called a *decision node*. The name in the decision node (box) indicates that it is that player's turn to move. The lines or branches extending out of the box represent a complete list of the possible actions that the player can make at that point of the game. On the left side of the figure, Dell Inc., the leader starts by picking one of the three output levels. In the middle of the figure, Apple Inc., the follower chooses one of the three quantities after learning the output level that Dell chose. The right side of the figure shows the profits that Dell and Apple earn, given that they sequentially took actions to reach this final branch, for instance, if Dell selects 75 and then Apple chooses 100, Dell earns $1.5 million profit per year and Apple earns $2.5 million. Two lines through an action line show that the firm rejects that action.

Within this game are *sub-games;* at a given stage, a subgame consists of all the subsequent decisions that players may make given the actions already taken. In the second stage where Apple makes a choice, there are three possible subgames. In Figure 8, if in the first stage Dell chooses Q_{Dell}, = 50, the relevant

Figure 8. Stackelberg game tree

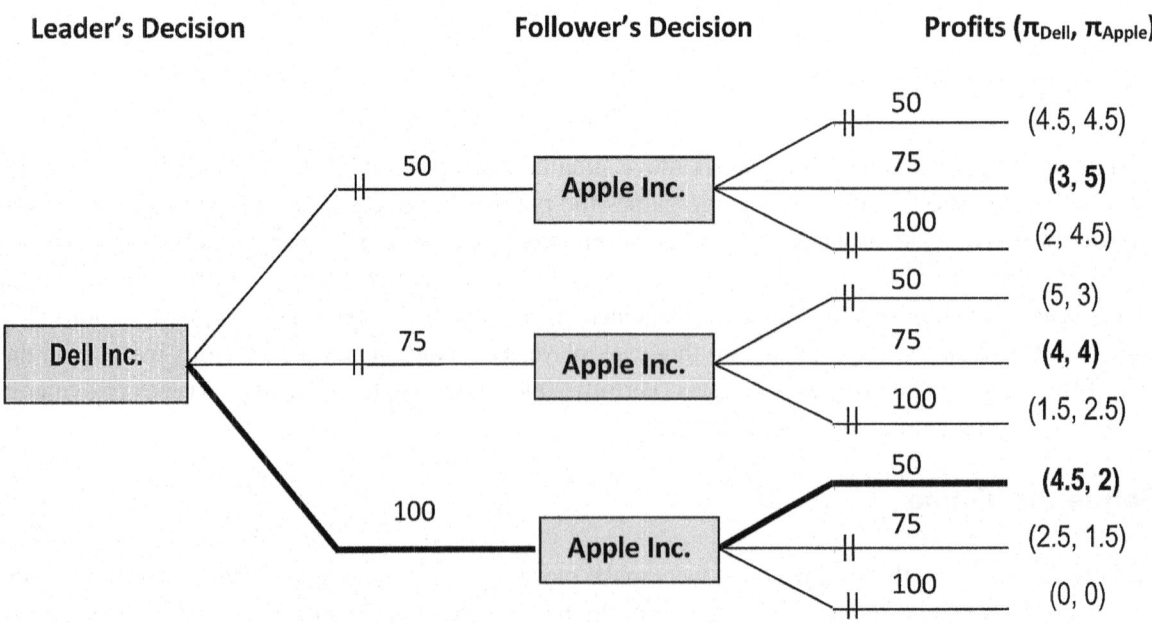

subgame is the top node in the second stage and its three branches. This game has four subgames: three subgames are at the second stage where Apple makes a decision given each of Dell's three possible first-stage actions, and the additional subgame at the time of the first-stage decision, which is actually the entire game.

Finding the Subgame Perfect Nash Equilibrium from a Game Tree

To predict the outcome of this sequential game, a stronger version of the Nash equilibrium concept; subgame perfect Nash equilibrium will be applied. A set of strategies forms a subgame perfect Nash equilibrium if the players' strategies form a Nash equilibrium in every subgame. As the entire dynamic game is a subgame, a subgame perfect Nash equilibrium is also a Nash equilibrium. In contrast, in a simultaneous-move game such as the static Prisoners' Dilemma, the only subgame is the game itself, so there is no important distinction between the Nash equilibrium and the subgame is in perfect Nash equilibrium (Nicholson & Snyder, 2008).

Figure 4 shows the normal-form representation of the game in which the Nash equilibrium to the simultaneous-move game is for each firm to choose 75. However, if the firms move sequentially, the subgame perfect Nash equilibrium results in a different outcome. The subgame perfect Nash equilibrium can be solved using backward induction, where the best response by the last player to move has to be determined first, next determine the best response for the player who made the next-to-last move, and then repeat the process until the move at the beginning of the game (Perloff, 2008). This backward process is applied in the Dell-Apple example, from the decision by the follower, Apple, to the decision by the leader, Dell, moving from right to the left side of the game tree.

How should Dell, the leader, select its output in the first stage? For each quantity it can produce, Dell predicts what Apple will do and picks the output level that maximizes its own profit. Thus, to predict its action in the first stage, Dell determines what Apple, the follower, will do in the second stage, given each possible output choice by Dell in the first stage. Using its conclusions about Apple's second-stage reaction, Dell makes its first-stage decision. Apple as a follower has no dominant strategy, the amount it chooses to produce depends on the quantity that Dell chose. If Dell chose 100, Apple's profit is $2 million if its output is 50, $1.5 million if it produces 75, and $0 if it produces 100. Thus, if Dell chose 100, Apple's best response is 50.

Using the same reasoning, Dell determines how Apple will respond to each of its possible actions, as the right-hand side of Figure 8 illustrates. Dell predicts that if it chooses 50, Apple will sell 75, so Dell's profit will be $3 million. If Dell chooses 75, Apple will sell 75, so Dell's profit will be $4 million. If Dell chooses 100, Apple will sell 50, so Dell's profit will be $4.5 million. Thus, to maximize its profit, Dell chooses 100 in the first stage. Apple's strategy is to make its best response to Dell's first-stage action: Apple selects 75 if Dell chooses 50 or 75, and it picks 50 if Dell chooses 100. Therefore, Apple responds in the second stage by selecting 50. In this subgame perfect Nash equilibrium, neither firm wants to change its strategy. Given that Dell selects 100 as its output, Apple is using a strategy that maximizes its profit, 50, so it does not want to change. Similarly, given how Apple will respond to each possible Dell's output level, Dell cannot make more profit than if it sells 100.

The subgame perfect Nash equilibrium requires players to believe that their opponents will act optimally, that is, in their own best interests. No player has an incentive to deviate from the equilibrium strategies. This subgame perfect Nash equilibrium, or Stackelberg equilibrium, differs from the simultaneous-move, Nash-Cournot equilibrium. Dell, the Stackelberg leader sells 33.3% more than the Cournot quantity, 75, and earns \$4.5 million, which is higher than the Cournot level of profit, \$4 million. Apple the Stackelberg follower sells a quantity, 50 and earns \$2 million, both of which are less than the Cournot levels. Although Apple has more information in the Stackelberg equilibrium than it does in the Cournot model (it knows Dell's output level), it is worse off than if both firms chose their actions simultaneously.

- **Credibility:** *Why do the simultaneous-move and sequential-move games have different outcomes?* Given the option to act first, Dell chooses a large output level to make it in Apple's best interest to pick a relatively small output level, 50. Dell benefits from moving first and choosing the Stackelberg leader quantity. *In the simultaneous move game, why doesn't Dell announce that it will produce the Stackelberg leader's output to induce Apple to produce the Stackelberg follower's output level?* The answer is that when the firms move simultaneously, Apple doesn't believe Dell's warning of producing a large quantity, because it is not in Dell's best interest to produce that large quantity of output.

For a firm's announced strategy to be a credible threat, rivals must believe that the firm's strategy is rational in the sense that it is in the firm's best interest to use it (Perloff, 2008). If Dell produced the leader's level of output and Apple produced the Cournot level, Dell's profit would be lower than if it too produced the Cournot level. Since Dell cannot be sure that Apple will believe its threat and reduce its output in the simultaneous-move game, it produces the Cournot output level. In contrast, in the sequential-move game, because Dell moves first, its commitment to produce a large quantity is credible. An example of commitment that makes a threat credible is that of "burning bridges". If the general burns the bridge behind the army so that the troops can only advance and not retreat, the army becomes a more fearsome foe. Similarly, by limiting its future options, a firm makes itself stronger.

Since not all firms can make commitments, it is not possible for all firms to make credible threats. For a threat to succeed, a firm must have an advantage that allows it to harm the other firm before that firm can retaliate. Identical firms that act simultaneously cannot credibly threaten each other. However, a firm may be able to make its threatened behavior believable if it is unique in a way. An important difference is the ability of one firm to act before the other. For example, an incumbent firm could lobby for the passage of a law that forbids further entry.

Advantages and Disadvantages of Moving First

Acting first in a sequential game can earn the firm the following advantages:

- If a firm introduces a product in a market first, it is likely to develop brand loyalties and the consumers may be able to associate the product with the firm in their minds.
- Using some products may require special skills. If consumers invest time and money to learn how to use the product of the first firm, they may become laidback to retool and use a similar product from another supplier. SPSS and STATA are good examples; users who are proficient in one program may become hesitant to switch to the other program unless it offers significant advantages.
- The downsides of entering early is that the cost of entering quickly is higher, the odds of miscalculating demand are greater and later entrants may build on the pioneer's research to produce a superior product.

Repeated Games: Dealing with Cheaters

Even if it is not possible to enforce agreements, firms may be able to escape the Prisoners' Dilemma if the action is repeated or if the game is played many times (Petersen & Lewis, 1999). For repeated games, in each period there is a single stage; both firms move simultaneously. Player 1's move in the first period precedes Players 2's move in the second period; hence, the earlier action may affect the later one, making the game to be a dynamic one. Here, the players have almost perfect information; they know all the moves from previous periods, but they do not know each other's moves within any single period (Perloff, 2008).

In a repeated game, a firm can influence its rival's behavior by signaling or threatening to punish. For instance adopting low advertising strategy or low output strategy for a couple of periods can signal to the other firm the desire of a firm that both of them should cooperate and hold down output or advertising. In single period games, cartels cannot form. Collusion is more likely in a multi period game than in a single period game. In a single period game, one firm cannot punish another for cheating on the cartel agreement, but if the firms meet period after period, a wayward firm can be punished by the other.

Consider the advertising game below (Figure 9). If the game is played once, neither firm will adopt a low advertising strategy because the other firm could select high advertising, capture more profits and the game would be over. As indicated in the payoff matrix, high ad is a dominant strategy for both firms; by adopting it each firm feels more secure and would make more profit if the rival used the low ad strategy ($4>$3). Even if the firms agreed to hold down advertising, if the agreement is not enforceable, the high advertising equilibrium is likely to occur.

If the advertising decision is made repeatedly, the outcome may change. A wayward firm that reneges on an agreement and heavily advertises the first time the game is played will realize that the other firm will respond accordingly by increasing its advertising in the second period. Thus, the cheater's advantage will be temporary and the profits for both firms will reduce in the second period ($2 each). Furthermore, since cheating will have occurred once, the other firm should be more cautious in the future. With repeated games, reputations are important in determining the games' outcome.

A common optimal (winning) strategy for firms playing non-cooperative repeated games is "tit-for-tat" (Axelrod, 1984). According to Robert Axelrod, each firm should mimic its rival's behavior from the previous period. If one firm cheats (say by cutting prices), the other firm responds by cutting prices in the next period. If one firm cooperates by raising prices, the other firm also raises prices.

Practically, the advantage of tit-for-tat is that it is embodies four principles that are important in any good strategy (Peterson & Lewis, 1999). These principles are:

Figure 9. Advertising and its profits (in millions of dollars)

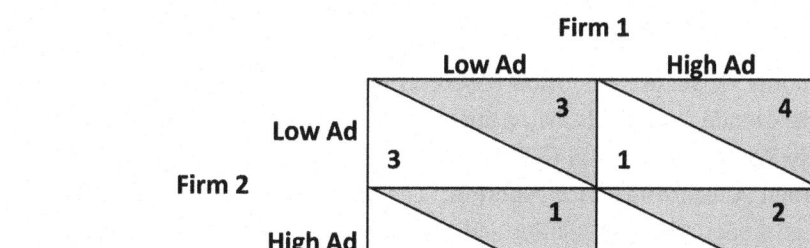

- It is simple, making it easily understood.
- It never initiates cheating which could cause failure in cooperation.
- It never rewards cheating; the cheaters will never go unpunished.
- Finally, it is forgiving because it allows cooperation to be quickly restored.

However, tit-for-tat can breakdown if the players clearly know the number of times the game will be repeated. This is because, as much as cooperation may increase profits, a firm can gain even more if it cheats the last time the game is played since there is no more chance for retaliation. Both firms could cheat on the last play of the game. If cheating will occur on the last round then there is no reason to co-operate on the next to the last round (Axelrod, 1984). Each play of the game is then likely to degenerate into a Prisoner's Dilemma.

AUCTIONS

In the preceding sections, the players in the games analyzed were mostly assumed to have complete information about payoff functions. In auction games, players formulate bidding strategies without knowing other players' payoff functions. An auction is a form of market where potential buyers bid for goods rather than simply pay the price posted by the seller. Often the good or service is sold to the highest bidder (Pearce, 1992).

Auctions have become very popular especially for awarding contracts by government departments or big private organizations. Goods or services often sold by auction include internet provision, telephone, houses, cars, timber, antiques, arts, wine, etc. Because the sellers assume that bidders will act strategically, an auction should be well designed. Auction design is a careful balance of encouraging bidders to reveal valuations, discouraging cheating or collusion, and maximizing revenues (Fine, 2008).

Elements of Auctions

It is very important that buyers understand the rules of the auction (game) as they decide on the strategies to use in bidding. A bid is an offer of payment which an individual or organization makes for possession or control of assets, inputs, goods, or services (Pearce, 1992).

Auctions have three important components: the number of units of the good/service being sold, the bidding format, and the value that potential bidders place on the good.

I.   **Number of Units:** Auctions can be used to sell one or many units of a good. This chapter focuses particularly on auctions where a single, indivisible item is sold. Recently, the U.S. Treasury auctioned off the Troubled Asset Relief Program (TARP) shares in some banks including Signature Bank (Souza, 2014).

II. **Format:** The taxonomy of auctions is often based on the order in which the auctioneer quotes prices and the bidders tender their bids. Most approaches are variants of the English auction, the Dutch auction, or the sealed-bid auction (Vikery, 1961).

 ◦ **English or Open Ascending Price Auction:** The auctioneer starts the bidding at the lowest price that is acceptable to the seller and then repeatedly encourages potential buyers to bid more than the previous highest bidder. The auction ends when no one is willing to bid more than the highest bid: "Going, going, gone" as they would announce. The good is sold to the last bidder for the highest bid. This type of auction is arguably the most common in use globally.

- ○ **Dutch or Open Descending Price Auction:** In the traditional Dutch auction the auctioneer begins with a high price, seeking to sell the items, the price is lowered until a participant is willing to accept the auctioneer's price for some quantity of the good in the lot or until the seller's reserve price is met. If the first bidder does not purchase the entire lot, the auctioneer continues lowering the price until all of the items have been bid for or the reserve price is reached. Items are allocated based on bid order; the highest bidder selects his/her item(s) first followed by the second highest bidder, and so forth.

- ○ **Sealed-Bid Auction:** In a *sealed-bid auction,* everyone submits a bid simultaneously without seeing anyone else's bid (for example, by submitting each bid in a sealed envelope), and the highest bidder wins. The price the winner pays depends on whether it is a first-price auction or a second-price auction.

  In a *first-price auction, also called blind auction* the winner pays his/her own, highest bid. Governments often use this type of auction. The *second-price auction,* is identical to the sealed first-price auction except that the winning bidder pays the second-highest bid rather than his or her own; it is sometimes known as the Vickery auction (Nicholson & Snyder, 2008).

III. **Value:** Auctioned goods are normally described as having *a private value* or a *common value.* Typically, this distinction turns on whether the good is unique or not.

- ○ **Private value:** If each potential bidder places a different personal value on the good, we say that the good has a *private value.* Individual bidders know how much the good is worth to them but not how much other bidders value it. A typical example is a second hand car where people differ greatly in the value they place to it.

- ○ **Common value:** Many auctions involve a good that has the same fundamental value to everyone, but no buyer knows exactly what that *common value* is. For example, in a timber auction, firms bid on all the trees in a given area. All firms know what the current price of lumber is; however, they do not know exactly how many board feet of lumber are contained in the trees.

In most auctions, goods have both private value and common value. For instance, in the tree auction, bidding firms may differ not only in their estimates of the amount of lumber in the trees (common value), but also in their costs of harvesting (private value).

Optimal Bidding in Private-Value Auctions

A potential buyer's optimal strategy depends on the number of units, the format, and the type of values in an auction. Consider an auction in which each bidder places a different private value on a single indivisible good. According to eBay, if you choose to bid on an item in its second-price auction, you should "enter the maximum amount you are willing to spend". *Is eBay's advice correct?*

In a traditional sealed-bid, second-price auction, bidding your highest value *weakly dominates* all other bidding strategies: bidding your maximum value is superior to bidding any other value. The amount that you bid affects whether you win, but it does not affect how much you pay if you win, which equals the second-highest bid.

Imagine that you value a used car at $1000. If the highest amount that any other participant is willing to bid is $750 and you place a bid higher than that, you will buy the car for $750 and receive $250 ($1000 — $750) of consumer surplus. Other bidders lose and miss the consumer surplus.

Is it beneficial to bid more than your value? Suppose that you bid $1,200. There are three possibilities. First, if the highest bid of your rivals is greater than $1,200, then you don't buy the good and receive no consumer surplus. This outcome is the same as what you would have received if you had bid $1000, so bidding higher than $1000 does not benefit you. Second, if the highest alternative bid is less that $1000 then you win and receive the same consumer surplus that you would have received had you bid $1000. Again, bidding higher does not affect the outcome. Third, if the highest bid by a rival was between $1000 and $1200, say $1,100, then bidding more than your maximum value makes you to win, but you purchase the good for more than you value it, so you receive negative consumer surplus: -$100 (= $1000 - $1,100). In contrast, if you had bid your maximum value, you would not have won, and your consumer surplus would have been zero – which is better than losing $100. Thus, bidding more than your maximum value can never make you better off than bidding your maximum value or it may even make you to suffer.

Should you ever bid less than your maximum value say, $900? No, because you only lower the odds of winning, without affecting the price that you pay if you do win. If the highest alternative bid is less than $900 or greater than your value, you receive the same consumer surplus by bidding $900 as you would by bidding $1,000. However, if the highest alternative bid lies between $900 and $1,000, you will lose the auction and give up positive consumer surplus as a result of underbidding. Thus, you do as well or even better by bidding your value than by over- or underbidding. This argument does not turn on whether or not you know other bidders' valuation. If you know your own value but not other bidders' values, bidding your value is your best strategy. By following this strategy, the person placing the highest value for the good wins and pays the second highest value (Perloff, 2008).

Revenue Maximization and Optimal Bidding in Auction

Bidding one's value is the dominant strategy in a sealed-bid, second- price auction. In sealed-bid second- price auctions, bids that exceed the bidder's value (overbids) are more common than underbids (Axelrod, 1984).

- **English Auction Strategy.** Consider a seller who uses an English auction to sell a used car to bidders with various private values. A buyer's best strategy is to raise his current highest bid as long as his bid is less than the value he places on the good, say $1,000. If the current bid is $750, the buyer should increase his bid by the smallest permitted amount, say to $800, which is less than his value. If no one raises his/her bid further, this buyer wins and receives a positive surplus of $200. By the same reasoning, it always pays to increase your bid as a buyer, say up to $1,000, where you receive zero surplus if you win. It is not worth to bid more than $1000, in the previous case, it is better for the buyer to lose and earn zero surplus than winning with a negative surplus. If all participants bid up to their values, the winner will pay slightly more than the value of the second-highest bidder. Thus, the outcome is essentially the same as in the sealed-bid, second-price auction.

- **Equivalence of Auction Outcomes.** For Dutch or first-price sealed-bid auctions, the participants may *shade* their bids to less than their value. The basic intuition is that a bidder does not know the values of the other bidders. Reducing one's bid reduces the probability of winning but increases ones consumer surplus if they win. The optimal bid that balances these *two* effects is lower than a bidder's actual value. One's bid depends on his/her beliefs about the strategies of the rivals. The best strategy is to bid an amount that is equal to or slightly greater than what one expects will be the second-highest bid, given that his/her value is the highest. Therefore, the expected outcome is the same under each format for private-value auctions: The winner is the person with the highest value, and he pays roughly the second-highest value.

According to the Revenue Equivalence Theorem (Klemperer, 2004), under certain plausible conditions we would expect the same revenue from any auction in which the winner is the person who places the highest value on the good. Once a seller has decided on a particular format of auction to use, he/she can use many variations within the auction to further manipulate the outcome so as to maximize revenue. These mechanisms may foster profound and often counterintuitive effects on bidding behavior, as well as on outcomes. The common mechanisms are reserve prices, entry fees, invited bidders only, closing rules, lot sizes, proxy bidding, bidding increment rules, and post-win payment rules.

- **Winner's Curse:** A phenomenon occurs in common-value auctions that does not occur in private-value auctions. The winner's curse is that the auction winner's bid exceeds the common- value of the item. Overbidding occurs when there is uncertainty about the true value of the good. Due to absence of clear information about the item being auctioned or purchased, the winner may be the person with the largest positive error in valuation, and he/she stands the risk of losing money. The higher one's estimate, the more likely that one will make the winning bid. If the average bid is accurate, then the high bid is probably excessive. Thus, the winner's curse is paying too much (Fine, 2008).

To minimize the likelihood of falling prey to the winner's curse a bidder should *shade* his/her bid by reducing his/her bid below his estimate. The amount by which a bidder should shade the bid depends on the number of other bidders; the more bidders, the more likely that the winning bid is an overestimate. Since intelligent bidders shade their bids, sellers can do better with an English auction than with a sealed-bid auction. In an English auction, bidders revise their views about the object's value as they watch others bid.

CONCLUSION AND RECOMMENDATIONS

Game theory is often applied to analyze conflicts and cooperation among players who decide strategically. Game theory attempts to solve two problems: 1) *how to describe a game; 2) how to predict the game's outcome.* A game is described in terms of the players; its rules; the outcome; the payoffs to players; and the information that players have about their rivals' moves. The outcome of a game can be predicted using the dominant strategies approach, iterated elimination of dominated strategies, or best response/Nash equilibrium.

Games may be static or dynamic, most of which are non-zero-sum. When analyzing static games, if it is not possible for the participants to negotiate or agree and enter into some form of binding agreements, the game is considered non cooperative, a popular example of which is the Prisoner's Dilemma. Non-cooperative games often result into outcomes that are undesirable or less beneficial for the participants, compared to what they would achieve if they cooperated in the game. Dynamic games may be sequential or repeated, and they are often analyzed in their extensive form. Unlike for static or dynamic games where the players are assumed to have complete information about payoff functions, in auction games, players formulate bidding strategies without knowing other players' payoff functions. Auctions are analyzed based on three important components: the number of units of the good/service being sold, the bidding format, and the value that bidders place on the good.

As a facet of neuroeconomics, game theory can highly underpin the comprehension of human decision making. However, valid evidences to show the convergence between economic theories and neuroscience are still scanty, yet the evidences would enhance better the understanding of the application of game theory in neuroeconomics. More researches should therefore focus on showing these links, particularly the relationship between neuroscience (both cognitive and behavioral) and strategic choices using appropriate data.

Economists, political scientists, and military analysts widely apply game theory to analyze players' strategic decision making. The model is often adopted to analyze oligopolistic firms' actions, legal and political negotiations, dating and mating strategies by couples, and competitive bidding in auctions. Game theory has often been presented in rather complex ways, making the model somewhat difficult to understand; however, in this chapter the author has attempted to present it in a very simple way to enhance its precision and easy understanding.

REFERENCES

Axelrod, R. (1984). *The evolution of cooperation*. New York: Basic books.

Breitmoser, Y. (2010). *A general model of oligopoly endogenizing Cournot, Bertrand, Stackelberg, and Allaz-Vila*. Retrieved March 30, 2015, from: http://mpra.ub.uni-muenchen.de/19998/1/MPRA_paper_19998.pdf

Cumbul, E. (2012). *Stackelberg versus Cournot Oligopoly with Private Information*. Retrieved March 30, 2015, from file:///C:/Users/DELL/Downloads/8480-17570-1-SMP.pdf

Fine, R. L. (2008). *The concise encyclopedia of economics*. Accessed March 2, 2015, from: http://www.econlib.org/library/Enc/Auctions.html

Halpern, J. Y., & Pass, R. (2015). Algorithmic rationality: Game theory with costly computation. *Journal of Economic Theory*, *156*, 246–268. doi:10.1016/j.jet.2014.04.007

Klemperer, P. (2004). *Auctions: Theory and Practice*. Economics Papers 2004-W09, Economics Group. Nuffield College, University of Oxford.

Koutsoyiannis, A. (1979). *Modern microeconomics* (2nd ed.). London: Macmillan Press Ltd. doi:10.1007/9781349160778

Nash, J. (1951). Non-cooperative games. *The Annals of Mathematics*, *54*(2), 289–295. doi:10.2307/1969529

Nicholson, W., & Snyder, C. (2008). *Microeconomic theory: Basic principles and extension* (10th ed.). Mason, OH: Thompson South-Western.

Pearce, D. W. (1992). *Macmillan dictionary of modern economics* (4th ed.). London, UK: Macmillan Press. doi:10.1007/978-1-349-22136-3

Perloff, J. M. (2008). *Microeconomics: Theory and applications with calculus*. Boston, MA: Pearson/Addison Wesley.

Petersen, H. C., & Lewis, W. C. (1999). *Managerial economics* (4th ed.). Singapore: Pearson Education Press.

Souza, K. (2014). *U.S. Treasury auctions off TARP shares in Signature Bank*. Accessed February 25, 2015, from: http://www.thecitywire.com/node/33754#.VO2U7nyUf84

The Economist. (2014). *Picking the World Champions of Trade*. Accessed May 1, 2014, from: http://www.economist.com/news/finance-and-economics/21594343-which-country-gets-most-out-international-commerce-trading-up

Vickery, W. (1961). Counter-speculation, auctions, and competitive sealed tenders. *The Journal of Finance*, *16*(1), 8–37. doi:10.1111/j.1540-6261.1961.tb02789.x

von Neumann, J., & Morgenstern, O. (1944). *Theory of games and economic behavior*. Princeton: Princeton University Press.

KEY TERMS AND DEFINITIONS

A Game: Any competition between players (individuals or firms) in which strategic behavior plays a major role.

A Strategy: A battle plan that specifies the course of action that a player will use in a game conditional on the information available at each move and for any possible contingency.

Action: A move that a player makes at a specified stage of a game, such as how much output a firm produces in the current period.

Auction: A form of market where potential buyers bid for goods rather than simply pay the price posted by the seller. Often the good or service is sold to the highest bidder.

Complete Information: A situation when each player knows the payoffs to all the players in the game for any possible combination of strategies.

Dominant Strategy: The best strategy a player can have regardless of what other players do. It produces a higher payoff for a player than any other strategy the player can use for every possible combination of its rivals' strategies.

Dominated Strategy: An alternative strategy that yields a lower payoff than some other strategy no matter what the other players in the game do.

Dynamic Game: Any game in which the players move either sequentially or repeatedly.

Game Theory: The set of tools that are applied to analyze conflict and cooperation among players (such as firms or individuals) who decide strategically. The techniques are often applied to evaluate situations where individuals or organizations have conflicting objectives.

Maximin Strategy: A strategy that maximizes for a player the minimum possible payoffs in a game. It is adopted by risk-averse players to ensure that the worst possible outcome is as beneficial as possible regardless of what other players do.

Minimax Strategy: A strategy that minimizes the undesirable outcome of a game.

Nash Equilibrium: The set of strategies such that none of the players in a game can improve their payoff, given the strategies of the other participant. If each player uses a Nash equilibrium strategy, then no player wants to deviate by choosing another strategy.

Perfect Information: When the player who is about to move knows the full history of the games' play to that point, and information is updated with each subsequent action.

Static Game: A game played once by players who act simultaneously and hence each of them do not know how other players will act at the time they must make a decision. In these games, firms have complete information about the payoff functions but imperfect information about rivals' moves.

Strategic Behavior: A set of actions a player takes to increase his or her payoff, while considering the possible actions of other players.

Chapter 15

Craving vs. Compulsion for Luxury Goods?
Trends and Patterns of Conspicuous Consumption Behavior in Asian Culture

Wan-Nurisma Ayu Wan-Ismail
University Utara Malaysia, Malaysia

Norhayati Zakaria
University Utara Malaysia, Malaysia

Asmat-Nizam Abdul-Talib
University Utara Malaysia, Malaysia

ABSTRACT

The purpose of this chapter is to examine why people are motivated to engage in luxury consumption, particularly in Asian countries. Purchases of global brands are increasingly popular among affluent society not only in Western nations, but also in other parts of the world. Global brands are normally associated with luxury brands from all categories of consumption goods such as cosmetics, handbags, electronic goods, cell phones and accessories, and watches among others. Previous studies have found that Western countries have clearly stated several key factors for consumers to purchase such luxury brands. Consumers in Asian markets are expected to engage in conspicuous consumption behavior to purchase global brands due to market demands and increasing income levels. Yet, such understanding is still much limited in the context of Asian consumers. Our work addresses this issue.

INTRODUCTION

The luxury market is growing worldwide from developed countries to developing countries due to the increasing in buying power of consumers from developing countries. An important factor for this changes is due to improvements in economic conditions (Kuisma, 2008) in some Asian countries such as China, Korea, Singapore, and Malaysia. As a result of encouraging economic situations, there are more demand of luxury goods from those countries with more new luxury brands are coming on the market than ever before.

DOI: 10.4018/978-1-4666-9989-2.ch015

Consumers are now more exposed to this type of goods – prestigious goods because they are more exposed to the prestige aspects of luxury goods and a new global phenomenon had emerged called as "luxury brand culture" especially in developing countries such as Asia (Chadha & Husband, 2006). This phenomenon takes slightly different form in developing countries where people who seldom spent money on luxuries in the past are now showing some interest to engage in luxury consumption and become conspicuous consumer. Previous studies have shown this conspicuous consumption behavior is applicable in situations where only rich people spend more of their money on luxury goods than other consumers classes (Chaudhuri & Majumdar, 2006). However, recent research have shown that people with limited financial capabilities also engage heavily on conspicuous consumption. Thus, it shown that luxury brand culture is not only limited to the rich but it can occur among all consumer groups of all ages.

Conspicuous consumption was first discussed more than 100 years ago by Thorstein Veblen (1899 republished in 1994) in his book, *The Theory of Leisure Class*. Veblen defined conspicuous consumption as the behavior characteristic of people who focus on the accumulation of wealth in order to show off their status and to be different from others. In this study, conspicuous consumption is defined as a buying of luxury products in order to show off the status and wealth to others in the society.

The influence of advertising may become an important aspects that influence consumers to behave conspicuously. Some advertising shows the important of material things where this material things can be used by consumers to portray their status and display their wealth among the society. Therefore, individuals who are concerned with their status and performance may showing some interest toward materialism. Thus, the primary objective of this study is to provide a better understanding of conspicuous consumption and its effect on consumer behavior, and specifically to explore the effects of material value to provide some useful information regarding consumer spending power and purchasing behavior towards conspicuousness.

Another objective of this study is to understand the growing interest in luxury products even when consumers are suffering financial difficulties. This behavior may partially be explained by the desire to display wealth and social status and their relationship towards material value. The demand for luxury products and services are expected to grow as the economic condition of consumers in emerging markets such as Malaysia, Singapore, China, Taiwan, Korea, Japan, India, and others are growing (Chadha & Husband, 2006).

This study will also explore the concept of conspicuous consumption and materialism where both concepts are originated from Western culture (Podoshen, Li, & Zhang, 2011). Much of the study on conspicuous consumption has focused primarily on Western culture (Podoshen & Andrzejewski, 2012); therefore, there is need to analyze it from the perspective of non-Western culture as this value and behavior are shaping consumers' lifestyles in many emerging economies such as China and India.

THE CONCEPT OF MATERIALISM

Many definitions of materialism have been offered in economic psychology and consumer research. The definitions showed in Table 1 are slightly different for both fields; however, they are similar in meaning.

Materialism can be divided into two types: terminal and instrumental (Csikszentmhalyi & Rochberg-Halton, 1981). Terminal materialism can be defined as a person who desires an object based on their own desire towards possession. Such people are likely to claim that they are not a materialistic, but they buy luxury goods because they want that particular product and/or because the product is high in quality.

Table 1. Summary of materialism's definition / concepts

Author	Definitions
Ward & Wackman (1971)	An orientation in which people view material goods and money as being important for personal happiness and social progress
Mochis & Churchill (1978)	An orientation that emphasize posessions and money for personal happiness and social progress
Belk (1985)	The importance a consumer attaches to worldly possessions
Rassuli & Hollander (1986)	An interest in getting and spending
Polanyi (1944), Sahlin (1987) & Mukerji (1983)	A culturak system in which material interests are not made subservient to other social goals.
Richins (1987)	The idea that goods are a means to happiness; that satisfaction in life is not achieved by religious contemplation, social interaction, or a simple life, but rather by possession of an interaction with goods.
Richins & Dawson (1992)	A value that guide people's choices and conduct in a variety of situation including consumption.

However, instrumental materialism is the desire of people towards possession because they believe that the objects they own can boost their self-actualization. In other words, people who are value their possessions for how those possessions make others see them. Such people buy luxury goods because they want others to see them as different and simultaneously they can highlight their status within the society.

There are two prevailing perspectives of conceptualizing materialism whether as personality trait or personal value (de Mooij & Hofstede, 2011). Each of the concepts comprised a number of variables. Belk (1985) referred to materialism as a combination of three personality traits: possessiveness, envy, and non-generosity. People with these three traits emphasize possessions and material things, and they are more focused on "product possession" or ownership of things and are envious if others have accumulated more possessions. This is because those who score higher on these three dimensions on the Belk scale (an indicator of emotional reactions and a measure of personality) tend to find the greatest sources of dissatisfaction and satisfaction in life from their possessions (Belk, 1985). These three dimensions measured the degree to which an individual values his or her material items, their willingness to share their items and whether they feel jealous or envious when others acquire more goods than themselves.

Richins and Dawson (1992) defined materialism as a personal value which guides people in decision making, especially regarding decisions about consumption. Materialism as a value consists of three components which are all based on "product acquisition": acquisition as a central goal in life, acquisition as a symbol of success, and acquisition as pursuit of happiness (Richins & Dawson, 1992). Richins and Dawson conceptualized materialism based on cognitive belief as opposed to emotional reactions. Therefore, the value-based definition of materialism is the extent to which people thinks that success is judged by the things people own and that happiness is having material possessions, and the degree to which material possession is at the center of their life. Belk's definition is based on possession while Richins and Dawson's definition is based on acquisition which is purchase behaviour.

When materialism becomes a part of a consumer's value system, it becomes part of their lifestyle: they make a high level of material consumption a main goal of their lives. This lifestyle can be influenced by their cultural system if material interests are a priority in a society. In this study, materialism is discussed as a value as suggested by Richins and Dawson (1992), and later Ahuvia and Wong (2002) who also define materialism as a value with the construct "personal value materialism". Materialism value scales by Richins and Dawson (1992) consisted of three components:

1. **Acquisition Centrality:** Centrality refers to people who are materialist place a possessions and acquisition at the center of their life (Richins & Dawson, 1992). People high in their level of materialism place possessions and acquisition as the most important part of life. This is supported by Daun (1983) who describes that materialism as a life-style which they set that material consumption as a goal.

2. **Acquisition as the Pursuit of Happiness:** Materialists place possessions and acquisition at the central of their life because they believe that possession and acquisition can bring them happiness. They view possessions and acquisition as essential part to the satisfaction and well-being of life. They think this value (emphasizing possessions and money) can bring happiness in their personal lives as well as social progress (Ward & Wackman, 1971 as cited in Richins & Dawson, 1992). The value of possessions that can bring happiness and enjoyment to the person's life have been study by several scholars such as Bloch and Bruce (1984), Holbrook (1994), Hirschman and LaBarbera (1990) and Kamptner (1991 as cited from Richins, 1994).

3. **Possession Defined Success:** Materialists considers material well-being as an evidence of success (Dubois & Paternault, 1995). Materialists also "tend to judge their own and other's success by the number and quality of possessions accumulated" (Richins & Dawson, 1992). Therefore, people who are materialist tend to judge their own and others' success on things people own.

LITERATURE REVIEW

Materialism is a set of value placed by consumer whose think that the acqusition of material objects is important in their life. Richins and Dawson (1992) study showed that this value have an influences on consumption in terms of the type of product and the quantity that people will purchased. Studies have found that materialist-oriented people are likely to use material goods as a mechanism for displaying their success, status, and prestige. They are likely to think of the acquisition of objects as a path to happiness in their life (Belk, 1985).

Materialistic people have certain motivations towards the purchase of luxury goods and believe that by acquiring luxury goods they can signal to others and themselves their achievement and status in society normally associated with power, wealth, and prestige. They employ luxury goods as visible evidence that they are successful or they rank higher in society (Eastman, Goldsmith, & Flynn, 1999). They also feel that by acquiring the best goods, the most expensive goods or the highest-status goods, they will confer a higher status on themselves and will communicate to others that they are wealthy and privileged (Fournier & Richins, 1991).

Materialistic people place a higher value on goods that can be recognized easily in public because they get additional pleasure from showing off the product, rather than from simply acquiring or using it (Richins, 1994). Therefore, materialist people tend to behave conspicuously as Herbig et al. (1993) stated that conspicuous consumption behaviour increased as the level of material values for each new generation increased (Bakewell & Mitchell, 2003b).

Conspicuous consumption behaviour can be defined as "the motivational process by which individuals strive to improve their social standing through consumption of consumer goods that confer or symbolize status for both the individual and surrounding others" (Eastman, Goldsmith, & Flynn, 1999, p. 310). Other studies have suggested that conspicuous consumption can be defined as a consumer's tendency to use conspicuous goods in order to impress others and display their wealth (Coleman, 1983) and portray their status in society (Hong & Zinkhan, 1995; Bagwell & Bernheim, 1996; Mason, 1998, 2001; O'Cass & Frost, 2002; O'Cass & Frost, 2004) through acquisition and expenditure (Shukla, 2008).

More recently, Chaudhuri and Majumdar (2006) gave the meaning of conspicuous as "eye-catching" and "prominent" or famous in addition to the previous meaning of "wasteful and lavish consumption" in order to enhance one's social prestige. In a recent article by Souiden et al. (2011), conspicuous consumption refers to the purchase of visually conspicuous brands that enable consumers to reflect their social status, convey their self-image, and boost their self-esteem. Generally, conspicuous consumption refers to the consumption of luxury items (Souiden et al., 2011).

There are two groups of conspicuous goods: visually conspicuous and verbally conspicuous. A visually conspicuous product is one that can be easily noticed and identified as a luxury item by others (e.g., a Coach handbag or a Rolls Royce automobile). A verbally conspicuous product is one that is highly attractive and interesting and that can be easily described to others (Schiffman & Kanuk, 2004; Souiden et. al., 2011). Therefore, we can see conspicuous consumption also relates to the concepts of status and luxury as well as to ostentation.

The most common mechanism for conspicuous consumption is the consumption of luxury goods. People buy conspicuous goods in order to acquire the prestige (Belk, 1988; Grubb & Grathwohl, 1967; Shukla, 2008) that comes with owning brand name luxury goods (Ziccardi, 2001; Dubois & Laurent, 1994). It has been shown that consumers are more likely to buy luxury goods because of their symbolic aspects, such as status and prestige, rather than because they wish to utilize the functionality (Amaldoss & Jain, 2005).

Materialism and conspicuous consumption behavior is well established in Western society, and has become a cultural orientation strongly associated with Western life (Swinyard, Kau, & Phua, 2001; Kilbourne & Pickett, 2008; Cleveland & Chang, 2009; de Mooij & Hofstede, 2011). However, because of globalization, consumption patterns are changing all over the world where people are sharing the same idea of consumption. Globalization also affects people's lifestyle where they are more exposed to the material lifestyle and valued well-known brands that carry a symbol of prestigious. Recently, materialism has become a truly global phenomenon in most non-Western countries, especially in Asia (Podoshen & Andrzejewski, 2012), and people in developing countries are beginning to imitate this Western-style material culture (Ger & Belk, 1996; Kilbourne & Pickett, 2008; Podoshen, Li & Zhang, 2011; Podoshen & Andrzejewski, 2012).

THEORETICAL FRAMEWORK AND PROPOSITIONS

Research suggests that people high in materialism believe that the possession of certain goods will provide the greatest satisfaction (Martin, 1993; Belk, 1985; Belk & Pollay, 1986). Materialistic people value things and achievement more than they value people or relationships (Wong, 1997). They are less likely to be involved in interpersonal associations (Richins, 1994), romantic relationships, and friendships because they put more priority on financial success (Kasser & Ahuvia, 2002). Richins and Dawson (1992) found that materialistic people value financial security more than "warm relationships with others." The researchers also found a negative correlation between materialism and relationships with friends and satisfaction with family (Richins & Dawson, 1992). Therefore, there is evidence that highly materialistic-oriented people place money and other material concerns at the center of their lives.

A person's success is often measured by their social status which refers to a situation in which people want to show off their success, wealth, and prestige to others (Marcoux, Filiatrault & Cheron, 1997). According to Smith, Speck, and Roy (2008), socioeconomic status is defined as "one's sense of position in a social system with respect to the portrayal in the media" (p.1200). Richins (1995) suggested that those high in materialism were more likely to value possessions, status, and utilitarian meanings. Other studies found that materialists were more involved with conspicuous consumption and the possessions they owned tended to be valued according to their price, prestige and public visibility (Wong, 1997).

According to Richins (1987) and Richins and Dawson (1992), low materialist-oriented people are more satisfied with their socioeconomic status than high materialistic-oriented people. The economic situation of a country also has a significant influence on the level of materialism among its people; some research on the influence of a country's economic situation on the level of materialism suggests that people in less affluent nations will be more materialistic than those from affluent nations (Inglehart & Abramson, 1994; Abramson & Inglehart, 1995).

Kamineni (2005 as cited by Seneca, 2009, p. 40) stated that "the crucial dimensions of possessions for any materialist are utility, appearance, financial worth, and the ability to convey status, success and prestige." People's need for appearance will result in increased materialism (Phau & Prendergast, 2000). As a consequence, there is an increasing demand for conspicuous and status goods in order to show their success to others.

As mentioned earlier, Richins and Dawson (1992) stated that materialist-oriented people use material goods to display their success, status or prestige to others. They also found that materialist-oriented people place a greater importance on the acquisition and possession of goods and services which can increase their social status. This finding is closely related to the idea that possession is a way of defining success. The most important point is that materialist-oriented people tend to buy more luxury goods than others (Belk, 1985). Seneca (2009, p.41) stated that "studies have shown that those high in materialism place a higher value on expensive items and associate such items with success". They place more value on the social meaning of goods and feel that goods (especially luxury goods) are more effective on communicating certain meanings to others and at the same time can project their identity to others (Fitzmaurice & Comegys, 2006).

A study from Chen, Aung, Zhou, and Kanetkar (2005) found that Chinese immigrants in Canada purchase luxury brands to meet the purposes of materialism, ostentation, and status. This complements existing literature which indicates that conspicuous consumption holds cultural meaning among East Asian peoples (Wong & Ahuvia, 1998; Piron, 2000).

In addition, materialistic consumer cultures are increasingly represented in Asia as evidenced by the growth of American and European branded houses in certain Asian countries (Phau & Prendergast, 2000). The implication of this argument is that materialist-oriented people can fulfill their need for happiness in several different dimensions by consuming a certain product/brand purchase. Therefore, it can be said that conspicuous consumption is a behaviour of accumulation, acquisition and possession used to bring attention to oneself and as a mark of how they want others to perceive them (Shukla, 2008). Thus, in this chapter, we proposed that materialism will be related to conspicuous consumption with the following proposition: *Materialism value will have positive influence on conspicuous consumption.*

PROPOSED RESEARCH METHOD

This study attempts to determine the relationship between materialism value with respect to conspicuous consumption. Malaysia – one of the Asian emerging countries is chosen in this study. Quantitative methods will be employed where the research hypothesis is based on the assumption that consumer engage in purchasing luxury goods are influence by their value toward materialism and therefore will behave conspicuously. The independent variable is materialism value and the dependent variable of this research is conspicuous consumption with multiple dimensions. The unit analysis of this study is the individual consumer.

The convenience sampling method is used for data collection procedure. The survey questionnaires will be distributed within the government entities, private companies, social gatherings, and other events. The instruments contain 18 items encompassing three factors of materialism value and 18 items of conspicuous consumption. Each of the measures was rated on a five-point Likert scale anchored on one extreme as: 1 –strongly disagree and on the other 5 – strongly agree. The suggested sample for the research consists of consumers who have purchased some form of luxury goods regardless of a specific brand name or product category.

To avoid response error, a screening question is required to identify whether an individual has purchased any form of luxury or imported goods within the past two-three years. It is important that the respondents should represent different ethnicities since Malaysia is composed of multi-ethnicities namely Malays, Chinese, and Indians.

THEORETICAL IMPLICATIONS

This study will contribute to both theoretical and managerial areas. Since luxury consumption has become a global phenomenon, it is clearly worthwhile to understand the behavior of conspicuous consumption and material value since it was originally seen only in affluent people from Western cultures (Chen, Aung, Zhou, & Kanetkar, 2005). Therefore, there is a need to understand the motivations behind conspicuous consumption for people from developing countries, especially Asian countries (Amaldoss & Jain, 2005). It is especially important to examine the values, practices, and attitudes surrounding conspicuous consumption, as these phenomena, once viewed as largely western, have begun to take hold in East Asian economies that are witnessing rapid changes in social structures and traditional values. This study will contribute to better understanding of established Western concepts of luxury foreign goods and conspicuous consumption in a different cultural context: Malaysia.

MANAGERIAL IMPLICATIONS

In terms of practical and managerial implications, this study will provide useful and relevant informations regarding how conspicuous consumers will behave and, therefore, will contribute an important implication for industry and marketers, especially product or brand managers. Domestic and international companies which hope to penetrate Asian markets will use this study as a basis for understanding the concept of conspicuous consumption more fully. It will give them a general understanding of how Asian consumers perceive foreign goods and luxury goods, and also provide information on the demand for these kinds of goods from other Asian countries besides China.

In addition, luxury retailers can use the information from this study in redesigning their marketing strategy by emphasizing the materialism concept so that it is better able to gain the attention of target consumers. This study will simultaneously also help global marketers in formulating strategic guidelines on how consumers in Asian markets will respond to their goods or services. Marketers should highlight the "prestige" that consumers may gain from purchasing their goods. As suggested by Souiden, M'Saad, and Pons (2011), marketers should redesign their strategy based on the markets and consumers in countries in which they want to gain a foothold. For example, if consumers in a particular market strongly engage in conspicuous consumption and value materialism, marketers should design an effective communication strategy so that consumers will be aware of their goods.

Therefore, foreign luxury goods manufacturers may wish to incorporate material value into their advertisements to Malaysian consumers, perhaps by showing the important aspects of possession of their goods that associate with status, wealth and success.

FUTURE RESEARCH AGENDA AND CONCLUSION

Since conspicuous consumption behavior is a universal phenomenon, there is a need to understand the motivation of conspicuous consumers, even though this behavior was originally observed in affluent Western cultures (Chen et. al., 2005). Our study aims to explore the reasons why developing countries such as Asia – especially Malaysia – have become conspicuous consumers even though they inhabit a different culture from Westerners (Amaldoss & Jain, 2005).

The concepts of materialism and conspicuous consumption are similar in that both are based on the concept of an individual displaying wealth through excessive expenditure on luxury goods and services (Trigg, 2001). People high in materialism value more expensive items and associate such items with success and power. The more materialistic an individual is, the more he/she values expensive possessions and the more he/she wants others to witness their ownership of such possessions. Materialistic people tend to show a positive attitude toward luxury purchases (Watson, 2003). In fact, they will even borrow money from others in order to fulfil their need/desire for luxury goods.

Future research should be conducted from several others aspects and dimensions. For example, although material value is one of the main predictors to understand whether people concern more on luxury brands culture, researchers can also investigage other aspects of values or people's attitude on purchasing behavior as the main determinant of conspicuous consumption.Secondly, futher research should be conducted using other concept of materialism rather than using Richins and Dawson (1992) personal value. Thirdly, future research should involve or include luxury brands services.

REFERENCES

Ahuvia, A. C., & Wong, N. Y. (2002). Personality and values based materialism: Their relationship and origins. *Journal of Consumer Psychology*, *12*(4), 389–402. doi:10.1207/15327660260382414

Amaldoss, W., & Jain, S. (2005). Conspicuous Consumption and Sophisticated Thinking. *Management Science, 51*(10), 1449–1466. doi:10.1287/mnsc.1050.0399

Bagwell, L. S., & Bernheim, D. B. (1996). Veblen effects in a Theory of Conspicuous Consumption. *The American Economic Review, 86*(3), 349–373.

Bakewell, C., & Mitchell, V.-W. (2003). Generation Y female consumer decision-making styles. *International Journal of Retail & Distribution Management, 31*(2), 95–106. doi:10.1108/09590550310461994

Belk, R. W. (1985). Materialism: Trait aspects of living in the material world. *The Journal of Consumer Research, 12*(3), 265–280. doi:10.1086/208515

Belk, R. W. (1988, September). Possessions and the Extended Self. *The Journal of Consumer Research*, 15.

Bloch, P. H., & Bruce, G. D. (1984). Product involvement as leisure behavior. *Advances in Consumer Research. Association for Consumer Research (U. S.), 11*, 197–202.

Chadha, R., & Husband, P. (2006). *The cult of the luxury brand: Inside Asia's love affair with luxury.* London: Nicholas Brealey International.

Chaudhuri, H. R., & Majumdar, S. (2006). Of diamonds and desires: Understanding conspicuous consumption from a contemporary marketing perspectives. *Academy of Marketing Science Review*, 11.

Chen, J., Aung, M., Zhou, L., & Kanetkar, V. (2005). Chinese Ethnic Identification and Conspicuous Consumption: Are There Moderators or Mediators Effect of Acculturation Dimensions? *Journal of International Consumer Marketing, 17*(2/3).

Cleveland, M., & Chang, W. (2009). Migration and materialism: The roles of ethnic identity, religiosity and generation. *Journal of Business Research, 62*(10), 963–971. doi:10.1016/j.jbusres.2008.05.022

Csikszentmihalyi, M., & Rochberg-Halton, E. (1981). *The meaning of things: Domestic symbols and the self.* Oxford, UK: Cambridge University Press. doi:10.1017/CBO9781139167611

Daun, A. (1983). The materialistic life-style: Some socio-psychological aspects. In Consumer behaviour and environmental quality. New York: St. Martin.

De Mooij, M., & Hofstede, G. (2011). Cross-Cultural Consumer Behavior : A Review of Research Findings. *Journal of International Consumer Marketing, 23*, 181–192. doi:10.1080/08961530.2011.578057

Dubois, B., & Paternault, C. (1995, July/August). Observations: Understanding the world of international luxury brands: The "Dream Formula". *Journal of Advertising Research*, 69–77.

Eastman, J. K., Goldsmith, R. E., & Flynn, L. R. (1999). Status consumption in consumer behavior: Scale development and validation. *Journal of Marketing Theory and Practice, 7*(3), 41–52. doi:10.108 0/10696679.1999.11501839

Eastman, J. K., Goldsmith, R. E., & Flynn, L. R. (1999). Status consumption in consumer behavior: Scale development and validation. *Journal of Marketing Theory and Practice, 7*(3), 41–52. doi:10.108 0/10696679.1999.11501839

Fitzmaurice, J., & Comegys, C. (2006). Materialism and Social Consumption. *Journal of Marketing Theory and Practice, 14*(4), 287–299. doi:10.2753/MTP1069-6679140403

Fournier, S., & Richins, M. L. (1991). Some theoretical and popular notions concerning materialism. *Journal of Social Behavior and Personality, 6*(6), 403–414.

Ger, G., & Belk, R. (1996). Cross-cultural differences in materialism. *Journal of Economic Psychology, 17*(1), 55–77. doi:10.1016/0167-4870(95)00035-6

Grubb, E. L., & Grathwohl, H. L. (1967). Consumer Self-Concept and Market Behavior : A Theoretical Symbolism Approach. *Journal of Marketing, 31*, 22–27. doi:10.2307/1249461

Herbig, P., Koehler, W., & Day, K. (1993). Marketing to the baby bust generation. *Journal of Consumer Marketing, 10*(1), 4–9. doi:10.1108/07363769310026520

Hirschman, E. C., & LaBarbera, P. A. (1990). Dimensions of importance. *Psychology and Marketing, 7*(Fall), 215–233. doi:10.1002/mar.4220070306

Holbrook, M. B. (1994). *The nature of customer value: An axiology of services in the consumption experience.* Thousand Oaks, CA: Sage Publications.

Hong, J. W., & Zinkan, G. M. (1995). Self-concept a advertising effectiveness: The influence of congruency, conspicuousness and response mode. *Psychology and Marketing, 12*(1), 53–78. doi:10.1002/mar.4220120105

Kasser, T., & Ahuvia, A. (2002). Materialistic values and well-being in business students. *European Journal of Social Psychology, 32*(1), 137–146. doi:10.1002/ejsp.85

Kilbourne, W., & Pickett, G. (2008). How materialism affects environmental beliefs, concern, and environmentally responsible behavior. *Journal of Business Research, 61*(9), 885–893. doi:10.1016/j.jbusres.2007.09.016

Kuisma, T. (2008). *Conspicuous consumption: a comparison between Finnish and Malaysian luxury good consumers.* Unpublished MBA Project Management Report, Universiti Sains Malaysia.

Marcoux, J.-S., Filiatrault, P., & Cheron, E. (1997). The attitudes underlying preferences of young urban educated polish consumers towards products made in Western countries. *Journal of International Consumer Marketing, 9*(4), 5–29. doi:10.1300/J046v09n04_02

Martin, A. S. (1993). Makers, buyers, and users: Consumerism as a material culture framework. *Winterthur Portfolio, 28*(2/3), 141–157. doi:10.1086/496612

O' Cass, A., & McEwen, H. (2004). Exploring consumer status and conspicuous consumption. *Journal of Consumer Behaviour, 4*(1), 25–39. doi:10.1002/cb.155

O'Cass, A., & Frost, H. (2002). Status brands: Examining the effects of non-product-related brand associations on status and conspicuous consumption. *Journal of Product and Brand Management, 11*(2), 67–88. doi:10.1108/10610420210423455

Phau, I., & Prendergast, G. (2000). Consuming luxury brands: The re;evance of the 'Rarity Principle'. *Brand Management, 8*(2), 122–138. doi:10.1057/palgrave.bm.2540013

Piron, F. (2000). Consumers' perceptions of the country-of-origin effect on purchasing intentions of (in) conspicuous products. *Journal of Consumer Marketing, 17*(4), 308–321. doi:10.1108/07363760010335330

Podoshen, J., Li, L., & Zhang, J. (2011). Materialism and conspicuous consumption in China: A cross-cultural examination. *International Journal of Consumer Studies, 35*(1), 17–25. doi:10.1111/j.1470-6431.2010.00930.x

Podoshen, J. S., & Andrzejewski, S. (2012). An examination of the relationships between materialism, conspicuous consumption, impulse buying and brand loyalty. *Journal of Marketing Theory and Practice, 20*(3), 319–334. doi:10.2753/MTP1069-6679200306

Richins, M. L. (1994). Special possessions and the expression of material values. *The Journal of Consumer Research, 21*(3), 522–533. doi:10.1086/209415

Richins, M. L., & Dawson, S. (1992). A consumer values orientation for materialism and its measurement: Scale development and validation. *The Journal of Consumer Research, 19*(3), 303–316. doi:10.1086/209304

Schiffman, L. G., & Kanuk, L. L. (2004). *Consumer behavior* (8th ed.). New York: Prentice Hall.

Seneca, P. J. (2009). *Measuring and manipulating materialism in the context of consumers' advertising responses.* (Unpublished Doctoral thesis). Graduate School of Southern Illinois University Carbondale, Department of Psychology.

Shukla, P. (2008). Conspicuous consumption among middle age consumers: Psychological and brand antecedents. *Journal of Product and Brand Management, 17*(1), 25–36. doi:10.1108/10610420810856495

Smith Speck, S. K., & Roy, A. (2008). The interrelationships between television viewing, values and perceived well-being: A global perspective. *Journal of International Business Studies, 39*(7), 1197–1219. doi:10.1057/palgrave.jibs.8400359

Souiden, N., M'Saad, B., & Pons, F. (2011). A Cross-Cultural Analysis of Consumers' Conspicuous Consumption of Branded Fashion Accessories. *Journal of International Consumer Marketing, 23*(5), 329–343. doi:10.1080/08961530.2011.602951

Swinyard, W. R., Kau, A.-K., & Phua, H.-Y. (2001). Happiness, materialism, and religious experience in the US and Singapore. *Journal of Happiness Studies, 2*(1), 13–32. doi:10.1023/A:1011596515474

Thorstein, V. (1994). *The theory of the leisure class.* New York: Prometheus Book.

Trigg, A. (2001). Veblen, Bourdiue and conspicuous consumption. *Journal of Economic Issues, 35*(1), 99–115. doi:10.1080/00213624.2001.11506342

Ward, S., & Wackman, D. (1971). Family and media influence on adolescent consumer learning. *The American Behavioral Scientist, 14*(3), 415–427. doi:10.1177/000276427101400315

Wong, N. Y. C. (1997). Suppose You Own the World and No One Knows? Conspicuous Consumption, Materialism and Self. *Advances in Consumer Research. Association for Consumer Research (U. S.), 24*, 18–22.

Ziccardi, D. P. (2001). Demonstrating the values of luxury brands. *Brandweek, 42*(44), 18–19.

Compilation of References

Abarbanell, J. S., & Bernard, V. L. (1992). Tests of Analysts' Overreaction/ Underreaction to Earnings Information as an Explanation for Anomalous Stock Price Behavior. *The Journal of Finance, 47*(3), 1181–1207. doi:10.1111/j.1540-6261.1992.tb04010.x

Adolphs, R. (2002). Neural systems for recognizing emotion. *Current Opinion in Neurobiology, 12*(2), 169–177. doi:10.1016/S0959-4388(02)00301-X PMID:12015233

Ahuvia, A. C., & Wong, N. Y. (2002). Personality and values based materialism: Their relationship and origins. *Journal of Consumer Psychology, 12*(4), 389–402. doi:10.1207/15327660260382414

Albarran, A. B. (2004). Media economics. In E.J.D. McQuail, P. Schlesinger, & D. Wartella (Eds.), *The SAGE handbook of media studies* (pp. 291–308). Sage.

Albarran, A. B. (1998). Media economics: Research paradigms, issues, and contributions to mass communication theory. *Mass Communication & Society, 1*(3-4), 117–129. doi:10.1080/15205436.1998.9677852

Albarran, A. B. (2010). *The Media Economy*. New York: Routledge.

Alchian, A., & Woodward, S. (1988). The firm is dead; long live the firm: A review of Oliver Williamson's The Economic Institutions of Capitalism. *Journal of Economic Literature, 26*(1), 65–79.

Alderson, W. (1957). *Marketing Behavior and Executive Action, A Functionalist Approach to Marketing Theory*. Homewood, IL: Richard D. Irwin, Inc.

Alexander, A., Owers, J., Carveth, R., Hollifield, C. A., & Greco, A. (2004). In A. Alexander, J. Owers, R. Carveth, C. A. Hollifield, & A. Greco (Eds.), *Media Economics Theory and Practice* (pp. 7–9). Mahwah, NJ: Lawrence Erlbaum Associates, Inc.

Alexander, G. E., DeLong, M. R., & Strick, P. L. (1986). Parietal organization of functionally segregated circuits linking basal ganglia and cortex. *Annual Review of Neuroscience, 9*(1), 357–381. doi:10.1146/annurev.ne.09.030186.002041 PMID:3085570

Alexander, W. H., & Brown, J. W. (2011). Medial prefrontal cortex as an action-outcome predictor. *Nature Neuroscience, 14*(10), 1338–1344. doi:10.1038/nn.2921 PMID:21926982

Allee, W. C. (1951). *Cooperation among animals, with human implications: A revised and amplified edition of the social life of animals*. New York: Schuman.

Allingham, M. G., & Sandmo, A. (1972). Income Tax Evasion: A Theoretical Analysis. *Journal of Public Economics, 1*(3-4), 323–338. doi:10.1016/0047-2727(72)90010-2

Allred, B. B., Snow, C. C., & Miles, R. E. (1996). Characteristics of managerial careers in the 21ˢᵗ century. *The Academy of Management Executive*, *10*(4), 17–27.

Alm, J. (1998). *Tax Compliance and Administration*. Working Paper. University of Colorado at Boulder.

Amaldoss, W., & Jain, S. (2005). Conspicuous Consumption and Sophisticated Thinking. *Management Science*, *51*(10), 1449–1466. doi:10.1287/mnsc.1050.0399

Ambrosino, A. (2014). A Cognitive Approach to Law and Economics: Hayek's Legacy. *Journal of Economic Issues*, *48*(1), 19–48. doi:10.2753/JEI0021-3624480102

Amin, A. (1999). An Institutionalist Perspective on Regional Economic Development. *International Journal of Urban and Regional Research*, *23*(2), 365–378. doi:10.1111/1468-2427.00201

Andersen, B., & Wong, D. (2013, February). *The new normal: Competitive advantage in the digital economy*. London: Big Innovation Centre. Retrieved on September 11, 2014, from: http://www.biginnovationcentre.com/Assets/Docs/The%20New%20Normal.pdf

Andersen, R. A., & Cui, H. (2009). Intention, action planning, and decision making in parietal–frontal circuits. *Neuron*, *63*(5), 568–583. doi:10.1016/j.neuron.2009.08.028 PMID:19755101

Angelides, M. C., & Sofokleous, A. A. (2013). A game approach to optimization of bandwidth allocation using MPEG-7 and MPEG-21. *Multimedia Tools and Applications*, *62*(1), 287–309. doi:10.1007/s11042-011-0981-0

Anich, I., & Larichev, O. I. (1996). The ELEKTRA Method and the Problem of Acyclicity of Relations of Alternatives. *Automatics and Telemechanics, 8*, 108–118.

Antkiewicz, S. (2008). Kryteria o podłożu behawioralnym a klasyczna teoria Markowitza. *Studia i Prace Wydziału Nauk Ekonomicznych i Zarządzania Uniwersytetu Szczecińskiego*, *9*, 362–377.

Anttila, M. (1990). *Consumer price perception and preferences: a reference price model of brand evaluation and a conjoint analysis of price utility structures*. Helsinki.

Ariely, D., & Berns, G. S. (2010). Neuromarketing: The Hope and Hype of Neuroimaging in Business. *Nature Reviews. Neuroscience*, *11*(4), 284–292. doi:10.1038/nrn2795 PMID:20197790

Arnold, V., & Sutton, S. G. (Eds.). (1997). *Behavioral Accounting Research: foundations and frontiers*. Sarasota, FL: American Accounting Association.

Arrow, K. J. (1986). Rationality of self and others in an economic system. *The Journal of Business*, *59*(4), S385–S399. doi:10.1086/296376

Artienwicz, N. (2011b). Sztuka pomiaru i komunikowania z perspektywy umiejętności księgowego. In Rachunkowość. Sztuka pomiaru i komunikowania (pp. 23-36). Warszawa: Oficyna Wydawnicza SGH.

Artienwicz, N. (2011a). Możliwości badania zachowania księgowych w świetle paradygmatów rachunkowości. *Prace i Materiały Wydziału Zarządzania Uniwersytetu Gdańskiego*, *1/2*, 355–364.

Artienwicz, N. (2013). Rachunkowość behawioralna jako interdyscyplinarny nurt rachunkowości i społecznych nauk o zachowaniu. *Zeszyty Teoretyczne Rachunkowości*, *71*(127), 7–23.

Ashton, R. H. (2013). Historical Perspective on Behavioral Accounting Research. In R.H. Ashton (Ed.), The Evolution of Behavioral Accounting Research: An Overview (pp. 113-119). London: Routledge.

Axelrod, R. (1984). *The evolution of cooperation*. New York: Basic books.

Ayton, P., & Fischer, I. (2004). The Hot Hand Fallacy and the Gambler's Fallacy: Two Faces of Subjective Randomness? *Memory & Cognition, 32*(8), 1369–1378. doi:10.3758/BF03206327 PMID:15900930

Babu, S. S., & Vidyasagar, T. P. (2012). Neuromarketing: Is Campbell in Soup? *The IUP Journal of Marketing Management, 9*(2), 76–100.

Babuśka, E. W. (2013). Teoria rachunkowości i jej miejsce w dyscyplinarnej strukturze nauk o kierowaniu organizacjami. *Zeszyty Teoretyczne Rachunkowości, 71*(71(127)), 25–37. doi:10.5604/16414381.1061632

Bachelier, L. (1964). Theory of Speculation. In The Random Character of Stock Market Price. Cambridge, MA: MIT Press. (Originally published in 1900.)

Bagwell, L. S., & Bernheim, D. B. (1996). Veblen effects in a Theory of Conspicuous Consumption. *The American Economic Review, 86*(3), 349–373.

Bailey, W. J., & Sawers, K. M. (2012, Spring). In GAAP We Trust: Examining How Trust Influences Nonprofessional Investor Decisions Under Rules-Based and Principles-Based Standards. *Behavioral Research in Accounting, 24*(1), 25–46. doi:10.2308/bria-50071

Bakewell, C., & Mitchell, V.-W. (2003). Generation Y female consumer decision-making styles. *International Journal of Retail & Distribution Management, 31*(2), 95–106. doi:10.1108/09590550310461994

Ballard, K., & Knutson, B. (2009). Dissociable neural representations of future reward magnitude and delay during temporal discounting. *NeuroImage, 45*(1), 143–150. doi:10.1016/j.neuroimage.2008.11.004 PMID:19071223

Ball, R., & Brown, P. (1968). An Empirical Evaluation of Accounting Income Numbers. *Journal of Accounting Research, 6*(2), 159–178. doi:10.2307/2490232

Bannock, G., Baxter, R. E., & Davis, E. (1987). *The Penguin Dictionary of Economics* (4th ed.). London: Penguin Books.

Bannon, L. J. (1991). From Human Factors to Human Actors: The Role of Psychology and Human Computer Interaction Studies in System Design. In J. Greenbaum & M. Kyng (Eds.), *Design At Work: Cooperative Design of Computer Systems* (pp. 25–44). Lawerence Erlbaum Associates Inc.

Barberis, N., & Thaler, R. (2003). A survey of behavioral finance. In G. M. Constantinides, M. Harris, & R. M. Stulz (Eds.), *Handbook of the Economics of Finance*. Amsterdam: Elsevier.

Barough, A. S., Shoubi, M. V., & Skardi, M. J. E. (2012). Application of game theory approach in solving the construction project conflicts. *Procedia: Social and Behavioral Sciences, 58*, 1586–1593. doi:10.1016/j.sbspro.2012.09.1145

Barreto, I., & Patient, D. L. (2013). Toward a theory of intraorganizational attention based on desirability and feasibility factors. *Strategic Management Journal, 34*(6), 687–703. doi:10.1002/smj.2029

Bartels, A., & Zeki, S. (2004). The neural correlates of maternal and romantic love. *NeuroImage, 21*(3), 1155–1166. doi:10.1016/j.neuroimage.2003.11.003 PMID:15006682

Barton, J., Berns, G. S., & Brooks, A. M. (2014). The Neuroscience Behind the Stock Market's Reaction to Corporate Earnings News. *Accounting Review, 89*(6), 1945–1977. doi:10.2308/accr-50841

Baumeister, R. F., Sparks, E. A., Stillman, T. F., & Vohs, K. D. (2008). Free will in consumer behavior: Self-control, ego depletion, and choice. *Journal of Consumer Psychology, 18*(1), 4–13. doi:10.1016/j.jcps.2007.10.002

Baumeister, R. F., Vohs, K. D., & Tice, D. M. (2007). The strength model of self-control. *Current Directions in Psychological Science, 16*(6), 351–355. doi:10.1111/j.1467-8721.2007.00534.x

Baumgartner, T., Heinrichs, M., Vonlanthen, A., Fischbacher, U., & Fehr, E. (2008). Oxytocin shapes the neural circuitry of trust and trust adaptation in humans. *Neuron, 58*(4), 639–650. doi:10.1016/j.neuron.2008.04.009 PMID:18498743

Bayer, H. M., & Glimcher, P. W. (2005). Midbrain dopamine neurons encode a quantitative reward prediction error signal. *Neuron, 47*(1), 129–141. doi:10.1016/j.neuron.2005.05.020 PMID:15996553

Beach, L. R., & Lipshitz, R. (1993). Why classical decision theory is an inappropriate standard for evaluating and aiding most human decision making. In G. A. Klein & J. Orasanu (Eds.), *Decision making in action: models and methods.* Westport, TX: Ablex Publishing.

Bechara, A., & Damasio, A. R. (2005). The somatic marker hypothesis: A neural theory of economic decision. *Games and Economic Behavior, 52*(2), 336–372. doi:10.1016/j.geb.2004.06.010

Bechara, A., Damasio, H., & Damasio, A. R. (2000). Emotion, decision-making, and the orbitofrontal cortex. *Cerebral Cortex, 10*(3), 295–307. doi:10.1093/cercor/10.3.295 PMID:10731224

Bechara, A., Tranel, D., & Damasio, A. R. (2002). The *somatic marker hypothesis and decision-making.* In F. Boller & J. Grafman (Eds.), *Handbook of neuropsychology: Frontal lobes, 7(2).* Amsterdam: Elsevier.

Becker, A., Deckers, T., Dohmen, T., Falk, A., & Kosse, F. (2012). *The Relationship Between Economic Preferences and Psychological Personality Measures.* Retrieved On January 8, 2015, from: http://www.iame.uni-bonn.de/people/thomas-dohmen/iza-dp-6470

Becker, B. E., & Huselid, M. A. (2006). Strategic human resources management: Where do we go from here? *Journal of Management, 32*(6), 898–925. doi:10.1177/0149206306293668

Becker, G. S. (1968). Crime and Punishment: An Economic Approach. *Journal of Political Economy, 76*(2), 169–217. doi:10.1086/259394

Becker, J. B., & Meisel, R. L. (2007). Neurochemistry and molecular neurobiology of reward. In A. Lajtha & J. D. Blaustein (Eds.), *Handbook of neurochemistry and molecular neurobiology* (pp. 739–774). New York, NY: Springer–Verlag. doi:10.1007/978-0-387-30405-2_20

Bedwell, W. L., Wildman, J. L., Diaz Granados, D., Salazar, M., Kramer, W. S., & Salas, E. (2012). Collaboration at work: An integrative multilevel conceptualization. *Human Resource Management Review, 22*(2), 128–145. doi:10.1016/j.hrmr.2011.11.007

Beersma, B., Hollenbeck, J. R., Humphrey, S. E., Moon, H., Conlon, D. E., & Ilgen, D. R. (2003). Cooperation, competition, and team performance: Toward a contingency approach. *Academy of Management Journal, 46*(5), 572–590. doi:10.2307/30040650

Beinhocker, E. D. (2006). The Origin of Wealth: Evolution, Complexity and the Radical Remaking of Economics. Boston: Harvard Business School Press.

Belkaoui, A. (1989). *Behavioral Accounting: The Research and Practical Issues.* New York: Quorum Books.

Belkaoui, A. (1996). *Accounting, a Multiparadigmatic Science.* Westport, CT: Greenwood Publishing Group.

Belkaoui, A. (2004). *Accounting theory.* London: Thomson Learning.

Belk, R. W. (1985). Materialism: Trait aspects of living in the material world. *The Journal of Consumer Research, 12*(3), 265–280. doi:10.1086/208515

Belk, R. W. (1988, September). Possessions and the Extended Self. *The Journal of Consumer Research, 15.*

Bell, D. E. (1995). Risk, return, and utility. *Management Science, 41*(1), 23–30. doi:10.1287/mnsc.41.1.23

Benartzi, S., & Thaler, R. H. (1995). Myopic loss aversion and the equity premium puzzle. *The Quarterly Journal of Economics, 110*(1), 73–92. doi:10.2307/2118511

Benkler, Y. (2011). The Unselfish Gene. *Harvard Business Review, 89*(7–8), 77–85. PMID:21800472

Bennett, L. L., Ragland, S. E., & Yolles, P. (1998). Facilitating international agreements through an interconnected game approach: The case of river basins. In Conflict and cooperation on trans-boundary water resources (pp. 61-85). New York: Kluwer Academic Publishers.

Bermejo, P. E., Dorado, R., Zea-Sevilla, M. A., & Menéndez, V. S. (2011). Neuroanatomy of financial decisions. *Neurologia (Barcelona, Spain), 26*(3), 173–181. doi:10.1016/j.nrl.2010.09.015 PMID:21163202

Berridge, K. C. (1999). Pleasure, pain, desire, and dread: Hidden core processes of emotion. In D. Kahneman, E. Diener, & N. Schwarz (Eds.), *Well-being: The foundations of hedonic psychology* (pp. 525–557). New York, NY: Russell Sage Foundation.

Berridge, K. C., & Kringelbach, M. L. (2008). Affective neuroscience of pleasure: Reward in humans and animals. *Psychopharmacology, 199*(3), 457–480. doi:10.1007/s00213-008-1099-6 PMID:18311558

Berridge, K. C., & Robinson, T. E. (1998). What is the role of dopamine in reward: Hedonic impact, reward learning, or incentive salience? *Brain Research Reviews, 28*(3), 309–369. doi:10.1016/S0165-0173(98)00019-8 PMID:9858756

Bhatnagar, S. (2004). *E-Government: From Vision to Implementation*. New Delhi: SAGE Publications.

Bickel, W. K., Jarmolowicz, D. P., Mueller, E. T., Gatchalian, K. M., & McClure, S. M. (2012). Are executive function and impulsivity antipodes? A conceptual reconstruction with special reference to addiction. *Psychopharmacology, 221*(3), 361–387. doi:10.1007/s00213-012-2689-x PMID:22441659

Bickel, W. K., Koffarnus, M. N., Moody, L., & Wilson, A. G. (2014). The behavioral- and neuro-economic process of temporal discounting: A candidate behavioral marker of addiction. *Neuropharmacology, 76*, 518–527. doi:10.1016/j.neuropharm.2013.06.013 PMID:23806805

Bickel, W. K., Miller, M. L., Yi, R., Kowal, B. P., Lindquist, D. M., & Pitcock, J. A. (2007). Behavioral and neuroeconomics of drug addiction: Competing neural systems and temporal discounting processes. *Drug and Alcohol Dependence, 90*, S85–S91. doi:10.1016/j.drugalcdep.2006.09.016 PMID:17101239

Bidlingmaier, J. (1973). *Unternehmerziele und Unternehmerstrategien*. Wiesbaden: Springer Verlag. doi:10.1007/978-3-322-87901-1

Bigoni, D. (2012). *Nonlinear Solid Mechanics: Bifurcation Theory and Material Instability*. New York: Cambridge University Press. doi:10.1017/CBO9781139178938

Birnberg, J. G., & Ganguly, A. R. (2012). Is Neuroaccounting Waiting in the Wings? An Essay. *Accounting, Organizations and Society, 37*(1), 1–13. doi:10.1016/j.aos.2011.11.004

Black, F., & Scholes, M. (1973). The Pricing of Options and Corporate Liabilities. *Journal of Political Economy, 81*(3), 637–654. doi:10.1086/260062

Blaškova, M., & Blaško, R. (2015).Tolerance and flexibility as crucial competences of multicultural team leader. In *Proceedings of Scientific Papers, 12th International Scientific Conference Human Potential Development*. Klaipeda: Klaipeda University Press. Retrieved on May 14, 2015, from: http://frcatel.fri.uniza.sk/hrme/ConfHPM/index.html\

Bloch, P. H., & Bruce, G. D. (1984). Product involvement as leisure behavior. *Advances in Consumer Research. Association for Consumer Research (U. S.)*, *11*, 197–202.

Bloomfield, R. (2011). Traditional Versus Behavioral Finance. In H. K. Baker & J. R. Nofsinger (Eds.), *Behavioral Finance: Investors, Corporations, and Markets*. New York: Wiley. doi:10.1002/9781118258415.ch2

Bohm, G., & Brun, W. (2008). Intuition and Affect in Risk Perception and Decision Making. *Judgment and Decision Making*, *3*(1), 1–4.

Booth, G. G., Kaen, F. R., & Koveos, P. E. (1982). R/S analysis of foreign exchange rates under two international monetary regimes. *Journal of Monetary Economics*, *10*(3), 407–415. doi:10.1016/0304-3932(82)90035-6

Borghans, L., Duckworth, A. L., Heckman, J. J., & Ter Weel, B. (2008). The Economics and Psychology of Personality Traits. *The Journal of Human Resources*, *43*(4), 972–1059. doi:10.3368/jhr.43.4.972

Boroditsky, L. (2001). Does Language Shape Thought? Mandaring and English speaker's conception of time. *Cognitive Psychology*, *43*(1), 1–22. doi:10.1006/cogp.2001.0748 PMID:11487292

Bourgeois-Gironde, S. (2010). Is neuroeconomics doomed by the reverse inference fallacy? *Mind & Society*, *9*(2), 229–249. doi:10.1007/s11299-010-0076-z

Bowles, S. (2006). Group competition, reproductive leveling, and the evolution of human altruism. *Science*, *314*(5805), 1569–1572. doi:10.1126/science.1134829 PMID:17158320

Boyd, R., & Richerson, P. J. (1982). Culture transmissionand the evolution of cooperative behavior *Human Ecology*, *10*(3), 325–351. doi:10.1007/BF01531189

Bradshaw, W. M. (2000). *How do analysts use their earnings forecasts in generating stock recommendations?* Harvard University Working Paper. Retrieved on November 10, 2014, from: www.researchgate.net

Braeutigam, S. (2005). Neuroeconomics: From neural systems to economic behaviour. *Brain Research Bulletin*, *67*(5), 355–360. doi:10.1016/j.brainresbull.2005.06.009 PMID:16216681

Brahmana, R. K., Hooy, C. W., & Ahmad, Z. (2012). Psychological Factors on Irrational Financial Decision Making. *Humanomics*, *28*(4), 236–257. doi:10.1108/08288661211277317

Brams, S. J. (1993). Theory of moves. *American Scientist*, 562–570.

Brams, S. J. (2004). *Game Theory and Politics*. Mineola, NY: Dover Publications, Inc.

Breiter, H. C., Aharon, I., Kahneman, D., Dale, A., & Shizgal, P. (2001). Functional imaging of neural responses to expectancy and experience of monetary gains and losses. *Neuron*, *30*(2), 619–639. doi:10.1016/S0896-6273(01)00303-8 PMID:11395019

Breitkreuz, R. (2009). *Behavioral Accounting vs. Behavioral Finance. A comparison of the related research disciplines*. Univeristat St. Gallen. Accessed December 13, 2014, from: http://www.grin.com/en/e-book/129284/behavioral-accounting-vs-behavioral-finance

Breitmoser, Y. (2010). *A general model of oligopoly endogenizing Cournot, Bertrand, Stackelberg, and Allaz-Vila*. Retrieved March 30, 2015, from: http://mpra.ub.uni-muenchen.de/19998/1/MPRA_paper_19998.pdf

Brenner, L., Rottenstreich, Y., Sood, S., & Bilgin, B. (2007). On the psychology of loss aversion: Possession, valence, and reversals of the endowment effect. *The Journal of Consumer Research*, *34*(3), 369–376. doi:10.1086/518545

Brett, J., Behfar, K., & Kern, M. (2006). Managing Multicultural Teams. *Harvard Business Review, 84*(11), 84–91. PMID:17131565

Brocas, I., & Carrillo, J. D. (2008). The brain as a hierarchical organization. *The American Economic Review, 98*(4), 1312–1346. doi:10.1257/aer.98.4.1312

Brown, G. R., & Richerson, P. (2014). Applying evolutionary theory to human behaviour: Past differences and current debates. *Journal of Bioeconomics, 16*(2), 105–128. doi:10.1007/s10818-013-9166-4

Bruhat Bangalore Mahanagara Palike. (2000). *Property Tax Self-Assessment Scheme: Golden Jubilee Year 2000*. Mahanagara Palike Council Resolution No. 194/99-2000.

Bruhat Bangalore Mahanagara Palike. (2007). *Assessment and Calculation of Property Tax Under the Capital Value System (New SAS): 2007- 2008*. Unpublished.

Bruni, L., & Sugden, R. (2007). The road not taken: How psychology was removed from economics, and how it might be brought back. *The Economic Journal, 117*(516), 146–173. doi:10.1111/j.1468-0297.2007.02005.x

Bryant, S. M., Stone, D., & Wier, B. (2011). An Exploration of Accountants, Accounting Work, and Creativity. *Behavioral Research in Accounting, 23*(1), 45–64. doi:10.2308/bria.2011.23.1.45

Buczek, S. (2006). Finanse behawioralne a inwestowanie w akcje. *Współczesne problemy finansów, bankowości i ubezpieczeń w teorii i praktyce, 1*, 293-306.

Buehler, R., McFarland, C., Spyropoulos, V., & Lam, K. C. H. (2007). Motivated prediction of future feelings: Effects of negative mood and mood orientation on affective forecasts. *Personality and Social Psychology Bulletin, 33*(9), 1265–1278. doi:10.1177/0146167207303014 PMID:17586732

Burton, E., & Shah, S. (2013). *Behavioral Finance: Understanding the Social, Cognitive, and Economic Debates*. New York: John Wiley & Sons.

Cai, X., Kim, S., & Lee, D. (2011). Heterogeneous coding of temporally discounted values in the dorsal and ventral striatum during intertemporal choice. *Neuron, 69*(1), 170–182. doi:10.1016/j.neuron.2010.11.041 PMID:21220107

Camara, E., Rodriguez-Fornells, A., & Münte, T. F. (2008). Functional connectivity of reward processing in the brain. *Frontiers in Human Neuroscience, 2*, 19. doi:10.3389/neuro.09.019.2008 PMID:19242558

Camara, E., Rodriguez-Fornells, A., Ye, Z., & Münte, T. F. (2009). Reward networks in the brain as captured by connectivity measures. *Frontiers in Neuroscience, 3*(3), 350–362. doi:10.3389/neuro.01.034.2009 PMID:20198152

Camerer, C. F. (2003). *Behavioral Game Theory: Experiments in Strategic Interaction*. Princeton, NJ: Princeton University Press.

Camerer, C. F. (2005). Three cheers—psychological, theoretical, empirical—for loss aversion. *JMR, Journal of Marketing Research, 42*(2), 129–133. doi:10.1509/jmkr.42.2.129.62286

Camerer, C. F. (2007). Neuroeconomics: Using neuroscience to make economic predictions. *The Economic Journal, 117*(519), C26–C42. doi:10.1111/j.1468-0297.2007.02033.x

Camerer, C. F. (2008). Neuroeconomics: Opening the gray box. *Neuron, 60*(3), 416–419. doi:10.1016/j.neuron.2008.10.027 PMID:18995815

Camerer, C. F. (2008). The Potential of Neuroeconomics. *Economics and Philosophy, 24*(03), 369–379. doi:10.1017/S0266267108002022

Camerer, C. F., Babcock, L., Loewenstein, G., & Thaler, R. (1997). Labor supply of New York City cabdrivers: One day at a time. *The Quarterly Journal of Economics*, *112*(2), 407–441. doi:10.1162/003355397555244

Camerer, C. F., Bhatt, M., & Ming, H. (2007). Neuroeconomics. In B. S. Frey & A. Stutzer (Eds.), *Economics and Psychology: A Promising New Cross-Disciplinary Field* (pp. 113–151). Boston, MA: MIT Press.

Camerer, C. F., Ho, T. H., & Chong, J. K. (2004). A cognitive hierarchy model of games. *The Quarterly Journal of Economics*, *119*(3), 861–898. doi:10.1162/0033553041502225

Camerer, C. F., & Loewenstein, G. (2004). Behavioral economics: Past, present, future. In C. F. Camerer, G. Loewenstein, & M. Rabin (Eds.), *Advances in behavioral economics* (pp. 3–51). Princeton, NJ: Princeton University Press.

Camerer, C., Loewenstein, G., & Prelec, D. (2005). Neuroeconomics: How neuroscience can inform economics. *Journal of Economic Literature*, *43*(1), 9–64. doi:10.1257/0022051053737843

Camille, N., Coricelli, G., Sallet, J., Pradat-Diehl, P., Duhamel, J.-R., & Sirigu, A. (2004). The involvement of the orbito-frontal cortex in the experience of regret. *Science*, *304*(5674), 1167–1170. doi:10.1126/science.1094550 PMID:15155951

Campion, A., Medsker, G. J., & Higgs, C. (1993). Relation between work group characteristics and effectiveness: Implications for designing an effective work group. *Personnel Psychology*, *46*(4), 823–850. doi:10.1111/j.1744-6570.1993.tb01571.x

Caplin, A., & Dean, M. (2008). Dopamine, reward prediction error, and economics. *The Quarterly Journal of Economics*, *123*(2), 663–701. doi:10.1162/qjec.2008.123.2.663

Carayon, P., Hoonakker, P., & Smith, M. J. (2012). Human Factors in Organizational Design and Management. In G. Salvendy (Ed.), *Handbook of Human Factors and Ergonomics* (4th ed.; pp. 534–552). John Wiley and Sons. doi:10.1002/9781118131350.ch18

Cardinal, R. N., Pennicott, D. R., Sugathapala, C. L., Robbins, T. W., & Everitt, B. J. (2001). Impulsive choice induced in rats by lesions of the nucleus accumbens core. *Science*, *292*(5526), 2499–2501. doi:10.1126/science.1060818 PMID:11375482

Carlsson, A. (2009). The forgotten pioneers of creative hacking and social networking–Introducing the demoscene. In *Re: live Media Art Histories 2009 conference proceedings*, (pp. 16-20).

Carter, C. S., Botvinick, M. M., & Cohen, J. D. (1999). The contribution of the anterior cingulate cortex to executive processes in cognition. *Reviews in the Neurosciences*, *10*(1), 49–57. doi:10.1515/REVNEURO.1999.10.1.49 PMID:10356991

Carter, C. S., & van Veen, V. (2007). Anterior cingulate cortex and conflict detection: An update of theory and data. *Cognitive, Affective & Behavioral Neuroscience*, *7*(4), 367–379. doi:10.3758/CABN.7.4.367 PMID:18189010

Cattin, P., & Wittink, D. R. (1982). Commercial Use of Conjoint Analysis: A Survey. *Journal of Marketing*, *46*(3), 44. doi:10.2307/1251701

Cayley, A. (1894). *The principles of book-keeping by double entry*. Cambridge University Press. Accessed April 1, 2015, from: https://archive.org/details/principlesofbook00caylrich

Cenoz, J., Hufeisen, B., & Jessner, U. (Eds.). (2001). *Cross-linguistic Influence in Third Language Acquisition: Psycholinguistic Perspectives*. Clevedon, UK: Multilingual Matters.

Chadha, R., & Husband, P. (2006). *The cult of the luxury brand: Inside Asia's love affair with luxury*. London: Nicholas Brealey International.

Chakravarty, S. R., Mitra, M., & Sarkar, P. (2015). *A Course on Cooperative Game Theory*. New Delhi: Cambridge University Press.

Chambers, R. J., & Dean, G. W. (2013). *Chambers on Accounting: Logic, Law and Ethics*. New York: Routledge.

Chander, P., & Wilde, L. (1992). Corruption in Tax Administration. *Journal of Public Economics, 49*(3), 333–349. doi:10.1016/0047-2727(92)90072-N

Chang, S. W. C., Barack, D. L., & Platt, M. L. (2012). Mechanistic classification of neural circuit dysfunctions: Insights from neuroeconomics research in animals. *Biological Psychiatry, 72*(2), 101–106. doi:10.1016/j.biopsych.2012.02.017 PMID:22440615

Chan, K. W., & Mauborgne, R. (2015). *Blue Ocean Strategy, Expanded Edition: How to Create Uncontested Market Space and Make the Competition Irrelevant*. Boston, MA: Harvard Business Review Press.

Chattopadhyay, P., Glick, W. H., & Huber, G. P. (2001). Organizational actions in response to threats and opportunities. *Academy of Management Journal, 44*(5), 937–955. doi:10.2307/3069439

Chaudhuri, H. R., & Majumdar, S. (2006). Of diamonds and desires: Understanding conspicuous consumption from a contemporary marketing perspectives. *Academy of Marketing Science Review, 11*.

Chenhall, R. H. (2004). The Role of Cognitive and Affective Conflict in Early Implementation of Activity-Based Cost Management. *Behavioral Research in Accounting, 16*(1), 19–44. doi:10.2308/bria.2004.16.1.19

Chen, J. (2011). The Entropy Theory of Mind and Behavioral Finance. *The IUP Journal of Behavioral Finance, 8*(4), 6–39.

Chen, J., Aung, M., Zhou, L., & Kanetkar, V. (2005). Chinese Ethnic Identification and Conspicuous Consumption: Are There Moderators or Mediators Effect of Acculturation Dimensions? *Journal of International Consumer Marketing, 17*(2/3).

Chiao, J. Y., & Blizinsky, K. D. (2010). Culture–gene coevolution of individualism–collectivism and the serotonintransporter gene. In *Proceedings of the Royal Society B: Biological Sciences* (vol. 277, pp. 529–537). Retrieved on September 11, 2013, from: http://rspb.royalsocietypublishing.org/content/277/1681/529

Chitturi, R., Raghunathan, R., & Mahajan, V. (2008). Delight by Design: The Role of Hedonic Versus Utilitarian Benefits. *Journal of Marketing, 72*(3), 48–63. doi:10.1509/jmkg.72.3.48

Chiu, C. M., Hsu, M. H., & Wang, E. T. (2006). Understanding Knowledge Sharing in Virtual Communities: An Integration of Social Capital and Social Cognitive Theories. *Decision Support Systems, 42*(3), 1872–1888. doi:10.1016/j.dss.2006.04.001

Chomsky, N. (1977). *Essays on Form and Interpretation*. Amsterdam: Elsevier Science, Ltd.

Chomsky, N. (2006). *Language and Mind* (3rd ed.). London: Cambridge University Press. doi:10.1017/CBO9780511791222

Chomsky, N. (2007). *Of Minds and Language*. London: Cambridge University Press.

Chorvat, T. R., & McCabe, K. (2005). Neuroeconomics and rationality. *Chicago-Kent Law Review, 80*(3), 1235–1255.

Cho, T. S., & Hambrick, D. C. (2006). Attention as the mediator between top management team characteristics and strategic change: The case of airline deregulation. *Organization Science, 17*(4), 453–469. doi:10.1287/orsc.1060.0192

Chu, C.Y.C. (1990). Income Tax Evasion with Venal Tax Officials - the Case of Developing Countries. *Public Finance = Finances Publiques, 45*(3), 392-408.

Clark, L. (2010). Decision-making during gambling: An integration of cognitive and psychobiological approaches. *Philosophical Transactions of the Royal Society of London. Series B, Biological Sciences*, *365*(1538), 319–330. doi:10.1098/rstb.2009.0147 PMID:20026469

Cleveland, M., & Chang, W. (2009). Migration and materialism: The roles of ethnic identity, religiosity and generation. *Journal of Business Research*, *62*(10), 963–971. doi:10.1016/j.jbusres.2008.05.022

Cloutier, J., & Gyurovski, I. (2014). Ventral medial prefrontal cortex and person evaluation: Forming impressions of others varying in financial and moral status. *NeuroImage*, *100*, 535–543. doi:10.1016/j.neuroimage.2014.06.024 PMID:24936688

Coello, Y., & Bartolo, A. (Eds.). (2013). *Language and Action in Cognitive Neuroscience*. New York: Psychology Press.

Cohen, J. D. (2005). The Vulcanization of the Human Brain: A Neural Perspective on Interactions between Cognition and Emotion. *The Journal of Economic Perspectives*, *19*(4), 3–24. doi:10.1257/089533005775196750

Cohen, J. R., & Lieberman, M. D. (2010). The common neural basis of exerting self-control in multiple domains. In *Society to Brain: The New Sciences of Self-Control* (pp. 141–162). New York: Oxford University Press. doi:10.1093/acprof:oso/9780195391381.003.0008

Cohen, S. G., & Ledford, G. E. (1994). The effectiveness of self-managing teams: A quasi-experiment. *Human Relations*, *47*(1), 13–43. doi:10.1177/001872679404700102

Cohen, S., Janicki-Deverts, D., & Miller, G. E. (2007). Psychological stress and disease. *Journal of the American Medical Association*, *298*(14), 1685–1687. doi:10.1001/jama.298.14.1685 PMID:17925521

Cole, S. W., Hawkley, L. C., Arevalo, J. M., & Cacioppo, J. T. (2011). Transcript origin analysis identifies antigen-presenting cells as primary targets of socially regulated gene expression in leukocytes. In *Proceedings of the National Academy of Sciences of the United States of America* (vol. 108, pp. 3080–3085). Retrieved on May 9, 2015, from: http://www.ncbi.nlm.nih.gov/pmc/articles/PMC3041107/

Cole, G. A. (1988). *Personnel Management. Theory and Practice* (2nd ed.). London: D.P. Publications, Ltd.

Coleman, S. (2005). Just how risky is online voting? *Information Polity*, *10*(1), 95–104.

Conen, K. E., & Padua-Schioppa, C. (2015). Neuronal variability in orbitofrontal cortex during economic decisions. *Journal of Neurophysiology*, *114*(3), 1367–1381. doi:10.1152/jn.00231.2015 PMID:26084903

Cook, K., Shortell, S., Conrad, B., & Morrisey, M. (1983). A theory of organizational response to regulation: The case of hospitals. *Academy of Management Review*, *8*(2), 193–205. PMID:10263058

Coricelli, G., Critchley, H. D., Joffily, M., O'Doherty, J. P., Sirigu, A., & Dolan, R. J. (2005). Regret and its avoidance: A neuroimaging study of choice behavior. *Nature Neuroscience*, *8*(9), 1255–1262. doi:10.1038/nn1514 PMID:16116457

Coricelli, G., & Nagel, R. (2009). Neural correlates of strategic reasoning in medial prefrontal cortex. *Proceedings of the National Academy of Sciences of the United States of America*, *106*(23), 9163–9168. doi:10.1073/pnas.0807721106 PMID:19470476

Corsani, A. (2013). Rent and Subjectivity in Neoliberal Cognitive Capitalism. *Knowledge Cultures*, *1*(4), 67–83.

Costa-Gomes, M., Crawford, V., & Broseta, B. (2001). Cognition behavior in normal-form games: An experimental study. *Econometrica*, *69*(5), 1193–1235. doi:10.1111/1468-0262.00239

Cote, J., Latham, C., & Sanders, D. (2013). Ethical Financial Reporting Choice: The Influence of Individual Characteristics. *Advances in Accounting Behavioral Research*, *16*, 115–148. doi:10.1108/S1475-1488(2013)0000016010

Council of Europe. (2010). *White Paper on Intercultural Dialogue: Living together as equals in dignity. Report of the Group of Eminent Persons of the Council of Europe.* Strasbourg: Council of Europe Publishing.

Craver, C. F., & Alexandrova, A. (2008). No Revolution Necessary: Neural Mechanism For Economics. *Economics and Philosophy, 24*(03), 381–406. doi:10.1017/S0266267108002034

Crozier, M., & Friedberg, E. (1980). *Actors and Systems.* Chicago, IL: University of Chicago Press.

Csikszentmihalyi, M., & Rochberg-Halton, E. (1981). *The meaning of things: Domestic symbols and the self.* Oxford, UK: Cambridge University Press. doi:10.1017/CBO9781139167611

Cumbul, E. (2012). *Stackelberg versus Cournot Oligopoly with Private Information.* Retrieved March 30, 2015, from file:///C:/Users/DELL/Downloads/8480-17570-1-SMP.pdf

Cushing, B. E., & Loebbecke, J. K. (1986). *Comparison of audit methodologies of large accounting firms.* Sarasota, FL: American Accounting Association.

Cyert, R., & March, J. (1963). *A Behavioral Theory of the Firm.* Englewood Cliffs, NJ: Prentice-Hall.

Czaja, S. J., & Nair, S. N. (2012). Human Factors Engineering and Systems Design. In G. Salvendy (Ed.), *Handbook of Human Factors and Ergonomics* (4th ed.; pp. 38–56). John Wiley and Sons. doi:10.1002/9781118131350.ch2

Czerwonka, M., & Gorlewski, B. (2008). *Finanse behawioralne: zachowania inwestorów i rynku.* Warszawa: Szkoła Główna Handlowa - Oficyna Wydawnicza.

Czerwonka, M., & Rzeszutek, M. (2011). Analiza zachowań inwestycyjnych inwestorów giełdowych oraz studentów kierunków ekonomicznych i psychologicznych z perspektywy finansów behawioralnych. *Studia i Prace Kolegium Zarządzania i Finansów, 107,* 28–44.

d'Acremont, M., & Bossaerts, P. (2008). Neurobiological studies of risk assessment: A comparison of expected utility and mean-variance approaches. *Cognitive, Affective & Behavioral Neuroscience, 8*(4), 363–374. doi:10.3758/CABN.8.4.363 PMID:19033235

D'Amour, D., Ferrada-Videla, M., Rodriguez, L. S. M., & Beaulieu, M. D. (2005). The conceptual basis for interprofessional collaboration: Core concepts and theoretical frame works. *Journal of Interprofessional Care, 19*(1), 116–131. doi:10.1080/13561820500082529 PMID:16096150

D'Andrade, R. G. (1992). Schemas and Motivation. In R. G. D'Andrade & C. Strauss (Eds.), *Human Motives and Cultural Modes* (pp. 23–24). Cambridge, UK: Cambridge University Press. doi:10.1017/CBO9781139166515.003

Dada, D. (2006). The Failure of E-Government in Developing Countries: A Literature Review. *The Electronic Journal on Information Systems in Developing Countries, 26*(7), 1–10.

Daft, R. L., & Weick, K. E. (1984). Toward a model of organizations as interpretation systems. *Academy of Management Review, 9*(2), 284–295.

Dagevos, H. (2005). Consumers as four-faced creatures: Looking at food consumption from the perspective of contemporary consumers. *Appetite, 45*(1), 32–39. doi:10.1016/j.appet.2005.03.006 PMID:15921822

Dalgleish, T. (2004). The emotional brain. *Nature Reviews. Neuroscience, 5*(7), 583–589. doi:10.1038/nrn1432 PMID:15208700

Daun, A. (1983). The materialistic life-style: Some socio-psychological aspects. In Consumer behaviour and environmental quality. New York: St. Martin.

D'Aveni, R., & MacMillan, I. (1990). Crisis and the content of managerial communications: A study of the focus of attention of top managers in surviving and failing firms. *Administrative Science Quarterly*, *35*(4), 634–657. doi:10.2307/2393512

Davis, J. B. (2010). Neuroeconomics: Constructing identity. *Journal of Economic Behavior & Organization*, *76*(3), 574–583. doi:10.1016/j.jebo.2010.08.011

Davis, L. (1989). Report format and the decision makers' task: An experimental investigation. *Accounting, Organizations and Society*, *14*(5-6), 495–508. doi:10.1016/0361-3682(89)90014-7

Davis, P. (2008). Book Review: The Origins of Wealth: Evolution, Complexity, and the Radical Remaking of Economics. *The FINSIA Journal of Applied Finance*, *1*(3), 48–50.

Dawkins, R. (2006). *The Selfish Gene (30th anniv. ed.)*. Oxford, UK: Oxford University Press.

de Angelis, G., & Dewaele, J. M. (2009). The development of psycholinguistic research on crosslinguistic influence. In L. Aronin & B. Hufeisen (Eds.), *The Exploration of Multilingualism*. Amsterdam: John Benjamins. doi:10.1075/aals.6.04ch4

De Bondt, W., & Thaler, R. H. (1985). Does the Stock Market Overreact. *The Journal of Finance*, *40*(3), 793–805. doi:10.1111/j.1540-6261.1985.tb05004.x

De Bondt, W., & Thaler, R. H. (1987). Further Evidence on Investor Overreaction and Stock Market Seasonality. *The Journal of Finance*, *42*(3), 557–581. doi:10.1111/j.1540-6261.1987.tb04569.x

de Bont, C. J. P. M. (1992). *Consumer Evaluations of Early Product-concepts*. Delft University Press.

de Cruz, H. (2009). Is Linguistic Determinism An Empirically Testable Hypothesis? *Logique & Analyse*, *208*, 327–341.

De Mooij, M., & Hofstede, G. (2011). Cross-Cultural Consumer Behavior : A Review of Research Findings. *Journal of International Consumer Marketing*, *23*, 181–192. doi:10.1080/08961530.2011.578057

de Quervain, D. J. F. et al.. (2004). The neural basis of altruistic punishment. *Science*, *305*(5688), 1254–1258. doi:10.1126/science.1100735 PMID:15333831

Deaner, R. O., Khera, A. V., & Platt, M. L. (2005). Monkeys pay per view: Adaptive valuation of social images by rhesus macaques. *Current Biology*, *15*(6), 543–548. doi:10.1016/j.cub.2005.01.044 PMID:15797023

Dębniewska, M., & Wojtowicz, K. (2014). Wpływ bieżących informacji na decyzje inwestorów w kontekście teorii finansów behawioralnych. *Prace Naukowe Wyższej Szkoły Bankowej w Gdańsku*, *32*, 105–116.

Decety, J., Jackson, P. L., Sommerville, J. A., Chaminade, T., & Meltzoff, A. N. (2004). The neural bases of cooperation and competition: An fMRI investigation. *NeuroImage*, *23*(2), 744–751. doi:10.1016/j.neuroimage.2004.05.025 PMID:15488424

Declerck, C. H., Boone, C., & Emonds, G. (2013). When do people cooperate? The neuroeconomics of prosocial decision making. *Brain and Cognition*, *81*(1), 95–117. doi:10.1016/j.bandc.2012.09.009 PMID:23174433

Dekker, P., & Van Rooy, R. (2000). Bi-directional optimality theory: An application of game theory. *Journal of Semantics*, *17*(3), 217–242. doi:10.1093/jos/17.3.217

Delgado, M. R. (2007). Reward-related responses in the human striatum. *Annals of the New York Academy of Sciences*, *1104*(1), 70–88. doi:10.1196/annals.1390.002 PMID:17344522

Delgado, M. R., Frank, R. H., & Phelps, E. A. (2005). Perceptions of moral character modulate the neural systems of reward during the trust game. *Nature Neuroscience*, *8*(11), 1611–1618. doi:10.1038/nn1575 PMID:16222226

Delgado, M. R., Nystrom, L. E., Fissell, C., Noll, D. C., & Fiez, J. A. (2000). Tracking the hemodynamic responses to reward and punishment in the striatum. *Journal of Neurophysiology, 84*, 3072–3077. PMID:11110834

Denktas-Sakar, G., Karatas-Cetin, C., & Saatcioğlu, O. Y. (2014). Discovering the Nexus between Market Orientation and Open Innovation: A Grounded Theory Approach. In B. Christiansen, S. Yıldız, & E. Yıldız (Eds.), *Transcultural Marketing for Incremental and Radical Innovation* (pp. 1–42). Hershey, PA: IGI Global. doi:10.4018/978-1-4666-4749-7.ch001

Deppe, M., Schwindt, W., Pieper, A., Kugel, H., Plassmann, H., Kenning, P., & Ringelstein, E. B. et al. (2007). Anterior cingulate reflects susceptibility to framing during attractiveness evaluation. *Neuroreport, 18*, 1119–1123. PMID:17589310

Depue, R. A., & Collins, P. F. (1999). Neurobiology of the structure of personality: Dopamine, facilitation of incentive motivation, and extraversion. *Behavioral and Brain Sciences, 22*(3), 491–569. doi:10.1017/S0140525X99002046 PMID:11301519

Depue, R. A., & Morrone-Strupinsky, J. V. (2005). A neurobehavioral model of affiliative bonding: Implications for conceptualizing a human trait of affiliation. *Behavioral and Brain Sciences, 28*(3), 313–395. doi:10.1017/S0140525X05000063 PMID:16209725

DeSarbo, W. S., Huff, L., Rolandelli, M. M., & Choi, J. (1994). Service Quality: New Directions in Theory and Practice. In *On the Measurement of Perceived Service Quality: A Conjoint Analysis Approach* (pp. 201–223). Thousand Oaks, CA: SAGE Publications, Inc.

Desmeules, R. (2002). Desmeules / The Impact of Variety on Consumer Happiness The Impact of Variety on Consumer Happiness: Marketing and the Tyranny of Freedom. *Academy of Marketing Science Review*, (12): 1–33.

Devine, C. (1960). Research methodology and accounting theory formation. *Accounting Review, 35*, 387–399.

Dickhaut, J., Basu, S., McCabe, K., & Waymire, G. (2010). Neuroaccounting: Consilience between the Biologically Evolved Brain and Culturally Evolved Accounting Principles. *Accounting Horizons, 24*(2), 221–255. doi:10.2308/acch.2010.24.2.221

Dickhaut, J., Rustichini, A., & Smith, V. (2009). A neuroeconomic theory of the decision process. *Proceedings of the National Academy of Sciences of the United States of America, 106*(52), 22145–22150. doi:10.1073/pnas.0912500106 PMID:20080787

Dillinger, W. (1988). *Urban Property Taxation in Developing Countries.* World Bank Policy Research Working Paper Series, no. 41, 1988. Retrieved on June 14, 2008, from: http://ideas.repec.org/p/wbk/wbrwps/41.html

Dixit, A., & Nalebuff, B. (1991). *Thinking Strategically.* New York: WW Norten & Company. Inc.

Dixit, A., & Skeath, S. (2004). *Games of Strategy* (2nd ed.). New York: W.W. Norton & Company, Inc.

Dobija, D., & Kucharczyk, M. (Eds.). (2009). *Rachunkowość zarządcza: teoria, praktyka, aspekty behawioralne.* Warszawa: Wydawnictwa Akademickie i Profesjonalne.

Donaldson, M. (1987). Labouring men: Love, sex and strife. *Journal of Sociology (Melbourne, Vic.), 23*(2), 165–184. doi:10.1177/144078338702300201

Downs, A. (1964). *Inside Bureaucracy.* Boston, MA: Little Brown.

Doyle, G. (2002). *Understanding Media Economics.* Thousand Oaks, CA: Sage. doi:10.4135/9781446279960

Doz, Y. L., & Hamel, G. (1998). *Alliance advantage: The art of creating value through partnering.* Boston: Harvard Business Press.

Druzhinin, A. G. (2005). *South of Russia in the late XX – early XXI century (economic-geographical aspects).* Rostov n/D: Publishing house of Rostov State University.

Druzhinin, A. G., & Ionov, A. C. (2001). *A Conceptual framework for the regionalization of the economy.* Rostov n/D: Publishing house of North-Caucasus scientific center of high school.

Duarte, P. B., Fadlullah, Z. M., Vasilakos, A. V., & Kato, N. (2012). On the partially overlapped channel assignment on wireless mesh network backbone: A game theoretic approach. *Selected Areas in Communications. IEEE Journal on, 30*(1), 119–127.

Dubois, B., & Paternault, C. (1995, July/August). Observations: Understanding the world of international luxury brands: The "Dream Formula". *Journal of Advertising Research,* 69–77.

Dudzińska-Baryła, R., & Michalska E. (2010). Efekt miesiąca a behawioralne aspekty podejmowania decyzji. *Metody i zastosowania badań operacyjnych, 10,* 54-75.

Dunleavy, P. (1991). *Democracy, Bureaucracy and Public Choice: Economic Explanations in Political Science.* London: Harvester Wheatsheaf.

Dutton, J. E., & Duncan, R. B. (1987). The creation of momentum for change through the process of strategic issue diagnosis. *Strategic Management Journal, 8*(3), 279–295. doi:10.1002/smj.4250080306

Dutton, J. E., Fahey, L., & Narayanan, V. K. (1983). Toward understanding strategic issue diagnosis. *Strategic Management Journal, 4*(4), 307–323. doi:10.1002/smj.4250040403

Dutton, J., & Jackson, S. (1987). Categorizing strategic issues: Links to organizational action. *Academy of Management Review, 12*(1), 76–90.

Dutton, W. H. (1992). The Ecology of Games Shaping Telecommunications Policy. *Communication Theory, 2*(4), 303–324. doi:10.1111/j.1468-2885.1992.tb00046.x

Dyckman, T. (1964). The Effects of Alternative Accounting Techniques on Certain Management Decisions. *Journal of Accounting Research, 2*(1), 91–107. doi:10.2307/2490158

Eastman, J. K., Goldsmith, R. E., & Flynn, L. R. (1999). Status consumption in consumer behavior: Scale development and validation. *Journal of Marketing Theory and Practice, 7*(3), 41–52. doi:10.1080/10696679.1999.11501839

Edwards, W. (1954). The theory of decision making. *Psychological Bulletin, 51*(4), 380–417. doi:10.1037/h0053870 PMID:13177802

Efferson, C., Lalive, R., & Fehr, E. (2008). The coevolution of cultural groups and in groupfavoritism. *Science, 321*(5897), 1844–1849. doi:10.1126/science.1155805 PMID:18818361

Egidi, G., Nusbaum, H. C., & Cacioppo, J. T. (2008). Neuroeconomics: Foundational issues and consumer relevance. In C. P. Haugtvedt, P. M. Herr, & F. R. Kardes (Eds.), *Handbook of consumer psychology* (pp. 1177–1214). New York, NY: Psychology Press.

Eisenhardt, K. M. (1989). Building Theories from Case Study Research. *Academy of Management Review, 14*(4), 532–550.

Elliott, R., Friston, K. J., & Dolan, R. J. (2000). Dissociable neural responses in human reward systems. *The Journal of Neuroscience, 20,* 6159–6165. PMID:10934265

Elliott, R., Newman, J. L., Longe, O. A., & Deakin, J. F. (2003). Differential response patterns in the striatum and orbitofrontal cortex to financial reward in humans: A parametric functional magnetic resonance imaging study. *The Journal of Neuroscience, 23*(1), 303–307. PMID:12514228

Engelmann, J. B., Capra, C. M., Noussair, C., & Berns, G. S. (2009). Expert Financial Advice Neurobiologically "Offloads" Financial Decision-Making under Risk. *PLoS ONE*, *4*(3), e4957. doi:10.1371/journal.pone.0004957 PMID:19308261

Engle-Warnick, J., & Slonim, R. L. (2006). Inferring repeated-game strategies from actions: Evidence from trust game experiments. *Economic Theory*, *28*(3), 603–632. doi:10.1007/s00199-005-0633-6

Enright, M. J. (2000). *Survey on the Characterization of Regional Clusters: Initial Results.* Working Paper, Institute of Economic Policy and Business Strategy. Hong Kong: University of Hong Kong.

Erev, I., Ert, E., & Yechiam, E. (2008). Loss aversion, diminishing sensitivity, and the effect of experience on repeated decisions. *Journal of Behavioral Decision Making*, *21*(5), 575–597. doi:10.1002/bdm.602

Eriksson, P., & Kovalainen, A. (2008). *Qualitative Methods in Business Research.* Thousand Oaks, CA: SAGE Publications, Ltd. doi:10.4135/9780857028044

Ernst, M., Bolla, K., Mouratidis, M., Contoreggi, C., Matochik, J. A., Kurian, V., & London, E. D. et al. (2002). Decision-making in a risk-taking task: A PET study. *Neuropsychopharmacology*, *26*(5), 682–691. doi:10.1016/S0893-133X(01)00414-6 PMID:11927193

Ernst, M., & Paulus, M. P. (2005). Neurobiology of decision making: A selective review from a neurocognitive and clinical perspective. *Biological Psychiatry*, *58*(8), 597–604. doi:10.1016/j.biopsych.2005.06.004 PMID:16095567

Eu, F. (1976). Foundations of Finance: Portfolio Decisions and Securities Prices. New York: Basic Books.

European Commission (2006). *Recommendation of the European Parliament and of the Council of 18 December 2006 on key competences for lifelong learning.* Official Journal 2006/962/EC.

Evans, K. L., & Hampson, E. (2015). Sex differences on prefrontally-dependent cognitive tasks. *Brain and Cognition*, *93*, 42–53. doi:10.1016/j.bandc.2014.11.006 PMID:25528435

Fabbro, F. (2001). The Bilingual Brain: Bilingual Aphasia. *Brain and Language*, *79*(2), 201–210. doi:10.1006/brln.2001.2480 PMID:11712844

Faber, R. J., & Vohs, K. D. (2004). To buy or not to buy?: Self-control and self-regulatory failure in purchase behavior. In R. F. Baumeister & K. D. Vohs (Eds.), *Handbook of self-regulation: Research, theory, and applications* (pp. 509–524). New York: Guilford Press.

Farrell, A. M., Goh, J. O., & White, B. J. (2014). The Effect of Performance-Based Incentive Contracts on System 1 and System 2 Processing in Affective Decision Contexts: fMRI and Behavioral Evidence. *Accounting Review*, *89*(6), 1979–2010. doi:10.2308/accr-50852

Fehr, E., & Camerer, C. F. (2007). Social neuroeconomics: The neural circuitry of social preferences. *Trends in Cognitive Sciences*, *11*(10), 419–427. doi:10.1016/j.tics.2007.09.002 PMID:17913566

Fehr, E., Fischbacher, U., & Kodfeld, M. (2005). Neuroeconomic Foundations of Trust and Social Preferences: Initial Evidence. *The American Review*, *95*(2), 346–351.

Fehr, E., & Gächter, S. (2002). Altruistic punishment in humans. *Nature*, *415*(6868), 137–140. doi:10.1038/415137a PMID:11805825

Fehr, E., & Rangel, A. (2011). Neuroeconomic Foundations of Economic Choice- Recent Advances. *The Journal of Economic Perspectives*, *25*(4), 3–30. doi:10.1257/jep.25.4.3 PMID:21595323

Fellows, L. K. (2007). Advances in understanding ventromedial prefrontal function. *Neurology*, *68*(13), 991–995. doi:10.1212/01.wnl.0000257835.46290.57 PMID:17389302

Ferguson, T. (2005). *Game theory: Games in coalitional form*. Retrieved July 24, 2015, from: http://www.math.ucla.edu /~tom/Game_Theory/coal.pdf

Fey, A. (1936). *Der Homo Oeconomicus in der klassischen Nationalökonomie und seine Kritik durch den Historismus*. Limburg: Limburger Vereindruckerei G.m.b.H.

Fiegenbaum, A., & Thomas, H. (1988). Attitudes towards risk and the risk-return paradox: Prospect theory explanations. *Academy of Management Journal, 31*(1), 85–106. doi:10.2307/256499

Field, J. (2003). *Psycholinguistics: A Resource Book for Students*. New York: Routledge.

Findlay, C. S., Hansell, R. I., & Lumsden, C. J. (1989). Behavioral evolution and biocultural games: Oblique and horizontal cultural transmission. *Journal of Theoretical Biology, 137*(3), 245–269. doi:10.1016/S0022-5193(89)80072-4 PMID:2811392

Fine, R. L. (2008). *The concise encyclopedia of economics*. Accessed March 2, 2015, from: http://www.econlib.org/library/Enc/Auctions.html

Fiorillo, C. D., Tobler, P. N., & Schultz, W. (2003). Discrete coding of reward probability and uncertainty by dopamine neurons. *Science, 299*(5614), 1898–1902. doi:10.1126/science.1077349 PMID:12649484

Firestone, W. A. (1989). Educational Policy as an Ecology of Games. *Educational Researcher, 18*(7), 18–24. doi:10.2307/1177165

Fischer, I., & Budescu, D. V. (2005). When do those who know more also know more about how much they know? The development of confidence and performance in categorical decision tasks. *Organizational Behavior and Human Decision Processes, 98*(1), 39–53. doi:10.1016/j.obhdp.2005.04.003

Fisher, K., & Statman, M. (2000). Cognitive bias in market forecasts. *Journal of Portfolio Management, 27*(1), 72–81. doi:10.3905/jpm.2000.319785

Fitzmaurice, J., & Comegys, C. (2006). Materialism and Social Consumption. *Journal of Marketing Theory and Practice, 14*(4), 287–299. doi:10.2753/MTP1069-6679140403

Flatters, F., & MacLeod, W. B. (1995). Administrative Corruption and Taxation. *International Tax and Public Finance, 2*(3), 397–417. doi:10.1007/BF00872774

Flavell, J. H. (1979). Metacognition and cognitive monitoring: A new area of cognitive-developmental inquiry. *The American Psychologist, 34*(10), 906–911. doi:10.1037/0003-066X.34.10.906

Flores, J., Baruca, A., & Saldivar, R. (2014). Is Neuromarketing Ethical? Consumers Say Yes, Consumers Say No. *Journal of Legal. Ethical and Regulatory Issues, 17*(2), 77–91.

Flynn, S., Foley, C., & Vinnitskaya, I. (2005). New Paradigm for the Study of Simultaneous vs. Sequential Bilingualism. *Proceedings of the 4th International Symposium on Bilingualism* (pp. 768-774). Somerville, MA: Cascadilla Press.

FOREX. (2014). Retrieved on February 2, 2015, from: http://ru.fxempire.com/currencies/eur-usd/tools/historical-data/

Forrester, J. W. (1961). *Industrial Dynamics*. Portland, OR: Productivity Press.

Fountain, J. E. (2001). *Building the Virtual State: Information Technology and Institutional Change*. Washington, DC: Brookings Institution Press.

Fountain, J. E. (2002). A Theory of Federal Bureaucracy. In E. Kamarck & J. S. Nye Jr., (Eds.), *Governance.com: Democracy in the Information Age* (pp. 117–140). Washington, DC: Brookings Institution Press.

Fountain, J. E., & Osorio-Urzua, C. A. (2001). Public sector: Early stage of a deep transformation. In R. Litan & A. Rivlin (Eds.), *The Economic Payoff from the Internet Revolution* (pp. 235–268). Washington, DC: Brookings Institution and Internet Policy Institute.

Fournier, S., & Richins, M. L. (1991). Some theoretical and popular notions concerning materialism. *Journal of Social Behavior and Personality, 6*(6), 403–414.

Frank, R. H. (2003). *Microeconomics and behavior*. London, UK: McGraw–Hill/Irwin.

Frederick, S., Lowenstein, G., & O'Donoghue, T. (2002). Discounting and Time Preference: A Critical Review. *Journal of Economic Literature, 40*(1), 351–401. doi:10.1257/jel.40.2.351

Freeman, D., & Freeman, J. (2008). *Paranoia: The Twenty-First Century Fear*. Oxford, UK: Oxford University Press.

Friedman, G. (2009). *The Next 100 Years: A Forecast for the 21st Century*. New York: Anchor Books.

Friston, K. J., Buechel, C., Fink, G. R., Morris, J., Rolls, E., & Dolan, R. J. (1997). Psychophysiological and modulatory interactions in neuroimaging. *NeuroImage, 6*(3), 218–229. doi:10.1006/nimg.1997.0291 PMID:9344826

Frith, U., & Frith, C. D. (2003). Development and Neurophysiology of Mentalizing. *Philosophical Transactions of the Royal Society of London. Series B, Biological Sciences, 358*(1431), 459–473. doi:10.1098/rstb.2002.1218 PMID:12689373

Fuchs, C. (2011). Foundations of critical media and information studies. *Routledge Advances in Sociology, 384*. doi:10.4324/9780203830864

Fudenberg, D., & Levine, D. K. (2006). A dual-self model of impulse control. *The American Economic Review, 96*(5), 1449–1476. doi:10.1257/aer.96.5.1449

Fukuyama, F. (1995). *Trust: The Social Virtues and the Creation of Prosperity*. New York: Free Press.

Gajdka, J. (2013). *Behawioralne finanse przedsiębiorstw: podstawowe podejścia i koncepcje*. Łódź: Wydawnictwo Uniwersytetu Łódzkiego.

Gallagher, H. L., & Frith, C. D. (2003). Functional Imaging of Theory of Mind. *Trends in Cognitive Sciences, 7*(2), 77–83. doi:10.1016/S1364-6613(02)00025-6 PMID:12584026

Gan, J. O., Walton, M. E., & Phillips, P. E. (2010). Dissociable cost and benefit encoding of future rewards by mesolimbic dopamine. *Nature Neuroscience, 13*(1), 25–27. doi:10.1038/nn.2460 PMID:19904261

Garcia-Mayo, M. D. P. (2012). Cognitive Approaches to L3 Acquisitions. *International Journal of English Studies*. Retrieved on July 4, 2015, from http://files.eric.ed.gov/fulltext/EJ975723.pdf

Gardner, R. (1995). *Games for business and economics*. New York: John Wiley & Sons.

Gardner, R., & Ostrom, E. (1991). Rules and games. *Public Choice, 70*(2), 121–149. doi:10.1007/BF00124480

Gascó, M. (2003). New Technologies and Institutional Change in Public Administration. *Social Science Computer Review, 21*(6), 6–14. doi:10.1177/0894439302238967

Gass, M. S., & Selinker, L. (2008). *Second Language Acquisition* (3rd ed.). New York: Routledge Press.

Gazzaniga, M., Ivry, R., & Mangun, G. (2002). *Cognitive neuroscience*. New York, NY: W. W. Norton & Company.

Gehring, J. W., & Willoughby, A. R. (2002). The medial frontal cortex and the rapid processing of monetary gains and losses. *Science, 295*(5563), 2279–2282. doi:10.1126/science.1066893 PMID:11910116

Ger, G., & Belk, R. (1996). Cross-cultural differences in materialism. *Journal of Economic Psychology, 17*(1), 55–77. doi:10.1016/0167-4870(95)00035-6

Gigerenzer, G., & Selten, R. (2002). *Bounded rationality: The adaptive toolbox.* Cambridge, MA: MIT Press.

Gilbert, D. T., & Osborne, R. E. (1989). Thinking backward: Some curable and incurable consequences of cognitive busyness. *Journal of Personality and Social Psychology, 57*(6), 940–949. doi:10.1037/0022-3514.57.6.940

Gintis, H. (2006). *The Economy as a Complex Adaptive System - A Review of Eric D. Beinhocker, The Origins of Wealth: Evolution, Complexity, and the Radical Remaking of Economics.* MacArthur Research Foundation Paper Series. Retrieved on September 30, 2011, from: http://www.umass.edu/preferen/Class%20Material/Readings%20in%20Market%20Dynamics/Complexity%20Economics.pdf

Gintis, H. (2010). Gene–culture coevolution and the nature of human sociality. In *Proceedings of the Royal Society B: Biological Sciences* (vol. 366, pp. 878–888). Retrieved on October 7, 2013, from: http://rspb.royalsocietypublishing.org

Gintis, H. (2000). *Game Theory Evolving: A Problem-Centered Introduction to Modeling Strategic Behavior.* Princeton, NJ: Princeton University Press.

Gintis, H. (2009). *Game Theory Evolving: A Problem-Centered Introduction to Modeling Strategic Interaction* (2nd ed.). Princeton, NJ: Princeton University Press.

Glimcher, P. W. Colin, Camerer, E. F., Fehr, E., & Poldrack, R. A. (2008). Introduction: A Brief History of Neuroeconomics. In P. Glimcher, E. Fehr, C. Camerer, & R. A. Poldrack (Eds.), Neuroeconomics: Decision Making and the Brain (pp. 1-12). London: Academic Press.

Glimcher, P. W. (2002). Decisions, decisions, decisions: Choosing a biological science of choice. *Neuron, 36*(2), 323–332. doi:10.1016/S0896-6273(02)00962-5 PMID:12383785

Glimcher, P. W. (2003). *Decisions, uncertainty and the brain: The science of neuroeconomics.* Cambridge, MA: MIT Press.

Glimcher, P. W. (2004). *Decisions, uncertainty, and the brain: The science of neuroeconomics.* Cambridge, MA: MIT Press.

Glimcher, P. W. (2008). Understanding risk: A guide for the perplexed. *Cognitive, Affective & Behavioral Neuroscience, 8*(4), 348–354. doi:10.3758/CABN.8.4.348 PMID:19033233

Glimcher, P. W. (2009). *Neuroeconomics: Decision making and the brain.* London, UK: Academic Press.

Glimcher, P. W. (2010). *Foundations of Neuroeconomic Analysis.* Oxford, UK: Oxford University Press. doi:10.1093/acprof:oso/9780199744251.001.0001

Glimcher, P. W. (2011). *Foundations of neuroeconomic analysis.* New York: Oxford University Press.

Glimcher, P. W., Camerer, C. F., Fehr, E., & Poldrack, R. A. (2008). Introduction: A brief history of neuroeconomics. In P. W. Glimcher, C. F. Camerer, E. Fehr, & R. A. Poldrack (Eds.), *Neuroeconomics: Decision making and the brain* (pp. 1–12). London, UK: Academic Press.

Glimcher, P. W., Camerer, C. F., Fehr, E., & Poldrack, R. A. (2009). Introduction: A Brief History of Neuroeconomics. In *Neuroeconomics Decision Making and The Brain* (pp. 1–12). San Diego, CA: Elsevier Inc.

Glimcher, P. W., & Rustichini, A. (2004). Neuroeconomics: The consilience of brain and decision. *Science, 306*(5695), 447–452. doi:10.1126/science.1102566 PMID:15486291

Godart, F. C., Maddux, W. W., Shipilov, A. V., & Galinsky, A. D. (2015). Fashion With a Foreign Flair: Professional Experiences Abroad Facilitate The Creative Innovations of Organizations. *Academy of Management Journal, 58*(1), 195–220. doi:10.5465/amj.2012.0575

Goel, V., Grafman, J., Tajik, J., Gana, S., & Danto, D. (1997). A study of the performance of patients with frontal lobe lesions in a financial planning task. *Brain, 120*(10), 1805–1822. doi:10.1093/brain/120.10.1805 PMID:9365372

Goldberg, M. F. (2002). *15 School questions and discussion: From class size, standards, and school safety to leadership and more*. Lanham, MD: Scarecrow.

Goodie, A. S., Doshi, P., & Young, D. L. (2012). Levels of Theory-of-Mind Reasoning in Competitive Games. *Journal of Behavioral Decision Making, 25*(1), 95–108. doi:10.1002/bdm.717

Gorelova, G. V., Verba, V. A., & Zakharova, E. N. (2004). Cognitive models in intelligent systems to support management decisions. Herald of TSURE, 5, 35 - 39.

Gorelova, G., Matveeva, L., & Nikitaeva, A. (2007). *Systematic approach and instruments of management in geographically localized economic systems of meso-level*. Rostov n/D: Publishing house of Southern Federal University.

Gorelova, G.V., Zakharova, E.N., & Radchenko., S.A. (2006). *The study semi-structured problems of socio-economic systems cognitive approach*. Rostov-on-Don: Publishing house of Southern Federal University.

Grace, J., Stout, J. C., & Malloy, P. F. (1999). Assessing frontal behavior syndromes with the Frontal Lobe Personality Scale. *Assessment, 6*(3), 269–284. doi:10.1177/107319119900600307 PMID:10445964

Granberg, A. G. (2005). *Strategy of development of macroregions of Russia*. Moscow: HSE.

Green, E. J., & Porter, R. H. (1984). Noncooperative collusion under imperfect price information. *Econometrica, 52*(1), 87–100. doi:10.2307/1911462

Greene, M. T., & Fielitz, B. D. (1977). Long-term Dependence in Common Stock Returns. *Journal of Financial Economics, 4*(3), 339–349. doi:10.1016/0304-405X(77)90006-X

Green, L., & Myerson, J. (2004). A discounting framework for choice with delayed and probabilistic rewards. *Psychological Bulletin, 130*(5), 769–792. doi:10.1037/0033-2909.130.5.769 PMID:15367080

Green, P. E. (1984). Hybrid Models for Conjoint Analysis: An Expository Review. *JMR, Journal of Marketing Research, 21*(2), 155. doi:10.2307/3151698

Green, P. E., Helsen, K., & Shandler, B. (1988). Conjoint Internal Validity under Alternative Profile Presentations. *The Journal of Consumer Research, 15*(3), 392–397. doi:10.1086/209177

Green, P. E., & Rao, V. R. (1971). Conjoint Measurement for Quantifying Judgmental Data. *JMR, Journal of Marketing Research, 8*(3), 355. doi:10.2307/3149575

Green, P. E., & Srinivasan, V. (1978). Conjoint Analysis in Consumer Research: Issues and Outlook. *The Journal of Consumer Research, 5*(2), 103–123. doi:10.1086/208721

Green, P. E., & Srinivasan, V. (1990). Conjoint Analysis in Marketing: New Developments with Implications for Research and Practice. *Journal of Marketing, 54*(4), 3. doi:10.2307/1251756

Grezes, J., & Decety, J. (2001). Functional Anatomy of Execution, Mental Simulation, Observation and Verb Generation of Actions: A Meta Analysis. *Human Brain Mapping, 12*(1), 1–19. doi:10.1002/1097-0193(200101)12:1<1::AID-HBM10>3.0.CO;2-V PMID:11198101

Griessinger, T., & Coricelli, G. (2015). The neuroeconomics of strategic interaction. *Current Opinion in Behavioral Sciences, 3*, 73–79. doi:10.1016/j.cobeha.2015.01.012

Grillon, C., & Davis, M. (1997). Effects of stress and shock anticipiation on prepulse Inhibition of the startle reflex. *Psychophysiology, 34*(5), 511–517. doi:10.1111/j.1469-8986.1997.tb01737.x PMID:9299905

Groome, D. (2014). *An Introduction to Cognitive Psychology: Processes and Disorders* (3rd ed.). New York: Psychology Press.

Grosenick, L., Greer, S., & Knutson, B. (2008). Interpretable classifiers for fMRI improve prediction of purchases. *IEEE Transactions on Neural Systems and Rehabilitation Engineering, 16*(6), 539–548. doi:10.1109/TNSRE.2008.926701 PMID:19144586

Grosjean, F. (1989). Neurolinguists, beware! The bilingual is not two monolinguals in one person. *Brain and Language, 36*(1), 3–15. doi:10.1016/0093-934X(89)90048-5 PMID:2465057

Grosjean, F. (1994). Individual bilingualism. In R. E. Asher (Ed.), *The encyclopedia of langauge and linguistics* (pp. 1656–1660). Oxford, UK: Pergamon Press.

Grover, R., & Vriens, M. (2006). *The Handbook of Marketing Research: Uses, Misuses, and Future Advances.* SAGE Publications.

Grubb, E. L., & Grathwohl, H. L. (1967). Consumer Self-Concept and Market Behavior : A Theoretical Symbolism Approach. *Journal of Marketing, 31*, 22–27. doi:10.2307/1249461

Grüne-Yanoff, T., & Lehtinen, A. (2010). Philosophy of game theory. *Philosophy of Economics, 13*, 467-513.

Gul, F., & Pesendorfer, W. (2008). The case for mindless economics. In A. Caplin & A. Shotter (Eds.), *The foundations of positive and normative economics* (pp. 3–39). Oxford, UK: Oxford University Press. doi:10.1093/acprof:oso/9780195328318.003.0001

Gutnik, L. A., Hakimzada, A. F., Yoskowitz, N. A., & Patel, V. L. (2006). The role of emotion in decision-making: A cognitive neuroeconomic approach towards understanding sexual risk behaviour. *Journal of Biomedical Informatics, 39*(6), 720–736. doi:10.1016/j.jbi.2006.03.002 PMID:16759915

Hageman, A. M. (2010). The role of confidence in tax return preparation using tax software. *Advances in Accounting Behavioral Research, 13*, 31–57. doi:10.1108/S1475-1488(2010)0000013006

Haile, P. A., Hortacsu, A., & Kosenok, G. (2008). On the empirical content of quantal response equilibrium. *The American Economic Review, 98*(1), 180–200. doi:10.1257/aer.98.1.180

Hall, P. A., & Taylor, R. C. R. (1996). *Political Science and the Three New Institutionalisms.* MPIFG Discussion Paper 96/9.

Halpern, J. Y., & Pass, R. (2015). Algorithmic rationality: Game theory with costly computation. *Journal of Economic Theory, 156*, 246–268. doi:10.1016/j.jet.2014.04.007

Harbaugh, W. T., Mayr, U., & Burghart, D. R. (2007). Neural responses to taxation and voluntary giving reveal motives for charitable donations. *Science, 316*(5831), 1622–1625. doi:10.1126/science.1140738 PMID:17569866

Hardie, B. G. S., Johnson, E. J., & Fader, P. S. (1993). Modeling loss aversion and reference dependence effects on brand choice. *Marketing Science, 12*(4), 378–394. doi:10.1287/mksc.12.4.378

Hare, T. A., Camerer, C. F., Knoepfle, D. T., & Rangel, A. (2010). Value computations in ventral medial prefrontal cortex during charitable decision making incorporate input from regions involved in social cognition. *The Journal of Neuroscience, 30*(2), 583–590. doi:10.1523/JNEUROSCI.4089-09.2010 PMID:20071521

Hare, T. A., Camerer, C. F., & Rangel, A. (2009). Self-control in decision-making involves modulation of the vmPFC valuation system. *Science, 324*(5927), 646–648. doi:10.1126/science.1168450 PMID:19407204

Hare, T. A., O'Doherty, J., Camerer, C. F., Schultz, W., & Rangel, A. (2008). Dissociating the role of the orbitofrontal cortex and the striatum in the computation of goal values and prediction errors. *The Journal of Neuroscience, 28*(22), 5623–5630. doi:10.1523/JNEUROSCI.1309-08.2008 PMID:18509023

Harley, A. T. (2008). *The Psychology Of Language* (3rd ed.). New York: Psychology Press.

Harlow, B., & Carter, M. (Eds.). (2003). *Archives of Empire-Volume II. The Scramble for Africa*. Durham, NC: Duke University Press. doi:10.1215/9780822385035

Harnick, F., van Dijk, E., van Beest, I., & Mersmann, P. (2007). When gains loom larger than losses: Reversed loss aversion for small amounts of money. *Psychological Science, 18*(12), 1099–1105. doi:10.1111/j.1467-9280.2007.02031.x PMID:18031418

Hartley, J. (2004). Case Study Research. In C. Cassell & G. Symon (Eds.), *Essential Guide to Qualitative Methods in Organisational Research* (pp. 323–333). London: SAGE Publications. doi:10.4135/9781446280119.n26

Hasik, W. (2008). Jakość informacji sprawozdawczych w kontekście rachunkowości behawioralnej a praktyka gospodarcza. *Prace Naukowe Akademii Ekonomicznej we Wrocławiu, 1199*, 20-27.

Hatfield, R. C., Jackson, S. B., & Vandervelde, S. D. (2011). The Effects of Prior Auditor Involvement and Client Pressure on Proposed Audit Adjustments. *Behavioral Research in Accounting, 23*(2), 117–130. doi:10.2308/bria-10064

Hayek, F. A. (1952). *The Sensory Order*. Chicago: Chicago University Press.

Haynie, J. M., Shepherd, D., Mosakowski, E., & Earley, P. C. (2010). A situated metacognitive model of the entrepreneurial mindset. *Journal of Business Venturing, 25*(2), 217–229. doi:10.1016/j.jbusvent.2008.10.001

Hechter, M., & Kanazawa, S. (1997). Sociological Rational Choice Theory. *Annual Review of Sociology, 23*(1), 191–214. doi:10.1146/annurev.soc.23.1.191

Hedgcock, W., & Rao, A. R. (2009). Trade-off aversion as an explanation for the attraction effect: A functional magnetic resonance study. *JMR, Journal of Marketing Research, 46*(1), 1–13. doi:10.1509/jmkr.46.1.1

Heeks, R. (2003). *Most eGovernment-for-Development Projects Fail: How Can the Risks be Reduced?* i-Government Working Paper Series, Paper No. 14, IDPM.

Heeks, R. (2002). Information Systems and Developing Countries: Failure, Success and Local Improvisations. *The Information Society, 18*(2), 101–112. doi:10.1080/01972240290075039

Hellmann, A. (2013). *Behavioral Accounting*. New York: Nova Science Publishers.

Helms, B. P., Kaen, F. R., & Rosenman, R. E. (1984). Memory in Commodity Futures Contracts. *Journal of Futures Markets, 4*(4), 559–567. doi:10.1002/fut.3990040408

Henrich, J. (2008). A cultural species. In M. Brown (Ed.), *Explaining Culture Scientifically* (pp. 184–210). Seattle, WA: University of Washington Press.

Henrich, J., Bowles, S., Boyd, R. T., Hopfensitz, A., Richerson, P. J., & Sigmund, K. (2003). Group report: The cultural and genetic evolution of human cooperation. In P. Hammerstein (Ed.), *Genetic and Cultural Evolution of Cooperation* (pp. 445–468). Cambridge, MA: MIT Press.

Henrich, J., & Boyd, R. (2002). On modeling cognition and culture. Why cultural evolution does not require replication of representations. *Journal of Cognition and Culture, 2*(2), 87–112. doi:10.1163/156853702320281836

Henrich, J., Boyd, R., Bowles, S., Camerer, C., Fehr, E., Gintis, H., & Tracer, D. et al. (2005). Economic man in cross-cultural perspective: Behavioral experiments in 15 small-scale societies. *Behavioral and Brain Sciences, 28*(6), 795–855. doi:10.1017/S0140525X05000142 PMID:16372952

Henrich, J., & Broesch, J. (2011). On the nature of cultural transmission networks: Evidence from Fijian villages for adaptive learning biases. *Philosophical Transactions of the Royal Society of London. Series B, Biological Sciences, 366*(1567), 1139–1148. doi:10.1098/rstb.2010.0323 PMID:21357236

Henrich, J., & Gil-White, F. (2001). The Evolution of Prestige: Freely conferred deference as a mechanism for enhancing the benefits of cultural transmission. *Evolution and Human Behavior, 22*(3), 165–196. doi:10.1016/S1090-5138(00)00071-4 PMID:11384884

Henrich, J., & McElreath, R. (2003). The Evolution of Cultural Evolution. *Evolutionary Anthropology, 12*(3), 123–135. doi:10.1002/evan.10110

Henrich, J., & McElreath, R. (2007). Dual Inheritance Theory: The Evolution of Human Cultural Capacities and Cultural Evolution. In R. Dunbar & L. Barret (Eds.), *Oxford Handbook of Evolutionary Psychology* (pp. 555–570). Oxford, UK: Oxford University Press. doi:10.1093/oxfordhb/9780198568308.013.0038

Henson, R. N. A. (2005). What can functional neuroimaging tell the experimental psychologist? *Quarterly Journal of Experimental Psychology, 58*(2), 193–233. doi:10.1080/02724980443000502 PMID:15903115

Henson, R. N. A., Rugg, M. D., Shallice, T., Josephs, O., & Dolan, R. (1999). Recollection and familiarity in recognition memory: An event-related fMRI study. *The Journal of Neuroscience, 19*(10), 3962–3972. PMID:10234026

Herbig, P., Koehler, W., & Day, K. (1993). Marketing to the baby bust generation. *Journal of Consumer Marketing, 10*(1), 4–9. doi:10.1108/07363769310026520

Heukelom, F. (2007). *Kahneman and Tversky and the Origin of Behavioral Economics.* Tinbergen Institute Discussion Paper, TI 2007-003/1. Retrieved on May 9, 2013, from: http://www.tinbergen.nl

Hickok, G. (2014). *The Myth of Mirror Neurons: The Real Neuroscience of Communication and Cognition.* New York: W.W. Norton & Company.

Hindriks, J., Keen, M., & Muthoo, A. (1999). Corruption, Extortion and Evasion. *Journal of Public Economics, 74*(3), 395–430. doi:10.1016/S0047-2727(99)00030-4

Hirschman, E. C., & LaBarbera, P. A. (1990). Dimensions of importance. *Psychology and Marketing, 7*(Fall), 215–233. doi:10.1002/mar.4220070306

Hodge, F., & Pronk, M. (2006). The impact of expertise and investment familiarity on investors' use of online financial reporting information. *Journal of Accounting, Auditing & Finance, 21*(3), 267–292.

Hoffman, M. B. (2004). The neuroeconomic path of the law. *Philosophical Transactions of the Royal Society of London. Series B, Biological Sciences, 359*(1451), 1667–1676. doi:10.1098/rstb.2004.1540 PMID:15590608

Hofstede, G. (2001). *Culture's Consequences: Comparing Values, Behaviors, Institutions and Organizations across Nations.* Thousand Oaks, CA: Sage Publications.

Hofstede, G., Hofstede, G. J., & Minkov, M. (2010). *Cultures and Organizations: Software of the Mind. Revised and expanded* (3rd ed.). New York: McGraw-Hill.

Holbrook, M. B. (1994). The Nature of Customer Value: An Axiology of Services in the Consumption Experience. In *Service Quality*. Thousand Oaks, CA: SAGE Publications. doi:10.4135/9781452229102.n2

Holbrook, M. B. (1994). *The nature of customer value: An axiology of services in the consumption experience*. Thousand Oaks, CA: Sage Publications.

Holland, P. C., & Gallagher, M. (1999). Amygdala circuitry in attentional and representational processes. *Trends in Cognitive Sciences*, 3(2), 65–73. doi:10.1016/S1364-6613(98)01271-6 PMID:10234229

Holt-Lunstad, J., Smith, T. B., & Layton, J. B. (2010). Social relationships and mortality risk: A meta-analytic review. *PLoS Medicine*, 7(7), e1000316. doi:10.1371/journal.pmed.1000316 PMID:20668659

Hong, J. W., & Zinkan, G. M. (1995). Self-concept a advertising effectiveness: The influence of congruency, conspicuousness and response mode. *Psychology and Marketing*, 12(1), 53–78. doi:10.1002/mar.4220120105

Hoskins, C., McFadyen, S., & Finn, A. (2004). *Media Economics: Applying Economics to New and Traditional Media*. http://doi.org/.<ALIGNMENT.qj></ALIGNMENT>10.4135/9781452233109

House, J. S. (2001). Social isolation kills, but how and why? *Psychosomatic Medicine*, 63(2), 273–274. doi:10.1097/00006842-200103000-00011 PMID:11292275

House, J. S., Landis, K. R., & Umberson, D. (1988). Social relationships and health. *Science*, 241(4865), 540–545. doi:10.1126/science.3399889 PMID:3399889

Houser, D., & Kevin, M. (2008). Introduction to Neuroeconomics. In D. Houser & M. Kevin (Eds.), *Neuroeconomics* (pp. 15–21). London, UK: Emerald Group Publishing Limited. doi:10.1016/S0731-2199(08)20014-2

Hsu, M., Bhatt, M., Adolphs, R., Tranel, D., & Camerer, C. F. (2005). Neural systems responding to degrees of uncertainty in human decision-making. *Science*, 310(5754), 1680–1683. doi:10.1126/science.1115327 PMID:16339445

Huber, J. (1987). Conjoint Analysis: How we got here and where we are. In *Proceedings of the Sawtooth Software Conference on Perpetual Mapping, Conjoint Analysis, and Computer Interviewing* (pp. 237–252). Ketchum, ID: Sawtooth Software.

Huber, J., & Hansen, D. (1986). Testing the impact of dimensional complexity and affective differences of paired concepts in adaptive conjoint analysis. *Advances in Consumer Research. Association for Consumer Research (U. S.)*, 14, 159–163.

Huber, J., Wittink, D. R., Fiedler, J. A., & Miller, R. (1993). The Effectiveness of Alternative Preference Elicitation Procedures in Predicting Choice. *JMR, Journal of Marketing Research*, 30(1), 105. doi:10.2307/3172517

Hubert, M. (2010). Does neuroeconomics give new impetus to economic and consumer research? *Journal of Economic Psychology*, 31(5), 812–817. doi:10.1016/j.joep.2010.03.009

Hubner, R., Steinhauser, M., & Lehle, C. (2010). A dual-stage two-phase model of selective attention. *Psychological Review*, 117(3), 759–784. doi:10.1037/a0019471 PMID:20658852

Hunter, M. (2013). Creativity and Making Connections: The Patchwork of Entrepreneurial Opportunity. *Psychological Issues in Human Resources Management*, 1(2), 7–51.

Hurford, J. R. (1991). The evolution of the critical period for language acquisition. *Cognition*, 40(3), 159–201. doi:10.1016/0010-0277(91)90024-X PMID:1786674

Hursh, S. R. (1984). Behavioral economics. *Journal of the Experimental Analysis of Behavior*, 42(3), 435–452. doi:10.1901/jeab.1984.42-435 PMID:16812401

Hurst, H. E. (1951). Long-term Storage of Reservoirs: An Experimental Study. *Transactions of the American Society of Civil Engineers, 116,* 770–799.

Hwang, J., Kim, S., & Lee, D. (2009). Temporal discounting and inter-temporal choice in rhesus monkeys. *Frontiers in Behavioral Neuroscience, 3*(9), 1–13. PMID:19562091

Immergut, E. M. (1998). The Theoretical Core of New Institutionalism. *Politics & Society, 26*(5), 5–34. doi:10.1177/0032329298026001002

Ingenhoff, D., & Koelling, A. M. (2012). Media governance and corporate social responsibility of media organizations: An international comparison. *Business Ethics (Oxford, England), 21*(2), 154–167. doi:10.1111/j.1467-8608.2011.01646.x

Innocenti, A., & Sbriglia, P. (2008). *Games, Rationality and Behaviour: Essays on Behavioural Game Theory and Experiments.* New York, NY: Palgrave Macmillan.

Inshakova, E. I., & Samokhin, A. V. (2008). Sustainable development of the macroregion: Methodological and theoretical aspects of research. *Herald of Volgograd State University. Series 3, 1*(12), 80–85.

Isaac-Henry, K. (1997). Development and Change in the Public Sector. In K. Isaac-Henry, C. Painter, & C. Barnes (Eds.), *Management in the Public Sector: Challenge and Change* (pp. 1–25). London: International Thomson Business Press.

Izuma, K., Saito, D. N., & Sadato, N. (2010). Processing of the incentive for social approval in the ventral striatum during charitable donation. *Journal of Cognitive Neuroscience, 22*(4), 621–631. doi:10.1162/jocn.2009.21228 PMID:19320552

Jacko, J. A., Yi, J. S., Sainfort, F., & McClellan, M. (2012). Human Factors and Ergonomic Methods. In G. Salvendy (Ed.), *Handbook of Human Factors and Ergonomics* (4th ed.; pp. 289–329). John Wiley and Sons. doi:10.1002/9781118131350.ch10

Jaruga, A. (1997). Jarosław Wiaczesławowicz Sokołow: Rachunkowość. Od źródeł do naszych dni. *Zeszyty Teoretyczne Rady Naukowej, 42,* 12–16.

Jason, P. (2014). Questions and Answers with Antonio Damasio. *MIT's Technology Review, 117*(4), 48–51.

Jaworska, E. (2014). Perspektywa behawioralna w rachunkowości w świetle wybranych teorii psychologii motywacji. *Zeszyty Naukowe Uniwersytetu Szczecińskiego. Finanse. Rynki finansowe. Ubezpieczenia, 70,* 49–58.

Jeankins, A., Neil Macrae, C., & Mitchell, J. (2008). Repetition suppression of ventromedial prefrontal activity during judgments of self and others. *Proceedings of the National Academy of Sciences of the United States of America, 105*(11), 4507–4512. doi:10.1073/pnas.0708785105 PMID:18347338

Johnson, R. M. (1987). Adaptive Conjoint Analysis. *Sawtooth Software Conference on Perpetual Mapping, Conjoint Analysis, and Computer Interviewing* (pp. 253–265). Ketchum, ID: Sawtooth Software.

Johnson, R. N., & Libecap, G. D. (1994). The Federal Civil Service System and the Problem of Bureaucracy. Chicago, IL: University of Chicago Press. doi:10.7208/chicago/9780226401775.001.0001

Johnson, E. J., & Goldstein, D. (2003). Do defaults save lives? *Science, 302*(5649), 1338–1339. doi:10.1126/science.1091721 PMID:14631022

Johnson, E. J., Shu, S. B., Dellaert, B. G. C., Fox, C., Goldstein, D. G., Häubl, G., & Weber, E. U. et al. (2012). Beyond Nudges: Tools of a Choice Architecture. *Marketing Letters, 23*(2), 487–504. doi:10.1007/s11002-012-9186-1

Kable, J.W., & Glimcher, P.W. (2009). The neurobiology of decision: Consensus and controversy. *Neuron, 63,* 733–745.

Kabalski, P. (2012). *Wybrane problemy stosowania Międzynarodowych Standardów Sprawozdawczości Finansowej w Polsce. Organizacja, kultura, osobowość, język.* Łódź: Wydawnictwo Uniwersytetu Łódzkiego.

Kabalski, P., Wyganowska, M., & Tobór-Osadnik, K. (2012). Międzynarodowe Standardy Sprawozdawczości Finansowej a homo sovieticus i postawy pracownicze polskich księgowych. *Zeszyty Teoretyczne Rachunkowości, 65,* 71–98.

Kable, J. W., & Glimcher, P. W. (2007). The neural correlates of subjective value during intertemporal choice. *Nature Neuroscience, 10*(12), 1625–1633. doi:10.1038/nn2007 PMID:17982449

Kahneman, D. (1994). New Challenges to the Rationality Assumption. *Journal of Institutional and Theoretical Economics, 150*(1), 18–44.

Kahneman, D. (2003a). Perspective on Judgment and Choice: Mapping Bounded Rationality. *The American Psychologist, 58*(9), 697–720. doi:10.1037/0003-066X.58.9.697 PMID:14584987

Kahneman, D. (2003b). Maps of Bounded Rationality: Psychology for Behavioral Economics. *The American Economic Review, 93*(5), 1449–1475. doi:10.1257/000282803322655392

Kahneman, D. (2011). *Thinking Fast And Slow - The Neuroscience Behind Good Decision-Making.* New York: Penguin Books.

Kahneman, D., & Lovallo, D. (1993). Timid choices and bold forecasts: A cognitive perspective on risk taking. *Management Science, 39*(1), 17–31. doi:10.1287/mnsc.39.1.17

Kahneman, D., Slovic, P., & Tversky, A. (1982). *Judgment under uncertainty: Heuristics and biases.* Cambridge, UK: Cambridge University Press. doi:10.1017/CBO9780511809477

Kahneman, D., & Thaler, R. (1991). Economic Analysis and the Psychology of Utility: Applications to Compensation Policy. *The American Economic Review, 81*(2), 341–346.

Kahneman, D., & Tversky, A. (1974). Judgment Under Uncertainty: Heuristics and Biases. *Science, 185*(4157), 1124–1131. doi:10.1126/science.185.4157.1124 PMID:17835457

Kahneman, D., & Tversky, A. (1979). Prospect theory: An analysis of decisions under risk. *Econometrica, 47*(2), 263–291. doi:10.2307/1914185

Kahneman, D., & Tversky, A. (1991). Loss Aversion in Riskless Choice: A Reference Dependent Model. *The Quarterly Journal of Economics, 106*(4), 1039–1061. doi:10.2307/2937956

Kahneman, D., & Tversky, A. (Eds.). (2000). *Choices, values and frames.* New York: Cambridge University Press.

Kahneman, D., & Tversky, A. (Eds.). (2002). *Choices, Values and Frames.* Cambridge, MA: Cambridge University Press.

Kahneman, D., Wakker, P. P., & Sarin, R. (1997). Back to Bentham? Explorations of experienced utility. *The Quarterly Journal of Economics, 112*(2), 375–405. doi:10.1162/003355397555235

Kajanova, J. (2006). The relationship between business finance and accounting. *VADYBA (Management), 2,* 58–64.

Kalenscher, T., & van Wingerden, M. (2011). Why we should use animals to study economic decision making: A perspective. *Frontiers in Neuroscience, 5*(82), 1–11. PMID:21731558

Kaplan, S. E., Pourciau, S., & Reckers, Ph. M. J. (1990). An Examination of the Effect of the President's Letter and Stock Advisory Service Information on Financial Decisions. *Behavioral Research in Accounting, 2,* 63–92.

Karabatsos, G. (2001). The Rasch model, additive conjoint measurement, and new models of probabilistic measurement theory. *Journal of Applied Measurement, 2*(4), 389–423. PMID:12011506

Karakaya, F., & Awasthi, A. (2014). Robustness and sensitivity of conjoint analysis versus multiple linear regression analysis. *International Journal of Data Analysis Techniques and Strategies, 6*(2), 121. doi:10.1504/IJDATS.2014.062461

Kardes, F. R. (1994). Consumer judgment and decision processes. In R. S. Wyer & T. K. Srull (Eds.), Handbook of social cognition (pp. 399–466). Hillsdale, NJ: Lawrence Erlbaum Associates.

Kasser, T., & Ahuvia, A. (2002). Materialistic values and well-being in business students. *European Journal of Social Psychology, 32*(1), 137–146. doi:10.1002/ejsp.85

Katsko, I. A., Krepishev, D.A., & Sennikova, A.E. (2011). Elements of the theory of multi-criteria decision making in system research. *Scientific Journal Proceedings of the Kuban State Agrarian University, 5*, 7-13.

Kauffman, S. A. (1993). *The origins of order: Self-organization and selection in evolution.* New York: Oxford University Press.

Kay, P., & Kempton, W. (1984). *What is the Sapir-Whorf Hypothesis?* Arlington, TX: American Anthropological Association.

Kebritchi, M., Hirumi, A., & Bai, H. (2010). The effects of modern mathematics computer games on mathematics achievement and class motivation. *Computers & Education, 55*(2), 427–443. doi:10.1016/j.compedu.2010.02.007

Kecskes, I., & Albertazzi, L. (Eds.). (2007). *Cognitive Aspects of Bilingualism.* Amsterdam: Springer. doi:10.1007/978-1-4020-5935-3

Keeney, R. L. (1996). Value-Focused Thinking: Identifying Decision Opportunities and Creating Alternatives. *European Journal of Operational Research, 92*(3), 537–549. doi:10.1016/0377-2217(96)00004-5

Kemp, C. (2009). Defining multilingualism. In L. Aronin & B. Hufeisen (Eds.), *The exploration of multilingualism* (pp. 11–26). Amsterdam: John Benjamins. doi:10.1075/aals.6.02ch2

Kenman, H. (1996). Konkordanzdemokratie und Korporatismus aus der Perspektive eines rationalen Institutionalismus. *Politische Vierteljahresschrift, 37*, 494–515.

Kenning, P., & Plassmann, H. (2005). NeuroEconomics: An overview from an economic perspective. *Brain Research Bulletin, 67*(5), 343–354. doi:10.1016/j.brainresbull.2005.07.006 PMID:16216680

Kenning, P., Plassmann, H., & Ahlert, D. (2007). Applications of functional magnetic resonance imaging for market research. *Qualitative Market Research, 10*(2), 135–152. doi:10.1108/13522750710740817

Kermer, D. A., Driver-Linn, E., Wilson, T. D., & Gilbert, D. T. (2006). Loss aversion is an affective forecasting error. *Psychological Science, 17*(8), 649–653. doi:10.1111/j.1467-9280.2006.01760.x PMID:16913944

Keršienė, K., & Savanevičienė, A. (2005). Defining and Understanding Organizational Multicultural Competence. *The Engineering Economist, 2*(42), 45–52.

Keynes, J. M. (1971). The collected writings of John Maynard Keynes: *The General Theory of Employment, Interest, and Money* (vol. 7). London: Macmilian.

Kicia, M. (2006). Cechy indywidualne a stosunek do ryzyka w świetle teorii finansów behawioralnych. *Współczesne problemy finansów, bankowości i ubezpieczeń w teorii i praktyce, 1*, 367-376.

Kida, T., Smith, J. F., & Maletta, M. (1998). The effects of encoded memory traces for numerical data on accounting decision making. *Accounting, Organizations and Society, 23*(5-6), 451–466. doi:10.1016/S0361-3682(98)00003-8

Kilbourne, W., & Pickett, G. (2008). How materialism affects environmental beliefs, concern, and environmentally responsible behavior. *Journal of Business Research*, *61*(9), 885–893. doi:10.1016/j.jbusres.2007.09.016

Kim, S., Hwang, J., & Lee, D. (2008). Prefrontal coding of temporally discounted values during intertemporal choice. *Neuron*, *59*(1), 161–172. doi:10.1016/j.neuron.2008.05.010 PMID:18614037

Kim, S., & Lee, D. (2011). Prefrontal cortex and impulsive decision making. *Biological Psychiatry*, *69*(12), 1140–1146. doi:10.1016/j.biopsych.2010.07.005 PMID:20728878

King-Casas, B. et al.. (2005). Getting to know you: Reputation and trust in a two-person economic exchange. *Science*, *308*(5718), 78–83. doi:10.1126/science.1108062 PMID:15802598

King-Casas, B., & Chiu, P. H. (2012). Understanding interpersonal function in psychiatric illness through multiplayer economic games. *Biological Psychiatry*, *72*(2), 119–125. doi:10.1016/j.biopsych.2012.03.033 PMID:22579510

King-Casas, B., Sharp, C., Lomax-Bream, L., Lohrenz, T., Fonagy, P., & Montague, P. R. (2008). The rupture and repair of cooperation in borderline personality disorder. *Science*, *321*(5890), 806–810. doi:10.1126/science.1156902 PMID:18687957

Kirby, K. N. (1997). Bidding on the future: Evidence against normative discounting of delayed rewards. *Journal of Experimental Psychology: General*, *126*(1), 54–70. doi:10.1037/0096-3445.126.1.54

Kirchler, E. (2007). *The Economic Psychology of Tax Behaviour*. Cambridge, UK: Cambridge University Press. doi:10.1017/CBO9780511628238

Kiselyova, N. N. (2007). *Sustainable development of socio-economic system of the region: methodology of research, model, management*. Rostov-on-Don: Publishing house of Southern Federal University.

Kjellberg, H., & Helgesson, C.-F. (2006). Multiple Versions of Markets: Multiplicity and Performativity in Market Practice. *Industrial Marketing Management*, *35*(7), 839–855. doi:10.1016/j.indmarman.2006.05.011

Kleiner, G. B. (Ed.). (2011). *Meso-economy of Development*. Moscow: Central Economics and Mathematics Institute RAS.

Klemperer, P. (2004). *Auctions: Theory and Practice*. Economics Papers 2004-W09, Economics Group. Nuffield College, University of Oxford.

Klucharev, V. A., Smidts, A., & Shestakova, A. N. (2011). Neuroeconomics. The Neurobiology of Decision-making. *Experimental Psychology*, *4*(2), 14–35.

Klyucharev, V. A., Smits, A., & Shestakova, A. N. (2011). Neuroeconomics: The neurobiology of Decision-making. *Experimental Psychology*, *4*(2), 14–25.

Knoll, M. A. Z. (2010). The Role of Behavioral Economics and Behavioral Decision- Making in Americans' Retirement Savings Decisions. *Social Security Bulletin*, *70*(4), 1–23. PMID:21261167

Knutson, B., Adams, C. M., Fong, G. W., & Hommer, D. (2001). Anticipation of increasing monetary reward selectively recruits nucleus accumbens. *The Journal of Neuroscience*, *21*, RC159. PMID:11459880

Knutson, B., Bhanji, J. P., Cooney, R. E., Atlas, L. Y., & Gotlib, I. H. (2008). Neural responses to monetary incentives in major depression. *Biological Psychiatry*, *63*(7), 686–692. doi:10.1016/j.biopsych.2007.07.023 PMID:17916330

Knutson, B., & Bossaerts, P. (2007). Neural antecedents of financial decisions. *The Journal of Neuroscience*, *27*(31), 8174–8177. doi:10.1523/JNEUROSCI.1564-07.2007 PMID:17670962

Knutson, B., & Peterson, R. (2005). Neurally reconstructing expected utility. *Games and Economic Behavior*, *52*(2), 305–315. doi:10.1016/j.geb.2005.01.002

Knutson, B., Rick, S., Wimmer, G. E., Prelec, D., & Loewenstein, G. (2007). Neural predictors of purchases. *Neuron*, *53*(1), 147–156. PMID:17196537

Knutson, B., Taylor, J., Kaufman, M., Peterson, R., & Glover, G. (2005). Distributed neural representation of expected value. *The Journal of Neuroscience*, *25*(19), 4806–4812. doi:10.1523/JNEUROSCI.0642-05.2005 PMID:15888656

Knutson, B., Westdorp, A., Kaiser, E., & Hommer, D. (2000). FMRI visualization of brain activity during a monetary incentive delay task. *NeuroImage*, *12*(1), 20–27. doi:10.1006/nimg.2000.0593 PMID:10875899

Knutson, B., Wimmer, G. E., Kuhnen, C. M., & Winkielman, P. (2008). Nucleus Accumbens Activation Mediates the Influence of Reward Cues on Financial Risk Taking. *Neuroreport*, *19*(5), 509–513. doi:10.1097/WNR.0b013e3282f85c01 PMID:18388729

Knyazeva, S. N., & Kurdyumov, S. P. (1999). Synergetics in the context of sustainable development of complex systems. In C. A. Koptyug, V. M. Matrosov, & V. K. Levashov (Eds.), *A new paradigm of development of Russia (the complex problems of sustainable development)* (pp. 340–344). Moscow: Publishing House Academy.

Koenigs, M., & Tranel, D. (2007). Prefrontal cortex damage abolishes brand-cued changes in cola preference. *Social Cognitive and Affective Neuroscience*, *3*(1), 1–6. doi:10.1093/scan/nsm032 PMID:18392113

Kolesnikov, Y.S. (2009). *Strategic planning for socio-economic development of region in the conditions of modernization*. Rostov-on-Don: Publishing house of Southern Federal University.

Kornai, J. (1998). *The System Paradigm*. William Davidson Institute Working Papers. Series 278. William Davidson Institute at the University.

Kosfeld, M., Heinrichs, M., Zak, P. J., Fischbacher, U., & Fehr, E. (2005). Oxytocin increases trust in humans. *Nature*, *435*(7042), 673–676. doi:10.1038/nature03701 PMID:15931222

Koutsoyiannis, A. (1979). *Modern microeconomics* (2nd ed.). London: Macmillan Press Ltd. doi:10.1007/9781349160778

Kozlowski, S. W. J., Gully, S. M., Nason, E. R., & Smith, E. M. (1999). Developing adaptive teams: A theory of compilation and performance across levels and time. In D. R. Ilgen & E. D. Pulakos (Eds.), *The changing nature of work performance: Implications for staffing, personnel actions, and development* (pp. 240–292). San Francisco, CA: Jossey-Bass.

Krajbich, I., Adolphs, R., Tranel, D., Denburg, N. L., & Camerer, C. F. (2009). Economic games quantify diminished sense of guilt in patients with damage to the prefrontal cortex. *The Journal of Neuroscience*, *29*(7), 2188–2192. doi:10.1523/JNEUROSCI.5086-08.2009 PMID:19228971

Krajbich, I., Armel, C., & Rangel, A. (2010). Visual fixations and the computation and comparison of value in simple choice. *Nature Neuroscience*, *13*(10), 1292–1298. doi:10.1038/nn.2635 PMID:20835253

Krawczyk, M. (2011). Pożytek z neuroekonomii. *Decyzje*, *15*, 43–59.

Kringelbach, M. L. (2005). The human orbitofrontal cortex: Linking reward to hedonic experience. *Nature Reviews Neuroscience*, *6*(9), 691–702. doi:10.1038/nrn1747 PMID:16136173

Kringelbach, M. L., & Berridge, K. C. (2010). *Pleasures of the brain*. New York, NY: Oxford University Press.

Kringelbach, M. L., & Rolls, E. T. (2004). The functional neuroanatomy of the human orbitofrontal cortex: Evidence from neuroimaging and neuropsychology. *Progress in Neurobiology*, *72*(5), 341–372. doi:10.1016/j.pneurobio.2004.03.006 PMID:15157726

Krishna, A., Wagner, M., Yoon, C., & Adaval, R. (2006). Effects of Extreme-Priced Products on consumer Reservation Prices. *Journal of Consumer Psychology*, *16*(2), 176–190. doi:10.1207/s15327663jcp1602_8

Krishnan, R., & Booke, M. (2002). Investors' use of analysts' recommendations. *Behavioral Research in Accounting*, *14*(1), 129–156. doi:10.2308/bria.2002.14.1.129

Kudryavtsev, A., Cohen, G., & Hon-Snir, S. (2013). Rational or Intuitive: Are Behavioral Biases Correlated Across Stock Market Investors? *Contemporary Economics*, *7*(2), 31–53. doi:10.5709/ce.1897-9254.81

Kuhnen, C. M., & Knutson, B. (2005). The neural basis of financial risk taking. *Neuron*, *47*(5), 763–770. doi:10.1016/j.neuron.2005.08.008 PMID:16129404

Kuhnen, C. M., & Knutson, B. (2011). The Influence of Affect on Beliefs, Preferences, and Financial Decisions. *Journal of Financial and Quantitative Analysis*, *46*(3), 605–626. doi:10.1017/S0022109011000123

Kuisma, T. (2008). *Conspicuous consumption: a comparison between Finnish and Malaysian luxury good consumers.* Unpublished MBA Project Management Report, Universiti Sains Malaysia.

Kurzban, R. (2011). *Why everyone (else) is a hypocrite: Evolution and the modular mind.* Princeton, NJ: Princeton University Press. doi:10.1515/9781400835997

Kuutti, K. (1996). Activity Theory as a Potential Framework for Human Computer Interaction Research. In B. A. Nardi (Ed.), *Context and Consciousness: Activity Theory and Human Computer Interaction* (pp. 17–44). Boston, MA: M.I.T. Press.

Lacy, S., & Bauer, J. M. (2006). Future Directions for Media Economics Research. In A. B. Albarran, S. M. Chan-Olmsted, & O. Wirth (Eds.), *Handbook of Media Management and Economics* (pp. 655–674). Mahwah, NJ: Lawrence Erlbaum Associates, Inc.

Lades, L. K. (2012). Towards an incentive salience model of intertemporal choice. *Journal of Economic Psychology*, *33*(4), 833–841. doi:10.1016/j.joep.2012.03.007

Laibson, D. (1997). Golden eggs and hyperbolic discounting. *The Quarterly Journal of Economics*, *112*(2), 443–477. doi:10.1162/003355397555253

Laland, K., Odling-Smee, J., & Myles, S. (2010). How culture shaped the human genome: Brinding genetics and the human sciences together. *Nature Reviews. Genetics*, *11*(2), 137–148. doi:10.1038/nrg2734 PMID:20084086

Lancaster, K. J. (1966). A New Approach to Consumer Theory. *Journal of Political Economy*, 74.

Laufs, H., & Tagliazucchi, E. (2014). Beware of sleep during resting state fMRI. *F1000Posters, 5*(806).

Laver, M., & Schofield, N. (1990). *Multiparty Government: The Politics of Coalition in Europe.* Oxford, UK: Oxford University Press.

Law, J., & Urry, J. (2004). Enacting the Social. *Economy and Society*, *33*(3), 390–410. doi:10.1080/0308514042000225716

Lee, N., Broderick, A. J., & Chamberlain, L. (2007). What is "neuromarketing"? A discussion and agenda for future research. *International Journal of Psychophysiology*, *63*(2), 199–204. doi:10.1016/j.ijpsycho.2006.03.007 PMID:16769143

Leigh, T. W., MacKay, D. B., & Summers, J. O. (1984). Reliability and Validity of Conjoint Analysis and Self-Explicated Weights: A Comparison. *JMR, Journal of Marketing Research*, *21*(4), 456. doi:10.2307/3151471

Leknes, S., & Tracey, I. (2008). A common neurobiology for pain and pleasure. *Nature Reviews Neuroscience*, *9*(4), 314–320. doi:10.1038/nrn2333 PMID:18354400

Lerner, J. S., Small, D. A., & Loewenstein, G. (2004). Heart strings and purse strings: Carryover effects of emotions on economic decisions. *Psychological Science*, *15*(5), 337–341. doi:10.1111/j.0956-7976.2004.00679.x PMID:15102144

Lerner, J. S., & Tiedens, L. Z. (2006). Portrait of the angry decision maker: How appraisal tendencies shape anger's influence on cognition. *Journal of Behavioral Decision Making*, *19*(2), 115–137. doi:10.1002/bdm.515

Lewis, B. L., Shields, M. D., & Young, S. M. (1983). Evaluating human judgements and decisions aids. *Journal of Accounting Research*, *13*(1), 271–285. doi:10.2307/2490947

Leyton, M. (2010). The neurobiology of desire: Dopamine and the regulation of mood and motivational states in humans. In M. L. Kringelbach & K. C. Berridge (Eds.), *Pleasures of the brain* (pp. 222–243). New York, NY: Oxford University Press.

Libby, R. (1985). Availability and the generation of hypotheses in analytic review. *Journal of Accounting Research*, *23*(2), 648–667. doi:10.2307/2490831

Liben, L. S., & Müller, U. (2015). *Handbook of Child Psychology and Developmental Science*. New York: Wiley & Sons, Inc.

Liberman, N., & Trope, Y. (1998). The role of feasibility and desirability considerations in near and distant future decisions: A test of temporal construal theory. *Journal of Personality and Social Psychology*, *75*(1), 5–18. doi:10.1037/0022-3514.75.1.5 PMID:11195890

Lindquist, M. A., Loh, J. M., Atlas, L. Y., & Wager, T. D. (2009). Modeling the Hemodynamic Response Function in fMRI: Efficiency, Bias and Mis-modeling. *NeuroImage*, *45*(1Suppl), S187–S198. doi:10.1016/j.neuroimage.2008.10.065 PMID:19084070

Lindstrom, M. (2010). *Buy Ology: Truth and Lies about Why We Buy*. New York: Broadway Books.

Ling, C., Na-na, Y., & Yun-shan, S. (2014). The application of game theory in the Hercynian economic development. In *Management Science & Engineering (ICMSE), 2014 International Conference on* (pp. 794-799). IEEE.

List, J. A. (2003). Does market experience eliminate market anomalies? *The Quarterly Journal of Economics*, *118*(1), 41–71. doi:10.1162/00335530360535144

Loasby, B. J. (2004). Hayek's Theory of the Mind. *Evolutionary Psychology and Economic Theory. Advances in Austrian Economics*, *7*, 101–134. doi:10.1016/S1529-2134(04)07006-1

Loewenstein, G. F. (1996). Out of control: Visceral influences on behavior. *Organizational Behavior and Human Decision Processes*, *65*(3), 272–292. doi:10.1006/obhd.1996.0028

Loewenstein, G. F., Rick, S., & Cohen, J. D. (2008). Neuroeconomics. *Annual Review of Psychology*, *59*(1), 647–672. doi:10.1146/annurev.psych.59.103006.093710 PMID:17883335

Loewenstein, G. F., Weber, E. U., Hsee, C. K., & Welch, N. (2001). Risk as feelings. *Psychological Bulletin*, *127*(2), 267–286. doi:10.1037/0033-2909.127.2.267 PMID:11316014

Long, N. E. (1958). The Local Community as an Ecology of Games. *American Journal of Sociology*, *64*(3), 251–261. doi:10.1086/222468

Lotov, A. V., Bushenkov, V. A., & Kamenev, G. K. (2004). *Interactive decision maps. Approximation and Visualization of Pareto Frontier. In Appl. Optimization* (Vol. 89). Boston: Kluwer Academic Publishers.

Louie, K., Khaw, M. W., & Glimcher, P. W. (2013). Normalization is a general neural mechanism for context-dependent decision making. *Proceedings of the National Academy of Sciences of the United States of America*, *110*(15), 6139–6144. doi:10.1073/pnas.1217854110 PMID:23530203

Luo, Y. (2004a). A coopetition perspective of MNC–host government relations. *Journal of International Management*, *10*(4), 431–451. doi:10.1016/j.intman.2004.08.004

Luo, Y. (2004b). *Coopetition in international business*. Copenhagen, Denmark: Copenhagen Business School Press.

Luo, Y. (2005). Toward coopetition within a multinational enterprise: A perspective from foreign subsidiaries. *Journal of World Business*, *40*(1), 71–90. doi:10.1016/j.jwb.2004.10.006

Lyttle, A. D. (2009). *Making Sense of Cultural Complexity: An Experimental Study of Third Culture Individuals' Interpersonal Sensitivity as a Result of Intercultural Adaptation*. (Unpublished Master's Thesis). University of Liberty.

Mac-Dermott, R., & Mornah, D. (2015). The Role of Culture in Foreign Direct Investment and Trade: Expectations from the GLOBE Dimensions of Culture. *Open Journal of Business and Management*, *3*(01), 63–74. doi:10.4236/ojbm.2015.31007

MacKillop, J. (2013). Integrating behavioral economics and behavioral genetics: Delayed reward discounting as an endophenotype for addictive disorders. *Journal of the Experimental Analysis of Behavior*, *99*(1), 14–31. doi:10.1002/jeab.4 PMID:23344986

Malabou, C. (2010). *Plasticity at the Dusk of Writing: Dialectic, Destruction, Deconstruction*. New York: Columbia University Press.

Malhotra, N. K. (1982). Structural Reliability and Stability of Nonmetric Conjoint Analysis. *JMR, Journal of Marketing Research*, *19*(2), 199–207. doi:10.2307/3151620

Mandelbrot, B. B., & van Ness, J. W. (1968). Fractional Brownian Motion, Fractional Noises, and Application. *SIAM Review*, *10*(4), 422–437. doi:10.1137/1010093

March, J. G. (1982). Theories of choice and making decisions. *Society*, *20*(1), 29–39. doi:10.1007/BF02694989

March, J. G., & Olsen, J. P. (1984). The New Institutionalism: Organisational Factors in Political Life. *The American Political Science Review*, *78*(3), 734–749. doi:10.2307/1961840

March, J. G., & Olsen, J. P. (1989). *Rediscovering Institutions: The Organisational Basis of Politics*. New York: The Free Press.

Marcoux, J.-S., Filiatrault, P., & Cheron, E. (1997). The attitudes underlying preferences of young urban educated polish consumers towards products made in Western countries. *Journal of International Consumer Marketing*, *9*(4), 5–29. doi:10.1300/J046v09n04_02

Markman, A. B., & Moreau, C. P. (2001). Analogy and analogical comparison in choice. In D. Gentner, K. J. Holyoak, & B. N. Kokinov (Eds.), *The Analogical Mind: Perspectives from Cognitive Science*. Cambridge, MA: MIT Press.

Markowitz, H. M. (1952). Portfolio Selection. *The Journal of Finance*, *7*(1), 77–91.

Martin, A. S. (1993). Makers, buyers, and users: Consumerism as a material culture framework. *Winterthur Portfolio*, *28*(2/3), 141–157. doi:10.1086/496612

Masicampo, E. J., & Baumeister, R. F. (2008). Toward a Physiology of Dual-Process Reasoning and Judgment: Lemonade, Willpower, and Expensive Rule-Based Analysis. *Psychological Science*, *19*(3), 255–260. doi:10.1111/j.1467-9280.2008.02077.x PMID:18315798

Maskin, E., & Tirole, J. (2004). The Politician and the Judge: Accountability in Government. *The American Economic Review, 94*(4), 1034–1054. doi:10.1257/0002828042002606

Matsumoto, D. (1990). Cultural Similarities and Differences in Display Rules. *Motivation and Emotion, 14*(3), 195–214. doi:10.1007/BF00995569

Maturana, H. R. (1978). Biology of Language: The Epistemology of Reality. In G. A. Miller & E. Lenneberg (Eds.), *Psychology and Biology of Language and Thought*. New York: Academic Press.

Matuska, E., & Landowska, A. (2015). Cooperation as a core competency. The neuro-economic approach. In *Proceedings of Scientific Papers, 12th International Scientific Conference Human Potential Development* (pp. 136-148). Klaipeda: Klaipeda University Press. Retrieved on June 2, 2015, from: http://frcatel.fri.uniza.sk/hrme/ConfHPM/index.html\

Matuska, E. (2015). Competence Management in frame of human capital management. In A. Sokół (Ed.), *Managing diversity in the organization. Creativity- Competence- Knowledge- Trust* (pp. 51–76). London: Sciemcee Publications.

McCabe, K. A. (2008). Neuroeconomics and the economic sciences. *Economics and Philosophy, 24*(3), 345–368. doi:10.1017/S0266267108002010

McCabe, K. A., Houser, D., Ryan, L., Smith, V., & Trouard, T. (2001). A functional imaging study of cooperation in two-person reciprocal exchange. *Proceedings of the National Academy of Sciences of the United States of America, 98*(20), 11832–11835. doi:10.1073/pnas.211415698 PMID:11562505

McClure, S. M., Laibson, D. I., Loewenstein, G., & Cohen, J. D. (2004). Separate Neural Systems Value Immediate and Delayed Monetary Rewards. *Science, 306*(5695), 503–507. doi:10.1126/science.1100907 PMID:15486304

McClure, S. M., York, M. K., & Montague, P. R. (2004). The neural substrates of reward processing in humans: The modern role of fMRI. *The Neuroscientist, 10*(3), 260–268. doi:10.1177/1073858404263526 PMID:15155064

McCubbins, M. D., & Sullivan, T. (1987). *Congress: Structure and Policy*. Cambridge, UK: Cambridge University Press.

McEntee, W. J., & Crook, T. H. (1991). Serotonin, memory, and the aging brain. *Psychopharmacology, 103*(2), 143–149. doi:10.1007/BF02244194 PMID:2027916

McKelvey, R., & Palfrey, T. (1995). Quantal response equilibria for normal form games. *Games and Economic Behavior, 10*(1), 6–38. doi:10.1006/game.1995.1023

McLure, S. M., Li, J., Tomlin, D., Cypert, K. S., Montague, L. M., & Montague, P. R. (2004). Neural Correlates of Behavioral Preference for Culturally Familiar Drinks. *Neuron, 44*(2), 379–387. doi:10.1016/j.neuron.2004.09.019 PMID:15473974

Mettler, T., & Rohner, P. (2009). E-procurement in hospital pharmacies: An exploratory multi-case study from Switzerland. *Journal of Theoretical and Applied Electronic Commerce Research, 4*(1), 23–38.

Miązek, A. (2014). Neurorachunkowość jako nowoczesne podejście w rachunkowości. *Studia Oeconomica Posnaniensia, 2*(5), 75–83.

Michaelson, Z. (2015). Biases in Choices About Fairness: Psychology and Economic Inequality. *Judgment and Decision Making, 10*(2), 198–203.

Miles, R. E., & Snow, C. C. (1978). *Organizational Strategy, Structure, and Process*. New York: McGraw-Hill.

Miller, E. K., & Cohen, J. D. (2001). An integrative theory of prefrontal cortex function. *Annual Review of Neuroscience, 24*(1), 167–202. doi:10.1146/annurev.neuro.24.1.167 PMID:11283309

Miller, K. D., & Lin, S. J. (2015). Analogical reasoning for diagnosing strategic issues in dynamic and complex environments. *Strategic Management Journal, 36*(13), 2000–2020. doi:10.1002/smj.2335

Minati, L., Grisoli, M., Seth, A. K., & Critchley, H. D. (2012). Decision-making under risk: A graph-based network analysis using functional MRI. *NeuroImage, 60*(4), 2191–2205. doi:10.1016/j.neuroimage.2012.02.048 PMID:22387471

Mintzberg, H., Ahlstrand, B., & Lampel, J. (2005). *Strategy Safari: A Guided Tour Through The Wilds of Strategic Managament.* New York: Simon and Schuster.

Mishra, H., Shiv, B., & Nayakankuppam, D. (2008). *The Blissful Ignorance Effect: Pre Versus Post Action Effects on Outcome-Expectancies Arising from Precise and Vague Information (SSRN Scholarly Paper No. ID 1158496).* Rochester, NY: Social Science Research Network.

Mitchell, J. R., Shepherd, D. A., & Sharfman, M. P. (2011). Erratic strategic decisions: When and why managers are inconsistent in strategic decision making. *Strategic Management Journal, 32*(7), 683–704. doi:10.1002/smj.905

Mohr, P. N. C., Li, S. C., & Heekeren, H. R. (2010). Neuroeconomics and aging: Neuromodulation of economic decision making in old age. *Neuroscience and Biobehavioral Reviews, 34*(5), 678–688. doi:10.1016/j.neubiorev.2009.05.010 PMID:19501615

Molinsky, A. (2007). Cross-Cultural Code-Switching: The Psychological Challenges of Adapting Behavior in Foreign Cultural Interactions. *Academy of Management Review, 32*(3), 622–640. doi:10.5465/AMR.2007.24351878

Montague, P. R. (2007). Neuroeconomics: A view from neuroscience. *Functional Neurology, 22*(4), 219–234. PMID:18182129

Montague, P. R., & Berns, G. S. (2002). Neural economics and the biological substrates of valuation. *Neuron, 36*(2), 265–284. doi:10.1016/S0896-6273(02)00974-1 PMID:12383781

Montague, P. R., Hyman, S. E., & Cohen, J. D. (2004). Computational roles for dopamine in behavioural control. *Nature, 431*(7010), 760–767. doi:10.1038/nature03015 PMID:15483596

Monterosso, J., Piray, P., & Luo, S. (2012). Neuroeconomics and the study of addiction. *Biological Psychiatry, 72*(2), 107–112. doi:10.1016/j.biopsych.2012.03.012 PMID:22520343

Montier, J. (2002). *Behavioural Finance. Insights into Irrational Minds and Markets.* New York: Wiley.

Moorhead, G., & Montanari, J. R. (1986). An Empirical Investigation of the Groupthink Phenomenon. *Human Relations, 39*(5), 399–410. doi:10.1177/001872678603900502

Morris, G., Nevet, A., Arkadir, D., Vaadia, E., & Bergman, H. (2006). Midbrain dopamine neurons encode decisions for future action. *Nature Neuroscience, 9*(8), 1057–1063. doi:10.1038/nn1743 PMID:16862149

Morrow, J. D. (1994). *Game Theory for Political Scientists.* Princeton, NJ: Princeton University Press.

Moulaert, F., & Mehmood, A. (2010). Analysing regional development and policy: A structural-realist approach. *Regional Studies, 44*(01), 103–118. doi:10.1080/00343400802251478

Murray, D. (1990). The Performance Effects of Participative Budgeting: An Integration of Intervening and Moderating Variables. *Behavioral Research in Accounting, 2*, 829–842.

Muzur, A., & Rinčić, I. (2013). Neurocriticism: A contribution to the study of the etiology, phenomenology, and ethics of the use and abuse of the prefix neuro. *JAHR-European Journal of Bioethics, 4*(7), 545–555.

Myerson, J., & Green, L. (1995). Discounting of delayed rewards: Models of individual choice. *Journal of the Experimental Analysis of Behavior, 64*(3), 263–276. doi:10.1901/jeab.1995.64-263 PMID:16812772

Nagpal, A., & Krishnamurthy, P. (2008). Attribute Conflict in Consumer Decision Making: The Role of Task Compatibility. *The Journal of Consumer Research, 34*(5), 696–705. doi:10.1086/521903

Nakagawa, S., Sugiura, M., Akitsuki, Y., Hosseini, S. M. H., Kotozaki, Y., & Miyauchi, C. M. et al. (2013). Compensatory Effort Parallels Midbrain Deactivation during Mental Fatigue: An fMRI Study. *PLoS ONE, 8*(2), e56606. doi:10.1371/journal.pone.0056606 PMID:23457592

Napoli, P. M. (2013). *Audience economics: Media institutions and the audience marketplace.* Columbia University Press.

Nardon, L., Steers, R. M., & Sanches-Runde, C. J. (2013, May 9). Developing Multicultural Competence. *The European Business Review.* Retrieved on November 11, 2014, from: http://www.europeanbusinessreview.com/?p=1386

Nash, J. (1951). Non-cooperative games. *The Annals of Mathematics, 54*(2), 289–295. doi:10.2307/1969529

Nash, J. F. Jr. (1950). Equilibrium Points in n-Person Games. *Proceedings of the National Academy of Sciences of the United States of America, 36*(1), 48–49. doi:10.1073/pnas.36.1.48 PMID:16588946

Neufeld, R. W. J. (2007). *Advances in Clinical Cognitive Science: Formal Modeling of Processes and Symptoms.* Washington, DC: American Psychological Association. doi:10.1037/11556-000

Newmark, R. I., & Karim, K. E. (2002). The effects of red-flag items, unfavorable projection errors, and time pressure on tax preparers' aggressiveness. *Advances in Accounting Behavioral Research, 5,* 213–243. doi:10.1016/S1474-7979(02)05043-3

Ng, Y.-K. (1986). *Meso-economics: A Micro-Macro Analysis.* London: Harvester.

Nicholson, W., & Snyder, C. (2008). *Microeconomic theory: Basic principles and extension* (10th ed.). Mason, OH: Thompson South-Western.

Nicolaou, A. I. (2011). Integrated Information Systems and Interorganizational Performance: The Role of Management Accounting Systems Design. *Advances in Accounting Behavioral Research, 14,* 117–141. doi:10.1108/S1475-1488(2011)0000014008

Nikitaeva, A.Y. (2007). *Theory and practice of management of interaction of the state and business: regional aspect.* Rostov-on-Don: Publishing house of Southern Federal University.

Nisbett, R. (2003). *The Geography of Thought: How Asians and Westerners Think Differently...and Why.* New York: Free Press.

Niyato, D., & Hossain, E. (2008). Competitive pricing for spectrum sharing in cognitive radio networks: Dynamic game, inefficiency of nash equilibrium, and collusion. Selected Areas in Communications. *IEEE Journal on, 26*(1), 192–202.

Nohria, N., & Gulati, R. (1996). Is slack good or bad for innovation? *Academy of Management Journal, 39*(5), 1245–1264. doi:10.2307/256998

North, D. C. (1994). Institutional Change: A Framework of Analysis. *Working Papers in Economics.* Retrieved on May 10, 2010, from: http://ideas.repec.org/p/wpa/wuwpeh/9412001.html#related

North, D. C. (1990). *Institutions, Institutional Change, and Economic Performance.* Cambridge, UK: Cambridge University Press. doi:10.1017/CBO9780511808678

Novemsky, N., & Kahneman, D. (2005). The boundaries of loss aversion. *JMR, Journal of Marketing Research, 42*(2), 119–128. doi:10.1509/jmkr.42.2.119.62292

Nowak, M. A. (2006). Five rules for the evolution of cooperation. *Science, 314*(5805), 1560–1563. doi:10.1126/science.1133755 PMID:17158317

Nye, J. S. (2002). Information technology and democratic governance. In E. Kamarck & J. S. Nye Jr., (Eds.), *Governance. com: Democracy in the Information Age* (pp. 1–16). Washington, DC: Brookings Institution Press.

O' Cass, A., & McEwen, H. (2004). Exploring consumer status and conspicuous consumption. *Journal of Consumer Behaviour, 4*(1), 25–39. doi:10.1002/cb.155

O'Cass, A., & Frost, H. (2002). Status brands: Examining the effects of non-product-related brand associations on status and conspicuous consumption. *Journal of Product and Brand Management, 11*(2), 67–88. doi:10.1108/10610420210423455

O'Doherty, J., Kringelbach, M. L., Rolls, E. T., Hornak, J., & Andrews, C. (2001). Abstract reward and punishment representations in the human orbitofrontal cortex. *Nature Neuroscience, 4*(1), 95–102. doi:10.1038/82959 PMID:11135651

Ocasio, W. (1997). Towards an attention-based view of the firm. *Strategic Management Journal, 18*(S1), 187–206. doi:10.1002/(SICI)1097-0266(199707)18:1+<187::AID-SMJ936>3.3.CO;2-B

Ohlin, J. D. (2012). Nash Equilibrium and International Law. *European Journal of International Law, 23*(4), 915–940. doi:10.1093/ejil/chs060

Ojemann, G. A. (1991). Cortical organization of language. *The Journal of Neuroscience.* PMID:1869914

Ordeshook, P. C. (1986). *Game Theory and Political Theory: An Introduction.* Cambridge, UK: Cambridge University Press. doi:10.1017/CBO9780511666742

Orphanides, G., & Reinberg, D. (2002, February22). A Unified Theory of Gene Expression. *Cell, 108*(4), 439–451. doi:10.1016/S0092-8674(02)00655-4 PMID:11909516

Osborne, M. F. M. (1964). Brownian Motion in the Stock Market. In P. Cootner (Ed.), *The Random Character of Stock Market Price.* Cambridge, MA: MIT Press.

Osińska, M., Pietrzak, M. B., & Żurek, M. (2011). Ocena wpływu czynników behawioralnych i rynkowych na postawy inwestorów indywidualnych na polskim rynku kapitałowym za pomocą modelu SEM. *Przegląd Statystyczny, 58*, 175–194.

Ostrom, E., Gardner, R., & Walker, J. (1994). *Rules, Games and Common-Pool Resources.* Ann Arbor, MI: University of Michigan Press.

Overskeid, G. (2000). The slave of the passions: Experiencing problems and selecting solutions. *Review of General Psychology, 4*(3), 284–309. doi:10.1037/1089-2680.4.3.284

Owers, J., Rod, C., & Alexander, A. (2004). An Introduction to Media Economics Theory. In N. G. Alison, J. Alexander, J. Owers, R. Carveth, C. Ann, & A. Hollifield (Eds.), *Media Economics Theory and Practice* (pp. 3–49). Mahwah, NJ: Lawrence Erlbaum Associates.

Ozanich, G. W., & Wirth, M. O. (2004). Structure and Change: A Communications Industry Overview. In A. Alison, J. Owers, R. Carveth, H. C. Ann, & N. G. Albert (Eds.), *Media Economics Theory and Practice* (pp. 69–85). Mahwah, NJ: Lawrence Erlbaum Associates.

Padoa-Schioppa, C., & Assad, J. A. (2006). Neurons in the orbitofrontal cortex encode economic value. *Nature, 441*(7090), 223–226. doi:10.1038/nature04676 PMID:16633341

Park, H., & Sohn, W. (2013). Behavioral Finance: A Survey of the Literature and Recent Development. *Seoul Journal of Business*, *19*(1), 3–42.

Parkin, M., Powell, M., & Matthews, K. (1997). *Economics* (3rd ed.). London: Addison-Wesley Longman.

Parkinson, J. A., Olmstead, M. C., Burns, L. H., Robbins, T. W., & Everitt, B. J. (1999). Dissociation in effects of lesions of the nucleus accumbens core and shell on appetitive pavlovian approach behavior and the potentiation of conditioned reinforcement and locomotor activity by D-amphetamine. *The Journal of Neuroscience*, *19*(6), 2401–2411. PMID:10066290

Park, S. Q., Kahnt, T., Rieskamp, J., & Heekeren, H. R. (2011). Neurobiology of value integration: When value impacts valuation. *The Journal of Neuroscience*, *31*(25), 9307–9314. doi:10.1523/JNEUROSCI.4973-10.2011 PMID:21697380

Parsaye, K. A. (1998). Characterization of Data Mining Technologies and Processes. *Journal of Data Warehousing*, *1*, 13–18.

Pascual-Leone, A., Amedi, A., Fregni, F., & Merabet, L. B. (2005). The Plastic Human Brain Cortex. *Annual Review of Neuroscience*, *28*(1), 377–401. doi:10.1146/annurev.neuro.27.070203.144216 PMID:16022601

Patton, J. H., Stanford, M. S., & Barratt, E. S. (1995). Factor structure of the Barratt impulsiveness scale. *Journal of Clinical Psychology*, *51*(6), 768–774. doi:10.1002/1097-4679(199511)51:6<768::AID-JCLP2270510607>3.0.CO;2-1 PMID:8778124

Pavlenko, A. (2005). *Emotions and Multilingualism*. Boston: Cambridge University Press.

Pearce, D. W. (1992). *Macmillan dictionary of modern economics* (4th ed.). London, UK: Macmillan Press. doi:10.1007/978-1-349-22136-3

Pei, B., Reckers, P., & Wyndelts, R. (1992). Tax professionals' Belief Revision: The Effects of Information Presentation Sequence, Client Preference and Domain Experience. *Decision Sciences*, *23*(1), 175–199. doi:10.1111/j.1540-5915.1992.tb00383.x

Perloff, J. M. (2008). *Microeconomics: Theory and applications with calculus*. Boston, MA: Pearson/Addison Wesley.

Perlovsky, L. (2009) Language and Emotions: Emotional Sapir-Whorf Hypothesis. *Article of Neural Networks,* 518-526. Retrieved on May 9, 2015, from, http://www.leonid-perlovsky.com/new-materials/9,%20NN,%20Emotional%20SWH.pdf

Peters, B. G. (2000). *Institutional Theory in Political Science: The New Institutionalism*. London: Continuum.

Peters, E. E. (1991). *Chaos and Order in the Capital Markets*. New York: John Wiley and Sons.

Peters, E. E. (1994). *Fractal Market Analysis: Applying Chaos Theory to Investment and Economics*. New York: John Wiley and Sons.

Petersen, H. C., & Lewis, W. C. (1999). *Managerial economics* (4th ed.). Singapore: Pearson Education Press.

Phau, I., & Prendergast, G. (2000). Consuming luxury brands: The re;evance of the 'Rarity Principle'. *Brand Management*, *8*(2), 122–138. doi:10.1057/palgrave.bm.2540013

Picard, R. G. (2006). Historical Trends and Patterns in Media Economics. In A. B. Albarran, S. M. Chan-Olmsted, & O. Wirth (Eds.), *Handbook of Media Management and Economics* (pp. 23–37). Mahwah, NJ: Lawrence Erlbaum Associates, Inc.

Pinsker, R. (2007). Long series of information and nonprofessional investors' belief revision. *Behavioral Research in Accounting*, *19*(1), 197–214. doi:10.2308/bria.2007.19.1.197

Pinto, M. B., Pinto, J. K., & Prescott, J. E. (1993). Antecedents and consequences of project team cross-functional co-operation. *Management Science, 39*(10), 1281–1297. doi:10.1287/mnsc.39.10.1281

Pirlot, M., & Bouyssou, D. (2009). *Analysing the correspondance between strict and non-strict concordance relations.* Bonn: Allemagne.

Piron, F. (2000). Consumers' perceptions of the country-of-origin effect on purchasing intentions of (in)conspicuous products. *Journal of Consumer Marketing, 17*(4), 308–321. doi:10.1108/07363760010335330

Plassman, H., Kenning, P., & Ahlert, A. (2007). Why Companies Should Make Their Customers Happy: The Neural Correlates of Customer Loyalty. *Advances in Consumer Research. Association for Consumer Research (U. S.), 34*, 735–739.

Plassmann, H., O'Doherty, J., & Rangel, A. (2007). Orbitofrontal cortex encodes willingness to pay in everyday economic transactions. *The Journal of Neuroscience, 27*(37), 9984–9988. doi:10.1523/JNEUROSCI.2131-07.2007 PMID:17855612

Plassmann, H., O'Doherty, J., Shiv, B., & Rangel, A. (2008). Marketing actions can modulate neural representations of experienced pleasantness. *Proceedings of the National Academy of Sciences of the United States of America, 105*(3), 1050–1054. doi:10.1073/pnas.0706929105 PMID:18195362

Platt, M. L., & Glimcher, P. W. (1999). Neural correlates of decision variables in parietal cortex. *Nature, 400*(6741), 233–238. doi:10.1038/22268 PMID:10421364

Platt, M. L., & Huettel, S. A. (2008). Risky business: The neuroeconomics of decision making under uncertainty. *Nature Neuroscience, 11*(4), 398–403. doi:10.1038/nn2062 PMID:18368046

Pletnyakov, V. A. (2012). *Research and analytical tools of strategic decision making in the economy.* Taganrog: Publishing house of TSURE.

Podoshen, J. S., & Andrzejewski, S. (2012). An examination of the relationships between materialism, conspicuous consumption, impulse buying and brand loyalty. *Journal of Marketing Theory and Practice, 20*(3), 319–334. doi:10.2753/MTP1069-6679200306

Podoshen, J., Li, L., & Zhang, J. (2011). Materialism and conspicuous consumption in China: A cross-cultural examination. *International Journal of Consumer Studies, 35*(1), 17–25. doi:10.1111/j.1470-6431.2010.00930.x

Politser, P. (2008). *Neuroeconomics: A Guide to the New Science of Making Choices.* New York: Oxford University Press. doi:10.1093/acprof:oso/9780195305821.001.0001

Pollock, D. (2001). *Third Culture Kids: The Experience of Growing Up Among Worlds.* London: Nicholas Brealey Publishing.

Poon, S., & Swatman, P. (1999). An exploratory study of small business Internet commerce issues. *Information & Management, 35*(19), 9–18. doi:10.1016/S0378-7206(98)00079-2

Popescu, G. H., & Nica, E. (2014). Neuroeconomic Models of Decision Making. *Knowledge Horizons – Economics, 6*(1), 63–66.

Porter, M. E. (2001). Regions and the new economics of competition. In *Global City-Regions: Trends, Theory, Policy.* Oxford, UK: Oxford University Press.

Pradeep, A. K. (2010). *The buying brain: Secrets for selling to the subconscious mind.* Hoboken, NJ: John Wiley & Sons.

Preston, S. D., & de Waal, F. B. M. (2002). Empathy: Its Ultimate and Proximate Bases. *Behavioral and Brain Sciences, 25*(1), 1–72. PMID:12625087

Preuschoff, K., Bossaerts, P., & Quartz, S. R. (2006). Neural differentiation of expected reward and risk in human sub-cortical structures. *Neuron, 51*(3), 381–390. doi:10.1016/j.neuron.2006.06.024 PMID:16880132

Previc, F. H. (2009). *The dopaminergic mind in human evolution and history.* Cambridge, UK: Cambridge University Press. doi:10.1017/CBO9780511581366

Proctor, R. W., & Vu, K.-P. L. (2012). Selection and Control of Action. In G. Salvendy (Ed.), *Handbook of Human Factors and Ergonomics* (4th ed.; pp. 95–116). John Wiley and Sons. doi:10.1002/9781118131350.ch4

Puppim de Oliveira, J. A., & Ali, S. H. (2011). Gemstone mining as a development cluster: A study of Brazil's emerald mines. *Resources Policy, 36*(2), 132–141. doi:10.1016/j.resourpol.2010.10.002

Quattrone, G. A., & Tversky, A. (1988). Contrasting rational and psychological analyses of political choice. *The American Political Science Review, 82*(3), 719–736. doi:10.2307/1962487

Rabin, M. (1998). Psychology and Economics. *Journal of Economic Literature, 36,* 11–46.

Rachlin, H., & Green, L. (1972). Commitment, choice, and self-control. *Journal of the Experimental Analysis of Behavior, 17*(1), 15–22. doi:10.1901/jeab.1972.17-15 PMID:16811561

Radner, R., Myerson, R., & Maskin, E. (1986). An example of a repeated partnership game with discounting and with uniformly inefficient equilibria. *The Review of Economic Studies, 53*(1), 59–69. doi:10.2307/2297591

Rajaniemi, P. (1992). *Conceptualization of product involvement as a property of a cognitive structure.* Acta Wasaensia, Vaasa.

Rangel, A., Camerer, C. F., & Montague, P. R. (2008). A framework for studying the neurobiology of value-based decision making. *Nature Reviews Neuroscience, 9*(7), 545–556. doi:10.1038/nrn2357 PMID:18545266

Rangel, A., & Hare, T. (2010). Neural computations associated with goal-directed choice. *Current Opinion in Neurobiology, 20*(2), 262–270. doi:10.1016/j.conb.2010.03.001 PMID:20338744

Rathje, S. (2007). Intercultural Competence: The Status and Future of a Controversial Concept. *Journal for Language and Intercultural Communication, 7*(4), 254–266. doi:10.2167/laic285.0

Rebele, J. E., & Michaels, R. E. (1990). Independent Auditors Role Stress: Antecedent, Outcome, and Moderating Variables. *Behavioral Research in Accounting, 2,* 124–153.

Reibstein, D., Bateson, J. E. G., & Boulding, W. (1988). Conjoint Analysis Reliability: Empirical Findings. *Marketing Science, 7*(3), 271–286. doi:10.1287/mksc.7.3.271

Reimann, M., & Bechara, A. (2010). The somatic marker framework as a neurological theory of decision-making: Review, conceptual comparisons, and future neuroeconomics research. *Journal of Economic Psychology, 31*(5), 767–776. doi:10.1016/j.joep.2010.03.002

Ricardo, C., Andrew, J. G., Gutman, D. A., & Kilts, C. D. (2015). Organization of intrinsic functional brain connectivity predicts decisions to reciprocate social behavior. *Behavioural Brain Research.* doi:10.1016/j.bbr.2015.07.008

Riccardi, V. (2004). *A Risk Perception Premier: A Narrative Research Review of the Risk Perception Literature in Behavioral Accounting and Finance.* Golden Gate University.

Richerson, P. J., Boyd, R., & Henrich, J. (2010). Gene-culture coevolution in the age of genomics. In *Proceedings of National Academy of Science of the United States of America.* Retrieved on January 22, 2013, from: http://www.pnas.org/content/107/Supplement_2/8985.full

Richerson, P. J., & Boyd, R. (2005). *Not by genes alone. How culture transformed human evolution.* Oxford, UK: Oxford University Press.

Richerson, P. J., Boyd, R., & Henrich, J. (2003). Cultural evolution of human cooperation. In P. Hammerstein (Ed.), *Genetic and Cultural Evolution of Cooperation* (pp. 357–388). Berlin: MIT Press.

Richins, M. L. (1994). Special possessions and the expression of material values. *The Journal of Consumer Research,* *21*(3), 522–533. doi:10.1086/209415

Richins, M. L., & Dawson, S. (1992). A consumer values orientation for materialism and its measurement: Scale development and validation. *The Journal of Consumer Research, 19*(3), 303–316. doi:10.1086/209304

Rich, P. (2015). Rethinking common belief, revision, and backward induction. *Mathematical Social Sciences, 75,* 102–114. doi:10.1016/j.mathsocsci.2015.03.001

Rick, S. (2011). Losses, gains, and brains: Neuroeconomics can help to answer open questions about loss aversion. *Journal of Consumer Psychology, 21*(4), 453–463. doi:10.1016/j.jcps.2010.04.004

Riedl, R., Hubert, M., & Kenning, P. (2010). Are there neural gender differences in online trust? An fMRI study on the perceived trustworthiness of eBay offers. *Management Information Systems Quarterly, 34*(2), 397–428.

Riether, W. (2014). *Business Cooperation cultural Integration as Key Factor.* Saarbruecken: AV Akademikerverlag.

Rilling, J. K., Gutman, D. A., Zeh, T. R., Pagnoni, G., Berns, G. S., Clint, D., & Kilts, C. D. (2002). A Neural Basis for Social Cooperation. *Neuron, 35*(2), 395–405. doi:10.1016/S0896-6273(02)00755-9 PMID:12160756

Rilling, J. K., Sanfey, A. G., Aronson, J. A., Nystrom, L. E., & Cohen, J. D. (2004). Opposing BOLD responses to reciprocated and unreciprocated altruism in putative reward pathways. *Neuroreport, 15*(16), 2539–2543. doi:10.1097/00001756-200411150-00022 PMID:15538191

Robalino, N., & Robson, A. (2012). The Economic Approach to theory of mind. *Philosophical Transactions of the Royal Society of London. Series B, Biological Sciences, 367*(1599), 2224–2233. doi:10.1098/rstb.2012.0124 PMID:22734065

Roberts, B. W. (2006). Personality Development and Organizational Behavior. In B. M. Staw (Ed.), *Research on Organizational Behavior* (pp. 1–41). Amsterdam: Elsevier Science/ JAI.

Robinson, T. E., & Berridge, K. C. (2003). Addiction. *Annual Review of Psychology, 54*(1), 25–53. doi:10.1146/annurev.psych.54.101601.145237 PMID:12185211

Rodríguez-Pose, A., & Comptour, F. (2011). Do clusters generate greater innovation and growth? An analysis of European regions. *Bruges European Economic Research Papers, 21.* Retrieved May 3, 2015, from: http://www.coleurope.eu/sites/default/files/research-paper/beer21.pdf

Romp, G. (1997). *Game Theory: Introduction and Applications.* New York: Oxford University Press.

Rosenbaum, M., Moore, D., Cotton, J., Cook, M., Heiser, R., Shovar, N., & Gray, M. (1980). Group productivity and process: Pure and mixed reward structures and task interdependence. *Journal of Personality and Social Psychology, 39*(4), 626–642. doi:10.1037/0022-3514.39.4.626

Rosengard, J. K. (1998). *Property Tax Reform in Developing Countries.* Boston, MA: Kluwer Academic Publications. doi:10.1007/978-1-4615-5667-1

Ross, C. T., & Richerson, P. J. (2014). New frontiers in the study of human cultural and genetic evolution. *Current Opinion in Genetics & Development, 29,* 102–109. doi:10.1016/j.gde.2014.08.014 PMID:25218864

Rotemberg, J. J., & Saloner, G. (1989). Tariffs vs quotas with implicit collusion. *The Canadian Journal of Economics. Revue Canadienne d'Economique, 22*(2), 237–244. doi:10.2307/135666

Rowland, N. E., Vaughan, C. H., Mathes, C. M., & Mitra, A. (2008). Feeding behavior, obesity, and neuroeconomics. *Physiology & Behavior, 93*(1/2), 97–109. doi:10.1016/j.physbeh.2007.08.003 PMID:17825853

Rubinstein, A. (2008). Comments on Neuroeconomics. *Economics and Philosophy, 24*(03), 485–494. doi:10.1017/S0266267108002101

Rushworth, M. F., & Behrens, T. E. (2008). Choice, uncertainty and value in prefrontal and cingulate cortex. *Nature Neuroscience, 11*(4), 389–397. doi:10.1038/nn2066 PMID:18368045

Rusko, R. (2005). The effects of a demand shock upon the market prices of the exported paper and pulp. *Forest Policy and Economics, 7*(3), 423–435. doi:10.1016/j.forpol.2003.08.002

Rusko, R. (2014a). Coopetition for Organizations. In M. Khosrow-Pour (Ed.), *Encyclopedia of Information Science and Technology* (3rd ed.). Hershey, PA: IGI Global.

Rusko, R. (2014b). Mapping the perspectives of coopetition and technology-based strategic networks: A case of smartphones. *Industrial Marketing Management, 43*(5), 801–812. doi:10.1016/j.indmarman.2014.04.013

Rusko, R. (2015). New business model: Intentional and unintentional degree one and degree two consumer coopetition in a branch of the Finnish game industry. *International Journal of Business Environment, 7*(3), 219. doi:10.1504/IJBE.2015.071221

Rustichini, A. (2009). Neuroeconomics: What have we found, and what should we search for. *Current Opinion in Neurobiology, 19*(6), 672–677. doi:10.1016/j.conb.2009.09.012 PMID:19896360

Rust, R. T., & Oliver, R. L. (Eds.). (1994). *Service quality: new directions in theory and practice*. Thousand Oaks, CA: Sage Publications.

Ryan, B., Scapens, R. W., & Theobald, M. (2002). *Research Method and Methodology in Finance and Accounting* (2nd ed.). Cornwall, UK: Mitcham Surrey International.

Saati, T. (2015). *Making decision with dependence and feedback links: Analytical network*. Moscow: LCI.

Sadeghnia, M., & Habibniko, A. (2013). Behavioral Finance and NeuroFinance and Research Conducted in This Area. *IJCRB, 4*(12), 793–801.

Salamone, J., Correa, M., Farrar, A., & Mingote, S. (2007). Effort-related functions of nucleus accumbens dopamine and associated forebrain circuits. *Psychopharmacology, 191*(3), 461–482. doi:10.1007/s00213-006-0668-9 PMID:17225164

Salas, E., Sims, D. E., & Burke, C. S. (2005). Is there "big five" in teamwork? *Small Group Research, 36*(5), 555–599. doi:10.1177/1046496405277134

Salvendy, G. (2012). *Handbook of Human Factors and Ergonomics* (4th ed.). John Wiley and Sons. doi:10.1002/9781118131350

Samelson, D., & Jeffrey, C. (2000). Accuracy and calibration in professional judgment: A study of tax practitioners. *Advances in Accounting Behavioral Research, 3*, 153–176. doi:10.1016/S1474-7979(00)03030-1

Sample, I., & Adam, D. (2003). *The brain can"t lie*. Retrieved June 11, 2015, from: http://www.theguardian.com/science/2003/nov/20/neuroscience.science

Samuelson, W., & Zeckhauser, R. (1988). Status quo bias in decision making. *Journal of Risk and Uncertainty, 1*(1), 7–59. doi:10.1007/BF00055564

Sanfey, A. G., & Chang, L. J. (2008). Multiple Systems in Decision Making. *Annals of the New York Academy of Sciences, 1128*(1), 53–62. doi:10.1196/annals.1399.007 PMID:18469214

Sanfey, A. G., Loewenstein, G., McClure, S. M., & Cohen, J. D. (2006). Neuroeconomics: Cross-currents in research on decision-making. *Trends in Cognitive Sciences, 10*(3), 108–116. doi:10.1016/j.tics.2006.01.009 PMID:16469524

Sanfey, A. G., Rilling, J. K., Aronson, J. A., Nystrom, L. E., & Cohen, J. D. (2003). The neural basis of economic decision-making in the ultimatum game. *Science, 300*(5626), 1755–1758. doi:10.1126/science.1082976 PMID:12805551

Santos, L. R., & Keith Chen, M. (2009). The evolution of rational and irrational economic behavior: evidence and insight from a non-human primate species. *Neuroeconomics–Decision Making and the Brain*, 81-93.

Sarin, R. K., & Weber, M. (1993). Risk-value models. *European Journal of Operational Research, 70*(2), 135–149. doi:10.1016/0377-2217(93)90033-J

Scharpf, F. W. (1997). *Games Real Actors Play: Actor-Centered Institutionalism in Policy Research*. Oxford, UK: Westview Press.

Schiff, M., & Lewin, A. Y. (Eds.). (1974). *Behavioral aspects of accounting*. Englewood Cliffs, NJ: Prentice Hall.

Schiffman, L. G., & Kanuk, L. L. (2004). *Consumer behavior* (8th ed.). New York: Prentice Hall.

Schoenbaum, G., Setlow, B., & Ramus, S. J. (2003). A systems approach to orbitofrontal cortex function: Recordings in rat orbitofrontal cortex reveal interactions with different learning systems. *Behavioural Brain Research, 146*(1/2), 19–29. doi:10.1016/j.bbr.2003.09.013 PMID:14643456

Schultz, W. (2002). Getting formal with dopamine and reward. *Neuron, 36*(2), 241–263. doi:10.1016/S0896-6273(02)00967-4 PMID:12383780

Schultz, W. (2006). Behavioral theories and the neurophysiology of reward. *Annual Review of Psychology, 57*(1), 87–115. doi:10.1146/annurev.psych.56.091103.070229 PMID:16318590

Schultz, W. (2011). Potential vulnerabilities of neuronal reward, risk, and decision mechanisms to addictive drugs. *Neuron, 69*(4), 603–617. doi:10.1016/j.neuron.2011.02.014 PMID:21338874

Schwartz, B. (2005). *The Paradox of Choice: Why More Is Less*. New York: Harper Perennial.

Schwartz, S. T., & Wallin, D. E. (2002). Behavioral Implications of Information Systems on Disclosure Fraud. *Behavioral Research in Accounting, 14*(1), 197–221. doi:10.2308/bria.2002.14.1.197

Schwarz, N., & Strack, F. (1999). Reports of subjective well-being: Judgmental processes and their methodological implications. In D. Kahneman, E. Diener, & N. Schwarz (Eds.), *Well-being: The foundations of hedonic psychology* (pp. 61–84). New York, NY: Russell Sage Foundation.

Scott, A. J., & Garofoli, G. (Eds.). (2007). Development on the Ground. Clusters, Networks and Regions in Emerging Economies. Routledge.

Scott, J. E., & Wright, P. (1976). Modeling an Organizational Buyer's Product Evaluation Strategy: Validity and Procedural Considerations. *JMR, Journal of Marketing Research, 13*(3), 211. doi:10.2307/3150730

Sebastian, V. (2014). New directions in understanding the decision-making process: Neuroeconomics and neuromarketing. *Procedia: Social and Behavioral Sciences, 127*, 758–762. doi:10.1016/j.sbspro.2014.03.350

Seneca, P. J. (2009). *Measuring and manipulating materialism in the context of consumers' advertising responses.* (Unpublished Doctoral thesis). Graduate School of Southern Illinois University Carbondale, Department of Psychology.

Seymour, B., & McClure, S. M. (2008). Anchors, scales and the relative coding of value in the brain. *Current Opinion in Neurobiology, 18*(2), 173–178. doi:10.1016/j.conb.2008.07.010 PMID:18692572

Shafir, E., Diamond, P., & Tversky, A. (1997). Money Illusion. *The Quarterly Journal of Economics, 112*(2), 341–355. doi:10.1162/003355397555208

Shane, S. (2009). Introduction to the focused issue on the biological basis of business. *Organizational Behavior and Human Decision Processes, 110*(2), 67–69. doi:10.1016/j.obhdp.2009.10.001

Shani, Y., Tykocinski, O. E., & Zeelenberg, M. (2008). When ignorance is not bliss: How feelings of discomfort promote the search for negative information. *Journal of Economic Psychology, 29*(5), 643–653. doi:10.1016/j.joep.2007.06.001

Sharot, T., Martino, B. D., & Dolan, R. J. (2009). How Choice Reveals and Shapes Expected Hedonic Outcome. *The Journal of Neuroscience, 29*(12), 3760–3765. doi:10.1523/JNEUROSCI.4972-08.2009 PMID:19321772

Sharp, C., Burton, P., & Ha, C. (2011). "Better the devil you know": A preliminary study of the differential modulating effects of reputation on reward processing for boys with and without externalizing behavior problems. *European Child & Adolescent Psychiatry, 20*(11/12), 581–592. doi:10.1007/s00787-011-0225-x PMID:22038344

Sharp, C., Monterosso, J., & Montague, P. R. (2012). Neuroeconomics: A bridge for translational research. *Biological Psychiatry, 72*(2), 87–92. doi:10.1016/j.biopsych.2012.02.029 PMID:22727459

Sharpe, W. F. (1964). Capital Asset Prices: A Theory of Market Equilibrium under Conditions of Risk. *The Journal of Finance, 19*(3), 425–442.

Shaver, M. A. (2004). The Economics of the Advertising Industry. In A. Alexander, J. Owers, R. Carveth, C. A. Hollifield, & A. N. Greco (Eds.), *Media Economics Theory and Practice* (pp. 249–265). Mahwah, NJ: Lawrence Erlbaum Associates, Inc.

Shefrin, H. (2000). *Beyond Greed and Fear: Understanding the Behavioral Finance and the Psychology of Investing.* Boston, MA: Harvard Business School Press.

Shefrin, H. (2007). *Behavioral Corporate Finance: Decisions that Create Value.* Boston: McGraw-Hill.

Shefrin, H. (2009). How Psychological Pitfalls Generated the Global Financial Crisis. In L. Siegel (Ed.), *Understanding the Global Financial Crisis.* Boston, MA: Harvard Business School Press. doi:10.2139/ssrn.1523931

Shiller, R. J. (2003). From Efficient Markets Theory to Behavioral Finance. *The Journal of Economic Perspectives, 17*(1), 83–104. doi:10.1257/089533003321164967

Shiv, B., Carmon, Z., & Ariely, D. (2005). Placebo Effects of Marketing Actions: Consumers may Get What They Pay For. *JMR, Journal of Marketing Research, 42*(4), 383–393. doi:10.1509/jmkr.2005.42.4.383

Shiv, B., Loewenstein, G., & Bechara, A. (2005). The Dark Side of Emotions? *Brain Research. Cognitive Brain Research, 23*(1), 85–92. doi:10.1016/j.cogbrainres.2005.01.006 PMID:15795136

Shubik, M. (1970). Game theory, behavior, and the paradox of the prisoner's dilemma: Three solutions. *The Journal of Conflict Resolution, 14*(2), 181–193. doi:10.1177/002200277001400204

Shukla, P. (2008). Conspicuous consumption among middle age consumers: Psychological and brand antecedents. *Journal of Product and Brand Management, 17*(1), 25–36. doi:10.1108/10610420810856495

Siegal, M., & Varley, R. (2002). Neural systems involved in "theory of mind.". *Nature Reviews Neuroscience*, *3*(6), 463–471. PMID:12042881

Simon, H. (1955). A Behavioral Model of Rational Choice. *The Quarterly Journal of Economics*, *69*(1), 99–188. doi:10.2307/1884852

Simon, H. A. (1967). The logic of heuristic decision making. In N. Rescher (Ed.), *The logic of decision and action* (pp. 1–20). Pittsburgh, PA: University of Pittsburgh Press.

Singer, T., & Fehr, E. (2005). Neuroscientific Foundations of Economic Decision Making – the Neuroeconomics of Mind Reading and Empathy. *The American Economic Review*, *95*(2), 34–345. doi:10.1257/000282805774670103

Singer, T., Seymour, B., O'Doherty, J. P., Kaube, H., Dolan, R. J., & Frith, C. D. (2004). Empathy for Pain Involves the Affective but not Sensory Components of Pain. *Science*, *303*(5661), 1157–1162. doi:10.1126/science.1093535 PMID:14976305

Singh, R. (2009). Behavioral Finance – The Basic Foundations. *ASBM Journal of Management*, *II*(1), 89–98.

Sinha, R. (2006). *Key Factors of Multicultural Team Management & Leadership*. Retrieved on April 1, 2010, from: http://ezinearticles.com/?Key-Factors-of-Multicultural-Team-Management-and-Leadership&id=293829

Sinha, R. (2008). *Managing Multicultural Teams*. Icfai University Press.

Skills and Functions Associated with the Lobes of the Brain. (n.d.). Retrieved on April 3, 2015, from: http://www.abi-ireland.ie/docs/BrainLaminate.pdf

Skuse, D. H., & Gallagher, L. (2008). Dopaminergic–neuropeptide interactions in the social brain. *Trends in Cognitive Sciences*, *13*(1), 27–35. doi:10.1016/j.tics.2008.09.007 PMID:19084465

Slavich, G. M., Way, B. M., Eisenberger, N. I., & Taylor, S. E. (2010). Neural sensitivity to social rejection is associated with inflammatory responses to social stress. In *Proceedings of the National Academy of Sciences of the United States of America* (vol. 107, pp. 14817–14822). Retrieved on July 4, 2013, from: http://www.ncbi.nlm.nih.gov/pmc/articles/PMC2930449/

Slavich, G. M., & Cole, S. W. (2013). The Emerging Field of Human Social Genomics. *Clinical Psychological Science*, *1*(3), 331–348. doi:10.1177/2167702613478594 PMID:23853742

Slovic, P. (1972). Psychological study of human judgment: Implications for investment decision making. *The Journal of Finance*, *27*(4), 779–799. doi:10.1111/j.1540-6261.1972.tb01311.x

Smith Speck, S. K., & Roy, A. (2008). The interrelationships between television viewing, values and perceived well-being: A global perspective. *Journal of International Business Studies*, *39*(7), 1197–1219. doi:10.1057/palgrave.jibs.8400359

Smith, K., Dickhaut, J., McCabe, K., & Pardo, J. V. (2002). Neuronal substrates for choice under ambiguity, risk, gains, and losses. *Management Science*, *48*(6), 711–718. doi:10.1287/mnsc.48.6.711.194

Snow, C. E., & Hoefnagel-Höhle, M. (1978, December). The Critical Period for Language Acquisition: Evidence from Second Language Learning. *Child Development*, *49*(4), 1114–1128. doi:10.2307/1128751

Soderberg, A. M., & Holden, N. (2002). Rethinking Cross Cultural Management in a Globalizing Business World. *International Journal of Cross Cultural Management*, *2*(1), 103–121. doi:10.1177/1470595802002001091

Soliwoda, M. (2014). Podejście behawioralne i eksperyment ekonomiczny w finansach rolnictwa. *Zagadnienia Ekonomiki Rolnej*, *1*, 57–77.

Souiden, N., M'Saad, B., & Pons, F. (2011). A Cross-Cultural Analysis of Consumers' Conspicuous Consumption of Branded Fashion Accessories. *Journal of International Consumer Marketing*, *23*(5), 329–343. doi:10.1080/08961530.2011.602951

Souza, K. (2014). *U.S. Treasury auctions off TARP shares in Signature Bank*. Accessed February 25, 2015, from: http://www.thecitywire.com/node/33754#.VO2U7nyUf84

Spinella, M., Yang, B., & Lester, D. (2007). Lester D. Prefrontal systems in financial processing. *Journal of Socio-Economics*, *36*(3), 480–489. doi:10.1016/j.socec.2006.12.008

Spinella, M., Yang, B., & Lester, D. (2008). Prefrontal cortex dysfunction and attitudes toward money: A study in neuroeconomics. *Journal of Socio-Economics*, *37*(5), 1785–1788. doi:10.1016/j.socec.2004.09.061

Staal, M. A., Bolton, A. E., Yaroush, R. A., & Bourne, L. E. Jr. (2008). Cognitive performance and resilience to stress. In B. J. Lukey & V. Tepe (Eds.), *Biobehavioral Resilience to Stress*. Boca Raton, FL: CRC Press.

Stahl, G. K., Mäkelä, K., Zander, L., & Maynevski, M. L. (2010). A Look at the Bright Side of Multicultural Team Diversity. *Scandinavian Journal of Management*, *26*(4), 439–447. doi:10.1016/j.scaman.2010.09.009

Staudinger, M. R., Erk, S., Abler, B., & Walter, H. (2009). Cognitive reappraisal modulates expected value and prediction error encoding in the ventral striatum. *NeuroImage*, *45*(3), 713–721. doi:10.1016/j.neuroimage.2009.04.095 PMID:19442745

Staw, B., Sandelands, L., & Dutton, J. (1981). Threat rigidity effects in organizational behavior: A multilevel analysis. *Administrative Science Quarterly*, *26*(4), 501–524. doi:10.2307/2392337

Stemmer, B. (2006). *Imaging Brain Lateralization, Words, Sentences, and Influencing Factors in Health, Pathological, and Special Populations*. Amsterdam: Elsevier, Ltd.

Stephan, K. E., Harrison, L. M., Kiebel, S. J., David, O., Penny, W. D., & Friston, K. J. (2007). Dynamic causal models of neural system dynamics: Current state and future extensions. *Journal of Biosciences*, *32*(1), 129–144. doi:10.1007/s12038-007-0012-5 PMID:17426386

Sterman, J. D. (2000). *Business Dynamics: Systems Thinking and Modeling for a Complex World*. Chicago: McGraw Hill.

Stewart, N., Chater, N., & Brown, G. D. A. (2006). Decision by sampling. *Cognitive Psychology*, *53*(1), 1–26. doi:10.1016/j.cogpsych.2005.10.003 PMID:16438947

Stoll, M., Baecke, S., & Kenning, P. (2008). What they see is what they get? An fMRI-study on neural correlates of attractive packaging. *Journal of Consumer Behaviour*, *7*(4-5), 342–359. doi:10.1002/cb.256

Stracke, Ch. M. (2011). Competence Modeling for Innovations and Quality Development in E-Learning: Towards learning outcome orientation by competence models. In *Proceedings of World Conference on Educational Multimedia, Hypermedia and Telecommunication 2011*. Retrieved on March 13, 2014, from: http://www.qed-info.de/downloads

Strambach, S. (2010). Path Dependence and Path Plasticity: The Co-evolution of Institutions and Innovation. In R. Boschma & R. Martin (Eds.), *The Handbook of Evolutionary Economic Geography* (pp. 406–431). Cheltenham, UK: Edward Elgar. doi:10.4337/9781849806497.00029

Strauss, C. (1992). Introduction. In R. G. D'Andrade & C. Strauss (Eds.), *Human Motives and Cultural Modes* (pp. 1–20). Cambridge, UK: Cambridge University Press. doi:10.1017/CBO9781139166515.002

Street, D. L., & Bishop, A. C. (1991). An Empirical Examination of the Need Profiles of Professional Accountants. *Behavioral Research in Accounting*, *2*, 97–116.

Suleiman, R., Troitzsch, K. G., & Gilbert, N. (2012). *Tools and Techniques for Social Science Simulation*. New York: Springer Science & Business Media.

Summerfield, C., & Tsetsos, K. (2015). Do humans make good decisions? *Trends in Cognitive Sciences*, *19*(1), 27–34. doi:10.1016/j.tics.2014.11.005 PMID:25488076

Sun, R. (2012). *Grounding Social Sciences in Cognitive Sciences*. Cambridge, MA: MIT Press.

Su, S., Chen, R., & Zhao, P. (2009). Do the size of consideration set and the source of the better competing option influence post-choice regret? *Motivation and Emotion*, *33*(3), 219–228. doi:10.1007/s11031-009-9127-3

Swinyard, W. R., Kau, A.-K., & Phua, H.-Y. (2001). Happiness, materialism, and religious experience in the US and Singapore. *Journal of Happiness Studies*, *2*(1), 13–32. doi:10.1023/A:1011596515474

Szyszka, A. (2009). *Finanse behawioralne: nowe podejście do inwestowania na rynku kapitałowym*. Poznań: Wydawnictwo Uniwersytetu Ekonomicznego.

Tabibnia, G., & Lieberman, M. D. (2007). Fairness and cooperation are rewarding: Evidence from social cognitive neuroscience. *Annals of the New York Academy of Sciences*, *1118*(1), 90–101. doi:10.1196/annals.1412.001 PMID:17717096

Tabibnia, G., Satpute, A. B., & Lieberman, M. D. (2008). The sunny side of fairness – reference for s activates self-control fairness activates reward circuitry (and disregarding unfairnescircuitry). *Psychological Science*, *19*(4), 339–347. doi:10.1111/j.1467-9280.2008.02091.x PMID:18399886

Taleb, N. (2011). *Der Schwarze Schwan, Die Macht höchst unwahrscheinlicher Ereignisse*. München: DTV.

Tekin, S., & Cummings, J. L. (2002). Frontal–subcortical neuronal circuits and clinical neuropsychiatry: An update. *Journal of Psychosomatic Research*, *53*(2), 647–654. doi:10.1016/S0022-3999(02)00428-2 PMID:12169339

Thaler, R. (1999). Mental Accounting Matters. *Journal of Behavioral Decision Making*, *12*(3), 183–206. doi:10.1002/(SICI)1099-0771(199909)12:3<183::AID-BDM318>3.0.CO;2-F

Thaler, R. H. (1980). Toward a positive theory of consumer choice. *Journal of Economic Behavior & Organization*, *1*(1), 39–60. doi:10.1016/0167-2681(80)90051-7

Thaler, R. H. (Ed.). (1993). *Advances in Behavioral Finance* (Vol. 1). New York: Princeton University Press.

Thaler, R. H., & Sunstein, C. R. (2009). *Nudge: Improving Decisions about Health, Wealth and Happiness*. London: Penguin Books, Ltd.

The Anatomy of the Brain. (2015). Retrieved on April 12, 2015, from: http://psychology.about.com/od/biopsychology/ss/brainstructure_2.htm

The Brain and Its Functions. (2015). Retrieved on April 9, 2015, from: http://mybrainonline.ca/?page=3

The Economist. (2014). *Picking the World Champions of Trade*. Accessed May 1, 2014, from: http://www.economist.com/news/finance-and-economics/21594343-which-country-gets-most-out-international-commerce-trading-up

Thomas, J. M., & Bennis, W. G. (1972). *The Management of Change and Conflict: Selected Readings*. Harmondsworth, UK: Penguin Books.

Thomas, J., Clark, S., & Gioia, D. (1993). Strategic sensemaking and organizational performance: Linkages among scanning, interpretation, action, and outcomes. *Academy of Management Journal*, *36*(2), 239–270. doi:10.2307/256522 PMID:10125120

Thorstein, V. (1994). *The theory of the leisure class*. New York: Prometheus Book.

Tirole, J. (1988). *The theory of industrial organization*. Cambridge, MA: MIT Press.

Tomasello, M., Carpenter, M., Call, J., Behne, T., & Moll, H. (2005). Understanding and sharing intentions: The ontogeny and phylogeny of cultural cognition. *Behavioral and Brain Sciences*, *28*(05), 675–735. doi:10.1017/S0140525X05000129 PMID:16262930

Tom, R., Tyler, T. R., & Blader, S. L. (2001). Identity and Cooperative Behavior in Groups. *Group Processes & Intergroup Relations*, *4*(3), 207–226. doi:10.1177/1368430201004003003

Tom, S. M., Fox, C. R., Trepel, C., & Poldrack, R. A. (2007). The neural basis of loss aversion in decision-making under risk. *Science*, *315*(5811), 515–518. doi:10.1126/science.1134239 PMID:17255512

Torgler, B. (2002). Speaking To Theorists and Searching for Facts: Tax Morale and Tax Compliance in Experiments. *Journal of Economic Surveys*, *16*(5), 657–683. doi:10.1111/1467-6419.00185

Touhami, Z. O., Benlafkih, L., Jiddane, M., Cherrah, Y., Malki, O. E., & Benomar, A. (2011). Neuromarketing: Where Marketing and Neuroscience Meet. *African Journal of Business Management, 5*(5), 1528-1532.

Tricomi, E. M., Delgado, M. R., & Fiez, J. A. (2004). Modulation of caudate activity by action contingency. *Neuron*, *41*(2), 281–292. doi:10.1016/S0896-6273(03)00848-1 PMID:14741108

Tricomi, E. M., Rangel, A., Camerer, C. F., & O'Doherty, J. P. (2010). Neural evidence for inequality-averse social preferences. *Nature*, *463*(7284), 1089–1091. doi:10.1038/nature08785 PMID:20182511

Trigg, A. (2001). Veblen, Bourdiue and conspicuous consumption. *Journal of Economic Issues*, *35*(1), 99–115. doi:10.1080/00213624.2001.11506342

Tsebelis, G. (1990). Nested Games: Rational Choice in Comparative Politics. Berkley, CA: University of California Press.

Tucker, R. G. (1999). A Global Perspective on Bilingualism and Bilingual Education. *Carnegie Mellon University Digest*. Retrieved on May 3, 2015, from: http://eric.ed.gov/?id=ED435168

Turner, B. S., Rowland, R., Connell, R. W., Waters, M., & Barbalet, J. M. (1995). Symposium: Human Rights and the Sociological Project. *Journal of Sociology (Melbourne, Vic.)*, *31*(2), 1–44. doi:10.1177/144078339503100201

Tversky, A., & Kahneman, D. (1981). The framing of decisions and the psychology of choice. *Science*, *211*(4481), 453–458. doi:10.1126/science.7455683 PMID:7455683

Tversky, A., & Kahneman, D. (1986). Rational Choice and the Framing of Decisions. *The Journal of Business*, *59*(4), S251–S278. doi:10.1086/296365

Vanwindekens, F. M., Stilmant, D., & Baret, Ph. V. (2013). Development of a broadened cognitive mapping approach for analysing systems of practices in social–ecological systems. *Ecological Modelling*, *250*, 352–362. doi:10.1016/j.ecolmodel.2012.11.023

Vázquez-Barquero, A. (2002). *Endogenous Development: Networking, Innovation, Institutions and Cities*. London: Routledge. doi:10.4324/9780203217313

Verplanken, R., & Holland, R. W. (2002). Motivated decision-making: Effects of activation and self-centrality of values on choices and behavior. *Journal of Personality and Social Psychology*, *82*(3), 434–447. doi:10.1037/0022-3514.82.3.434 PMID:11902626

Vickery, W. (1961). Counter-speculation, auctions, and competitive sealed tenders. *The Journal of Finance*, *16*(1), 8–37. doi:10.1111/j.1540-6261.1961.tb02789.x

Virchow, R. (2006). Report on the typhus outbreak of Upper Silesia. *Social Medicine, 1*(1), 11–27. (Original work published 1848).

Virkar, S. (2011). *The Politics of Implementing e-Government for Development: The Ecology of Games Shaping Property Tax Administration in Bangalore City, India.* (Unpublished Doctoral Thesis). University of Oxford.

Virkar, S. (2013) Designing and Implementing e-Government Projects: Actors, Influences, and Fields of Play. In S. Saeed & C. G. Reddick (Eds.), Human-Centered Design for Electronic Government (pp. 88-110). Hershey, PA: IGI Global, Inc.

Virmani, A. (1987). *Indirect Tax Evasion and Production Efficiency. Development Research Department, Economics and Research Staff.* Washington, DC: World Bank.

Vogel, J. J., Vogel, D. S., Cannon-Bowers, J. A. N., Bowers, C. A., Muse, K., & Wright, M. (2006). Computer gaming and interactive simulations for learning: A meta-analysis. *Journal of Educational Computing Research, 34*(3), 229–243. doi:10.2190/FLHV-K4WA-WPVQ-H0YM

Volk, S., Thoni, C., & Ruigrok, W. (2012). Temporal stability and psychological Foundations of cooperation preferences. *Journal of Economic Behavior & Organization, 81*(2), 664–676. doi:10.1016/j.jebo.2011.10.006

von Neumann, J., & Morgenstern, O. (1944). *Theory of games and economic behavior.* Princeton: Princeton University Press.

Vromen, J. J. (2007). Neuroeconomics as a natural extension of bioeconomics: The shifting scope of standard economic theory. *Journal of Bioeconomics, 9*(2), 145–167. doi:10.1007/s10818-007-9021-6

Wallis, J. D., & Kennerley, S. W. (2010). Heterogeneous reward signals in prefrontal cortex. *Current Opinion in Neurobiology, 20*(2), 191–198. doi:10.1016/j.conb.2010.02.009 PMID:20303739

Wansink, B. (2004). Environmental factors that increase the food intake and consumption volume of unknowing consumers. *Annual Review of Nutrition, 24*(1), 455–479. doi:10.1146/annurev.nutr.24.012003.132140 PMID:15189128

Ward, S., & Wackman, D. (1971). Family and media influence on adolescent consumer learning. *The American Behavioral Scientist, 14*(3), 415–427. doi:10.1177/000276427101400315

Weber, B., Rangel, A., Wibral, M., & Falk, A. (2009). The medial prefrontal cortex exhibits money illusion. Proceedings of the National Academy of Sciences, pnas.0901490106. doi:10.1073/pnas.0901490106

Weber, E. U., & Johnson, E. J. (2009). Mindful judgment and decision making. *Annual Review of Psychology, 60*(1), 53–85. doi:10.1146/annurev.psych.60.110707.163633 PMID:18798706

Wegner, D. M. (1995). A computer network model of human transactive memory. *Social Cognition, 13*(3), 319–339. doi:10.1521/soco.1995.13.3.319

West-Eberhard, M. J. (1989). Phenotypic Plasticity and the Origins of Diversity. *Annual Review of Ecology and Systematics, 20*(1), 249–278. doi:10.1146/annurev.es.20.110189.001341

White, M., Hill, S., McGovern, P., Mills, C., & Smeaton, D. (2003). High performance – management practices, working hours and work-life balance. *British Journal of Industrial Relations, 41*(2), 175–195. doi:10.1111/1467-8543.00268

Wildman, S. S. (2006). Paradigms and Analytical Frameworks in Modern Economics and Media Economics. In Handbook of Media Management and Economics (pp. 67–90). Mahwah, NJ: Lawrence Erlbaum Associates, Inc.

William, B. (2003).Cross-Cultural and Intercultural Communication. Thousand Oaks, CA: Sage.

Williams, K. C. (2013). *Introduction to Game Theory: A Behavioral Approach* (International Edition). New York, NY: Oxford University Press.

Winkielman, P., & Berridge, K. C. (2003). Irrational wanting and subrational liking: How rudimentary motivational and affective processes shape preferences and choices. *Political Psychology, 24*(4), 657–680. doi:10.1046/j.1467-9221.2003.00346.x

Winkielman, P., Knutson, B., Paulus, M., & Trujil, J. L. (2007). Affective influence on judgments and decisions: Moving towards core mechanisms. *Review of General Psychology, 11*(2), 179–192. doi:10.1037/1089-2680.11.2.179

Winter, E. (2014). *Feeling Smart: Why Our Emotions Are More Rational Than We Think*. New York: Public Affairs.

Wirth, M. O., & Bloch, H. (1995). Industrial organization theory and media industry analysis. *Journal of Media Economics, 8*(2), 15–26. doi:10.1207/s15327736me0802_3

Wiseman, R. L. (2003). Intercultural Communication Competence. In W. B. Gudykunst (Ed.), *Cross-Cultural and Intercultural Communication* (pp. 191–208). Thousand Oaks, CA: Sage.

Wiseman, R., & Gomez-Mejia, L. (1998). A behavioral agency model of managerial risk taking. *Academy of Management Review, 23*(1), 133–153.

Witte, A. (2012). Making the Case for a Post-National Cultural Analysis of Organizations. *Journal of Management Inquiry, 21*(2), 141–159. doi:10.1177/1056492611415279

Witt, U., & Binder, M. (2013). Disentangling motivational and experiential aspects of "utility" – A neuroeconomics perspective. *Journal of Economic Psychology, 36*(1), 27–40. doi:10.1016/j.joep.2013.02.001

Wolfram, E., Torsten, H., & Henning, Sch. (2015). The Size Dimension of Complex Economies—Towards a Meso-Economics: The Size of Interaction Arenas and the Emergence of Meso-Platforms of Institutional Coordination. In *The Microeconomics of Complex Economies* (pp. 419–447). Bremen, Germany: University of Bremen.

Wolk, H. I., Dodd, J. L., & Rozycki, J. J. (2012). *Accounting theory. Conceptual Issues in a Political and Economic Environment* (8th ed.). London: Sage Publishing.

Wong, N. Y. C. (1997). Suppose You Own the World and No One Knows? Conspicuous Consumption, Materialism and Self. *Advances in Consumer Research. Association for Consumer Research (U. S.), 24*, 18–22.

Wood, D. J. (1988). *How Children Think and Learn*. Oxford, UK: Blackwell.

Wood, J. C., & Kates, S. (2000). *Jean-Baptiste Say: critical assessments of leading economists* (Vol. 5). Taylor & Francis.

Yacubian, J., Gläscher, J., Schroeder, K., Sommer, T., Braus, D. F., & Büchel, C. (2006). Dissociable systems for gain- and loss-related value predictions and errors of prediction in the human brain. *The Journal of Neuroscience, 26*(37), 9530–9537. doi:10.1523/JNEUROSCI.2915-06.2006 PMID:16971537

Yin, R. K. (1983). *Case Study Research: Design and Methods* (3rd ed.). Thousand Oaks, CA: Sage Publications.

Yin, Z., Jiang, A. X., Tambe, M., Kiekintveld, C., Leyton-Brown, K., Sandholm, T., & Sullivan, J. P. (2012). TRUSTS: Scheduling randomized patrols for fare inspection in transit systems using game theory. *AI Magazine, 33*(4), 59–72.

Young, L., & Koenigs, M. (2007). Investigating emotion in moral cognition: A review of evidence from functional neuroimaging and neuropsychology. *British Medical Bulletin, 84*(1), 69–79. doi:10.1093/bmb/ldm031 PMID:18029385

Yule, G. (2010). *The Study of Language* (4th ed.). London: Cambridge University Press. doi:10.1017/CBO9780511757754

Zak, P. J. (2004). Neuroeconomics. *Philosophical Transactions of the Royal Society of London. Series B, Biological Sciences*, *359*(1451), 1737–1748. doi:10.1098/rstb.2004.1544 PMID:15590614

Zaleśkiewicz, T. (2003). *Psychologia inwestora giełdowego. Wprowadzenie do behawioralnych finansów*. Sopot: Gdańskie Wydawnictwo Psychologiczne.

Zaleśkiewicz, T. (2008). Neuroekonomia. *Decyzje*, *9*, 29–56.

Zaltman, G., LeMasters, K., & Heffring, M. (1982). *Theory construction in marketing: some thoughts on thinking*. Toronto: John Wiley & Sons Canada, Limited.

Zamora-López, G., Zhou, C., & Kurths, J. (2010). Cortical hubs forma module formulti sensory integration on top of the hierarchy of cortical networks. *Frontiers in Neuroinformatics*, *4*, 1. PMID:20428515

Zeithaml, V. A. (2009). *Delivering Quality Service*. New York: Free Press.

Zeithaml, V. A., Parasuraman, A., & Berry, L. L. (1990). *Delivering Quality Service: Balancing Customer Perceptions and Expectations*. London: Simon and Schuster.

Zhang, Y., & Fishbach, A. (2005). The role of anticipated emotions in the endowment effect. *Journal of Consumer Psychology*, *15*(4), 316–324. doi:10.1207/s15327663jcp1504_6

Ziccardi, D. P. (2001). Demonstrating the values of luxury brands. *Brandweek*, *42*(44), 18–19.

Zielonka, P. (2003). *Czym są finanse behawioralne, czyli krótkie wprowadzenie do psychologii rynków finansowych*. Warszawa: Narodowy Bank Polski.

Zielonka, P., & Tyszka, T. (1999). Nowoczesne finanse: Efektywność rynku czy finanse behawioralne? *Bank i Kredyt*, *11*, 8–19.

Zollo, M., & Winter, S. G. (2002). Deliberate learning and the evolution of dynamic capabilities. *Organization Science*, *13*(3), 339–351. doi:10.1287/orsc.13.3.339.2780

Zurawicki, L. (2010). *Neuromarketing: Exploring the brain of the consumer*. Berlin, Germany: Springer–Verlag. doi:10.1007/978-3-540-77829-5

About the Contributors

Bryan Christiansen, since 2004, has progressively held the positions of President, CEO, and then Chairman in PryMarke, LLC, a Michigan, USA-based Business Analytics and Management Consultancy. Bryan has also been an Adjunct Business Professor at Capella University, DeVry University, and Ellis University (formerly Ellis College of New York Institute of Technology) in the USA, and a Senior Business Lecturer at Gumushane University in Turkey. Born in Washington, DC and raised in Asia, Bryan is fluent in Chinese, Japanese, Spanish, and Turkish, and has traveled to 40 countries during his 28-year business career involving Global 1000 firms. Bryan holds a Bachelor's degree in Marketing from the University of the State of New York and an MBA degree from Capella University. Bryan will complete his Doctor of Business Administration degree (DBA) from Middlesex University in London, England in 2020.

Ewa Lechman is an Assistant Professor of Economics at the Faculty of Management and Economics, Gdansk University of Technology. Her extensive research interests concentrate on economic development, ICT, and its role in reshaping social and economic systems and various aspects of poverty and economics in developing countries. She coordinates and participates in international research and educational projects and also works as an independent expert assisting with innovation assignments, including the evaluation of small and medium enterprise proposals, EU-financed programmes, and policy design regarding innovativeness, digitalization, education and social exclusion. She was the 2013 winner of an Emerald Literati Network Award for Excellence and is a member of the editorial boards of international journals on technology diffusion, the digital economy and economic development.

* * *

Asmat-Nizam Abdul-Talib teaches international business and international marketing at the Universiti Utara Malaysia and he is recently attached to the Department of International Business, College of Law, Government and International Studies. He receives his PhD in International Marketing from Aston Business School, Aston University, UK, MBA in International Business from Cardiff University, UK, and a Bechelor Degree in Business and Economics from Concordia University, Canada. At current, his academic research has received financial support or support in kind from various institutions. He is also the recipient of Universiti Utara Malaysia Outstanding Research Award and Universiti Utara Malaysia Most Promising Researcher Award. His research interests lie primarily in international marketing and strategic marketing, especially in export market intelligence, and the use of export market intelligence in the firm's export decision process. He has also been appointed as an Associate Professor in International Business in Tashkent State University, Uzbakistan, a research fellow at Honda Foundation, Japan, and Faculty Associate at Aston Business School, UK, teaching international marketing and international business.

William Amone, from 2006 to date, has been working at Gulu University in Uganda as a Lecturer of Economics. Since 2012 to date, he also serves as a Consultant in Business Management at Uganda Management Institute. William has been involved in many researches and trainings in Uganda, Kenya, Tanzania and Canada. He is currently a PhD candidate at Mbarara University of Science and Technology in Uganda and a researcher in Development Economics. William is the author of "Global Market Trends", a chapter in the Handbook of Research on Global Business Opportunities.

Nelli Artienwicz (Ph.D) is a lecturer at the Faculty of Business Administration at University of Gdansk in Poland. Her research interests concern understanding and application of basic accounting concepts and also cognitive errors and biases in accounting processes. She is also accounting practitioner (accountant and accountancy advisor) and translator.

Dincer Atli is an Asst. Prof. at Uskudar University in Turkey. Dr. Dincer Atli joined Labor and Employment Relations at Pennsylvania State University, USA as a Post-doctoral visiting scholar for academic year 2014/2015. After completing his military service he moved on working as a Human Resources specialist on Turkcell Group and also attended P.h.D program in Marmara University. He gained a scholarship during his PhD education from the Istanbul Chamber Of Commerce (ITO). This scholarship has been granted due to his position as the highest ranked student during his master's education. His PhD thesis (Human Resources Managements' New Vision: Talent Management and a Research On Media Companies), the first in Turkey to focus on the subject of Talent Management, was submitted in 2010. Dr. Atli's enhanced PhD dissertation was published in 2012 as a book which was the first of its kind regarding Talent Management in Turkey. (2nd edition 2013) His research interests are human resources, talent management, corporate culture, employer branding, employer attractiveness, media organizations, social media, neuro marketing and virtual worlds.

Duygu Buğa graduated from English Language Teaching division of Istanbul University. She just has a bachelor degree, but she is interested in linguistics and especially psycholinguistics and neurolinguistics. That's why she approaches language and life in a critical way. She wants to propose academic/experimental studies on psycholinguistics and neurolinguistics.

Harish C. Chandan is Professor of Business at Argosy University, Atlanta. He was interim chair of the business program in 2011. He received President's award for excellence in teaching in 2007, 2008 and 2009. His teaching philosophy is grounded in the learner needs and life-long learning. His research interests include research methods, leadership, marketing, and organizational behavior. He has published 20 peer-reviewed articles in business journals and five chapters in business reference books. Dr. Chandan has presented conference papers at Academy of Management, International Academy of Business and Management, Southeast Association of Information Systems, and Academy of International Business. Prior to joining Argosy, Dr. Chandan managed optical fiber and cable product qualification laboratories for Lucent Technologies, Bell Laboratories. During his career with Lucent, he had 40 technical publications, a chapter in a book and five patents.

Jarmo Heinonen (PhD/Education LicSc/Marketing, MSc/Food Economy) of Laurea University of Applied Sciences has ample experience of consumer science. His experience lies particularly in Conjoint methodology applied to consumers preferences. He has also assisted many Finnish and international research groups in the capacity of an expert statistician. He has published many neuroeconomics and neuromarketing papers as conference proceedings, such as Annual meeting of Neuroeconomics and NeuroPsychoEconomics. Heinonen has been studying in University of Helsinki (-1998), University of Tampere (-2007), University of Rhode Island (1987-1988) and University of California Davis (1995-1996).

Oxana Karnaukhova – PhD in Cultural Studies, associate professor in the Institute of History and International Relations, Southern Federal University (Russia), executive director of the Centre of European Union in the South West Russia. Research interests concern exploitation of cultural approach to socio-economic development of multicultural agglomerations and investigation of communicative strategies within cooperation accounts. Publication list includes articles on intercultural communications in transnational corporations, communicative strategies and entrepreneurship performance, multicultural policies and practices in the EU states etc.

Kijpokin Kasemsap received his BEng degree in Mechanical Engineering from King Mongkut's University of Technology Thonburi, his MBA degree from Ramkhamhaeng University, and his DBA degree in Human Resource Management from Suan Sunandha Rajabhat University. He is a Special Lecturer at Faculty of Management Sciences, Suan Sunandha Rajabhat University based in Bangkok, Thailand. He is a Member of International Association of Engineers (IAENG), International Association of Engineers and Scientists (IAEST), International Economics Development and Research Center (IEDRC), International Association of Computer Science and Information Technology (IACSIT), International Foundation for Research and Development (IFRD), and International Innovative Scientific and Research Organization (IISRO). He also serves on the International Advisory Committee (IAC) for International Association of Academicians and Researchers (INAAR). He has numerous original research articles in top international journals, conference proceedings, and book chapters on business management, human resource management, and knowledge management published internationally.

Wiboon Kittilaksanawong is Professor of Strategy and International Business in the Graduate School of Humanities and Social Sciences, Faculty of Economics, Saitama University (Japan). He received his PhD in Management from National Taiwan University. His research interests include global business and strategy, business strategies in emerging markets, and international entrepreneurship.

Salim Lahmiri is full professor at ESCA School of Management in Casablanca, Morocco. He holds a Ph.D degree in Cognitive Informatics from University of Quebec at Montreal and a master of engineering (M. Eng) degree within the department of electrical engineering at École de Technologie Supérieure, Montreal, Canada. His research interests are in pattern recognition, intelligent decision systems, and times series analysis and forecasting.

Alina Maria Landowska is a PhD candidate in Cultural Anthropology at SWPS University of Social Sciences and Humanities (Warsaw, Poland). Her doctoral research related, in particular, to cognitive anthropology seeks to explore attitudes to co-operation and its formation in different cultures with special focus on unique social-cognitive abilities of humans. Landowska holds a Master of Science in Management, as well as she graduated PhD program in Economics.

Ewa Matuska - PhD in Psychology, graduate of Gdansk University (Poland) and Charles' University in Praque (Czech Rep.). Assistant Professor at Hanseatic Academy of Management in Slupsk, Poland, cooperatin with scientific Institute for Development in Sopot, (Poland). Experienced manager and HR practitioner. A member of Polish Association of Human Resources Management and a vice - president of the board in international academic network "Human Potential Development in Central and Eastern EU", joining higher schools from Poland, Slovakia, Lithuania, Czech Rep. and Hungary. About 60 scientific publications in area of HRM and labor market. Scientific interests: change management, competence & talent management, soft innovations, social innovations, local development via human capital engagement.

Inna Nekrasova is Associate Professor in Economics Department of Economics, at Southern Federal University. Nekrasova I. V. defended her dissertation in 1992, at the Russian State Pedagogical University in St. Petersburg. She has been working in the Southern Federal University from 1993 to the present. She had Training Course in Economics and Management in context of TACIS Project, in the Piraeus University, in 1996. Nekrasova I. V. lectures in the following disciplines - Investment, Financial Market and Financial Institutes, Financial Management, Mergers and Acquisitions in the Banking Sector.

Anastasia Nikitaeva is Professor of the Department of Information Economics, Head of Research interdisciplinary laboratory "Innovative processes in economy" of Faculty of Economics of Southern Federal University. In 2009 she has become a Doctor of Science in Economics, specialization "Economic and Social Systems Management". Fields of Interests: Interaction of Government and Business in the Economy System, Models and technologies of decision making support, Public-Private Partnership, Project Management. Anastasia Nikitaeva has about 150 publications.

Rauno Rusko is Lecturer at the University of Lapland. His research activities focus on cooperation, coopetition, strategic management, supply chain management and entrepreneurship mainly in the branches of information communication technology, forest industry and tourism. In addition to several published book chapters, his articles appeared in the European Management Journal, Forest Policy and Economics, International Journal of Business Environment, Industrial Marketing Management, International Journal of Innovation in the Digital Economy and International Journal of Tourism Research among others.

Shefali Virkar is research student at the University of Oxford (UK), currently reading for a D.Phil. in Politics. Her doctoral research seeks to explore the growing use of Information and Communication Technologies (ICTs) to promote better governance in the developing world, with special focus on the political, behavioural, and institutional impacts associated with the deployment of ICTs on local public administration reform and institution building in India.Shefali holds an M.A. in Globalisation, Governance and Development from the University of Warwick (UK). Her Master's dissertation analysed the concept of the Digital Divide within the context of a globalising world, its impact on developing countries, and the ensuing policy implications. At Oxford, Shefali is a member of Keble College.

Wan-Nurisma Ayu Wan-Ismail received her BA in International Business Management from University Utara Malaysia and M.B.A from National University of Malaysia. She just complete her PhD in Culture and International Marketing from University Utara Malaysia, Malaysia. Her major research interests are in cross cultural management, consumer behavior and international marketing. She is now as a lecturer in University Utara Malaysia.

Mehmet Yilmazata is an economic researcher, working with the Undersecretariat of Treasury at the Embassy of the Republic of Turkey in Berlin. Mehmet Yilmazata was born in Berlin in 1977. After gaining his diploma in history at the Faculty of Letters, Istanbul University (2002) he enrolled at Freie Universitat Berlin, finishing the BA programme in Political Science (2006), Mehmet Yilmazata also studied economics at Berlin Technical University and finished his MA at Marmara University Istanbul, writing a thesis on the Bosnian Annexation thesis of 1908. After serving with the Turkish Armed Forces in 2006, he continued his PhD studies at Istanbul University, finishing his thesis on Turkish-German relations between 1930-44 in 2014. In 2009 he worked at the United Nations Headquarters' Department of Political Affairs (MEWAD Division), focusing on security issues in Iraq and Central Asia. Since 2010 he is working as an economic researcher with the Undersecretariat of Turkish Treasury, currently at the Embassy of the Republic of Turkey in Berlin. Mehmet has participated as a speaker at several economic and academic conferences and published several research papers and two books.

Norhayati Zakaria is an Associate Professor at School of International Studies at College of Law, Government, and International Studies, Universiti Utara Malaysia. Dr. Zakaria earned her Ph.D in Information Science and Technology and MPhil. of Information Transfer, both at Syracuse University and MSc. Management at Rensselaer Polytechnic Institute, Troy. Her research expertise combines several interdisciplinary fields, including cross-cultural management, international business, and computer-mediated communication technology. For more than a decade, Dr. Zakaria has established international research collaborations with global scholars from the United States, Japan, and Canada. As a principal investigator, she has obtained international research grants from the Asian Office of Aerospace Research & Development (AOARD). From 2006 till now, she serves as a Senior Research Faculty Associate at the Center for Research on Collaboratories and Technology Enhanced Learning Communities (COTELCO) under American University where she led projects using global virtual teams. Additionally, she has worked at two Universities in the Gulf region (4 years)--University of Wollongong in Dubai and Saudi Electronic University, Riyadh.

Index

Lightning Source UK Ltd.
Milton Keynes UK
UKOW04n0611260517

302059UK00015B/225/P